THE HOME BOOK OF
MODERN VERSE

THE HOME BOOK OF MODERN VERSE

AN EXTENSION OF

THE HOME BOOK OF VERSE

BEING A SELECTION FROM AMERICAN
AND ENGLISH POETRY OF THE
TWENTIETH CENTURY

COMPILED AND ARRANGED BY
BURTON EGBERT STEVENSON

FIRST EDITION
REVISED

NEW YORK
HENRY HOLT AND COMPANY

Printed in
United States of America

TO THE MEMBERS OF
THE LIBRARY OVERSEAS FELLOWSHIP
THIS BOOK IS DEDICATED
IN MEMORY OF STIRRING DAYS TO-
GETHER AND A LOYALTY AND
DEVOTION NEVER TO BE
FORGOTTEN

COPYRIGHT ACKNOWLEDGMENTS

Mary Aldis, from *Flashlights;* "I Know," and six sonnets from "The Spirit and the Bride," by Elsa Barker, from *The Book of Love;* "At the Front," and "Apparition," by John Erskine, from *Collected Poems.*

E. P. Dutton & Co.: "Christmas Island," by Katherine Lee Bates, from *Yellow Clover;* the poems by Helen Gray Cone, from *A Chant of Love for England,* and *The Coat Without a Seam;* "The Night Will Never Stay," by Eleanor Farjeon, from *Gypsy and Ginger;* the poems by Louis Golding, from *Prophet and Fool;* the poems by Benjamin R. C. Low, from *Broken Music;* the poems by Siegfried Sassoon, from *Counterattack and Other Poems,* and *Picture Show;* the poems by Leonora Speyer, from *A Canopic Jar;* the poems by W. J. Turner, from *The Dark Wind;* the poems by Willard Wattles, from *Lanterns in Gethsemane;* the poems by Clement Wood, from *The Earth Turns South;* the poems by Francis Brett Young, from his *Poems.*

The Four Seas Co.: The poems by Conrad Aiken, from *The Charnel Rose,* and *The Jig of Forslin;* "The Poplar," and "Choricos," by Richard Aldington, from *War and Love,* and *Images;* the poems by Joseph Campbell, from *The Mountainy Singer;* the poems by Elinor Chipp, from *The City and Other Poems;* "My April," by Preston Clark, from *Poems;* the poems by Edwin Curran, from *Poems;* "Since Youth is all for Gladness," by Glenn Ward Dresbach, from *Morning, Noon and Night.*

Harcourt, Brace & Co.: The poems by John Freeman, from *Music;* the poems by Helen Hoyt, from *Apples Here in My Basket;* the poems by Alfred Kreymborg, from *Less Lonely;* the poems by Edwin Meade Robinson, from *Piping and Panning;* the poems by Carl Sandburg, from *Smoke and Steel;* "Beauty," and "Italian Poppies" by Joel Elias Spingarn, from *Poems;* "Little Things," and "Frightened Face," by Marion Strobel, from *Once in a Blue Moon;* the poems by Louis Untermeyer, from *The New Adam;* the poems by Anna Wickham, from *The Contemplative Quarry;* the poems by Margaret Widdemer, from *Cross Currents;* the poems by George Edward Wooderry, from *The Roamer;* the poems by Elinor Wylie, from *Nets to Catch the Wind.*

Harvard University Press: "Sonnets," and "To a Scarlatti Passepied," by Robert Hillyer, from *Sonnets and other Lyrics.*

Henry Holt & Company: "The Retort Discourteous," by Stephen Vincent Benét, from *Heavens and Earth;* "Piccadilly," by Thomas Burke, from *Street of Pain;* the poems by Francis Carlin, from *My Ireland,* and *The Cairn of Stars;* the poems by Sarah N. Cleghorn, from *Portraits and Protests;* the poems by Padraic Colum, from *Poems;* The poems by Grace Hazard Conkling, from *Wilderness Songs;* the poems by Walter de la Mare, from his *Collected Poems;* "Life and Death," and "An Autumn Road," by Glenn Ward Dresbach, from *In Colors of the West;* the poems by Robert Frost, from *New Hampshire, Mountain Interval, A Boy's Will,* and *North of Boston;* the poems by H. D., from *Hymen;* "Glimpses," and "In Passing," by Roy Helton, from *Outcasts in Beulah Land;* the poems by Carl Sandburg, from *Cornhuskers;* the poems by Lew Sarett, from *Many, Many Moons;* "Saul," by George Sterling, from *Selected Poems;* the poems by Edward Thomas, from *Poems;* the poems by Louis Untermeyer, from *And Other Poets,* and *These Times;* the poems

fornia Troubadour; the poems by George Sterling, from *The House of Orchids.*

Charles Scribner's Sons: The poems by Struthers Burt, from *Songs and Portraits;* "Toil Away," by John Jay Chapman, from *Songs and Poems;* the poems by Olive Tilford Dargan, from *Lute and Furrow;* "Devon to Me," by John Galsworthy, from *Songs, Moods, and Doggerels;* the poems by Alice Meynell, from *The Poems of Alice Meynell,* copyright 1923, by Wilfrid Meynell; the poems by Corinne Roosevelt Robinson, from *Poems;* the poems by Edwin Arlington Robinson, from *The Town Down the River,* and *Children of the Night;* the poems by John Hall Wheelock, from *Dust and Light,* and *The Caged Panther and Other Poems.*

Thomas Seltzer, Inc.: The poems by Laura Benét, from *Fairy Bread;* "Of Nicolette," by E. E. Cummings, from *Tulips and Chimneys;* the poems by Charles Divine, from *Gypsy Gold;* the poems by Douglas Goldring, from *Streets and Other Verses;* "Prisoners," by Nancy Barr Mavity, from *A Dinner of Herbs;* the poems by William Kean Seymour, from *Cæsar Remembers and Other Poems;* "The Enamel Girl," and "First Miracle," by Genevieve Taggard, from *For Eager Lovers;* the poems by Robert L. Wolf, from *After Disillusion.*

Ralph Fletcher Seymour: The poems by Alice Corbin, from *Red Earth.*

Frank Shay: The poems by Henry Martyn Hoyt, from *Dry Points.*

Sherman, French & Co.: "Songs of Ballyshannon," by Jeanne Robert Foster, from *Wild Apples;* "The Secret," by Arthur Wallace Peach, from *Hill Trails.*

Small, Maynard & Co.: "Willy and the Lady," by Gelett Burgess, from *The Gage of Youth;* the poems by Bliss Carman, from *Echoes from Vagabondia;* the poems by Laurence Housman, from *Heart of Peace;* the poems by J. Corson Miller, from *Veils of Samité;* the poems by Edward J. O'Brien, from *Distant Music,* and *White Fountains.*

Frederick A. Stokes Co.: "John-John," and "Wishes for My Son," by Thomas MacDonagh, from *Poems;* the poems by Robert Nichols, from *Ardours and Endurances;* the poems by Cecil Roberts, from *Poems.*

Harold Vinal: "Flail," and "Finite," by Power Dalton, from *Turning Earth;* "Men Are the Devil," by Mary Carolyn Davies, from *Marriage Songs.*

The Yale University Press: "The Spell," "Some Day," and "G. G. H.," by Medora C. Addison, from *Dreams and a Sword;* "I Love the Friendly Faces of Old Trees," "I Shall be Loved as Quiet Things," "Burning Bush," "Creeds," and "A Silver Lantern," by Karle Wilson Baker, from *Burning Bush, Blue Smoke,* and *Casements;* the poems by William Rose Benét, from *Merchants from Cathay and Other Poems,* and *Perpetual Light;* "May," and "The Silent Ranges," by Stephen Moyland Bird, from *In The Sky Garden;* "To One Older," and "White Dusk," by Marion M. Boyd, from *Silver Wands;* "Hope," by Gamaliel Bradford, from *Shadow Verses;* "Fate," by James Fenimore Cooper, Jr., from *Afterglow;* "Come, Let Us Find," by William H. Davies, from *The Captive Lion;* the poems by Brian Hooker, from *Poems;* "The Silence," "Dusk," and "The Reed Player," by Archibald

TABLE OF CONTENTS

PART I

POEMS OF YOUTH AND AGE

PART II

POEMS OF LOVE

Table of Contents

Table of Contents

THE TRAGEDY OF LOVE

Table of Contents

Table of Contents

WOOD AND FIELD AND RUNNING BROOK

Table of Contents

Table of Contents

PART IV

FAMILIAR VERSE AND POEMS HUMOROUS AND SATIRIC

THE KINDLY MUSE

Table of Contents

PART V

POEMS OF PATRIOTISM, HISTORY AND LEGEND

PART VI

POEMS OF SENTIMENT AND REFLECTION

Table of Contents xxxvii

IN PRAISE OF BEAUTY

ROMANCE

SHADOW-LAND

Table of Contents

HEARTH AND HOME

NARRATIVE AND DESCRIPTIVE POEMS

PART VII

POEMS OF SORROW, DEATH, AND IMMORTALITY

IN THE SHADOW

THE DARK CAVALIER

Table of Contents   xliii

INTRODUCTION

WHEN THE HOME BOOK OF VERSE was first projected some sixteen years ago, there was a tentative agreement between publisher and compiler that it should be revised and enlarged from time to time, as occasion might require, provided there was a continued demand for it sufficient to justify the expenditure. It was assumed that the need for such revision would be infrequent and that the book would never be greatly enlarged, since, in all probability, little of the new poetry would be sufficiently important to demand inclusion. As a matter of fact, the future of the book was so much in doubt that neither party to the agreement was inclined to take it very seriously.

There was unquestionably a place for a general anthology, since no new one had been published in this country for many years and the old ones were hopelessly antiquated, but how far the public could be interested in such a book was extremely uncertain. Opinions from the trade were decidedly pessimistic, for it had become an aphorism that nobody read poetry, and it is perhaps not too much to say that had either publisher or compiler foreseen the difficulties and discouragements which lay ahead, the task would never have been undertaken. But, once started, it had to be carried through.

The book had been planned on an ambitious scale—it was to be the most comprehensive collection of American and English verse ever brought together in one volume; but Mr. Holt has recorded in his memoirs how dubiously he regarded it on the day of publication, and its compiler is not ashamed to confess that he had become acutely aware of his limitations as the work progressed, and was anything but confident of the result.

To everyone's amazement, the book was a success almost from the start. This was partly due, no doubt, to its own merits, and yet in spite of them it might easily have stranded,

as many notable books have done before and since, but for
the fact that it was launched, by great good fortune, at
the very moment when a remarkable poetic revival was
gathering force, and when public interest in poetry was
being stimulated to an astonishing degree. It caught this
rising tide, and was soon so firmly established that its future
could be forecast with considerable certainty.

But it was also almost immediately out of date, for a new
generation of poets had suddenly arisen and was hammering
at its portals. John Masefield, Robert Frost, Alfred Noyes,
Vachel Lindsay, Edwin Arlington Robinson, and Walter
de la Mare—to mention only those who come first to mind—
were producing work of such significance that no anthology
could afford to disregard them. It was therefore necessary
within five years not only to revise the book completely,
but also to enlarge it far beyond expectations. Nearly
six hundred poems were added to the third edition, and
succeeding revisions have brought it to a total of over
four thousand pages. It was a big book to start with, and
it grew into a bulky, if not actually ungainly, one, for there
is a limit to the thinness even of India paper!

It has been evident for a long time that it could be made
no larger if it were to be kept in its single-volume form,
and experiments with other forms had been distinctly
discouraging. Meanwhile many of the older poets were
doing better and better work, while a still younger generation, after some youthful gambollings in pursuit of various
will-o'-the-wisps, was settling down to solid achievement.
These developments could not be ignored, if THE HOME
BOOK OF VERSE were to continue to fulfill its mission, and
there was much prayerful consideration of how the problem
could be solved. It was finally agreed that the only feasible
solution was to extend the book by a supplementary volume,
devoted exclusively to recent verse, to which all future
revisions and enlargements should be confined.

It is, then, as an extension of the older book that THE
HOME BOOK OF MODERN VERSE must be considered. It
is composed entirely of new material, which is designed
to supplement and round out the selections previously

used from the work of the older generation of present-day poets and to give a fair taste of the quality of the younger ones who here appear for the first time; but no attempt whatever has been made to indicate their relative importance by the number of selections used. Poets whose work is principally dramatic or narrative never bulk very large in an anthology which is essentially a collection of lyrics, and even lyric poets vary surprisingly in quotability.

In the course of a fairly comprehensive survey of current verse, continued through the greater part of the past three years, such poems were chosen as seemed suitable for the new book. In this way three or four times as much material was assembled as could be used, so that the poems finally selected have survived repeated readings and repeated winnowings. But their survival has been due solely to their content, and not at all to their authorship. In a few cases, the number of selections was limited by copyright conditions, and two or three poets are altogether missing for the same reason, but these omissions are comparatively unimportant. For the rest, the compiler had a free hand, and the poems here included were chosen for one reason only—because they seemed worth while.

It was realized that to make this volume a worthy companion of the older one it must be planned in a large way, and it has been possible to carry out this plan solely because of an extraordinary generosity on the part of both authors and publishers—a generosity quite unexampled, which is here most gratefully acknowledged. The compiler is also indebted to many authors for a personal interest in the development of the book and for various helpful suggestions, nor must he neglect to acknowledge his obligation to Mr. Braithwaite, Mr. Untermeyer, Miss Rittenhouse, Miss Monroe, Mrs. Wilkinson, and other anthologists who have done pioneer labor in the same field.

As in the older volume, the poems have been classified by subject, and the classification previously used has been followed very closely, with only such modifications as the nature of the material rendered necessary. No apologies are offered for this system of arrangement. It is the only system by which an anthology can be given a sort of individuality. If it is intelligently carried out, one poem enhances the interest of the next, there is an interplay of thought between them, and the effect of all of them is heightened. It might be added that anthologizing would be a dreary task, in the opinion of the present writer at least, but for the pleasure of working out these interesting problems of juxtaposition.

This arrangement, too, enables one to take a sort of bird's-eye view of the tendencies of modern verse. It will be seen that there is a dearth of notable verse for children, and that no poets have arisen to take the place of Eugene Field and James Whitcomb Riley, with the possible exception of Walter de la Mare. Love, as always, is a favorite theme, but present-day poets are concerned with its tragic and ironic phases rather than with its tender ones, and write about it with a frankness and absence of sentimentality almost unknown a generation ago—there are no longer any serenades, and very little time is wasted in celebrating eyebrows. A great deal of good nature poetry is being written, with wanderlust much in the foreground, especially among the women. There is also a fair volume of humorous verse, almost all of it the work of the newspaper columnists. Patriotic and historical verse has taken a decided slump, and war is no longer celebrated with drums and trumpets. The verse evoked by the World War is largely elegiac in character, and has to do with its agony and futility, rather than with its glory. Not a single battle nor a single leader has been commemorated in a noteworthy poem. To anyone familiar with the older patriotic poetry, especially with Civil War verse, the contrast is positively startling—and most refreshing, for it indicates that poets, at least, are agreed that war should be outlawed!

Where the output bulks largest is in verse of a philosophic, reflective and satiric character, and here there was an actual embarrassment of material. How present-day poets react to the world about them is abundantly shown in the section where this verse is gathered together, and it will be seen that the reaction is by no means so gloomy as might have been imagined. Of religious poetry, in the old sense, there is very little, but if the poets have, for the most part, turned definitely away from the Fundamentalist conception of God and the universe, it is evident that they have come closer to Him as the source of being, and that they still tread confidently among the stars!

B. E. S.

Chillicothe, Ohio,
  January 17, 1925.

PART I

POEMS OF YOUTH AND AGE

O YOUTH WITH BLOSSOMS LADEN

O YOUTH with blossoms laden,
  Hast not a rose for Age,
A bit of bloom to brighten
  A lonely pilgrimage?

O Youth with song and laughter,
  Go not so lightly by.
Have pity—and remember
  How soon thy roses die!

Arthur Wallace Peach

RHYMES OF CHILDHOOD

THE HUNTSMEN

THREE jolly gentlemen,
  In coats of red,
Rode their horses
  Up to bed.

Three jolly gentlemen
  Snored till morn,
Their horses champing
  The golden corn.

Three jolly gentlemen,
  At break of day,
Came clitter-clatter down the stairs
  And galloped away.
                    Walter de la Mare

THE LION

THE Lion is a kingly beast.
He likes a Hindu for a feast.
And if no Hindu he can get,
The lion-family is upset.

He cuffs his wife and bites her ears
Till she is nearly moved to tears.
Then some explorer finds the den
And all is family peace again.
                    Vachel Lindsay

MIRROR, MIRROR

MIRROR, mirror, tell me,
  Am I pretty or plain?
Or am I downright ugly,
  And ugly to remain?

Shall I marry a gentleman?
　Shall I marry a clown?
Or shall I marry old knives-and-scissors
　Shouting through the town?

Robert Graves

VARIATIONS ON AN OLD NURSERY RHYME

THE King of China's daughter
　So beautiful to see
With her face like yellow water,
　Left her nutmeg tree.

Her little rope for skipping
　She skipped and gave it me—
Made of painted notes of singing-birds
　Among the fields of tea.

I skipped across the nutmeg grove,—
　I skipped across the sea;
But neither sun nor moon, my dear,
　Has yet caught me.

Edith Sitwell

WISHES

WHAT do you look for, what do you seek?
　A silver bird with a golden beak.

What do you long for, what do you crave?
　Golden gems in a silver cave.

What do you lack, and what do you need?
　A silver sword and a golden steed.

What do you want, of what do you dream?
　A golden ship on a silver stream.

What do you have, and what do you own?
　A silver robe and a golden crown.

What would you be? Oh, what would you be?
　Only the king of the land and the sea.

Norman Ault

JIM JAY

Do diddle di do,
  Poor Jim Jay
Got stuck fast
  In Yesterday.
Squinting he was,
  On cross-legs bent,
Never heeding
  The wind was spent.
Round veered the weathercock,
  The sun drew in—
And stuck was Jim
  Like a rusty pin. . . .
We pulled and we pulled
  From seven till twelve,
Jim, too frightened
  To help himself.
But all in vain.
  The clock struck one,
And there was Jim
  A little bit gone.
At half-past five
  You scarce could see
A glimpse of his flapping
  Handkerchee.
And when came noon,
  And we climbed sky-high,
Jim was a speck
  Slip-slipping by.
Come to-morrow,
  The neighbors say,
He'll be past crying for;
  Poor Jim Jay.

Walter de la Mare

WIND'S WORK

KATE rose up early as fresh as a lark,
Almost in time to see vanish the dark;
Jack rather later, bouncing from bed,
Saw fade on the dawn's cheek the last flush of red:

Yet who knows
When the wind rose?

Kate went to watch the new lambs at their play
And stroke the white calf born yesterday;
Jack sought the woods where trees grow tall
As who would learn to swarm them all:
Yet who knows
Where the wind goes?

Kate has sown candy-tuft, lupins and peas,
Carnations, forget-me-not and heart's-ease;
Jack has sown cherry-pie, marigold,
Love-that-lies-bleeding and snap-dragons bold;
But who knows
What the wind sows?

Kate knows a thing or two useful at home,
Darns like a fairy, and churns like a gnome;
Jack is a wise man at shaping a stick,
Once he's in the saddle the pony may kick.
But hark to the wind how it blows!
None comes, none goes,
None reaps or mows,
No friends turn foes,
No hedge bears sloes,
And no cock crows,
But the wind knows!

T. Sturge Moore

CONTRARY MARY

From " Zodiac Town "

You ask why Mary was called contrary?
Well, this is why, my dear:
She planted the most outlandish things
In her garden every year:
She was always sowing the queerest seed,
And when advised to stop,
Her answer was merely, "No, indeed—
Just wait till you see the crop!"

And here are some of the crops, my child
(Although not nearly all):
Bananarcissus and cucumberries,
And violettuce small;
Potatomatoes, melonions rare,
And rhubarberries round,
With porcupineapples prickly-rough
On a little bush close to the ground.

She gathered the stuff in mid-July
And sent it away to sell—
And now you'll see how she earned her name,
And how she earned it well.
Were the crops hauled off in a farmer's cart?
No, not by any means,
But in little June-buggies and automobeetles
And dragonflying machines!

Nancy Byrd Turner

AUNT SELINA

WHEN Aunt Selina comes to tea
She always makes them send for me,
And I must be polite and clean
And seldom heard, but always seen.
I must sit stiffly in my chair
As long as Aunt Selina's there.

But there are certain things I would
Ask Aunt Selina if I could.
I'd ask when she was small, like me,
If she had ever climbed a tree.
Or if she'd ever, ever gone
Without her shoes and stockings on
Where lovely puddles lay in rows
To let the mud squeege through her toes.
Of if she'd coasted on a sled,
Or learned to stand upon her head
And wave her feet—and after that
I'd ask her how she got so fat.

These things I'd like to ask, and then—
I hope she would not come again!

Carol Haynes

MANNERS

I HAVE an uncle I don't like,
   An aunt I cannot bear:
She chucks me underneath the chin,
   He ruffles up my hair.

Another uncle I adore,
   Another aunty, too:
She shakes me kindly by the hand,
   He says, How do you do?

Mrs. Schuyler Van Renssellaer

MR. WELLS

ON Sunday morning, then he comes
   To church, and everybody smells
The blacking and the toilet soap
   And camphor balls from Mr. Wells.

He wears his whiskers in a bunch,
   And wears his glasses on his head.
I mustn't call him Old Man Wells—
   No matter—that's what Father said.

And when the little blacking smells
   And camphor balls and soap begin,
I do not have to look to know
   That Mr. Wells is coming in.

Elizabeth Madox Roberts

THE HENS

THE night was coming very fast;
It reached the gate as I ran past.

The Rabbit

The pigeons had gone to the tower of the church,
And all the hens were on their perch

Up in the barn, and I thought I heard
A piece of a little purring word.

I stopped inside, waiting and staying,
To try to hear what the hens were saying.

They were asking something, that was plain,
Asking it over and over again.

One of them moved and turned around,
Her feathers made a ruffled sound,

A ruffled sound, like a bushful of birds,
And she said her little asking words.

She pushed her head close into her wing,
But nothing answered anything.

Elizabeth Madox Roberts

THE RABBIT

Brown bunny sits inside his burrow
  Till everything is still,
Then out he slips along the furrow,
  Or up the grassy hill.

He nibbles all about the bushes
  Or sits to wash his face,
But at a sound he stamps, and rushes
  At a surprising pace.

You see some little streaks and flashes,
  A last sharp twink of white,
As down his hidy-hole he dashes
  And disappears from sight.

Edith King

THE MILK JUG

(*The Kitten Speaks*)

THE Gentle Milk Jug blue and white
　　I love with all my soul;
She pours herself with all her might
　　To fill my breakfast bowl.

All day she sits upon the shelf,
　　She does not jump or climb—
She only waits to pour herself
　　When 'tis my supper-time.

And when the Jug is empty quite,
　　I shall not mew in vain,
The Friendly Cow, all red and white,
　　Will fill her up again.

Oliver Herford

"FOUR–PAWS"

FOUR-PAWS, the kitten from the farm,
Is come to live with Betsey-Jane,
Leaving the stack-yard for the warm
Flower-compassed cottage in the lane,
To wash his idle face and play
Among chintz cushions all the day.

Under the shadow of her hair
He lies, who loves him nor desists
To praise his whiskers and compare
The tabby bracelets on his wrists,—
Omelet at lunch and milk at tea
Suit Betsey-Jane and so fares he.

Happy beneath her golden hand
He purrs contentedly nor hears
His Mother mourning through the land,
The old gray cat with tattered ears
And humble tail and heavy paw
Who brought him up among the straw.

Never by day she ventures nigh,
But when the dusk grows dim and deep
And moths flit out of the strange sky
And Betsey has been long asleep—
Out of the dark she comes and brings
Her dark maternal offerings;—

Some field-mouse or a throstle caught
Near netted fruit or in the corn,
Or rat, for this her darling sought
In the old barn where he was born;
And all lest on his dainty bed
Four-paws were faint or under-fed.

Only between the twilight hours
Under the window-panes she walks
Shrewdly among the scented flowers
Nor snaps the soft nasturtium stalks,
Uttering still her plaintive cries
And Four-paws, from the house, replies,

Leaps from his cushion to the floor,
Down the brick passage scantly lit,
Waits wailing at the outer door
Till one arise and open it—
Then from the swinging lantern's light
Runs to his Mother in the night.

Helen Parry Eden

THE GARDENER'S CAT

THE gardener's cat's called Mignonette,
She hates the cold, she hates the wet,
She sits among the hothouse flowers
And sleeps for hours and hours and hours.

She dreams she is a tiger fierce
With great majestic claws that pierce,
She sits by the hot-water pipes
And dreams about a coat of stripes;

And in her slumbers she will go
And stalk the sullen buffalo,
And when he roars across the brake
She does not wink, she does not wake.

It must be perfectly immense
To dream with such magnificence,
And pass the most inclement day
In this indeed stupendous way.

She dreams of India's sunny clime,
And only wakes at dinner-time,
But even then she does not stir
But waits till milk is brought to her.

How nice to be the gardener's cat,
She troubles not for mouse or rat,
But, when it's coming down in streams,
She sits among the flowers and dreams.

The gardener's cat would be the thing,
Her dreams are so encouraging;
She dreams that she's a tiger, yet
She's just a cat called Mignonette!

.   .   .   .

The moral's this, my little man—
Sleep 'neath life's hailstones when you can,
And if you're humble in estate,
Dream splendidly, at any rate!

Patrick Chalmers

NICHOLAS NYE

THISTLE and darnell and dock grew there,
    And a bush, in the corner, of may,
On the orchard wall I used to sprawl
    In the blazing heat of the day;

Half asleep and half awake,
  While the birds went twittering by,
And nobody there my lone to share
  But Nicholas Nye.

Nicholas Nye was lean and gray,
  Lame of a leg and old,
More than a score of donkey's years
  He had seen since he was foaled;
He munched the thistles, purple and spiked,
  Would sometimes stoop and sigh,
And turn to his head, as if he said,
  "Poor Nicholas Nye!"

Alone with his shadow he'd drowse in the meadow,
  Lazily swinging his tail,
At break of day he used to bray,—
  Not much too hearty and hale;
But a wonderful gumption was under his skin,
  And a clear calm light in his eye,
And once in a while: he'd smile:—
  Would Nicholas Nye.

Seem to be smiling at me, he would,
  From his bush in the corner, of may,—
Bony and ownerless, widowed and worn,
  Knobble-kneed, lonely and gray;
And over the grass would seem to pass
  'Neath the deep dark blue of the sky,
Something much better than words between me
  And Nicholas Nye.

But dusk would come in the apple boughs,
  The green of the glow-worm shine,
The birds in nest would crouch to rest,
  And home I'd trudge to mine;
And there, in the moonlight, dark with dew,
  Asking not wherefore nor why,
Would brood like a ghost, and as still as a post,
  Old Nicholas Nye.

                    Walter de la Mare

THE TERRIBLE ROBBER MEN

O! I WISH the sun was bright in the sky,
　And the fox was back in his den, O!
For always I'm hearing the passing by
　Of the terrible robber men, O!
　　The terrible robber men.

O! what does the fox carry over the rye
　When it's bright in the morn again, O!
And what is it making the lonesome cry
　With the terrible robber men, O!
　　The terrible robber men.

O! I wish the sun was bright in the sky,
　And the fox was back in his den, O!
For always I'm hearing the passing by
　Of the terrible robber men, O!
　　The terrible robber men.

Padraic Colum

THERE ARE NO WOLVES IN ENGLAND NOW

THERE are no wolves in England now, nor any grizzly bears;
You could not meet them after dark upon the attic stairs.

When Nanna goes to fetch the tea there is no need at all
To leave the nursery door ajar in case you want to call.

And mother says, in fairy tales, those bits are never true
That tell you all the dreadful deeds that wicked fairies do.

And wouldn't it be silly for a great big girl like me
To be the leastest bit afraid of things that couldn't be?

Rose Fyleman

THE SLEEPYTOWN EXPRESS

JUST beyond the rainbow's rim a river ripples down
Beneath a bridge, around a bend, and flows through Sleepy-
　　town—
Through Sleepytown, where goblins toil to fashion wondrous
　　toys
And make up fascinating games for little girls and boys.

And automobiles, just the size for little hands to drive,
Await to whirl you all about as soon as you arrive.
But no one ever is allowed in Sleepytown, unless
He goes to bed in time to take the Sleepytown Express!

I know a foolish little boy who always starts to whine
When he is asked to trot upstairs before it's half-past nine.
And often he will stamp his feet and shake his tousled head,
And make a racket, even then, when he is sent to bed.
Of course, when he has said his prayers it always is too
    late
To catch the Sleepytown Express—it starts at half-past
    eight.
And so, in all his long, long life—he's five years old this fall—
That little boy has never been to Sleepytown at all.

But other wiser little boys, and little girls as well,
As soon as eight o'clock has struck rush right upstairs, pell-
    mell,
Get off their clothes and say their prayers, just of their own
    accord,
And, when the train comes rolling in, they're there to climb
    aboard.
Then through a long, delightful night they wander up and
    down
And have a most exciting time in queer old Sleepytown;
And not for cake or anything that children could possess
Would any of them ever miss the Sleepytown Express!

James J. Montague

POOR HENRY

THICK in its glass
    The physic stands,
Poor Henry lifts
    Distracted hands;
His round cheek wans
    In the candlelight,
To smell that smell!
    To see that sight!

Finger and thumb
   Clinch his small nose,
A gurgle, a gasp,
   And down it goes;
Scowls Henry now;
   But mark that cheek,
Sleek with the bloom
   Of health next week!

Walter de la Mare

TONGUES

Tongues there are that naught can say;
Tongues there are that run away;
Tongues that lure the fairies nigher;
Tongues that set the world on fire;
Bad's the tongue that rules his master;
Such lead ever to disaster.

Early make your tongue obey;
Always know what it will say;
Bid it say what you think best,
Hold it in for all the rest:
Fairies ban all tittle-tattle,
Wise men shun the tongues that rattle.

T. Sturge Moore

HENRY KING

The Chief Defect of Henry King
Was chewing little bits of String.
At last he swallowed some which tied
Itself in ugly Knots inside.

Physicians of the Utmost Fame
Were called at once; but when they came
They answered, as they took their Fees,
"There is no Cure for this Disease.

Henry will very soon be dead."
His Parents stood about his Bed
Lamenting his Untimely Death,
When Henry, with his Latest Breath,

Cried, "Oh, my Friends, be warned by me,
That Breakfast, Dinner, Lunch, and Tea
Are all the Human Frame requires . . ."
With that, the Wretched Child expires.

Hilaire Belloc

JIM

THERE was a Boy whose name was Jim;
His Friends were very good to him.
They gave him Tea, and Cakes, and Jam,
And slices of delicious Ham,
And Chocolate with pink inside
And little Tricycles to ride,
And read him Stories through and through,
And even took him to the Zoo—
But there it was the dreadful Fate
Befell him, which I now relate.

You know—at least you ought to know,
For I have often told you so—
That Children never are allowed
To leave their Nurses in a Crowd;
Now this was Jim's especial Foible,
He ran away when he was able,
And on this inauspicious day
He slipped his hand and ran away!

He hadn't gone a yard when—Bang!
With open Jaws, a Lion sprang,
And hungrily began to eat
The Boy: beginning at his feet.
Now, just imagine how it feels
When first your toes and then your heels,

And then by gradual degrees,
Your shins and ankles, calves and knees,
Are slowly eaten, bit by bit.
No wonder Jim detested it!
No wonder that he shouted "Hi!"

The Honest Keeper heard his cry,
Though very fat he almost ran
To help the little gentleman.
"Ponto!" he ordered as he came
(For Ponto was the Lion's name),
"Ponto!" he cried, with angry Frown,
"Let go, Sir! Down, Sir! Put it down!"
The Lion made a sudden stop,
He let the Dainty Morsel drop,
And slunk reluctant to his Cage,
Snarling with Disappointed Rage.
But when he bent him over Jim,
The Honest Keeper's Eyes were dim.
The Lion having reached his Head,
The Miserable Boy was dead!

When Nurse informed his Parents, they
Were more Concerned than I can say:—
His Mother, as She dried her eyes,
Said, "Well—it gives me no surprise,
He would not do as he was told!"
His Father, who was self-controlled,
Bade all the children round attend
To James's miserable end,
And always keep a-hold of Nurse
For fear of finding something worse.

Hilaire Belloc

CHRISTMAS ISLAND

Fringed with coral, floored with lava,
Three-score leagues to south of Java,
So is Christmas Island charted
By geographers blind-hearted,

—Just a dot, by their dull notion,
On the burning Indian Ocean;
Merely a refreshment station
For the birds in long migration;
Its pomegranates, custard-apples
That the dancing sunshine dapples,
Cocoanuts with milky hollows
Only feast wing-weary swallows
Or the tropic fowl there dwelling.
Don't believe a word they're telling!
Christmas Island, though it seem land,
Is a floating bit of dreamland
Gone adrift from childhood, planted
By the winds with seeds enchanted,
Seeds of candied plum and cherry:
Here the Christmas Saints make merry.

Even saints must have vacation;
So they chose from all creation
As a change from iceberg castles
Hung with snow in loops and tassels,
Christmas Island for a summer
Residence. The earliest comer
Is our own saint, none diviner,
Santa Claus. His ocean-liner
Is a sleigh that's scudding fast.
Mistletoe climbs up the mast,
And the sail, so full of caper,
Is of tissue wrapping-paper.
As he steers, he hums a carol;
But instead of fur apparel
Smudged with soot, he's spick and spandy
In white linen, dear old dandy.
With a Borealis sash on,
And a palm-leaf hat in fashion
Wreathed about with holly berry.
Welcome, Santa! Rest you merry!

Next, his chubby legs bestriding
Such a Yule-log, who comes riding

Overseas, the feast to dish up,
But—aha!—the boys' own bishop,
Good St. Nicholas! And listen!
Out of Denmark, old Jule-nissen,
Kindly goblin, bent, rheumatic,
In the milk-bowl set up attic
For his Christmas cheer, comes bobbing
Through the waves. He'll be hob-nobbing
With Knecht Clobes, Dutchman true,
Sailing in a wooden shoe.
When the sunset gold enamels
All the sea, three cloudy camels
Bear the Kings with stately paces,
Taking islands for oases,
While a star-boat brings Kriss Kringle.
Singing *Noël* as they mingle,
Drinking toasts in sunshine sherry,
How the Christmas Saints make merry!

While a gray contralto pigeon
Coos that loving is religion,
How they laugh and how they rollick,
How they fill the isle with frolic.
Up the Christmas Trees they clamber,
Lighting candles rose and amber,
Till the sudden moonbeams glisten.
Then all kneel but old Jule-nissen,
Who, a heathen elf stiff-jointed,
Doffs his night-cap, red and pointed;
For within the moon's pale luster
They behold bright figures cluster;
Their adoring eyes look on a
Silver-throned serene Madonna,
With the Christ-Child, rosy sweeting,
Smiling to their loyal greeting.
Would that on this Holy Night
We might share such blissful sight,
—We might find a fairy ferry
To that isle where saints make merry!

Katherine Lee Bates

THE FAIRIES HAVE NEVER A PENNY TO SPEND

THE Fairies have never a penny to spend,
    They haven't a thing put by,
But theirs is the dower of bird and of flower
    And theirs are the earth and the sky.
And though you should live in a palace of gold
    Or sleep in a dried-up ditch,
You could never be poor as the fairies are,
      And never as rich.

Since ever and ever the world began
    They have danced like a ribbon of flame,
They have sung their song through the centuries long
    And yet it is never the same.
And though you be foolish or though you be wise,
    With hair of silver or gold,
You could never be young as the fairies are,
      And never as old.

Rose Fyleman

FAIRIES

THERE are fairies at the bottom of our garden!
    It's not so very, very far away;
You pass the gardener's shed and you just keep straight
    ahead—
    I do so hope they've really come to stay.
There's a little wood, with moss in it and beetles,
    And a little stream that quietly runs through;
You wouldn't think they'd dare to come merry-making
        there—
        Well, they do.

There are fairies at the bottom of our garden!
    They often have a dance on summer nights;
The butterflies and bees make a lovely little breeze,
    And the rabbits stand about and hold the lights.

Did you know that they could sit upon the moonbeams
    And pick a little star to make a fan,
And dance away up there in the middle of the air?
          Well, they can.

There are fairies at the bottom of our garden!
    You cannot think how beautiful they are;
They all stand up and sing when the Fairy Queen and King
    Come gently floating down upon their car.
The King is very proud and *very* handsome;
    The Queen—now can you guess who that could be
(She's a little girl all day, but at night she steals away)?
          Well—it's *Me!*

                                        Rose Fyleman

IN THE MOONLIGHT

            THE Fairies dance the livelong night
            Across the moonlit hill;
            The moonbeams dance along the lake;
            The western wind is still.
            The waters make a little sound
            More sweet than music far—
            Oh, let me fly across the world
            To where the Fairies are!

                          Norreys Jephson O'Conor

THE DANCE

WHEN good-nights have been prattled, and prayers have
        been said,
And the last little sunbeam is tucked up in bed,
Then, skirting the trees on a carpet of snow,
The elves and the fairies come out in a row.
    With a preening of wings
    They are forming in rings;
Pirouetting and setting they cross and advance
In a ripple of laughter, and pair for a dance.

And it's oh for the boom of the fairy bassoon,
And the oboes and horns as they strike up a tune,

And the twang of the harps and the sigh of the lutes,
And the clash of the cymbals, the purl of the flutes;
    And the fiddles sail in
    To the musical din,
While the chief all on fire, with a flame for a hand,
Rattles on the gay measure and stirs up his band.

With a pointing of toes and a lifting of wrists
They are off through the whirls and the twirls and the twists;
Thread the mazes of marvelous figures, and chime
With a bow to a curtsey, and always keep time:
    All the gallants and girls
    In their diamonds and pearls,
And their gauze and their sparkles, designed for a dance
By the leaders of fairy-land fashion in France.

But the old lady fairies sit out by the trees,
And the old beaux attend them as pert as you please.
They quiz the young dancers and scorn their display,
And deny any grace to the dance of to-day;
    "In Oberon's reign,"
    So they're heard to complain,
"When we went out at night we could temper our fun
With some manners in dancing, but now there are none."

But at last, though the music goes gallantly on,
And the dancers are none of them weary or gone,
When the gauze is in rags and the hair is awry,
Comes a light in the East and a sudden cock-cry.
    With a scurry of fear
    Then they all disappear,
Leaving never a trace of their gay little selves
Or the winter-night dance of the fairies and elves.

                                        R. C. Lehmann

ADVENTURE

BLACK wave the trees in the forest
    And a rough wind hurries by,
But the swineherd's toddling daughter
    Knows where fallen pine-cones lie.

And girt in a snowy apron
　　She scampers, alert and gay,
To the hidden pool in the hollow
　　Where the wan witch people play.

They smile, the wee wrinkled women,
　　They creep to her pinafore;
And lay in her lap strange treasures
　　Trolls brought from the ocean's floor.

And they marvel at her blonde tresses
　　And braid them with scented fern;
And they lave her dusty, brown ankles
　　With snow water from the burn.

But nobody listens, or heeds them,
　　The swineherd hews a new trail,
The swineherd's wife in the cottage
　　Pours the sour milk from the pail.

And little Gerta lags homeward
　　Dream-shod through the shadows deep;
Her eyelids heavy with wonder—
　　They whisper, "She's been asleep."

Laura Benét

LULLABY

SLEEP, little baby, sleep and rest,
The moon hangs low in the crimson west;
As the Christ-child slept at Mary's breast,
Sleep, little baby, sleep!

Hush, little baby, hush and dream
Of golden boats on a silver stream,
And let my love creep in between.
Hush, little baby, hush!

Rest, little baby, rest and sleep,
Far in the fields are the little white sheep.
Safe in my arms in slumber deep
　Rest, little baby, rest!

Elinor Chipp

AT BEDTIME

DARLING, my darling!—It was mother singing low,
And I heard the little fishes through the water come and go;
I saw the little tree-leaves fluttering in the sky,
Green amid the blueness where the little clouds go by.

There are many, many darlings for the mothers far and wide,
But my only mother sings to me, to me and none beside;
I shut my eyes to hear her and she sings me far away,
I open them to see her and I know that she will say:

Darling, my darling!—I was down among the grass,
The clover-blossoms nodded, so the daisies let me pass;
I was up among the tree-tops and flying with a bird,
But when he sang his song for me, 'twas *Darling* that I heard.
                    Mrs. Schuyler Van Renssellaer

IN A LOW ROCKING–CHAIR

HEAVEN is a fine place, a fine place entirely.
Oh, like Killarney in rose-time 'twill be,
With Mary in a blue gown flowered like the meadow,
And Little Christ as like a rose
As any rose you'd see.

Himself is high upon a throne; but Herself sits a-rocking
In a low rocking-chair, her babe on her knee.
Sure, now he'd go to sleep at once, and Herself a-crooning,
And not lie with his eyes wide
The way you'd treat me.

Now fasten down your eyelids and get you gone a-sleeping,
And in a little heart-beat in heaven you'll be,
And when you've bowed to Himself, and made Herself a
        curtsey,
And kissed the Little Rose o' Heaven,
Come back along to me.
                    Helen Coale Crew

SLUMBER SONG

DROWSILY come the sheep
From the place where the pastures be,
  By a dusty lane
  To the fold again,
First one, and then two, and three:
  First one, then two, by the paths of sleep
  Drowsily come the sheep.

Drowsily come the sheep,
And the shepherd is singing low:
  After eight comes nine
  In the endless line,
They come, and then in they go.
  First eight, then nine, by the paths of sleep
  Drowsily come the sheep.

Drowsily come the sheep
And they pass through the sheepfold door;
  After one comes two,
  · After one comes two,
Comes two and then three and four.
  First one, then two, by the paths of sleep,
  Drowsily come the sheep.

Louis V. Ledoux

NOD

SOFTLY along the road of evening,
  In a twilight dim with rose,
Wrinkled with age, and drenched with dew,
  Old Nod, the shepherd, goes.

His drowsy flock streams on before him,
  Their fleeces charged with gold,
To where the sun's last beam leans low
  On Nod the shepherd's fold.

The hedge is quick and green with briar,
   From their sand the conies creep;
And all the birds that fly in heaven
   Flock singing home to sleep.

His lambs outnumber a noon's roses,
   Yet, when night's shadows fall,
His blind old sheep-dog, Slumber-soon,
   Misses not one of all.

His are the quiet steeps of dreamland,
   The waters of no-more-pain,
His ram's bell rings 'neath an arch of stars,
   "Rest, rest, and rest again."

Walter de la Mare

THE CHILDREN

A LETTER TO ELSA

ROSE-RED, russet-brown,
Were there elves in your town?
When you breathed little words
Would they flock in like birds?
Did you eat magic fruit
For your supper to suit
The spiced garden, the dew,
And the sweetness of you?
Had the elf-mother spread
A low table with bread
And milk white as the moon?
Did you find very soon
A bed white as the milk,
Smooth and tender with silk,
Where you laid your tired head,
Russet-brown, rose-red?

Russet-eyes, rose-mouth,
When the wind's from the south,
When he rustles and stirs
In the plumed junipers,
Does he bring coaxing words
From the sly mocking-birds?
Do they call you to come
Where the wind is at home
When he rests from his trips?
Elf-locks, scarlet-lips,
I am wiser than they.
Hearken now what *I* say!

I will build you a house
Velvet-gray like a mouse,
Snug and shy among trees.
There shall be if you please

Peacocks pacing the walks,
And a fountain that talks,
And a playmate for you,
And a green cockatoo.
Bees shall dwell in the phlox
And the gay hollyhocks,
And their honey will be
In the sycamore tree.
Every dusk I will spread
A low table with bread
And a brown honey-comb
(When the bees have gone home),
And heaped mulberry-fruit,
(While the thrush tries his flute),
And milk white as the moon.
Then if bed-time come soon,
You shall lay your dear head
On a smooth silken bed
To the thrush-lullabies,
Russet-brown, rose-red,
Rose-mouth, russet-eyes!

Grace Hazard Conkling

HAROLD AT TWO YEARS OLD

OPEN your gates for him
    Eager and new!
All the world waits for him;
    What will he do?

Dear incompletenesses
    Blossoming hours!
Feed him with sweetnesses!
    Heap him with flowers!

See how he crumbles them,
    Shouts like a man!
Tosses and tumbles them
    Wide as he can!

Vain is admonishment,
    Sermons in vain:—
Gleeful astonishment!
    At it again!

Wildness of babyhood!
    Passion of play!
Who but a baby would
    Wish it away?

Rapt from the Mystery,
    Reft from the whole,
Hast thou a history,
    Innocent soul?

Gaze we with wondering,
    Baby, on thee;—
Sped o'er what sundering
    Strait of the sea?

Borne to us hitherward,
    Ah! from what shore?
Voyaging whitherward,
    Child, evermore?

Little he'll tell for us!
    Nothing he knows!
Clear like a bell for us
    Laughs as he goes!

Powers supersensible
    Breathe through the boy
Incomprehensible
    Promise of joy!

Frederick W. H. Myers

THE DAUGHTER AT EVENING

BEFORE her supper where she sits
    With every favored toe she plays,
Singing whatever ballad fits
    The past romances of her days.

To Betsey-Jane 31

The dusk comes softly to her room,
  The night winds in the branches stir;
That nations battle to their doom
  Across the seas, is naught to her.

For what she does not know, she eats,
  A worm, a twig, a block, a fly,
And every novel thing she meets
  Is bitten into bye and bye.

She, from the blankets of her bed,
  Holds no opinion on the war,
But munches on her thumb instead,
  This being what a thumb is for.

The troubles that invade the day,
  On some remote to-morrow creep;
Comes Bertha with the supper tray,
  And—now I laymen down ee beep.

Robert Nathan

TO BETSEY–JANE, ON HER DESIRING TO GO IN-CONTINENTLY TO HEAVEN

My Betsey-Jane, it would not do,
For what would Heaven make of you,
A little, honey-loving bear,
Among the Blessèd Babies there?

Nor do you dwell with us in vain
Who tumble and get up again
And try, with bruisèd knees, to smile—
Sweet, you are blessèd all the while

And we in you: so wait, they'll come
To take your hand and fetch you home,
In Heavenly leaves to play at tents
With all the Holy Innocents.

Helen Parry Eden

A LITTLE PERSON

Sunny hair and eyes of wonder,
    Baby-lips apart,
Vivid mother-breast, whereunder
    Laughs a childish heart—
What have you to do with learning
    Wiser bliss or woe?
Take our gold; the cost of earning
    You shall never know.

You shall joy as for another,
    Find it strange to weep,
Play at being wife and mother,
    Dream, and fall asleep;
All we toil for, all we doubt of,
    All we yearn to see,
All our hopes have sneered us out of—
    You shall prove, and be.

You shall purify deceiving
    With a glad disdain,
Beautifully unbelieving
    Meet the eyes of pain,
Dance through hells undreamed-of, bringing
    Benefits unguessed:
Unto shame, a sound of singing,
    Unto passion, rest.

Sunny hair and eyes of wonder,
    Baby-lips apart,
Vivid mother-breast, whereunder
    Laughs a childish heart,
Soul unsinful, unforgiven,
    Voice of dawn and dew—
God one morning, glad of heaven,
    Laughed—and that was you!

                                        Brian Hooker

TO MY LITTLE SON

In your face I sometimes see
Shadowings of the man to be,
And eager, dream of what my son
Will be in twenty years and one.

But when you are to manhood grown,
And all your manhood ways are known,
Then shall I, wistful, try to trace
The child you once were in your face?

Julia Johnson Davis

WISHES FOR MY SON

Now, my son, is life for you,
And I wish you joy of it,—
Joy of power in all you do,
Deeper passion, better wit
Than I had who had enough,
Quicker life and length thereof,
More of every gift but love.

Love I have beyond all men,
Love that now you share with me—
What have I to wish you then
But that you be good and free,
And that God to you may give
Grace in stronger days to live?

For I wish you more than I
Ever knew of glorious deed,
Though no rapture passed me by
That an eager heart could heed,
Though I followed heights and sought
Things the sequel never brought.

Wild and perilous holy things
Flaming with a martyr's blood,
And the joy that laughs and sings
Where a foe must be withstood,

Joy of headlong happy chance
Leading on the battle dance.

But I found no enemy,
No man in a world of wrong,
That Christ's word of charity
Did not render clean and strong—
Who was I to judge my kind,
Blindest groper of the blind?

God to you may give the sight
And the clear, undoubting strength
Wars to knit for single right,
Freedom's war to knit at length,
And to win through wrath and strife,
To the sequel of my life.

But for you, so small and young,
Born on Saint Cecilia's Day,
I in more harmonious song
Now for nearer joys should pray—
Simple joys: the natural growth
Of your childhood and your youth,
Courage, innocence, and truth:
These for you, so small and young,
In your hand and heart and tongue.

Thomas MacDonagh

WITH A FIRST READER

DEAR little child, this little book
   Is less a primer than a key
To sunder gates where wonder waits
   Your "Open Sesame!"

These tiny syllables look large;
   They'll fret your wide, bewildered eyes:
But "Is the cat upon the mat?"
   Is passport to the skies.

For, yet awhile, and you shall turn
   From Mother Goose to Avon's swan;
From Mary's lamb to grim Khayyám
   And Mancha's mad-wise Don.

You'll writhe at Jean Valjean's disgrace;
   And D'Artagnan and Ivanhoe
Shall steal your sleep; and you shall weep
   At Sidney Carton's woe.

You'll find old Chaucer young once more,
   Beaumont and Fletcher fierce with fire;
At your demand, John Milton's hand
   Shall wake his ivory lyre.

And learning other tongues, you'll learn
   All times are one; all men, one race;
Hear Homer speak, as Greek to Greek;
   See Dante, face to face.

Arma virumque shall resound;
   And Horace wreathe his rhymes afresh;
You'll rediscover Laura's lover,
   Meet Gretchen in the flesh.

Oh, could I find for the first time
   The Churchyard Elegy again!
Re-taste the sweets of new-found Keats;
   Read Byron now as then!

Make haste to wander these old roads,
   O envied little parvenue;
For all things trite shall leap alight
   And bloom again for you!

                      Rupert Hughes

TO A CHILD

WITH A COPY OF THE AUTHOR'S "HANSEL AND GRETEL"

HERE, Nancy, let me take your hand,
And lead you back to Fairyland,
In this famed tale of long ago,
Told often in the sunset glow

By mothers, lest their children roam
In the dark forest, far from home.
This lesson learn: that mothers know
Where lurks, perchance, a hidden foe;
And though you may not understand
The reason in each kind command,
It is to keep you from the fear
That terrified the children here.
Learn, too, how God's own angels keep
Your ways by day, your dreams, asleep.

Norreys Jephson O'Conor

THE LITTLE BOY TO THE LOCOMOTIVE

Big iron horse with lifted head,
Panting beneath the station shed,
You are my dearest dream come true;—
I love my Dad; I worship you!

Your noble heart is filled with fire,
For all your toil, you never tire,
And though you're saddled-up in steel,
Somewhere, inside, I *know* you feel.

All night in dreams when you pass by,
You breathe out stars that fill the sky,
And now, when all my dreams are true,
I hardly dare come close to you.

Benjamin R. C. Low

THE LOCOMOTIVE TO THE LITTLE BOY

Boy, whose little, confiding hand
Your father holds, why do you stand
Staring in wonderment at me,—
Poor thing of iron that I be?

Your unsophisticated eyes
Are full of beautiful surprise;
And oh, how wonderful you are,
You little, golden morning-star!

Poor thing of iron that I be,
A mortal man imagined me;
But you—you drop of morning dew—
God and His heaven are globed in you.

Benjamin R. C. Low

BABYLON

THE child alone a poet is:
Spring and Fairyland are his.
Truth and Reason show but dim,
And all's poetry with him.
Rhyme and music flow in plenty
For the lad of one-and-twenty,
But Spring for him is no more now
Than daisies to a munching cow;
Just a cheery pleasant season,
Daisy buds to live at ease on.
He's forgotten how he smiled
And shrieked at snowdrops when a child,
Or wept one evening secretly
For April's glorious misery.
Wisdom made him old and wary
Banishing the lords of Faery.
Wisdom made a breach and battered
Babylon to bits: she scattered
To the hedges and the ditches
All our nursery gnomes and witches.
Lob and Puck, poor frantic elves,
Drag their treasures from the shelves.
Jack the Giant-killer's gone,
Mother Goose and Oberon,
Bluebeard and King Solomon.
Robin, and Red Riding Hood
Take together to the wood,
And Sir Galahad lies hid
In a cave with Captain Kidd.
None of all the magic hosts,
None remain but a few ghosts

Of timorous heart, to linger on
Weeping for lost Babylon.

Robert Graves

TO A CHILD

THE greatest poem ever known
Is one all poets have outgrown:
The poetry, innate, untold,
Of being only four years old.

Still young enough to be a part
Of Nature's great impulsive heart,
Born comrade of bird, beast and tree
And unselfconscious as the bee—

And yet with lovely reason skilled
Each day new paradise to build,
Elate explorer of each sense,
Without dismay, without pretence!

In your unstained transparent eyes
·There is no conscience, no surprise:
Life's queer conundrums you accept,
Your strange divinity still kept.

Being, that now absorbs you, all
Harmonious, unit, integral,
Will shred into perplexing bits,—
Oh, contradiction of the wits!

And Life, that sets all things in rhyme,
May make you poet, too, in time—
But there were days, O tender elf,
When you were Poetry itself!

Christopher Morley

QUANTITY AND QUALITY

THE poor have childher and to spare,
But with the quality they're rare,
Where money's scarce the childher's many,
Where money's thick you'll scarce find any,
Some wanted here, too many there—
    It's quare.

Now, if the rich and poor could share,
There'd soon be childher everywhere;
But God have pity on the mother
That gives her child up to another;
An' so you'll find a mansion bare,
A cabin rich in all that's fair—
    It's quare.

Winifred M. Letts

BOYS

I DO be thinking God must laugh
The time He makes a boy;
All element the creatures are,
And divilmint and joy.
Careless and gay as a wad in a window,
Swift as a redshanks, and wild as a hare;
Heartscalds and torments—but sorra a mother
Has got one to spare.

Winifred M. Letts

IF I SHOULD EVER BY CHANCE

IF I should ever by chance grow rich
I'll buy Codham, Cockridden, and Childerditch,
Roses, Pyrgo, and Lapwater,
And let them all to my elder daughter.
The rent I shall ask of her will be only
Each year's first violets, white and lonely,
The first primroses and orchises—
She must find them before I do, that is.

But if she finds a blossom on furze
Without rent they shall all for ever be hers,
Codham, Cockridden, and Childerditch,
Roses, Pyrgo and Lapwater,—
I shall give them all to my elder daughter.

Edward Thomas

EXPERIENCE

DEBORAH danced, when she was two,
As buttercups and daffodils do;
Spirited, frail, naïvely bold,
Her hair a ruffled crest of gold,
And whenever she spoke her voice went singing
Like water up from a fountain springing.

But now her step is quiet and slow;
She walks the way primroses go;
Her hair is yellow instead of gilt,
Her voice is losing its lovely lilt,
And in place of her wild, delightful ways
A quaint precision rules her days.

For Deborah now is three, and oh,
She knows so much that she did not know.

Aline Kilmer

AMBITION

KENTON and Deborah, Michael and Rose,
These are fine children as all the world knows,
But into my arms in my dreams every night
Come Peter and Christopher, Faith and Delight.

Kenton is tropical, Rose is pure white,
Deborah shines like a star in the night,
Michael's round eyes are as blue as the sea
And nothing on earth could be dearer to me.

But where is the baby with Faith can compare?
What is the color of Peterkin's hair?

Who can make Christopher clear to my sight,
Or show me the eyes of my daughter, Delight?

When people inquire I always just state,
"I have four nice children and hope to have eight.
Though the first four are pretty and certain to please,
Who knows but the rest will be nicer than these?"

Aline Kilmer

APOCRYPHA

WHEN John the Baptist was so young
That he had not yet learned to speak
A syllable of his native tongue,
The voice must have been shrill and weak
Wherewith his mother's heart was wrung.

When Jesus' fists uncurled to clutch
The shavings in his father's beard,
Before he learned to like to touch
The screws and nails his mother feared,
Small wandering hands had hurt her much.

When Judas was so frail a child
He sucked and slept, and little more,—
His mother, patient still, beguiled
The baby she must needs adore.
He shaped a kiss: all day she smiled.

Babette Deutsch

THE BACCHANTE TO HER BABE

Scherzo

COME, sprite, and dance! The sun is up,
The wind runs laughing down the sky
That brims with morning like a cup;
Sprite, we must race him,
We must chase him,
You and I!
And skim across the fuzzy heather,
You and joy and I together
Whirling by!

You merry little roll of fat!
Made warm to kiss, and smooth to pat,
And round to toy with, like a cub,
To put one's nozzle in and rub
And breathe you in like breath of kine,
Like juice of vine,
That sets my morning heart a-tingling,
Dancing, jingling,
All the glad abandon mingling
Of wind and wine!

Sprite, you are love, and you are joy,
A happiness, a dream, a toy,
A god to laugh with,
Love to chaff with,
The sun come down in tangled gold,
The moon to kiss and spring to hold.

There was a time once, long ago,
Long, oh, long since . . . I scarcely know;
Almost I had forgot . . .
There was a time when you were not,
You merry sprite, save as a strain,
The strange dull pain
Of green buds swelling
In warm straight dwelling
That must burst to the April rain.
A little heavy I was then,
And dull, and glad to rest.   And when
The travail came
In searing flame . . .
But, sprite, that was so long ago!
A century!   I scarcely know.
Almost I had forgot
When you were not.

So, little sprite, come dance with me!
The sun is up, the wind is free!
Come now and trip it,
Romp and skip it;

Earth is young and so are we.
Sprite, you and I will dance together
On the heather,
Glad with all the procreant earth,
With all the fruitage of the trees,
And golden pollen on the breeze;
With plants that bring the grain to birth,
With beast and bird
Feathered and furred,
With youth and hope and life and love
And joy thereof,
While we are part of all, we two,
For my glad burgeoning in you!

So, merry little roll of fat,
Made warm to kiss and smooth to pat
And round to toy with, like a cub,
To put one's nozzle in and rub;
My god to laugh with,
Love to chaff with,
Come and dance beneath the sky,
You and I!
Look out with those round wondering eyes,
And squirm, and gurgle—and grow wise!

Eunice Tietjens

MOTHER–PRAYER

"Lord, make my loving a guard for them
    Day and night,
Let never pathway be hard for them;
    Keep all bright!
Let not harsh touch of a thorn for them
    Wound their ease—
All of the pain I have borne for them
    Spare to these!"

So I would pray for them,
Kneeling to God
Night and day for them.

"Lord, let the pain life must bring to them
   Make them strong,
Keep their hearts white though grief cling to them
   All life long,
Let all the joys Thou dost keep from them
   At Thy will
Give to them power to reap from them
   Courage still!"

So I must ask for them,
Leaving to God
His own task for them.

                Margaret Widdemer

PRAYER

She cannot tell my name
Nor whence I came
But when at night she hears my voice below
My little girl runs quickly down the hall,
Peers through the stair bars, laughing at my call,
Yet who or what I am she does not know.
Nor can she understand
All that for her I've planned;
That the day's work without her would be vain,
Or how her laughter clears the troubled brain;
That her small hands, soft as the white rose leaf,
Can ward off grief.
Then as she runs to me, each faltering word
Seems the divinest music I have heard.
She does not know the father's love I feel,
That were she gone, her death would pierce the heart like
   steel.

O God, thy ways are dark.
Man cannot mark
Thy path upon the mountain or the sea.
We cannot read thy will or know thy mind,
Baffled by one small world thou hast designed,
Awed by the grandeur of infinity.

He who can trace
The marching stars through space,
Measure the oceans, lift the mountains up,
Scatter the perfume in the lily's cup,
Planning for æons, measuring each year,
Will this God hear?
Yes; if we call to Him in joy, dismay,
(For that is prayer) He cannot turn away,
A Father dwelling with us, not apart.
When my child's call I hear, I catch her to my heart.

Edward Bliss Reed

IDYLL

In Switzerland one idle day,
As on the grass at noon we lay,
Came a grave peasant child and stood
Watching the strangers eat their food.
And what we offered her she took
In silence, with her quiet look,
And when we rose to go, content
Without a word of thanks she went.

Another day in sleet and rain
I chose the meadow path again,
And partly turning chanced to see
My little guest-friend watching me
With eyes half hidden by her hair,
Blowing me kisses, unaware
That I had seen, and still she wore
The same grave aspect as before.

And some recall for heart's delight
A sunrise, some a snowy height,
And I a little child who stands
And gravely kisses both her hands.

Hugh Macnaghten

PORTRAIT OF A CHILD

UNCONSCIOUS of amused and tolerant eyes,
He sits among his scattered dreams, and plays.
True to no one thing long; running for praise
With something less than half begun.   He tries
To build his blocks against the furthest skies.
They fall; his soldiers tumble; but he stays
And plans and struts and laughs at fresh dismays—
Too confident and busy to be wise.
His toys are towns and temples; his commands
Bring forth vast armies trembling at his nod.
He shapes and shatters with impartial hands. . . .
And, in his crude and tireless play, I see
The savage, the creator, and the god:
All that man was and all he hopes to be.

Louis Untermeyer

PORTRAIT OF A BOY

AFTER the whipping, he crawled into bed;
Accepting the harsh fact with no great weeping.
How funny uncle's hat had looked striped red!
He chuckled silently.   The moon came, sweeping
A black frayed rag of tattered cloud before
In scorning; very pure and pale she seemed,
Flooding his bed with radiance.   On the floor
Fat motes danced.   He sobbed; closed his eyes and dreamed.
Warm sand flowed round him.   Blurts of crimson light
Splashed the white grains like blood.   Past the cave's
      mouth
Shone with a large fierce splendor, wildly bright,
The crooked constellations of the South;

Here the Cross swung; and there, affronting Mars,
The Centaur stormed aside a froth of stars.
Within, great casks like wattled aldermen
Sighed of enormous feasts, and cloth of gold
Glowed on the walls like hot desire.   Again,
Beside webbed purples from some galleon's hold,

A black chest bore the skull and bones in white
Above a scrawled "Gunpowder!" By the flames,
Decked out in crimson, gemmed with syenite,
Hailing their fellows by outrageous names
The pirates sat and diced. Their eyes were moons.
"Doubloons!" they said. The words crashed gold.
    " Doubloons!"

Stephen Vincent Benét

WEE HUGHIE

HE's gone to school, wee Hughie,
    An' him not four,
Sure I saw the fright was in him
    When he left the door.

But he took a hand o' Denny,
    An' a hand o' Dan,
Wi' Joe's owld coat upon him—
    Och, the poor wee man!

He cut the quarest figure,
    More stout nor thin;
An' trottin' right an' steady
    Wi' his toes turned in.

I watched him to the corner
    O' the big turf stack,
An' the more his feet went forrit,
    Still his head turned back.

He was lookin', would I call him—
    Och, my heart was woe—
Sure it's lost I am without him,
    But he be to go.

I followed to the turnin'
    When they passed it by,
God help him, he was cryin',
    An', maybe, so was I.

Elizabeth Shane

YOUTH AND AGE

BARGAIN

With his unspent youth
Like a penny in his hand,
See him stand!
There's a look on his face
Like a child that comes
To the market-place
After tops and drums.

With his youth—his youth
As a thing that he can spend—
See him run!
And what will he have for
His bargain at the end
When it's done?

I have asked old men
With their empty purses,
I have heard the tale
Each one rehearses,
And on the last page
They have all bought age.
They have all bought age.

When youth is spent
A penny at a fair,
The old men tell
Of the bargains there.
There was this and that
For a price and a wage,
But when they came away
They had all bought age.

Louise Driscoll

48

TO ONE OLDER

MOCKING the water with their wings
The blue kingfishers scream,
Where willows bend, like silver flames,
Along the curving stream.
　I cannot be as calm as you,
　Seeing the sky so deeply blue.

On arching sprays of goldenrod
The nervous warblers sing,
Drunk with the lavish sunlight
The yellow daisies fling.
　How can you keep from dancing, now
　Gold butterflies have taught you how?

To-day the world is blue and gold,
A chain of rich surprise,
You glimpse the hidden glory
Of the pain that underlies.
　I see but colors gaily strung,
　Forgive me that I am so young.

Marion M. Boyd

A GIRL'S MOOD

I LOVE a prayer-book;
I love a thorn-tree
That blows in the grass
As white as can be.

I love an old house
Set down in the sun,
And the windy old roads
That thereabout run.

I love blue, thin frocks;
Green stones one and all;
A sky full of stars,
A rose at the fall.

A lover I love;
Oh, had I but one,
I would give him all these,
Myself, and the sun!

Lizette Woodworth Reese

A SONG OF DILIGENCE

BE still, my little, dancing feet
  That would go satin-shod!
The road that leads to Workaday
  Is long, and straight, and broad.

Be still, my little, eager hands
  That clutch at wing and bloom!
The dust-cloth needs a quiet grip,
  And steady hands, a broom.

Be still, my little, singing voice
  That reaches for a word!
The diligent and competent
  Are seen, and never heard.

Be still, my little, restless heart
  That flutters at a glance!
What would a little kitchen maid
  Be doing with romance?

Helen Frazee-Bower

DISCOVERY

UNTIL my lamp and I
Stood close together by the glass,
I had not ever noticed
I was a comely lass.

My aunts have always nodded,
"Sweet child,
She has a gentle soul
And mild."

And so, one night,
I took my lamp and said
"I'll look upon my gentle soul
Before I go to bed."

I could not find it; no,
But gazing hard I spied
Something much more near to me,
White-armed and amber-eyed.

And as I looked I seemed to feel
Warm hands upon my breast,
Where never any hands but mine
Were known to rest.

And as I looked my startled thoughts
Winged up in happy flight,
And circled like mad butterflies
About the light.

I went to bed without my soul,
And I had no mind to care,
For a joyful little sin
Slept pillowed on my hair.

I went to bed without my soul—
What difference to me?—
I had a joyful little sin
For company.

And that is what came of listening
To aunts who always lied.
They never told me that I was
White-armed and amber-eyed.

Hildegarde Flanner

IMOGEN

A LADY OF TENDER AGE

LADIES, where were your bright eyes glancing,
  Where were they glancing yesternight?
Saw ye Imogen dancing, dancing,
  Imogen dancing all in white?
  Laughed she not with a pure delight,
  Laughed she not with a joy serene,
Stepped she not with a grace entrancing,
  Slenderly girt in silken sheen?

All through the night from dusk to daytime
  Under her feet the hours were swift,
Under her feet the hours of playtime
  Rose and fell with a rhythmic lift:
  Music set her adrift, adrift,
  Music eddying towards the day
Swept her along as brooks in Maytime
  Carry the freshly falling may.

Ladies, life is a changing measure,
  Youth is a lilt that endeth soon;
Pluck ye never so fast at pleasure,
  Twilight follows the longest noon.
  Nay, but here is a lasting boon,
  Life for hearts that are old and chill,
Youth undying for hearts that treasure
  Imogen dancing, dancing still.

Henry Newbolt

A NEW HAMPSHIRE BOY

UNDER Monadnock,
  Fold on fold,
The world's fat kingdoms
  Lie unrolled.

Far in the blue south
  City-smoke, swirled,
Marks the dwellings
  Of the kings of the world.

Old kings and broken,
  Soon to die,
Once you had little,
  As little as I.

Smoke of the city,
  Blow in my eyes—
Blind me a little,
  Make me wise.

Dust of the city,
  Blow and gust—
Make me, like all men,
  Color of dust.

I stand on Monadnock,
  And seem to see
Brown and purple kingdoms
  Offered to me.

Morris Bishop

YOUTH

I NEVER thought that youth would go
  Who was so blithe and fain,
Or if he strayed I thought a song
  Would call him back again.

But knowledge came one April day
  And woke me with a start—
When I walked alone in a wooded lane
  With perfect peace of heart.

Jessie B. Rittenhouse

LITTLE DIRGE

As hearts have broken, let young hearts break;
   Let slow feet tread a measure feet have trod before.
Here gleams a pathway I shall never take;
   Here dies a grief will trouble me no more.

Only swift feet may overtake desire,
   Only young hearts can soar.
My goal is beckoning from a safe hearth-fire;
   My youth is slipping out the door.

Jean Starr Untermeyer

SINCE YOUTH IS ALL FOR GLADNESS

SINCE Youth is all for gladness,
   And dreams and rainbow-skies,
For rapture and moon-madness,
   Why are Youth's eyes so wise?

Since Youth is all for vaunting
   Adventures, scorning fears—
Is there not something haunting
   In Youth's incongruous tears?

O Youth must bleed and measure
   The days and span the sea—
But Age will keep for pleasure
   What Youth thought misery.

Glenn Ward Dresbach

YOUTH

THE glory of the sunset and the night
Adorned our kingly castles and our halls,
And as we dreamed we heard with grave delight
The homage of the waves beneath our walls.

When the end came or how we do not know;
Others are wearing scarlet that was ours,
And in our castles others come and go,
Dreaming our dreams and watching from our towers.
Preston Clark

UNBELIEVER

THEY say that old age
   Is gentle and fair . . .
Why do I shiver
   At a gray hair?

Pagan, I pray to
   Beauty alone.
Ugly things leave me
   Cold as a stone.

See how my throat curves?
   How then, unstirred,
Shall I behold it
   Wrinkled and blurred?

Peace may enfold me
   Misty and bright . . .
What of my shoulders,
   Will they stay white?

It may be, old age
   Is gentle and fair . . .
Still I shall tremble
   At a gray hair.
Dorothy Dow

COMES FALL

COMES fall, and with a sound of leaves,
The wind's incorrigible stroke
Blows out the insufficient sleeves
Of my forlorn and ancient cloak.

Expect no tenement, my friend,
Beneath this scant and threadbare vest;
Alone, to my indifferent end
I go my way, and God knows best.

Robert Nathan

FAREWELL TO TOWN

Now with gray hair begins defeat,
   Our sap is running downward;
So turn we from the hurrying street,
   And look no further townward.

'Mid yonder crowds, o'er roof and mart,
   A hundred clocks are striking
The hour for us who played a part
   Which was not to their liking.

And this is wisdom: not to carp
   With wasted breath grown wordy;
For if you harp too long your harp
   Becomes a hurdy-gurdy.

For wearied hand and labored head
   That fail to gain their guerdon,
Farewell, when once the word is said
   Makes light the lifted burden.

Farewell! Far harder was the word
   To beg what men deny us.
We harped our best; a few have heard,
   And others have passed by us!

Leave strumming at the doors of inns
   To vagabonds and sharpers.
Where men seek minstrels for their sins
   They shall not lack for harpers.

So take the hint, the hands of Time
   Are pointing, not unkindly,
Back to the hills we used to climb
   While prospects beckoned blindly;

Come, Captain Age 57

To where, by wood-tracks roughly laid,
 With hoofs and cart-ruts dinted,
Some hamlet lies too still for trade,
 Where coin was never minted:

Where, cresting lone, a wind-vane stands
 High on a time-worn steeple,
And blesses with its circling hands
 A still untravelled people.

There let's away, while blood runs warm,
 Before the heart's beat weakens,
And roam again with cloud and storm
 Along the windy beacons,

And watch by field and wooded coast,
 While flying autumn yellows,
The starling gather up his host,
 The swallow call his fellows.

No need is now for looking back;
 If any wish to find us,
They, too, can follow in our track
 The road we leave behind us.

Or if they liefer would forget,
 'Tis easy to ignore us;
Farther and farther from them yet
 The road that lies before us.

Laurence Housman

COME, CAPTAIN AGE

Come, Captain Age,
With your great sea-chest full of treasure!
Under the yellow and wrinkled tarpaulin
Disclose the carved ivory
And the sandalwood inlaid with pearl;
Riches of wisdom and years.

Unfold the India shawl
With its border of emerald and orange and crimson and
    blue
Weave of a lifetime!
I shall be rich and splendid
With the spoils of the Indies of Age.

Sarah N. Cleghorn

GARDEN–SONG

" Adieu, nous n'irons plus aux champs."—CHARLES GARNIER

FAREWELL to Fields and Butterflies
And levities of Yester-year!
For we espy, and hold more dear,
The Wicket of our Destinies.

Whereby we enter, once for all,
A Garden which such Fruit doth yield
As, tasted once, no more afield
We fare where Youth holds carnival.

Farewell, fair Fields, none found amiss
When laughter was a frequent noise
And golden-hearted girls and boys
Appraised the mouth they meant to kiss.

Farewell, farewell! but for a space
We, being young, Afield might stray,
That in our Garden nod and say,
Afield is no unpleasant place.

James Branch Cabell

I'VE WORKED FOR A SILVER SHILLING

I'VE worked for a silver shilling!
I've slaved for a friend;
And ever the work was willing,
Though much to mend.

Yet of the years' achieving
Little I find
Worth pride, or hope, or grieving,
Or calling to mind.

But love and laughing youth
And a rain-washed spring:
These were truth,
And a memorable thing.

Charles W. Kennedy

TWO VOICES

THERE is a country full of wine
And liquor of the sun,
Where sap is running all the year,
And spring is never done,
Where all is good as it is fair,
And love and will are one.
Old age may never come there,
But ever in today
The people talk as in a dream
And laugh slow time away.

But would you stay as now you are,
Or as a year ago?
Oh, not as then, for then how small
The wisdom we did owe!
Or if forever as today,
How little we could know!

Then welcome age, and fear not sorrow;
Today's no better than tomorrow.
Or yesterday that flies.
By the low light in your eyes,
By the love that in me lies,
I know we grow more lovely
Growing wise.

Alice Corbin

LET ME GROW LOVELY

Let me grow lovely, growing old—
    So many fine things do:
Laces, and ivory, and gold,
    And silks need not be new;

And there is healing in old trees,
    Old streets a glamour hold;
Why may not I, as well as these,
    Grow lovely, growing old?

Karle Wilson Baker

MIDDLE–AGE

Now the last drop, both sweet and fierce,
Of passion's essence is distilled,
Ah, need we grieve?—For there is scarce
A grayness that dreams cannot gild.

The pools of art and memory keep
Reflections of our fallen towers,
And every princess there asleep,
Whom once we kissed, is always ours.

We have strange visions, and we bear
Their faint light on our brows and cheeks;
And when the silence grows more rare
It seems a lovely phantom speaks;

And shadows which at evening come
Have grace not only for the eye,
And sometime water gushes from
Fountains that have long been dry.

E. B. C. Jones

TO EARTHWARD

Love at the lips was touch
    As sweet as I could bear;
And once that seemed too much;
    I lived on air

That crossed me from sweet things,
The flow of—was it musk
From hidden grapevine springs
Down hill at dusk?

I had the swirl and ache
From sprays of honeysuckle
That when they're gathered shake
Dew on the knuckle.

I craved strong sweets, but those
Seemed strong when I was young;
The petal of the rose
It was that stung.

Now no joy but lacks salt
That is not dashed with pain
And weariness and fault;
I crave the stain

Of tears, the aftermark
Of almost too much love,
The sweet of bitter bark
And burning clove.

When stiff and sore and scarred
I take away my hand
From leaning on it hard
In grass and sand,

The hurt is not enough:
I long for weight and strength
To feel the earth as rough
To all my length.

Robert Frost

IN SUMMER

THE days drift by—as ships drift out to sea:
Morning, high noon, twilight's tranquility.

And then—the peace the honeyed evening brings
With the large moon and old rememberings.

Old memories, old raptures, old desires,
Old joys return, and Youth's immortal fires;

Old loves that still around the spirit lie
And whisper of long Summer days gone by.

O rapture of the world that crowds to-night
About my soul, and brings back lost delight,

Bid me farewell when the last stars awake,
Or else my wounded heart will break, will break!

Charles Hanson Towne

SAND DUNES AND SEA

BLUE skies and bluer sea with its white teeth showing,
Gold dunes made sweet by yellow jasmine growing,
And over sand and sea a keen wind blowing.

Gray skies and grayed days and the years swift going,
Youth's golden dunes all white with winter's snowing . . .
And in my heart the bitter wind of memory blowing.

John Richard Moreland

CONTENTED AT FORTY

SINCE more than half my hopes came true
    And more than half my fears
Are but the pleasant laughing-stock
    Of these my middle years:—

Since busy are my brain and hand
    With not ignoble aim:
Since neighbors on my help rely
    And render me the same:—

Since in our village councils deep,
    The quest of public weal,
I weigh my wits and heave my turn
    With shoulder to the wheel:—

Since early friends have weathered well,
   And triumphed o'er the tongue
That jesting told how brief should prove
   The friendship of the young:—

Since ardent youth is justified
   Of many a hope forlorn,
Now bulwarked in the very hearts
   That laughed it once to scorn:

Since still the blooming fields of May
   And burning autumn glen
Delight the eyes that these have seen
   Half threescore times and ten:—

Since children near me grow and thrive,
   Whom friendly parents lend,
That I may taste the darling joy
   Their small, sweet forms to tend:—

Shall I not bless the middle years?
   Not I for youth repine
While warmly round me cluster lives
   More dear to me than mine.

Sarah N. Cleghorn

A MINUET

ON REACHING THE AGE OF FIFTY

OLD Age, on tiptoe, lays her jeweled hand
Lightly in mine. Come, tread a stately measure,
Most gracious partner, nobly poised and bland;
   Ours be no boisterous pleasure,
But smiling conversation, with quick glance,
And memories dancing lightlier than we dance—
   Friends, who a thousand joys
Divide and double, save one joy supreme
   Which many a pang alloys.
   Let wanton girls and boys
   Cry over lovers' woes and broken toys.

Our waking life is sweeter than their dream.
Dame Nature, with unwitting hand,
  Has sparsely strewn the black abyss with lights,
Minute, remote, and numberless. We stand
  Measuring far depths and heights,
Arched over by a laughing heaven,
  Intangible and never to be scaled.
If we confess our sins, they are forgiven;
  We triumph, if we know we failed.

Tears that in youth you shed,
  Congealed to pearls, now deck your silvery hair;
Sighs breathed for loves long dead
  Frosted the glittering atoms of the air
  Into the veils you wear
Round your soft bosom and most queenly head;
  The shimmer of your gown
Catches all tints of autumn, and the dew
Of gardens where the damask roses blew;
  The myriad tapers from these arches hung
  Play on your diamonded crown;
  And stars, whose light angelical caressed
Your virgin days,
Give back in your calm eyes their holier rays.
  The deep past living in your breast
  Heaves these half-merry sighs;
  And the soft accents of your tongue
  Breathe unrecorded charities.

Hasten not; the feast will wait.
  This is a master-night without a morrow.
  No chill and haggard dawn, with after-sorrow,
  Will snuff the spluttering candle out
Or blanch the revelers homeward straggling late.
  Before the rout
Wearies or wanes, will come a calmer trance.
  Lulled by the poppied fragrance of this bower,
  We'll cheat the lapsing hour
And close our eyes, still smiling, on the dance.

George Santayana

A GENTLEMAN OF FIFTY SOLILOQUIZES

I

SOME ten or twelve old friends of yours and mine,
  If we spoke truly, are not friends at all.
They never were. That accident divine,
  A friendship, not so often may befall!

But as the dull years pass with dragging feet
  Within them waxes, in us wanes, esteem;
For weakly, and half conscious of deceit,
  We gave them cause an equal love to dream.

Could we have told some fool with haggard face
  Who bared his soul, so sure we'd understand,
His little tragedy was commonplace? . . .
  We lied. We stretched to him a brother's hand;

He loved us for it, and mere ruth has kept
Our jaws from yawning while he drooled and wept.

II

The valor cold to be ourselves we lack;
  And so from strands of kindness misconstrued
And lenient moments, careless threads and slack,
  We're meshed within a web of habitude.

And often these are worthier men than we;
  But that itself, in time, becomes offense;
We're burdened with this damned nobility
  That's forced on us, which we must recompense.

We loathe ourselves for being insincere,
  And lavish generous deeds to hide the fact:
For who could wound these hearts? Thus we appear
  Thrice loyal friends in word and look and act!

And golden lies with which we save them pain
But serve to make their true regard more fain.

III

Should chance strike out of me some human heat,
 Leap not at that and think to grasp my soul!
I flee new bonds. My self must still retreat
 Down devious ways to keep me free and whole.

Give me your mind, and I will give you mine.
 Then should it change no heart will bleed or burn.
Give me your wits. I want no heart of thine.
 You'll ask too much of life-blood in return.

There was a golden lad in years long gone. . . .
 We twain together left the ways of men
And roamed the starry heights, the fields of dawn,
 In youth and gladness. This comes not again.

Give me your mirth. It bores me when you weep.
My loves you cannot touch. They're buried deep.

Don Marquis

FIFTY YEARS SPENT

Fifty years spent before I found me
Wind on my mouth and the taste of the rain,
Where the great hills circled and swept around me
And the torrents leapt to the mist-drenched plain;
Ah, it was long this coming of me
Back to the hills and the sounding sea.

Ye who can go when so it tideth
To fallow fields when the Spring is new,
Finding the spirit that there abideth,
Taking fill of the sun and the dew;
Little ye know of the cross of the town
And the small pale folk who go up and down.

Fifty years spent before I found me
A bank knee-deep with climbing rose,
Saw, or had space to look around me,
Knew how the apple buds and blows;
And all the while that I thought me wise
I walked as one with blinded eyes.

Scarcely a lad who passes twenty
But finds him a girl to balm his heart;
Only I, who had work so plenty,
Bade this loving keep apart:
Once I saw a girl in a crowd,
But I hushed my heart when it cried aloud.

City courts in January,—
City courts in wilted June,
Often ye will catch and carry
Echoes of some straying tune:
Ah, but underneath the feet
Echo stifles in a street.

Fifty years spent, and what do they bring me?
Now I can buy the meadow and hill:
Where is the heart of the boy to sing thee?
Where is the life for thy living to fill?
And thirty years back in a city crowd
I passed a girl when my heart cried loud!

Struthers Burt

GRAMPA SCHULER

GRAMPA SCHULER, when he was young,
Had a crest of hair, and shining eyes.
He wore red-flowered waistcoats,
Wild Byronic ties.
The whole land of Germany
Wasn't wide enough!—
He ran away one night, when winter
Seas were fierce and rough.

He has a sleek farm here
With already a settled air.
He's patriarchal, with his sons
And daughters round him everywhere.
His son's son Jim has fiery eyes—
He wants to go where the land is new!
Grampa bitterly wonders: "What are
Young fools coming to!"

Ruth Suckow

SPINNERS AT WILLOWSLEIGH

THE YOUNG GIRL PASSES

THE old women sit at Willowsleigh and spin,
And sing and shout above the humming din.

They are so very old, and brown and wise,
One is afraid to look them in the eyes.

Their bony fingers make a crackling sound,
Like dead bones shaking six feet underground,

Their toothless singing mocks; it seems to say:
"What I was yesterday, you are to-day.

"Stars kissed our eyes, the sunlight loved our brow,
You'll be to-morrow, lass, what we are now."

They sing and talk, they are so old and lean;
And the whole earth is young, and fresh, and green.

Once they were flowers, and flame and living bread;
Now they are old and brown and all but dead!

                                    Marya Zaturenska

OLD WOMEN

OLD women sit, stiffly, mosaics of pain,
Framed in drab doorways looking on the dark.
Rarely they rouse to gossip or complain
As dozing bitches break their dream to bark.
And then once more they fold their creaking bones
In silence, pulled about them like a shawl.
Their memories: a heap of tumbling stones,
Once builded stronger than a city wall.
Sometimes they mend the gaps with twitching hand,—
Because they see a woman big with child,
Because a wet wind smells of grave-pocked land,
Because a train wailed, because troops defiled.

Sometimes old women limp through altered streets
Whose hostile houses beat them down to earth;
Now in their beds they fumble at the sheets
That once were spread for bridal, once for birth,
And now are laid for women who are cold
With difficult plodding or with sitting still.
Old women, pitying all that age can kill,
Lie quiet, wondering that they are old.

Babette Deutsch

SHE SEWS FINE LINEN

SHE sews fine linen
    With trembling fingers,
Thin, withered hands
    Where no bloom lingers.

The sun glints on
    A worn gold ring,—
Granddaughter marries
    Her man this spring.

They go to the church
    On an April day,
That other April,—
    How far away!

Julia Johnson Davis

AUTUMN LEAVES

THE dear old ladies whose cheeks are pink
In spite of the years of Winter's chill,
Are like the Autumn leaves I think,
A little crumpled, but lovely still.

Janie Screven Heyward

THE OLD WOMAN

As a white candle
    In a holy place,
So is the beauty
    Of an aged face.

As the spent radiance
  Of the winter sun,
So is a woman
  With her travail done.

Her brood gone from her,
  And her thoughts as still
As the waters
  Under a ruined mill.

Joseph Campbell

STRANGE, IS IT NOT

STRANGE, is it not, that youth will always sing
With heart so filled, and with such bitter grief,
Of birds that fly from autumn's withered leaf,
Of dying summer, born of dying spring?
Not for the leaf, but for the withering;
Not for the age, but for the growing old;
The winter's coming, not the winter's cold,
And the bird never, but the taking wing.
Yet being old, and finding place among
The walkers in the dusk, he sings no more
Of all dear beauty that has gone before—
The death of youth by youth alone is sung.
Is age a sorrow, then, too great to share?
Or to be old, perhaps, is not to care.

Edward D. Kennedy

THE WHISPERER

STILL by meadow and stream
When I saunter and muse and dream,
A mocking whisper I hear—
"Old Age draweth a-near."

When fancy would be weaving
Gay hopes for my deceiving,
The Whisperer bids " Remember:
Rake not a dying ember."

It shall not me dismay
That I've grown old and gray;
Nor tell-tale glass I chide
That will not wrinkles hide:

The visionary gold
That in my heart I hold
Doth far in worth outshine
All metal from the mine.
                    Arthur Bullen [1857-1920]

ON GROWING OLD

BE with me Beauty for the fire is dying,
My dog and I are old, too old for roving,
Man, whose young passion sets the spindrift flying
Is soon too lame to march, too cold for loving.

I take the book and gather to the fire,
Turning old yellow leaves; minute by minute,
The clock ticks to my heart; a withered wire
Moves a thin ghost of music in the spinet.

I cannot sail your seas, I cannot wander
Your cornland, nor your hill-land nor your valleys,
Ever again, nor share the battle yonder
Where the young knight the broken squadron rallies.

Only stay quiet while my mind remembers
The beauty of fire from the beauty of embers.

Beauty, have pity, for the strong have power,
The rich their wealth, the beautiful their grace,
Summer of man its sunlight and its flower,
Spring time of man all April in a face.

Only, as in the jostling in the Strand,
Where the mob thrusts or loiters or is loud
The beggar with the saucer in his hand
Asks only a penny from the passing crowd,

So, from this glittering world with all its fashion,
Its fire and play of men, its stir, its march,
Let me have wisdom, Beauty, wisdom and passion,
Bread to the soul, rain where the summers parch.

Give me but these, and though the darkness close
Even the night will blossom as the rose.

John Masefield

PART II

POEMS OF LOVE

THE PASSING FLOWER

In Baalbec there were lovers
   Who plucked the passing flower;
In Sidon and Palmyra
   Each flushed, immortal hour

Was gathered in the passing;
   In Greece and Rome they knew
That from the living Present
   The whitest blossoms grew.

The countless generations
   Like Autumn leaves go by:
Love only is eternal,
   Love only does not die. . . .

I hear the dying nations
   Go by on phantom feet—
But still the rose is fragrant,
   And still a kiss is sweet!

Harry Kemp

THE WEB OF EROS

IS LOVE, THEN, SO SIMPLE

Is love, then, so simple, my dear?
  The opening of a door,
And seeing all things clear?
  I did not know before.

I had thought it unrest and desire
  Soaring only to fall,
Annihilation and fire:
  It is not so at all.

I feel no desperate will,
  But I think I understand
Many things, as I sit quite still,
  With Eternity in my hand.

Irene Rutherford McLeod

I KNOW

OH! I know why the alder trees
  Lean over the reflecting stream;
And I know what the wandering bees
  Heard in the woods of dream.

I know how the uneasy tide
  Answers the signal of the moon,
And why the morning-glories hide
  Their eyes in the forenoon.

And I know all the wild delight
  That quivers in the sea-bird's wings,
For in one little hour last night
  Love told me all these things.

Elsa Barker

SONG

IF love were but a little thing—
   Strange love which, more than all, is great—
One might not such devotion bring,
   Early to serve and late:

If love were but a passing breath—
   Wild love—which, as God knows, is sweet—
One might not make of life and death
   A pillow for love's feet!

Florence Earle Coates

A PRAYER

UNTIL I lose my soul and lie
   Blind to the beauty of the earth,
Deaf though a shouting wind goes by,
   Dumb in a storm of mirth;

Until my heart is quenched at length
   And I have left the land of men,
Oh, let me love with all my strength
   Careless if I am loved again.

Sara Teasdale

TOO SOON THE LIGHTEST FEET

TOO soon the lightest feet are lead,
   All tongues of silver cease:
Even Shakespeare with a word half said
   Is pledged to hold his peace!

So artlessly kings fall asleep,
   Wearing their crowns awry.
Their hands forget what they would keep
   And loosen as they lie.

And lovers mellow to the sound
   Of meadow larks in spring
Grow inattentive underground
   Nor heed them when they sing.

I dare not say my joy is great,
    Time presses on me so.
Counting the early hour as late
    What space I have to go.

But faint for rapture like the rest
    Life chooses so to mock
Speechless, I hold love to my breast
    And listen to the clock!
                        Amanda Benjamin Hall

TO AN OLD TUNE

You cannot choose but love, lad,
    From dawn till twilight dreary;
You cannot choose but love, lad,
    Though love grows weary, weary.

For, lad, an if you love not,
    You'd best have slept unwaking;
But, O, an if you love, lad,
    Your heart is breaking, breaking.

Though friends and lovers only
    Fill life with joyous breath,
Yet friend or lover only
    Can make you pray for death.

Throw open wide your heart then,
    Love's road-house for a mile!
And if one turns to leave you
    Or stab you—smile, lad, smile.
                        William Alexander Percy

LOOK NOT TO ME FOR WISDOM

Look not to me for wisdom,
    There's naught you shall be told;
I make the moon my loving cup
    And toast the spilling gold.

Look not to me for wisdom—
    The cup is warm above,
And I shall drink of kisses,
    So look to me for love.

When love speaks well of wisdom,
    Watch out, and guard your heart,
Oh, do not give it wholly,
    Or happiness depart.

For love with me is courage,
    A vagabond, a road,
Two roving underneath the moon,
    And on their hearts no load.

For love with me is madness—
    Go to, who would be wise!—
For oh, she talks of wisdom
    With challenge in her eyes.

Charles Divine

I THOUGHT JOY WENT BY ME

I THOUGHT Joy went by me,
    I thought Love was dead—
They did it but to try me;
    Laughingly Love said:

"We are crazy fellows,
    All the roads we roam;
When you come to find us,
    We are not at home.

"Then some winter evening
    We will straggle in,
Set the rafters rocking
    With the old familiar din.

"Stay not hands to hold us
    When we're bowsed and fed,
We are crazy fellows," . . . .
    Laughingly Love said.

Willard Wattles

STRING STARS FOR PEARLS

STRING stars for pearls on a ribbon of whim
    And fling it about her shoulders,
Carve cups from coral and crust each brim
    Till the whole gem smokes and smoulders;
Bring gold for beating in thick bright rings
    And honey from hearts of clover:
But love will long for the absent things,
    Ever the old earth over.

Go, ride the world in a glory of wars
    And startle the gods to wonder;
Break men to follow triumphant cars
    With a rose-paved road thereunder;
Pile stone on stone for the bruit of a name
    When a thousand years dissever:
But love will lean to a smaller flame
    Forever and forever.

                                        J. U. Nicolson

WHERE LOVE IS KING

WHERE love is king,
Ah, there is little need
To dance and sing,
With bridal-torch to flare
Amber and scatter light
Across the purple air,
To sing and dance
To flute-note and to reed.

Where love is come
(Ah, love is come indeed!)
Our limbs are numb
Before his fiery need;
With all their glad
Rapture of speech unsaid,
Before his fiery lips
Our lips are mute and dumb.

Ah, sound of reed,
Ah, flute and trumpet wail,
Ah, joy decreed—
The fringes of her veil
Are seared and white;
Across the flare of light,
Blinded the torches fail.
(Ah, love is come indeed!)

H. D.

THE WEB OF EROS

WITHIN your magic web of hair lies furled
The fire and splendor of the ancient world;
The dire gold of the comet's wind-blown hair;
The songs that turned to gold the evening air
When all the stars of heaven sang for joy.
The flames that burnt the cloud-high city Troy;
The mænad fire of spring on the cold earth;
The myrrh-lit flame that gave both death and birth
To the soul Phœnix; and the star-bright shower
That came to Danaë in her brazen tower . . .
Within your magic web of hair lies furled
The fire and splendor of the ancient world.

Edith Sitwell

WINDS OF EROS

I LOVE to think this fragrant air
 I breathe in the deep-bosomed night
Has mixed with beauty and may bear
 The burden of a heart's delight.

This may have been the burning breath
 That uttered Deirdre's love. It may
Have been a note outlasting death
 As Sappho sang her heart away.

It may have fanned a joy so deep
 That Ilium must pay the price,
And under desert sand must sleep
 Heroes and towers in sacrifice.

And this rich air, it may have been—
  To bring these dreams, so sweet a throng—
Sighed by the lovely listening queen
  While Solomon had sung his song.

So it will take from me, from thee,
  Ere from our being it departs,
And keep for lovers yet to be
  All the enchantment of our hearts.

A. E.

THE CROWNING GIFT

I HAVE had courage to accuse;
And a fine wit that could upbraid;
And a nice cunning that could bruise;
And a shrewd wisdom, unafraid
Of what weak mortals fear to lose.

I have had virtue to despise
The sophistry of pious fools;
I have had firmness to chastise;
And intellect to make me rules,
To estimate and exorcise.

I have had knowledge to be true;
My faith could obstacles remove.
But now, by failure taught anew,
I would have courage now to love,
And lay aside the strength I knew.

Gladys Cromwell

MEN LOVED WHOLLY BEYOND WISDOM

MEN loved wholly beyond wisdom
Have the staff without the banner.
Like a fire in a dry thicket
Rising within women's eyes
Is the love men must return.
Heart, so subtle now, and trembling,
What a marvel to be wise,

To love never in this manner!
To be quiet in the fern
Like a thing gone dead and still,
Listening to the prisoned cricket
Shake its terrible, dissembling
Music in the granite hill.

Louise Bogan

GLIMPSES

LAST night, as through the crowd on Market Street
  A new-made soldier proudly swung along,
Guiding that gray-eyed wonder called his girl,
  Whose face turned up to him in silent song:

I marked, above those gay young hearts atune,
The unimportant beauty of the moon.

Roy Helton

AT A WINDOW

GIVE me hunger,
O you gods that sit and give
The world its orders.
Give me hunger, pain and want;
Shut me out with shame and failure
From your doors of gold and fame,
Give me your shabbiest, weariest hunger.

But leave me a little love,
A voice to speak to me in the day end,
A hand to touch me in the dark room
Breaking the long loneliness.
In the dusk of day-shapes
Blurring the sunset,
One little wandering, western star
Thrust out from the changing shores of shadow.
Let me go to the window,
Watch there the day-shapes of dusk,
And wait and know the coming
Of a little love.

Carl Sandburg

COOL TOMBS

WHEN Abraham Lincoln was shoveled into the tombs, he
    forgot the copperheads and the assassin . . . in the
    dust, in the cool tombs.

And Ulysses Grant lost all thought of con men and Wall
    Street, cash and collateral turned ashes . . . in the
    dust, in the cool tombs.

Pocahontas' body, lovely as a poplar, sweet as a red haw in
    November or a pawpaw in May—did she wonder?
    does she remember? . . . in the dust, in the cool tombs?

Take any streetful of people buying clothes and groceries,
    cheering a hero or throwing confetti and blowing tin
    horns . . . tell me if the lovers are losers . . . tell me
    if any get more than the lovers . . . in the dust . . .
    in the cool tombs.

Carl Sandburg

PLAINTS AND PROTESTATIONS

IN PHÆACIA

HAD I that haze of streaming blue,
    That sea below, the summer faced,
I'd work and weave a dress for you
    And kneel to clasp it round your waist,
And broider with those burning bright
    Threads of the Sun across the sea,
And bind it with the silver light
    That wavers in the olive tree.

Had I the gold that like a river
    Pours through our garden, eve by eve,
Our garden that goes on forever
    Out of the world, as we believe;
Had I that glory on the vine
    That splendor soft on tower and town,
I'd forge a crown of that sunshine,
    And break before your feet the crown.

Through the great pinewood I have been
    An hour before the lustre dies,
Nor have such forest-colors seen
    As those that glimmer in your eyes.
Ah, misty woodland, down whose deep
    And twilight paths I love to stroll
To meadows quieter than sleep
    And pools more secret than the soul!

Could I but steal that awful throne
    Ablaze with dreams and songs and stars
Where sits Night, a man of stone,
    On the frozen mountain spars.

I'd cast him down, for he is old,
    And set my Lady there to rule,
Gowned with silver, crowned with gold,
    And in her eyes the forest pool.

James Elroy Flecker

SONG AT SANTA CRUZ

WERE there lovers in the lanes of Atlantis:
Meeting lips and twining fingers
In the mild Atlantid Springtime?
    How should I know
If there were lovers in the lanes of Atlantis,
When the dark sea drowned her mountains
    Many years ago?

Were there poets in the paths of Atlantis:
Eager poets, seeking beauty
To adorn the women they worshipped?
    How can I say
If there were poets in the paths of Atlantis?
For the waters that drowned her mountains
    Washed their beauty away.

Were there women in the ways of Atlantis:
Foolish women who loved, as I do,
Dreaming that mortal love was deathless?
    Ask me not now
If there were women in the ways of Atlantis:
There was no woman in all her mountains
    Wonderful as thou!

Francis Brett Young

IN MISTY BLUE

IN misty blue the lark is heard
Above the silent homes of men;
The bright-eyed thrush, the little wren,
The yellow-billed sweet-voiced blackbird
Mid sallow blossoms blond as curd

Or silver oak boughs, carolling
With happy throat from tree to tree,
Sing into light this morn of spring
That sang my dear love home to me.

Be starry, buds of clustered white,
Around the dark waves of her hair!
The young fresh glory you prepare
Is like my ever-fresh delight
When she comes shining on my sight
With meeting eyes, with such a cheek
As colors fair like flushing tips
Of shoots, and music ere she speaks
Lies in the wonder of her lips.

Airs of the morning, breathe about
Keen faint scents of the wild wood side
From thickets where primroses hide
Mid the brown leaves of winter's rout.
Chestnut and willow, beacon out
For joy of her, from far and nigh,
Your English green on English hills:
Above her head, song-quivering sky,
And at her feet the daffodils.

Because she breathed, the world was more,
And breath a finer soul to use,
And life held lovelier hopes to choose:
But O, today my heart brims o'er,
Earth glows as from a kindled core,
Like shadows of diviner things
Are hill and cloud and flower and tree—
A splendor that is hers and spring's,—
The day my love came home to me.

Laurence Binyon

THE POET DESCRIBES HIS LOVE

So tall she is, and slender, and so fair,
So like a child for play, a queen for grace,
So pale and proud she is, with that bright hair
Blown in a storm of gold about her face;

So gay she is, and with such pretty words,
So like a thrush for making a sweet note,
And then her hands, like little anxious birds—
My heart to watch her trembles in my throat.
So that I am all wonder to behold her,
I being I, she being what she is,
And dare in reverence alone to fold her,
And touch her cheek and forehead with a kiss;
All loveliness she is, the whole world over,
All joy, all grief, all beauty to her lover.

Robert Nathan

HER BEAUTY

I HEARD them say, "Her hands are hard as stone,"
And I remembered how she laid for me
The road to heaven. They said, "Her hair is gray."
Then I remembered how she once had thrown
Long plaited strands, like cables, into the sea
I battled in—the salt sea of dismay.
They said, "Her beauty's past." And then I wept,
That these, who should have been in love adept,
Against my fount of beauty should blaspheme,
And hearing a new music, miss the theme.

Max Plowman

BODILY BEAUTY

Her curving bosom images
    A tender-folded thought
Whose grace, too exquisite for speech,
    Was in her body wrought.

The shining vale between her breasts
    Is like a quiet joy,
Such as no malison can harm
    Nor any shade annoy.

Yea, all her bodily beauty is
    A subtle-fashioned scroll,
Where God has written visibly
    Brave hintings of her soul.

George Rostrevor

TO L. C.

When every lip invokes young loveliness,
Whom, whom but you shall I commemorate?
I cannot praise you as you were, create
With borrowed words, your parts, and bright excess.

When for our pleasure, at the long week's ending,
An idle story springs to every tongue
Of saddest Fate, and Fortune lost, among
All piteous souls, you rise, you, comprehending
All sorrows in the loss of you, and turning
Your pretty head to me, set the old fires new burning.

Lucy Hawkins

SO BEAUTIFUL YOU ARE, INDEED

So beautiful you are, indeed,
 That I am troubled when you come,
And though I crave you for my need,
 Your nearness strikes me blind and dumb.

And when you bring your lips to mine
 My spirit trembles and escapes,
And you and I are turned divine,
 Bereft of our familiar shapes.

And fearfully we tread cold space,
 Naked of flesh and winged with flame,
. . . Until we find us face to face,
 Each calling on the other's name!

Irene Rutherford McLeod

HER FAIRNESS, WEDDED TO A STAR

Her fairness, wedded to a star,
Is whiter than all lilies are,
And flowers within her eyes more white
Than moonlight on an April night.

Her wonder like a wind doth sing,
Wedded to the heart of spring,
And April, dawning in her eyes,
Reflects the wonder of the skies.

Her beauty lights the April day
With radiance of her chastity,
And innocence doth slumber now
Upon her candid April brow.

Edward J. O'Brien

CAROL

THE month can never forget the year;
   The moth can never forget the fire;
And I can never forget my dear
   Lady of High Desire.

The earth can never forget the sun;
   The day can never forget the night;
And I can never forget the one
   Lady of My Delight.

John McClure

CHANSON NAÏVE

I SHALL steal upon her
   Where she sits so white,
Creep-mouse, creep-mouse,
   In the twilight.

She sits in the shadows,
   Dreamy, dreamy—
I shall go stealthily
   So she cannot see me.

I shall steal behind her
   And kiss her on the cheek
And cover up her wee mouth
   So she cannot speak.

> I would fain surprise her
>   If so be I might,
> Creep-mouse, creep-mouse,
>   In the twilight!

John McClure

GOLDENHAIR

> LEAN out of the window,
>   Goldenhair,
> I hear you singing
>   A merry air.
>
> My book was closed,
>   I read no more,
> Watching the fire dance
>   On the floor.
>
> I have left my book,
>   I have left my room,
> For I heard you singing
>   Through the gloom.
>
> Singing and singing
>   A merry air,
> Lean out of the window,
>   Goldenhair.

James Joyce

AFTER STORM

> I KNOW how it would be . . . a rainy moon
> Would make an arching loveliness of sky,
> And we would note again how strangely soon
> The heavens are stilled of storm gone loudly by,—
> And how is left, along the storm's late way,
> Thin veils of cloud that let the moon look through
> In sad, white beauty . . . and then I would say:
> "Nothing of this is beautiful as you;

For you are strange with storm that swept your skies
And left you sad as moons in a sad place,
With old, remembered sorrow in your eyes". . . .
And you would smile, and turn away your face,
But I would say, there where the moon looked through:
"Nothing of this is beautiful as you."

David Morton

CATALOGUE

WHY all these fears and feigned alarms
    That never can pretend to blind me?
Let me enumerate the charms
        With which you bind me.

First, I shall list one pair of eyes,
    Like flame beneath some mouldering fuel;
A mouth that's witty if not wise,
        Half kind, half cruel.

Thirdly, there are two tapering hands,
    So delicate and diamond-spangled;
And there's your hair, in whose bright strands
    I lie entangled.

Your breast, all rose and silk and pearl;
    Your laugh, a bright and sharpened sickle;
Your whims, dear and distracting girl,
        Footloose and fickle.

Your kiss, a wine that has no dregs;
    Your love, a bird that seldom perches.
And I must add your lyric legs—
        Two dancing birches.

But most of all I love your pride,
    As firm as mine that I believe in.
Stubborn and selfish; hard inside . . .
        That makes us even.

Louis Untermeyer

THE GIFT

I THOUGHT, beloved, to have brought to you
A gift of quietness and ease and peace,
Cooling your brow as with the mystic dew
        Dropping from twilight trees.

Homeward I go not yet; the darkness grows;
Not mine the voice to still with peace divine:
From the first fount the stream of quiet flows
        Through other hearts than mine.

Yet of my night I give to you the stars,
And of my sorrow here the sweetest gains,
And out of hell, beyond its iron bars,
        My scorn of all its pains.

A. E.

RHYME FOR REMEMBRANCE OF MAY

REMEMBER May?
O, till no more a color tincts the spray,
And Life's last branch goes bloomless; aye, my Dear,
So long I shall remember that sweet year
And sweeter meeting, that divine soft day.

    Remember you?
What glamoury of May I listen to
Or see, must have your voice, plead from your eyes.
I swear that month was dropped from Paradise
To date our dream, and bring the dreaming true!
        May means remembering you!

Richard Burton

VOYAGER'S SONG

WHAT if I coasted near the shore
    Of ultimate utter sleep—
You were the tide that swung me back
    Into the living deep.

I did not heed what all the world
   Held in its proud embrace;
But it was life to hear you speak,
   And heaven to see your face.

Clement Wood

OBLATION

'TIS little I can give you, yet I can give you these . . .
A little naked dwelling to dress it as you please,
And a low moon, a gold moon, swinging in the trees.

And maybe in the quiet, when the stars out-throng,
Your beating heart will tell you how you were not wrong
To count nor gold nor silver sweeter than my song.

So fare you well or stay you, and I will go or stay;
'Tis little I can give you, save love for every day,
And little golden heads for when your head is gray.

A. Newberry Choyce

COME MICHAELMAS

IF I could stand, gel, goldenly,
Like glinting dandelions do,
I would go grandly down the lane,
And knock, and ask your dad for you.

When I clomp heavy home at night,
They glim like guineas on the way,
Until the fairies thieve their gold,
And spend it all on clocks next day.

But seven-and-forty pounds I have,
Come Michaelmas I'll make three more,
And then, belike, your dad will hear
An ash-stick tapping on his door.

A. Newberry Choyce

COME, LET US FIND

Come, let us find a cottage, love,
   That's green for half a mile around;
To laugh at every grumbling bee,
   Whose sweetest blossom's not yet found.
Where many a bird shall sing for you,
   And in our garden build its nest:
They'll sing for you as though their eggs
    Were lying in your breast,
      My love—
    Were lying warm in your soft breast.

'Tis strange how men find time to hate,
   When life is all too short for love;
But we, away from our own kind,
   A different life can live and prove.
And early on a summer's morn,
   'As I go walking out with you,
We'll help the sun with our warm breath
    To clear away the dew,
      My love,
    To clear away the morning dew.

William H. Davies

RAINY SONG

Down the dripping pathway dancing through the rain,
Brown eyes of beauty, laugh to me again!

Eyes full of starlight, moist over fire,
Full of young wonder, touch my desire!

O like a brown bird, like a bird's flight,
Run through the rain drops lithely and light.

Body like a gypsy, like a wild queen,
Slim brown dress to slip through the green—

The little leaves hold you as soft as a child,
The little path loves you, the path that runs wild.

Who would not love you, seeing you move,
Warm-eyed and beautiful through the green grove?

Let the rain kiss you, trickle through your hair,
Laugh if my fingers mingle with it there,

Laugh if my cheek too is misty and drips—
Wetness is tender—laugh on my lips

The happy sweet laughter of love without pain,
Young love, the strong love, burning in the rain.

Max Eastman

WE MET ON ROADS OF LAUGHTER

WE met on roads of laughter,
    Both careless at the start,
But other roads came after
    And wound around my heart.

There are roads a wise man misses,
    And roads where fools will try
To say farewell with kisses,
    Touch love and say good-bye.

We met on roads of laughter;—
    Now wistful roads depart,
For I must hurry after
    To overtake my heart.

Charles Divine

SUPPLICATION

TAKE away your soft hair and your softer lips,
  Loose me from your twining fingers; turn away your eyes.
For I loved this earth, and now a greater passion slips
    All its earthly ties.

I can wait for heaven, if that is to be;
　　Let me have these common days and know their simple
　　　worth.
Do not make the quiet-colored moments dull to me—
　　　　Let me keep the earth.

There is much I long to look at, much I long to taste.
　　You have mocked a thousand raptures with contemptuous
　　　power.
Do not let your beauty lay all other beauty waste;
　　　　Spare a casual hour.

Let old music thrill me to my finger tips;
　　Bring me back the glamour of the things I used to prize;
Lift this cloudy radiance where I only see your lips—
　　　　Turn away your eyes!

　　　　　　　　　　　　　　　Louis Untermeyer

I LAY MY LUTE BESIDE THY DOOR

WHAT was it Colin gave to thee?—
A blossom from the hawthorne tree?
A flower of song is all I own,
A little dreamland rose, half blown.
Oh, deck thy tresses, I implore—
I lay my lute beside thy door!

What was it Damon sent to thee?—
A gleaming pearl from eastern sea?
A gem of song is all I own,
A tiny, glistening, tear-stained stone.
Oh, wear it—'twill my peace restore—
I lay my lute beside thy door!

What was it Lubin brought to thee?—
A falcon from the dewy lea?
A bird of song is all I own,
And to thy heart it now has flown.
Oh, cage it, let it roam no more—
I lay my lute beside thy door!

　　　　　　　　　　　　　　　Clarence Urmy

THIS IS THE SHAPE OF THE LEAF

From " Priapus and the Pool "

THIS is the shape of the leaf, and this of the flower,
And this the pale bole of the tree
Which watches its bough in a pool of unwavering water
In a land we never shall see.

The thrush on the bough is silent, the dew falls softly,
In the evening is hardly a sound.
And the three beautiful pilgrims who come here together
Touch lightly the dust of the ground,

Touch it with feet that trouble the dust but as wings do,
Come shyly together, are still,
Like dancers who wait, in a pause of the music, for music
The exquisite silence to fill. . . .

This is the thought of the first, and this of the second,
And this the grave thought of the third:
"Linger we thus for a moment, palely expectant,
And silence will end, and the bird

"Sing the pure phrase, sweet phrase, clear phrase in the
    twilight
To fill the blue bell of the world;
And we, who on music so leaflike have drifted together,
Leaflike apart shall be whirled

"Into what but the beauty of silence, silence forever?" . . .
. . . This is the shape of the tree,
And the flower, and the leaf, and the three pale beautiful
    pilgrims;
This is what you are to me.

Conrad Aiken

DESIDERAVI

LEST, tortured by the world's strong sin,
    Her little bruisèd heart should die—
Give her your heart to shelter in,
    O earth and sky!

Kneel, sun, to clothe her round about
    With rays to keep her body warm;
And, kind moon, shut the shadows out
    That work her harm.

Yes, even shield her from my will's
    Wild folly—hold her safe and close!—
For my rough hand in touching spills
    Life from the rose.

But teach me, too, that I may learn
    Your passion classical and cool;
To me, who tremble so and burn,
    Be pitiful!

Theodore Maynard

THE UNLOVED TO HIS BELOVED

COULD I pluck down Aldebaran
And have the Pleiades in your hair
I could not add more burning to your beauty
Or lend a starrier coldness to your air.

If I were cleaving terrible waters
With death ahead on the visible sands
I could not turn and stretch my hands more wildly,
More vainly turn and stretch to you my hands.

William Alexander Percy

LAD'S LOVE

LAD'S love and lavender,
    Rosemary and rue,
I picked them in a posy
    And I offered them to you.

It was only lad's love
    But surely it was true,
Only wild gray lavender,
    But fragrant as it grew.

I plucked the sprig of rosemary
  For memory of you,
And was it to complete the tale
  I tied it up with rue?

Lad's love and lavender
  Rosemary and rue,
I picked them in a posy
  And I offered it to you.

Esther Lilian Duff

NEVER WILL YOU HOLD ME

Never will you hold me
  With puddings and cake
Or even the threat
  Of a heart to break.

Never will you hold me
  With knife, fork, and spoon
As long as the road lies
  Under the moon.

Nor phantoms at fireside
  With grief in the room,
Nor obvious candles
  To jewel the gloom.

But a song satyr-footed,
  A mood of gowns of gold,
And laughter like a wine-cup—
  These things hold.

A song within a song
  And eyes upon the door—
And you will always hold me
  One day more.

Charles Divine

HOW TO GO AND FORGET

I KNOW how to hold
As the lovers of old—
How to cling to you, sing to you,
Let all the world know the song that I bring to you.
  But I do not know yet
  How to go and forget!

I know how to call
To the God over all—
How to sigh for you, cry for you,
Fight down the terrible dark till I die for you.
  But I do not know yet
  How to go and forget!

Edwin Markham

IN AN AUTUMN WOOD

THOU, too, O bronze-eyed darling of the feast,
Under the deep, brown leaves and faded sky
    At last wilt lie,
Forgetful of the joy thy beauty leased.

But ere that time, how many times, alas,
Wilt thou with careless hand sweep all the vain,
    Taut strings of pain
That are my heart nor hear the hurt chords pass.

Almost I wish to-day that thou didst lie
Beyond the leaves, unsummonably still—
    So well, so ill
I love thy loveliness that hears no cry.

William Alexander Percy

ON THE HEIGHT

THE foot-hills called us, green and sweet.
  We dallied, but we might not stay,
And all day long we set our feet
  In the wind's way.

We climbed with him the wandering trail
   Up to the last keen, lonely height
Where snow-peaks clustered, sharp and frail,
   Swimming in light.

Sheer on the edge of heaven we dwelt,
   And laughed above the blue abyss,
While on my happy lips I felt
   Your windy kiss.

You were the spirit of the height,
   The breath of sun and air . . .
A bird dipped wing, and, swift and white,
   Peace brooded there.

Eunice Tietjens

SONGS

I WOULD make songs for you:
Of slow suns weighing
Through pale mist to the river, overlaying
Gold upon silver tissue; or the hush
Of winter twilight when the bushes quiver
Blooming with birds;
Of the easy snow;
Of patient streets, or the theatric glow
Of lamps on crowding faces in the night;
Of sudden gay encounters without words;
Of sorrow quiet in a huddled fight;
Of the release of April winds;
Of death,
That is a stillness without peace,—
Like love, wherefor I am so dumb to you.

Babette Deutsch

DAVID

DAVID was a shepherd lad, beautiful as you,
   Sang within a shadowed tent to soothe a king's unrest.
Oh, the bashful years in which he made the songs and
     hoarded them,
   By the other shepherd lads all unguessed.

David's song is in a book, for stupid folk to bow before,
   Folk who think it wisdom, which is only lovely song.
You are kin to him, you see beauty in a little moon,
   In branches bent to lash you, with each faint gray thong.

David, when he found his songs—did he use to practice them
   For a little shepherd maid who marveled at each line?
When he left his humble task, and drew the king from
      weariness—
   She who heard the songs first, was her pride like mine?
                              Mary Carolyn Davies

CHANSON D'OR

      I SHALL have a gold room
         When I am a queen,
      With a poppy-perfume
         And a jewelled screen;

      You may come and see me
         Any time you will
      If you wear a green coat
         And a gold frill;

      I shall keep a black slave
         Hidden in the wall,
      Waiting to admit you
         When you come to call,

      And if you displease me
         So that I am bored,
      I will have him kill you
         With a gold sword.
                              Ann Hamilton

CAPRICCIO

   I SHALL have pearls blacker than caviar,
   Rubies such as a ripe pomegranate bleeds,
   Gold pale as honey dripping from a star,
   Brought me by slaves like snow and apple-seeds.

I shall have linen smooth as pigeons' throats,
I shall have purple more than sunset-red,—
The velvet leap of leopards to my boats,—
The fragrance of the cedars to my bed.

I shall have music stronger than the wind
And sweeter than a Chinese apricot.
In gardens like translucent melon-rind
I shall have dreams as sharp as bergamot.

Before my throning presence, emperors
Will stand abashed as troubled children do.
I shall not smile though every knee defers,
But bid them go, bid them bring night, and you.

Babette Deutsch

LITTLE THINGS

LITTLE things I'll give to you—
Till your fingers learn to press
Gently
On a loveliness;

Little things and new—
Till your fingers learn to hold
Love that's fragile,
Love that's old.

Marion Strobel

A PAIR OF LOVERS

(VERSES FOR JAPANESE PRINTS.—MORONOBO)

I SHALL be shapen
Out of the dust of your heart
At the Last Day.
The resurrection will be
Finding myself yours again.

Jeanne Robert Foster

THE GOWN

BENEATH the curious gaze of all the dead,
To enter heaven (O my beads unsaid!
Sins unconfessed!)
Dressed
In a gown woven of your fealty!
Oh, poor and lone and frighted I may be,
—But every woman there will look at me.

Mary Carolyn Davies

POSSESSIONS

AN old and quiet house set down
A windy field or two from town.

And a great clump of lavender,
All day with cross, small bees astir.

Larkspur, hot-blue as with a sting;
And mist, so brief and sharp a thing.

Tall, well-thumbed books upon a shelf;
A green, white-flowered jug of delf.

Old friends, who from the village walk
On Sunday afternoons, to talk

Of the new shop; the guests from town;
The wind that blew the apples down.

They go; the dusk comes from afar,
Like music blown from out a star.

Those others drift across the dew;
My early love—and you—and you!

Lizette Woodworth Reese

INSCRIPTION

It is not hard to tell of a rose
That in another's garden grows,

Or the green shadow of a tree
That has cooled others, but not me,

Or the star-radiance of a sky
That heaven possesses, but not I;

The rose is a scent, the tree a shade,
The sky a temple God has made,

But you are mine—a flame that endures
To warm my soul as it warms yours—

How can I praise it when its light
Is the fierce pen with which I write?

Back to the rose. I cannot see
When sunlight is so close to me.

Ann Hamilton

DEBTS

My debt to you, Belovèd,
  Is one I cannot pay
In any coin of any realm
  On any reckoning day;

For where is he shall figure
  The debt, when all is said,
To one who makes you dream again
  When all the dreams were dead?

Or where is the appraiser
  Who shall the claim compute
Of one who makes you sing again
  When all the songs were mute?

Jessie B. Rittenhouse

TRANSFORMATION

I SHALL be beautiful when you come back,
  With beauty that is not of lips nor eyes,
  And you will look at me with swift surprise
Seeing in me that loveliness I lack.

And you will wonder how this beauty grew,
  In all the restless clamor of the days,
  Not knowing that I walk in cloistered ways
Bearing within one rapt, still thought of you.

Jessie B. Rittenhouse

CERTAINTY ENOUGH

I AM not sure that earth is round
Nor that the sky is really blue.
The tale of why the apples fall
May or may not be true.
I do not know what makes the tides
Nor what tomorrow's world may do,
But I have certainty enough
For I am sure of you.

Amelia Josephine Burr

THE SPELL

LONG have I dreamed of love's adventure,
  Long have I sung of love's desire,
Songs that I sang with red lips laughing,
  Hot with the flame of borrowed fire.

Now I have felt your arms about me,
  Now that my lips on your lips have lain,
Mute with the memory of your kisses,
  How shall I sing of love again?

Medora C. Addison

REPARATION

You are my song come true
　That I sang unbelieving;
You are my hope made new
　That I tarnished with grieving.

More than the losses of love
　With which love denied me,
More than the shadows of love
　With which love belied me,

Is the reward of this love
　That now love has given—
All of the earth of love
　And love's high heaven!

Helen Hoyt

THE WHITE DREAM

My little bed is wide enough
　To hold the dream of you;
And O! its sheets are silken stuff,
　Its covering silk-spun too,
When I reach out my arms about
　That fancy's perfect hue!

And every night when first I creep
　Into its white-wove rest,
Before I shut my eyes in sleep
　I build that dream a nest,
With thoughts and hands and hope's demands
　Against my cheek and breast.

Sometimes adown that lilied dell
　Of exquisite desire
A little wind of want will swell
　In sudden-breathing fire,
And bid my heart a-trembling start,
　As though 'twere Orpheus' lyre.

Three roses in that virgin bower
 The vows of Eden paint;
One is my mouth's deep-honeyed flower;
 Two on my bosom faint,
As white and sweet from head to feet
 I lie in dumb complaint.

And always ere the darkness seals
 My lips till light's new day,
After my hallowed body kneels,
 For all your needs to pray,
Like shy, screened birds, low-whispered words
 Sing to that dream their lay.

All night does my soul's angel guard
 That bower for your dear sake;
All night by his wide wings are barred
 Those flowers, till morning-break,
And like a thrush whose quick notes rush,
 I greet you when I wake.

May Doney

SONG

I COULD make you songs
 Beautiful and frail;
Since you will not listen
 What will these avail?

I could paint my mouth—
 Brush and curl my hair;
Why should I be lovely
 Since you do not care?

Lights have beckoned me
 Uselessly.   My Dear—
How can I be happy
 While you are not here?

Dorothy Dow

IF YOU SHOULD TIRE OF LOVING ME

IF you should tire of loving me
  Some one of our far days,
Oh, never start to hide your heart
  Or cover thought with praise.

For every word you would not say
  Be sure my heart has heard,
So go from me all silently
  Without a kiss or word;

For God must give you happiness. . . .
  And oh, it may befall
In listening long to Heaven-song
  I may not care at all!

Margaret Widdemer

LOVE ME AT LAST

LOVE me at last, or if you will not,
  Leave me;
Hard words could never, as these half-words,
  Grieve me:
Love me at last—or leave me.

Love me at last, or let the last word uttered
  Be but your own;
Love me, or leave me—as a cloud, a vapor,
  Or a bird flown.
Love me at last—I am but sliding water
  Over a stone.

Alice Corbin

COME, LET US MAKE LOVE DEATHLESS

COME, let us make love deathless, thou and I,
  Seeing that our footing on the Earth is brief—
Seeing that her multitudes sweep out to die
  Mocking at all that passes our belief.

For standard of our love not theirs we take:
 If we go hence to-day,
Fill the high cup that is so soon to break
 With richer wine than they!

Ay, since beyond these walls no heavens there be,
 Joy to revive or wasted youth repair,
I'll not bedim the lovely flame in thee,
 Nor sully the sad splendor that we wear.
Great be the love, if with the lover dies
 Our greatness past recall,
And nobler for the fading of those eyes
 The world seen once for all.

Herbert Trench

THE HUMOR OF LOVE

TO THE GOD OF LOVE

COME to me, Eros, if you needs must come
    This year, with milder twinges;
Aim not your arrow at the bull's-eye plumb,
But let the outer pericardium
    Be where the point impinges.

Garishly beautiful I watch them wane
    Like sunsets in a pink west,
The passions of the past; but O their pain!
You recollect that nice affair with Jane?
    We nearly had an inquest.

I want some mellower romance than these,
    Something that shall not waken
The bosom of the bard from midnight ease,
Nor spoil his appetite for breakfast, please,
    (Porridge and eggs and bacon).

Something that shall not steep the soul in gall,
    Nor plant it *in excelsis,*
Nor quite prevent the bondman in its thrall
From biffing off the tee as good a ball
    As anybody else's.

But rather, when the world is dull and gray
    And everything seems horrid,
And books are impotent to charm away
The leaden-footed hours, shall make me say,
    "My hat!" (and strike my forehead)

"I am in love, O circumstance how sweet!
    O ne'er-to-be-forgot knot!"
And praise the damsel's eyebrows, and repeat
Her name out loud, until it's time to eat,
    Or go to bed, or what not.

This is the kind of desultory bolt,
  Eros, I bid you shoot me;
One with no barb to agitate and jolt,
One where the feathers have begun to moult—
  Any old sort will suit me.

                                        E. G. V. Knox

THE TRYST

ACCORDING to tradition
  The place where sweethearts meet
Is meadowland and hillside,
  And not the city street.
Love lingers when you say it
  By lake and moonlight glow:
The poets all O. K. it—
  It may be better so!

And yet I keep my trysting
  In the department stores;
I always wait for Emma
  At the revolving doors.
It might dismay the poets,
  And yet it's wholly true—
My heart leaps when I know it's
  My Emma, pushing through!

It may be more romantic
  By brook or waterfall,
Yet better meet on pavement
  Than never meet at all;
I want no moon beguiling,
  No dark and bouldered shore,
When I see Emma smiling
  And twirling through the door!

                                    Christopher Morley

MAC DIARMOD'S DAUGHTER

THERE is much to be said
    For Mac Diarmod's young daughter,
And much to be sung
    Were a poet about;
Since her eye is a mirror
    Of Ulster's Blackwater,
When ripples shine over
    The dark-dappled trout.

And much might be said
    For his daughter's fair dower
Of heifers and bullocks
    And meadowy grass;
But my head might be hanging
    From Omagh gaol's tower
For all the concern
    That the heart of her has.

So I'll not spend a thought
    On Mac Diarmod's young daughter,
But much might be sung
    Of her land and her looks;
Since her fields are the fairest
    Near Ulster's Blackwater,
And her eyes are dark-dappled
    Like trout in the brooks.

                              Francis Carlin

VIRGINS

IT was after hearing the parish priest
On the Gospel of the Wedding Feast
In Cana, of the Wine and Water—
And I on the road with MacSorley's daughter—

That a snowy bud on a hawthorn bush,
Aware of the sun, began to flush;
While the sunny beauty of blushing water
Came over the cheeks of MacSorley's daughter.

                              Francis Carlin

BEYOND RATHKELLY

As I went over the Far Hill,
    Just beyond Rathkelly,
        —Och, to be on the Far Hill
    O'er Newtonstewart Town!
As I went over the Far Hill
    With Marget's daughter Nellie,
The night was up and the moon was out,
    And a star was falling down.

As I went over the Far Hill,
    Just beyond Rathkelly,
        —Och, to be on the Far Hill
    Above the Bridge o' Moyle!
As I went over the Far Hill,
    With Marget's daughter Nellie,
I made a wish before the star
    Had fallen in the Foyle.

As I went over the Far Hill,
    Just beyond Rathkelly,
        —Och, to be on the Far Hill
    With the hopes that I had then!
As I went over the Far Hill,
    I wished for little Nellie,
And if a star were falling now
    I'd wish for her again.

Francis Carlin

WET OR FINE

As I was on the high-road
That leads to Miller's Run,
I met my lover Barney
Riding in the sun.
He lifted me so tenderly
And sat me on his mare,
And as we sauntered up the hill
He strove to woo me there.

A bonny house had Barney
And many lands he had,
Of all his wealthy family
He was the only lad.
He courted me so grandly
With many a sigh and moan,
Why could I think of nothing
But—"How long his teeth have grown!"

As I was on the high-road
That leads to Somerset,
I met my lover Sandy
Walking through the wet.
He asked me very shyly
If I would walk a way,
And when I asked him why, he said,
"It's such a lovely day."

Then all the beauty of the day
Went tingling through my brain;
The high-road seemed a magic thing,
All muddy in the rain.
And as we panted up the hill
And through the soaking grass,
Why could I think of nothing
But—"What darling eyes he has!"

Amory Hare

POT AND KETTLE

COME close to me, dear Annie, while I bind a lover's knot.
A tale of burning love between a kettle and a pot.
The pot was stalwart iron and the kettle trusty tin,
And though their sides were black with smoke they bubbled
    love within.

Forget that kettle, Jamie, and that pot of boiling broth;
I know a dismal story of a candle and a moth.
For while your pot is boiling and while your kettle sings
My moth makes love to candle flame and burns away his
    wings.

Your moth I envy, Annie, that died by candle flame,
But here are two more lovers, unto no damage came.
There was a cuckoo loved a clock and found her always true.
For every hour they told their hearts, "Ring! ting!
    Cuckoo! Cuckoo!"

As the pot boiled for the kettle, as the kettle for the pot,
So boils my love within me till my breast is glowing hot.
As the moth died for the candle, so could I die for you.
And my fond heart beats time with yours and cries,
    "Cuckoo! Cuckoo!"

Robert Graves

THE KERRY LADS

My eyes were all too wary,
    My heart was none too gay
Until the lads from Kerry
    Came tramping through this way
And lodged about the village
    And helped us with the hay.

The lads that come from Kerry
    Are not like lads at home;
They show you where the fairie
    Dance circles on the loam
And tell old tales and sing old songs
    That lift your heart like foam.

The lads that come from Kerry,
    They never stay for long;
But oh, their mouths are merry!
    And oh, their arms are strong!
And what's a careless kiss or so
    To one remembered song?

Theodosia Garrison

SPANISH SONG

Under my window Dolores sings,
    Polishing pots of brass,
Rose in her hair and ears with rings,
    Voice of the wind in the grass.

Whine of Arabian minor strains,
 Drone of a soul that thrills,
Crying of mountains that love will leap,
 Princes who ride from the hills.

Down in the garden Dolores sings,
 Under catalpa trees;
All of the lovers who fill her songs,
 Only Dolores sees.

 O lover of mine
  From the south of Spain,
 With kisses of wine
  And lips of pain.

Thus with your pots and your candlesticks,
 Sing, Dolores, at ease!
Though never a lover step out of the songs,
 Under catalpa trees;
Though never a prince or a mountain man,
You can always sing to a copper pan.

Charles Divine

TO ATALANTA

You, Atalanta, were so fleet,
Lend the magic of your feet,
Lend your rushing sandals slim
That I may outdistance him.

I would race with him, and show
How much faster I can go.

Then, when he, all wearily
Stops to rest beneath a tree,
Whisper to him that I will
Wait . . . beyond the farthest hill.

Dorothy Dow

THE CONTEMPLATIVE QUARRY

My love is male and proper-man
And what he'd have he'd get by chase,
So I must cheat as women can
And keep my love from off my face.
'Tis folly to my dawning, thrifty thought
That I must run, who in the end am caught.

Anna Wickham

MARKET DAY

It follows up the hill and down—
The road that takes me into town;

And, oh, it's many lads I meet
With smiles and glances bold or sweet;

Eyes that are blue maybe, or black—
But I am never smiling back.

I have to hold my tongue and go
As prim as if I didn't know.

Ah, dear, it's hard—this being good—
I don't like doing what I should.

My basket's always heavy, too—
I need a man's strong arm, I do!

I wonder why there's any harm,
When all the air's so kind and warm,

When smiling lads swing down the road
And ask to help me with my load,

In smiling back at them again—
Not every time, but now and then?

Abigail Cresson

TAM I' THE KIRK

O JEAN, my Jean, when the bell ca's the congregation
O'er valley an' hill wi' the ding frae its iron mou',
When a' body's thoughts is set on his ain salvation,
    Mine's set on you.

There's a reid rose lies on the Buik o' the Word afore ye
That was growin' braw on its bush at the keek o' day,
But the lad that pu'd yon flower i' the mornin's glory,
    He canna pray.

He canna pray; but there's nane i' the kirk will heed him
Whaur he sits sae still his lane at the side o' the wa',
For nane but the reid rose kens what my lassie gie'd him—
    It and us twa!

He canna sing for the sang that his ain he'rt raises,
He canna see for the mist that's afore his een,
An' a voice drowns the hale o' the psalms an' the para-
    phrases,
    Cryin' " Jean, Jean, Jean!"

                  Violet Jacob

OF A CERTAIN GREEN–EYED MONSTER

CHARLES gave Elizabeth a Dodo,
    Charles never offered one to me—
The loveliest lemon-colored Dodo,
    With the greenest eyes that you could wish to see.

Now it isn't that I'm doubting if Charles loves me,
    And I know that he would ask me out to tea,
But he *did* give Elizabeth a Dodo
    And he never even offered one to me.

                  Esther Lilian Duff

TO NATALIE

ALTHOUGH your charms are many,
    Although you're sweet and cute,
Although you equal any
    Magnetic little beaut,
I'm sick of reading matter
    Your many beaux turn out
In re your charming chatter,
    In re your pretty pout.

I wish they'd stop their praising
    Your eyes, your nose, your smile;
And cut their lyric phrasing
    For just a little while.
I know their verses grip you—
    But put them on the shelf! . . .
You see, I want to slip you
    A verse or two myself.

Morrie Ryskind

WILLY AND THE LADY

LEAVE the lady, Willy, let the racket rip,
She is going to fool you, you have lost your grip,
Your brain is in a muddle and your heart is in a whirl,
Come along with me, Willy, never mind the girl!

    Come and have a Man-Talk,
    Come with those who *can* talk,
Light your pipe and listen, and the boys will see you through;
    Love is only chatter,
    Friends are all that matter,
Come and talk the Man-Talk, that's the cure for you!

Leave the lady, Willy, let her letter wait!
You'll forget your troubles when you get it straight,
The world is full of women, and the women full of wile;
Come along with me, Willy, we can make you smile!

Come and have a Man-Talk,
A rousing black-and-tan talk,
There are plenty there to teach you, there's a lot for you to
do;
Your head must stop its whirling
Before you go a-girling,
Come and talk the Man-Talk, that's the cure for you!

Leave the lady, Willy, the night is good and long,
Time for beer and 'baccy, time to have a song;
Where the smoke is swirling, sorrow if you can—
Come along with me, Willy, come and be a man!

Come and have a Man-Talk,
Come and hear the clan talk,
We've all of us been there before, and jolly glad it's through!
We'll advise you confidently,
And we'll break it to you gently,
Come and talk the Man-Talk, that's the cure for you!

Leave the lady, Willy, you are rather young;
When the tales are over, when the songs are sung,
When the men have made you, try the girl again;
Come along with me, Willy, you'll be better then!

Come and have a Man-Talk,
Forget your girl-divan talk,
You've got to get acquainted with another point of view!
Girls will only fool you,
We're the ones to school you,
Come and talk the Man-Talk, that's the cure for you!

Gelett Burgess

THE IRONY OF LOVE

THE WISE WOMAN

HIS eyes grow hot, his words grow wild;
　　He swears to break the mold and leave her.
She smiles at him as at a child
　　That's touched with fever.

She smooths his ruffled wings, she leans
　　To comfort, pamper and restore him.
And when he sulks or scowls she preens
　　His feathers for him.

He hungers after stale regrets,
　　Nourished by what she offers gaily;
And all he thinks he never gets
　　She feeds him daily.

He lusts for freedom, cries how long
　　Must he be bound by what controlled him;
Yet he is glad the chains are strong
　　And that they hold him.

She knows he feels all this but she
　　Is far too wise to let him know it;
He likes to nurse the agony
　　That fits a poet.

He grins to see her shape his life,
　　When she half-coaxes, half-commands him.
And groans it's hard to have a wife
　　Who understands him.

Louis Untermeyer

LOVE

YOU close your book and put it down,
　　As one might drop a tiresome task;
And, with what tries to be a frown,
　　You turn and ask:

"How can you care one hour for me
  Unless your love is all a sham?
'Childish and cheap'—but can I be
  More than I am?

"Your poet knows that love delights
  Only its equals, near or far . . .
'*We love the things we love,*' he writes,
  '*For what they are.*'"

You serious child, how can you place
  Such utter credence in a song?
It is, I grant, a lovely phrase;
  But it is wrong.

Why look, my darling, at the world
  Rolling in blood and murderous flame.
And what's this life? A brief torch hurled
  To darkness, whence it came.

The world is easy to revile
  Where much is false and little true.
And yet we live in it, and smile.
  —And love it, too.

Cease, then, to talk of wrong or right;
  Finalities are cold and far.
We love the things we love in spite
  Of what they are.

                         Louis Untermeyer

SINFONIA DOMESTICA

WHEN the white wave of a glory that is hardly I
  Breaks through my mind and washes it clean,
I know at last the meaning of my ecstasy,
  And know at last my wish and what it can mean.

To have sped out of life that night—to have vanished
  Not as a vision, but as something touched, yet grown
Radiant as the moonlight, circling my naked shoulder;
  Wrapped in a dream of beauty, longed for, but never
    known!

For how with our daily converse, even the sweet sharing
  Of thoughts, of food, of home, of common life,
How shall I be that glory, that last desire
  For which men struggle?   Is Romance in a wife?

Must I bend a heart that is bowed to breaking
  With a frustration, inevitable and slow,
And bank my flame to a low hearth fire, believing
  You'll come for warmth and life to its tempered glow?

Shall I mould my hope anew, to one of service,
  And tell my uneasy soul "Behold, this is good."
And meet you (if we do meet), even at Heaven's threshold,
  With ewer and basin, with clothing and with food?

Jean Starr Untermeyer

THE RED–HAIRED MAN'S WIFE

I HAVE taken that vow—
And you were my friend
But yesterday—now
All that's at an end,
And you are my husband, and claim me, and I must depend.

Yesterday I was free,
Now you, as I stand,
Walk over to me
And take hold of my hand.
You look at my lips, your eyes are too bold, your smile is
    too bland.

My old name is lost,
My distinction of race:
Now the line has been crossed,
Must I step to your pace?
Must I walk as you list, and obey, and smile up in your face?

All the white and the red
Of my cheeks you have won;
All the hair of my head,
And my feet, though they run,
Are yours, and you own me and end me just as I begun.

Must I bow when you speak,
Be silent and hear,
Inclining my cheek
And incredulous ear
To your voice, and command, and behest, hold your lightest
    wish dear?

I am woman, but still
Am alive, and can feel
Every intimate thrill
That is woe or is weal.
I, aloof, and divided, apart, standing far, can I kneel?

O if kneeling were right,
I should kneel nor be sad,
And abase in your sight
All the pride that I had,
I should come to you, hold to you, cling to you, call to you,
    glad.

If not, I shall know,
I shall surely find out,
And your world will throw
In disaster and rout;
I am woman and glory and beauty, I mystery, terror, and
    doubt.

I am separate still,
I am I and not you:
And my mind and my will,
As in secret they grew,
Still are secret, unreached and untouched and not subject
    to you.

                                    James Stephens

THE FARMER'S BRIDE

Three Summers since I chose a maid,
Too young maybe—but more's to do
At harvest-time than bide and woo.
    When us was wed she turned afraid

Of love and me and all things human;
Like the shut of a winter's day.
Her smile went out, and 'twasn't a woman—
    More like a little frightened fay.
    One night, in the Fall, she runned away.

"Out 'mong the sheep, her be," they said,
'Should properly havê been abed;
    But sure enough she wasn't there
    Lying awake with her wide brown stare.
So over seven-acre field and up-along across the down
We chased her, flying like a hare
Before our lanterns.   To Church-Town
All in a shiver and a scare
    We caught her, fetched her home at last
    And turned the key upon her, fast.

She does the work about the house
As well as most, but like a mouse:
    Happy enough to chat and play
    With birds and rabbits and such as they,
    So long as men-folk keep away.
"Not near, not near!" her eyes beseech
When one of us comes within reach.
    The women say that beasts in stall
    Look round like children at her call.
    I've hardly heard her speak at all.

Shy as a leveret, swift as he,
Straight and slight as a young larch tree,
Sweet as the first wild violets, she,
To her wild self.   But what to me?
The short days shorten and the oaks are brown,
    The blue smoke rises to the low gray sky,
One leaf in the still air falls slowly down,
    A magpie's spotted feathers lie
On the black earth spread white with rime,
The berries redden up to Christmas-time.
    What's Christmas-time without there be
    Some other in the house than we!

She sleeps up in the attic there
Alone, poor maid.   'Tis but a stair
Betwixt us.   Oh, my God!—the down,
The soft young down of her; the brown,
    The brown of her—her eyes, her hair, her hair!

Charlotte Mew

NEEDS

Silk I have for you, Madonna—you shook your small dear
    head—
"Silk I have and silk enough, a store of it," you said,
Content I laid the web away; you lacked some cotton thread.

A cup I filled for you, Madonna, but other hands than mine,
More meet, had given you to know the magic of the vine.
I poured within my empty cup fresh water for the wine.

A song I made for you, Madonna—it was my very best—
But your heart had heard the melody that will not let us
    rest,
Yet your lips had need of laughter, so I sang it for a jest.

Love I had for you, Madonna, because I looked on you,
But long ago your love was gone to pay its happy due;
Love you had, and love enough, and yet your friends were
    few.

My days are sweet, Madonna—sweet to their farthest end.
You, rich beyond all telling, had need that I should send
Cotton threads and clear clean water and jesting and a
    friend.

Elizabeth Rendall

THE IDOL

If you had asked of me
    All that I had,
I would have given it
    And been glad.

But you made of me
   A dream thing
That you pleased yourself
   By worshipping.

You looked at my face
   And never knew
What in my heart
   I asked of you.

And so I said,
   "It is only a game
To give to a dream
   A face and name,

"While the woman I am
   And the man you are
Are as far apart
   As star and star."

Louise Driscoll

DIALOGUE

IT is my own door that is shut,
   Shut fast within am I,
Since you, who were a guest, are but
   A passer-by.

Was I your guest? Oh, long ago
   I did come hurrying by;
We did exchange a word or so—
   How the years fly!

You visited my heart, and took
   Welcome I ill could spare—
Once only.   Did your casual look
   Find the house bare?

By no means!   You were more than kind,
   But I was called away;
Youth, and the world, and love to find—
   How could I stay?

Youth called you once, and it was I,
 Ashamed to call so loud,
Just once—for you made no reply,
 And I was proud.

Were you indeed? Ah, if again
 We had our lives to choose!
I thought a voice was calling then,
 I wondered whose.

Oh, why insult the heart you broke?
 Where love was, well you knew!
Even then the liar in you woke,
 The traitor grew!

Quite right, my fault, as I recall;
 Bitter it is, but true!
Reason to hate me—none at all
 For loving you.

John Erskine

TALK TO ME TENDERLY

TALK to me tenderly, tell me lies;
I am a woman and time flies,
I am a woman and out of the door
Beauty goes to come no more.

Talk to me tenderly, take my hand;
I am a woman and understand,
I am a woman and must be told
Lies to warn me when I am old.

Vivian Yeiser Laramore

THE DREAM–TELLER

I WAS a dreamer: I dreamed
A dream at the dark of dawn,
When the stars hung over the mountains
 And morn was wan.

I dreamed my dream at morn,
At noon, at the even-light,
But I told it to you, dark woman,
    One soft glad night.

And the sharing of my dream
Has brought me only this:
The gnawing pain of loss, the ache
    For your mouth to kiss.

I walked the high hills last night,
And lo, where the pale stars gleam,
God's cold Voice spake: "If you dream again,
    Tell none your dream;
    Tell none your dream!"

Padraic Gregory

TRIUMPH

ATHENS, a fragile kingdom by the foam,
Assumed the stranger's yoke; but then behold how meek
Those unbred Cæsars grew, who spent their fruits of Rome
For ever after, trying to be Greek.

I too shook out my locks like one born royal;
For she dissolved in tears, and said my barbarous name,
And took my oath, she was so piteous and loyal:
Vote the young Cæsar triumph, spread his fame!

But oh, I find my captive was not caught.
It was her empty house that fell before my legions;
Of where her soul inhabits I have conquered naught;
It is so far from these my Roman regions!

John Crowe Ransom

THE VICTOR

BLARE of trumpet and roll of drum!
Hath the day of my fancy come?

Dimly the house-tops seem to sway
Over the mile-long crowded way

To the palace portals: and hark!—the cry,
"Hail to the victor who passes by!"

Banner and pennon flutter red,
Dyed with the blood that my hands have shed;

And red and white are the roses strewn
Under my horse's silver shoon:

But O, for the face that I do not see
In casement, or in balcony!

Hides she there, where the shadows lurk,
Under the awnings of needle-work?—

Silent and pale, with her white hands pressed
Over the tumult of her breast?—

Stands she to gaze?—And her eyes, forlorn,
Look they in hatred, or pride, or scorn?

Onward! neither to left nor right
Let me glance in the rabble's sight!

Neither by word nor sign reveal
The sad, sick brain in the casque of steel!

Empty pageant and passing show!
Thus doth the day of my fancy go!

These, the guerdons of love's duress—
Pain, and peril, and weariness!

Better, mayhap, if the foeman's spear
Under my cuirass were buried here!

Better if now, through the gala town,
Heralded thus, I was riding down,

As the sweet Saints grant that I soon may ride,
Shrouded, and shriven, and satisfied!

Yea, that I never had heard the cry,
"Hail to the victor who passes by!"

William Young

THE CARVER

From "Priapus and the Pool"

SEE, as the carver carves a rose,
A wing, a toad, a serpent's eye,
In cruel granite, to disclose
The soft things that in hardness lie,

So this one, taking up his heart,
Which time and change had made a stone,
Carved out of it with dolorous art,
Laboring yearlong and alone,

The thing there hidden—rose, toad, wing?
A frog's hand on a lily pad?
Bees in a cobweb?—no such thing!
A girl's head was the thing he had,

Small, shapely, richly crowned with hair,
Drowsy, with eyes half closed, as they
Looked through you and beyond you, clear
To something farther than Cathay:

Saw you, yet counted you not worth
The seeing, thinking all the while
How, flower-like, beauty comes to birth;
And thinking this, began to smile.

Medusa! For she could not see
The world she turned to stone and ash.
Only herself she saw, a tree
That flowered beneath a lightning-flash.

Thus dreamed her face—a lovely thing,
To worship, weep for, or to break. . . .
Better to carve a claw, a wing,
Or, if the heart provide, a snake.

Conrad Aiken

ECCLESIASTES

IN the smoke-blue cabaret
    She sang some comic thing:
I heeded not at all
    Till "Sing! " she cried, "Sing! "
So I sang in tune with her
    The only song I know:
"The doors shall be shut in the streets,
    And the daughters of music brought low."

Her eyes and working lips
    Gleamed through the cruddled air—
I tried to sing with her
    Her song of devil-may-care.
But in the shouted chorus
    My lips would not be stilled:
"The rivers run into the sea,
    Yet the sea is not filled."

Then one came to my table
    Who said, with a laughing glance,
"If that is the way you sing,
    Why don't you learn to dance?"
But I said: "With this one song
    My heart and lips are cumbered—
'The crooked cannot be made straight,
    Nor that which is wanting numbered.'

"This song must I sing,
    Whatever else I covet—
Hear the end of my song,
    Hear the beginning of it:
'More bitter than death the woman
    (Beside me still she stands)
Whose heart is snares and nets,
    And whose hands are bands.'"

Morris Bishop

A WOMAN

You would give your red lips to press
On mine forever—would caress
Me with your white, unusèd arms
And fill me with the sweet alarms
Love sends through Man;

And you would nail your heart to mine,
And with your laughter would entwine
My soul and body, till the two
Were one—and always one—for you.
This is your plan.

Mary Dixon Thayer

MEN ARE THE DEVIL

Men are the devil—that's one thing sure.
Close your windows and lock your door,
Shut your eyes and shake your head.
Get your fun somewhere else, she said.

Men are the devil—they all bring woe.
In winter it's easy to say just "No."
Men are the devil, that's one sure thing,
But what are you going to do in spring?

Mary Carolyn Davies

TRAPS

A trap's a very useful thing:
Nature in our path sets Spring.
It is a trap to catch us two,
It is planned for me and you.
Do not think my cheeks are warm,
Do not wonder if my arm
Would make a pillow sweet for rest.
Not to speak or glance is best—
To smother the thing that calls so clear
Deep in our thoughts at the spring of the year.

If we stop, if we look, if we speak, if we care,
Nature will snatch us unaware,
Will put us in a home with four
Chairs, a table, and a door
To enslave us evermore.
She means to tie you firm and tight
To a desk from dawn till night
To make you strain and make you sweat
Till you forget, till you forget
All that is good and fine and high.
She will give you fear to keep till you die.
She means to tear my flesh to make
A child to steal my hours awake,
To break my hours asleep, to be
Slayer of the youth in me,
Slayer of the youth in you,
Slayer of that which makes us sing.
Let us never look at Spring;
It is a trap to catch us two.

Mary Carolyn Davies

SPRING

Spring! and the buds against the sky;
Heart, forget that you saw
The little brown bird that fluttered by—
    The bird with the wisp of straw.

Caroline Giltinan

THE FREE WOMAN

Women who do not love are free;
All day their thoughts go carelessly.
I know they do not fear at all
When the nights come and the snows fall.

But those who love—their thoughts must trace
All day the well-belovèd face,
And they are fearful and grow chill
At the snow's fall and the night's ill.

And they would fire their hearts to burn
Like a bright light at the road's turn,
And flay their souls to keep him warm
In the cold night and the white storm.

Surely I may be glad that I
Softly a night of storms may lie,
For I have watched a woman's face
A black night at a window's space.

Surely I should be happier,
Nor envy—envy—envy her;
But I have heard the word she spoke
In her man's arms as the dawn broke.

Theodosia Garrison

SPRING NIGHT

THE park is filled with night and fog,
    The veils are drawn about the world,
The drowsy lights along the paths
    Are dim and pearled.

Gold and gleaming the empty streets,
    Gold and gleaming the misty lake,
The mirrored lights like sunken swords,
    Glimmer and shake.

Oh, is it not enough to be
Here with this beauty over me?
My throat should ache with praise, and I
Should kneel in joy beneath the sky.
O beauty, are you not enough?
Why am I crying after love
With youth, a singing voice, and eyes
To take earth's wonder with surprise?
Why have I put off my pride,
Why am I unsatisfied,—
I, for whom the pensive night
Binds her cloudy hair with light,—

I, for whom all beauty burns
Like incense in a million urns?
O beauty, are you not enough?
Why am I crying after love?

Sara Teasdale

IN THE PARK

HE whistled soft whistlings I knew were for me,
Teasing, endearing.
Won't you look? was what they said,
But I did not turn my head.
(Only a little I turned my hearing.)

My feet took me by;
Straight and evenly they went:
As if they had not dreamed what he meant:
As if such a curiosity
Never was known since the world began
As woman wanting man!

My heart led me past and took me away;
And yet it was my heart that wanted to stay.

Helen Hoyt

ET SA PAUVRE CHAIR

THE moonlight filled them both with sundry glamors,
    Filtered silver in between white birches,
Blood whispered, like the stream, with urgent clamors,
    And bells were struck that never rang in churches.

She would not when he wished, and so the scene
    Progressed as aimless as the wind-blown sands:
He bit a box-bush leaflet tart and green
    She disciplined a rosebud with white hands.

When he had soothed this war to some accord
    What then remained of what was quick or breathless?
What came of scorn?   What of the bitten word?
    What of the wings, the flight they two called deathless?

The breaking of a smile when day was dim,
And her poor flesh awake, adoring him.

Alec Brock Stevenson

INTERVALS

I SHALL make offering in a new basket of marsh-grass
Curved like a conch-shell, sharp with salt echoes,
With two long handles like looped arms.
Untamed things shall I bring to the god of gardens,
Plum-blossom, sweet-olive and thyme,
Tang of small figs, gone wild in deserted gardens,
Most subtle of trees as the serpent is subtlest of beasts,
Slouched on the sun-soaked walls. . . .
I shall lay them under the weary, appraising eyes,
The cynical, musical fingers
That rest on the goat-thighs.
Let me give him, O Pan,
All in the way of love—
The new, keen edge of difference,
The wonder of being together,
And the wild taste of immemorial marsh-grass.
But in the intervals,
When the lover is gone and only the comrade remains,
Pan, have mercy!
Teach me to talk like a man!

Beatrice Ravenel

THE MODERN WOMAN TO HER LOVER

I SHALL not lie to you any more,
    Flatter or fawn to attain my end—
I am what never has been before,
    Woman—and Friend.

I shall be strong as a man is strong,
    I shall be fair as a man is fair,
Hand in locked hand we shall pass along
    To a purer air:

I shall not drag at your bridle-rein,
  Knee pressed to knee shall we ride the hill;
I shall not lie to you ever again—
  Will you love me still?
Margaret Widdemer

THE FLIGHT

Look back with longing eyes and know that I will follow,
Lift me up in your love as a light wind lifts a swallow,
Let our flight be far in sun or windy rain—
But what if I heard my first love calling me again?

Hold me on your heart as the brave sea holds the foam,
Take me far away to the hills that hide your home;
Peace shall thatch the roof and love shall latch the door—
But what if I heard my first love calling me once more?
Sara Teasdale

THE GOLDEN HEART

I had a heart as good as gold
For spending or for buying;
It bought me many a hand to hold
And many a breath for sighing.

It bought me many a mouth to kiss,
And many a secret token—
But what's the good of all of this
Now that my heart is broken!

My heart that once, as good as gold,
Bought anything that mattered
Is like a tale completely told,
Like golden money scattered. . . .

But somewhere there's a heart so young
It still can spare for spending
Will sing the song that I have sung,
Beginning with my ending.
Witter Bynner

CHANSON UN PEU NAÏVE

WHAT body can be ploughed,
Sown, and broken yearly?
She would not die, she vowed,
But she has nearly.
    Sing, heart, sing;
    Call and carol clearly.

And since she could not die,
Care would be a feather,
A film over the eye
Of two that lie together.
    Fly, song, fly,
    Break your little tether.

So from strength concealed
She makes her pretty boast:
Pain is a furrow healed
And she may love you most.
    Cry, song, cry,
    And hear your crying lost.

Louise Bogan

SILVER WEDDING

IN the middle of the night he started up
At a cry from his sleeping Bride,
A bat from some ruin in a heart he'd never searched,
Nay, hardly seen inside:

"Want me and take me for the woman that I am,
And not for her that died,
The lovely chit Nineteen I one time was,
And am no more," she cried.

Ralph Hodgson

TAMPICO

OH, cut me reeds to blow upon,
    Or gather me a star,
But leave the sultry passion-flowers
    Growing where they are.

I fear their sombre yellow deeps,
   Their whirling fringe of black,
And he who gives a passion-flower
   Always asks it back.

               Grace Hazard Conkling

FRIGHTENED FACE

CHILD of the frightened face,
   Trying to understand
The little bit of love
   Under your hand,

Holding the little love
   Under fingers that crush
That which is soft as the
   Throat of a thrush,

Holding your hand upon
   The wonder of the thing,
Crushing out the song that
   Wanted to sing:

Child of the frightened face,
   Why do your fingers try
To kill the little love?
   Soon it would die.

               Marion Strobel

BLACK AND WHITE

DID love sojourn with you long,
   Many days or few?
It was one with Time itself,
   That was all I knew.

Was it sacred or profane,
   Was it false or true?
It was bitter at the core,
   That was all I knew.

               Esther Lilian Duff

LOVE-FAITH

Now that you would leave me
  And another woo,
Was it you that told me once
  Lovers should be true?

Was it you that told me
  Lovers should be true?—
Dear, I still believe in love,
  But no more—in you!

Harry Kemp

ALIENATION

Go, I will shut the windows
  And draw the blinds for gloom.
Go, for the flower has fallen
  That filled two lives with bloom.

For me wait other women,
  For you wait other men . . .
But the ghosts of our old madness
  Will rise and walk again.

Harry Kemp

LITERARY LOVE

I BROKE my heart because of you, my dear;
I wept full many an unmanly tear—
But as in agony I lay awake
I thought, "What lovely poems this will make!"

Harry Kemp

AS HELEN ONCE

THE east unrolled a sheet of gold,
  Gold for river and flower and limb;
As Helen once to Paris was
  Was I to him.

All things gold fade gray and old,
  Even the sun of love grows dim;
As Helen now to Paris is
  Am I to him.

Muna Lee

A FAREWELL

GOOD-BYE!—no, do not grieve that it is over,
  The perfect hour;
That the winged joy, sweet honey-loving rover,
  Flits from the flower.

Grieve not—it is the law. Love will be flying—
  Yes, love and all.
Glad was the living—blessed be the dying.
  Let the leaves fall.

Harriet Monroe

MAN'S WAY

JANE, she could not:
  Fay, she could.
Mary would not,
  Kitty would.

My curse on Mary,
  Tears for Jane.
Kitty I'll love
  And love again.

Yet in the end
  I'll marry Fay.
Forgive it, Kitty,
  'Tis man's way.

L. A. G. Strong

THE CYNIC

I SAY it to comfort me over and over,
  Having a querulous heart to beguile,
Never had woman a tenderer lover—
  For a little while.

Oh, there never were eyes more eager to read her
   In her saddest mood or her moments gay,
Oh, there never were hands more strong to lead her—
   For a little way.

There never were loftier promises given
   Of love that should guard her the ages through,
As great, enduring and steadfast as Heaven—
   For a week or two.

Well, end as it does, I have had it, known it,
   For this shall I turn me to weep or pray?
Nay, rather I laugh that I thought to own it
    For more than a day.

Theodosia Garrison

LIGHT LOVER

Why don't you go back to the sea, my dear?
   I am not one who would hold you;
The sea is the woman you really love,
   So let hers be the arms that fold you.
Your bright blue eyes are a sailor's eyes,
   Your hungry heart is a sailor's, too.
   And I know each port that you pass through
Will give one lass both bonny and wise
Who has learned light love from a sailor's eyes.

If you ever go back to the sea, my dear,
   I shall miss you—yes, can you doubt it?
But women have lived through worse than that,
   So why should we worry about it?
Take your restless heart to the restless sea,
   Your light, light love to a lighter lass
   Who will smile when you come and smile when you pass.
Here you can only trouble me.
Oh, I think you had better go back to sea!

Aline Kilmer

COUNSEL

Love, like Ulysses,
Is a wanderer,
For new fields always
And new faces yearning. . . .
Put by, O waiting ones,
Put by your weaving,
Unlike Ulysses,
Love is unreturning.

Roselle Mercier Montgomery

THE BEATEN PATH

Ἰυγξ, ἕλκε τὺ τῆνον εμὸν ποτὶ δῶμα τὸν ἄνδρα.

Theocritus: Idyl II.

Dido with the driven hair
And with the salt sea spray
Upon those undesired lips,
And eyes that follow fading ships,—
It is no use to wander there
Along the shore
All day,
Or hope to see him any more;—
The way
He went is the old way!

Calypso, let the wanderer go
And weave your web and sing your song;
You knew you could not hold him long,
Though lost and shipwrecked on those shores,
And how can curses keep him yours
When kisses could not make him so?
There is no help from winds that blow,
No seas so strange or so unkind
That they can make him stay behind;—
The way he came he doesn't know,
But there's one way they all can find!

Fond Simætha, turning, turning
The bird upon your wheel and burning
Laurel leaves and barley grain,—
It will not draw him back again.
The moon above the lemon tree
Will watch with you, but watch in vain,
Nor are the dead of Hecate
Gone more utterly than he,—
Fled along a pathway fleet
Worn smooth by many feet. . . .

They make a long procession, sweeping
Relentlessly
Through all the past,—
These hearts that were not meant for keeping
And failed too fast;
And ships with windy sails at sea
And flowery lanes in Sicily
Alike led lovers down the track
That knows no turning back.

Anne Goodwin Winslow

PERMANENCE

THERE is no power to change
    One act, one word.
We move in time: these range
    Immortal. I have heard

Egypt and her Antony,
    With their love first fulfilled,
Cry out, and again cry—
    Nor ever are they stilled.

And Sheba I have seen
    Bare for her love her breast.
The silken Lesbian queen
    Leaves nothing unconfessed.

Though Helen's lips are dust
  The kisses of her lips
Must burn the towers, and must
  Still launch the thousand ships.

Unspaced, untimed, held fast
  Are all things done or undone.
Eternity knows no haste—
  In Babylon, or London.

Though they have never moved
  These hundred hundred years,
Their rhythm when they loved
  Lives ever, and their tears.

When your love's flight shall falter,
  Shall fall like a wounded bird,
You too cannot alter
  The said or unsaid word.

O passion of wisdom, this
  (Helen held it for such):
You cannot unkiss that kiss,
    You cannot untouch that touch.

Francis Meynell

JOHN–JOHN

I DREAMT last night of you, John-John,
  And thought you called to me;
And when I woke this morning, John,
  Yourself I hoped to see;
But I was all alone, John-John,
  Though still I heard your call:
I put my boots and bonnet on,
  And took my Sunday shawl,
And went, full sure to find you, John,
    To Nenagh fair.

The fair was just the same as then,
  Five years ago today,
When first you left the thimble men
  And came with me away;
For there again were thimble men
  And shooting galleries,
And card-trick men and Maggie men
  Of all sorts and degrees,—
But not a sight of you, John-John,
      Was anywhere.

I turned my face to home again,
  And called myself a fool
To think you'd leave the thimble men
  And live again by rule,
And go to Mass and keep the fast
  And till the little patch:
My wish to have you home was past
  Before I raised the latch
And pushed the door and saw you, John,
      Sitting down there.

How cool you came in here, begad,
  As if you owned the place!
But rest yourself there now, my lad,
  'Tis good to see your face;
My dream is out, and now by it
  I think I know my mind:
At six o'clock this house you'll quit,
  And leave no grief behind;—
But until six o'clock, John-John,
      My bit you'll share.

The neighbors' shame of me began
  When first I brought you in;
To wed and keep a tinker man
  They thought a kind of sin;
But now this three year since you're gone
  'Tis pity me they do,

And that I'd rather have, John-John,
  Than that they'd pity you.
Pity for me and you, John-John,
      I could not bear.

Oh, you're my husband right enough,
  But what's the good of that?
You know you never was the stuff
  To be the cottage cat,
To watch the fire and hear me lock
  The door and put out Shep—
But there now, it is six o'clock
  And time for you to step.
God bless and keep you far, John-John!
      And that's my prayer.
                              Thomas MacDonagh

THE TURN OF THE ROAD

Now my thick years bend your back.
Cut the thongs that hold the pack
      Merrily, merrily . . .

I will not be sad again.
I will strip myself of pain
And go singing as of old.
Though my hands are thin to hold,
Though my hair is pale as sand,
And I shiver as I stand,
I am not so short of breath
As to strangle you to death. . . .

Why should you go crook'd for me?
Shake yourself and run! run free!
No. It's long enough you ache
Borrowing years for my stiff sake.
No. I do not need you now. . . .

Toss the wild hair from your brow:
Run! while roads and city-smoke
Beckon young dream-worthy folk,

Why should I be lonely? See,
The old sun shines to comfort me,
And the small old hours dance
Lovely with all lost romance.
I have needed time to dream,—
But you must run, and grow, and gleam,
      Merrily! Merrily!

And if you come back to find
No one here but sun and wind,
Think, "He did not fail away
Cringing like a beast at bay,
But like an eagle or a star,
Lost by flying far,—so far!"

(God forgive me if I lie. . . .
All I love in life, good-bye. . . .)

Look! the long road and the sky! . . .
      Merrily! Merrily!

Fannie Stearns Gifford

THE TRAGEDY OF LOVE

CERTAINTIES

WHETHER you live by hut or throne,
  Whether your feet tread stone or grass,
Comes the one lad you shall never own,
  Or the one lass;

Whether you've pence to spend or gold,
  Whether you've toil or time to weep,
Comes the one pain that may never be told
  And may never sleep;

Whether you weep or mock in pride,
  Whether you tell or still deny,
Comes the one scar that your heart shall hide
  Till the day you die!

Margaret Widdemer

THE UNKNOWN BELOVED

I DREAMED I passed a doorway
  Where, for a sign of death,
White ribbons one was binding
  About a flowery wreath.

What drew me so I know not,
  But drawing near I said,
"Kind sir, and can you tell me
  Who is it here lies dead?"

Said he, "Your most belovèd
  Died here this very day,
That had known twenty Aprils
  Had she but lived till May."

151

Astonished I made answer,
  "Good sir, how say you so!
Here have I no belovèd,
  This house I do not know."

Quoth he, "Who from the world's end
  Was destined unto thee
Here lies, thy true belovèd,
  Whom thou shalt never see."

I dreamed I passed a doorway
  Where, for a sign of death,
White ribbons one was binding
  About a flowery wreath.

John Hall Wheelock

I PASS A LIGHTED WINDOW

I PASS a lighted window
  And a closed door—
And I am not troubled
  Any more.

Though the road is murky,
  I am not afraid,
For a shadow passes
  On the lighted shade.

Once I knew the sesame
  To the closed door;
Now I shall not enter
  Any more;

Nor will people, passing
  By the lit place,
See our shadows marry
  In a gray embrace.

Strange, a passing shadow
  Has a long spell!
What can matter, knowing
  She does well?

How could life annoy me
  Any more?
Life: a lighted window
  And a closed door.

Clement Wood

MAN TO MAN

BETTER it were, my brother,
  You twain had never met,
Then were no hearts broken
  And no dream to forget.

Now you must not remember,
  After you are gone,
The mystic magic of her eyes
  At twilight nor at dawn.

Now you must not remember
  The songs her red lips sing
Of love and lovers' ecstasy
  At dawn or evening.

John McClure

A PRAYER

GOD, is it sinful if I feel
His arms about me when I kneel
To pray? His arms that thrilled and drew
Me along paths the world's youth knew?

Or is it sin if I mistake
Eternity for time—and break
One instant from the dust of years
To mix with ecstasy, and tears?

God, oh my God, the way is long
Alone. Can it be very wrong
To dream of ways I did not tread?
To weep for words I never said?

Mary Dixon Thayer

GESTURE

My arms were always quiet,
    Close, and never freed.
I was furled like a banner,
    Enfolded like a seed.

I thought, when Love shall strike me,
    Each arm will start and spring,
Unloosen like a petal,
    And open like a wing.

O Love—my arms are lifted,
    But not to sway and toss;
They strain out wide and wounded,
    Like arms upon a cross.
             Winifred Welles

LOVE SONG FROM NEW ENGLAND

In every solemn tree the wind
    Has rung a little lonesome bell,
As sweet and clear, as cool and kind
    As my voice bidding you farewell.

This is an hour that gods have loved
    To snatch with bare, bright hands and hold.
Mine, with a gesture, gray and gloved,
    Dismiss it from me in the cold.

Closely as some dark-shuttered house
    I keep my light.   How should you know,
That, as you turn beneath brown boughs,
    My heart is breaking in the snow?
             Winifred Welles

FROM A CAR–WINDOW

Pines, and a blur of lithe young grasses;
    Gold in a pool, from the western glow;
Spread of wings where the last thrush passes—
    And thoughts of you as the sun dips low.

Quiet lane, and an irised meadow . . .
  (*How many summers have died since then?*) . . .
I wish you knew how the deepening shadow
    Lies on the blue and green again!

Dusk, and the curve of field and hollow
    Etched in gray when a star appears:
Sunset, . . . twilight, . . . and dark to follow, . . .
    And thoughts of you through a mist of tears.

Ruth Guthrie Harding

SONG

    GOING down the old way
        When the day's through,
    If I met my old love
        What should I do?

    Greet him with a light word,
        Pass with a sigh?
    Give pain for pain he gave
        In times gone by?

    Nay—laugh for happiness,
        Cling and forget
    How he left my heart sore
        And my eyes wet!

Margaret Widdemer

THE CAUSE OF THIS I KNOW NOT

    THE cause of this I know not,
        Whither they went nor why,
    But I still remember the laughter
        And the bright eyes flashing by,
    The day the girls were kissing
        The boys who had to die.

I search in vain for the reason—
    What does a poet know?—
Only that youth is lovely,
    Only that youth must go;
And hearts are made to be broken
    And love is always woe.

Haniel Long

SONG

ONLY a little while since first we met,
    And soon the sea, with many a weary mile,
Shall sever us forever, Sweet . . . and yet,
Will it be very easy to forget?—
        Only a little while!

Only a little while that I may claim
    The whole soul's breath of you without denial,
And see your eyes grow golden with a flame
That is not Love, yet hath no other name—
        Only a little while!

Only a little while to use my art
    So that some day you may look back, and smile
Out of a joy wherein I have no part
On that old self of yours that filled my heart
        Only a little while!

Brian Hooker

I SHALL NOT WEEP

" Or, to be old, perhaps, is not to care."—EDWARD D. KENNEDY

    I SHALL not weep when you are gone;
    I shall not miss you over-much.
    I shall not grieve for kiss or touch
    Or speech with you.   These, in the dawn
    Of love's awakening, held back wan
    Terror, fear of loss, mad jealousy,
    And mutinous flutterings to be free
    From fetters, e'er so gently drawn.

They'll say I am too old to care;
That trivial things my days beguile;
Youth knows so little. I shall smile,
Remembering jokes we used to share,
Unending argument, and flare
Of sudden temper; all the ways of Love
To prove its strength, to grow above
The need to see you sitting there.

I shall not weep when you are gone,
Nor shall I miss you . . . over-much.

Belle MacDiarmid Ritchey

I SHALL NOT BE AFRAID

I SHALL not be afraid any more,
  Either by night or day.
What would it profit me to be afraid
  With you away?

Now I am brave. In the dark night alone
  All through the house I go,
Locking the doors and making windows fast
  When sharp winds blow.

For there is only sorrow in my heart;
  There is no room for fear.
But how I wish I were afraid again,
  My dear, my dear!

Aline Kilmer

WHERE YOU PASSED

ALONG the woodland path we took
I walk alone today,
Between white drifts of loveliness
New flowered by the way.
Lightly did we meet, my dear,
And smiling did we part—
But where you passed there is a trail
Of blossoms in my heart.

Amelia Josephine Burr

THE RAINBOW

WHOSE doorway was it, in the sordid street,
　That gave us shelter from the sudden rain,—
Two vagrant sparrows on a dripping branch,
　Waiting a moment to spread wing again?

The beggar children danced through pavement pools
　Barefoot and joyous, splashing at their will;
The rain washed green that dusty sycamore
　And straws swirled wildly down the gutter's rill.

Fast-breathing from the run, our hands still clasped,
　We leaned out laughing, shaking free our hair
Of dewy drops, while still the clouds poured down
　A freshness that made heavenly the air.

Then we both saw, above the sodden world,
　The Rainbow like a miracle appear,
And you said, whispering, "Oh, kiss me once
　Before it fades! "—"Kiss me then quickly, Dear! "

One warm sweet touch of lips—then forth we went
　Oblivious of all the rain and wet.
To-day I saw a rainbow after rain. . . .
　My heart remembered then—does yours forget?
                                            Vine Colby

VISTAS

　　As I walked through the rumorous streets
　　Of the wind-rustled, elm-shaded city
　　Where all the houses were friends
　　　And the trees were all lovers of her,
　　The spell of its old enchantment
　　Was woven again to subdue me
　　With magic of flickering shadows,
　　　Blown branches and leafy stir.

Street after street, as I passed,
Lured me and beckoned me onward
With memories frail as the odor
   Of lilac adrift on the air.
At the end of each breeze-blurred vista
She seemed to be watching and waiting,
With leaf shadows over her gown
   And sunshine gilding her hair.

For there was a dream that the kind God
Withheld, while granting us many—
But surely, I think, we shall come
   Sometime, at the end, she and I,
To the heaven He keeps for all tired souls,
The quiet suburban gardens
Where He Himself walks in the evening
   Beneath the rose-dropping sky
And watches the balancing elm trees
Sway in the early starshine
When high in their murmurous arches
   The night breeze ruffles by.

Odell Shepard

NOT UNTO THE FOREST

(REMEMBRANCE)

Not unto the forest—not unto the forest, O my lover!
Why do you lead me to the forest!
  Joy is where the temples are
  Lines of dancers swinging far
    Drums and lyres and viols in the town—
(It is dark in the forest.)
  And the flapping leaves will blind me
  And the clinging vines will bind me
    And the thorny rose-boughs tear my saffron gown—
And I fear the forest.

Not unto the forest—not unto the forest, O my lover!
Long since one led me to the forest. . . .
  Hand in hand we wandered mute
  Where was neither lyre nor flute

Little stars were bright above the dusk
  And the thickets of wild rose
  Breathed across our lips locked close
    Perfumings of spikenard and musk. . . .
I am tired of the forest.

Not unto the forest—not unto the forest, O my lover!
Take me from the silence of the forest!
  I will love you by the light
  And the beat of drums at night
    And the echoing of laughter in my ears,
But here in the forest
  I am still, remembering
  A forgotten, useless thing,
    And my eyelids are locked down for fear of tears. . . .
There is memory in the forest.
                              Margaret Widdemer

TO BUTTERFLY

Do you remember how the twilight stood
  And leaned above the river just to see
If still the crocus buds were in her hood,
  And if her robes were gold or shadowy?
Do you remember how the twilight stood
When we were lovers and the world our wood?

And then, one night, when we could find no word,
  But silence trembled like a heart—like mine!—
And suddenly that moon-enraptured bird
  Awoke and all the darkness turned to wine?
How long ago that was! And how absurd
For us to own a wood that owned a bird!

They tell me there are magic gardens still,
  And birds that sleep to wake and dream to sing,
And streams that pause for crocus skies to fill;
  But they that told were lovers and 'twas spring.
Yet why the moon to-night's a daffodil
When it is March—Do you remember, still?
                              William Alexander Percy

NOCTURNE OF REMEMBERED SPRING

I

MOONLIGHT silvers the shaken tops of trees,
Moonlight whitens the lilac-shadowed wall;
And through the soft-starred evening fall
Clearly as if through enchanted seas
Footsteps passing an infinite distance away,
In another world, and another day.
Moonlight turns the purple lilacs to blue,
Moonlight leaves the fountain hoar and old,
Moonlight whitens the sleepy dew,
And the boughs of elms grow green and cold. . . .
Our footsteps echo on gleaming stones;
The leaves are stirred to a jargon of muted tones. . . .
This is the night we have kept, you say;
This is the moonlight night that never will die. . . .
Let us return there, let us return, you and I,—
Through the gray streets our memories retain
Let us go back again.

II

Mist goes up from the river to dim the stars,
The river is black and cold; so let us dance
To a tremor of violins and troubled guitars,
And flare of horns, and clang of cymbals, and drums;
And strew the glimmering floor with petals of roses
And remember, while rich music yawns and closes,
With a luxury of pain, how silence comes. . . .
Yes, we have loved each other, long ago;
We moved like wind to a music's ebb and flow
At a phrase from the violins you closed your eyes,
And smiled, and let me lead you . . . how young we were!
Waves of music beneath us dizzied to rise.
Your hair, upon that music, seemed to stir. . . .
Let us return there, let us return, you and I.
Through changelesss streets our memories retain
Let us go back again.

III

Mist goes up from the rain-steeped earth, and clings
Ghostly with lamplight among drenched maple trees,
We walk in silence, and see how the lamplight flings
Fans of shadow upon it . . . the music's mournful
    pleas
Die out behind us, the door is closed at last,
A net of silver silence is softly cast
Over our dreams . . . slowly and softly we walk,
Quietly, with delicious pause, we talk,
Of foolish trivial things, of life and death,
Time and forgetfulness, and dust and truth,—
Lilacs and youth.
You laugh, I hear the after-taken breath,
You darken your eyes and turn away your head
At something I have said—
Some tremulous intuition that flew too deep,
And struck a plangent chord . . . to-night, to-night,
You will remember it as you fall asleep,
Your dream will suddenly blossom with sharp de-
    light. . . .
Good-night! you say. . . .
The leaves of the lilac softly dip and sway,
The purple spikes of bloom
Nod their sweetness upon us, and lift again,
Your white face turns away,—I am caught with pain,—
And silence descends . . . and the dripping of dew from
    the eaves
And jewelled points of leaves.

IV

I walk in a pleasure of sorrow along the street
And try to remember you . . . the slow drops patter,
The mist upon the lilacs has made them sweet,
I brush them with my sleeve, the cool drops scatter,
And suddenly I laugh . . . and stand and listen
As if another had laughed . . . a fragrant gust
Rustles the laden leaves, the wet spikes glisten,
A shower of drops goes down on stones and dust.

And it seems as though it were you who had shaken the
    bough,
And spilled the fragrance—I pursue your face again,
It grows more vague and lovely, it eludes me now.
I remember that you are gone, and drown in pain.
Something there was I said to you, I recall,
Something, just as the music seemed to fall,
That made you laugh, and burns me still with pleas-
    ure. . . .
What were the words—the words like dripping fire? . . .
I remember them now, and smile, and in sweet leisure
Rehearse the scene, more exquisite than before,
And you more beautiful, and I more wise. . . .
Lilacs, and spring, and night, and your clear eyes,
And you, in white, by the darkness of a door. . . .
These things, like voices weaving to richest music,
Flow and fall in the cool night of my mind,
I pursue your ghost among green leaves that are ghostly,
I pursue you, but cannot find. . . .
And suddenly, with a pang that is sweetest of all,
I become aware that I cannot remember you;
The beautiful ghost I knew
Has silently plunged in the shadows, shadows that stream
    and fall.

v

Let us go in and dance once more
On the dream's glimmering floor,
Beneath the balcony festooned with roses.
Let us go in and dance once more. . . .
The door behind us closes
Against an evening purple with stars and mist. . . .
Let us go in and keep our tryst
With music and white roses, and spin around
In lazy swirls of sound.
Do you foresee me, married and grown old? . . .
And you, who smile about you at this room
Dizzy with whirling dancers—is it foretold
That you must step from tumult into a gloom,
Forget me, love another, grow white and cold?

No, you are Cleopatra, fiercely young,
Laughing upon the topmost stair of night;
Roses upon the desert must be flung,
It is your wish. . . . Above us, light by light,
Weaves the delirious darkness, petals fall,
They fall upon your jewelled hands, they tremble upon
　　your hair,—
And music breaks in waves on the pillared wall,
And you are Cleopatra, and do not care. . . .
And so, in memory, you will always be—
Young, and foolish, a thing of dream and mist;
And so, perhaps, when all is disillusioned,
And eternal spring returns once more,
Bringing a ghost of lovelier springs remembered,
You will remember me.

VI

Yet when we meet we seem in silence to say,
Pretending serene forgetfulness of our youth,
"Do you remember . . . but then, why, should you re-
　　member! . . .
Do you remember a certain day,
Or evening, rather,—spring evening long ago,—
We talked of death, and love, and time, and truth. . . .
And said such wise things, things that amused us so . . .?
How foolish we were, who thought ourselves so wise!"
And then we laugh, with shadows in our eyes.

Conrad Aiken

THRESHOLD

If I knocked in this dead night,
She would know, as fate had told,
Who stood in the streaming light,
Though the young look had grown old.
Years have gone since last we two
Met in the lane and parted wide,
There by the fire I see her new,
Perhaps a lover or a bride;

There, it is but tap the pane
And what might be? dare I so?
Rouse the sleeping past again
And tangle now with long ago?

What would pass, a riddle lies,
But not time, for all he tries,
Could darken the awakened gleam
Of love's early primrose dream—
Primroses, how we hailed their peeping,
Under the black-barked woodsides creeping,
And kingcups by the cold lost rill
And other flowers our hats to fill—
But hawthorn flowers she'd have me leave,
They cross a threshold but to grieve;
'Twas primrose all our journeys through,
Her love, air's beams, earth's faëry too.

For with what joyful starry drops
Those primrose buds bedewed each copse!
And all the new-born air excelled
To show what long had been withheld.
And though in pale offence she turned
And latched the door and left me spurned
She could not choose but weep anon,
She, to her life's noon blossoming on,
And think as I do, where's joy gone?
Finding in some unbidden tears
That there are buds no winter sears,
And when time comes, for old time's sake
Primrosing in our earliest brake.

Edmund Blunden

THE RETURN

A LITTLE hand is knocking at my heart,
    And I have closed the door.
"I pray thee, for the love of God, depart:
    Thou shalt come in no more."

"Open, for I am weary of the way.
  The night is very black.
I have been wandering many a night and day.
  Open. I have come back."

The little hand is knocking patiently;
  I listen, dumb with pain.
"Wilt thou not open, any more to me?
  I have come back again."

"I will not open any more. Depart.
  I, that once lived, am dead."
The hand that had been knocking at my heart
  Was still. "And I?" she said.

There is no sound, save in the winter air,
  The sound of wind and rain.
All that I loved in all the world stands there,
  And will not knock again.

                                        Arthur Symons

JERKED HEARTSTRINGS IN TOWN

I HAVE heard echoes and seen visions of you
Often of late. Once yawning at a play
A sad keen rapture suddenly pierced me through
Because one puppet moved and sighed your way;

An omnibus-conductor fixed your glance
—Intense, preoccupied—upon my fare;
I saw your stooping shoulders, at a dance,
Lean by a doorway: but you were not there.

Down Oxford Street, in the slow shopping crowd,
Hearing your very voice, "Ah, that's superb!"
I turned,—a tawdry simpering little dowd
Passed by, and left me trembling on the curb.

                                        E. B. C. Jones

THE WANDERER

HE's such a wanderer in his thoughts
That no one can keep pace;
So strangely he will talk of Crete,
Of Candia and Thrace!

He will not take me where he goes,
He's deaf to me and blind.
Always, I am left at home,
Sitting in my mind. . . .

Amanda Benjamin Hall

PARTING AFTER A QUARREL

YOU looked at me with eyes grown bright with pain,
   Like some trapped thing's.   And then you moved your
      head
Slowly from side to side, as though the strain
   Ached in your throat with anger and with dread.

And then you turned and left me, and I stood
   With a queer sense of deadness over me,
And only wondered dully that you could
   Fasten your trench-coat up so carefully

Till you were gone.   Then all the air was thick
   With my last words that seemed to leap and quiver;
And in my heart I heard the little click
   Of a door that closes—quietly, forever.

Eunice Tietjens

SPINSTER SONG

IT's a mournful tune the rain is making,
   Over and over, over and over.
Will it never have done at my window?
   Where is your lover?   Where is your lover?

And why should I know or care where he is?
  Except for the rain I'd not be thinking
Of him. "Good riddance," my people said,
  "He with his lights o' love, and his drinking."

"Good riddance," they said. Lord, Lord, how it rains!
  I should be thankful enough for a cover
Above my head, and a fire to warm me,—
  Over and over. Where is your lover?

I had my pride as a girl should have.
  I have it still. If I am crying,
It's the rain. I'd shed no tears for him,
  And his smiling lips that were made for lying.

It's a mournful tune the rain is making.
  Over and over, over and over.
While the fire burns low, and the ashes fall.
  Where is my lover? Where is my lover?
                                    Virginia Lyne Tunstall

SEVEN TIMES THE MOON CAME

  SEVEN times the moon came
    When you were gone from me,
  Casting on the mountain land
    Its old sorcery.

  Seven times the river caught
    Its cold silver fire,
  And the ancient hooded bridge
    Arched above it higher.

  All was lovely as before,
    But I could only see
  That seven times the moon had come
    And you were gone from me.
                          Jessie B. Rittenhouse

THE WIND'S WAY

THE winds of the world for a little season
  Blew us together heart to heart,
But now, alas! with the wind's unreason,
  The winds of the world must blow us apart.

And thou to the north, and I to the south,
  Must wander away into loveless lands,
With a last long anguish of mouth on mouth,
  And a last despair of dissevered hands.

O winds of the world that blew us together,
  Winds of the world that blow us apart,
Will it ever again be lovers' weather,
  Shall we ever again be heart to heart?
                              Richard Le Gallienne

JOHN O' DREAMS

WHAT a world that was you planned us—
  Made of Summer and the sea,
Where the very wind that fanned us
  Drifted down from Arcady.
There where never Fate might sunder
  Rose your castle's shining beams.
Are you there to-day I wonder,
  John o' Dreams?

That was but a trick Life played you
  When this planet knew your birth,
When she trapped your soul and made you
  One of us on dreary earth.
Since for you what fancies crossed it,
  Lures of alien stars and streams,
Have you found the path or lost it,
  John o' Dreams?

Just a little day in May-time
　　Once I took the road with you;
Just a boy and girl in play-time
　　With a vision to pursue.
I but glimpsed the glow around it
　　Ere I turned, and yet it seems
Sometimes that you surely found it,
　　John o' Dreams.

Theodosia Garrison

"MARY, HELPER OF HEARTBREAK"

WELL, if the thing is over, better it is for me,
The lad was ever a rover, loving and laughing free,
Far too clever a lover not to be having still
A lass in the town and a lass by the road and a lass by the
　　farther hill—
Love on the field and love on the path and love in the
　　woody glen—
(Lad, will I never see you, never your face again?)

Ay, if the thing is ending now I'll be getting rest,
Saying my prayers and bending down to be stilled and
　　blest,
Never the days are sending hope till my heart is sore
For a laugh on the path and a voice by the gate and a step
　　on the shieling floor—
Grief on my ways and grief on my work and grief till the
　　evening's dim—
(Lord, will I never hear it, never a sound of him?)

Sure if it's done forever, better for me that's wise,
Never the hurt, and never tears in my aching eyes,
No more the trouble ever to hide from my asking folk
Beat of my heart at click o' the latch, and throb if his
　　name is spoke;
Never the need to hide the sighs and the flushing thoughts
　　and the fret,
And after awhile my heart will hush and my hungering
　　hands forget . . .

Peace on my ways, and peace in my step, and maybe my
    heart grown light—
(*Mary, helper of heartbreak, send him to me to-night!*)
                              Margaret Widdemer

EMERGENCY

REGULATION-skirted,
Throat framed in fur,
Poised . . . and disconcerted
To the soul of her.

Modish from her taxi,
The last word of art . . .
And the fires of Cotopaxi
In her shaken heart.

Fortunate her manner,
On the Mayfair curb;
But her stricken banner
Would high heaven disturb:

Trivial her cover,
Judge it as you must,
Yesterday her lover
Turned her dream to dust.

Tragedy is roguish
To the point of shame
When it is the voguish
Thing to play the game:

Touch of rouge for masking,
Flippancy of skirt,
Meanwhile eyes are asking
Remedy for hurt.

Here's no cause for pity
Seen from fashion's pave,—
But from another City,
How they rush to save!

                          Isabel Fiske Conant

LOSS

SHE went about accustomed tasks
  As quietly as before,
Put roses in the yellow bowl,
  New curtains at the door.

Folding the sheets, she laid some sprigs
  Of lavender inside,
But in her room . . . an empty room . . .
  She had no pride.

Julia Johnson Davis

DECENT BURIAL

THOSE nights we said "Goodbye! goodbye!" and then
Returned to say "Goodbye . . . goodbye—" again,
Did not a parting but a greeting tell,
Close-wrapping us in darkness and farewell.

The night we dared no kissed goodbye to say
But buried hope, and took the lonely way,
That was a parting all the world might see—
The grave is neatly kept by you and me.

Lois Seyster Montross

I SAT AMONG THE GREEN LEAVES

I SAT among the green leaves, and heard the nuts falling,
  The broadred butterflies were gold against the sun,
But in between the silence and the sweet birds calling
  The nuts fell one by one.

Why should they fall and the year but half over?
  Why should sorrow seek me and I so young and kind?
The leaf is on the bough and the dew is on the clover,
  But the green nuts are falling in the wind.

Oh, I gave my lips away and all my soul behind them.
  Why should trouble follow and the quick tears start?
The little birds may love and fly with only God to mind
    them,
  But the green nuts are falling on my heart.

Marjorie L. C. Pickthall

THE DREAM HOUSE

I STEAL across the sodden floor
  And dead leaves blow about,
Where once we planned an iron door
  To shut the whole world out;

I find the hearth, its fires unlit,
  Its ashes cold—to-night
Only the stars give warmth to it,
  Only the moon gives light.

And yonder on our spacious bed
  Fashioned for love and sleep
The Autumn goldenrod lies dead,
  The maple-leaves lie deep.

Marjorie Allen Seiffert

LET IT BE FORGOTTEN

LET it be forgotten, as a flower is forgotten,
  Forgotten as a fire that once was singing gold,
Let it be forgotten for ever and ever,
  Time is a kind friend, he will make us old.

If anyone asks, say it was forgotten
  Long and long ago,
As a flower, as a fire, as a hushed footfall
  In a long forgotten snow.

Sara Teasdale

DOUBT

WHAT can I give my dear
   Who has given his heart to me,
That I may keep his love
   Safe under lock and key?

Oh, I can give him a singing voice,
   And a body white and fine;
But what if he asked for an old, old dream
   That once in the past was mine?

What if he came to seek for love,
   Where never love might win?
What if he knocked at my empty heart
   And said, "Sweet, let me in!"

Elinor Chipp

BEFORE DAWN

LAST night you stirred in your sleep as the night went
      through
And I knew you were thinking far off, invisible things,
And my heart cried out with the ache of its love for you
Till I longed to be free of its spell and the pain that it
      brings.

There came to me, out of the night, the hum of the city
      street,
The honking of horns and the rattle of passing cars,
And ever the sound of restless and hurrying feet;
But my heart was alone and crying under the stars.

My heart was alone, though you that I love the best
Crept into my arms, and your slumber grew peaceful
      again;
You smiled in your sleep, and your head drooped over my
      breast,
But I lay awake; and my heart was heavy with pain.

Elinor Chipp

RED MAY

OUT of the window the trees in the Square
Are covered with crimson may—
You, that were all of my love and my care,
Have broken my heart to-day.

But though I have lost you and though I despair
Till even the past looks gray—
Out of the window the trees in the Square
Are covered with crimson may.

A. Mary F. Robinson

RISPETTO

I

WHAT good is there, ah me, what good in Love?
　Since, even if you love me, we must part;
And since for either, an you cared enough,
　There's but division and a broken heart?

And yet, God knows, to hear you say: My Dear!
I would lie down and stretch me on the bier.
And yet would I, to hear you say: My Own!
With mine own hands drag down the burial stone.

II

Let us forget we loved each other much,
　Let us forget we ever have to part,
Let us forget that any look or touch
　Once let in either to the other's heart.

Only we'll sit upon the daised grass
And hear the larks and see the swallows pass;
Only we'll live awhile, as children play,
Without to-morrow, without yesterday.

III

Ah, Love, I cannot die, I cannot go
  Down in the dark and leave you all alone;
Ah, hold me fast, safe in the warmth I know,
  And never shut me underneath a stone.

Dead in the grave!   And I can never hear
If you are ill, or if you miss me, dear;
Dead, oh, my God! and you may need me yet,
While I shall sleep, while I—while I—forget!

                              A. Mary F. Robinson

WILL YOU, ONE DAY

WILL you, one day when I am dead,
  See what you see not now?
Say "This was love, although it fled
  Without a vow?"
Will you? one day?

Will you, one day when life and love
  Have taught you all I know,
Say "Could the time return, I'd prove
  I could love so?"
Will you? one day?

Will you, when I have long been dead,
  Look on a daughter near
To your dear heart and say, "She said
  Thus was I dear?"
Will you? one day?

Will you one day, oh sweetest heart,
  Know that beyond command
Is love that ever seems of life a part,
  And understand?
Try to.—One day?

                              Marian Ramie

COMPENSATION

HERE, in the field, last year,
   I saw a seagull die,
Flying inland, for fear
   Of change in the sky.

Seagulls six and seven
   Flew inland, and cried:
And one fell out of Heaven
   Here, and died.

I found no scar or stain:
   He was white and gray, like smoke.
He flew, and was in pain,
   And his heart broke.

Now, when I come this way,
   I remember his beauty and pride,
And how from the hollow of day
   He fell, and died.

Then, I too was proud;
   I was angry to see death.
The hour, that was warm and loud,
   Drew one cold breath.

Again the gulls are flying.
   My heart, that then was a lover
Hot and high, is dying—
   But the gulls fly over.

Gerald Gould

SONG

IF I had only loved your flesh
   And careless damned your soul to Hell,
I might have laughed and loved afresh,
   And loved as lightly and as well,
      And little more to tell.

But since to clasp your soul I strove
  (That mountebank, that fugitive),
And poured the river of my love
  Through meshes that, like Danaë's sieve,
    Drained all I had to give,

Now nightly by the tamarisks
  I pace, and watch the risen moon
Litter the sea with silver disks;
  And pray of night one only boon:
    Let my release be soon.

V. Sackville-West

SPLENDID AND TERRIBLE

SPLENDID and terrible your love.
The searing pinions of its flight
Flamed but a moment's space above
The place where ancient memories keep
Their quiet; and the dreaming deep
Moved inly with a troubled light,
And that old passion woke and stirred
Out of its sleep.

Splendid and terrible your love.
I hold it to me like a flame;
I hold it like a flame above
The empty anguish of my breast.
There let it stay, there let it rest—
Deep in the heart whereto it came
Of old as some wind-wearied bird
Drops to its nest.

Seumas O'Sullivan

TO——

ASLEEP within the deadest hour of night
And turning with the earth, I was aware
How suddenly the eastern curve was bright,
As when the sun arises from his lair.
But not the sun arose: it was thy hair
Shaken up heaven in tossing leagues of light.

Since then I know that neither night nor day
May I escape thee, O my heavenly hell!
Awake, in dreams, thou springest to waylay;
And should I dare to die, I know full well
Whose voice would mock me in the mourning bell,
Whose face would greet me in hell's fiery way.

Robert Nichols

THE KLEPTOMANIAC

SHE stole his eyes because they shone,
Stole the good things they looked upon;
—They were no brighter than her own.

She stole his mouth—her own was fair—
She stole his words, his songs, his prayer;
His kisses too, since they were there.

She stole the journeys of his heart,
—Her own, their very counterpart—
His seas, his sails, his course, his chart.

She stole his strength so fierce and true,
—Perhaps for something brave to do—
Wept at his weakness, stole that too.

But she was caught one early morn!
She stood red-handed and forlorn,
And stole his anger and his scorn.

Upon his breast she laid her head,
Refusing to be comforted;
"Unkind! Unkind!" was all she said;

Denied she stole; confessed she did;
Glad of such plunder to be rid;
—Clutching the place where it was hid.

As he forgave, she snatched his soul;
She did not want it . . . but she stole.

Leonora Speyer

LITTLE LOVER

You made your little lover kind,
   And quick of word and kiss and tear,
   And everything a woman craves;
   You could not make him big, my dear.

And so you made your great self small,
   As only a great woman can,
   Nor cared a jot; but he, he knew,
   And cared a lot, the little man.

He knew, and hated you at last. . . .
   Let me be fair! He left you then.
   That one big, generous thing he did;
   Left you to grieve to heights again.

Leonora Speyer

THE WITCH

You cannot build again what you have broken,
You cannot bind the words your lips have spoken.

You broke the golden bowl and shattered it,
You put away Remembrance in a pit.

You sprinkled earth, you wove a spell and sang,
And on its grave certain red lilies sprang.

You watered them with a betrayed man's tears,
And found them fair. God sent you sighs and fears.

You bent them to your lust and made them be
Food for your Hell-imagined ecstasy.

You took Remorse and strangled it by night,
And sank it in a well. You bound Delight

And brought it home: the cord that held it fast
Was the forgetfulness of kindness past.

You took the price of him you had betrayed
And bought you toys and decked yourself and played

Like any child: you were all soft and sweet;
Your lovers watched your little dancing feet

With glowing eyes, too lover-blind to see
In your white hands clasped close the Judas-fee.

You took the price and you have held it still;
And now, far off, you see Heaven on a hill,

And dream of peace and gates of pearl unlocked—
Poor fool! be not deceived, God is not mocked.

Alfred Bruce Douglas

JACK ROSE

WITH crafty brooding life turned to Jack Rose
And made him heroin-peddler, and his pose
Was sullenly reflective since he feared
That life, regarding him, had merely jeered.
His vanity was small and could not call
His egoism to the dubious hall
Of fame, where average artists spend their hour.
Doubting his powers he was forced to cower
Within the shrill, damp alleys of his time,
Immersed in that brisk midnight known as crime.
He shunned the fiercely shrewd stuff that he sold
To other people, and derived a cold
Enjoyment from the writhing of their hearts.
A speechless artist, he admired the arts
Of blundering destruction, like a monk
Viewing a play that made him mildly drunk.
And so malicious and ascetic Jack
Bent to his trade with a relentless back
Until he tapped an unexpected smile—
A woman's smile as smooth and hard as tile.
May Bulger pawned her flesh to him and gave
His heroin to her brother, with a grave
Reluctance fumbling at her painted lips.
Though angry at herself, she took the whips
Of undesired love, to quiet a boy
Who wept inanely for his favorite toy.

She hated Jack because he failed to gloss
And soften the rough surface of her loss,
His matter-of-fact frown biting at her heart.
He hated her because her smiling guess
Had robbed him of ascetic loneliness,
And when her brother died, Jack sat beside
Her grief and played a mouth-harp while she cried.
But when she raised her head and smiled at him—
A smile intensely stripped and subtly grim—
His hate felt overawed and in a trap,
And suddenly his head fell to her lap.
For some time she sat stiffly in the chair,
Then slowly raised her hand and stroked his hair.

Maxwell Bodenheim

NEWPORT STREET, E.

Down Newport Street, last Sunday night,
    Bill stabbed his sweetheart in the breast:
She screamed and fell, a dreadful sight,
    And Bill strode on like one possessed.

O Love's a curse to them that's young;
    'Twas all because of love and drink;
Why couldn't the silly hold her tongue,
    Or stop, before she spoke, to think?

She played with fire, did pretty Nell,
    So Bill must hang ere summer's here:
Christ, what a crowd are sent to Hell
    Through love, and poverty and beer!

Douglas Goldring

TWO WAYS

Oncet in the museum
    We seen a little rose
In a jar of alcohol—
    You turns up your nose:
"That's the way people think
    Love ought to be—
Last forever!   Pickled roses!—
    None o' that for me!"

That night was fireworks
   Out to Riverview—
Gold and red and purple
   Bustin' over you.
"Beautiful! " you says then,
   "That's how love should be!
Burn wild and die quick—
   That's the love for me! "

Now you're gone for good . . . say,
Wasn't they no other way?
John V. A. Weaver

NOCTURNE

"Nothin' or everythin' it's got to be,"
You says, and hides your face down on my arm.
"If it meant nothin', 'twouldn't do no harm,
Or either everythin'—but this way—see? . . ."

I feel your tremblin' heart against my coat,
An' the big arc-light moon grins down so cool,
"Go on! " I think it says, "you softie fool! " . . .
I love you so it hurts me in my throat. . . .

"Don't make me kiss you; sure, I know you could,"
You're pleadin', "an' we gone too far for play;
I care a lot . . . but yet not so's to say
I love you yet. . . . Aw, help me to be good! " . . .

O darlin', darlin', can't you let it be
Nothin' to you, an' everythin' to me?
John V. A. Weaver

SARAH THREENEEDLES

(Boston, 1698)

By the grim grace of the Puritans she had been brought
   Into their frigid meeting-house to list
Her funeral sermon before the rope ran taut.
   Soft neck that he had kissed!

Through the narrow window her dazed blue eyes could see
   The rope.   Like a glittering icicle it hung
From the hoar cross-beam of the horrible gallows-tree.
   His arms about her flung!

Two captive Indians and one Guinea slave,
   Hating at heart the merciless white God,
In the stubborn ground were hacking her shallow grave.
   Sweet April path they trod!

Her shivering neighbors thrilled to the fierce discourse
   Of the minister, who thundered the dire sting
Of a sinner's death till his vehement voice went hoarse.
   She heard love's whispering.

And still she stood while the frozen communion bread,
   That the preacher broke ere he poured the chilly wine,
Rattling into the plates, her judges fed.
   Her food was more divine.
                      Katherine Lee Bates

KIT LOGAN AND LADY HELEN

HERE is Kit Logan with her love-child come
      To Lady Helen's gate:
Then down sweeps Helen from the Italian room,
      She with her child of hate.

Kit's boy was born of violent hot desire,
      Helen's of hate and dread:
Poor girl, betrayed to union with the Squire,
      Loathing her marriage bed.

Kit Logan, who is father to your boy?
      But Helen knows, too well:
Listen what biting taunts they both employ,
      Watch their red anger swell.

Yet each would give her undying soul to be
      Changed to the other's place.
Kit from the wet road's tasking cruelty
      Looks up to silk and lace,

Helen looks down at rags, her fluttering pride
    Caught in this cage of glass,
Eager to trudge, thieve, beg by the road-side,
    Or starving to eat grass. . . .

Silence. Wrath dies. For Woman's old good name
    Each swears a sister's oath;
Weeping, they kiss; to the Squire's lasting shame,
    Who broke the heart in both.
                    Robert Graves

TERESINA'S FACE

HE saw it last of all before they herded in the steerage,
   Dark against the sunset where he lingered by the hold—
The tear-stained, dusk-rose face of her, the little Teresina,
   Sailing out to lands of gold.

Ah, his days were long, long days, still toiling in the vine-
       yard,
   Working for the gold to set him free to go to her,
Where gay there glowed the flower-face of little Teresina,
   Where all joy and riches were. . . .

Hard to find one rose-face where the dark rose-faces cluster,
   Where the outland laws are strange and outland voices
       hum—
Only one lad's hoping, and the word of Teresina,
   Who would wait for him to come:

  .   .   .   .

God grant he may not find her, since he may not win her
     freedom,
   Nor yet be great enough to love, in such marred, captive guise,
The patient, painted face of her, the little Teresina,
   With its cowed, all-knowing eyes!
                   Margaret Widdemer

LOVE AND DEATH

DREAM TRYST

She was as lovely as a flower,
   And, like a flower, she passed away,
And yet, as in that morning hour
   I saw her first, I still to-day
Her unforgotten face behold,
Tender as dew, and bright as gold.

Shed from her gown the old perfume,
   She steals like blossom to my side,
Sweetens my thoughts, and fills the room,
   And leaves me glad and sanctified;
She still about me comes and goes,
Soft as the shadow of a rose.

I know she only seemed to die,
   'Tis all the happier for me
That no one sees her face but I—
   So would we have it, I and she—
That no one sees us meet and part,
And hold each other heart to heart.

What trysts are ours, what moments rare,
   What happy laughter side by side,
While no one dreams that she is there,
   Because they think that she has died—
They'd call it dreams, were I to tell,
And so we keep our secret well.

And now it is this many a year
   Since they have missed her from her place,
Healed is the wound, and dried the tear
   That fell once for her vanished face;
And only I remember her,
Once so beloved and once so fair.

Once!—ah! beloved, if they could know!
  If they as I could see you still,
And watch your beauty lovelier grow,
  And feast their eyes and drink their fill
Of all that breath and bloom of you—
Ah! I might lose you, if they knew.

But now no eyes but mine can see,
  No hands can touch, no ears can hear,
And none can come 'twixt you and me,
  No other lover hold you dear;
And Time that other beauty mars
Can reach you not among the stars.

Richard Le Gallienne

HER WAY

You loved the hay in the meadow,
  Flowers at noon,
The high cloud's long shadow,
  Honey of June,
The flaming woodways tangled
  With Fall on the hill,
The towering night star-spangled
  And winter-still.

And you loved firelit faces,
  The hearth, the home,—
Your mind on golden traces,
  London or Rome,—
On quaintly-colored spaces
  Where heavens glow
With his quaint saints' embraces,—
  Angelico.

In cloister and highway
  (Gold of God's dust!)
And many an elfin byway
  You put your trust,—

A crock and a table,
    Love's end of day,
And light of a storied stable
    Where kings must pray.

Somewhere there is a village
    For you and me,
Hayfield, hearth and tillage,—
    Where can it be?
Prayers when birds awake,
    Daily bread,
Toil for His sunlit sake
    Who raised us dead.

With this in mind you moved
    Through love and pain.
Hard though the long road proved,
    You turned again
With a heart that knew its trust
    Not ill-bestowed.
With this you light the dust
    That clouds my road.

William Rose Benét

ON SUNDAY IN THE SUNLIGHT

On Sunday in the sunlight
With brightness round her strown
And murmuring beauty of the sky
At last her very own,
She who had loved all children
And all high things and clean
Turned away to silentness
And bliss unseen.

Rending, blinding anguish,
Is all a man can know;
Yet still I kneel beside her
For she would have it so,

Kneel and pray beside her
In Light she left behind—
Light and love in silentness,
Sight to the blind.

Oh living light burn through me!
Oh speak, as spoke to me
Her deep sweet eyes and faithful,
Voice on Calvary!
Oh light be near and shining,
Nearer than I can guess,
And teach me that true language
Of silentness!

William Rose Benét

INDIAN SUMMER

From "Two Lives"

(O Earth-and-Autumn of the Setting Sun,
She is not by, to know my task is done!)

In the brown grasses slanting with the wind,
Lone as a lad whose dog's no longer near,
Lone as a mother whose only child has sinned,
Lone on the loved hill . . . and below me here
The thistle-down in tremulous atmosphere
Along red clusters of the sumach streams;
The shriveled stalks of golden-rod are sere,
And crisp and white their flashing old racemes.
(. . . forever . . . forever . . . forever . . .)
This is the lonely season of the year,
This is the season of our lonely dreams.

(O Earth-and-Autumn of the Setting Sun,
She is not by, to know my task is done!)

The corn-shocks westward on the stubble plain
Show like an Indian village of dead days;
The long smoke trails behind the crawling train,
And floats atop the distant woods ablaze

With orange, crimson, purple.   The low haze
Dims the scarped bluffs above the inland sea,
Whose wide and slaty waters in cold glaze
Await yon full-moon of the night-to-be,
(. . . far . . . and far . . . and far . . .)
These are the solemn horizons of man's ways,
These the horizons of solemn thought to me.

   (*O Earth-and-Autumn of the Setting Sun,
   She is not by, to know my task is done!*)

And this the hill she visited, as friend;
And this the hill she lingered on, as bride—
Down in the yellow valley is the end:
They laid her . . . in no evening autumn tide. . . .
Under fresh flowers of that May morn, beside
The queens and cave-women of ancient earth. . . .

This is the hill . . . and over my city's towers,
Across the world from sunset, yonder in air,
Shines, through its scaffoldings, a civic dome
Of pilèd masonry, which shall be ours
To give, completed, to our children there. . . .
And yonder far roof of my abandoned home
Shall   house   new   laughter. . . . Yet   I   tried . . . I
      tried . . .
And, ever wistful of the doom to come,
I built her many a fire for love . . . for mirth. . . .
(When snows were falling on our oaks outside,
Dear, many a winter fire upon the hearth) . . .
(. . . farewell . . . farewell . . . farewell . . .)
We dare not think too long on those who died,
While still so many yet must come to birth.

                              William Ellery Leonard

SOME DAY

   Some day perhaps I too may speak your name
      As others speak it now,
   In just that tone of low-voiced sorrowing
      Well-ordered griefs allow.

And when the years have dimmed my flaming grief
  To embers of regret
Then may I too find words to voice your praise—
  But oh, not yet, not yet.

Medora C. Addison

KEEN

WEEP him dead and mourn as you may,
  Me, I sing as I must:
Blessed be death, that cuts in marble
  What would have sunk to dust!

Blessed be death, that took my love
  And buried him in the sea,
Where never a lie nor a bitter word
  Will out of his mouth at me!

This I have to hold to my heart,
  This to take by the hand:
Sweet we were for a summer month
  As the sun on the dry, white sand;

Mild we were for a summer month
  As the wind from over the weirs;
And blessed be death, that hushed with salt
  The harsh and slovenly years!

Who builds her a house with love for timber,
  Builds her a house of foam;
And I'd rather be bride to a lad gone down
  Than widow to one safe home.

Edna St. Vincent Millay

HOME–COMING

I AM come home again
  Back to the old gray town,
  Battling with wind and rain
  As I go up and down.

I am come from the South,
With never a greeting said,
And no one to kiss my mouth
Now that my love is dead.

As I go up and down
In the loud wind and rain,
Through the familiar town
He walks with me again.

A woman robbed of her youth—
The ghost of a lad long dead,
With never a kiss on my mouth.
And never a greeting said.

Isobel Hume

À QUOI BON DIRE

SEVENTEEN years ago you said
　　Something that sounded like Good-bye;
And everybody thinks that you are dead,
　　　　But I.

So I, as I grow stiff and cold
　　To this and that say Good-bye too;
And everybody sees that I am old
　　　　But you.

And one fine morning in a sunny lane
　　Some boy and girl will meet and kiss and swear
That nobody can love their way again
　　　　While over there
　　You will have smiled, I shall have tossed your hair.

Charlotte Mew

WHEN I AM DEAD

WHEN I am dead and nervous hands have thrust
My body downward into careless dust;
I think the grave cannot suffice to hold
My spirit 'prisoned in the sunless mould!

Some subtle memory of you shall be
A resurrection of the life of me.
Yea, I shall be, because I love you so,
The speechless spirit of all things that grow.
You shall not touch a flower but it shall be
Like a caress upon the cheek of me.
I shall be patient in the common grass
That I may feel your footfall when you pass.
I shall be kind as rain and pure as dew,
A loving spirit 'round the life of you.
When your soft cheeks by perfumed winds are fanned,
'Twill be my kiss—and you will understand.
But when some sultry, storm-bleared sun has set,
I will be lightning if you dare forget!

John G. Neihardt

UNREGENERATE

I SHALL come back in ways I think you'll know:
A cocky, strutting robin where you pass,
Perhaps a flake of sudden, stinging snow,
A cricket mocking at you from the grass;
A gusty little wind will whirl your hat
(And laugh to watch your funny, pompous wrath).
I'll be an April rain and drench it flat,
Then stand, a prickly hedge, straight in your path.
I shall not come a sentimental thing:
A star, a cloud, a Wordsworth daffodil;
A woodpecker, red-topped, will light and bring
Her maddening racket to your window-sill
At five A. M.   And when you've waked and heard,
She'll *love* to hear you mutter: "Damn that bird! "

Jacqueline Embry

GHOST

I'M comin' back and haunt you, don't you fret.
  What if I get as far as Hell away?
  They's things of me that just can't help but stay—
Whether I want or not, you can't forget.

Just when you think you got me wiped out clear,
  Some bird that's singin'—moonlight on a hill—
  Some lovely thing'll hurt like it would kill,
And you'll hear somethin' whisperin', "He's here!"

And when somebody holds you closte, like this,
  And you start in to feel your pulses race,
  The face that's pressin' yours'll be my face . . .
My lips'll be the ones your lips'll kiss.
Don't cry . . . which do you think it'll hurt most?—
Oh, God!   You think I want to be a ghost? . . .

John V. A. Weaver

THE MASTERS

You have taught me laughter,
  Joyousness and light,
How the day is rosy-wild,
  Star-enthrilled the night:

Maybe God can teach me
  After you are gone
How to bear the blackened night
  And the dreadful dawn.

Margaret Widdemer

THE SLEEPER

Under white eyelids
The dreams come and go,
Kiss her on her rosy mouth,
  And wake her so.

Under white eyelids
The dreams are all done,
Fold her hands across her breast—
  Let her sleep on.

Isobel Hume

NIRVANA

SLEEP on, I lie at heaven's high oriels,
    Over the stars that murmur as they go
    Lighting your lattice-window far below.
And every star some of the glory spells
    Whereof I know.

I have forgotten you, long, long ago;
    Like the sweet silver singing of thin bells
Vanished, or music fading faint and low.
    Sleep on, I lie at heaven's high oriels,
Who loved you so.

John Hall Wheelock

BED–TIME

I MIND, love, how it ever was this way:
    That I would to my task; and soon I'd hear
Your little fluttering sigh, and you would say,
    "It's bed-time, dear."

So you would go and leave me at my work;
    And I would turn to it with steady will,
And wonder why the room had grown so dark,
    The night so chill.

Betimes I'd hear the whisper of your feet
    Upon the stair; and you would come to me,
All rosy from your dreams, and take your seat
    Upon my knee.

"Poor, tired boy!" you'd say.   But I would miss
    The lonely message of your eyes, and so
Proffer the hasty bribery of a kiss,
    And let you go.

But now, dear heart, that you have scaled the stair
    To that dim chamber far above the sun,
I fumble with my futile task, nor care
    To get it done.

For all is empty since you said good-night
  (So spent you were, and weary with the day!)
And on the hearth the ashes of delight
  Lie cold and gray.

Ah, sweet my love, could I but wish you down
  In that white raiment which I know you wear;
And hear once more the rustle of your gown
  Upon the stair;

Could I but have you, drowsily-sweet, to say
  The tender little words that once I knew—
How gaily would I put my work away
  And go with you.

Ralph M. Jones

I'LL BE YOUR EPITAPH

OVER your dear dead heart I'll lift
As lightly as a bough,
Saying, "Here lies the false, high song,
Cruelly quiet now."

I'll say, "Here lies the lying sword,
Still dripping with my truth;
Here lies the lovely sheath I made,
Embroidered with my youth."

I'll sing: "Here lies, here lies, here lies!"
—*Ah, rust in peace below!*—
Passers will wonder at my words,
But your dark dust will know.

Leonora Speyer

RECONCILIATION

WHEN I am dead and deep in dust,
  So you but plant a rose-tree there,
Get back to labor and to lust
  And weep no more nor greatly care.

The quick they have so much to learn,
    The dead they have so much to do,
If but your roses bloom and burn,
    There shall be peace between us two.

J. U. Nicolson

SOMEHOW, SOMEWHERE, SOMETIME

SOMEHOW, but God knows how, we'll meet again,
You'll see the firelight on the pane,
Knock at the door, call "Come, my dear."
You'll hear the bolt drawn,—"You, love, here?"
And answer, "Yes—no partings now,
For all things have come right somehow."

Somewhere beyond the furthest, western sea,
My boat will reach a sun-washed quay,
White birds, brown sails, a topaz sky,
Your smile of welcome. You and I
Together with all time to spare,
A brave new shining world—somewhere!

Sometime . . . but now, how long we have to wait,
Gray hair, deaf ears, slow feeble gait,
The dull monotony of age,
The book of life spelt page by page
Till sight fails, hope fails, then sublime
The great surprise of death—sometime!

Winifred M. Letts

RESURGAM

Now is a great and shining company,
Choired like stars before the break of day,
So radiant, their silence is like singing,
Like mist of music down the Milky Way;
And they who wake, hearing the dawn wind bringing
Comfort of voices, are content and stay
A little while their tears, forbear the clinging
Of hands that hinder youth at last made free.

There is no death, nor change, nor any ending,
Only a journey, and so many go,
That we who stay at length discern the blending
Of the two roads, two breaths, two lives, and so
Come to the high and quiet knowledge that the dead
Are but ourselves made beautiful instead.

And you, O best beloved of them all,
How is it with you?   It is well indeed?
Or is there in the vivid quiet need
Of some familiar task; yet does the call
Of the warm earth, the rise and fall
Of accents you held dear, when in the night
They talk of you, trouble the wingèd light?
O foolish question wisdom should forestall!
Now are you most immediate: so near,
That there is left no thing between us; no,
Nor veil of life.   Ah dear, my very dear,
Only the dead are close and never apart,
Speaking in lucid sentences, and so,
Can find their way unhampered to a heart.

There is a wind that blows from earth when dusk is coming,
Laden with richness of the stored up day;
The secret warmth of hidden paths; the humming
Of pollened bees; the sweetness of damp hay;
And mist along a shining valley stream;
And green cool reaches where the bending trees,
After the hot noon, listen for the breeze:
All this, I know, is part of your new dream.
And when I wake, and death seems most unfair,
Even then is some new mystery on the air,
Of scent, or sound, or loveliness of hue,
Stirring my heart and making me aware
I cannot grasp the rapture now of you,
Who were so close to dawn, and trees, and dew.

Struthers Burt

LOVE'S FULFILMENT

THE HAWTHORN TREE

Across the shimmering meadows—
Ah, when he came to me!
In the spring-time,
In the night-time,
In the starlight,
Beneath the hawthorn tree.

Up from the misty marshland—
Ah, when he climbed to me!
To my white bower,
To my sweet rest,
To my warm breast,
Beneath the hawthorn tree.

Ask of me what the birds sang,
High in the hawthorn tree;
What the breeze tells,
What the rose smells,
What the stars shine—
Not what he said to me!

Willa Cather

KNOCKING AT THE DOOR

Great winds may blow now
But I will go now
Down to her cottage on the shore,
And drawing near her
I shall hear her
Singing as I knock at the door.

Blow high or low then
The winds, I shall know then

She's happy when I hear her sing.
Then at my knocking
The quick rain mocking
She'll pause, and to her wild heart cling.

And I shall stand there
In the blown sand there,
Listening as she listens too,
And the dark fir-trees
And autumn bare trees
Hush, then shake their bones anew.

I knock again and
Again like rain and
Softly as rain, till she laughs to hear.
"I thought it was rain-drops
That when the rain stops
Patter the pane with tapping clear."

—In, in, in now!
There's fire within now,
And a voice whose song is heard in speech. . . .
But if that knocking
Were the rain's mocking
And she opened but to an empty beach;

Or if that singing
Were but the wind's ringing
Faint senseless bells hung in my brain;
How would the night then
Lack all light then,
And she and I each listen in vain!

John Freeman

THE TWO LOVES

WHEN curfew-bells begin,
    And the log-fire hisses,
I covered Jeannie in
    From head to foot with kisses.

There, in the glow
  And flicker of the ingle,
I gave her for to know
  How a man loves single:

I gave her for to know,
  When the heart needs mating,
How hard a road to go
  Was the long lone waiting.

Her face was all a mist,
  Her dear eyes tear-laden,
To find herself so kissed,
  And man so love a maiden.

Ah! but she did love!
  With kind lips so quiet,
While my heart above
  Was all storm and riot.

And looking deep I saw,
  In all its woman's meaning,
How her heart would draw
  My heart to have its leaning.

For my heart was fain,
  Oh, fain to be a-mating;
But hers saw the pain
  Of the long lone waiting.

So there, in the light,
  Beside the dying ember,
I gave her all that night
  My kisses to remember.

   .   .   .   .

A cold dawn came;
  Then parted our embraces;
We blew the ash to flame
  On tear-wet faces;

We drank the last cup
   And we shared the last platter;
And pale the light went up,
   And the birds began to chatter.

And then she oped the door,
   And there I left her standing,
As I went down to the shore
   To the ship beside the landing.

And far out from the sea
   I saw the white shawl flutter,
As her hand waved to me
   The thoughts she could not utter.

Oh! a man's love is strong
   When fain he comes a-mating.
But a woman's love is long
   And grows when it is waiting.

Laurence Housman

ALONE IN APRIL

" In un boschetto trovai pastorella "—? GUERZO DI MONTECANTI

RUSTLING leaves of the willow-tree
Peering downward at you and me,
And no man else in the world to see.

Only the birds, whose dusty coats
Show dark in the green—whose throbbing throats
Turn joy to music and love to notes.

Lean your body against the tree,
Lifting your red lips up to me,
Ettarre, and kiss with no man to see!

And let us laugh for a little.—Yea,
Let love and laughter herald the day
When laughter and love will be put away.

Then you will remember the willow-tree
And this very hour, and remember me,
Ettarre,—whose face you will no more see!

So swift, so swift the glad time goes,
And Eld and Death with their countless woes
Draw near, and the end thereof no man knows.

Lean your body against the tree,
Lifting your red lips up to me,
Ettarre, and kiss, with no man to see!

James Branch Cabell

MY DELIGHT

THICK and stormy was the night,
    Not a single star,
When I climbed to my delight,
    Where the roses are;

Where the roses are and love,
    In a bower warm,
Climbing up to heaven above
    Night and wind and storm.

Gamaliel Bradford

THE NIGHTS REMEMBER

THE nights remember lovely things they knew,
    The words of lovers, tremulous and wise,
And kisses blown and laughter and the beauty
    Of glowing eyes.

The nights remember hours white with wonder,
    Lipped with red stars and strangely luminous;
Perchance, belovèd, when the years have lengthened—
    They will remember us.

Harold Vinal

CHARIOTS

I NEVER saw the morning till to-day;
I never knew how soon night went away—
Day merely came a regular event;
　　　Night merely went. . . .

Now day and night are chariots for me,
Since I have learned their mystery from you:
Day holding one and moving solemnly—
　　　Night holding two.

Witter Bynner

FULFILMENT

HAPPY: yea, happy for ever and aye!
Scarlet bursts through the eastern gray
　　　And the night is past;
For a woman's lips and a woman's hair,
And the soul of her womanhood, wonderful, fair,
　　　Are mine at last.

Dawn was near, but no whisper told
Why the stars went out and the world grew cold
　　　As the void above;
When suddenly out of the darkness sprang
My passionate rose, and the whole world sang
　　　Of love, of love.

Now happy, yea, happy for ever I stand,
The rose of passion within my hand,
　　　And the day may close
With the dust of worlds on the midnight strown,
For I hold forever, forever my own,
　　　The passionate rose.

Louis V. Ledoux

THE HAPPY NIGHT

I HAVE loved to-night; from love's last bordering steep
I have fallen at last with joy and forgotten the shore;
I have known my love to-night as never before,
I have flung myself in the deep, and drawn from the deep,

And kissed her lightly, and left my belovèd to sleep.
And now I sit in the night and my heart is still:
Strong and secure; there is nothing that's left to will,
There is nothing to win but only a thing to keep.
And I look to-night, completed and not afraid,
Into the windy dark where shines no light;
And care not at all though the darkness never should fade,
Nor fear that death should suddenly come to-night.
Knowing my last would be surely my bravest breath,
I am happy to-night: I have laughed to-night at death.

J. C. Squire

O SWEETHEART, HEAR YOU

O SWEETHEART, hear you
   Your lover's tale;
A man shall have sorrow
   When friends him fail.

For he shall know then
   Friends be untrue
And a little ashes
   Their words come to.

But one unto him
   Will softly move
And softly woo him
   In ways of love.

His hand is under
   Her smooth round breast;
So he who has sorrow
   Shall have rest.

James Joyce

SHEPHERD'S HOLIDAY

Too honest for a Gipsy, too lazy for a farmer,
What should you be but a shepherd on the hills,
Herding sheep with sad faces
Over grass-grown places,
High above a web of streams and willow-trees and mills?

Too tame for a Gipsy, too wild for a dairy-maid,
What could I be but a silly goose-girl,
Tending hissing white snakes
By weed-green lakes,
Crying in the dew-fall with my hair out of curl?

Too silent for the neighbors, too simple for the townspeople,
What shall we do who love each other so?
I'll teach your gray sheep
To guard you from the steep,
You'll catch me back from drowning where my dark lake
    lies deep,
I'll pluck a feather pillow that shall sing you to sleep
Up among the rocks where the blueberries grow.

Elinor Wylie

DEER ON THE MOUNTAIN

Deer are on the mountain, deer!
A hunter spied one browsing near
And the little girl who lives below
Saw beside her cabbage-field a running doe.
But I have never seen them though I used to wait
And wander, and come home weary and late.
No, I have never seen them stand a-quiver,
Then turn and bound and go,
Nor have I started as they loomed above me,
Sudden, bright, upon a hill,
Nor turned to find them, kneeling, breathless, still.
But now—at last—I know you love me,
For now at last I know
How the noble deer leaps, how leaps the doe!
O I lie locked and lone and white
In my little room all night
And toss and laugh and have no peace of mind,
For deer are plunging through the thickets and they stop
    and sniff the wind,
They break and dash for cover with the hounds far be-
    hind.

Swift runs the deer and close to him the doe—
Now they have found the glen, now they are crouching
    low—
I have never seen them, but now—at last—I know. . . . .

Grace Fallow Norton

CONQUERED

O PALE! O vivid! dear!
   O disillusioned eyes
Forever near!
   O dream, arise!

I will not turn away
   From the face I loved again.
Your beauty may sway
   My life with pain.

I will drink the wine you pour,
   I will seek to put asunder
Our ways no more—
   O love! O wonder!

Zoë Akins

THE DOOR

THE littlest door, the inner door,
   I swing it wide.
Now in my heart there is no more
   To hide.

The farthest door—the latch at last
   Is lifted; see.
I kept the little fortress fast.
   —Be good to me.

Mary Carolyn Davies

THE MYSTERY

YOUR eyes drink of me,
   Love makes them shine,
Your eyes that lean
   So close to mine.

We have long been lovers
    We know the range
Of each other's moods
    And how they change.

But when we look
    At each other so,
Then we feel
    How little we know.

The spirit eludes us,
    Timid and free—
Can I ever know you
    Or you know me?

                                        Sara Teasdale

RAIN, RAIN

RAIN, rain—fall, fall,
    In a heavy screen—
    That my lover be not seen!

Wind, wind,—blow, blow,
    Till the leaves are stirred—
    That my lover be not heard!

Storm, storm,—rage, rage,
    Like a war around—
    That my lover be not found!

. . . Lark, lark,—hush . . . hush . . .
    Softer music make—
    That my lover may not wake . . .

                                        Zoë Akins

BEFORE DAWN IN THE WOODS

UPON our eyelids, dear, the dew will lie,
    And on the roughened meshes of our hair,
While little feet make bold to scurry by
    And half-notes shrilly cut the quickened air.

Our clean, hard bodies, on the clean, hard ground
  Will vaguely feel that they are full of power,
And they will stir, and stretch, and look around,
  Loving the early, chill, half-lighted hour.

Loving the voices in the shadowed trees,
  Loving the feet that stir the blossoming grass—
Oh, always we have known such things as these,
  And knowing, can we love and let them pass?

Marguerite Wilkinson

GOLDEN BOUGH

LET it not be, love, underneath a roof,
  Closed in with furniture and four walls round;
But we will find a place wild, far aloof,
  Our room the woods, our bed the sweet-smelled ground.

There at the soft foot of some friendly tree
  With grass and leaves and flowers we will lie
Where all is wide and beautiful and free—
  Free as when love first loved beneath the sky.

No lock or curtain need we in the shade
  And silence of the forest's inmost fold:
And none save us shall know where we are laid
  Or guess what nuptial day those woodlands hold.

There fitly may we bring our loves to greet
  That ancient love, more old than wind or sod;
Fitly where beasts and flowers wed shall meet
  Our lips, our limbs, beneath the look of God.

Helen Hoyt

FAUN–TAKEN

WHO was it then that lately took me in the wood?
  And was it I that lay twice seven nights on leaves,
    With musky hair against my side!
That cruel hair that kept me kindly from the cold!

Gold, gold!
 Of yellow eyes that glance and hide!
 Am I the maddened one that goes—and grieves
  For lack of laughter laughing till I died?

Oh, drouth of grapey laughter, dearth and drouth!
 Twice seven days are but a blurring ring
That circles round the corner of a mouth!
 Oh, wide, wide mouths that bellow so, or fling
That fluting up to birds like spurted wine!
  But, ah, no more, those sounds without a name—
   No more that ambiguous grace of god and ape,
   Where strange feet dance upon the dripping grape—
Those feet one must not see—that wounded mine!

Let me but once look back again and pass.
 Once only see him again—and groan and go—
The lips that laugh in the grass—
 And kiss in a way one must not know:
The lips that cling the mouths of pipes and suck
The roots of frightened flowers too pale to pluck;
 The curls that vine o'er what one must not see—
 Those horney hiders that so gorèd me!
Then, run and run—again to the hearths, the roofs!
But close behind,—the pipes, the pipes,—the hoofs!
        Rose O'Neill

COMPLETION

My heart has fed to-day.
My heart, like hind at play,
Has grazed in fields of love, and washed in streams
Of quick, imperishable dreams.

In moth-white beauty shimmering,
Lovely as birches in the moon glimmering,
From coigns of sleep my eyes
Saw dawn and love arise.

And like a bird at rest,
Steady in a swinging nest,

My heart at peace lay gloriously
While wings of ecstasy
Beat round me and above.

I am fulfilled of Love.

Eunice Tietjens

TWO NOCTURNES

I

THE ARABIAN SHAWL

"It is cold outside, you will need a coat—
    What! this old Arabian shawl!
Bind it about your head and throat,
    These steps . . . it is dark . . . my hand . . . you
        might fall."

What has happened—what strange, sweet charm
    Lingers about the Arabian shawl? . . .
Do not tremble so! There can be no harm
    In just remembering—that is all.

"I love you so—I will be your wife,"
    Here, in the dark of the terrace wall,
Say it again.—Let that other Life
    Fold us like the Arabian shawl.

"Do you remember?" . . . "I quite forget,
    Some childish foolishness, that is all,
To-night is the first time we have met. . . .
    Let me take off my Arabian shawl."

II

SLEEPING TOGETHER

Sleeping together . . . how tired you were . . .
How warm our room . . . how the firelight spread
On walls and ceiling and great, white bed!
We spoke in whispers as children do,
And now it was I—and then it was you
Slept a moment, to wake—"My dear,
I'm not at all sleepy," one of us said . . .

Was it a thousand years ago?
I woke in your arms—you were sound asleep—
And heard the pattering sound of sheep.
Softly I slid to the floor and crept
To the curtained window, then, while you slept,
I watched the sheep pass by in the snow.

O flock of thoughts with their shepherd Fear
Shivering, desolate, out in the cold,
That entered into my heart to fold!
A thousand years . . . was it yesterday
When we, two children of far away,
Clinging close in the darkness, lay
Sleeping together? . . . How tired you were. . . .

Katherine Mansfield

BABYLON

THE blue dusk ran between the streets: my love was winged within my mind,
It left to-day and yesterday and thrice a thousand years behind.
To-day was past and dead for me, for from to-day my feet had run
Through thrice a thousand years to walk the ways of ancient Babylon.
On temple top and palace roof the burnished gold flung back the rays
Of a red sunset that was dead and lost beyond a million days.
The tower of heaven turns darker blue, a starry sparkle now begins;
The mystery and magnificence, the myriad beauty and the sins
Come back to me.   I walk beneath the shadowy multitude of towers;
Within the gloom the fountain jets its pallid mist in lily flowers.
The waters lull me and the scent of many gardens, and I hear
Familiar voices, and the voice I love is whispering in my ear.

Oh real as in dream all this; and then a hand on mine is laid:
The wave of phantom time withdraws; and that young
    Babylonian maid,
One drop of beauty left behind from all the flowing of
    that tide,
Is looking with the self-same eyes, and here in Ireland
    by my side.
Oh light our life in Babylon, but Babylon has taken wings,
While we are in the calm and proud possession of eternal
    things.

                                                    A. E.

CHRISTMAS EVE

On Christmas Eve I lay abed,
    With the still night more still
For all the pluming snows that spread
    Along our sparkling hill,
And while again to Jesu' stall
    Walked wisdom from afar,
I heard another shepherd call
    Under the Christmas star.

Along the lane his carol came,
    But not of Bethlehem,
A burning boy, he knew a flame,
    But not the flame of them:
"This Christmas Eve from courting home
    I am a bachelor,
But soon the snows again will come,
    And I'll be wed before."

All one with kings from Bible-page,
    And holy shepherds old,
Went yeoman love in pilgrimage
    Across the Christmas wold.
"Goodwill," he sang, "Goodwill, Goodwill,"
    Or seemed to me to sing,
While some glad girl beyond the hill
    Dreamt of a new-born king.

                                        John Drinkwater

WHITENESS

The little betrothed has washed her linen—
   And hung it out to dry
It puffs and blows into mists and cloudlets
   Under the April sky.

Her arms are white as the white pear-blossom—
   Her throat is as white as may;
And her heart, like a song on a sunny morning,
   New-born and sweet as they.

She will walk in white to church on Sunday
   Through orchards where birds sing:
And the bridegroom, taking her home at evening,
   Will think he weds the Spring.

Isobel Hume

PROTHALAMION

When the evening came my love said to me:
  Let us go into the garden now that the sky is cool,
The garden of black hellebore and rosemary,
  Where wild woodruff spills in a milky pool.

Low we passed in the twilight, for the wavering heat
  Of day had waned, and round that shaded plot
Of secret beauty the thickets clustered sweet:
  Here is heaven, our hearts whispered, but our lips spake
    not.

Between that old garden and seas of lazy foam
  Gloomy and beautiful alleys of trees arise
With spire of cypress and dreamy beechen dome,
  So dark that our enchanted sight knew nothing but the
    skies

Veiled with soft air, drenched in the roses' musk
  Or the dusky, dark carnation's breath of clove;
No stars burned in their deeps, but through the dusk
  I saw my love's eyes, and they were brimmed with love.

No star their secret ravished, no wasting moon
  Mocked the sad transience of those eternal hours:
Only the soft, unseeing heaven of June,
   The ghosts of great trees, and the sleeping flowers.

For doves that crooned in the leafy noonday now
  Were silent; the night-jar sought his secret covers,
Nor even a mild sea-whisper moved a creaking bough—
  Was ever a silence deeper made for lovers?

Was ever a moment meeter made for love?
  Beautiful are your closed lips beneath my kiss;
And all your yielding sweetness beautiful—
  Oh, never in all the world was such a night as this!

Francis Brett Young

CAPTURED

Under an elm tree where the river reaches
They watched the evening deepen in the sky,
They watched the westward clouds go towering by
Through lakes of blue toward those shining beaches,
Those far enchanted strands where blowing tides
Break into light along the shallow air:
They watched how like a tall ship's lantern there
Over that stormy surf the faint star rides.
Ship of a dream, he thought—O dreamed-of shore
Beyond all oceans and all earthly seas!
Now would they never call him any more;
Now would they never hurt him with unease.
She was that ship, that sea, that siren land,
And she was here, her hand shut in his hand.

Archibald MacLeish

THE ROAD'S END

Sometimes the road was a twisted riddle
  Where one might stray for a crooked mile,
But O, she danced to the pipes and fiddle
  Most of the while, most of the while.

Sometimes the wind and the rain together
　　Blurred the hill that she needs must climb,
But O, she tripped it in primrose weather
　　Most of the time, most of the time.

Who may say that the journey tried her?
　　Never a Romany went as gay,
Seeing that true love walked beside her
　　All of the way, all of the way.

Theodosia Garrison

THE ALTAR

THERE were estrangements on the road of love:
Betrayals and false passions, angers, lusts.
There were keen nights and sated noons and trusts
Grudgingly given and held light to prove
Your self-sufficiency, your manhood's dower,
And mockery at my faith,—my single power.

There were renewals all along the way,
Of pledges and of weeping, new delights.
But no new meaning till that night of nights
You groped beyond to where my meaning lay.
And when you knelt to me you found me kneeling,
Proud of love's pain and humble to its healing.

Jean Starr Untermeyer

CLICK O' THE LATCH

THE silence holds for it, taut and true,
The young moon stays for it, wistful white;
Winds that whimpered the sunset through
　　Sigh for it, low and light,—

Click o' the latch and he'll come home—
A stir in the dusk at the little gate.
Hush, my heart,—be still, my heart—
　　Surely it's sweet to wait!

The tall skies lean for it, listening—
Never a star but lends an ear—
The passionate porch-flowers stoop and cling—
　　Stilling their leaves to hear

Click o' the latch and him come home,—
A step on the flags, a snatch of song,
Hurry, my heart, be swift, my heart,—
 How did we wait so long!

Nancy Byrd Turner

TOGETHER

You and I by this lamp with these
Few books shut out the world. Our knees
Touch almost in this little space.
But I am glad. I see your face.
The silences are long, but each
Hears the other without speech.
And in this simple scene there is
The essence of all subtleties,
The freedom from all fret and smart,
The one sure sabbath of the heart.

The world—we cannot conquer it,
Nor change the mind of fools one whit.
Here, here alone do we create
Beauty and peace inviolate;
Here night by night and hour by hour
We build a high impregnable tower
Whence may shine, now and again,
A light to light the feet of men
When they see the rays thereof:
And this is marriage, this is love.

Ludwig Lewisohn

THE GIRL TAKES HER PLACE AMONG THE MOTHERS

"To link the generations each to each."—Tennyson

I wake in the night with such uncertain gladness,
Fearing the little pain beneath my heart,
The little pains that cease again and start,
Delicious fear that aches with a strange madness.

"And is this I," I say, seeing my shadowed face
In the old mirror where I laughing saw
So long ago, beautiful without flaw,
Its delicate young lines, and careless grace.

This pain, these happy pains that seem to blend
In my young blood with old forgotten mothers,
Daughters of my race and unremembered others,
The pain that foretells life's beginning and end.

"And is this I," I say, beholding my body's line,
Fragile and young and sweet but not the body I knew,
Now I am drunken with the ancient wine—
"Child, as it was with others, so with you."

Marya Zaturenska

UNBORN

LITTLE body I would hold,
Little feet my hands enfold,
Little head my tears have blessed,
Little mouth that seeks my breast,
Little shining soul that cries
From the worship of his eyes,
I must wait that I may be
Great enough to mother thee.

Irene Rutherford McLeod

BABY

POOH—men!
We are done with them now,
Who had need of them then,—
I and you!

Rounding face,
Little feet,
Hair to love,
You sweet!

Men!
I shall laugh at them now
Who had sighed moon-sick then.
I have you!

Florence Kiper Frank

LOVE SONNETS

PAUSE

Quick, for the tide is sifting down the shore,
Water and wind and vapory lift of spray—
Flowing of light with darkness through the door,
Sun or moon at the window, night and day—
Quick, while the shadow tangles in and out
Over this threshold that the rain has worn,
Whisper or threaten, trust or pray or doubt,
Still will some men be dead, and some be born;
Give me your eyes unmasked, and wonder well
How we are brief antagonists of Fate.
Friendship?   But what is friendship?   Can you tell?
Look at the hinges rusting on the gate;
Quick then, this breath, while we believe we know—
Kiss through your laughter, kiss again—and go.

Ann Hamilton

LOVER TO LOVER

Leave me a while, for you have been too long
A nearness that is perilous and sweet:
Loose me a little from the tightening thong
That binds my spirit, eyes and hands and feet.
For there are old communions I would hold,
To mind my heart what field and sky may be:
Earth bears her fruit . . . November has a gold . . .
And stars are still high points in constancy.
Loose me a little, now. . . . I have a need
Of standing in an open, windy place,
Of saying names again, of giving heed
To these companions of man's lonely race . . .
Loose me to these, between one dusk and dawn;—
I shall have need of them, when you are gone.

David Morton

219

COMPENSATION

ALL day I bar you from my slightest thought;
Make myself clear of you or any mark
Of our wrecked dawn and the uprising lark;
Am stern and strong and do the thing I ought.
Yet ever are there moments with you fraught:
I hear you like some glad sound in the dark;
You wait like bloom outside my branches stark;
I dare not heed; else were my fight unfought.
But when the clamor and the heat are done,
And spent with both I come unto that door
Sleep opens for me every setting sun,
The bitter lies behind, the sweet before.
We that are twain by day, at night are one.
A dream can bring me to your arms once more.

Lizette Woodworth Reese

NIGHT OF RAIN

BETTER the empty sorrow in the dark,
The crying heart, the crying eyes that stare
Blindly till morning, than the bitter flare
Of rainy street-lights, threaded spark to spark
To lure me from this room in my distress,
Out where you pass—far out beyond my sight.
Better to grope in this small space of night
For sleep, or peace, or any nothingness.
You are not here, and you will not return;
And if you came—the door is shut,.and locked,
And sealed with pride, and barred across with pain;
And now it is for quiet that I yearn. . . .
I should but lie and listen, if you knocked—
Rain in my heart, and at my window rain.

Bernice Lesbia Kenyon

CERTAINTY

WHAT wisdom have I that I surely know
Your going from me is a temporal thing?
What woman's intuition, strange and slow,
Fills me with patience like a quiet Spring?

I tell you I am like a mariner,
Weary of wind and rain and open sky,
Who feels himself no more a wanderer,
Knowing the long-desired land is nigh.
Give me no chill advice nor solace cold,
All you who see me laugh and judge me wrong,
I am not yet so comfortless and old
That I am stripped of mirth, bereft of song.
You will come back; I care not what the time,
Be it the green of Spring or Winter's rime.

Evelyn Hardy

IF I HAD RIDDEN HORSES

IF I had ridden horses in the lists,
Fought wars, gone pilgrimage to fabled lands,
Seen Pharaoh's drinking-cups of amethysts,
Held dead queens' secret jewels in my hands—
I would have laid my triumphs at your feet,
And worn with no ignoble pride my scars . . .
But I can only offer you, my sweet,
The songs I made on many a night of stars.
Yet have I worshipped honor, loving you;
Your graciousness and gentle courtesy,
With ringing and romantic trumpets blew
A mighty music through the heart of me,
A joy as cleansing as the wind that fills
The open spaces on the sunny hills.

Theodore Maynard

WHEN THERE IS MUSIC

WHENEVER there is music, it is you
Who come between me and the sound of strings:
The cloudy portals part to let you through,
Troubled and strange with long rememberings.
Your nearness gathers ghostwise down the room,
And through the pleading violins they play,
There drifts the dim and delicate perfume
That once was you, come dreamily astray.

Behind what thin and shadowy doors you wait
That such frail things as these should set you free!
When all my need, like armies at a gate,
Would storm in vain to bring you back to me;
When in this hush of strings you draw more near
Than any sound of music that I hear.

David Morton

MOTHER OF MEN

Dear wanton, when the moon made light our bed
Last night, and drenched our passion with its gold,
I asked no dream to lay beside the dead
Dreams that had crumbled to a little mould.
And then I caught a trembling tenderness
Soften your lips, that was not of desire;
And my hot blood, that sought one more caress,
Poured to my brows with a transfigured fire.
So that I hid my face where your heart beat,
Feeling your cool breath through my hair.   Confest,
And shameful, like a child, I would not meet
Your eyes, but very quiet on your breast
I lay until I slept; and when the day
Found us, my soul knelt at your feet to pray.

Stephen Southwold

I DO NOT LOVE TO SEE YOUR BEAUTY FIRE

I do not love to see your beauty fire
The light of eager love in every eye,
Nor the unconscious ardor of desire
Mantle a cheek when you are passing by;
When in the loud world's giddy thoroughfare
Your holy loveliness is noised about—
Lips that my love has prayed to—the gold hair
Where I have babbled all my secrets out—
O then I would I had you in my arms,
Desolate, lonely, broken, and forlorn,
Stripped of your splendor, spoiled of all your charms;
So that my love might prove her haughty scorn—

So I might catch you to my heart, and prove
'Tis not your beauty only that I love!

John Hall Wheelock

THE IMAGE OF DELIGHT

O HOW came I that loved stars, moon, and flame,
And unimaginable wind and sea,
All inner shrines and temples of the free,
Legends and hopes and golden books of fame;
I that upon the mountain carved my name
With cliffs and clouds and eagles over me,
O how came I to stoop to loving thee—
I that had never stooped before to shame?
O 'twas not thee!   Too eager of a white
Far beauty and a voice to answer mine,
Myself I built an image of delight,
Which all one purple day I deemed divine—
And when it vanished in the fiery night,
I lost not thee, nor any shape of thine.

William Ellery Leonard

SOMEWHERE I CHANCED TO READ

SOMEWHERE I chanced to read how love may die
From too large giving; so I mused thereon:
"Haply in this our utmost fear should lie?"
And mindful of this caution, I read on;
Then saw these words: "Yet love may equally
Abate through long neglect."   But thereupon
I smiled, believing hereof we were free
And would be ever till our days were done.
Now love is dead, but how I cannot tell—
Whether from too large giving, or neglect.
First dimmed the flame, and after that there fell
The fated silence.   Yet I should elect
Neither of these as cause, but say love died
Out of a cold and calculating pride.

Gustav Davidson

SOLITUDE

THERE is the loneliness of peopled places:
Streets roaring with their human flood; the crowd
That fills bright rooms with billowing sounds and faces,
Like foreign music, overshrill and loud.
There is the loneliness of one who stands
Fronting the waste under the cold sea-light,
A wisp of flesh against the endless sands,
Like a lost gull in solitary flight.
Single is all up-rising and down-lying;
Struggle or fear or silence none may share;
Each is alone in bearing, and in dying;
Conquest is uncompanioned as despair.
Yet I have known no loneliness like this,
Locked in your arms and bent beneath your kiss.

Babette Deutsch

THE LADDER

I HAD a sudden vision in the night—
I did not sleep, I dare not say I dreamed—
Beside my bed a pallid ladder gleamed
And lifted upward to the sky's dim height:
And every rung shone strangely in that light,
And every rung a woman's body seemed,
Outstretched, and down the sides her long hair streamed,
And you—you climbed that ladder of delight!
You climbed, sure-footed, naked rung by rung,
Clasped them and trod them, called them by their name,
And my name too I heard you speak at last;
You stood upon my breast the while and flung
A hand up to the next! And then—oh shame—
I kissed the foot that bruised me as it passed.

Leonora Speyer

THE FLOWERS OF APOLLO

THE flowers of Apollo that will heal
Are laid across my anger and my eyes.
Oh, once-belovèd, where they set their seal,
I have grown merry and I shall grow wise.

But lest my merriment should flutter out
And wisdom fall in shadows and in night,
I must forget what I grow wise about,
And why I laugh must be forgotten quite.
And so my memory on whispering feet
Goes nowhere in a dim processional,
While I (with Lenten eyes) along the street
Come homeward from a dumb confessional.
I will not tell how many times I break
The flowers of Apollo for your sake.

Hildegarde Flanner

BELOVÈD, FROM THE HOUR THAT YOU WERE BORN

BELOVÈD, from the hour that you were born
I loved you with the love whose birth is pain;
And now, that I have lost you, I must mourn
With mortal anguish, born of love again;
And so I know that Love and Pain are one,
Yet not one single joy would I forego.—
The very radiance of the tropic sun
Makes the dark night but darker here below.
Mine is no coward soul to count the cost;
The coin of love with lavish hand I spend,
And though the sunlight of my life is lost
And I must walk in shadow to the end,—
I gladly press the cross against my heart,
And welcome Pain, that is Love's counterpart!

Corinne Roosevelt Robinson

IN THAT DIM MONUMENT WHERE TYBALT LIES

IN that dim monument where Tybalt lies
I would that we lay sleeping side by side,
And that the loveliness that never dies
There in our silent effigies had died.
For now your living beauty too much stirs
Across my sight, and I grow dumb with tears;
And I am homesick for old sepulchres
Now that your lips wake the forgotten years.

Love that is perfect comes thus to the land
Within whose borders only death can be.
Wherefore I say, hold out to me your hand
And set me free, set me forever free,
And come, with terrible silence in your eyes,
To that dim monument where Tybalt lies.

Arthur Davison Ficke

THE SILENCE

A SONG between two silences Life sings,
A melody 'twixt night and patient night.
He strums his lute against the fading light
To gild the shadow that the gloaming brings,
And Love is but a plucking of the strings,
A throb of music staying music's flight,
A little note that hardly shall requite
Thine outstretched hand that mars Life's lute-playings.
Yet, when the last faint echo of that note
Has stirred the cypress-leaves at eventide,
When night has stilled forever Life's white throat,
And his gold lute lies shattered by his side,
We two shall follow through a world remote
The silence whereinto Love's music died.

Archibald MacLeish

DUSK

THINK not I may not know thee kneeling there
For all I lie so silently in death;
Ay, ever as the candle flickereth,
I watch the light weave shadow in thy hair,
I see thy white hands eloquent in prayer,
I hear the agony of sobbing breath;
And words of faith thy sorrow whispereth
Upon thy lips are echoes of despair.
I hear—and wonder how one time we played
At this; called Death's reflection to Love's glass,
And blurred the image with a laugh, afraid.
Now Death is come and gone, the solemn mass

Low sung, the mirror shattered; fancies pass,
And heart in heart we weep Love's body laid.

Archibald MacLeish

SEVEN SAD SONNETS

I

THE HAPPENING

It had to be. She from his weariness
Discerned a world of unsuspected things;
And though she leapt to meet his swift caress
She feared a trail of dim imaginings.
He drew to him her half-unwilling eyes,
And gazing, learned of wistfulness for joy:
Her singing words gave him desired surprise,
Waking his memory of a lyric boy.
She thought they loved. At any rate they lay
A moment in each other's arms and parted:
He unbereft, and, in his fashion, gay;
She, startled and undone and sorry-hearted.
But if she gave to his satiety
To no avail, what then? It had to be.

II

THE OTHER ONE COMES TO HER

At last her face was turned to him who knew
Only the mockery of an old denial,
And though he sensed no single word was true
He sunned him in the strangeness of her smile.
Wondering why she suddenly was kind,
He thought his faithfulness had found her heart.
He did not see the path that lay behind,
Nor guess what kept them ever wide apart.
She held him lightly, so he held her high,
Jumping to answer each amused behest;
She tried to make I love you not a lie,
To take him to her soft deserted breast.

But when the hour came—to his surprise
She sent him from her with remorseful eyes.

III

THE WANDERING ONE

While he to whom her vexing thoughts still clung
Went wearily philandering on his way:
He tried them slightly worn, he tried them young,
He tried them sorrowful, he tried them gay.
He said, and thought, he had not loved before;
He shrined a picture on his memory-shelf;
And as each loved one left his closing door
He took grave counsel with his puzzled self:
"There is no love. We for a moment stand
And hold at bay inevitable pain,
Aghast and passionate, hand in eager hand,
Before we face our loneliness again."
Perhaps he made a rhyme; but quite forgot
Before another came that love was not.

IV

SHE REMEMBERS

From far she watched his wanderings, and sighed
To know herself so soft, so warm a thing;
And laughed recalling with what pain she tried
To pipe the tune that he had bade her sing.
For he had told her in those golden days,
When all her hope lay trembling on his breast,
That she must watch him go his vagrant ways—
For him there was no peace, there was no rest.
His words had shown her all she feared, and when
He slept she lay beside him silently.
Up in the morning, gayly serene again,
She told him she had found Philosophy.
This made him comfortable, and though she died
He should not know how bitterly she lied.

V

SHE THINKS OF THE FAITHFUL ONE

And when her broken thoughts went following after
That other one, she saw a sorry thing;
For all she had for him was vainest laughter,
And all he had for her was comforting.
So, sadly then, and with no mockery
She called him to her, touched his hand, and pled
That he forgive. As in humility
He listened to the words his lady said,
He saw her hiding something gone amiss,
And knew her dreadful gentleness portended
Worse than her raillery. Her quiet kiss
Told him his living dream of her was ended.
Next day, forlorn, she questioned wonderingly
Why, since she needs must love, it was not he.

VI

THE WANDERING ONE MAKES MUSIC

The years sped onward. He who forever sought
The unseeable light beyond the western skies
Made mighty music. In his work he wrought
All that he knew, all that man might surmise,
Until a vast and intricate design
Awoke and spoke—a living, new-born thing.
He watched it grow in beauty, line on line,
And yielded it his only worshipping.
At last she saw why he had gone his way—
His endless quest; even, she could rejoice,
For like a whispering wind at close of day
Faintly she heard the echo of her voice.
Not one but every kind of song she found
In that great diapason of sweet sound.

VII

THEY MEET AGAIN

It chanced one day they met. Each in surprise
Was extra glad, and unto each the other
Spoke ardently with lighting lips and eyes,
Bandying synonyms for "long lost brother."

A café then and tea, and much to tell
Of this and that and what the years had brought:
She held again a mystery, for well
He knew that she had found what he had sought.
Gravely he questioned, saw her oddly gay,
Uncovered guarded memories, and so
Prayed that they meet again another day,
Prayed that she would not lightly let him go.
She shook her head: Alack, it might not be!
She had, she said, embraced Philosophy.

Mary Aldis

ULYSSES RETURNS

I

PENELOPE SPEAKS

Ulysses has come back to me again!
I listen when he tells me of the sea,
But he has strange reserves . . . and strangely he
Stares in the fire . . . I question him, and then
He tells me more of arms . . . and men—
But there is something. . . . *Heart, what can it be
He sees there that he will not tell to me?*
What swift withdrawal makes him alien?
Oh, there are many things that women know,
That no one tells them, no one needs to tell;
And that they know, their dearest never guess!
Because the woman heart is fashioned so.
*I know that he has loved another well,
Still his remembering lips know her caress!*

II

CIRCE SPEAKS

So swift to bloom, so soon to pass, Love's flower!
The sea that brought him, took him back again—
Ah, well, so is the world and so are men!
But he was happy with me here an hour,

Or almost happy, here within my bower!
He had his silences, his moments when
A strange abstraction took him . . . *I knew then*
That he remembered . . . slipped beyond my power!
I brought him strange, bright blossoms that were grown
In emerald gardens, underneath the sea,
We rode white horses, far beyond the shore—
I would not let him sit and think alone!
One day he held me long and tenderly . . .
I knew, I knew that he would come no more!

III

ULYSSES SPEAKS

Was it I, was it I who dallied there
With a strange, sweet woman beside the sea?
Did she race the wind on the beach with me?
Was it I who kissed her and called her fair?
Was it I who fondled her soft, gold hair—
While she wove and waited me patiently
The woman I love, my Penelope?
Was it I who lingered in Circe's snare?
Now my foot again in my hall is set,
And my keel is dry and my sails are furled:
Beside me, the face I could not forget,
That called me back from across the world—
But there in the fire . . . those red lips wet,
And that soft, gold hair by the sea-mist curled!

IV

PENELOPE SEWS

Oh, the hearts of men, they are rovers, all!
And men will go down to the sea in ships,
And they stop when they hear the sirens call,
And lean to the lure of their red, wet lips!
But never a Circe has snared one yet,
In a green, cool cavern beside the sea,
Who could make the heart of him quite forget
A patiently waiting Penelope!

Yet—there's never a roving one returns
But will sit him down in his easy chair,
While Penelope sews and the fire burns,
And into the depths of it stare . . . *and stare.*
The fire burns and Penelope sews . . .
He never tells—*but Penelope knows!*

Roselle Mercier Montgomery

TWO MARRIED

THE HEIGHTS

Do you remember how we came that day,
Breathless with love, unto a hill and stood,
My lips athirst to drink the wine of play,
Before I must fulfill my womanhood?
Your hand on mine was sudden secret fire,
It promised wonder, fear and ecstasy;
Our dreams were high and white as stars, yea higher—
They were the hope of things we shall not see.
Do you recall how, even going down,
Our spirits seemed to soar?　The dusk that came
And hung a cold gray silence on the town,
For us was leaping glory and a flame.
You drew me close, your hands caressed my head;
And "All our days shall be as this," you said.

DESCENT

Sometimes that promised glory haunts my sleep,
Who all day long in dull monotony
Traverse with you the common days and keep
The steady pace your footsteps set for me.
Above the deadly level of our lives,
Somewhere, I know, are other heights to climb;
But all the little tasks of husbands, wives,
Forbid the quest—we no more have the time.
I fear, I fear sometimes when nights are still,
That something in my heart will rise and break.
I dare not look too long upon a hill,
Or think on beauty, sleeping or awake—

Lest you should find me some tempestuous June,
Crying my mad white hunger to the moon.

FLIGHT

All night between my dreams the thought of you
Was daybreak falling from a green-gold tree,
Was beauty mirrored in a drop of dew.
It woke an old, old urge; it troubled me.
Somewhile before the dawn I left your bed,
Nor bound the soft confusion of my hair,
More still than silence from your side I fled—
You, dreaming of a desk, an easy chair.
The world was waking wonder where I ran,
Gray pools of shadow leapt beneath my feet;
And at the dawn's edge, where the woods began,
I found you waiting, eager and most sweet—
Your laughter sunlight, and the wind your kiss.
Long in the woods I drank remembered bliss.

CERTAINTIES

My heart is young—the breath of blowing trees
Is more than all the wisdom I have known.
How shall I hedge myself with certainties:
A dinner gong, the mail, a telephone?
How shall I move among these common things
And decently observe my household rites,
When love is calling, calling for its wings,
When all my heart is thirsting for the heights?
When we are dust, these daily tasks will move
As well without us. Dear, how soon, how soon
We have forgotten what it is to love!
The moon, that was high hope, is just the moon,
The stars are stars; no wonder stirs a tree.
And life itself is one more certainty.

Helen Frazee-Bower

RETRACTIONS

—AFTER THEODORE PASSERAT

YOU ASK A SONNET?—WELL, IT IS YOUR RIGHT.
I GRANT IT, LAUGH, SHRUG, SET ABOUT THE TASK,
AND MAKE A SEQUENCE, SINCE IT IS MY RIGHT
NO MORE TO GIVE YOU ONLY WHAT YOU ASK.

I

Although as yet my cure be incomplete,
Yet love of you, time-lulled and vigorless,
Engenders now no more unhappiness,
Not even discontent. And now we meet
Unmoved—half-waggish,—and my pulses beat
Quite calmly as I wonder now, *Is he
As proud as I was? and—as once to me—
To him is her love lovely and very sweet?*
Nor do I grudge him any joy of his
Who follows on a road that I have trod,
And sues for love where I was wont to sue;
I am contented by remembrances,
And know that neither fate, nor time, nor God,
Robs me of that first mastery of you.

II

I am contented by remembrances,—
Dreams of dead passions, wraiths of vanished times,
Fragments of vows, and by-ends of old rhymes,—
Flotsam and jetsam tumbling in the seas
Whereon, long since, put forth our argosies
Which, launched for traffic in the Isles of Love,
Lie foundered somewhere in some firth thereof,
Encradled by eternal silences.
Thus, having come to naked bankruptcy,
Let us part friends, as thrifty tradesmen do
When common ventures fail; for it may be
These battered oaths and rhymes may yet ring true
To some fair woman's hearing, so that she
Will listen and think of love, and I of you.

V

It is in many ways made plain to us
That love must grow like any common thing,
Root, bud, and leaf, ere ripe for garnering
The mellow fruitage front us; even thus
Must Helena encounter Thesëus
Ere Paris come, and every century
Spawn divers queens who die with Antony
But live a great while first with Julius.
Thus I have spoken the prologue of a play
Wherein I have no part, and laugh, and sit
Contented in the wings, whilst you portray
An amorous maid with gestures that befit
This lovely rôle,—as who knows better, pray,
Than I that helped you in rehearsing it?

VI

With Love I garnered mirth, and dreams, and shame;
And half his playmate, half his worshipper,
I flouted him, and yet might not demur
To do his bidding, or in aught defame
Love's tutorage,—not even when you came,
And at the portal of Love's golden house
We hazarded stray kisses, sighs and vows,
And lightly staked them in a hackneyed game.
And now the game is ended, dear; and we
May not re-enter that august domain
Which we, encoasting, lost eternally;
And now, although beloved by many men,
You may love no man as you have loved me,
Who have loved you as I may not love again.

XII

Cry *Kismet!* and take heart. Erôs is gone,
Nor may we follow to that loftier air
Olympians breathe. Take heart, and enter where
A lighter love-lord takes a heatless sun,

Oblivious of tangled webs ill-spun
By ancient wearied weavers, for it may be
His guidance leads to lovers of such as we
And hearts so credulous as to be won.
Cry *Kismet!* Put away vain memories
Of all old sorrows and of all old joys,
And learn that life is never quite amiss
So long as unreflective girls and boys
Remember that young lips were meant to kiss,
And hold that laughter is a seemly noise.

XIV

So, let us laugh,—lest vain rememberings
Breed, as of old, some rude bucolic cry
Of awkward anguishes, of dreams that die
Without decorum, of Love lacking wings
Yet striving you-ward in his flounderings
Eternally,—as now, even when I lie
As I lie now, who know that you and I
Exist and heed not lesser happenings.
I was. I am. I will be. Eh, no doubt
For some sufficient cause, I drift, defer,
Equivocate, dream, hazard, grow more stout,
Age, am no longer Love's idolater,—
And yet I could and would not live without
Your faith that heartens and your doubts which spur.

XV

Nightly I mark and praise, or great or small,
Such stars as proudly struggle one by one
To heaven's highest place, as Procyon,
Antarês, Naös, Tejat and Nibal
Attain supremacy, and proudly fall,
Still glorious, and glitter, and are gone
So very soon;—whilst steadfast and alone
Polaris gleams, and is not changed at all.
Daily I find some gallant dream that ranges
The heights of heaven; and as others do,
I serve my dream until my dream estranges
Its errant bondage, and I note anew

That nothing dims, nor shakes, nor mars, nor changes
Fond faith in you and in my love of you.

AND THEREFORE PRAISE I EVEN THE MOST HIGH
LORD CHANCE,—THAT, BEING OF KIN WITH SETEBOS,
IN ORDERING LIFE'S LABOR, STRIFE AND LOSS,
ORDAINED THAT YOU BE YOU, AND I BE I.

James Branch Cabell

SONNETS

FOREWORD

WHAT other form were worthy of your praise
But this lute-voice mocking the centuries
In many a silvery phrase that hallowed is
By love not faltering with length of days?
A lute that I have little worth to raise
And little skill to sound!—Yet not amiss
Your love may find it, since my heart in this
Only one thing for your heart only says.
These are no perfect blossoms I offer you.
No rose whose crimson cup all longing slakes,
Not moonflowers, sunflowers, flowers bold of hue,
Nor silver lilies mystical with dew—
No more than bluets, blown when April takes
Millions of them to make one meadow blue.

III

I make no question of your right to go—
Rain and swift lightning, thunder, and the sea,
Sand and dust and ashes are less free!
Follow all paths that wings and spread sails know,
Unheralded you came, and even so,
If so you will, you may take leave of me.
Yours is your life, and what you will shall be.
I ask no questions: hasten or be slow!
But I who would not hold you—I who give
Your freedom to you with no word to say,
And, watching quietly, with my prayers all dumb,
Speed you to any life you choose to live—

Shall ask God's self, incredulous, some day,
Why in the name of Christ He let you come!

IV

I have a thousand pictures of the sea—
Snatches of song and things that travelers say.
I know its glimmerings from green to gray;
At dawn and sunset it is real to me.
Like something known and loved for years will be
That sight of it when I shall come some day
Where little waves and great waves war and play,
And little winds and great winds fly out free.
Of love I made no pictures: Love would come
Like any casual guest whom I could greet
Serenely, and serenely let depart—
Love that came like fire and struck me dumb,
That came like wind and swept me from my feet,
That came like lightning shattering my heart!

V

Life of itself will be cruel and hard enough:
There will be pain and loss enough to bear;
Battles to wage, sorrow and tears to share.
We must know grief and the salt taste thereof;
Must mark the Shadow towering above;
Must shut our eyes to gain the strength to dare
And force tired hearts to face the noise and glare,
Though it is dusk and silence that we love.
Life has no need of stones that we might heap
To build up walls between; no need of tears
That we seek out and proudly make our own.
Oh my belovèd, since we have alone
These brief hours granted from the hurrying years,
Be patient—life itself will make us weep!

XI

It will be easy to love you when I am dead—
Shadowed from light and shut away from sound,
Held deeper than the wild roots underground,
Where nothing can be changed and no more said.

All will be uttered then: beyond the dread
Of failure in you or me, I shall have found
Most perfect quietness to wrap me round,
Where I can dream while all Time's years are sped.
But now Life roars about me like a sea,
Sears me like flame, is thunder in my ears.
There is no time for song, no space for tears,
And every vision has forsaken me.
In a world earthquake-shaken, lightning-charred,
Love is the hardest where all things are hard.

XII

Along my ways of life you never came—
You would be alien to the paths I take.
These orchards never reddened for your sake,
This larkspur never rustled with your name.
Startled alike by sound and sudden flame,
Swept centerward like clouds when tempests break,
We knew such unity as storms may make
Before returning calm shows earth the same.
I am not I who come back to old ways—
Not I, but what a dream has made of me,
Beyond earth's power to alter or undo.
And if I must walk quietly all my days,
As once I walked, content that this should be,
God must remake the world, or me, or you!

Muna Lee

SONNETS

From "Ideal Passion"

I NEVER muse upon my lady's grace,
Nor dream upon her bounty, what may be
Largess or guerdon at the last to me,
Who serve far off and in a lowly place.
I was not fashioned of the suitor-race
Who give their labor and their hearts for fee;
No recompense of my fidelity
I meditate,—not even to see her face.

Only always invisible tenderness,
Hanging about me like a spiritual cloud,
Holds me obscure, and undivulged doth bless
My soul, and in this world doth strangely shroud;
Whereof the meaning I but faintly guess,
Save that it keeps me private in life's crowd.

In what a glorious substance did they dream
Who first embodied immortality,
And in warm marble gave this world to see
The earthly art that lifts heaven-high its beam!
Of things that only to the spirit seem
They wrought the eternal stuff of memory,
And the invisible divinity
That they so loved, did in their temples gleam.
I have no art to deify the stone,
Nor genius, later born, to limn or paint;
No instrumental music do I own,
Of choiring angel or ecstatic saint;
Best by its frailties here is true love known,
That in the heavenly presence waxes faint.

"An evil thing is honor," once of old
The saddest of Italian shepherds sang,
And on his mouth the immortal lyric sprang
That through all ages pours the age of gold:
"Not that the earth untilled her harvests rolled,
The rose no thorn, the serpent had no fang,
The sea no furrow, nowhere ever rang
The battle, but that love was uncontrolled."
The reminiscence of all lost desire
That love-defrauded hearts dream on for aye,
Hangs in the words, and rises from the lyre,
Whose ecstasy fails not unto this day.
O Song of Gold! O all-consuming fire!
Victorious flame! O lover-hearted lay!

Oh, how with brightness hath Love filled my way,
And with his glory hath beset my road!
It seemeth that to him alone I owed
Dawn, and the sweet salvation of the day.

Enlightenment upon my soul held sway,
And all my faculties of man o'erflowed
With inward light, that, unobservèd, showed
The path, more brilliant than noon's burning ray.
I did not know it then,—that gift divine,
The beam wherein my spirit walked secure;
I thought the clarity of nature mine,
Which only in him shines, and doth endure;
The track of light behind me crystalline
With truth eternal, he made bright and pure.

Why, Love, beneath the fields of asphodel
Where youth lies buried, goest thou wandering,
And like a rainbow droops thy irised wing
Above the dead on whom sweet passion fell?
There thy eternal incarnations dwell;
There bends Narcissus o'er the beauteous spring;
There to the lovely soil doth Hyacinth cling.
Ay me! when young, I breathed the Ægean spell.
Once voyaged I—Europe, Asia on each hand—
To the inaccessible, dim, holy main;
Beautiful Ida wooed me, misty, grand;
Scamander shouted music in my brain;
And in the darkness, in the Trojan land,
I heard my horses champing golden grain.

Between my eyes and hers so thin the screen
Grows with the passage of my mortal years
That almost to my human sight appears
The holy presence of the life serene.
The skies of Perugino, golden-green,
Encompass it; and like an angel nears,
Through cypress lights, she whom my soul reveres
And dim through veils of nature I have seen.
Most like the coming of the evening star,
When dawns the night with that sweet miracle,
Her apparition is, from me how far!
But so doth love within my bosom swell,
And in my eyes such wondrous tidings are,
I kneel, expectant of what heaven shall tell.

Immortal Love, too high for my possessing,—
Yet, lower than thee, where shall I find repose?
Long in my youth I sang the morning rose,
By earthly things the heavenly pattern guessing!
Long fared I on, beauty and love caressing,
And finding in my heart a place for those
Eternal fugitives; the golden close
Of evening folds me, still their sweetness blessing.
Oh, happy we, the first-born heirs of nature,
For whom the Heavenly Sun delays his light!
He by the sweets of every mortal creature
Tempers eternal beauty to our sight;
And by the glow upon love's earthly feature
Maketh the path of our departure bright.

Farewell, my Muse! for, lo, there is no end
Of singing of the winged and soaring choir,
Whose flights mount up, and, circling high and higher,
My heavenly salutations to her send.
I found her upon earth my only friend;
She fed my boyhood with thy holy fire;
She drew my manhood from the world's desire.
Oh, unto my frail state may she yet lend
Her strength, stay my faint heart, and still console
A little longer; with a poor man's bread
Succor my poverty; and pay my toll
To Charon, when to Lethe I am led!
And ever round her shine the aureole
Of my sad verses, after I am dead!

George Edward Woodberry

SONNETS

From "Sonnets of a Portrait Painter"

IX

HER PEDIGREE

Your beauty is as timeless as the earth;
All storied women live again in you:—
Yet with some element of later birth,
Some savor strange, some light troubling and new.

You were not possible until to-day;
For in your soul the risen Celtic wind
Breathes audible; and tragic shadows gray
From dark Norwegian winters tinge your mind.
The pulse of the world's dreamers who have been
Lemans of beauty, and grown faint thereby,—
The fierce unrest of toilers who have seen
Life as a cage of steam-shot agony,—
Have woven round you, in the burning Now,
A lure unknown to Helen's Phidian brow.

X

TROUBADOURS

Did not each poet amorous of old
Plead the sweet pretext of the wingèd time
To urge his lady that she be not cold
To the dissolving master of that rhyme?
I with no new importunings address
One not less proud and beautiful than they
Whose lovers breathed—"Fleet is thy loveliness;
Let not its treasure slip unused away."
Light hearts! Light words! Here in my transient Spring
Let them suffice to hide the things unsaid.
No shadow from the lonely deeps I bring.
Nay, I with gayest flowers will wreathe your head.
Here in the sun I put apart from me
Cassandra, Helen, and Persephone.

XI

APRIL MOMENT

Come forth! for Spring is singing in the boughs
Of every white and tremulous apple-tree.
This is the season of eternal vows;
Yet what are vows that they should solace me?
For on the winds wild loveliness is crying,
And in all flowers wild joy its present worth
Proclaims, as from the dying to the dying—
"Seize, clasp your hour of sun upon the earth!"

Then never dream that fire or beauty stays
More than one April moment in its flight
Toward regions where the sea-drift of all days
Sinks in a vast, desireless, lonely night.
What are eternal vows!—oh, give me breath
Of one white hour here on the marge of death!

XII

SPRING LANDSCAPE

Take you my brushes, child of light, and lay
Your colors on the canvas as you choose:—
Paint me the soft glow of this crystal day;
My harder touch would grasp them but to lose
The rose-hung veils, the liquid golden flood,—
I who with palette-knife must pry and strain
To wrench from attitude, face, figure, mood,
A living soul and limn its riddle plain.
What need you teachings of my labored art?
The brush will serve your April winsomeness.
Yet . . . rather lay your hand upon my heart—
Draw me to you in a supreme caress,—
That one day, as I paint some throat or hair,
Spring's whole delight bloom like a marvel there!

XIII

VIEW FROM HEIGHTS

I am in love with high far-seeing places
That look on plains half-sunlight and half-storm,—
In love with hours when from the circling faces
Veils pass, and laughing fellowship glows warm.
You who look on me with grave eyes where rapture
And April love of living burn confessed—
The gods are good! The world lies free to capture!
Life has no walls. O take me to your breast!
Take me,—be with me for a moment's span!—
I am in love with all unveilèd faces.
I seek the wonder at the heart of man;
I would go up to the far-seeing places.
While youth is ours, turn to me for a space
The marvel of your rapture-lighted face!

XIV

SUMMONS

Ah, life is good! and good thus to behold
From far horizons where their tents are furled
The mighty storms of Being rise, unfold,
Mix, strike, and crash across a shaken world:—
Good to behold their trailing rearguards pass,
And feel the sun renewed its sweetness send
Down to the sparkling leaf-blades of the grass,
And watch the drops fall where the branches bend.
I think to-day I almost were content
To hear some bard life's epic story tell,—
To view the stage through some small curtain-rent,
Mere watcher at this gorgeous spectacle.
But now the curtain lifts:—my soul's swift powers
Rise robed and crowned—for lo! the play is ours!

Arthur Davison Ficke

SONNETS

SWEET, when I think how summer's smallest bird
May better sing of Love than I who love you,
That I can sing no note you have not heard
More purely sung by larks in skies above you,
I am downcast, forswearing my dull pen—
Did I not pause to think how birds go wooing,
How envious shame kills not the little wren
Because the ring-dove thrills the glade with cooing;
Nor does the speedwell fail to lift her blue,
Small face to match the glory of the sky;
Content to know her tiny worship true,
She smiles on boundless heaven steadfastly:
Then, dearest, I, your speedwell and your wren,
Learning from these, take back my banished pen.

Shall I be fearful thus to speak my mind
Lest certainty steal virtue from our joy?
More common men prize all their greed may bind
Save love, whose sweets possessed they dread must cloy.

Possessed! Who speaks that word of love blasphemes,
Or else, too dull, he merits not our scorn.
Such fools, save when they sleep, are shut from dreams;
In custom are they bred, of custom born,
And daily rise to earth's beneficence
With eyes by long assurance turned to stone,
To every natural wonder hugely dense,
And most to love, whose peace they dare not own!
Could I have chosen you from this poor flock?
And, loving, shall we fear to build on rock?

When sane men gather in to talk of Love,
Sometimes I lend an ear to their discourse,
Holding my tongue while those more learnèd prove
How this experience that creed must endorse;
How human nature—wretched scapegoat—shows
Monogamy in males is nature's freak;
How marriage laws—as every woman knows—
Were framed by men to render women meek;
How men own nobler brains, or women, souls;
How sexual education still is rotten—
And so the mossless pebble onward rolls:
All these are true—but somehow Love's forgotten!
Let them that know not Love apologize!
We lovers know ourselves the only wise!

In heaven there is a star I call my own—
Some other name she has which I ignore—
Most bright she is, and somewhat moves alone,
With this peculiar grace which I adore—
She has a look of my beloved's eyes,
When they, so steadfast, meditate on me,
And, like his love, no comfort she denies,
But lights my saddest darkness faithfully.
Another grace to this she adds, moreover:
Living so high, she owns us both her wards,
Our separate griefs her common beams discover,
And, war and death surmounting, say "Love guards!"
O gentle star, thy lovely vigil keeping,
Draw up my love to shower on him sleeping!

Between my love and me there runs a thread,
So light that some would say it scarce could bind,
Nor does it serve this use, which hearts too dead
For love's sweet grafting, profitable find.
O, not for chains our airy thread was spun
From fair material of our delight,
When, ever keeping noon, our summer sun
Betrayed no shadow of approaching night;
But that through fear's illimitable hell,
Through dangerous seas of griefs and pains unknown,
We be not wholly lost, but still may tell
Faintly, each where the other moves alone.
When wilt thou backwards spin, O faithful twine,
Until no space divides his heart from mine?

Irene Rutherford McLeod

SONNETS

From "The Spirit and the Bride"

CONSUMMATION

Look in mine eyes, Belovèd!   Is it true
That you and I have found each other now?
And when I smooth the dear hair from your brow,
Do I touch you, and not the shadow of you
That I have known in dreams the slow years through?
My soul made long ago its maiden vow
Before no other than its mate to bow
In spiritual submission; for it knew—
Belovèd brother of the Inner Shrine!—
That in the long procession of the years,
Slow, weighted down with destiny's arrears,
One laurel-crowned would bring me what was mine.
Now I will melt the pearl that was my tears,
And pledge you in Love's sweet and bitter wine.

THE INSCRIPTION

Sealed with the seal of Life, thy soul and mine
Are one this day and we have graven our date
Of recognition on Time's ponderous gate,
Staining the letters deep with love-spilled wine.

Neither the fire of death nor the strong brine
Of the world's waters can obliterate
That record, and the steady hand of Fate
Under the words has drawn a strange design.
They are an incantation, justified
Upon our lips by the incarnate Breath.
The measure of their potency is wide
As the world's orbit; for God promiseth
Unto all love-inscriptions that abide,
Power and dominion over life and death.

CARESSES

The sweet caresses that I give to you
Are but the perfume of the Rose of Love,
The color and the witchery thereof,
And not the Rose itself. Each is a clue
Merely, whereby to seek the hidden, true,
Substantial blossom. Like the Jordan dove,
A kiss is but a symbol from above—
An emblem the Reality shines through.
The Rose of Love is ever unrevealed
In all its beauty, for the sight of it
Were perilous to the purpose of the world.
The hand of Life has cautiously concealed
The pollen-chambers of the infinite
Flower, and its petals only half uncurled.

FULFILMENT

I am so empty and so incomplete,
Save when your lips on my lips realize
For me my own fulfilment. Life denies
Its own abundance save when two lives meet.
Within your arms is all I know of sweet,
And all I need of heaven. When I rise
From your embrace, I feel a vague surprise—
A sundering from my forehead to my feet.
You are the key of every kind event,
You open all the doors of joy to me.
Your being and my being, interblent
As the sea and the saltness of the sea,

Are one inevitable element
In the great crucible of Destiny.

CONFESSION

Yea, Dear, lay bare thy lovely soul, nor fear
That any wraith of shame can enter in
This guarded house of faith, nor any sin
Darken for me Love's mirror, crystal-clear
For all thy revelations. Thou art peer
Now of Love's lofty ones, whose heights begin
Always in humbleness, and thou shalt win
A pearl of rapture for thine every tear.
My love is reverent as the virgin prayer
Whose power the gate of paradise unbars;
My love is tender as the ecstasy
Of the young mother as she grows aware;
And full of understanding as the stars
That shone in wonder over Galilee.

LOVE'S IMMORTALITY

Among those things that make our love complete,
And high beyond all others I have known,
This knowledge is not least: That we have sown
Together seeds of beauty, that shall greet
Strange years in blossoms which the reckless feet
Of Death shall not destroy; that we have shown
To blinded eyes the visions of our own,
Making our blood in others' veins to beat.
Why should we yearn for immortality
In some imagined heaven, when on the earth
Our flowers of song perfume the dusty road,
And speak to passers-by of you and me?
Enough that we have jusified our birth,
Ere entering the inscrutable abode.

Elsa Barker

SONNETS

I

QUICKLY and pleasantly the seasons blow
Over the meadows of eternity,
As wave on wave the pulsings of the sea
Merge and are lost, each in the other's flow.
Time is no lover; it is only he
That is the one unconquerable foe,
He is the sudden tempest none can know,
Winged with swift winds that none may hope to flee.
Fair child of loveliness, these endless fears
Are nought to us; let us be gods of stone,
And set our images beyond the years
On some high mount where we can be alone;
And thou shalt ever be as now thou art,
And I shall watch thee with untroubled heart.

II

The golden spring redeems the withered year,
And wherefore should my spirit be afraid
Though autumn winds wail through the smoky shade
And chill me like the fleeting ghost of fear?
Sweet love of youth, I know that thou must fade,
I know what nameless spectres hover near,
And that the loveliness I hold so dear,
Borrowed from dust, to ashes must be paid.
Yet linger still over these wasted meadows
Faint shreds of song, and scattered scents of flowers,
And from the heart's abyss of deepening shadows
Rise the young passions of immortal hours.
The golden spring its withered year redeems;
Sleep comes at last, but sleep made rich with dreams.

III

Then judge me as thou wilt, I cannot flee,
I cannot turn away from thee forever,
For there are bonds that wisdom cannot sever,
And slaves with souls far freer than the free.

Such strong desires the Universal Giver
With unknown plan has buried deep in me,
That the passionate joy of watching thee
Has dominated all my life's endeavor.
Thou weariest of having me so near,
I feel the scorn thou hast within thy heart,
And yet, thy face has never seemed so dear
As now, when I am minded to depart.
Though thou shalt drive me hence, I love thee so
That I shall watch thee when thou dost not know.

XII

I will fling wide the windows of my soul
Under the deep hush of nocturnal skies,
When the white legions of the stars arise
And write their secrets of the Master's scroll.
I will go forth and watch with slumberous eyes
The languid billows of the ocean roll
In silver rhythms on some hidden shoal,
Swelling with laughter, falling back with sighs.
And in the tranquil twilight of that place,
The lovely solitude of lonely sands,
Will flash the pale resplendence of thy grace
In sudden beauty out of other lands,
And I will kneel and kiss thine ivory hands
Beneath the flowered music of thy face.

XIV

Let all men see the ruins of the shrine
That I, with passionate and holy care,
Built long ago from laughter and despair
That godly love might have a fane divine.
Let the wide wings of darkness hover where
The god of youth once drank his rarest wine,
And let the rank breath of some poisoned vine
Choke the last sigh that lingers on the air.
Hurl the white sanctuary down, and bare
Its inmost secrets to the gaze of men,
Unveil the altar to the vulgar stare,
And let none seek to build it up again;—

Ah, when the last wall crumbles, stone by stone,
I shall go hence that I may weep alone.

XVI

Even as love grows more, I write the less,
Impelled to speak, unable still to voice
The lyric thoughts like angels that rejoice
Attendant on thy godly loveliness.
Stay the bright swallow high in airy poise,
Carve out of stone an infinite caress,
Garner the fruits of tears and happiness,
Make bloom forever what an hour destroys,
Then shamed by such unprecedented skill
I may find words to name thee, and to sing
Such praises of thy beauty as shall fill
The listening world with floods of carolling;
Till then thou art like starlight on the air,
Or clouds at dawn, unutterably fair.

XXIII

Over the waters but a single bough
Stretches in silhouette against the moon,
The little dark waves haunt the dim lagoon
And splash against the languid-moving prow.
I should have left thee when the afternoon
Surrendered to pursuing night, for now
Too perilously dear and fair art thou,
And love too soon invoked shall die too soon.
I fear the very floods of happiness
That swell the narrow chambers of my heart,
Knowing indeed that with our first caress,
Contentment and my soul forever part;
O night of love and beauty, all the years
Shall pay for thy brief ecstasy with tears.

Robert Hillyer

SONNETS

I KNOW I am but summer to your heart,
And not the full four seasons of the year;
And you must welcome from another part
Such noble moods as are not mine, my dear.
No gracious weight of golden fruits to sell
Have I, nor any wise and wintry thing;
And I have loved you all too long and well
To carry still the high sweet breast of Spring.
Wherefore I say: O love, as summer goes,
I must be gone, steal forth with silent drums,
That you may hail anew the bird and rose
When I come back to you, as summer comes.
Else will you seek, at some not distant time,
Even your summer in another clime.

Say what you will, and scratch my heart to find
The roots of last year's roses in my breast;
I am as surely riper in my mind
As if the fruit stood in the stalls confessed.
Laugh at the unshed leaf, say what you will,
Call me in all things what I was before,
A flutterer in the wind, a woman still;
I tell you I am what I was and more.
My branches weigh me down, frost cleans the air,
My sky is black with small birds bearing south;
Say what you will, confuse me with fine care,
Put by my word as but an April truth,—
Autumn is no less on me than a rose
Hugs the brown bough and sighs before it goes.

What lips my lips have kissed, and where, and why,
I have forgotten, and what arms have lain
Under my head till morning; but the rain
Is full of ghosts to-night, that tap and sigh
Upon the glass and listen for reply;
And in my heart there stirs a quiet pain
For unremembered lads that not again
Will turn to me at midnight with a cry.

Thus in the winter stands the lonely tree,
Nor knows what birds have vanished one by one,
Yet knows its boughs more silent than before:
I cannot say what loves have come and gone;
I only know that summer sang in me
A little while, that in me sings no more.

Oh, my belovèd, have you thought of this:
How in the years to come unscrupulous Time,
More cruel than Death, will tear you from my kiss,
And make you old, and leave me in my prime?
How you and I, who scale together yet
A little while the sweet, immortal height
No pilgrim may remember or forget,
As sure as the world turns, some granite night
Shall lie awake and know the gracious flame
Gone out forever on the mutual stone;
And call to mind that on the day you came
I was a child, and you a hero grown?—
And the night pass, and the strange morning break
Upon our anguish for each other's sake!

Not with libations, but with shouts and laughter
We drenched the altars of Love's sacred grove,
Shaking to earth green fruits, impatient after
The launching of the colored moths of Love.
Love's proper myrtle and his mother's zone
We bound about our irreligious brows,
And fettered him with garlands of our own,
And spread a banquet in his frugal house.
Not yet the god has spoken; but I fear
Though we should break our bodies in his flame,
And pour our blood upon his altar, here
Henceforward is a grove without a name,
A pasture to the shaggy goats of Pan,
Whence flee forever a woman and a man.

Edna St. Vincent Millay

PART III

POEMS OF NATURE

INVOCATION

As pools beneath stone arches take
    Darkly within their deeps again
Shapes of the flowing stone, and make
    Stories anew of passing men,

So let the living thoughts that keep,
    Morning and evening, in their kind,
Eternal change in height and deep,
    Be mirrored in my happy mind.

Beat, world, upon this heart, be loud
    Your marvel chanted in my blood.
Come forth, O sun, through cloud on cloud
    To shine upon my stubborn mood.

Great hills that fold above the sea,
    Ecstatic airs and sparkling skies,
Sing out your words to master me—
    Make me immoderately wise.

                                John Drinkwater

MOTHER NATURE

EARTH

GRASSHOPPER, your fairy song
And my poem alike belong
To the dark and silent earth
From which all poetry has birth;
All we say and all we sing
Is but as the murmuring
Of that drowsy heart of hers
When from her deep dream she stirs:
If we sorrow, or rejoice,
You and I are but her voice.

Deftly does the dust express
In mind her hidden loveliness,
And from her cool silence stream
The cricket's cry and Dante's dream:
For the earth that breeds the trees
Breeds cities, too, and symphonies.
Equally her beauty flows
Into a saviour, or a rose,—
Looks down in dream, and from above
Smiles at herself in Jesus' love.
Christ's love and Homer's art
Are but the workings of her heart;
Through Leonardo's hand she seeks
Herself, and through Beethoven speaks
In holy thunderings around
The awful message of the ground.

The serene and humble mould
Does in herself all selves enfold—
Kingdoms, destinies, and creeds,
Great dreams and dauntless deeds,

Science that metes the firmament,
The high, inflexible intent
Of one for many sacrificed—
Plato's brain, the heart of Christ:
All love, all legend, and all lore
Are in the dust forevermore.

Even as the growing grass
Up from the soil religions pass,
And the field that bears the rye
Bears parables and prophecy.
Out of the earth the poem grows
Like the lily, or the rose;
And all Man is, or yet may be,
Is but herself in agony
Toiling up the steep ascent
Toward the complete accomplishment
When all dust shall be (the whole
Universe,) one conscious soul.

Yea, the quiet and cool sod
Bears in her breast the dream of God.

If you would know what earth is, scan
The intricate, proud heart of man,
Which is the earth articulate,
And learn how holy and how great,
How limitless and how profound
Is the nature of the ground—
How without terror or demur
We may entrust ourselves to her
When we are wearied out, and lay
Our faces in the common clay.

For she is pity, she is love,
All wisdom she, all thoughts that move
About her everlasting breast
Till she gathers them to rest:
All tenderness of all the ages,
Seraphic secrets of the sages,

Vision and hope of all the seers,
All prayer, all anguish, and all tears
Are but the dust, that from her dream
Awakes, and knows herself supreme—
Are but earth when she reveals
All that her secret heart conceals
Down in the dark and silent loam,
Which is ourselves, asleep, at home.

Yea, and this my poem, too,
Is part of her as dust and dew,
Wherein herself she doth declare
Through my lips, and say her prayer.

John Hall Wheelock

DUST

I HEARD them in their sadness say,
  "The earth rebukes the thought of God;
We are but embers wrapped in clay,
  A little nobler than the sod."

But I have touched the lips of clay,
  Mother, thy rudest sod to me
Is thrilled with fire of hidden day,
  And haunted by all mystery.

A. E.

THE OLD LOVE

Out of my door I step into
The country, all her scent and dew,
Nor travel there by a hard road,
Dusty and far from my abode.

The country washes to my door
Green miles on miles in soft uproar,
The thunder of the woods, and then
The backwash of green surf again.

Beyond the feverfew and stocks,
The guelder-rose and hollyhocks;
Outside my trellised porch a tree
Of lilac frames a sky for me.

A stretch of primrose and pale green
To hold the tender Hesper in;
Hesper that by the moon makes pale
Her silver keel and silver sail.

The country silence wraps me quite,
Silence and song and pure delight;
The country beckons all the day
Smiling, and but a step away.

This is that country seen across
How many a league of love and loss,
Prayed for and longed for, and as far
As fountains in the desert are.

This is that country at my door,
Whose fragrant airs run on before,
And call me when the first birds stir
In the green wood to walk with her.

Katherine Tynan Hinkson

REFUGE

WHEN stars ride in on the wings of dusk,
    Out on the silent plain,
After the fevered fret of day,
    I find my strength again.

Under the million friendly eyes
    That smile in the lonely night,
Close to the rolling prairie's heart,
    I find my heart for the fight.

Out where the cool long winds blow free,
    I fling myself on the sod;
And there in the tranquil solitude
    I find my soul,—and God.

Lew Sarett

OUT OF THE EARTH

OUT of the earth, and out of the tree
Strength comes flowing into me;
Out of the brook comes quietude,
Down from the sky comes wisdom's food.

As oft as on the earth I've lain
I've died and come to life again
For only men who are brave and good
Can come out changeless from a wood.

Mary Carolyn Davies

AMENDS TO NATURE

I HAVE loved colors, and not flowers;
    Their motion, not the swallow's wings;
And wasted more than half my hours
    Without the comradeship of things.

How is it, now, that I can see,
    With love and wonder and delight,
The children of the hedge and tree,
    The little lords of day and night?

How is it that I see the roads,
    No longer with usurping eyes,
A twilight meeting-place for toads,
    A mid-day mart for butterflies?

I feel, in every midge that hums,
    Life, fugitive and infinite,
And suddenly the world becomes
    A part of me and I of it.

Arthur Symons

THE GREEN INN

I SICKEN of men's company,
    The crowded tavern's din,
Where all day long with oath and song
    Sit they who entrance win,
So come I out from noise and rout
    To rest in God's Green Inn.

Here none may mock an empty purse
　　Or ragged coat and poor,
But Silence waits within the gates,
　　And Peace beside the door;
The weary guest is welcomest,
　　The richest pays no score.

The roof is high and arched and blue,
　　The floor is spread with pine;
On my four walls the sunlight falls
　　In golden flecks and fine;
And swift and fleet on noiseless feet
　　The Four Winds bring me wine.

Upon my board they set their store—
　　Great drinks mixed cunningly,
Wherein the scent of furze is blent
　　With odor of the sea;
As from a cup I drink it up
　　To thrill the veins of me.

It's I will sit in God's Green Inn
　　Unvexed by man or ghost,
Yet ever fed and comforted,
　　Companioned by mine host,
And watched at night by that white light
　　High swung from coast to coast.

Oh, you who in the House of Strife
　　Quarrel and game and sin,
Come out and see what cheer may be
　　For starveling souls and thin,
Who come at last from drought and fast
　　To sit in God's Green Inn.

Theodosia Garrison

PRELUDE

STILL south I went and west and south again,
　　Through Wicklow from the morning till the night,
And far from cities and the sights of men,
　　Lived with the sunshine and the moon's delight.

I knew the stars, the flowers, and the birds,
  The gray and wintry sides of many glens,
And did but half remember human words,
  In converse with the mountains, moors and fens.

J. M. Synge

THE FULL HEART

ALONE on the shore in the pause of the night-time
I stand and I hear the long wind blow light;
I view the constellations quietly, quietly burning;
I hear the wave fall in the hush of the night.

Long after I am dead, ended this bitter journey,
Many another whose heart holds no light
Shall your solemn sweetness hush, awe and comfort,
O my companions, Wind, Waters, Stars, and Night.

Robert Nichols

THREE THINGS

THREE things filled this day for me,
Three common things filled this day;
Each had, for me, a word to say;
Said it in beauty, and was done:
Cows on a hillside all one way,
A buttercup tilted seductively,
And a lark arguing with the sun.

These three things, merely these three,
Were enough to cry the world
Out of my heart: the buttercup curled
Where some gorgeous ruffian plundered;
The skylark's dizzy flag unfurled;
The placid cows pensively
Wondering why they wondered.

Joseph Auslander

A B C'S IN GREEN

THE trees are God's great alphabet:
With them He writes in shining green
Across the world His thoughts serene.

He scribbles poems against the sky
With a gay, leafy lettering,
For us and for our bettering.

The wind pulls softly at His page,
And every star and bird
Repeats in dutiful delight His word,
And every blade of grass
Flutters to class.

Like a slow child that does not heed,
I stand at summer's knees,
And from the primer of the wood
I spell that life and love are good,
I learn to read.

Leonora Speyer

STRINGS IN THE EARTH

STRINGS in the earth and air
   Make music sweet;
Strings by the river where
   The willows meet.

There's music along the river
   For Love wanders there,
Pale flowers on his mantle,
   Dark leaves on his hair.

All softly playing,
   With head to the music bent,
And fingers straying
   Upon an instrument.

James Joyce

VOICES OF THE AIR

BUT then there comes that moment rare
   When, for no cause that I can find,
The little voices of the air
   Sound above all the sea and wind.

The sea and wind do then obey
   And sighing, sighing double notes
Of double basses, content to play
   A droning chord for the little throats—

The little throats that sing and rise
   Up into the light with lovely ease,
And a kind of magical sweet surprise
   To hear and know themselves for these—

For these little voices: the bee, the fly,
   The leaf that taps, the pod that breaks,
The breeze on the grass-tops bending by,
   The shrill quick sound that the insect makes.

Katherine Mansfield

A PAINTER IN NEW ENGLAND

DID you ever note the beauty of the soft New England
      grasses,
   All the ochres, reds and browns;
And the flowers: the purple asters and the goldenrod's rich
      masses
   With the cardinals' flaming gowns,
Dots of blood against the tangle of the reedy lone morasses
Where the nodding cat-tails rustle under every wind that
      passes?
   Ah! what reticent depth of color,
   Growing brighter, growing duller,
As a smile of sunlight broadens or a gloomy storm-cloud
      frowns.

Have you read the blazoned glory of the sunset's revela-
      tions,
   Glowing scarlet streaked with gold;
Or observed the crumbling sky-towers cleft by radiant
      fulgurations,
   Ruins gorgeous to behold?
While the East is hung with tapestries in dove-serene grada-
      tions
And the naked vault of heaven is touched with vivid varia-
      tions,

Where in all the world resplendent
Or the poet's mind transcendent
Can such miracles be imaged, form so grand or hue so bold?

Have you watched the dreamy progress of a gray New England schooner
Drifting seaward with the tide
Darkly down a line of radiance, dawn-bright gold or silvery lunar,
Ribbon narrow or ocean wide?
Such a boat in such a background I will paint you ten times sooner
Than a lily-perfect yacht with drooping topsail and ballooner.
No, for me the old-time vessel
In a land-locked bay to nestle
Till the light breeze flaps her stay-sail and the light wave laps her side.

Have you shrunk before the grimness of the rugged 'longshore ledges
Where the groundswell surf rolls in
Round the battlemented coast-line with its walls and bastion wedges?
Hark! the cave-resounded din
As a breaker smites the granite with the strength of giant sledges
And a swaying fringe of foam enfolds the dark cliff's dripping edges.
Readily will other nations
Yield a sheaf of sharp sensations,
But the landscape of New England holds a rapture hard to win.

Charles Wharton Stork

LIFE OR DEATH

From "In Western Mountains"

He stood a moment at the edge
Of that cliff, looking out with me
Upon great valleys ending in the haze,
And mountains that from hazes drove a wedge

Of snow in skies of lapis lazuli.
Then something of the littleness of days
His life could span came to him dizzily
And he, who boasted of his might with men,
Turned back and grasped a little cedar tree
Nearby, for safety and he shut his eyes,
Shaken, and would not turn to look again. . . .
Back from that cliff-edge jutting out to skies
He climbed and spoke at last with heavy breath,
"God, what a place! What is it? Life or Death?"

Glenn Ward Dresbach

THE STRANGER

I HEDGE rebellious grasses in,
But where shall ownership begin?

The spider spins her silvery bars
Between me and the cosmos' stars,

And ere I waken is astir
To write revolt in gossamer!

With beady and forboding eye
The turtle peers as I go by:

The shell that shuts him in is stout—
Stronger the code that shuts me out!

What dauntless and primeval stock
Makes yonder stone its council-rock?

What old, indomitable breed
Takes this low bush for Runnymede?

Races whose titles run from God
Dispute my warrant to the sod!

I am Intrusion! I am Danger!
Familiar, but for aye—the Stranger!

Daniel Henderson

A HILLSIDE FARMER

DAWN—and the mist across the silent lane;
Each day its little round of petty tasks.
"Are you not very lonely?" someone asks,
"Here where the old folks stay, and no one new
Comes in to start a farm? You should go, too;
Valleys grow better grain."

This may seem still and lonely, but for me
Hill-tops are wider than the open land.
Maybe you never could quite understand
How dear it is to me—this loneliness.
You think the hills are narrowing, I guess;
But, oh, how far we see!

John Farrar

SOWING

IT was a perfect day
For sowing; just
As sweet and dry was the ground
As tobacco-dust.

I tasted deep the hour
Between the far
Owl's chuckling first soft cry
And the first star.

A long stretched hour it was;
Nothing undone
Remained; the early seeds
All safely sown.

And now, hark at the rain,
Windless and light,
Half a kiss, half a tear,
Saying good-night.

Edward Thomas

PLOUGHMAN AT THE PLOUGH

He behind the straight plough stands
Stalwart, firm shafts in firm hands.

Naught he cares for wars and naught
For the fierce disease of thought.

Only for the winds, the sheer
Naked impulse of the year,

Only for the soil which stares
Clean into God's face he cares.

In the stark might of his deed
There is more than art or creed;

In his wrist more strength is hid
Than in the monstrous Pyramid;

Stauncher than stern Everest
Be the muscles of his breast;

Not the Atlantic sweeps a flood
Potent as the ploughman's blood.

He, his horse, his ploughshare, these
Are the only verities.

Dawn to dusk with God he stands,
The Earth poised on his broad hands.

Louis Golding

THE PLOUGHMAN

I wandered on through field and fold,
  The way was lone and chill.
Towards the East a mist lay rolled
  Upon a distant hill—

That hill which once with boyish stride
 I oft would climb to see
The dawn unfold the portals wide
 Into infinity.

And from infinity no breath
 Wakened my soul this morn;
As in a dream that whispereth
 Vaguely of things forlorn,
I stumbled on—till lo, above
 A gleam of sunlight kissed
The shoulder of the hill, and clove
 A pathway through the mist.

And in that sudden cleft of light
 Hewn through a world of cloud,
My trembling eyes beheld a sight
 That made my heart beat loud;
For toiling there unseen till now
 And toiling gently still,
A ploughman drove his early plough
 In patience on the hill.

Oh sudden gleam too swiftly past!
 Oh sudden gleam of red!
A moment now it seemed to cast
 A halo round his head.
But now it flickered and grew dim,
 Grew dim and died away;
Once more the mist enveloped him
 Within its trackless gray.

Yet light of heart I journeyed now;
 For, though once more the hill
Was lost, that unsuspected plough
 Was surely plodding still—
As, in the mists of doubt that coil
 Around the soul's high slope,
Unseen, undreamt, there still may toil
 The patient plough of Hope.

Gilbert Thomas

THE PLOUGHER

SUNSET and silence!   A man: around him earth savage,
    earth broken;
Beside him two horses—a plough!

Earth savage, earth broken, the brutes, the dawn man
    there in the sunset,
And the Plough that is twin to the Sword, that is founder of
    cities!

"Brute-tamer, plough-maker, earth-breaker!   Can'st hear?
    There are ages between us.
Is it praying you are as you stand there alone in the sunset?

"Surely our sky-born gods can be naught to you, earth
    child and earth master?
Surely your thoughts are of Pan, or of Wotan, or Dana?

"Yet why give thought to the gods?   Has Pan led your
    brutes where they stumble?
Has Dana numbed pain of the child-bed, or Wotan put
    hands to your plough?

"What matter your foolish reply!   O man, standing lone
    and bowed earthward,
Your task is a day near its close.   Give thanks to the
    night-giving God."
. . . .
Slowly the darkness falls, the broken lands blend with the
    savage;
The brute-tamer stands by the brutes, a head's breadth
    only above them.

A head's breadth?   Ay, but therein is hell's depth, and the
    height up to heaven,
And the thrones of the gods and their halls, their chariots,
    purples, and splendors.

                              Padraic Colum

GO, PLOUGHMAN, PLOUGH

Go, ploughman, plough
The mearing lands,
The meadow lands,
The mountain lands:
All life is bare
Beneath your share,
All love is in your lusty hands.

Up, horses, now!
And straight and true
Let every broken furrow run:
The strength you sweat
Shall blossom yet
In golden glory to the sun.

Joseph Campbell

MOWING

THERE was never a sound beside the wood but one,
And that was my long scythe whispering to the ground.
What was it it whispered? I knew not well myself;
Perhaps it was something about the heat of the sun,
Something, perhaps, about the lack of sound—
And that was why it whispered and did not speak.
It was no dream of the gift of idle hours,
Or easy gold at the hand of fay or elf:
Anything more than the truth would have seemed too weak
To the earnest love that laid the swale in rows,
Not without feeble-pointed spikes of flowers
(Pale orchises), and scared a bright green snake.
The fact is the sweetest dream that labor knows.
My long scythe whispered and left the hay to make.

Robert Frost

HOME–COMING

WHEN I stepped homeward to my hill
    Dusk went before with quiet tread;
The bare laced branches of the trees
    Were as a mist about its head.

Upon its leaf-brown breast, the rocks
  Like great gray sheep lay silent-wise;
Between the birch trees' gleaming arms,
  The faint stars trembled in the skies.

The white brook met me half-way up
  And laughed as one that knew me well,
To whose more clear than crystal voice
  The frost had joined a crystal spell.

The skies lay like pale-watered deep.
  Dusk ran before me to its strand
And cloudily leaned forth to touch
  The moon's slow wonder with her hand.

Léonie Adams

THE FLOCK AT EVENING

SUNSET is golden on the steep,
  And all our little valleys lie
Golden and still and full of sleep
  To watch the flocks go by.
Down through the winding leaf-hung lane,
Now blurred in shade, now bright again,
They trail in splendor, aureoled
And mystical in clouded gold.

As insubstantial as a dream
  They huddle homeward past my door . . .
From what Theocritean stream,
  Or what Thessalian shore?
An ancient air surrounds them still,
As though from some Arcadian hill
They shuffled through the afterglow
Across the fields of long ago.

Is this the flock Apollo kept
  From straying by his reed-soft tunes
While the long ilex shadow crept
  Through ancient afternoons?

In some dim legendary wood,
Ages ago, have they not stood
Wondering, circle-wise and mute,
Round some remote Sicilian flute?

I think that they have gazed across
   The dazzle of Ionian seas
From the green capes of Tenedos
   Or wave-washed Cyclades,
And wandered through the twilight down
The hills that gird some Attic town
Dim-shining in the purple gloam
Beside the whispering of pale foam.

What dream is this? I know the croft,
   Deep in this vale, where they were born;
I know their wind-swept fields aloft
   Among the waving corn.
Yet, while they glimmer slowly by,
A fairer earth and earlier sky
Seem round them, and they move sublime
Among the dews of dawning time.

Odell Shepard

THE HOMECOMING OF THE SHEEP

THE sheep are coming home in Greece,
Hark the bells on every hill!
Flock by flock, and fleece by fleece,
Wandering wide a little piece
Through the evening red and still,
Stopping where the pathways cease,
Cropping with a hurried will.

Through the cotton-bushes low
Merry boys with shouldered crooks
Close them in a single row,
Shout among them as they go
With one bell-ring o'er the brooks.
Such delight you never know
Reading it from gilded books.

Before the early stars are bright
Cormorants and sea-gulls call,
And the moon comes large and white
Filling with a lovely light
The ferny curtained waterfall.
Then sleep wraps every bell up tight
And the climbing moon grows small.

Francis Ledwidge

THE SHEPHERD BOY

I saw him naked on a hill
Above a world of gold,
And coming by, so still, so still,
The sheep within his fold.

He strode along that golden air,
A rosy-bodied fool,
With wonder-dripping dreams as fair
As starlight in a pool.

He sang of old, forgotten springs
Of worship in the sky,
And longing passionate with wings,
And vision that must die.

His body and his spirit glowed
For joy that they were one,
And from his heart the music flowed
Into the setting sun.

I hurried as the light grew dim,
And left him far behind,
Yet still I heard his joyous hymn
Come faintly down the wind.

Edward J. O'Brien

THE HERD BOY

The night I brought the cows home
   Blue mist was in the air,
And in my heart was heaven
   And on my lips a prayer.

I raised my arms above me,
   I stretched them wide apart,
And all the world was pressing
   In beauty on my heart.

The lane led by a river
   Along an ancient wood,
And ancient thoughts came softly,
   As with the leaves they should.

I hung the cows with garlands,
   And proud they walked before;
While mother-naked after
   A laurel branch I bore.

Haniel Long

SHEPHERD

EVENING has brought the glow-worm to the green,
And early stars to heaven, and joy to men;
The sun is gone, the shepherd leaves the pen
And hobbles home, while we for leisure lean
On garden pales.   O shepherd old and kind,
Sweet may your musings and your slumbers prove!—
Where the rude chairs, of untanned osiers wove,
Creak to the dead of night, his rest he'll find:
And at his feet well pleased his dog will doze,
And not a traveller passes but he knows.

A country god to every childish eye—
Who sees the shepherd save when he comes home,
With untrimmed staff, smock stitched like honeycomb,
With great-tongued boots, and buskins to the thigh?
A seer, a country god—so thought conceives
His oracles of seasons foul or fair,
His weather-bitten looks and wild white hair
That on his shoulders thatches like an eaves:
And he himself, proud of his antique toil,
Gossips with none that might such honor soil.

Sleep comes upon the village, the rich bee
From honeyed bells of balsams high is gone;
The windows palely shine; the owls whoop on,
But bats have slunk into their hollow tree.

The shepherd hours before has closed his eyes,
But he unseen will take his staff in hand
And walk to wake the morning through the land
Before the cockerel knows 'tis time to rise.
High on the hill he dares the mist and dew
And sings before a sunbeam ventures through.

Now when the morning ripens and unfolds
Like beds of flowers the glories of the plain,
His heart leaps up at every steeple vane
And barn and kiln and windmill on the wolds;
For boyhood knew them all, and not a brook
But he has bathed and played the miller there;
By every green he's hurried to the fair
And tended sheep in every whitethorn nook.
Thus dreaming does he hurdle up the pen
And thinks how soon comes clipping-time agen.

His sheep his children are, each one he knows,
And well might know, who lay through winter storm
In cramping hulks with bracken scarce kept warm
While each one came from the poor frightened yoes.
He never bids or wants for holiday,
His sheep his children are and his delight:
That shepherds'-harvest makes the May so bright
When round his feet the lambs so frisk and play
And nuzzle in his sleeve and twitch his hand—
The prettiest dears, he calls them, in the land.

But May when music grows on every tree
Too quickly passes, shepherd's-roses die—
New dipt and shorn, they still delight the eye:
How fast they gather to his "Cub-burree!"
Even crows and jackdaws scrambling for the beans
Among their troughs are of his rustic clan
And know him king of bird and sheep and man;
And where he breaks his bread the emmet gleans.
The great sun gives him wisdom, the wind sings
Clear to his simple heart the hardest things.

The stubble browsing comes, and grand and grave
Autumn in shadow swathes the rolling weald,
The blue smoke curls with mocking stealth afield,
And far-off lights, like wild eyes in a cave,
Stare at the shepherd on the bleaching grounds.
Deeply he broods on the dark tide of change,
And starts when echo sharp and sly and strange
To his gap-stopping from the sear wood sounds.
His very sheep-bells seem to bode him ill
And starling whirlwinds strike his bosom chill.

Then whispering all his eighty years draw nigh,
And mutter like an Advent wind, and grieve
At perished summer, bid him take his leave
Of toil and take some comfort ere he die.
The hounded leaf has found a tongue to warn
How fierce the fang of winter, the lead rain
Brings him old pictures of the drowning plain,
When even his dog sulks loath to face the morn.
The sun drops cold in a watery cloud, the briars
Like starved arms still snatch at his withered fires.

But shepherd goes to warm him in his chair,
And in the blaze his dog growls at his dreams,
And on the hearth the leaping firelight gleams
That makes him think of one with ruddy hair
Who kept the sheep in ancient Bethlehem.
With trusting tears he takes his Bible, reads
Once more of still green banks and glittering meads
Where storms are not, nor ever floods to stem;
Where the kind shepherd never takes them wrong,
And gently leads the yoes that are with young.

                                        Edmund Blunden

BEATUS VIR

HAPPY is the man who loves the woods and waters,
    Brother to the grass, and well-beloved of Pan;
The earth shall be his, and all her laughing daughters—
    Happy the man.

Never grows he old, nor shall he taste of sorrow,
    Happy at the day's end as when the day began,
Yesterday forgotten, unshadowed by To-morrow,—
    Happy the man.

Fellowed by the mountains, ne'er his heart is lonely,
    Talked to all day by rivers as they ran,
The earth is his love, as he who loves one only—
    Happy the man.

His gossips are the stars, and the moon-rise his tavern;
    He who seeks a better find it if he can—
And O his sweet pillow in the ferny cavern!
    Happy the man.

Richard Le Gallienne

DAWN AND DARK

THE WAKERS

THE joyous morning ran and kissed the grass
And drew his fingers through her sleeping hair,
 And cried, "Before thy flowers are well awake
 Rise, and the lingering darkness from thee shake.

"Before the daisy and the sorrel buy
Their brightness back from that close-folding night,
 Come, and the shadows from thy bosom shake,
 Awake from thy thick sleep, awake, awake! "

Then the grass of that mounded meadow stirred
Above the Roman bones that may not stir
 Though joyous morning whispered, shouted, sang:
 The grass stirred as that happy music rang.

Oh, what a wondrous rustling everywhere!
The steady shadows shook and thinned and died,
 The shining grass flashed brightness back for brightness,
 And sleep was gone, and there was heavenly lightness.

As if she had found wings, light as the wind,
The grass flew, bent with the wind, from east to west,
 Chased by one wild gray cloud, and flashing all
 Her dews for happiness to hear morning call. . . .

But even as I stepped out the brightness dimmed,
I saw the fading edge of all delight.
 The sober morning waked the drowsy herds,
 And there was the old scolding of the birds.

John Freeman

THE TRUMPET

Rise up, rise up,
And, as the trumpet blowing
Chases the dreams of men,
As the dawn glowing
The stars that left unlit
The land and water,
Rise up and scatter
The dew that covers
The print of last night's lovers—
Scatter it, scatter it!

While you are listening
To the clear horn,
Forget, men, everything
On this earth newborn,
Except that it is lovelier
Than any mysteries.
Open your eyes to the air
That has washed the eyes of the stars
Through all the dewy night:
Up with the light,
To the old wars;
Arise, arise!

Edward Thomas

WINGS AT DAWN

Dawn is dense with twitter,
    And the white air swims and sings
In rapid wings that glitter,
    And the flashing of wings—
    Delicate and fugitive shiverings.

The dews curl up in haze,
    While the sun from his hive
Like a giant bee ablaze
    Bursts dizzily alive—
    And through the glow a thousand swallows dive.

Light like a storm
  Deluges the grass,
And birds in a swarm
  Wheel, dwindle and mass—
  And their wings are split silver as they pass.
                              Joseph Auslander

GLORY, GLORY TO THE SUN

GLORY, glory to the sun
who spends his being
caring not what he shines upon
nor for whose seeing.

In the furrow swells the wheat
and the chestnut leaf respires,
quickened to life by the heat
of his innocent fires.

Small thanks the farmer allows,
turning his hay,
but watches with reckoning brows
the fall of the day.

Clouds flame in the upper air;
the fields slip to the night;
but the rugged horsemen of Thibet stir
to a finger of light.

They wrap their skins about
and spear in hand,
round up their flocks and shout
and scour the land.
                              John Alford

THE GUERDON OF THE SUN

OF all the fonts from which man's heart has drawn
  Some essence of the majesty of earth,
  Some intimation of the human worth,
I reckon first the sunset and the dawn.

For those were fires whose splendor smote his clay
  With witness of a light beyond the clod;
  Enshrined, he made of radiance a god,
And found his benediction in the day.

And all his eager hands have found to do,
  And all his tireless hope and love unite,
  In some wise take their symbol from the light,
Our very heaven based on heaven's blue.

Tilth beyond tilth, he waits upon the sun,
  The first to goad, the last to calm his breast,
  With dawns that like a clarion break his rest,
And after-glows that crown his labor done.

George Sterling

THE EARLY MORNING

THE moon on the one hand, the dawn on the other:
The moon is my sister, the dawn is my brother.
The moon on my left and the dawn on my right.
My brother, good morning: my sister, good night.

Hilaire Belloc

FOG

THE fog comes
on little cat feet.

It sits looking
over harbor and city
on silent haunches
and then, moves on.

Carl Sandburg

WHITE DUSK

THE fog is freezing on the trees and shrubs;
Each tendril of the larch is edged with lace;
The tiniest twigs are filigreed with frost;
There is faint movement through an open space—
And lovely white ghosts wake mysteriously
Like white thoughts smiling through gray memory.

Marion M. Boyd

TWILIGHT

TIPTOEING twilight,
Before you pass,
Bathe light my spirit
As dew bathes grass.

Quiet the longing
Of my hands that yearn,
As you fold the flower
And hush the fern.

Guard me with shadows
To fortify
My failing purpose,
My tired eye,

That in your stillness
I may relight
My faith's frail candle
Before the night.

Hazel Hall

BY THE MARGIN OF THE GREAT DEEP

WHEN the breath of twilight blows to flame the misty skies,
All its vaporous sapphire, violet glow and silver gleam
With their magic flood me through the gateway of the eyes;
    I am one with the twilight's dream.

When the trees and skies and fields are one in dusky mood,
Every heart of man is rapt within the mother's breast:
Full of peace and sleep and dreams in the vasty quietude,
    I am one with their hearts at rest.

From our immemorial joys of hearth and home and love
Strayed away along the margin of the unknown tide,
All its reach of soundless calm can thrill me far above
    Word or touch from the lips beside.

Aye, and deep and deep and deeper let me drink and draw
From the olden fountain more than light or peace or dream,
Such primeval being as o'erfills the heart with awe,
   Growing one with its silent stream.

                                        A. E.

TWILIGHT

STILL glowing from the red-lipped kiss of noon,
Your perfumed hands caress the night and dare
To deck your breast with stars . . . to steal a moon
And set it rose-like in your tawny hair.

                                Virginia McCormick

AT THE EDGE OF THE DAY

SEE Twilight standing on the brink
   That skirts the dark abyss of night;
The dew-wet roses in her hair
   Shed incense through the waning light,
Low in the west one lonely star
   Shines tremulous and white.

Across the far, dim edge of day,
   The task of morn and toil of noon
Slip noiselessly adown the tide
   With dusky shadows thickly strewn,
And o'er the lately purple hills
   Rises the yellow moon.

Go, Twilight, trembling on the verge
   'Twixt shadowy earth and shadowy air,
Fold peaceful hands on peaceful breast,
   Spread starlit wings and gently bear
To Heaven's gate a burden sweet—
   The World's low vesper prayer.

                                Clarence Urmy

EVENING ON THE HARBOR

THE shining daggers of the harbor lights
   Stab the smooth waters of the quiet bay,
As dusk comes in, like a belated guest,
   Waited and hoped for all the weary day.

The swaying fringes of the shadows droop
  To catch and tangle in the huddled spars:
The day is gone, and all the restless night
  Is bound about with ribbons of pale stars.

Virginia Lyne Tunstall

BESIDE THE BLACKWATER

With life forever old yet new,
Changed not in kind but in degree
The instant made eternity.—ROBERT BROWNING

I hear a young girl singing,
  Herself I cannot see:
The twilight time is bringing
  Shadows and mystery.

The clouds lie close together—
  Sheep folded for the night—
True omens of the weather
  For him who reads aright.

The patch of light is fading
  From Knockaroura's brow
Green trees and foliage shading
  Into the evening glow.

A hungry trout is leaping
  In the dark, winding stream,
Where low-bent trees are sweeping
  Waters that whirl and gleam.

O wondrous hour of even,
  When all the world is peace;
Earth were exchanged for heaven,
  Could Time his passing cease!

Norreys Jephson O'Conor

CHECK

THE night was creeping on the ground;
She crept and did not make a sound
Until she reached the tree, and then
She covered it, and stole again
Along the grass beside the wall.

I heard the rustle of her shawl
As she threw blackness everywhere
Upon the sky and ground and air,
And in the room where I was hid:
But no matter what she did
To everything that was without,
She could not put my candle out.

So I stared at the night, and she
Stared back solemnly at me.

James Stephens

A NIGHT PIECE

COME out and walk. The last few drops of light
Drain silently out of the cloudy blue;
The trees are full of the dark-stooping night,
    The fields are wet with dew.

All's quiet in the wood, but, far away,
Down the hillside and out across the plain,
Moves, with long trail of white that marks its way,
    The softly panting train.

Come through the clearing. Hardly now we see
The flowers, save dark or light against the grass,
Or glimmering silver on a scented tree,
    That trembles as we pass.

Hark now! So far, so far . . . that distant song . . .
Move not the rustling grasses with your feet.
The dusk is full of sounds, that all along
    The muttering boughs repeat.

So far, so faint, we lift our heads in doubt.
Wind, or the blood that beats within our ears,
Has feigned a dubious and delusive note,
    Such as a dreamer hears.

Again . . . again! The faint sounds rise and fail.
So far the enchanted tree, the song so low . . .
A drowsy thrush? A waking nightingale?
    Silence. We do not know.

Edward Shanks

THANKS FROM EARTH TO HEAVEN

God pours for me His draught divine,—
Moonlight, which is the poet's wine,
He has made this perfect night
For my wonder and delight.

What is it He would declare
In this beauty everywhere—
What dearest thought of His is heard
In the moonlight's secret word?

To the human, the Supreme
Poet speaks in wind and stream,
Tenderly He does express
His meaning in each loveliness.

Simply does He speak and clear,
As man to man, His message dear—
Aye—and well enough He knows
Who shall understand His rose!

Night is but His parable
Secretly where He would tell,
As to an intimate of His,
The mystery of all that is;

Nor humblest, nor most exquisite
Detail or phrase does He omit
From His great poem, confident
It shall be noted what He meant.

And cunningly doth still devise
New Aprils for His poet's eyes
For whose joy all things were wrought,
That without him were as nought.

Holy Poet, I have heard
Thy lost music, Thy least word;
Not Thy beauty's tiniest part
Has escaped this loving heart!

While the great world goes its way
I watch in wonder all the day,
All the night my spirit sings
For the loveliness of things.

But for lonely men like me
It were wasted utterly
All this beauty, vainly spent,—
Unavailing lavishment.

Little cricket, never fear,
There is one who waits to hear—
Nor is there loveliness so shy
It shall escape a poet's eye.

For the world enough it were
To have a useful earth and bare,
But for poets it is made
All in loveliness arrayed.

For his eye the little moth
Wears her coat of colored cloth,
And to please his ear the deep
Ocean murmurs in her sleep.

Rustle gently in the breeze
For his delight the poplar trees,
And in the song within his head
The thanks from earth to heaven is said.

John Hall Wheelock

JUNE NIGHT

INTO my room to-night came June,
A band of stars caught up her hair,
And woven of the mist of moon,
And patterned from the leaf-laced air,
Her garments spread a soft perfume
Over the shadows of my room.

But hardly had her coming stirred
My darkness with a hope like dawn,
Or had my anxious silence heard
Her faint footfall, than she was gone.
She went as though with a quick fear
Of the eternal winter here.

Hazel Hall

I HAVE CARED FOR YOU, MOON

I HAVE cared for you, Moon,
Cold as you are,
Frozen on the sky
With your dandling star.

It is not your shape,
Nor your lure of light,
Holding the sun
On your breast all night:

It is not your voice,
I have never heard
Your glittering cry,
Your wandering word.

Yet you are romance
And you are song.
I have cared for you, Moon,
Long, long

Since I first paid toll
With a coin of dream
On the road you silver.
You peer and gleam

With a wistful look
On your haunted face,
As though Earth were
A wonderful place.

Grace Hazard Conkling

I LOOK INTO THE STARS

Stars have ways I do not know,
  Enormity that checks my thought,
Yet on the loom of their fine glow
  The fabric of my dreams is wrought.

I look into the stars and one
  After one, convictions die,
While more than I have lost is spun
  Delicately across the sky.

I look into the stars, and all
  The fuming purposes life gives
Pass, like mists of evening fall,
  And all life never has been, lives.

Jane Draper

STARS

Alone in the night
  On a dark hill
With pines around me
  Spicy and still,

And a heaven full of stars
  Over my head,
White and topaz
  And misty red;

Myriads with beating
  Hearts of fire
That æons
  Cannot vex or tire;

Up the dome of heaven
  Like a great hill,
I watch them marching
  Stately and still,

And I know that I
  Am honored to be
Witness
  Of so much majesty.

Sara Teasdale

THE NIGHT WILL NEVER STAY

THE night will never stay,
The night will still go by,
Though with a million stars
You pin it to the sky,
Though you bind it with the blowing wind
And buckle it with the moon,
The night will slip away
Like sorrow or a tune.

Eleanor Farjeon

THE CHANGING YEAR

EASTER, 1923

ONCE more the Ancient Wonder
    Brings back the goose and crane,
Prophetic Sons of Thunder,
    Apostles of the Rain.

In many a battling river
    The broken gorges boom.
Behold, the Mighty Giver
    Emerges from the tomb!

Now robins chant the story
    Of how the wintry sward
Is litten with the glory
    Of the Angel of the Lord.

His countenance is lightning,
    And still his robe is snow,
As when the dawn was brightening
    Two thousand years ago.

O who can be a stranger
    To what has come to pass?
The Pity of the Manger
    Is mighty in the grass!

Undaunted by Decembers,
    The sap is faithful yet.
The giving Earth remembers
    And only men forget!

                John G. Neihardt

SPRING MARKET

IT'S foolish to bring money
    To any spring wood,
Jewels won't help you,
    Gold's no good.

Silver won't buy you
   One small leaf.
You may bring joy here,
   You may bring grief.

You should look for
   Tufted moss,
Marked where a light foot
   Ran across.

Where the old rose hips
   Shrivel brown
And dried clematis
   Bloom hangs down.

There you'll find what
   Everyman needs,
Wild religion
   Without any creeds,

Green that lifts its
   Blossoming head,
New life springing
   Among the dead.

You needn't bring money
   To this market place,
Or think you can bargain for
   Wild flower grace.

Louise Driscoll

SPRINGTIME IN COOKHAM DEAN

How marvellous and fair a thing
It is to see an English spring,
He cannot know who has not seen
The cherry trees at Cookham Dean,
Who has not seen the blossom lie
Like snowdrifts 'gainst a cloudless sky

And found the beauty of the way
Through woodlands odorous with may;
It is a rare, a holy sight
To see the hills with blossom white,
To feel the air about one flowing
With the silent rapture growing
In the hidden heart of things
That yearn, that flower, put forth wings
And show their splendors one by one
Beneath the all-rejoicing sun.

Perhaps the joy of all the earth
Moved through us on that day of mirth
When in the morning air we trod
Hills sacred to the woodland god,
And heard behind us as we ran
The laughter of a hidden Pan,
Who dropped his flute because he heard
The artless cadence of a bird;
And we, who love the southern sky,
One moment ceased to wonder why
A poet in his exile cried
To see an English spring, and sighed
Because a chaffinch from the bough
Sings and shakes the blossom now.
For who would sigh for southern skies
Who once had seen the paradise
Of this new Eden where the flowers
Drench the woods with odorous showers,
And give delight till the sense sickens
With the rapture that it quickens?
This heaven where petals fall as stars,
This paradise where beauty bars
Its petaled, white, inviolable portals
'Gainst the clamoring of mortals,
And from green altars in dim shrines
Calls to the driven soul that pines
For leafy solitude, and prayer
That whispers through the branches there.

When Spring, in her ascension, fills
The chalice of the sacred hills
With blossoms like the driven snow,
And longing takes the heart, then go
On pilgrimage to Cookham Dean
And through dim aisles of shadowed green,
Diapered with the light that trembles
Round each tree till it resembles
A maiden letting fall her hair
In cataracts of gold—draw near
The secret that brings Englishmen,
Faithful through exile, home again,
And watch the wonder of the morn
And hear the lark with wings upborne
Into the cloudless empyrean
Pour his lucent, quenchless pæan,
Or feel the quickened senses start
In rapture at the artless art
Of orchards all in blossom showing
Against the blue of heaven glowing
Through its depths of luminous light;
Then from the windy woodland height
Through dim ravines where tall trees wait
For day's decline to gild their state
And thrill them with caressing fingers
Of the sun-god whose touch lingers
Upon their limbs—by paths that wind
Into the valley go,—and find
The village by the water's edge
And listen to the rustling sedge
That by the churchyard whispers; go—
And tread the woodland paths I know
For whosoever has not seen
The cherry trees at Cookham Dean,
Who has not roamed its hills and found
Delight in that enchanted ground,
He cannot know, he cannot tell
Where Spring performs her miracle.

Cecil Roberts

SPRING IN ENGLAND

THE green Spring tide has risen, until its crest
Fragrant with cowslips, flecked with tiny spray
Of small white daisies, laps the warm Earth's breast
And ripples on the hedge-reefs of the may.

Across the wood the mournful cuckoo cries;
Across the downs, the sheep slow-moving pass;
The skylark flutters, singing, from the skies
To drop in sudden silence in the grass.

I hear the robin piping in the hedge—
The murmur of the drowsy wakening bee—
The song of winds, low-fluting in the sedge,
That blends with organ pedals of the sea.

Oh, land enriched with life-blood and with tears
Of people after people, churl and king!
The haunting stories of a thousand years
Waken to fragrance in the English Spring!

Charles Buxton Going

SPRING GOETH ALL IN WHITE

SPRING goeth all in white,
    Crowned with milk-white may:
In fleecy flocks of light
    O'er heaven the white clouds stray:

White butterflies in the air;
    White daisies prank the ground:
The cherry and hoary pear
    Scatter their snow around.

Robert Bridges

SONG

SPRING lights her candles everywhere,
But death still hangs upon the air;
The celandine through dusk is lit,
The redbreasts from the holly flit,

At night the violets spring to birth
Out of the mute, encrusted earth.

The wind has cast his winding sheet
(Which is the sky) and he goes fleet
Over the country in the rain,
Singing how all the world is vain
And how, of all things vainest, he
Journeys above both land and sea.

Fredegond Shove

CAROLINA SPRING SONG

AGAINST the swart magnolias' sheen
Pronged maples, like a stag's new horn,
Stand gouted red upon the green,
In March when shaggy buds are shorn.

Then all a mist-streaked, sunny day
The long sea-islands lean to hear
A water harp that shallows play
To lull the beaches' fluted ear.

When this same music wakes the gift
Of pregnant beauty in the sod,
And makes the uneasy vultures shift
Like evil things afraid of God,

Then, then it is I love to drift
Upon the flood-tide's lazy swirls,
While from the level rice fields lift
The spiritu'ls of darky girls.

I hear them singing in the fields
Like voices from the long-ago;
They speak to me of somber worlds
And sorrows that the humble know;

Of sorrow—yet their tones release
A harmony of larger hours
From easy epochs long at peace
Amid an irony of flowers.

So if they sometimes seem a choir
That cast a chill of doubt on spring,
They have still higher notes of fire
Like cardinals upon the wing.

Hervey Allen

WONDER AND A THOUSAND SPRINGS

ALONG the just-returning green
That fledges field and berm and brake
The purple-veined white violets lean,
    Scarcely awake;

And pear and plum and apple trees,
Evoked to bloom before they leaf,
Lift cloudy branches filled with bees
    Strange as new grief.

A thousand springs will poise and pass
And leave no track beneath the sun:
Some gray-eyed lad, cool-cheeked as grass,
    Will watch each one,

And wonder, as I wonder here,
And find no clue I have not found,
And smile before he joins me, near
    But underground.

William Alexander Percy

APRIL

ALL night the small feet of the rain
    Within my garden ran,
And gentle fingers tapped the pane
    Until the dawn began.

The rill-like voices called and sang
    The slanting roof beside;
"The children of the clouds have come;
    Awake! Awake!" they cried.

"Weep no more the drooping rose,
    Nor mourn the thirsting tree;
The little children of the storm
    Have gained their liberty."

All night the small feet of the rain
    About my garden ran;
Their rill-like voices called and cried
    Until the dawn began.

Dora Sigerson Shorter

APRIL

SOMETHING tapped at my window-pane,
    Someone called me without my door,
Someone laughed like the tinkle o' rain,
    The robin echoed it o'er and o'er.

I threw the door and the window wide;
    Sun and the touch of the breeze and then—
"Ah, were you expecting me, dear?" she cried,
    And here was April come back again.

Theodosia Garrison

APRIL WEATHER

OH, hush, my heart, and take thine ease,
    For here is April weather!
The daffodils beneath the trees
    Are all a-row together.

The thrush is back with his old note;
    The scarlet tulip blowing;
And white—ay, white as my love's throat—
    The dogwood boughs are growing.

The lilac bush is sweet again;
    Down every wind that passes,
Fly flakes from hedgerow and from lane;
    The bees are in the grasses.

And Grief goes out, and Joy comes in,
   And care is but a feather;
And every lad his love can win,
   For here is April weather.

Lizette Woodworth Reese

WHILE APRIL RAIN WENT BY

UNDER a budding hedge I hid
   While April rain went by,
But little drops came slipping through,
   Fresh from a laughing sky:

A-many little scurrying drops,
   Laughing the song they sing,
Soon found me where I sought to hide,
   And pelted me with Spring.

And I lay back and let them pelt,
   And dreamt deliciously
Of lusty leaves and lady-blossoms
   And baby-buds I'd see,

When April rain had laughed the land
   Out of its wintry way,
And coaxed all growing things to greet
   With gracious garb the May.

Shaemas O Sheel

AN APRIL MORNING

ONCE more in misted April
   The world is growing green,
Along the winding river
   The plumey willows lean.

Beyond the sweeping meadows
   The looming mountains rise,
Like battlements of dreamland
   Against the brooding skies.

In every wooded valley
    The buds are breaking through,
As though the heart of all things
    No languor ever knew.

The golden wings and bluebirds
    Call to their heavenly choirs.
The pines are blued and drifted
    With smoke of brushwood fires.

And in my sister's garden
    Where little breezes run,
The golden daffodillies
    Are blowing in the sun.

Bliss Carman

MAY

THE Pan-thrilled saplings swayed in sportive bliss,
Longing to change their roots to flying feet,
And, where the buds were pouting for Pan's kiss,
The high lark sprinkled music, dewy sweet.

I wandered down a golden lane of light,
And found a dell, unsoiled by man, untrod,
And, with the daffodil for acolyte,
I bared my soul to all the woods, and God.

Stephen Moylan Bird

TELL ALL THE WORLD

TELL all the world that summer's here again
    With song and joy; tell them, that they may know
How, on the hillside, in the shining fields
    New clumps of violets and daisies grow.

Tell all the world that summer's here again,
    That white clouds voyage through a sky so still
With blue tranquillity, it seems to hang
    One windless tapestry, from hill to hill.

Tell all the world that summer's here again:
  Folk go about so solemnly and slow,
Walking each one his grooved and ordered way—
  I fear that, otherwise they will not know!

Harry Kemp

JUNE

Broom out the floor now, lay the fender by,
And plant this bee-sucked bough of woodbine there,
And let the window down. The butterfly
Floats in upon the sunbeam, and the fair
Tanned face of June, the nomad gipsy, laughs
Above her widespread wares, the while she tells
The farmers' fortunes in the fields, and quaffs
The water from the spider-peopled wells.

The hedges are all drowned in green grass seas,
And bobbing poppies flare like Elmor's light,
While siren-like the pollen-stainèd bees
Drone in the clover depths. And up the height
The cuckoo's voice is hoarse and broke with joy.
And on the lowland crops the crows make raid,
Nor fear the clappers of the farmer's boy,
Who sleeps, like drunken Noah, in the shade.

And loop this red rose in that hazel ring
That snares your little ear, for June is short
And we must joy in it and dance and sing,
And from her bounty draw her rosy worth.
Ay! soon the swallows will be flying south,
The wind wheel north to gather in the snow,
Even the roses spilt on youth's red mouth
Will soon blow down the road all roses go.

Francis Ledwidge

JUNE RAPTURE

Green! What a world of green! My startled soul
Panting for beauty long denied,
Leaps in a passion of high gratitude
To meet the wild embraces of the wood;

Rushes and flings itself upon the whole
Mad miracle of green, with senses wide,
Clings to the glory, hugs and holds it fast,
As one who finds a long-lost love at last.
Billows of green that break upon the sight
In bounteous crescendos of delight,
Wind-hurried verdure hastening up the hills
To where the sun its highest rapture spills;
Cascades of color tumbling down the height
In golden gushes of delicious light—
God! Can I bear the beauty of this day,
Or shall I be swept utterly away?

Hush—here are deeps of green, where rapture stills,
Sheathing itself in veils of amber dusk;
Breathing a silence suffocating, sweet,
Wherein a million hidden pulses beat.
Look! How the very air takes fire and thrills
With hint of heaven pushing through her husk.
Ah, joy's not stopped! 'Tis only more intense,
Here where Creation's ardors all condense;
Here where I crush me to the radiant sod,
Close-folded to the very nerves of God.
See now—I hold my heart against this tree.
The life that thrills its trembling leaves thrills me.
There's not a pleasure pulsing through its veins
That does not sting me with ecstatic pains.
No twig or tracery, however fine,
Can bear a tale of joy exceeding mine.

Praised be the gods that made my spirit mad;
Kept me aflame and raw to beauty's touch;
Lashed me and scourged me with the whip of fate;
Gave me so often agony for mate;
Tore from my heart the things that make men glad—
Praised be the gods! If I at last, by such
Relentless means may know the sacred bliss,
The anguished rapture of an hour like this.
Smite me, O life, and bruise me if thou must;
Mock me and starve me with thy bitter crust,

But keep me thus aquiver and awake,
Enamoured of my life for living's sake!
This were the tragedy—that I should pass,
Dull and indifferent through the glowing grass.
And this the reason I was born, I say—
That I might know the passion of this day!

Angela Morgan

THE HOUND

Some are sick for Spring and warm winds blowing
Over close-sheathed buds and a patch of old snow,
With the early arc-lamps delicately bowing
Across thin sunshine that hesitates to go.

But it's not for any April promises I sicken,
Though their stammering sweetness be a plucked string;
My mind is bent toward Autumn, I am shaken
More by her denials than by all the hopes of Spring.

The curt cold days, the blue and windy weather,
The smoke of burning brushwood keener than a frost,
An orchard full of odors night is wise to gather,
The fur-collared stubble where the flower is lost.

A clear green sunset and a pale moon showing,
A sense of dawning ends, like the light in the sky.
Autumn is a hound that shrills, my heart is for her gnawing,
The quarry goes to Autumn, let Spring die.

Babette Deutsch

AUTUMN

The music of the autumn winds sings low,
Down by the ruins of the painted hills,
Where death lies flaming with a marvelous glow,
Upon the ash of rose and daffodils.
But I can find no melancholy here
To see the naked rocks and thinning trees;
Earth strips to grapple with the winter year—
I see her gnarled hills plan for victories!

I love the earth who goes to battle now,
To struggle with the wintry whipping storm
And bring the glorious spring out from the night.
I see earth's muscles bared, her battle brow,
And am not sad, but feel her marvelous charm
As splendidly she plunges in the fight.

Edwin Curran

SEPTEMBER

CRICKETS are making
   The merriest din,
All the fields waking
   With shrill violin.

Now all the swallows
   Debate when to go;
In the valleys and hollows
   The mists are like snow.

Dahlias are glowing
   In purple and red
Where once were growing
   Pale roses instead.

Piled up leaves smoulder,
   All hazy the noon,
Nights have grown colder,
   The frost will come soon.

Early lamps burning,
   So soon the night falls,
Leaves, crimson turning,
   Make bright the stone walls.

Summer recalling
   At turn of the year,
Fruit will be falling,
   September is here.

Edward Bliss Reed

RONDEL FOR SEPTEMBER

You thought it was a falling leaf we heard;
I knew it was the summer's gypsy feet;
A sound so reticent it scarcely stirred
The ear so still a message to repeat,—
"I go, and lo, I make my going sweet,"
What wonder you should miss so soft a word?
You thought it was a falling leaf we heard;
I knew it was the Summer's gypsy feet.
With slender torches for her service meet
The golden-rod is coming; softer slurred
Midsummer noises take a note replete
With hint of change; who told the mocking bird?
I knew it was the Summer's gypsy feet—
You thought it was a falling leaf we heard.

Karle Wilson Baker

HOME THOUGHTS

October in New England,
  And I not there to see
The glamour of the goldenrod,
  The flame of the maple tree!

October in my own land. . . .
  I know what glory fills
The mountains of New Hampshire
  And Massachusetts hills.

I know what hues of opal
  Rhode Island breezes fan,
And how Connecticut puts on
  Colors of Hindustan.

Vermont, in robes of splendor,
  Sings with the woods of Maine
Alternate hallelujahs
  Of gold and crimson stain.

The armies of the asters,
    Frail hosts in blue and gray,
Invade the hills of home—and I
    Three thousand miles away!

I shall take down the calendar
    And from the rounded year
Blot out one name, October,
    The loveliest and most dear.

For I would not remember,
    While she is marching by
The pomp of her stately passing,
    The magic of her cry.

Odell Shepard

FIRST FROST

A SPARKLING sunset, oranged to gold,
Rings like a bell of sorrow told,
Across the night of whistling cold;
For now an arm swings near and far
The brittle lamp of every star.
The flowers grow in the garden pied
Velvet, imperial, laughing-eyed,
While on them all hovers a breath,
The whistling frost of silver death.
I grieve to see the wine-red crowd
And watch and watch them, tall and proud,
And tell them that tonight death comes,
Beating the stars like kettle drums.
For the last time I kiss their breasts,
The lovely golden fleeting guests,
Made sad to think on morning's shore
Their beauty will be nevermore.
I grieve to see them fall and die
Where kindled, burning, sparkling high
The stars make mirrors of the sky.
I bid them farewell in their sleep,
Wrapped now in snowy silver seas,
For they, immortal, will but leap
Like us, to a more marvelous peace.

And here I sit by them and view
The solid sky as white frost comes,
Knocking the winds to silver dew,
Beating the stars like kettle drums.

Edwin Curran

THE LAST DAYS

THE russet leaves of the scyamore
Lie at last on the valley floor—
By the autumn wind swept to and fro
Like ghosts in a tale of long ago.
Shallow and clear the Carmel glides
Where the willows droop on its vine-walled sides.

The bracken-rust is red on the hill;
The pines stand brooding, somber and still;
Gray are the cliffs, and the waters gray,
Where the seagulls dip to the sea-born spray.
Sad November, lady of rain,
Sends the goose-wedge over again.

Wilder now, for the verdure's birth,
Falls the sunlight over the earth;
Kildees call from the fields where now
The banding blackbirds follow the plow;
Rustling poplar and brittle weed
Whisper low to the river-reed.

Days departing linger and sigh;
Stars come soon to the quiet sky;
Buried voices, intimate, strange,
Cry to body and soul of Change;
Beauty, eternal fugitive,
Seeks the home that we cannot give.

George Sterling

MY NOVEMBER GUEST

MY Sorrow, when she's here with me,
    Thinks these dark days of autumn rain
Are beautiful as days can be;
She loves the bare, the withered tree;
    She walks the sodden pasture lane.

Her pleasure will not let me stay.
  She talks and I am fain to list:
She's glad the birds are gone away,
She's glad her simple worsted gray
  Is silver now with clinging mist.

The desolate deserted trees,
  The faded earth, the heavy sky,
The beauties she so truly sees,
She thinks I have no eye for these,
  And vexes me for reason why.

Not yesterday I learned to know
  The love of bare November days
Before the coming of the snow,
But it were vain to tell her so,
  And they are better for her praise.

Robert Frost

WHERE IT IS WINTER

Now there is frost upon the hill
And no leaf stirring in the wood;
The little streams are cold and still;
Never so still has winter stood.
Never so held as in this hollow,
Beneath these hemlocks dark and low,
Brooding this hour that hours must follow
Burdened with snow. . . .

Now there is nothing, no confusion,
To shield against the silence here;
And spirits, barren of illusion,
To whom all agonies are clear,
Rush on the naked heart and cry
Of every poignant shining thing
Where there is little left to die
And no more Spring.

George O'Neil

LATE WINTER

I am content with latticed sights:
A lean gray bough, a frill
Of filmy cloud, the shadow-lights
Upon a window-sill.

I am content in wintered days
With all my eyes may meet.
*April, when you dance down these ways
Hush your awakening feet.*

Hazel Hall

FEBRUARY

The robin on my lawn,
He was the first to tell
How, in the frozen dawn,
This miracle befell,
Waking the meadows white
With hoar, the iron road
Agleam with splintered light,
And ice where water flowed:
Till, when the low sun drank
Those milky mists that cloak
Hanger and hollied bank,
The winter world awoke
To hear the feeble bleat
Of lambs on downland farms:
A blackbird whistled sweet;
Old beeches moved their arms
Into a mellow haze
Aërial, newly-born:
And I, alone, agaze,
Stood waiting for the thorn
To break in blossom white
Or burst in a green flame. . . .
So, in a single night,
Fair February came,

Bidding my lips to sing
Or whisper their surprise,
With all the joy of spring
And morning in her eyes.

Francis Brett Young

INFANT SPRING

Soft and pure fell the snow,
Pure, soft, the new lamb lay.
February in the field,
Sun's heat far away,
Wave's cry sad and strange,
Lamb's cry weak and wild,
No buds in the bleak thorn hedge:
Spring is but a tiny child.

Fredegond Shove

WOOD AND FIELD AND RUNNING BROOK

STOPPING BY WOODS ON A SNOWY EVENING

WHOSE woods these are I think I know.
His house is in the village though;
He will not see me stopping here
To watch his woods fill up with snow.

The little horse must think it queer
To stop without a farmhouse near
Between the woods and frozen lake
The darkest evening of the year.

He gives his harness bells a shake
To ask if there is some mistake.
The only other sound's the sweep
Of easy wind and downy flake.

The woods are lovely, dark and deep.
But I have promises to keep,
And miles to go before I sleep,
And miles to go before I sleep.

Robert Frost

BE DIFFERENT TO TREES

THE talking oak
To the ancients spoke.

But any tree
Will talk to me.

What truths I know
I garnered so.

313

But those who want to talk and tell,
    And those who will not listeners be,
Will never hear a syllable
    From out the lips of any tree.

Mary Carolyn Davies

BIRCHES

WHEN I see birches bend to left and right
Across the lines of straighter darker trees,
I like to think some boy's been swinging them.
But swinging doesn't bend them down to stay.
Ice-storms do that. Often you must have seen them
Loaded with ice a sunny winter morning
After a rain. They click upon themselves
As the breeze rises, and turn many-colored
As the stir cracks and crazes their enamel.
Soon the sun's warmth makes them shed crystal shells
Shattering and avalanching on the snow-crust—
Such heaps of broken glass to sweep away
You'd think the inner dome of heaven had fallen.
They are dragged to the withered bracken by the load,
And they seem not to break; though once they are bowed
So low for long, they never right themselves:
You may see their trunks arching in the woods
Years afterwards, trailing their leaves on the ground
Like girls on hands and knees that throw their hair
Before them over their heads to dry in the sun.
But I was going to say when Truth broke in
With all her matter-of-fact about the ice-storm
(Now am I free to be poetical?)
I should prefer to have some boy bend them
As he went out and in to fetch the cows—
Some boy too far from town to learn baseball,
Whose only play was what he found himself,
Summer or winter, and could play alone.
One by one he subdued his father's trees
By riding them down over and over again
Until he took the stiffness out of them,
And not one but hung limp, not one was left

For him to conquer. He learned all there was
To learn about not launching out too soon
And so not carrying the tree away
Clear to the ground. He always kept his poise
To the top branches, climbing carefully
With the same pains you use to fill a cup
Up to the brim, and even above the brim.
Then he flung outward, feet first, with a swish,
Kicking his way down through the air to the ground.
So was I once myself a swinger of birches.
And so I dream of going back to be.
It's when I'm weary of considerations,
And life is too much like a pathless wood
Where your face burns and tickles with the cobwebs
Broken across it, and one eye is weeping
From a twig's having lashed across it open.
I'd like to get away from earth awhile
And then come back to it and begin over.
May no fate wilfully misunderstand me
And half grant what I wish and snatch me away
Not to return. Earth's the right place for love:
I don't know where it's likely to go better.
I'd like to go by climbing a birch tree,
And climb black branches up a snow-white trunk
Toward heaven, till the tree could bear no more,
But dipped its top and set me down again.
That would be good both going and coming back.
One could do worse than be a swinger of birches.

Robert Frost

BIRCH TREES

THE night is white,
    The moon is high,
The birch trees lean
    Against the sky.

The cruel winds
    Have blown away
Each little leaf
    Of silver gray.

O lonely trees
　　As white as wool . . .
That moonlight makes
　　So beautiful.

　　　　　　　　John Richard Moreland

THE ELM

THE mountain pine is a man at arms
　　With flashing shield and blade,
The willow is a dowager,
　　The birch is a guileless maid,
But the elm tree is a lady
　　In gold and green brocade.

Broad-bosomed to the meadow breeze
　　The matron maple grows,
The poplar plays the courtesan
　　To every wind that blows,
But who the tall elm's lovers are
　　Only the midnight knows.

And few would ever ask it
　　Of such a stately tree,
So lofty in the moonlight,
　　So virginal stands she,
Snaring the little silver fish
　　That swim her silent sea.

But hush!   A hum of instruments
　　Deep in the night begins,
Along those dusky galleries
　　Low music throbs and thins—
A whispered sound of harps and flutes
　　And ghostly violins.

For what mysterious visitor
　　Do all her windy bells
Ring welcome in the moonlight
　　And amorous farewells? . . .
The elm tree is a lady.
　　The midnight never tells.

　　　　　　　　Odell Shepard

THE WIND IN THE ELMS

THE sunset's kiss, with lingering desire,
Unheeded, falls upon the elms asleep;
They are as lovers, sick of passion's fire,
And crave the Moon that rules the starry deep.

But when that haughty Queen rides down the lane,
And blows them kisses in a silver throng,
A gush of music floods the elms again,
And every leaf is exquisite with song.

J. Corson Miller

PEAR TREE

SILVER dust
lifted from the earth,
higher than my arms reach,
you have mounted.
O silver,
higher than my arms reach
you front us with great mass;

no flower ever opened
so staunch a white leaf,
no flower ever parted silver
from such rare silver;

O white pear,
your flower-tufts,
thick on the branch,
bring summer and ripe fruits
in their purple hearts.

H. D.

THE POPLAR

WHY do you always stand there shivering
Between the white stream and the road?

The people pass through the dust
On bicycles, in carts, in motor-cars;

The wagoners go by at dawn;
The lovers walk on the grass path at night.
Stir from your roots, walk, poplar!
You are more beautiful than they are.

I know that the white wind loves you,
Is always kissing you and turning up
The white lining of your green petticoat.
The sky darts through you like blue rain,
And the gray rain drips on your flanks
And loves you.
And I have seen the moon
Slip his silver penny into your pocket
As you straightened your hair;
And the white mist curling and hesitating
Like a bashful lover about your knees.

I know you, poplar;
I have watched you since I was ten.
But if you had a little real love,
A little strength,
You would leave your nonchalant idle lovers
And go walking down the white road
Behind·the wagoners.

There are beautiful beeches down beyond the hill.
Will you always stand there shivering?

Richard Aldington

POPLARS

THE poplar is a lonely tree,
It has no branches spreading wide
Where birds may sing or squirrels hide.
It throws no shadow on the grass
Tempting the wayfarers who pass
To stop and sit there quietly.

The poplar is a slender tree,
It has no boughs where children try
To climb far off into the sky,

To hold a swing, it's far too weak,
Too small it is for hide-and-seek,
Friendless, forsaken it must be.

The poplar is a restless tree,
At every breeze its branches bend
And signal to the child, "Come, friend."
Its leaves forever whispering
To thrush and robin, "Stay and sing,"
They pass. It quivers plaintively.

Poplars are lonely. They must grow
Close to each other in a row.

Edward Bliss Reed

THE POPLARS

My poplars are like ladies trim,
Each conscious of her own estate;
In costume somewhat over prim,
In manner cordially sedate,
Like two old neighbors met to chat
Beside my garden gate.

My stately old aristocrats—
I fancy still their talk must be
Of rose-conserves and Persian cats,
And lavender and Indian tea;—
I wonder sometimes as I pass—
If they approve of me.

I give them greeting night and morn,
I like to think they answer, too,
With that benign assurance born
When youth gives age the reverence due,
And bend their wise heads as I go,
As courteous ladies do.

Long may you stand before my door,
Oh, kindly neighbors garbed in green,
And bend with rustling welcome o'er
The many friends who pass between;

And where the little children play
Look down with gracious mien.

Theodosia Garrison

BLACK POPLAR–BOUGHS

BLACK poplar-boughs are bare, and comb
  With their sharp spines the stooping cloud.
Rain falls in gusts, like the torn foam
  When the west wind is loud.

The heavens stoop low and, broken, sweep
  Still with rough seas the water meads,
And shake long furrow-pools where sleep
  The slowly rotting seeds.

Not Cornwall's cliffs more bold that take
  The mass and number of the seas,
Than boughs that comb swift heavens and shake
  Rain upon rainy leas.

John Freeman

WILD PLUM

THEY are unholy who are born
  To love wild plum at night,
Who once have passed it on a road
  Glimmering and white.

It is as though the darkness had
  Speech of silver words,
Or as though a cloud of stars
  Perched like ghostly birds.

They are unpitied from their birth
  And homeless in men's sight,
Who love, better than the earth,
  Wild plum at night.

Orrick Johns

THE WILLOWS

By the little river,
  Still and deep and brown,
Grow the graceful willows,
  Gently dipping down;

Dipping down and brushing
  Everything that floats—
Leaves and logs and fishes,
  And the passing boats.

Were they water maidens
  In the long ago,
That they lean out sadly
  Looking down below?

In the misty twilight
  You can see their hair,
Weeping water maidens
  That were once so fair.
              Walter Prichard Eaton

THE THREE HILLS

THERE were three hills that stood alone
  With woods about their feet.
They dreamed quiet when the sun shone
  And whispered when the rain beat.

They wore all three their coronals
  Till men with houses came
And scored their heads with pits and walls
  And thought the hills were tame.

Red and white the clay shines bright,
  They hide the green for miles,
Where are the old hills gone? At night
  The moon looks down and smiles.

She sees the captors small and weak,
    She knows the prisoners strong,
She hears the patient hills that speak:
    "Brothers, it is not long:

"Brothers, we stood when they were not
    Ten thousand summers past.
Brothers, when they are clean forgot
    We shall outlive the last;

"One shall die and one shall flee
    With terror in his train,
And earth shall eat the stones, and we
    Shall be alone again."

                                    J. C. Squire

THE GRANITE MOUNTAIN

I know a mountain, lone it lies
Under wide blue Arctic skies.

Gray against the crimson rags
Of sunset loom its granite crags.

Gray granite are the peaks that sunder
The clouds, and gray the shadows under.

Down the weathered gullies flow
Waters from its crannied snow,

Tumbling cataracts that roar
Cannonading down the shore;

And rivulets that hurry after
With a sound of silver laughter.

Up its ramparts winds a trail
To a clover-meadowed vale,

High among the hills and woods
Locked in lonely solitudes.

Only wild feet can essay
The perils of that cragged way.

And here beneath the rugged shoulders
Of the granite cliffs and boulders,

In the valley of the sky
Where tranquil twilight shadows lie,

Hunted creatures in their flight
Find a refuge for the night.

Lew Sarett

THE SILENT RANGES

GIVE me the hills, that echo silence back,
    Save the harp-haunted pines' wild minstrelsy,
And white peaks, lifting rapt Madonna gaze
    To where God's cloud-sheep roam the azure lea.

Give me the Lethe of the harebell's wine,
    And in the fleece of silence folded deep,
Let half-heard echoes of an Oread's song
    Breathe on the drowsy lyre of my sleep.

Stephen Moylan Bird

THE BLUE RIDGE

STILL and calm,
In purple robes of kings,
The low-lying mountains sleep at the edge of the world.
The forests cover them like mantles;
Day and night
Rise and fall over them like the wash of waves.

Asleep, they reign.
Silent, they say all.
Hush me, O slumbering mountains—
Send me dreams.

Harriet Monroe

AFTER SUNSET

I HAVE an understanding with the hills
At evening when the slanted radiance fills
Their hollows, and the great winds let them be,
And they are quiet and look down at me.
Oh, then I see the patience in their eyes
Out of the centuries that made them wise.
They lend me hoarded memory and I learn
Their thoughts of granite and their whims of fern,
And why a dream of forests must endure
Though every tree be slain; and how the pure
Invisible beauty has a word so brief,
A flower can say it or a shaken leaf,
But few may ever snare it in a song,
Though for the quest a life is not too long.
When the blue hills grow tender, when they pull
The twilight close with gesture beautiful,
And shadows are their garments, and the air
Deepens, and the wild veery is at prayer,
Their arms are strong around me: and I know
That somehow I shall follow when you go
To the still land beyond the evening star,
Where everlasting hills and valleys are,
And silence may not hurt us any more,
And terror shall be past, and grief, and war.

Grace Hazard Conkling

FIELDS AT EVENING

THEY wear their evening light as women wear
Their pale, proud beauty for a lover's sake,
Too quiet-hearted evermore to care
For moving worlds and musics that they make.
And they are hushed as lonely women are,
So lost in dreams they have no thought to mark
How the wide heavens blossom, star by star,
And the slow dusk is deepening to the dark.

The moon comes like a lover from the hill,
Leaning across the twilight and the trees,
And finds them grave and beautiful and still,
And wearing always, on such nights as these,
A glimmer less than any ghostly light,
As women wear their beauty in the night.

David Morton

RAIN

I NEVER knew how words were vain
    Until I strove to say
The thoughts that fell like the gray rain
    Upon my heart today.

The April rain falls on the earth,
    That waits a while for words,
And then becomes articulate
    In buds and bees and birds.

The thoughts that rain upon my heart
    Bring nothing fair to birth;
O God, I kneel before the art,
    Of this great lyrist, earth.

Kenneth Slade Alling

RAIN

THE golden sun is garish
    On the white wall of the day.
I close my eyes against it
    For a vision cool and gray.

Gray-fissured and gray-skirted,
    She sweeps across the plain
And wraps me in her softness—
    O Rain, my mother Rain!

Frances Shaw

FIRST RAIN

WHEN Eve walked in her garden,
With Adam by her side,
And God was still the warden,
And she was still a bride,

How great was her amazement
To see when twilight died,
The first moon at the casement
Of evening, open wide!

But greater than her wonder
At star or bird or tree,
Or afterward at thunder,
Or delicate deer or bee,

Was her flushed awe one morning,
When down the clouded air
With freshened winds for warning,
Came water—everywhere!

Zoë Akins

WHO LOVES THE RAIN

WHO loves the rain
And loves his home,
And looks on life with quiet eyes,
Him will I follow through the storm;
And at his hearth-fire keep me warm;
Nor hell nor heaven shall that soul surprise,
Who loves the rain,
And loves his home,
And looks on life with quiet eyes.

Frances Shaw

LITTLE PONDS

WHERE balsams droop their fragrant boughs
And ferns their fronds,
Below Katahdin idly drowse
The little ponds,

Until the southwind calls, "Awake!"
  Or paddles ply,
Or trout come flashing up to take
  The scarlet fly.

The little ponds are bright and clear
  And soft of brink;
And after twilight when the deer
  Come down to drink,

And in their mirrors, coldly pure
  The moon is shown,
The moon, each little pond is sure
  Loves it alone.

Let not the little ponds be told
  That every night
On countless ponds as clear and cold
  Their moon is bright!

They do not guess that such things are
  For good or ill—
The strange high ways of moon and star;—
  And still, and still,

When hushed feet cross the beaver-dike
  And stars are strewn,
Each little pond, Endymion-like,
  Enfolds the moon.

And so the little ponds are glad:
  They keep their dream
From wintertime when chained is mad
  Katahdin Stream,

Through autumn when the maple-tree
  Is crimson-leaved.
Oh, happy little ponds to be
  So well deceived!

Arthur Guiterman

THE CANAL

No dip and dart of swallows wakes the black
Slumber of the canal:—a mirror dead
For lack of loveliness rememberèd
From ancient azures and green trees, for lack
Of some white beauty given and flung back,
Secret, to her that gave: no sun has bled
To wake an echo here of answering red;
The surface stirs to no leaf's wind-blown track.
Between unseeing walls the waters rest,
Lifeless and hushed, till suddenly a swan
Glides from some broader river blue as day,
And with the mirrored magic of his breast
Creates within that barren water-way
New life, new loveliness, and passes on.

Aldous Huxley

AS RIVERS OF WATER IN A DRY PLACE

LONELY, lonely lay the hill,
Not a bird was there to sing,
Not a bee was there to drone;
The sky, unbrushed of any wing,
Hung above me like a stone,
And scarce my feet obeyed my will
As heavily I walked alone.

Then, like a tender memory,
Crept up from off the lifeless ground
The low, melodious lovely sound
Of water lapsing secretly.
A little sunken stream I found,
And all the way was sweet to me.

O ancient music earliest heard
Ere tune was born or any bird,
When first above the chaos wild
The brooding spirit breathed and stirred;

O first-born music, undefiled,
Clear as the laughter of a child,
Fresh as God's latest word!

Anna Bunston de Bary

SINGING WATER

I HEARD—'twas on a morning, but when it was and where,
Except that well I heard it, I neither know nor care—
I heard, and oh, the sunlight was shining in the blue,
A little water singing as little waters do.

At Lechlade and at Buscot, when Summer days are long,
The tiny rills and ripples they tremble into song;
And where the silver Windrush brings down her liquid gems,
There's music in the wavelets she tosses to the Thames.

The eddies have an air too, and brave it is and blithe;
I think I may have heard it that day at Bablockhythe;
And where the Eynsham weir-fall breaks out in rainbow
    spray
The Evenlode comes singing to join the pretty play.

But where I heard that music I cannot rightly tell;
I only know I heard it, and that I know full well:
I heard a little water, and oh, the sky was blue,
A little water singing as little waters do.

R. C. Lehmann

THE WHOLE DUTY OF BERKSHIRE BROOKS

To build the trout a crystal stair;
To comb the hillside's thick green hair;
To water jewel-weed and rushes;
To teach first notes to baby thrushes;
To flavor raspberry and apple
And make a whirling pool to dapple
With scattered gold of late October;
To urge wise laughter on the sober
And lend a dream to those who laugh;
To chant the beetle's epitaph;

To mirror the blue dragonfly,
Frail air-plane of a slender sky;
Over the stones to lull and leap
Herding the bubbles like white sheep;
The claims of worry to deny,
And whisper sorrow into sleep!

Grace Hazard Conkling

GOING FOR WATER

THE well was dry beside the door,
    And so we went with pail and can
Across the fields behind the house
    To seek the brook if still it ran;

Not loth to have excuse to go,
    Because the autumn eve was fair
(Though chill) because the fields were ours,
    And by the brook our woods were there.

We ran as if to meet the moon
    That slowly dawned behind the trees—
The barren boughs without the leaves,
    Without the birds, without the breeze.

But once within the wood, we paused
    Like gnomes that hid us from the moon,
Ready to run to hiding new
    With laughter when she found us soon.

Each laid on other a staying hand
    To listen ere we dared to look,
And in the hush we joined to make
    We heard, we knew we heard the brook.

A note as from a single place,
    A slender tinkling fall that made
Now drops that floated on the pool
    Like pearls, and now a silver blade.

Robert Frost

THE ROAD TO THE POOL

I KNOW a road that leads from town,
A pale road in a Watteau gown
Of wild-rose sprays, that runs away
All fragrant-sandaled, slim and gray.

It slips along the laurel grove
And down the hill, intent to rove,
And crooks an arm of shadow cool
Around a willow-silvered pool.

I never travel very far
Beyond the pool where willows are:
There is a shy and native grace
That hovers all about the place,

And resting there I hardly know
Just where it was I meant to go,
Contented like the road that dozes
In panniered gown of briar roses.

Grace Hazard Conkling

"RIVERS UNKNOWN TO SONG"

WIDE waters in the waste; or, out of reach,
 Rough Alpine falls where late a glacier hung;
Or rivers groping for an alien beach,
 Through continents, unsung.

Nay, not these nameless, these remote, alone;
 But all the streams from all the watersheds—
Peneus, Danube, Nile—are the unknown,
 Young in their ancient beds.

Man has no tale for them. Oh! travelers swift
 From secrets to oblivion! Waters wild
That pass in act to bend a flower or lift
 The bright limbs of a child!

For they are new, they are fresh; there's no surprise
　Like theirs on earth. Oh, strange forevermore!
This moment's Tiber with his shining eyes
　Never saw Rome before.

Man has no word for their eternity—
　Rhine, Avon, Arno, younglings, youth uncrowned!
Ignorant, innocent, instantaneous, free,
　Unwelcomed, unrenowned.

Alice Meynell

SEA BORN

My mother bore me in an island town,
So I love windy water and the sight
Of luggers sailing by in thin moonlight—
I wear the sea as others wear a crown!
My mother bore me near the spinning water,
Water was the first sound upon my ears,
And near the sea her mother bore her daughter,
Close to a window looking on the weirs.
Ever a wind is moaning where I go,
I never stand at night upon a quay,
But I must strain my eyes for sails that blow,
But I must strain my ears to hear the sea.
My mother bore me in a seaport town,
I wear the sea as others wear a crown!

So I have loved the sea as other men
Have loved the way of women who were dear;
Think it not strange that I should turn again
Back to the water and a windy pier.
For men turn back to women and so I,
Turn to the sea that I have loved the best,
Back to the waves and salty spume flung high,
Back to the furious beating of her breast.
So am I stifled now by streets and trees,
That have no space for breathing; I would wear
The splendid look of ships and breathe sea air,
Vessels and schooners, I am one with these.

My mother bore me in an island town,—
I wear the sea as others wear a crown!

Harold Vinal

THE FISHING FLEET

BROWN sails of fishing boats
On a sea of jade,
Startled at early dawn,
Fleeing unafraid.
Far as the eye can see
Into the sun,
Count we their endless fleet
One by one.
Dun foreign hills in sight
There on the beam;
Voices now close aboard,
Like ghosts they seem.
Brown sails of fishing boats
On a sea of jade,
Leaving on either hand
The wake we made.
Yellow foam of breaking waves
On a jade-green sea;
Brown junks with brown sails
Windward and lee.

Lincoln Colcord

OLD SHIPS

BESIDE dim wharves, the battered ships are dreaming,—
The worn ships, the torn ships, with many a draggled mast.
The gray old ships are musing of those creaming
Waters that weltered in the days long past.

Maybe they dream of how the idle ocean,
A glittering dragon, with rippling scales of gold,
Would writhe and twist with sleepy crafty motion,
Suddenly frothing where the hushed bark rolled.

How still they sway and think upon the glories
Of shimmering lagoons that lit the tranquil morn!
How soft they sigh, remembering the stories
Of Africa, Bermuda, and the far Cape Horn!

By what fierce tempests were they hurled and harried?
Or did they groan on any foamy shoal?
And what strange freight or cargoes have they carried:
Bulging green bananas or the bins of coal?

But now they creak and startle from their napping,—
These worn old ships with many a draggled mast;
And while they listen to the waves lip-lapping,
They fall to dreaming of the days long past.

Louis Ginsberg

SKETCH

THE shadows of the ships
Rock on the crest
In the low blue lustre
Of the tardy and the soft inrolling tide.

A long brown bar at the dip of the sky
Puts an arm of sand in the span of salt.

The lucid and endless wrinkles
Draw in, lapse and withdraw.
Wavelets crumble and white spent bubbles
Wash on the floor of the beach.

Rocking on the crest
In the low blue lustre
Are the shadows of the ships.

Carl Sandburg

IN PRAISE OF GARDENS

MAY GARDEN

A SHOWER of green gems on my apple-tree
   This first morning of May
Has fallen out of the night, to be
   Herald of holiday—
Bright gems of green that, fallen there,
Seem fixed and glowing on the air.

Until a flutter of blackbird wings
   Shakes and makes the boughs alive,
And the gems are now no frozen things,
   But apple-green buds to thrive
On sap of my May garden, how well
The green September globes will tell.

Also my pear-tree has its buds,
   But they are silver-yellow,
Like autumn meadows when the floods
   Are silver under willow,
And here shall long and shapely pears
Be gathered while the autumn wears.

And there are sixty daffodils
   Beneath my wall. . . .
And jealousy it is that kills
   This world when all
The spring's behavior here is spent
To make the world magnificent

John Drinkwater

THE SUNKEN GARDEN

SPEAK not—whisper not;
Here bloweth thyme and bergamot;
Softly on the evening hour,
Secret herbs their spices shower.

Dark-spiked rosemary and myrrh,
Lean-stalked, purple lavender;
Hides within her bosom, too,
All her sorrows, bitter rue.

Breathe not—trespass not;
Of this green and darkling spot,
Latticed from the moon's beams,
Perchance a distant dreamer dreams;
Perchance upon its darkening air,
The unseen ghosts of children fare,
Faintly swinging, sway and sweep,
Like lovely sea-flowers in its deep;
While, unmoved, to watch and ward,
Amid its gloomed and daisied sward,
Stands with bowed and dewy head
That one little leaden Lad.

Walter de la Mare

THE GARDEN

WHAT makes a garden?
Flowers, grass and trees,
Odor, grace and color:
Lovely gifts like these.

What makes a garden
And why do gardens grow?
Love lives in gardens—
God and lovers know!

Caroline Giltinan

THE LORD GOD PLANTED A GARDEN

THE Lord God planted a garden
In the first white days of the world,
And He set there an angel warden
In a garment of light enfurled.

Bloom 337

So near to the peace of Heaven,
  That the hawk might nest with the wren,
For there in the cool of the even
  God walked with the first of men.

And I dream that these garden-closes
  With their shade and their sun-flecked sod
And their lilies and bowers of roses,
  Were laid by the hand of God.

The kiss of the sun for pardon,
  The song of the birds for mirth,—
One is nearer God's heart in a garden
  Than anywhere else on earth.

Dorothy Frances Gurney

BLOOM

WHEN flowers thrust their heads above the ground
in showers pale as raindrops, and as round,
who would suspect that such, before they're gone,
could hold the sun?

So fine a pressure from above can bring
so frail a thing to push its way aloft?—
through clay, a woman might consider cloth
for constant stitching?

Right straight down and right straight up again,
through holes so close, no manly eye can see
the bloom come out of needles—or can she
be using rain?

And now that she still labors in the gloom,
her room just lighted by the sun turned moon—
need any man be told what flowers are,
that hold a star?

Alfred Kreymborg

THE ROSE IS A ROYAL LADY

THE rose is a royal lady
    That loves the lordly sun;
The violet haunts the shady
    Cool cloisters of the nun.

I would not wed with roses,
    And nuns they never wed;
I love the country posies
    Where I was born and bred!

I love the gorse and heather,
    And bluebells close beside—
I'll find my cap a feather,
    And kiss a Highland bride!

Charles G. Blanden

BARBERRIES

YOU say I touch the barberries
As a lover his mistress?
What a curious fancy!
One must be delicate, you know—
They have bitter thorns.
You say my hand is hurt?
Oh no, it was my breast—
It was crushed and pressed.
I mean—why yes, of course, of course—
There is a bright drop—isn't there?—
Right on my finger;
Just the color of a barberry,
But it comes from my heart.

Do you love barberries?—
In the autumn
When the sun's desire
Touches them to a glory of crimson and gold?
I love them best then.
There is something splendid about them:

They are not afraid
Of being warm and glad and bold;
They flush joyously,
Like a cheek under a lover's kiss;
They bleed cruelly
Like a dagger-wound in the breast;
They flame up madly for their little hour,
Knowing they must die.
Do you love barberries?

Mary Aldis

BLUEBELLS

TO-NIGHT from deeps of loneliness I wake in wistful wonder
  To a sudden sense of brightness, an immanence of blue—
O are there bluebells swaying in a shadowy coppice yonder,
  Shriven with the dawning and the dew?

For little silver echoes are all about me ringing,
  A crystal chime of waters where a wayward brooklet
    strays,
Faint robin-trills and dove-calls and happy children's
    singing
  And merriment of long-forgotten Mays.

And then my heart remembers a shady reach of wildwood
  Sweet with bloom and innocence, with joy of bird and
    stream
Where bluebells rang their fragrant chimes in sunny springs
    of childhood
  Calling me to fairyland and dream.

And so I know across the years that disenchant and harden,
  Through midnight's alien silence and the black wind's
    mockery,
Down from some paradisal glade, some green, immortal
    garden
  The souls of bluebells come to comfort me.

Lucia Clark Markham

CROCUS

WHEN trees have lost remembrance of the leaves
that spring bequeaths to summer, autumn weaves
and loosens mournfully—this dirge, to whom
does it belong—who treads the hidden loom?

When peaks are overwhelmed with snow and ice,
and clouds with crepe bedeck and shroud the skies—
nor any sun or moon or star, it seems,
can wedge a path of light through such black dreams—

All motion cold, and dead all trace thereof:
what sudden shock below, or spark above,
starts torrents raging down till rivers surge—
that aid the first small crocus to emerge?

The earth will turn and spin and fairly soar,
that couldn't move a tortoise-foot before—
and planets permeate the atmosphere
till misery depart and mystery clear!

And yet, so insignificant a hearse?—
who gave it the endurance so to brave
such elements?—shove winter down a grave?—
and then lead on again the universe?

Alfred Kreymborg

DAFFODILS

THERE flames the first gay daffodil
    Where winter-long the snows have lain;
Who buried Love, all spent and still?
There flames the first gay daffodil.
    Go, Love's alive on yonder hill,
    And yours for asking, joy and pain,
There flames the first gay daffodil
    Where winter-long the snows have lain!

Ruth Guthrie Harding

LILAC

O LILAC,
Whiter than swan's down,
Among your soft-green leaves,
Purer than snow
New fallen on the boughs,
The white butterfly fluttering
Over your fragrance
Is happy.
I watch you from my window,
And feel on my face and hair
The warm wind blowing across London.

I have many things to hurt me,—
Youth gone and life and friends uncertain;
And no god will take me
And turn me into a lilac-tree,—
With the world beneath me
For my roots, and each springtime
A myriad tender hearts
For the winds to fondle,
And the startling candor of my blossom
For men to love.

Some god has done this to you,
O lilac,
And the butterfly does not fear you.

F. S. Flint

TALL NETTLES

TALL nettles cover up, as they have done
These many springs, the rusty harrow, the plough
Long worn out, and the roller made of stone:
Only the elm butt tops the nettles now.

This corner of the farmyard I like most:
As well as any bloom upon a flower
I like the dust on the nettles, never lost
Except to prove the sweetness of a shower.

Edward Thomas

A YELLOW PANSY

To the wall of the old green garden
  A butterfly quivering came;
His wings on the sombre lichens
  Played like a yellow flame.

He looked at the gray geraniums,
  And the sleepy four-o'-clocks;
He looked at the low lanes bordered
  With the glossy-growing box.

He longed for the peace and the silence,
  And the shadows that lengthened there,
And his wee wild heart was weary
  Of skimming the endless air.

And now in the old green garden,—
  I know not how it came,—
A single pansy is blooming,
  Bright as a yellow flame.

And whenever a gay gust passes,
  It quivers as if with pain,
For the butterfly-soul that is in it
  Longs for the winds again!

Helen Gray Cone

ITALIAN POPPIES

WHEREVER on Italian ground,
  Carried by whim, I chance to go,
The poppy follows me around
  Palace and pasture, high and low.
Rich in her red, she decks my heart
  Like her own meadows; sick of soul,
I watch the whirl of crowded art,
  Till her pure passion makes me whole.

O simple flower, you speak the tongue
　　That tear-drops answer; North and South,
The lips of lovers as they clung,
　　Spake your sweet language, mouth to mouth:
Francesca, ere she found her doom,
　　Planted you on Paolo's lips;
And Roman Antony saw you bloom,
　　Flaming, on Cleopatra's ships.

Joel Elias Spingarn

THE ROSE AND GOD

MEDITATIONS OF A PERSIAN MYSTIC

What are you, rose?—lips that lean back to meet
The June-long kiss of the sun? or fervid wine
Born of dark pangs, though trod out by the feet

Of spring's wild votaries; will the breeze incline
His waving curls and drink with tremulous hand,
Then lurch away to drowse at last supine

On yielding grasses? As your leaves expand,
Rose, you repay the dower that nature brought:
The sun begot you, and the warm breeze fanned

Your widening buds; till earth, whose womb was fraught
So patiently, might flaunt in recompense
A living ruby. Deeper must be sought

Your soul, that perfume of the inward sense
Which men call beauty, that red kiss of joy
Which bathes my being,—who knows how or whence?—

Till I am steeped in rapture. No mere toy
Of subterranean looms are you, sweet rose,
That frost or drouth or canker may destroy.

The color that exhales, the scent that glows,
Your many-petaled indivisible grace;—
Like mists the dawn-light wears but later throws

Aside—what were they but a withered face,
A starless night, a chord that felt no thrill
Of passion's fingers; could I neither trace

The light that from your bosom throbs to fill
Your emerald shrine with awe, nor dream some tone
From which your deep thoughts limpidly distil

As music. Love is roused by love alone;
You, rose, unbarring paradise to me,
Are therefore God. How could He else be known

To mortals than in sensuous rhapsody?
Naught that is told us may we comprehend
Until we taste and breathe and hear and see

And handle. Rose, in you the ineffable Friend
Has three persuasive voices: perfume, touch
And color. Though your song may seem to end

To-night, your petals whirled off in the clutch
Of winds, like wounded doves that hawks pursue;
Your beauty shall for me be ever such

As at this moment, when love speaks in you.
You blossom in my breast, as warm, as red
As my own heart. And my heart blossoms, too,

In God's heart. Through all time and space are spread
Roses unfading, ever-fragrant, more
And more; across the earth, and overhead,

Reflected on the ocean's tranquil floor;
Until the universe is one vast rose,
Nature and man, with God the flaming core
Whence love to every crimson petal flows.

Charles Wharton Stork

THE SNOWDROP

CLOSE to the sod
  There can be seen
A thought of God
  In white and green.

Unmarred, unsoiled
  It cleft the clay,
Serene, unspoiled
  It views the day.

It is so holy
And yet so lowly.
  Would you enjoy
    Its grace and dower
  And not destroy
    The living flower?
Then you must, please,
Fall on your knees.

Anna Bunston de Bary

BLUE SQUILLS

How many million Aprils came
  Before I ever knew
How white a cherry bough could be,
  A bed of squills, how blue!

And many a dancing April
  When life is done with me,
Will lift the blue flame of the flower
  And the white flame of the tree.

Oh burn me with your beauty, then,
  Oh hurt me, tree and flower,
Lest in the end death try to take
  Even this glistening hour.

O shaken flowers, O shimmering trees,
    O sunlit white and blue,
Wound me, that I, through endless sleep,
    May bear the scar of you.

Sara Teasdale

SUNFLOWERS

My tall sunflowers love the sun,
Love the burning August noons
When the locust tunes its viol,
And the cricket croons.

When the purple night draws in,
With its planets hung on high,
And the attared winds of slumber
Wander down the sky,·

Still my sunflowers love the sun,
Keep their ward and watch and wait
Till the rosy key of morning
Opes the Eastern Gate.

Then, when they have deeply quaffed
From the brimming cups of dew,
You can hear their golden laughter
All the garden through!

Clinton Scollard

WHITE VIOLETS

Tears that never quite touched earth,
    Passion-buds that lie
Stillborn of a fruitless birth,—
    Stars from a dead sky.

Not with purple pulses borne
    Down wild tides of play;
Ages since, an elfin horn
    Witched their youth away.

Blanched with their own beauty; pale,
    Much as maids might be,
Looking long for one soft sail
    Swallowed by the sea.

Much as they who, stooped with years,
    Listen all alone,
Hearing faint, through far-off ears,
    Voices they have known.

Children of too gentle birth,
    Here these flowers lie;
Love that never quite touched earth,—
    They . . . and thou and I.

Benjamin R. C. Low

ROADSIDE FLOWERS

WE are the roadside flowers,
    Straying from garden grounds;
Lovers of idle hours,
    Breakers of ordered bounds.

If only the earth will feed us,
    If only the wind be kind,
We blossom for those who need us,
    The stragglers left behind.

And lo, the Lord of the Garden,
    He makes His sun to rise,
And His rain to fall like pardon
    On our dusty paradise.

On us He has laid the duty—
    The task of the wandering breed—
To better the world with beauty,
    Wherever the way may lead.

Who shall inquire of the season,
    Or question the wind where it blows?
We blossom and ask no reason,
    The Lord of the Garden knows.

Bliss Carman

LITTLE CREATURES EVERYWHERE

LITTLE THINGS

LITTLE things that run and quail
  And die in silence and despair;

Little things that fight and fail
  And fall on sea and earth and air;

All trapped and frightened little things,
  The mouse, the coney, hear our prayer:

As we forgive those done to us,
  The lamb, the linnet, and the hare,

Forgive us all our trespasses,
  Little creatures everywhere.

James Stephens

THE SNARE

I HEAR a sudden cry of pain!
There is a rabbit in a snare:
Now I hear the cry again,
But I cannot tell from where.

But I cannot tell from where
He is calling out for aid;
Crying on the frightened air,
Making everything afraid.

Making everything afraid,
Wrinkling up his little face,
As he cries again for aid;
And I cannot find the place!

348

And I cannot find the place
Where his paw is in the snare:
Little one! Oh, little one!
I am searching everywhere.

James Stephens

CANTICLE

DEVOUTLY worshipping the oak
Wherein the barred owl stares,
The little feathered forest folk
Are praying sleepy prayers:

Praying the summer to be long
And drowsy to the end,
And daily full of sun and song,
That broken hopes may mend.

Praying the golden age to stay
Until the whippoorwill
Appoints a windy moving-day,
And hurries from the hill.

William Griffith

FIREFLIES

LITTLE lamps of the dusk,
    You fly low and gold
When the summer evening
    Starts to unfold,
So that all the insects,
    Now, before you pass,
Will have light to see by
    Undressing in the grass.

But when night has flowered
    Little lamps a-gleam,
You fly over tree-tops
    Following a dream.

Men wonder from their windows
  That a firefly goes so far—
They do not know your longing
  To be a shooting star.

Carolyn Hall

THE NIGHT MOTHS

Out of the night to my leafy porch they came,
A thousand moths. Did He who made the toad
Give them their wings upon the starry road?
Restless and wild, they circle round the flame,
Frail wonder-shapes that man can never tame—
Whirl like the blown flakes of December snows,
Tinted with amber, violet and rose,
Marked with hieroglyphs that have no name.
Out of the summer darkness pours the flight:
Unknown the wild processional they keep.
What lures them to this rush of mad delight?
Why are they called from nothingness and sleep?
Why this rich beauty wandering the night?
Do they go lost and aimless to the deep?

Edwin Markham

THE TREE–TOAD

A tiny bell the tree-toad has,
  I wonder if he knows
The charm it is to hear him
  Ringing as he goes.

He can't have gone the journeys
  He tells me to go on,
Here in the darkness
  Of the cool, cropped lawn.

He cannot know the thrill
  Of the soft spring wind,
Or the wonder, when you walk,
  What will come behind.

He hasn't seen the places
　　I'd break my heart to win,
Nor heard the city calling
　　When the cold comes in.

He sings away contented
　　And doesn't leave his tree,
But he sets my blood a-going
　　Where his song will never be.

Orrick Johns

THE BIRDS

WITHIN mankind's duration, so they say,
Khephren and Ninus lived but yesterday.
Asia had no name till man was old
And long had learned the use of iron and gold;
And æons had passed, when the first corn was planted,
Since first the use of syllables was granted.

Men were on earth while climates slowly swung,
Fanning wide zones to heat and cold, and long
Subsidence turned great continents to sea,
And seas dried up, dried up interminably,
Age after age; enormous seas were dried
Amid wastes of land.　And the last monsters died.

Earth wore another face.　O since that prime
Man with how many works has sprinkled time!
Hammering, hewing, digging tunnels, roads;
Building ships, temples, multiform abodes.
How, for his body's appetites, his toils
Have conquered all earth's products, all her soils;
And in what thousand thousand shapes of art
He has tried to find a language for his heart!

Never at rest, never content or tired:
Insatiate wanderer, marvellously fired,
Most grandly piling and piling into the air
Stones that will topple or arch he knows not where.

And yet did I, this spring, think it more strange,
More grand, more full of awe, than all that change,
And lovely and sweet and touching unto tears,
That through man's chronicled and unchronicled years,
And even into that unguessable beyond
The water-hen has nested by a pond,
Weaving dry flags into a beaten floor,
The one sure product of her only lore.
Low on a ledge above the shadowed water
Then, when she heard no men, as nature taught her,
Plashing around with busy scarlet bill
She built that nest, her nest, and builds it still.

O let your strong imagination turn
The great wheel backward, until Troy unburn, .
And then unbuild, and seven Troys below
Rise out of death, and dwindle, and outflow,
Till all have passed, and none has yet been there:
Back, ever back.   Our birds still crossed the air;
Beyond our myriad changing generations
Still built, unchanged, their known inhabitations.
A million years before Atlantis was
Our lark sprang from some hollow in the grass,
Some old soft hoof-print in a tussock's shade;
And the wood-pigeon's smooth snow-white eggs were
     laid,
High amid green pines' sunset-colored shafts,
And rooks their villages of twiggy rafts
Set on the tops of elms, where elms grew then,
And still the thumbling tit and perky wren
Popped through the tiny doors of cosy balls
And the blackbird lined with moss his high-built walls;
A round mud cottage held the thrush's young,
And straws from the untidy sparrow's hung.
And, skimming forktailed in the evening air,
When man first was were not the martens there?
Did not those birds some human shelter crave,
And stow beneath the cornice of his cave
Their dry tight cups of clay?   And from each door
Peeped on a morning wiseheads three or four.

Yes, daw and owl, curlew and crested hern,
Kingfisher, mallard, water-rail and tern,
Chaffinch and greenfinch, wagtail, stonechat, ruff,
Whitethroat and robin, fly-catcher and chough,
Missel-thrush, magpie, sparrow-hawk and jay,
Built, those far ages gone, in this year's way.
And the first man who walked the cliffs of Rame,
As I this year, looked down and saw the same
Blotches of rusty red on ledge and cleft
With gray-green spots on them, while right and left
A dizzying tangle of gulls were floating and flying,
Wheeling and crossing and darting, crying and crying,
Circling and crying, over and over and over,
Crying with swoop and hover and fall and recover.
And below on a rock against the gray sea fretted,
Pipe-necked and stationary and silhouetted,
Cormorants stood in a wise, black, equal row
Above the nests and long blue eggs we know.

O delicate chain over all the ages stretched,
O dumb tradition from what far darkness fetched:
Each little architect with its one design
Perpetual, fixed and right in stuff and line,
Each little ministrant who knows one thing,
One learnèd rite to celebrate the spring.
Whatever alters else on sea or shore,
These are unchanging: man must still explore.

J. C. Squire

THE MAKING OF BIRDS

God made Him birds in a pleasant humor;
    Tired of planets and suns was He.
He said, "I will add a glory to summer,
    Gifts for my creatures banished from Me!"

He had a thought and it set Him smiling,
    Of the shape of a bird and its glancing head,
Its dainty air and its grace beguiling:
    "I will make feathers," the Lord God said.

He made the robin: He made the swallow;
　His deft hands moulding the shape to His mood;
The thrush, the lark, and the finch to follow,
　And laughed to see that His work was good.

He who has given men gift of laughter,
　Made in His image; He fashioned fit
The blink of the owl and the stork thereafter,
　The little wren and the long-tailed tit.

He spent in the making His wit and fancies;
　The wing-feathers He fashioned them strong;
Deft and dear as daisies and pansies,
　He crowned His work with the gift of song.

"Dearlings," He said, "make songs for my praises!"
　He tossed them loose to the sun and wind,
Airily sweet as pansies and daisies;
　He taught them to build a nest to their mind.

The dear Lord God of His glories weary—
　Christ our Lord had the heart of a boy—
Made Him birds in a moment merry,
　Bade them soar and sing for his joy.
                              Katherine Tynan Hinkson

OVERTONES

I HEARD a bird at break of day
　Sing from the autumn trees
A song so mystical and calm,
　So full of certainties,
No man, I think, could listen long
　Except upon his knees.
Yet this was but a simple bird,
　Alone, among dead trees.
                              William Alexander Percy

TO AN IRISH BLACKBIRD

WET your feet, wet your feet,
  This is what he seems to say,
Calling from the dewy thicket
  At the breaking of the day.

Wet your feet, wet your feet,
  Silver toned he sounds the call
From his bramble in the thicket
  When the dew is on the fall.

Many times in lands far distant,
  In my dreams I hear him play
On his flute within the thicket,
  Ere the showers have passed away.

Years have passed since last I heard him,
  Since I said a sad adieu
To the early Irish morning
  With the rainbow-tinted dew.

And I still can hear him calling
  And the call come clear and sweet,
And I still can see the mornings
  With the dew about my feet.

Wet your feet, wet your feet,
  Silver toned he sounds the call
From his bramble in the thicket
  When the dew is on the fall.

James MacAlpine

THE BLACKBIRD

  IN the far corner
  close by the swings,
  every morning
  a blackbird sings.

His bill's so yellow,
his coat's so black,
that he makes a fellow
whistle back.

Ann, my daughter,
thinks that he
sings for us two
especially.

Humbert Wolfe

ADVICE TO A BLUE–BIRD

WHO can make a delicate adventure
Of walking on the ground?
Who can make grass-blades
Arcades for pertly careless straying?
You alone, who skim against these leaves,
Turning all desire into light whips
Moulded by your deep blue wing-tips,
You who shrill your unconcern
Into the sternly antique sky.
You to whom all things
Hold an equal kiss of touch.

Mincing, wanton blue-bird,
Grimace at the hoofs of passing men.
You alone can lose yourself
Within a sky, and rob it of its blue!

Maxwell Bodenheim

THE BUZZARDS

WHEN evening came and the warm glow grew deeper,
And every tree that bordered the green meadows
And in the yellow cornfields every reaper
And every corn-shock stood above their shadows
Flung eastward from their feet in longer measure,
Serenely far there swam in the sunny height
A buzzard and his mate who took their pleasure
Swirling and poising idly in golden light.

On great pied motionless moth-wings borne along,
So effortless and so strong,
Cutting each other's paths together they glided,
Then wheeled asunder till they soared divided
Two valleys' width (as though it were delight
To part like this, being sure they could unite
So swiftly in their empty, free dominion),
Curved headlong downward, towered up the sunny steep,
Then, with a sudden lift of the one great pinion,
Swung proudly to a curve, and from its height
Took half a mile of sunlight in one long sweep.

And we, so small on the swift immense hillside,
Stood tranced, until our souls arose uplifted
On those far-sweeping, wide,
Strong curves of flight—swayed up and hugely drifted,
Were washed, made strong and beautiful in the tide
Of sun-bathed air. But far beneath, beholden
Through shining deeps of air, the fields were golden
And rosy burned the heather where cornfields ended.

And still those buzzards whirled, while light withdrew
Out of the vales and to surging slopes ascended,
Till the loftiest flaming summit died to blue.

Martin Armstrong

WHITE DOVE OF THE WILD DARK EYES

WHITE Dove of the wild dark eyes
Faint silver flutes are calling
From the night where the star-mists rise
  And fire-flies falling
  Tremble in starry wise.
  Is it you they are calling?

White Dove of the beating heart
Shrill golden reeds are thrilling
In the woods where the shadows start,
  While moonbeams, filling
  With dreams the floweret's heart
  Its dreams are thrilling.

White Dove of the folded wings,
Soft purple night is crying
With the voice of fairy things
    For you, lest dying
    They miss your flashing wings,
    Your splendorous flying.

Joseph M. Plunkett

THE FISH-HAWK

ON the large highway of the awful air that flows
    Unbounded between sea and heaven, while twilight
        screened
The majestic distances, he moved and had repose;
    On the huge wind of the Immensity he leaned
His steady body in long lapse of flight—and rose

Gradual, through broad gyres of ever-climbing rest,
    Up the clear stair of the eternal sky, and stood
Throned on the summit!   Slowly, with his widening breast,
    Widened around him the enormous Solitude,
From the gray rim of ocean to the glowing west.

Headlands and capes forlorn of the far coast, the land
    Rolling her barrens toward the south, he, from his throne
Upon the gigantic wind, beheld: he hung—he fanned
    The abyss for mighty joy, to feel beneath him strown
Pale pastures of the sea, with heaven on either hand—

The world with all her winds and waters, earth and air,
    Fields, folds, and moving clouds.   The awful and adored
Arches and endless aisles of vacancy, the fair
    Void of sheer heights and hollows hailed him as her lord
And lover in the highest, to whom all heaven lay bare!

Till from that tower of ecstasy, that baffled height,
    Stooping, he sank; and slowly on the world's wide way
Walked, with great wing on wing, the merciless, proud
        Might,
    Hunting the huddled and lone reaches for his prey
Down the dim shore—and faded in the crumbling light.

Slowly the dusk covered the land. Like a great hymn
  The sound of moving winds and waters was; the sea
Whispered a benediction, and the west grew dim
  Where evening lifted her clear candles quietly . . .
Heaven, crowded with stars, trembled from rim to rim.
John Hall Wheelock

THE HUMMINGBIRD

THE sunlight speaks, and its voice is a bird:
It glimmers half-guessed, half-seen, half-heard,
Above the flowerbed, over the lawn . . .
A flashing dip, and it is gone,
And all it lends to the eye is this—
A sunbeam giving the air a kiss.
Harry Kemp

THE LARK

(SALISBURY, ENGLAND)

A CLOSE gray sky,
And poplars gray and high,
The country-side along;
The steeple bold
Across the acres old—
And then a song!

Oh, far, far, far,
As any spire or star,
Beyond the cloistered wall!
Oh, high, high, high,
A heart-throb in the sky—
Then not at all!
Lizette Woodworth Reese

THE LINNET

UPON this leafy bush
With thorns and roses in it,
Flutters a thing of light,
A twittering linnet.

And all the throbbing world
Of dew and sun and air
By this small parcel of life
Is made more fair;
As if each bramble-spray
And mounded gold-wreathed furze,
Harebell and little thyme,
Were only hers;
As if this beauty and grace
Did to one bird belong,
And, at a flutter of wing,
Might vanish in song.

Walter de la Mare

THE LOON

A LONELY lake, a lonely shore,
A lone pine leaning on the moon;
All night the water-beating wings
Of a solitary loon.

With mournful wail from dusk to dawn
He gibbered at the taunting stars—
A hermit-soul gone raving mad,
And beating at his bars.

Lew Sarett

NIGHTINGALES

BEAUTIFUL must be the mountains whence ye come,
And bright in the fruitful valleys the streams, wherefrom
    Ye learn your song:
Where are those starry woods? O might I wander there,
  Among the flowers, which in that heavenly air
      Bloom the year long!

Nay, barren are those mountains and spent the streams:
Our song is the voice of desire, that haunts our dreams,
    A throe of the heart,
Whose pining visions dim, forbidden hopes profound,
  No dying cadence nor long sigh can sound,
      For all our art.

Alone, aloud in the raptured ear of men
We pour our dark nocturnal secret; and then,
         As night is withdrawn
From these sweet-springing meads and bursting boughs of
      may,
   Dream, while the innumerable choir of day
         Welcome the dawn.

Robert Bridges

NIGHTINGALES

AT sunset my brown nightingales
Hidden and hushed all day,
Ring vespers, while the color pales
And fades to twilight gray:
The little mellow bells they ring,
The little flutes they play,
Are soft as though for practising
The things they want to say.
It's when the dark has floated down
To hide and guard and fold,
I know their throats that look so brown,
Are really made of gold.
No music I have ever heard
Can call as sweet as they!
I wonder if it *is* a bird
That sings within the hidden tree,
Or some shy angel calling me
To follow far away?

Grace Hazard Conkling

THE NIGHTINGALE NEAR THE HOUSE

HERE is the soundless cypress on the lawn;
It listens, listens.   Taller trees beyond
Listen.   The moon at the unruffled pond
      Stares.   And you sing, you sing.

That star-enchanted song falls through the air
From lawn to lawn down terraces of sound,
Darts in white arrows on the shadowed ground;
      And all the night you sing.

My dreams are flowers to which you are a bee
As all night long I listen, and my brain
Receives your song; then loses it again
    In moonlight on the lawn.

Now is your voice a marble high and white,
Then like a mist on fields of paradise,
Now is a raging fire, then is like ice,
    Then breaks, and it is dawn.

Harold Monro

TO A PHŒBE-BIRD

UNDER the eaves, out of the wet,
    You nest within my reach;
You never sing for me and yet
    You have a golden speech.

You sit and quirk a rapid tail,
    Wrinkle a ragged crest,
Then pirouette from tree to rail
    And vault from rail to nest.

And when in frequent, dainty fright
    You grayly slip and fade,
And when at hand you re-alight
    Demure and unafraid,

And when you bring your brood its fill
    Of iridescent wings
And green legs dewy in your bill,
    Your silence is what sings.

Not of a feather that enjoys
    To prate or praise or preach,
O Phœbe, with so little noise,
    What eloquence you teach!

Witter Bynner

ROOKS

THERE, where the rusty iron lies,
   The rooks are cawing all the day.
Perhaps no man, until he dies,
   Will understand them, what they say.

The evening makes the sky like clay.
   The slow wind waits for night to rise.
The world is half content.   But they

Still trouble all the trees with cries,
   That know, and cannot put away,
The yearning to the soul that flies
   From day to night, from night to day.
Charles Hamilton Sorley

THE SANDPIPER

ALONG the sea-edge, like a gnome
Or rolling pebble in the foam,
As though he timed the ocean's throbbing,
Runs a piper, bobbing, bobbing.

Now he stiffens, now he wilts,
Like a little boy on stilts!
Creatures burrow, insects hide,
When they see the piper glide.

You would think him out of joint,
Till his bill begins to point.
You would doubt if he could fly,
Till his straightness arrows by.

You would take him for a clown,
Till he peeps and flutters down,
Vigilant among the grasses,
Where a fledgling bobs and passes.
Witter Bynner

TO A SPARROW

Because you have no fear to mingle
Wings with those of greater part
So like me, with song I single
Your sweet impudence of heart.

And when prouder feathers go where
Summer holds her leafy show,
You still come to us from nowhere
Like gray leaves across the snow.

In back ways where odd and end go
To your meals you drop down sure,
Knowing every broken window
Of the hospitable poor.

There is no bird half so harmless,
None so sweetly rude as you,
None so common and so charmless,
None of virtues nude as you.

But for all your faults I love you,
For you linger with us still,
Though the wintry winds reprove you,
And the snow is on the hill.

Francis Ledwidge

A THRUSH BEFORE DAWN

A voice peals in this end of night
    A phrase of notes resembling stars,
Single and spiritual notes of light.
        What call they at my window-bars?
            The South, the past, the day to be,
                An ancient infelicity.

Darkling, deliberate, what sings
    This wonderful one, alone, at peace?
What wilder things than song, what things
        Sweeter than youth, clearer than Greece,
            Dearer than Italy, untold
                Delight, and freshness centuries old?

And first first-loves, a multitude,
  The exaltation of their pain;
Ancestral childhood long renewed;
  And midnights of invisible rain;
    And gardens, gardens, night and day,
    Gardens and childhood all the way.

What Middle Ages passionate,
  O passionless voice!   What distant bells
Lodged in the hills, what palace state
  Illyrian!   For it speaks, it tells,
    Without desire, without dismay,
    Some morrow and some yesterday.

All-natural things!   But more—Whence came
  This yet remoter mystery?
 How do these starry notes proclaim
  A graver still divinity?
    This hope, this sancity of fear?
    O innocent throat!   O human ear!
                                    Alice Meynell

THE THRUSH

God bade the birds break not the silent spell
    That lay upon the wood.
Longing for liquid notes that never fell
    Ached the deep solitude.

The little birds obeyed.   No voice awoke.
    Dwelling sedate, apart,
Only the thrush, the thrush that never spoke,
    Sang from her bursting heart.
                                    Laura Benét

THE DARKLING THRUSH

I leant upon a coppice gate
    When Frost was spectre-gray,
And Winter's dregs made desolate
    The weakening eye of day.

The tangled bine-stems scored the sky
　Like strings from broken lyres,
And all mankind that haunted nigh
　Had sought their household fires.

The land's sharp features seemed to be
　The Century's corpse outleant,
His crypt the cloudy canopy,
　The wind his death-lament.
The ancient pulse of germ and birth
　Was shrunken hard and dry,
And every spirit upon earth
　Seemed fervorless as I.

At once a voice burst forth among
　The bleak twigs overhead
In a full-hearted evensong
　Of joy illimited;
An agèd thrush, frail, gaunt, and small,
　In blast-beruffled plume,
Had chosen thus to fling his soul
　Upon the growing gloom.

So little cause for carollings
　Of such ecstatic sound
Was written on terrestrial things
　Afar or nigh around,
That I could think there trembled through
　His happy good-night air
Some blessèd Hope, whereof he knew
　And I was unaware.

Thomas Hardy

WILD GEESE

I HEARD the wild geese flying
　In the dead of the night,
With beat of wings and crying
I heard the wild geese flying.

Wild Geese 367

And dreams in my heart sighing
Followed their northward flight.
I heard the wild geese flying
In the dead of the night.

Elinor Chipp

GYPSY–HEARTS

THE HUNTER

"But there was one land he dared not enter."

BEYOND the blue, the purple seas,
Beyond the thin horizon's line,
Beyond Antilla, Hebrides,
Jamaica, Cuba, Caribbees,
There lies the land of Yucatan.

The land, the land of Yucatan,
The low coast breaking into foam,
The dim hills where my thoughts shall roam,
The forests of my boyhood's home,
The splendid dream of Yucatan!

I met thee first long, long ago
Turning a printed page, and I
Stared at a world I did not know
And felt my blood like fire flow
At that strange name of Yucatan.

O those sweet, far-off Austral days
When life had a diviner glow,
When hot suns whipped my blood to know
Things all unseen, then I could go
Into thy heart, O Yucatan!

I have forgotten what I saw,
I have forgotten what I knew,
And many lands I've set sail for
To find that marvellous spell of yore,
Never to set foot on thy shore,
O haunting land of Yucatan!

But sailing I have passed thee by,
And leaning on the white ship's rail
Watched thy dim hills till mystery
Wrapped thy far stillness close to me,
And I have breathed "'Tis Yucatan!"

"'Tis Yucatan, 'tis Yucatan!"
The ship is sailing far away,
The coast recedes, the dim hills fade,
A bubble-winding track we've made,
And thou'rt a Dream, O Yucatan!

W. J. Turner

THE ROAD TO ANYWHERE

Across the places deep and dim,
    And places brown and bare,
It reaches to the planet's rim—
    The Road to Anywhere.

Now east is east, and west is west,
    But north lies in between,
And he is blest whose feet have pressed
    The road that's cool and green.

The road of roads for them that dare
    The lightest whim obey,
To follow where the moose or bear
    Has brushed his headlong way.

The secrets that these tangles house
    Are step by step revealed,
While, to the sun, the grass and boughs
    A store of odors yield.

More sweet these odors in the sun
    Than swim in chemists' jars;
And when the fragrant day is done,
    Night—and a shoal of stars.

Oh, east is east, and west is west,
But north lies full and fair;
And blest is he who follows free
The Road to Anywhere.

Bert Leston Taylor

THE BEST ROAD OF ALL

I LIKE a road that leads away to prospects white and fair,
A road that is an ordered road, like a nun's evening prayer;
But, best of all, I love a road that leads to God knows where.

You come upon it suddenly—you cannot seek it out;
It's like a secret still unheard and never noised about;
But when you see it, gone at once is every lurking doubt.

It winds beside some rushing stream where aspens lightly
quiver,
It follows many a broken field by many a shining river;
It seems to lead you on and on, forever and forever!

You tramp along its dusty way, beneath its shadowy trees,
And hear beside you chattering birds or happy booming
bees,
And all around you golden sounds, the green leaves' litanies.

And here's a hedge, and there's a cot; and then—strange,
sudden turns;
A dip, a rise, a little glimpse where the red sunset burns;
A bit of sky at eveningtime, the scent of hidden ferns.

A winding road, a loitering road, a finger-mark of God
Traced when the Maker of the world leaned over ways
untrod.
See! Here He smiled His glowing smile, and lo, the golden-
rod!

I like a road that wanders straight; the King's highway is
fair,
And lovely are the sheltered lanes that take you here and
there;
But, best of all, I love a road that leads to God knows where.

Charles Hanson Towne

NEW HORIZONS

NEVER was there path our childhood used to roam
So long it led not in the evening home;

Nor could the magic of the unknown track
Prevail against the hearth that called us back.

Over the same hill-tops, wild-rose or gray,
Our evening and our twilight always lay;

And when the night fell all the unknown stars
Grew homely shining through our window bars.

Now we have fared to the country o'er the hill,
And unknown journeys lie beyond us still;—

Ways unadventured, countless paths to roam,
But none that leads us in the evening home.

Onward, not homeward, some adventure calls
With every dawn, and every evening falls

Over new horizons, wild-rose or gray,
And old stars shining on the unknown way

Strange look and far, not those we saw of old
Safe moored in haven skies above our fold.

S. R. Lysaght

NEEDLE TRAVEL

I SIT at home and sew,
I ply my needle and thread,
But the trip around the garment's hem
Is not the path I tread;
My stitches neat,
With their rhythmic beat,
Keep time to very different feet,
On a different journey sped.

Now, glad heart
Tip-toe, tip-toe,

They must not hear you,
They must not know,
They must not follow where you go.

Bare, brown feet on the dusty road,
Unbound body free of its load,
Limbs that need no stinging goad
Step, step out on the dusty road.

Friends to greet on the jolly road,
Lopeing rabbit, and squatting toad,
Beetle, trundling along with your load;
Hey, little friends,
Good-day, good-morrow,
You see me to-day,
You forget me to-morrow.

Time to chase you across the road,
Lopeing rabbit, and poke you, toad,
Upset you, beetle with your load;
Hey, little friends,
Good-day.

Bare, brown feet in the shelving pool,
Unbound body, relaxed and cool,
Limbs lying bare and beautiful;
Hey, green pool,
Good-day, good-morrow,
You hold me to-day,
You forget me to-morrow.

Time to float in you, rapt and cool,
Swim the rapids above you, pool,
Dive in your waters bountiful;
Hey, sweet friend,
Good-day.

I sit at home and sew,
I ply my needle and thread,
But the trip around the garment's hem
Is not the path I tread.

Margaret French Patton

THE TICKET AGENT

LIKE any merchant in a store
Who sells things by the pound or score,

He deals with scarce perfunctory glance
Small pass-keys to the world's Romance.

He takes dull money, turns and hands
The roadways to far distant lands.

Bright shining rail and fenceless sea
Are partners to his wizardry.

He calls off names as if they were
Just names to cause no heart to stir.

For listening you'll hear him say
" . . . and then to Aden and Bombay . . ."

Or " . . . 'Frisco first and then to Nome,
Across the Rocky Mountains—Home . . ."

And never catch of voice to tell
He knows the lure or feels the spell.

Like any salesman in a store,
He sells but tickets—nothing more.

And casual as any clerk
He deals in dreams, and calls it—work!

Edmund Leamy

THE TRAVEL BUREAU

ALL day she sits behind a bright brass rail
Planning proud journeyings in terms that bring
Far places near; high-colored words that sing,
"The Taj Mahal at Agra," "Kashmir's Vale,"

Spanning wide spaces with her clear detail,
"Sevilla or Fiesole in spring,
Through the fiords in June." Her words take wing.
She is the minstrel of the great out-trail.
At half past five she puts her maps away,
Pins on a gray, meek hat, and braves the sleet,
A timid eye on traffic. Dully gray
The house that harbors her in a gray street,
The close, sequestered, colorless retreat
Where she was born, where she will always stay.

Ruth Comfort Mitchell

PRISONERS

I SIT in my garden among the roses.
They are gracious, and stately, and delicately fragrant;
And the wall is high behind them.

I who long for bare hills and deep forests,
And roads that find no town at twilight-time,
And streams that have no name,
And high sea-winds—
I sit in my garden among the roses.

O God, when I with wandering soul
Have adventured into death,
Re-fashion me into a sea-gull or wisp of wind
Or a tree on a high crag—
Not a rose in a walled garden!

Nancy Barr Mavity

WILDNESS

LOVE forged for me a golden chain
    To bind my straying feet.
I dwelt in scented rose-leaf rain
    And found the young years sweet.

But when I hear the wind sweep by
    Or see the white clouds pass–
The spaces of the open sky—
    Birds soaring o'er the grass—

There is a little place in me
   That cries like any child
To be as forest things are, free,
   Lonely, and strange and wild!
           Blanche Shoemaker Wagstaff

AN AUTUMN ROAD

DOWN a hill, then up a hill
   And then a vast of sea!
A wedge of wild geese crying
   Passes over me—
And now my dreams are flying
   Where I may never be. . . .

Down a hill and up a hill,
   Then level lands again!
Far off the sea is speaking
   A longing that is pain—
My eyes are weary seeking
   For my lost ship from Spain.

Down a hill and up a hill,
   Oh, so long ago,
There was a princess singing—
   Where, I do not know. . . .
There were arms that, clinging,
   Would not let me go.
           Glenn Ward Dresbach

MORNING SONG

THERE'S a mellower light just over the hill,
And somewhere a yellower daffodil,
And honey, somewhere, that's sweeter still.

And some were meant to stay like a stone,
Knowing the things they have always known,
Sinking down deeper into their own.

But some must follow the wind and me,
Who like to be starting and like to be free,
Never so glad as we're going to be!

Karle Wilson Baker

I WAS MADE OF THIS AND THIS

(I WAS made of this and this—
An angel's prayer, a gipsy's kiss.)

My mother bore me prayerfully
   And reared me sweet as a gift for God,
And taught me to look shudderingly
   On ways my father trod.

They buried him long and long ago
   (I just remember his eyes were blue),
He always did—they say who know—
   Things it was wrong to do.

He prayed no saints but the Little Folk,
   Pan was his only god; ah me,
The times he laughed when my mother spoke
   The beads on her rosary!

(I tend my roof-tree and I pray
   The Maid who knew a mother's woe
To keep my feet in the gentle way
   Her Son would have me go.)

He swore round oaths and drank black gin;
   He held four things to his heart's delight:
The hills, the road, his violin,
   An open sky at night.

He told strange tales that were never true
   (They buried him long and long ago!)
It always seemed the things he knew
   Were things it was wrong to know.

He scoffed at walls and a garden plot;
   He held three things to his heart's desire:
The river's song, an open spot,
    The smoke from a driftwood fire.

(I wonder would I greatly care—
   Mary, keep my heart from sin!—
If babe of mine should come to swear
    Round oaths and drink black gin?)

I grieve for my mother's every tear,
   I weep for the hurt in my mother's breast,
But ever and ever at bud o' year
    I love my father best.

(That I had never been made of this—
The angel's prayer, or the gipsy's kiss!)
                 Gertrude Robison Ross

GRANDSER

My Grandser was a fearsome man!
   He died before I came;
But I have watched my Granny's face
    That withered at his name.

And I have spied the scared gaze
   And lips as white as chalk
Of slender aunts whose dreams he haunts
    With his terrible sailor-talk.

Only my Mother always said
   With wistful looks at me—
"His eyes were blue like the eyes of you,—
    And he ran away to sea!"

Oh, the wild sea-thirst in the blood,
   Her rhythm in the heart!
The mighty urge of the tide's surge,
    The salty sting and smart!

Of course he fled the dull town
    When the magic grew too strong.
A lad will go; (but a lassie, no!
    She has to bide and long).

He sailed thrice over the round world,
    To ports as strange as hell;
A thousand curious things he saw,
    A thousand haps befell.

Till he docked at last in the home port,
    And married a gentle maid
With a land grace and a flower face,
    Whom the sea-wind blew afraid.

Oh, squalls are rough, the combers rough,
    And sailors rough as the sea.
But Grandser was as soft as silk
    To the daughter on his knee;

Growling her talks of serpents, whales,
    And mermaids green as waves;
Of tropical girls festooned with pearls;
    Of palms and coraline caves;

She did not fear the strange oaths,
    Nor the blue fire of his glance,
Nor his callous hand.   She could understand,
    And so can I, by chance!

My Grandser was a fearsome man,
    But a hero to her and me.
If I had a son I know he'd run
    Like a brook away to sea!

Abbie Farwell Brown

GOING UP TO LONDON

    "As I went up to London,"
    I heard a stranger say—
    Going up to London
    In such a casual way!

He turned the magic phrase
That has haunted all my days
As though it were a common thing
For careless lips to say.
As he went up to London!
I'll wager many a crown
He never saw the road that I
Shall take to London town

When I go up to London
'Twill be in April weather.
I'll have a riband on my rein
And flaunt a scarlet feather;
The broom will toss its brush for me;
Two blackbirds and a thrush will be
Assembled in a bush for me
And sing a song together.
And all the blossomy hedgerows
Will shake their hawthorn down
As I go riding, riding
Up to London town.

Halting on a tall hill
Pied with purple flowers,
Twenty turrets I shall count,
And twice as many towers;
Count them on my finger-tip
As I used to do,
And half a hundred spires
Pricking toward the blue.
There will be a glass dome
And a roof of gold,
And a latticed window high
Tilting toward the western sky,
As I knew of old.
London, London,
They counted me a fool—
I could draw your skyline plain
Before I went to school!

Riding, riding downward
By many a silver ridge
And many a slope of amethyst,
I'll come to London Bridge—
London Bridge flung wide for me,
Horses drawn aside for me,
Thames my amber looking-glass
As I proudly pass;
Lords and flunkies, dukes and dames,
Country folk with comely names
Wondering at my steadfast face,
Beggars curtsying,
Footmen falling back a space;—
I would scarcely stay my pace
If I met the King!
If I met the King himself
He'd smile beneath his frown:
"Who is this comes travelling up
So light to London Town?"

Riding, riding eagerly,
Thrusting through the throng,
(Travelling light, Your Majesty,
Because the way was long),
I'll hurry fast to London gate,
(The way was long, and I am late),
I'll come at last to London gate,
Singing me a song—
Some old rhyme of ancient time
When wondrous things befell.
And there the boys and girls at play,
Understanding well,
Quick will hail me, clear and sweet,
Crowding, crowding after;
Every little crooked street
Will echo to their laughter;
Lilting, as they mark my look,
Chanting, two and two,
Dreamed it, dreamed it in a dream
And waked and found it true!

Sing, you rhymes, and ring, you chimes
And swing, you bells of Bow!
When I go up to London
All the world shall know!

Nancy Byrd Turner

REFUGE

I SHALL go down from the stark, gray-stone towers,
Out from this town—the dogs howl at its gates—
The sad clocks strike the eternal hours
And my refuge waits.

I shall go forth with sandals and a crust,
Before the evil, stupid, friendly feet
Have stopped my singing mouth with choking dust,
Stamped from the common street.

For hope has planted vineyards in a place
Of valleys where a heart may lie at ease,
And dreams can dally with a shy, young thought,
Naked among the silver birchen trees.

There Æolus will play a willow harp,
Soft as the autumn light upon a hill,
And dipping swallows leave tight water rings
Which widen with a motion that is still.

Hervey Allen

THE VAGRANT

I WILL leave the dust of the City street and the noise of the
    busy town
For the windy moor and the high hill and the peat-stream
    flowing brown;
I will keep my watch by the camp-fires where the white
    cliffs lean to the sea,
And dawn shall wake me with golden hands and the rain
    shall walk with me.

I will seek the place where gypsies roam and strange, wild
    songs are sung;
I will find once more the magic paths I knew when earth was
    young,
And the stars will give me comradeship and the wind will
    be my friend,
And I will send you the faëry gold that lies at the rainbow's
    end.

Stretch not your hands nor bid me stay, I hear the white
    road's call,
The sun hath kissed the buds from sleep, and I am one
    with them all;
But I will send you a golden cloak and a pair of silver shoon,
And a dream that the fairies spin from stars on the other
    side of the moon.

Pauline Slender

GYPSY–HEART

THE April world is misted with emerald and gold;
    The meadow-larks are calling sweet and keen;
Gypsy-heart is up and off for woodland and for wold,
    Roaming, roaming, roaming through the green.
        Gypsy-heart, away!
       Oh, the wind—the wind and the sun!
    Take the blithe adventure of the fugitive to-day;
       Youth will soon be done.

From buds that May is kissing there trembles forth a soul;
    The rosy boughs are whispering the white;
Gypsy-heart is heedless now of thrush and oriole,
    Dreaming, dreaming, dreaming of delight.
        Gypsy-heart, beware!
       Oh, the song—the song in the blood!
    Magic walks the forest; there's bewitchment on the air.
      Spring is at the flood.

The wings of June are woven of fragrance and of fire;
    Heap roses, crimson roses, for her throne.
Gypsy-heart is anguished with tumultuous desire,
    Seeking, seeking, seeking for its own.

Gypsy-heart, abide!
Oh, the far—the far is the near!
'Tis a foolish fable that the universe is wide.
All the world is here.

Katharine Lee Bates

BEGGARS

You of the painted wagons, folk of the shimmering eye,
What do you stretch your wrinkled hands, wide for the
    passer-by?
You that are rich with your legends, you with your wisdom
    of old,
What do you ask of the west-world, land that has only gold?

You of the moors at nightfall, you of the smoking fire,
What have the dreary town-folk fit for your hearts' desire?
You that have rain for your brother, riding with wind and
    sun,
What would you ask of the west-world, weary and over-
    done?

You with the galloping ponies' clatter and shimmer of hoofs,
What do you stand at our houses, gape at our motionless
    roofs?
Bread you may have, and pennies; but in turn, for a gift
    ere you rise,
Toss me the wind of your homeland, the world-old dream
    in your eyes.

Rhys Carpenter

GORGIO LAD

Gorgio lad, my tribe are waiting.
Here at your garden's gate we part.
The Romany heart with the road is mating,
The caravan's ready to start,
And it's I that must wander, wander, wander.
Gardens a-many with never a wall
Are blossoming back of the skyline yonder.
Gorgio lad, they call!

Strong are your arms, but the wind is stronger.
It blows me out as the dust is blown.
Love as I may, I can stay no longer.
Dreaming at dusk alone
It's I will be sighing, sighing, sighing
Seeing your eyes in the campfire's glow,
But—this is the call there is no denying.
Gorgio lad, I go.

Heart to my heart once more—then let me
Slip from your world as the sunset goes.
Just as a falling star, regret me,
Just as a fading rose,
For it's I must be roving, roving, roving
At the will of the wind between earth and sky.
There are butterfly wings on a gypsy's loving.
Gorgio lad, good-bye.

Amelia Josephine Burr

THE BRIDE

Farewell to Himself
That I left in his sleep,
And God save him kindly
And let him sleep deep;

And more shame to me,
Creeping out like a mouse—
A seven-weeks' bride—
From my husband's house.

But I was born of the eastern world
And I'll never be knit to the western places,
And the hunger's on me, fierce and keen,
For the morning look of the eastern faces;
And oh, my grief, but Himself is queer,
With his cold, soft words and his cold, hard caring!
(It must have been I was daft itself
With the thought of the silks I would be wearing.)

Well there'll be staring to see me home,
And there'll be clack and a nine-days' talking;
But for all the binding book and bell,
This is the road that I must be walking.

And when they will ask him—
"But where is your bride?"
Then he will be weeping
The slow tears of pride.

And when they are prying—
"But where was the blame?"
It's he will be blushing
The thin blush of shame.

But I'm destroyed with a homesick heart,
And the likes of me would best bide single!
I'll step it brisk till the evening damp,
And I'll sleep snug in a deep, soft dingle.
And I'll win back to the eastern world
By a way Himself could never follow;
And I'll be lepping the streams for joy
And lifting a tune by hedge and hollow.
And if they'll look on the morning's morn,
Rising up in the sweet young weather,
Then they'll see me and the darling day
Footing it over the Hill together!

Ruth Comfort Mitchell

THE FIDDLER

DONAL o' Dreams has no bed for his sleeping,
No gold in his keeping, no glove for his hand;
But the birds understand his wild music's leaping
And the children follow his fiddle's command.
He is sib to the winds and the wandering streams
And the stars are the kinsfolk of Donal o' Dreams.

When day goes over the edge of the dark
The grandsires hark to his songs of old,
And on dreams of gold do the lads embark
While the lassies beckon him in from the cold;

But he's heeding no hearth where the firelight gleams
For the voices are calling to Donal o' Dreams.

Playing o' nights by the fairy rings
The brown fiddle swings a dancing song;
Nor right nor wrong in the music sings—
(O, the light feet whirling the leaves along!)
Soulless as moon's light and soft as her beams
Sounds the fairy music of Donal o' Dreams.

Gold cannot stay him nor maidens' sighs—
Stars fleck the skies or the fiddle's croon
Softens the noon on his way that lies
To the East of the Sun and the West of the Moon—
Always in search of that Land he is roaming
And he follows its Gleam from the dawn to the gloaming.

Edna Valentine Trapnell

A SONG OF TWO WANDERERS

DEAR, when I went with you
To where the town ends,
Simple things that Christ loved—
They were our friends;
Tree shade and grass blade
And meadows in flower;
Sun-sparkle, dew-glisten,
Star-glow and shower;
Cool-flowing song at night
Where the river bends,
And the shingle croons a tune—
These were our friends.

Under us the brown earth
Ancient and strong,
The best bed for wanderers
All the night long;
Over us the blue sky
Ancient and dear,
The best roof to shelter all
Glad wanderers here;

And racing between them there
Falls and ascends
The chantey of the clean winds—
These were our friends.

By day on the broad road
Or on the narrow trail,
Angel wings shadowed us,
Glimmering pale
Through the red heat of noon;
In the twilight of dawn
Fairies broke fast with us;
Prophets led us on,
Heroes were kind to us
Day after happy day;
Many white Madonnas
We met on our way—
Farmer and longshoreman,
Fisherman and wife,
Children and laborers
Brave enough for Life,
Simple folk that Christ loved—
They were our friends. . . .

Dear, we must go again
To where the town ends. . . .
                         Marguerite Wilkinson

ROMANY GOLD

THERE's a crackle of brown on the leaf's crisp edge
And the goldenrod blooms have begun to feather.
We're two jolly vagabonds under a hedge
By the dusty road together.

Could an emperor boast such a house as ours,
The sky for a roof and for couch the clover?
Does he sleep as well under silken flowers
As we, when the day is over?

He sits at ease at his table fine
With the richest of meat and drink before him.
I eat my crust with your hand in mine,
And your eyes are cups of a stronger wine
Than any his steward can pour him.

What if the autumn days grow cold?
Under one cloak we can brave the weather.
A comrade's troth is the Romany gold,
And we're taking the road together.

Amelia Josephine Burr

PART IV

FAMILIAR VERSE AND POEMS
HUMOROUS AND SATIRIC

TO PUCK

I HEAR you, little spirit, in the bushes,
  Laughing where the heather blossoms low,
Where the tiny fieldmouse softly pushes
  Nose inquisitive and eyes aglow.
Little sprite of laughter and derision,
  Tender-hearted spirit of good luck,
Pranking through the dream of days Elysian,
    Teach me laughter, Puck!

Puck, you elf, you wisely merry fairy,
  What have you to do with solemn men?
You so foot it, airiest of airy,
  That we only catch you now and then.
Earnest, sombre-browed, we follow after
  You, who fly a-mocking from the ruck;
O we have a desperate need of laughter!
    Give us laughter, Puck!

Beatrice Llewellyn Thomas

THE KINDLY MUSE

THE BIRD IN THE ROOM

A ROBIN skimmed into the room,
  And blithe he looked and jolly,
A foe to every sort of gloom,
  And, most, to melancholy.
He cocked his head, he made no sound,
  But gave me stare for stare back,
When, having fluttered round and round,
  He perched upon a chair-back.

I rose; ah, then, it seemed, he knew
  Too late his reckless error:
Away in eager haste he flew,
  And at his tail flew terror.
Now here, now there, from wall to floor,
  For mere escape appealing,
He fled and struck against the door
  Or bumped about the ceiling.

I went and flung each window wide,
  I drew each half-raised blind up;
To coax him out in vain I tried;
  He could not make his mind up.
He flew, he fell, he took a rest,
  And off again he scuffled
With parted beak and panting breast
  And every feather ruffled.

At length I lured him to the sill,
  All dazed and undivining;
Beyond was peace o'er vale and hill,
  And all the air was shining.

I stretched my hand and touched him; then
   He made no more resistance,
But left the cramped abode of men
   And flew into the distance.

.   .   .   .

Is life like that?   We make it so;
   We leave the sunny spaces,
And beat about, or high or low,
   In dark and narrow places;
Till, worn with failure, vexed with doubt,
   Our strength at last we rally,
And the bruised spirit flutters out
   To find the happy valley.

                     R. C. Lehmann

IN THE CAVES OF AUVERGNE

He carved the red deer and the bull
   Upon the smooth cave rock,
Returned from war, with belly full,
   And scarred with many a knock,
He carved the red deer and the bull
   Upon the smooth cave rock.

The stars flew by the cave's wide door,
   The clouds' wild trumpets blew,
Trees rose in wild dreams from the floor,
   Flowers with dream faces grew
Up to the sky, and softly hung
   Golden and white and blue.

The woman ground her heap of corn,
   Her heart a guarded fire;
The wind played in his trembling soul
   Like a hand upon a lyre,
The wind drew faintly on the stone
   Symbols of his desire:

The red deer of the forests dark,
　Whose antlers cut the sky,
That vanishes into the mirk
　And like a dream flits by,
And by an arrow slain at last
　Is but the wind's dark body.

The bull that stands in marshy lakes
　As motionless and still
As a dark rock jutting from a plain
　Without a tree or hill,
The bull that is the sign of life,
　Its sombre, phallic will.

And from the dead, white eyes of them
　The wind springs up anew,
It blows upon the trembling heart,
　And bull and deer renew
Their flitting life in the dim past
　Which that dead Hunter drew.

I sit beside him in the night,
　And, fingering his red stone,
I chase through endless forests dark
　Seeking that thing unknown,
That which is not red deer or bull,
　But which by them was shown:

By those stiff shapes in which he drew
　His soul's exalted cry,
When flying down the forest dark
　He slew and knew not why,
When he was filled with song, and strength
　Flowed to him from the sky.

The wind blows from red deer and bull,
　The clouds' wild trumpets blare,
Trees rise in wild dreams from the earth,
　Flowers with dream-faces stare—
O Hunter, your own shadow stands
　Within your forest lair!

                              W. J. Turner

TO A ROMAN

I

You died two thousand years ago, Catullus,
    Myriads since then have walked the earth you knew
All their long lives and faded into nothing,
    And still across that waste men think of you.

You loved your Sirmio, and loved your brother,
    You gave a pitiless woman all your heart;
You wrote for her, you mourned a sparrow for her,
    Served like a slave: and suffering made your art.

Some fiery songs, a few soft elegies,
    Perfect—you said you used a pumice-stone:
Coarse little squibs, a rosy song for a wedding,
    What else you did, it never will be known.

A proud young man of fashion, whom a woman
    Played with and dropped: nothing remains beside;
Only we know, about a certain year,
    You went away, out of the glare, and died;

And all your world died after, all the towers
    Fell, and the temples mouldered, and the games
Left the great circus empty, and the dust
    Buried the Cæsars, senators, and dames.

II

I see you lying under marble arches,
    Above the bright blue meadow of a bay,
With certain supercilious gross companions
    Talking their filth more cleverly than they.

Amusing them, one of them, seeming with them:
    They are pleased to find Catullus of their kind;
They sprawl and drink and sneer and jest of wenches,
    Pose to you: but they do not hear your mind.

You share debauch, debauch does not distract you,
    You wine is tasteless, pleasureless your ease;
Behind your brutal talk you are cold and lonely,
    Sick of the laughter of such men as these.

And even they at times perceive you moody,
    Bid you cheer up, are vaguely tired of you,
Damper of pleasure, hypocrite, prig, superior,
    Too cranky and vain to think as others do.

For, suddenly, your answers grow abstracted,
    Empty, or rough; your eyes go over sea,
Watching a distant sail that seems unmoving,
    The symbol of some lost tranquillity;

A silent sail that cuts the clear horizon,
    A warm blue sea, a tranquil, cloudless sky,
You sit and gaze, and, as you stare, they guess you
    Indifferent though the whole of them should die.

III

"The poet should be chaste, his verses——" well,
    It wasn't Lesbia's view, she did her best,
Tempting and spurning, to weary and degrade you,
    To callous you and make you like the rest.

Disliking, piqued by, that strange difference in you,
    Contemptuous and curious, she would dare
And then deny, provoke and then repel you,
    Yet could not make you other than you were.

The soft-pressed foot, the glance that hinted heat,
    The scanty favors always auguring more,
The haughty, cold indifference, mingling twin
    Frigidities of the vestal and the whore

Still could not even more than wound, cloud over,
    The eager boy in you she so despised,
The love of fineness, sweetness, loyalty, candor,
    The innocent country memories you prized.

IV

A flower in a garden grew, Catullus,
  Some time you saw it, and the memory stayed,
One flower of all the flowers you ever glanced at,
  A perfect thing of dew and radiance made:

Emblem of youth, plucked, carried away and drooping,
  Out of the garden; emblem of your lot,
Perplexed, bewildered, languishing, an alien
  Who was born to cherish all his world forgot.

                                        J. C. Squire

IN A COPY OF BROWNING

Browning, old fellow, your leaves grow yellow,
  Beginning to mellow as seasons pass.
Your cover is wrinkled and stained and sprinkled,
  And warped and crinkled from sleep on the grass.

Is it a wine stain or only a pine stain,
  That makes such a fine stain on your dull blue—
Got as we numbered the clouds that lumbered
  Southward and slumbered when day was through?

What is the dear mark there like an earmark?
  Only a tear mark a woman let fall,
As, bending over, she bade me discover,
  "Who *plays* the lover, he loses all!"

With you for teacher, we learned love's feature
  In every creature that roves or grieves;
When winds were brawling, or birds were calling,
  Or leaves were falling about our eaves.

No law must straiten the ways they wait in,
  Whose spirits greaten and hearts aspire.
The world may dwindle, and summer brindle,
  So love but kindle the soul to fire.

Here many a red line, or pencilled headline,
  Shows love could wed line to perfect sense;
And something better than wisdom's fetter
  Has made your letter dense to the dense.

You made us farers and equal sharers
   With homespun-wearers in home-made joys;
You sent the chary Contemporary,
   To make us wary of dust and noise.

Long thoughts were started, when youth departed
   From the half hearted Riccardi's bride;
For, saith your fable, great Love is able
   To slip the cable and take the tide.

When Fate was nagging, and days were dragging,
   And fancy lagging, you gave it scope,
(When eaves were drippy, and pavements slippy,)
   From Lippo Lippi to Evelyn Hope.

When winter's arrow pierced to the marrow,
   And thought was narrow, you gave it room;
We guessed the warder on Roland's border,
   And helped to order the Bishop's Tomb.

When winds were harshish, and ways were marshish,
   We found with Karshish escape at need;
Were bold with Waring in far seafaring,
   And strong in sharing Ben Ezra's creed.

We felt dark menace intrigue and pen us,
   Afloat in Venice, devising fibs;
And little mattered the rain that pattered,
   While Blougram chattered to Gigadibs.

Or truth compels us with Paracelsus,
   Till nothing else is of worth at all.
Del Sarto's vision is our own mission,
   And art's ambition is God's own call.

We two have waited, with heart elated
   And breathing bated, for Pippa's song;—
Seen Satan hover with wings to cover
   Porphyria's lover, Pompilia's wrong.

Through all the seasons, you gave us reasons
   For splendid treasons to doubt and fear;
Bade no foot falter, though weaklings palter,
   And friendships alter from year to year.

Since first I sought you, found you and bought you,
　　Hugged you and brought you home from Cornhill,
While some upbraid you, and some parade you,
　　Nine years have made you my master still.

Bliss Carman

A LIKENESS

(PORTRAIT BUST OF AN UNKNOWN, CAPITOL, ROME)

In every line a supple beauty—
　　The restless head a little bent—
Disgust of pleasure, scorn of duty,
　　The unseeing eyes of discontent.
I often come to sit beside him,
　　This youth who passed and left no trace
Of good or ill that did betide him,
　　Save the disdain upon his face.

The hope of all his House, the brother
　　Adored, the golden-hearted son,
Whom Fortune pampered like a mother;
　　And then—a shadow on the sun.
Whether he followed Cæsar's trumpet,
　　Or chanced the riskier game at home
To find how favor played the strumpet
　　In fickle politics at Rome;

Whether he dreamed a dream in Asia
　　He never could forget by day,
Or gave his youth to some Aspasia,
　　Or gamed his heritage away—
Once lost, across the Empire's border
　　This man would seek his peace in vain;
His look arraigns a social order
　　Somehow entrammelled with his pain.

"The dice of gods are always loaded";
　　One gambler, arrogant as they,
Fierce, and by fierce injustice goaded,
　　Left both his hazard and the play.

Incapable of compromises,
  Unable to forgive or spare,
The strange awarding of the prizes
  He had no fortitude to bear.

Tricked by the forms of things material,—
  The solid-seeming arch and stone;
The noise of war, the pomp Imperial,
  The heights and depths about a throne—
He missed, among the shapes diurnal,
  The old, deep-travelled road from pain,
The thoughts of men, which are eternal,
  In which, eternal, men remain.

Ritratto d'ignoto; defying
  Things unsubstantial as a dream—
An empire, long in ashes lying—
  His face still set against the stream—
Yes, so he looked, that gifted brother
  I loved, who passed and left no trace,
Not even,—luckier than this other—
  His sorrow in a marble face.

                              Willa Cather

AN ITALIAN CHEST

LORENZO DESIGNS A BAS-RELIEF

Lust is the oldest lion of them all,
And he shall have first place;
With a malignant growl satirical
To curve in foliations prodigal
Round and around his face,
Extending till the echoes interlace
With Pride and Prudence, two cranes gaunt and tall.

Four lesser lions crouch and malign the cranes.
Cursing and gossiping, they shake their manes,
While from their long tongues leak
Drops of thin venom as they speak.

The cranes, unmoved, peck grapes and grains
From a huge cornucopia, which rains
A plenteous meal from its antique
Interior—a note quite curiously Greek.

And nine long serpents twist
And twine, twist and twine—
A riotously beautiful design
Whose elements consist
Of eloquent spirals, fair and fine,
Embracing cranes and lions, who exist
Seemingly free, yet tangled in that living vine.

And in this chest shall be
Two cubic meters of space—
Enough to hold all memory
Of you and me. . . .
And this shall be the place
Where silence shall embrace
Our bodies, and obliterate the trace
Our souls made on the purity
Of night. . . .
            Now lock the chest, for we
Are dead, and lose the key!

Marjorie Allen Seiffert

CASTILIAN

Velasquez took a pliant knife
And scraped his palette clean;
He said, "I lead a dog's own life
Painting a king and queen."

He cleaned his palette with oily rags
And oakum from Seville wharves;
"I am sick of painting painted hags
And bad ambiguous dwarves.

"The sky is silver, the clouds are pearl,
Their locks are looped with rain.
I will not paint Maria's girl
For all the money in Spain."

He washed his face in water cold,
His hands in turpentine;
He squeezed out color like coins of gold
And color like drops of wine.

Each color lay like a little pool
On the polished cedar wood;
Clear and pale and ivory-cool
Or dark as solitude.

He burnt the rags in the fireplace
And leaned from the window high;
He said, "I like that gentleman's face
Who wears his cap awry."

This is the gentleman, there he stands,
Castilian, sombre-caped,
With arrogant eyes, and narrow hands
Miraculously shaped.

Elinor Wylie

MONSEIGNEUR PLAYS

MONSEIGNEUR plays his new gavotte—
    Within her gilded chair the Queen
    Listens, her rustling maids between;
        A very tulip-garden stirred
        To hear the fluting of a bird;
    Faint sunlight on the casement falls
    On cupids painted on the walls
        At play with doves.   Precisely set
        Awaits the slender legged spinet
    Expectant of its happy lot,
        The while the player stays to twist
        The cobweb ruffle from his wrist.
A pause, and then—(Ah, whisper not)
Monseigneur plays his new gavotte.

Monseigneur plays his new gavotte—
    Hark, 'tis the faintest dawn of Spring,
    So still the dew drops whispering
        Is loud upon the violets;
        Here in this garden of Pierette's

Where Pierrot waits, ah, hasten, Sweet,
And hear; on dainty, tripping feet
　　She comes—the little, glad coquette.
　　"Ah thou, Pierrot?"　"Ah thou, Pierrette?"
A kiss, nay, hear—a bird wakes, then
A silence—and they kiss again,
"Ah, Mesdames, have you quite forgot—"
　　(So laughs his music) "Love's first kiss?
　　Let this note lead you then, and this
Back to that fragrant garden-spot."
Monseigneur plays his new gavotte.

Monseigneur plays his new gavotte—
　　Ah, hear—in that last note they go
　　The little lovers laughing so;
　　　　Kissing their finger-tips, they dance
　　　　From out this gilded room of France.
Adieu!　Monseigneur rises now
Ready for compliment and bow,
　　Playing about his mouth the while
　　Its cynical, accustomed smile,
Protests and, hand on heart, avers
The patience of his listeners.
"A masterpiece?　Ah, surely not."
　　A gray-eyed maid of honor slips
　　A long-stemmed rose across her lips
And drops it; does he guess her thought?
Monseigneur plays his new gavotte.
　　　　　　　　　　　Theodosia Garrison

FRENCH CLOCK

TIME is a heavy legend to be told
By this slight clock, shapely and full of guile,
With brilliants at its throat, the sun in gold,
Louis' own seal—above its painted smile.
Some clocks have souls; they grow into a wall,
Become a part of lives they tick away,
This is a toy, perfect, sufficient all
Unto itself—a butterfly at bay!

Hours and years? They change but do not pass.
In this light world of gold and ormolu,
Time is one splendid moment under glass!
Mad little clock! So gay it never knew
Blood on the hours—a lifted pike—a head—
And hot throats roaring that the King is dead!

Hortense Flexner

THE ROMNEY

THEY lived alone
Under the portraits of their ancestors—
Two elderly spinsters slowly graying away.
They cooked thin little meals,
And ate them on Lowestoft china
At the banquet-table no longer served by slaves.
Year by year
Their shadowy income dwindled.

One portrait was a Romney—
Two brave young lads in velvet.
A London dealer heard of it and came over,
And politely, insinuatingly, asked to see.
Reluctantly they showed the stranger in.

Twenty thousand dollars he offered,
Sure of the prize—
Were they not visibly starving, these ladies,
In the ashes of grandeur?

The sisters stirred a little
In pained surprise.
"You quite mistake us," the elder said;
"We cannot sell our family portraits."
And the dealer, in pained surprise,
Bowed himself out.

A few days later came a letter
Offering thirty thousand.
But the dealer waited in vain for an answer.

Then forty thousand.

A young nephew,
Blowing in from the U. of S. C.,
Was paying a duty call on his aunts.
"By the Lord, I'd take it!" he said.

The ladies shrank like gray moths frosted,
And the elder said:
"Great-aunt Millicent, whose name I bear,
Left the picture to Father.
They were stepsons of old Simeon Hugea,
Her grandfather—
His wife had been the widow of an Italian."

"Yes, and so not of our line—
They don't belong here."

The younger sister turned her eyes inward:
"Old Simeon could make nothing of those boys.
He gave them the grand tour
And ordered this portrait,
And they never came back—
Took to fiddling and painting like their father.
Millicent, do you think—"

"I am in doubt," said the elder sister;
"They were collateral."

So a family council gathered in the ashen-coated drawing-
          room
And argued acrimoniously.
And it was decided that the half-Italian collaterals,
Who were not of the blood,
Might well be sold and forgotten.
And the deal was closed.

"It is a great deal of money," said the elder sister,
"But I am not quite sure—"

And the younger,
"Who was this Romney?"

                              Harriet Monroe

ST. SWITHIN

"Bury me," the bishop said,
"Close to my geranium bed;
Lay me near the gentle birch.
It is lonely in the church,
And its vaults are damp and chill!
Noble men sleep there, but still
House me in the friendly grass!
Let the linnets sing my mass!"

Dying Swithin had his whim
And the green sod covered him.

Then what holy celebrations
And what rapturous adorations,
Joy no worldly pen may paint—
Swithin had been made a saint!
Yet the monks forgot that he
Craved for blossom, bird and bee,
And, communing round his tomb,
Vowed its narrow earthen room
Was unworthy one whose star
Shone in Peter's calendar.
"Who," they asked, "when we are gone
Will protect this sacred lawn?
What if time's irreverent gust
Should disperse his holy dust?"
Troubled by a blackbird's whistle,
Vexed by an invading thistle,
They resolved to move his bones
To the chaste cathedral stones.

But the clouds grew black and thick
When they lifted spade and pick,
And they feared that they had blundered
By the way it poured and thundered.
Quoth the abbot: "Thus, I deem,
Swithin shows us we blaspheme!
He was fond of wind and rain;
Let him in their clasp remain!"

Forty days the heavens wept,
But St. Swithin smiled and slept.

Daniel Henderson

THE COBBLER IN WILLOW STREET

UNLESS you knew just where to look
You couldn't find it out of a book,—
Willow Street . . . close-walled and still,
Short and shadowed in every nook
And hour as day goes up the hill.

The dark shapes slant to west at nine
And creep at one up to a line
Measuring eastern walls again,
And close the gloried morning vine
That they have touched enough to stain.

The cobbler's house is half the height
The pigeons measure in a flight
From bottom of the hill to top . . .
And where his one doorstep is white
The cobbler sings and keeps his shop.

Mornings, he makes a bluebird tune
For dreams and things that go too soon,
And in a song he's half forgot
Of Willow Street, in afternoon,
He sings of people who are not . . .

Of people who no longer care
About the houses in the square
Above the street and at its end,
Or do not see the willow bare
When rain drips from the boughs and bend.

He hums his quiet song about
The houses with their shutters out
Or folded in . . . of men who talked
Of plans and faith and hope and doubt,
And those that whispered while they walked . . .

Where houses kneel around the church
The pigeons flutter from their perch
Down to the narrow spotless street
To strut and stand and flash and lurch,
Crowding about the cobbler's feet.

Some day the cobbler's sound will beat—
When evening threnody is sweet
With old bells shaking sprays of chime—
A song of us and Willow Street,
Tapping a heel all out of time. . . .

George O'Neil

HANSOM CABBIES

WHEN I was a lad there were hansoms in London,
    With drivers on top of a little back stair
And horses that ran under silver-tipt harness
    Or stood by the curb-stone awaiting a fare,
    And tossed in the air
        Their nose-bags of corn for the sparrows to share.

And sometimes in Spring when the nose-bags were leaking,
    And sparrows were loud amid loot of spilt corn,
Old Cabby reached over the slender Park railings
    And stole a rosette of the double red thorn
    His mare to adorn,
        With "Fares may be few, but we won't be forlorn."

The spokes they were pointed with red and with yellow;
    The brass was like gold where the reins threaded through;
There was sometimes a crest on the old leather blinkers,
    A crown on the horse-cloth of crimson and blue
    That said "It's for you
        We're waiting, my Lord, and a crown is our due."

Now where are they gone to, the weather-worn cabbies
    That drove us alertly through all the dense shoals
That filled the strait Fleet from St. Paul's to St. Martin's,
    Or over the bridge where big Benjamin tolls?
    O! somewhere their souls
        Still murmur "Where to, Sir?" through tiny peep-holes.

Elysian fields show them pasturing fillies
   Sure-footed and shapely—just built for a yoke;
They comb their silk manes and they wheedle and drive
      them
   Down roads without mud where the fogs never choke,
   And rain's a rare joke
     To cheerful night-watchmen with cressets of coke.

The fares that they find there are born in the purple;
   Their talk is of Dizzy and Toole and Bend Or;
Their manners are suave and their tips are all golden;
   They dwell between Mayfair and Kensington Gore;
   And flunkeys galore
     Poll-powdered, receive them at Paradise door.

Wilfrid Thorley

HOW TO CATCH UNICORNS

ITS cloven hoofprint on the sand
Will lead you—where?
Into a phantasmagoric land—
Beware!

There all the bright streams run up-hill.
The birds on every tree are still.
But from stocks and stones clear voices come
That should be dumb.

If you have taken along a net,
A noose, a prod,
You'll be waiting in the forest yet . . .
Nid—nod!

In a virgin's lap the beast slept sound,
They say . . . but I—
I think (is anyone around?)
That's just a lie!

If you have taken a musketoon
To flinders 'twill flash 'neath the wizard moon.

So *I* should take browned batter-cake,
Hot-buttered inside, like foam to flake.

And I should take an easy heart
And a whimsical face,
And a tied-up lunch of sandwich and tart,
And spread a cloth in the open chase.

And then I should pretend to snore.
And I'd hear a snort, and I'd hear a roar,
The wind of a mane and a tail, and four
Wild hoofs prancing the forest-floor.

And I'd open my eyes on a flashing horn—
And see the Unicorn!

Paladins fierce and virgins sweet . . .
But he's never had anything to eat!
Knights have tramped in their iron-mong'ry . . .
But nobody thought—that's all!—*he's hungry!*

ADDENDUM

Really hungry! Good Lord, deliver us,
The Unicorn is not *carnivorous!*

William Rose Benét

STAR–TALK

"ARE you awake, Gemelli,
    This frosty night?"
"We'll be awake till reveillé,
Which is Sunrise," say the Gemelli,
"It's no good trying to go to sleep:
If there's wine to be got we'll drink it deep,
    But rest is hopeless to-night,
    But rest is hopeless to-night."

"Are you cold too, poor Pleiads,
    This frosty night?"
"Yes, and so are the Hyads:
See us cuddle and hug," say the Pleiads,

"All six in a ring: it keeps us warm:
We huddle together like birds in a storm:
    It's bitter weather to-night,
    It's bitter weather to-night."

"What do you hunt, Orion,
    This starry night?"
"The Ram, the Bull and the Lion,
And the Great Bear," says Orion,
"With my starry quiver and beautiful belt
I am trying to find a good thick pelt
    To warm my shoulders to-night,
    To warm my shoulders to-night."

"Did you hear that, Great She-bear,
    This frosty night?"
"Yes, he's talking of stripping *me* bare,
Of my own big fur," says the She-bear.
"I'm afraid of the man and his terrible arrow:
The thought of it chills my bones to the marrow,
    And the frost so cruel to-night!
    And the frost so cruel to-night!"

"How is your trade, Aquarius,
    This frosty night?"
"Complaints is many and various,
And my feet are cold," says Aquarius,
"There's Venus objects to Dolphin-scales,
And Mars to Crab-spawn found in my pails,
    And the pump has frozen to-night,
    And the pump has frozen to-night."

Robert Graves

DOROTHEA

Young is she, and slight to view
    In her home-made cambric dresses:
Are her sweet eyes gray or blue?
    Shade of twilight are her tresses.
Fairy-fine at first she seems;
    But a longer look confesses
She's more wholesome stuff than dreams!

(Yet I mind an April moon
   Shining down an orchard alley:
From one book, companions boon,
   There we read "Love in the Valley";
And I saw bright phantoms race,
   Thousand phantoms fleet and rally
All across her lighted face.)

Once, within that ancient ground
   Where her fathers all lie sleeping,
She, beside a recent mound,
   Still and tender, but not weeping,
Stood: that picture on my heart
   Fair am I forever keeping:
With that look I would not part.

O but in her maiden days
   How she led the children trooping
Through the old familiar plays!
   Up her sash and flounces looping,
If the tiniest lost his cue,
   To his side she ran and stooping,
Caught his hand and danced him through.

Met you her in Hemlock Wood
   In the white midwinter weather,
When the pine's a tufted hood,
   And the fern's a crystal feather?
Heard you then her yodel sweet
   And a far reply, together
Float in echo where they meet?

Ariel voice, from range to range
   Lightly tossed and sweetly flying!
All her notes to murmurs change
   When the winter light is dying:
All in magic murmurs she
   Laps and lulls the wee one lying,
Pearl of twilight, on her knee.

Sarah N. Cleghorn

ELIZABETH

SHE has the strange sweet grace of violets
That stand in slender vases in the dusk
When fire-flies weave their unseen fairy nets
About an unreal world of rose and musk.
She has the glad young smile that poppies wear
In quiet gardens when the day comes in
With dewy cobwebs tangled in her hair
And laughing eyes that bid the dance begin!
Her path's a trail of beauty down the years,
And where she steps the dust is touched with flame;
A genius, as of hills when night appears,
Clings to her from the silence whence she came.
She passes me, and there remains behind
A sense of flowers drifting down the wind.

George Brandon Saul

SILENCE

SHE was a quiet little body
    In a quaint silk shawl,
Who sat and sewed and listened,
    But hardly spoke at all.

She let her copper kettle
    And her bright-as-copper fire,
Wag like tongues and hum like voices
    In a cozy little choir.

She was quieter with others
    Than they could be alone,
But the flashing of her fingers
    Was a wit all its own.

And while we talked her needle
    Like a swift dragon fly,
Was sewing seeds of summer
    Into squares as blue as sky.

I have taken tea from many,
    And talk from many more,
But a blue bag of lavender
    I never had before
Or since from any woman
    When I left her at her door.

Now that her fire, her kettle,
    And herself are still,
Hearths seem merely hissing,
    Spouts only shrill.

So I never stop from talking,
    So I always keep astir—
I would be afraid of silence
    That was not a gift from her
In shiny bits like ribbons,
    Sweet, like lavender.

                        Winifred Welles

IN AN OLD NURSERY

A PRIM old room where memories stir
Through faded chintz and wall-paper,
Like bees along the lavender
    Of some dim border;
Bay-windowed, whence at close of day
You see the roosty starlings sway
High on the elm-tree's topmost spray
    In gossip order.

In its quaint realm how soon one slips
Back to the edge of treasure-ships,
The atmosphere of cowboy-trips
    And boundless prairies;
And when the red logs fret and fume
(They're lit to-night to air the room)
Here come a tip-toe in the gloom
    Old nursery fairies.

Here come dear ghosts to him who sees—
Fat ghosts of long digested teas,
Thin little ghosts of "saying please,"
     Big ghosts of birthdays,
And sundry honorable sprites
To whisper those foredone delights
Of hallowe'ens and stocking-nights
     And other mirth-days.

Its walls are full of musics drawn
From twitterings in the eaves at dawn,
From swish of scythe on summer lawn,
     From Shetlands pawing
The gravel by the front-door yew,
And, wind-tossed from the avenue,
Fugues of first February blue
     And rooks a-cawing.

Old room, the years have galloped on,
The days that danced, the hours that shone
Have turned their backs on you and gone
     By ways that harden;
But you—in you their gold and myrrh
And frankincense of dreams still stir
Like bees that haunt the lavender
     Of some walled garden!

                              Patrick R. Chalmers

EPITAPHIUM CITHARISTRIÆ

Stand not uttering sedately
     Trite oblivious praise above her!
Rather say you saw her lately
     Lightly kissing her last lover.

Whisper not "There is a reason
     Why we bring her no white blossom:"
Since the snowy bloom's in season,
     Strow it on her sleeping bosom:

Oh, for it would be a pity
    To o'erpraise her or to flout her:
She was wild, and sweet, and witty—
    Let's not say dull things about her.

Victor Plarr

LAVENDER'S FOR LADIES

LAVENDER'S for ladies, an' they grows it in the garden;
Lavender's for ladies, an' it's sweet an' dry an' blue;
But the swallows leave the steeple an' the skies begin to
        harden,
For now's the time o' lavender, an' now's the time o' rue!

"Lavender, lavender, buy my sweet lavender,"
All down the street an old woman will cry;
        But when she trundles
        The sweet-smellin' bundles,
When she calls lavender—swallows must fly!

Lavender's for ladies (Heaven love their pretty faces);
Lavender's for ladies, they can sniff it at their ease,
An' they puts it on their counterpins an' on their pillow-
        cases,
An' dreams about their true-loves an' o' ships that cross
        the seas!

"Lavender, lavender, buy my sweet lavender,"
Thus the old woman will quaver an' call
        All through the city—
        It's blue an' it's pretty,
But brown's on the beech-tree an' mist over all!

Lavender's for ladies, so they puts it in their presses;
Lavender's for ladies, Joan an' Mary, Jill and Jane;
So they lays it in their muslins an' their lawny Sunday
        dresses,
An' keeps 'em fresh as April till their loves come 'ome again!

"Lavender, lavender, buy my sweet lavender,"
Still the old woman will wheeze and will cry.

Give 'er a copper
An' p'r'aps it will stop 'er,
For when she calls lavender summer must die!

Patrick R. Chalmers

EARLY MORNING MEADOW SONG

Now some may drink old vintage wine
    To ladies gowned with rustling silk,
But we will drink to dairymaids,
    And drink to them in rum and milk—
O, it's up in the morning early,
    When the dew is on the grass,
And St. John's bell rings for matins,
    And St. Mary's rings for mass!

The merry skylarks soar and sing,
    And seem to Heaven very near—
Who knows what blessed inns they see,
    What holy drinking songs they hear?
O, it's up in the morning early,
    When the dew is on the grass,
And St. John's bell rings for matins,
    And St. Mary's rings for mass!

The mushrooms may be priceless pearls
    A queen has lost beside the stream;
But rum is melted rubies when
    It turns the milk to golden cream!
O, it's up in the morning early,
    When the dew is on the grass,
And St. John's bell rings for matins,
    And St. Mary's rings for mass!

Charles Dalmon

THE MAY DAY GARLAND

THOUGH folks no more go Maying
    Upon the dancing-green
With ale and cakes and music loud
    To crown the fairest queen,

Yet little ones to each gate go
  Before the clock tells noon,
And there the prettiest garlands show
  That e'er Love smiled upon.

Their garlands are of peagles
  That flaunt their yellow heads
By dykesides where the pigeon broods
  And the nuzzling hedgehog beds—
Their ladysmocks shall nod in the sun
  And kingcups scent like mead,
And blue bell's misty flame be spun
  With daisies' glittering brede.

And one will make her garland
  A crown for such a day,
And one a harp, and one a heart
  (Lest hers be stolen away);
Cart-wheels never meant to turn
  And chip-hats never worn
And petal-tambourines shall earn
  A largess this May morn.

And for these little children
  And my love like a child,
The May should never fade to-night
  Could Time but be beguiled,
Could Time but see the beauty of
  These singing honied hours,
And lie in the sun adream while we
  Hid up his scythe in flowers!

Edmund Blunden

A WOODLAND REVEL

HITHER, Strephon, Chloe, Phyllis,
Corydon and Amaryllis;
Hasten, Lubin and Lysander,
Daphne, Colin, and Sylvander;
Come, Jocunda, Delia, Doris,
Let us dance the merry morris;

Play up, pipers! Bee and cricket,
All ye minstrels of the thicket,
Tune up, strike up to the measure
Of the golden wand of pleasure;
Dance, ye rustics, swain and yokel,
Making all the greenwood vocal,
Filling joy's glad cup completely,
As we sing and foot it featly.

Now what dear delight to wander
While our hearts grow fond and fonder,
Breathing incense, balm, and spices,
Gazing on the fair devices
Arabesqued by shade and shimmer
Through the tree-tops, dim and dimmer;
Up the hill and down the hollow,
Through the paths deer love to follow,
With a bubbling spring for ending
Under redwood boughs low-bending;
Filling fardels with pomander
Of the wildwood oleander;
Laurel-wreaths our brows entwining,
Love-light in our eyes soft shining!

Shepherds, rest! Ye shepherdesses,
Here are crispy water-cresses,
Ripe-red berries sunlight-basking,
To be had without the asking;
And in high and dim seclusion
Hazel-nuts in rare profusion;
Nectar from a fairy fountain
Hidden in a misty mountain,
Spread in wondrous rich libation
For our ease and delectation.
See, the shadows deeply darting
Bid us sing a song of parting;
Hey for home! Lo, for our guiding,
Hesper in the dusk abiding!

Clarence Urmy

THE BRIDE

THE book was dull, its pictures
As leaden as its lore,
But one glad, happy picture
Made up for all and more;
'Twas that of you, sweet peasant,
Beside your grannie's door—
I never stopped so startled
Inside a book before.

Just so had I sat spell-bound,
Quite still with staring eyes,
If some great shiny hoopoe
Or moth of song-bird size
Had drifted to my window
And trailed its fineries—
Just so had I been startled,
Spelled with the same surprise.

It pictured you when springtime
In part had given place
But not surrendered wholly
To summer in your face;
When still your slender body
Was all a childish grace,
Though woman's richest glories
Were building there apace.

'Twas blissful so to see you,
Yet not without a sigh
I dwelt upon the people
Who saw you not as I,
But in your living sweetness,
Beneath your native sky;
Ah, bliss to be the people
When you went tripping by!

I sat there, thinking, wondering,
About your life and home,

The happy days behind you,
The happy days to come,
Your grannie in her corner,
Upstairs the little room
Where you wake up each morning
To dream all day—of Whom?

That ring upon your finger,
Who gave you that to wear?
What blushing smith or farm lad
Came stammering at your ear
A million-time-told story
No maid but burns to hear
And went about his labors
Delighting in his dear!

I thought of you sweet lovers,
The things you say and do,
The pouts and tears and partings
And swearings to be true,
The kissings in the barley—
You brazens, both of you!
I nearly burst out crying
With thinking of you two.

It put me in a frenzy
Of pleasure nearly pain,
A host of blurry faces
'Gan shaping in my brain,
I shut my eyes to see them
Come forward clear and plain;
I saw them come full flower,
And blur and fade again.

One moment so I saw them,
One sovereign moment so,
A host of girlish faces
All happy and aglow
With Life and Love it dealt them
Before it laid them low,

A hundred years, a thousand,
Ten thousand years ago.

One moment so I saw them
Come back with time full tide,
The host of girls, your grannies,
Who lived and loved and died
To give your mouth its beauty,
Your soul its gentle pride,
Who wrestled with the ages
To give the world a bride.

Ralph Hodgson

THE BARCAROLE OF JAMES SMITH

WITH willing arms I row and row
So dear a freight that I must know
The moment is the point of time
When James Smith changes, grows sublime,
And hurries to the flaming tryst
Of Love, that ancient alchemist,
And grows into his thoughts and comes
To half awaked millenniums.

I could imagine madrigals
With curiously dying falls
To creep into your little ears
And lift you with me through the years.
But you would barely understand
Why you were lifted, long for land,
And tell me to row back again
From heaven to the Vast Inane.

Meanwhile I sit and row the boat
And catch your laughter, watch your throat
And mouth sway perilously near
And burn away the atmosphere.
The sunset shakes me almost free
From river, boat and lunacy.
You say it's rather like a fish
Of crimson on a golden dish?

It may be so. It may be I
Have other thoughts that signify
A closer meaning for us two. . . .
But I must row and what's to do?
If you could see yourself and be
The rower, look through eyes of me
Not knowing what was hid inside
Your little head—but that's denied.

You'll be the freight until the end:
I'll be the rower—and the friend.
And you will never know the thought
That makes you curiously wrought
In other substance than you are:
And I will steer by some vague star
That is not even lit for you,
And I daresay the star will do.

If I were not James Smith but one
Not haunted by the desert sun
Of too excessive visioning
Perhaps you'd be a different thing
And quite unusual, but that
At most is but conjectured at. . . .
So willingly I row and row
And let you wonder while I know.

Herbert S. Gorman

THE TRUE ROMANCE

ALL that I know of you is that you wore
    A light blue dress.
Your age fifteen, perhaps a little more
    (This is a guess).

I found you on a forest road, in pain,
    And rescued you;
And felt like Galahad, and thought, "It's plain,
    Romance is true."

And meant to read, while yet my heart was stout,
   The Faerie Queen,
To see if Spenser knew so much about
   A rescue-scene.

I doubt if any of the knights who won
   Their spurs that way,
Found in the doing even half the fun
   I did, that day—

Because, not being rigidly encased
   In frigid steel,
The arms that carried you, however chaste,
   Your charm could feel.

And I have left the Faerie Queen unread,
   For it appears
Far better to remember, in her stead,
   Your fifteen years.

Herbert Jones

WESTLAND ROW

EVERY Sunday there's a throng
Of pretty girls, who trot along
In a pious, breathless state
(They are nearly always late)
To the Chapel, where they pray
For the sins of Saturday.

They have frocks of white and blue,
Yellow sashes they have too,
And red ribbons show each head
Tenderly is ringleted;
And the bell rings loud, and the
Railway whistles urgently.

After Chapel they will go,
Walking delicately slow,

Telling still how Father John
Is so good to look upon,
And such other grave affairs
As they thought of during prayers.

James Stephens

STORY OF THE FLOWERY KINGDOM

"La belle Sou-Chong-Thé, au claire de pleine Lune."—PAUL VERVILLE

FAIR Sou-Chong-Tee, by a shimmering brook
Where ghost-like lilies loomed tall and straight,
Met young Too-Hi, in a moonlit nook,
Where they cooed and kissed till the hour was late:
Then, with lanterns, a mandarin passed in state,
Named Hoo-Hung-Hoo of the Golden Band,
Who had wooed the maiden to be *his* mate,—
For these things occur in the Flowery Land.

Now, Hoo-hung-Hoo had written a book,
In seven volumes, to celebrate
The death of the Emperor's thirteenth cook:
So, being a person whose power was great,
He ordered a herald to indicate
He would blind Too-Hi with a red-hot brand
And marry Sou-Chong at a quarter-past eight,—
For these things occur in the Flowery Land.

Whilst the brand was heating, the lovers shook
In their several shoes,—when by lucky fate
A Dragon came, with his tail in a crook,—
A Dragon out of a Nankeen Plate,—
And gobbled the hard-hearted potentate
And all of his servants, and snorted, *and*
Passed on at a super-cyclonic rate,—
For these things occur in the Flowery Land.

The lovers were wed at an early date,
And lived for the future, I understand,
In one continuous tête-à-tête,—
For these things occur . . . in the Flowery Land.

James Branch Cabell

LADY GODIVA

(A third version)

If the truth were but known, when she came at last
To the bower's low door and the journey was past,
Godiva slid from her palfrey and said:
Only one with a curious eye in his head?

For why had she gone with not even a shift
Through the still gray streets, where her hair's gold drift
On shoulder and breast and side made one
With the bright veil cast on her by the sun?

O surely it had been braver, and sweet,
To have lavished her beauty along the street,
To have ridden in the eyes and the smiles of the crowd
And to have heard their praises, muttered or loud.

For else her ride was only a ride,
Nothing done, nothing given, nothing beside,
No shame, no sacrifice made, no pain,
But a fresh, cool journey and home again.

She frowned as she stood up bare in her bower,
White as a pearl and fresh as a flower,
Then smiled as she thought that there had been one
And that Peeping Tom was better than none.

Edward Shanks

AT THE LAVENDER LANTERN

I wonder who is haunting the little snug café,
That place, half restaurant and home, since we have gone
        away;
The candled dimness, smoke and talk, and tables brown
        and bare—
But no one thinks of tablecloths when love and laughter's
        there.

I wonder if it's crowded still, three steps below the street,
Half hidden from the passing town, where even poets eat;
I wonder if the girls still laugh, the girls whose art was
 play,
I wonder who the fellows are that try to make them gay.

Some said it was Bohemia, this little haunt we knew,
Where hearts were high and fortunes low, and onions in
 . the stew,
I wonder if it's still the same, the after dinner ease—
Bohemia is in the heart, and hearts are overseas.

Oh, great were all the problems that we settled there, with
 wine,
And fates of many nations were disposed of, after nine,
But France has braved a fate that brought us swarming
 to her shore—
I wonder who is sitting at the table near the door.

I wonder who is haunting the little snug café,
That place, half restaurant and home, since we have gone
 away;
I wonder if they miss me, I don't suppose they do,
As long as there are art and girls, and onions in the stew.

Charles Divine

THE GREEN ESTAMINET

The old men sit by the chimney-piece and drink the good
 red wine
And tell great tales of the *soixante-dix* to the men from
 the English line,
And Madame sits in her old armchair and sighs to herself
 all day—
So Madeleine serves the soldiers in the Green Estaminet.

For Madame wishes the war was won and speaks of a strange
 disease,
And Pierre is somewhere about Verdun, and Albert on the
 seas;
Le Patron, 'e is *soldat*, too, but long time *prisonnier*—
So Madeleine serves the soldiers in the Green Estaminet.

She creeps downstairs when the black dawn scowls and
helps at a neighbor's plow,
She rakes the midden and feeds the fowls and milks the
lonely cow,
She mends the holes in the *Padre's* clothes and keeps his
billet gay—
And she also serves the soldiers in the Green Estaminet.

The smoke grows thick and the wine flows free and the
great round songs begin,
And Madeleine sings in her heart, maybe, and welcomes the
whole world in;
But I know that life is a hard, hard thing, and I know that
her lips look gray,
*Though she smiles as she serves the soldiers in the Green Es-
taminet.*

But many a tired young English lad has learned his lesson
there,
To smile and sing when the world looks bad, for, "*Mon-
sieur, c'est la guerre;*"
Has drunk her honor and made his vow to fight in the same
good way
That Madeleine serves the soldiers in the Green Estaminet.

A big shell came on a windy night and half of the old house
went,
But half of the old house stands upright, and Mademoiselle's
content;
The shells still fall in the Square sometimes, but Madeleine
means to stay,
So Madeleine serves the soldiers still in the Green Estaminet.

A. P. Herbert

BLONDEL

WITHIN my heart I long have kept
A little chamber cleanly swept,
Embroidered with a *fleur-de-lis,*
And lintel boughs of redwood tree;
A bed, a book, a crucifix,
Two little copper candlesticks

With tapers ready for the match
The moment I his footfall catch,
That when in thought he comes to me
He straightway at his ease may be.
This guest I love so to allure—
Blondel, King Richard's troubadour!

He often comes, but sings no more
(He says his singing days are o'er!);
Still, sweet of tongue and filled with tales
Of knights and ladies, bowers and vales,
He caps our frugal meal with talk
Of *langue d'oïl* and *langue d'oc*,
Of Picardy and Aquitaine,
Blanche of Castile and Charlemagne,
Of *ménestrel, trouvère, conteur,*
Mime, histrion, and old *harpeur*—
Small wonder that I love him well,
King Richard's troubadour, Blondel!

Still, as he comes at candle-light
And goes before the east is bright,
I have no heart to beg him keep
Late hour with me when wooed by sleep;
But one request I ever make,
And ever no for answer take:
He will not make the secret mine,
What song he sang at Dürrenstein!
Sleep, troubadour! Enough that thou
With that sweet lay didst keep thy vow
And link thy name by deathless art
With Richard of the Lion Heart!

Clarence Urmy

I WEAR A CRIMSON CLOAK TO-NIGHT

I WEAR a crimson cloak to-night,
    Villon, Villon, look down and see
    I wander insolent and free,
Free as the wind in Montfaucon—

And is thy droll ghost there, Villon,
Thy spirit as my flesh bedight?
   Ah, would I might lock arms with thee,
I wear a crimson cloak to-night.

Marlowe, in doublet slashed with gold,
   Insouciant as a drunken star,
   Surely no Lethean mandates bar
This life from death, as dark from light?
I wear a crimson cloak to-night,
Bold is my heart, my trappings bold—
   Thy rich, bright laugh I hear afar,
Marlowe, in doublet slashed with gold.

I wear a crimson cloak to-night,
   Dowson, Baudelaire, Verlaine!
   I, too, have seen Octobers wane
And watched decadent Love pass by
With naked feet and drooping eye,
With throat of laughter, lips of light
   Trembling to hear thy songs again,
I wear a crimson cloak to-night.

The fainting moon is wan and white,
   Our silken courtesan, the moon—
   Ah, brothers, hast thou watched her swoon?
Over the stars ye lean to tell:
Death is an endless villanelle
That Life frees poet-hands to write . . .
   I'll join thy vagabondia soon,
   I wear the crimson cloak to-night!

Lois Seyster Montross

A BALLADE–CATALOGUE OF LOVELY THINGS

I WOULD make a list against the evil days
   Of lovely things to hold in memory:
First, I set down my lady's lovely face,
   For earth has no such lovely thing as she;

And next I add, to bear her company,
The great-eyed virgin star that morning brings;
  Then the wild-rose upon its little tree—
So runs my catalogue of lovely things.

The enchanted dog-wood, with its ivory trays,
  The water-lily in its sanctuary
Of reeded pools, and dew-drenched lilac sprays,
  For these, of all fair flowers, the fairest be;
  Next write I down the great name of the sea,
Lonely in greatness as the names of kings;
  Then the young moon that hath us all in fee—
So runs my catalogue of lovely things.

Imperial sunsets that in crimson blaze
  Along the hills, and, fairer still to me,
The fireflies dancing in a netted maze
  Woven of twilight and tranquillity;
  Shakespeare and Virgil, their high poesy;
Then a great ship, splendid with snowy wings,
  Voyaging on into eternity—
So runs my catalogue of lovely things.

ENVOI

Prince, not the gold bars of thy treasury,
  Not all thy jewelled sceptres, crowns and rings,
Are worth the honeycomb of the wild bee—
  So runs my catalogue of lovely things.

Richard Le Gallienne

BALLADE OF THE DREAMLAND ROSE

WHERE the waves of burning cloud are rolled
  On the further shore of the sunset sea,
In a land of wonder that none behold,
  There blooms a rose on the Dreamland Tree
That stands in the Garden of Mystery
  Where the River of Slumber softly flows;
And whenever a dream has come to be,
  A petal falls from the Dreamland Rose.

In the heart of the tree, on a branch of gold,
  A silvern bird sings endlessly
A mystic song that is ages old,
  A mournful song in a minor key,
Full of the glamor of faëry;
  And whenever a dreamer's ears unclose
To the sound of that distant melody,
  A petal falls from the Dreamland Rose.

Dreams and visions in hosts untold
  Throng around on the moonlit lea:
Dreams of age that are calm and cold,
  Dreams of youth that are fair and free—
Dark with a lone heart's agony,
  Bright with a hope that no one knows—
And whenever a dream and a dream agree,
  A petal falls from the Dreamland Rose.

ENVOI

Princess, you gaze in a reverie
  Where the drowsy firelight redly glows;
Slowly you raise your eyes to me . . .
  A petal falls from the Dreamland Rose.

Brian Hooker

THE NINEPENNY FIDIL

  My father and mother were Irish,
  And I am Irish, too;
  I bought a wee fidil for ninepence,
  And it is Irish, too.
  I'm up in the morning early
  To meet the dawn of day,
  And to the lintwhite's piping
  The many's the tune I play.

  One pleasant eve in June time
  I met a lochrie-man;
  His face and hands were weazen,
  His height was not a span.

He boored me for my fidil—
"You know," says he, "like you,
My father and mother were Irish,
And I am Irish, too!"

He took my wee red fidil,
And such a tune he turned—
The Glaise in it whispered,
The Lionan in it mourned.
Says he, "My lad, you're lucky—
I wisht I was like you:
You're lucky in your birth-star,
And in your fidil, too!"

He gave me back my fidil,
My fidil-stick also,
And stepping like a mayboy,
He jumped the Leargaidh Knowe.
I never saw him after,
Nor met his gentle kind;
But, whiles, I think I hear him
A-wheening in the wind!

My father and mother were Irish,
And I am Irish, too;
I bought a wee fidil for ninepence,
And it is Irish, too.
I'm up in the morning early
To meet the dawn of day,
And to the lintwhite's piping
The many's the tune I play.

Joseph Campbell

CONFESSION IN HOLY WEEK

TAKING a charity
    To Mrs. McBride,
What do you think, then,
    I plainly espied?
A small, darksome leprechaun,
    Wishful, gray-eyed!

Leprechaun, leprechaun,
  Where are you faring?
Out in an Easter wind
  Just for an airing?

Did I say *gray*-eyed?
  I'm still a bit muddled;
Sure in the clear of them
  Gold lights were puddled,
And, very likely, a glint of the green
(Like leafshine in hedges, when sun slips between).

Halted? I gapped there! The dapperest baggage!
  (A she of them, too: as you know, it is rare).
And in spite of its queer little toss of defiance
  There was something distressful, I thought, in its air.

Leprechaun, leprechaun,
  What are you doing?
Would you expose yourself
  To a man's wooing?

Lord, but the comical, tempting small creature,
  Dainty and eager, and soft as a cat:
Womanlike, too, in each curving and feature,
  The brooch on her kerchief unfastened, at that!

Leprechaun, leprechaun,
  Golden or gray,
Big winds can blow
  Little people away.

What might she do (was my thought, in a tingle)
  Paddling cold hedges, on rainywet nights?
Sure, let her have just the jog of my ingle,
  Which could be irksome to nobody's rights.

Fool, then, and fool, then! I must have been tipsy.
  I should have crossed myself. Clumsily mannish,
Putting my hand out to snare the wee gypsy. . . .
  I'd ought have known. If you touch them—they vanish.

And that, Father Daly, explains why I lied
To tell how the milk soured on Mrs. McBride.

Christopher Morley

THE GRAND MATCH

DENNIS was hearty when Dennis was young,
High was his step in the jig that he sprung,
He had the looks an' the sootherin' tongue—
  An' he wanted a girl wid a fortune.

Nannie was gray-eyed an' Nannie was tall,
Fair was the face hid inunder her shawl,
Troth! an' he liked her the best o' them all—
  But she'd not a *traneen* to her fortune.

He be to look out for a likelier match,
So he married a girl that was counted a catch,
An' as ugly as need be, the dark little patch—
  But that was a trifle, he told her.

She brought him her good-lookin' gold to admire,
She brought him her good-lookin' cows to his byre,
But far from good-lookin' she sat by his fire—
  An' paid him that " thrifle " he told her.

He met pretty Nan when a month had gone by,
An' he thought, like a fool, to get round her he'd try;
Wid a smile on her lip an' a spark in her eye,
  She said, " How is the woman that owns ye?"

Och, never be tellin' the life that he's led!
Sure, many's the night that he'll wish himself dead,
For the sake of two eyes in a pretty girl's head,—
  An' the tongue of the woman that owns him.

Moira O'Neill

IN SERVICE

LITTLE Nellie Cassidy has got a place in town,
  She wears a fine white apron,
  She wears a new black gown,
An' the quarest little cap at all with straymers hanging
    down.

I met her one fine evening stravagin' down the street,
 A feathered hat upon her head,
 And boots upon her feet.
"Och, Mick," says she, "may God be praised that you and
 I should meet.

"It's lonesome in the city with such a crowd," says she;
 "I'm lost without the bog-land,
 I'm lost without the sea,
An' the harbor an' the fishing-boats that sail out fine and
 free.

"I'd give a golden guinea to stand upon the shore,
 To see the big waves lepping,
 To hear them splash and roar,
To smell the tar and the drying nets, I'd not be asking more.

"To see the small white houses, their faces to the sea,
 The childher in the doorway,
 Or round my mother's knee;
For I'm strange and lonesome missing them, God keep
 them all," says she.

Little Nellie Cassidy earns fourteen pounds and more,
 Waiting on the quality,
 And answering the door—
But her heart is some place far away upon the Wexford
 shore.

      Winifred M. Letts

THE DEATH OF PUCK

I

I FEAR that Puck is dead—it is so long
Since men last saw him—dead with all the rest
Of that sweet elfin crew that made their nest
In hollow huts, where hazels sing their song;
Dead and for ever, like the antique throng
The elves replaced; the Dryad that you guessed
Behind the leaves; the Naiad weed-bedressed;
The leaf-eared Faun that loved to lead you wrong.

Tell me, thou hopping Robin, hast thou met
A little man, no bigger than thyself,
Whom they call Puck, where woodland bells are wet?
Tell me, thou Wood-Mouse, hast thou seen an elf
Whom they call Puck, and is he seated yet,
Capped with a snail-shell, on his mushroom shelf?

II

The Robin gave three hops, and chirped, and said:
"Yes, I knew Puck, and loved him; though I trow
He mimicked oft my whistle, chuckling low;
Yes, I knew Cousin Puck; but he is dead.
We found him lying on his mushroom bed—
The Wren and I—half covered up with snow,
As we were hopping where the berries grow.
We think he died of cold.   Ay, Puck is fled."

And then the Wood-Mouse said: "We made the Mole
Dig him a little grave beneath the moss,
And four big Dormice placed him in the hole.
The Squirrel made with sticks a little cross;—
Puck was a Christian elf, and had a soul;—
And all we velvet-jackets mourn his loss."

Eugene Lee-Hamilton

SENSE AND NONSENSE

A DISAGREEABLE FEATURE

SHE has a bright and clever mind,
  Her cheek with health and beauty glows;
I wish she had a more refined
  Nose.

I like the saucy retroussé,
  Admire the Roman, love the Greek;
But her's is none of these—It's a
  Beak.

Soon as the sun of summer sets,
  Or ever winter's snows are shed,
That hapless feature always gets
  Red.

The hints that beauty sharps indite
  Account for this in many ways;
Some say it comes from wearing tight
  Stays.

O lady fair, let such be shunned!
  A larger waist, a looser boot   *were better*
Were better than a rubicund
  Snoot!

And you'd improve its shape, God wot,
  And look less like a pink pug pup
If you would wipe it down, and not
  Up.

Farewell! That love cannot endure
  Though you have every other grace
Is plain as is the nose on your
  Face.
                              Edwin Meade Robinson

IT HAPPENS, OFTEN

THERE was a man in our town
  Whose Christian name was Jim;
He stepped into a pot of glue,
  And fell and broke his limb.

The doctors tried to set it,
  But still it would not mend;
He limped about, and would, no doubt,
  Be limping to the end,

But on a day it happened
  He walked abroad, and then
He stepped into some other glue,
  And broke his leg again.

And when his leg was mended,
  And he was out once more,
Both leg and man were stronger than
  They'd ever been before!

So, when I broke my heart, once,
  I thought of Mister Jim—
I went and broke it once again,
  Now I'm as well as him!

Edwin Meade Robinson

VILLANELLE OF A VILLANESS

SHE was the daughter of Glubstein the Glover,
  Sooner or later, you'd hear about that.
I wooed with poems, a lyrical lover.

"We two shall dwell where the humming birds hover!"
  Thus did I go with the Muse to the mat.
She was the daughter of Glubstein the Glover.

"Oh, for a home in the haunts of the plover!"
  (Knowing not plover from Angora cat,
I wooed with poems, a lyrical lover!)

Then came the day when she chanced to discover
  What was my wage—and she got me my hat!
"She was the daughter of Glubstein the Glover—

"Had I the nerve to take *her* and to shove her
  Into some dingy old fifth-story flat?"
I wooed with poems! A lyrical lover!

"Go!" and the chandelier rattled above her!
  Out on the sidewalk was where I was at!
(She was the daughter of Glubstein the Glover;
I wooed with poems—a lyrical lover.)

Edwin Meade Robinson

DE SENECTUTE

WHEN as a young and budding pote
I gazed upon the stuff I wrote,
I knew that stuff so weak and poor
Would never rank as Literature.

And yet, I thought, what I have sung
Is not so bad for one so young;
When years and ripeness shall be mine,
I may achieve the Mighty Line.

And in that withered yesteryear
I used to take unwonted cheer
In that De Morgan was a man
Of seventy when he began.

But now that years have bowed my bean
And I am more than seventeen,
I tell myself the bitter truth
And know I was a lying youth.

Now of my verse so thin and cold
I say, Not bad for one so old;
When I was twenty-four or -five
Then, then my verses were alive.

Now I, as creeping age defeats
Me, think of Chatterton or Keats,
And say, Look at the stuff he did,
When he was nothing but a kid!

But Time has taught me this, to wit:
That Age has naught to do with it,
That plenty be the years or scant,
Some can be poets, and some can't.

Franklin P. Adams

POETRY AND THOUGHTS ON SAME

I SIT here at the window
    This Tuesday afternoon,
In the editorial room
    Of the New York *Tribune*.

I hear upon the cobbles
    The tramp of horses' feet;
The newsboys' loud obscenenesses
    Here in Frankfort Street.

The echoes of their voices
    Back to me are hurled
From the brownstone walls of the building
    Of the New York *World*.

I see the business office,
    And I see the floor above it.
I see and hear a lot of things.
    Suppose I do.   What of it?

"What of it?" Ignoramus!
    That obviously shows
How little I know of Poetry,
    How all my thoughts are Prose.

"What of it?" If I said that,
    Were I so analytic
About the Modern Poetry,
    You'd cry, "A rotten critic!"

Yet that is what I think about
  This Tuesday afternoon
In the editorial room
  Of the New York *Tribune*.

Franklin P. Adams

REGARDING (1) THE U. S. AND (2) NEW YORK

BEFORE I was a travelled bird,
  I scoffed, in my provincial way,
At other lands; I deemed absurd
  All nations but these U. S. A.

And—although Middle-Western born—
  Before I was a travelled guy,
I laughed at, with unhidden scorn,
  All cities but New York, N. Y.

But now I've been about a bit—
  How travel broadens! How it does!
And I have found out this, to wit:
  How right I was! How right I was!

Franklin P. Adams

THOUGHTS ON THE COSMOS

I

I DO not hold with him who thinks
The world is jonahed by a jinx;
That everything is sad and sour,
And life a withered hothouse flower

II

I hate the Pollyanna pest
Who says that All Is for the Best,
And hold in high, unhidden scorn
Who sees the Rose, nor feels the Thorn.

III

I do not like extremists who
Are like the pair in (1) and (II);

But how I hate the wabbly gink,
Like me, who knows not what to think!

Franklin P. Adams

BALLADE OF SCHOPENHAUER'S PHILOSOPHY

WISHFUL to add to my mental power,
　　Avid of knowledge and wisdom, I
Pondered the Essays of Schopenhauer,
　　Taking his terrible hills on high.
　　Worried I was, and a trifle shy,
Fearful I'd find him a bit opaque!
　　Thus does he say, with a soul-sick sigh:
"The best you get is an even break."

Life, he says, is awry and sour;
　　Life, he adds, is sour and awry;
Love, he says, is a withered flower;
　　Love, he adds, is a dragon-fly;
　　Love, he swears, is the Major Lie;
Life, he vows, is the Great Mistake;
　　No one can beat it, and few can tie.
The best you get is an even break.

Women, he says, are clouds that lower;
　　Women dissemble and falsify.
(Those are things that The Conning Tower
　　Cannot asseverate or deny.)
　　Futile to struggle, and strain, and try;
Pleasure is freedom from pain and ache;
　　The greatest thing you can do is die—
The best you get is an even break.

L'ENVOI

Gosh! I feel like a real good cry!
　　Life, he says, is a cheat, a fake.
Well, I agree with the grouchy guy—
　　The best you get is an even break.

Franklin P. Adams

TO THE POLYANDROUS LYDIA

HORACE: BOOK I, ODE 13

"Cum tu, Lydia, Telephi—"

Oh Lydia, when I hear you rave
About the arms, the rosy neck
Of Telephus, the vamping knave,
I cry, "Oh heck!"

No longer can I check mine ire;
Unheeded rise the tears that flow
Over my features, with the fire
Of passion's woe.

I weep when on your shoulders white
I see the marks of drunken grips;
The traces of the madman's bite
Upon your lips.

Lydia, my love, attend my song;
Simple it is, nor hieroglyph:
He used you rough, he done you wrong—
The great big stiff!

Thrice happy Jack that holds his Jill
Close to his unpolygamous heart!
Thrice blessèd they who cleave until
Death do them part!
                        Franklin P. Adams

HORACE THE WISE

BOOK I, ODE 5

"Quis multa gracilis te puer in rosa—"

Or, Pyrrha, tell me who's the guy,
   The boob, the simp you've got a date with?
(Well I recall what time 'twas *I*
   You'd tête-à-tête with!)

I saw him in the barber's chair:
  His face perfumed with scented water,
And oil upon his shoes and hair—
  Dressed for the slaughter!

I do not know this kid whose goat
  You've got by saying you adore him.
But, take it from this famous pote,
  I'm sorry for him!

The fates deal kindly with the lad!
  This crush of his—how he will rue it!
He'll call you everything that's Bad—
  Ain't *I* been through it?

                              Morrie Ryskind

OLD STUFF

IF I go to see the play,
  Of the story I am certain;
Promptly it gets under way
  With the lifting of the curtain.
Builded all that's said and done
  On the ancient recipe—
'Tis the same old Two and One:
  A and B in love with C.

If I read the latest book,
  There's the mossy situation;
One may confidently look
  For the trite triangulation.
Old as time, but ever new,
  Seemingly, this tale of Three—
Same old yarn of One and Two:
  A and C in love with B.

If I cast my eyes around,
  Far and near and middle distance,
Still the formula is found
  In our everyday existence.

Everywhere I look I see—
    Fact or fiction, life or play—
Still the little game of Three:
    B and C in love with A.

While the ancient law fulfills,
    Myriad moons shall wane and wax.
Jack must have his pair of Jills,
    Jill must have her pair of Jacks.

                              Bert Leston Taylor

ATARAXIA

To purge what I am pleased to call my mind
    Of matters that perplex it and embarrass,
I get a glass, and seek until I find,
    High in the heaven, southward from Polaris,
A wisp of cloud—a nebula by name:
Andromeda provides a starry frame.

It's quite remote. I hesitate to say
    How many million light-years it is distant.
But I can make the journey any day,
    When earthly cares become a bit insistent—
Propelled by thought-waves—through the star-frame pass
Like little Alice through the Looking-Glass.

There, gazing back, I see our flock of stars
    Shine palely in the void, a patch of vapor.
Far from the madding crowd's ignoble jars,
    Sequestered from the clamant daily paper
I breathe awhile in measureless content—
Alone at last, 'neath a new firmament!

If you would cultivate a soul serene,
    A mind emancipated from emotion,
There's nothing like entire change of scene—
    Some far-off isle in space's shoreless ocean.
It's well, at times, to change your universe:
The new one, if not better, can't be worse.

                              Bert Leston Taylor

THE BARDS WE QUOTE

Whene'er I quote I seldom take
From bards whom angel hosts environ;
But usually some damned rake
   Like Byron.

Of Whittier I think a lot,
My fancy to him often turns;
But when I quote 'tis some such sot
   As Burns.

I'm very fond of Bryant, too,
He brings to me the woodland smelley;
Why should I quote that "village roo,"
   P. Shelley?

I think Felicia Hemans great,
I dote upon Jean Ingelow;
Yet quote from such a reprobate
   As Poe.

To quote from drunkard or from rake
Is not a proper thing to do.
I find the habit hard to break,
   Don't you?

Bert Leston Taylor

THE VAMP PASSES

Vamp plays are no longer popular with photo-play audiences—A Movie Scout.

No longer the wife of the hero
   Need swallow a piteous sigh,
And stifle the storm that convulses her form
   As she kisses her husband good-by.
No longer her wife's intuition
   Can waken the fear in her breast
That he's going to decamp with a red-headed Vamp
   On the nine-fifty train for the West.

Oh! The Vamp was a merciless creature,
   Whenever she met a young wife
She would powder her nose, strike an insolent pose
   And sneer (and they sneer like a knife!)
And the kindest and lovingest husbands
   Who never before had backslid
Would lamp at the Vamp like a rah-rahing scamp,
   And coyly observe, "Oh, you kid!"

No opulent home could be happy;
   The Vamp's subterranean stealth
In the very first reel never failed to reveal
   That the husband was rolling in wealth,
And, putting her gauziest dress on,
   She looked and she looked and she looked
At the poor millionaire, who would never beware
   Until he was hopelessly hooked.

I grieve that the Vamp has departed,
   Though of course I could never approve
When she harrowed the lives of those innocent wives
   Still she *did* keep events on the move,
And, watching her witching behavior,
   I have frequently hankered to see
Just how hard I'd resist if a Vamp should insist,
   On working the Vamp stuff on me!

                     James J. Montague

"AND WHEN THEY FALL"

WHERE is the Grand Duke Ruffanuff, who stole the Czar's
    first wife?
  Who used to shoot and burn and loot,
  While all his suite would follow suit,
  And never gave a single hoot
    For threats upon his life?
He's mandatory of a mule just out of Teheran;
He's working for Bazouk Pasha as second hired man!

Where is Graf von Gipfelstein, that man of noble rank,
  Who when he sat at baccarat,
  Would bet a million with éclat,
  And with rare nonchalance stand pat
    Until he broke the bank?
You'll find him down in old Stamboul, if you are passing
    by,
He's mandatory of the pigs in Izzak-Issik's sty!

Where is Countess von der Schtuff, that ravishing brunette
  Whose wiles and arts broke scores of hearts,
  Who raided all the jewel marts—
  The belle of many foreign parts—
    Is she in Europe yet?
Across the Turkish moors she bears a bucket full of corn;
She's mandatory of a cow beside the Golden Horn!

                      James J. Montague

THE SAME OLD STORY

WHEN Julius Cæsar went to town
  To purchase steaks and chops and such,
He tried to beat the butchers down
  And swore their prices were too much.
"Two cents a pound for steak," he roared,
  "Why, man, that's nothing short of crime.
You butchers are a greedy horde,
  It cost but one in Noah's time!"

When Ollie Cromwell went to shop
  For beef and mutton and the like,
He said if prices didn't drop
  He'd spit the butchers on a spike.
"Six cents a pound for steak," he said.
  "It's more than honest men can pay.
You folks are robbers, on the dead,
  It cost but two in Cæsar's day!"

Today when we go out and find
  That beef is eighty cents a pound,
We tarry there and speak our mind
  And scatter savage words around.

'Twas ever thus, in every age,
  In every time and clime and season
The price of meat has made men rage
  And always with abundant reason.

James J. Montague

KING COPHETUA AND THE BEGGAR MAID

COPHETUA was a merry King,
  And slightly sentimental;
His morals were (if anything)
  What some call "Oriental."

Zenelophon, the Beggar Goil,
  Was innocent and careful;
She had been reared to Honest Toil
  By parents poor and prayerful,

For Papa peddled lemonade
  While Mamma laundered laundry,
And she had been a solder maid
  Within a muzzle foundry;

But, oh! the foreman of the staff
  Had tried to Make Advances . . .
The Villain used to smirk and chaff
  And ask her out to dances!

And so she quit the Hellish Place
  And went salvationarming
A careful smile upon her face
  So innocent and charming.

While begging in a Beer Saloon
  Right opposite the palace
She saw the King one afternoon
  Drink chalice after chalice—

(He dallied daily with the Jug,
  He hit the pipe and gambled,
He introduced the bunny-hug
  As round his realm he rambled)—

Eftsoons the Monarch, reeling by
　　Imperially laden,
Remarked, iniquitous and sly,
　　"Pray, buss me, Beggar Maiden!"

"Not I!" she cried, "I'd rather go
　　Right back to making muzzles
Than kiss a King that roisters so
　　And gambles, flirts, and guzzles!"

The Regal Cut-up, in a mood
　　Majestically reckless,
Then offered her a samite snood,
　　A duchy and a necklace.

"Oh, keep your Royal Gauds," she said,
　　"And buss your legal spouses!
I won't kiss none until I'm wed,
　　Especial if they're souses!"

With that he laid his sceptre down
　　Beneath her footsy-wootsies—
"Oh, wed me, and I'll fling muh crown
　　Before them pretty tootsies!"

"O King!" says she, "you *have* some queens!"
　　Says he, "They're soon beheaded!"
That day his headsman reaped their beans,
　　The next the King was wedded.

And Mrs. King Cophetua made
　　All parties quit their vices,
And Papa's private lemonade
　　Soon rose to fancy prices,

And Mamma laundered for the King
　　As happy as a linnet—
Oh, Virtue always wins, I sing,
　　If Wisdom's mingled in it!

Don Marquis

TRISTRAM AND ISOLT

SIR Tristram was a Bear, in listed field
Or lady's bower, Champeen with sword or song;
All that life's traffic could be made to yield
Trist took; He'd tell some Sweet Thing, "You belong!"
And with that word he'd cop her from the throng.
Boudoir or tourney, tea or dancing green,
He never kept them waiting very long;
Nor Foe nor Frail had really turned his bean
Until he lamped King Mark of Cornwall's sprightly Queen.

Mark was a Pill. His little Dame had Class . . .
One of those Unions that neglect to Une . . .
She was a Saint! He was a Hound! Alas,
That such a Peach should marry such a Prune!
Why did she stick? Who knows the inward tune
To which these women march? We know, at least,
Mark had a Wad, and bought her gowns and shoon . . .
Also, one eats or one is soon deceased. . . .
Mayhap it was a case of Booty and the Beast!

Tristram rode by her palace on a day
When some young angel leaned from Paradise
And loved the earth and laughed and made it May;
And Izzy saw his lovely purple eyes—
Not the young angel's: Tristram's; otherwise
She might have flagged the angel for her Beau
Instead of Tristram. Ah! what tears and sighs
Were saved if women never looked below
The angels . . . yet, no doubt, at times they'd find it slow.

As she gave him the rapt Once Over, he
Felt all his bounding pulses pause, then fill
With love as tidal creeks flood from the sea. . . .
Sir Tristram, if you get me, got Some Thrill. . . .
One jump and he was at her window-sill,
The Sudden Cuss! "Divinity!" he said,
"Newly descended from th' Olympian Hill,
I'm yourn! Say, are you single? Are you wed?
If so, where is your Spouse?—I'll go and chop his head!"

"I'm not Olympian sir," she said, "but only
Of this hick realm the melancholy Queen.
You love me, Stranger?   Thanks!   I get *so* lonely!
As for your kindly offer to unbean
My liege lord, 'Ataboy!   I *loathe* a Scene,
As all Nice Women should, but this is Fate—
No girl can dodge her destiny, I ween . . .
Or do I dream?   Pinch me—Ouch!   *Don't!*   I'd *hate*
To have you get some Horrid Notion in your pate!

"I know you'll think me Unconventional!"—
"What are conventions 'twixt Affinities?"—
"I always thought love was more gradual!"
"Let Temperate Zones grow warmer by degrees,
But why should we Equators think of these?"—
"Why does your mustache taste that funny way?"—
"Something   the   barber   does."—"Stop him!"—"Say
      please!"
"Please, then—and *could* you murder Mark *to-day!*"
"I'll cut his throat 'mid the sweet twilight's tender gray!"—

Ah, pretty prattle, innocent and artless!
Sweet interchange as when lute answers lute!
These cooing doves! what Fiend could be so heartless
As wish to make their happy murmurs mute?
What Fiend but Mark!   That wicked, sly old brute,
Whenever his fair wife would kiss a stranger,
Would scowl at her and even stamp his boot,
Or read her lectures on A Young Wife's Danger—
When Home is Hell what wonder if Love proves a Ranger!

The Spoilsport crept behind them as they kissed
And slammed the window down across their necks,
Nor any guardian spirit grabbed his wrist,
And in one instant both of them were Wrecks!
The sad tale's Moral goes for either sex:
Don't spoon beneath a giddy guillotine
If any one's about whom it may vex—
Make love quite out of windows or quite in
If you aspire to keep a chest below your chin.

And so they died, in Cornwall by the sea,
Where tides asthmatic ever wheeze and snortle,
And the damp tin miners going home to tea
Still hear sometimes old Mark's complacent chortle
As his lean ghost by a ghostly window-portal
Slams phantom sashes down and gloats and gloats. . . .
And so they died, and so they are immortal,
And in Elysian meadows feel their oats
Forever! Death can never get true lovers' goats!

Don Marquis

A HOT–WEATHER SONG

I FEEL so exceedingly lazy,
  I neglect what I oughtn't to should!
My notion of work is so hazy
    That I couldn't to toil if I would!

I feel so exceedingly silly
    That I say all I shouldn't to ought!
And my mind is as frail as a lily;
    It would break with the weight of a thought!

Don Marquis

ODE TO WORK IN SPRINGTIME

OH, would that working I might shun,
    From labor my connection sever,
That I might do a bit—or none
    Whatever!

That I might wander over hills,
    Establish friendship with a daisy,
O'er pretty things like daffodils
    Go crazy!

That I might at the heavens gaze,
    Concern myself with nothing weighty,
Loaf, at a stretch, for seven days—
    Or eighty.

Why can't I cease a slave to be,
 And taste existence beatific
On some fair island, hid in the
  Pacific?

Instead of sitting at a desk
 'Mid undone labors grimly lurking—
Oh, say, what is there picturesque
 In working?

But no!—to loaf were misery!—
 I love to work! Hang isles of coral!
(To end this otherwise would be
  Immoral!)

Thomas R. Ybarra

A RONDEAU OF REMORSE

UNHAPPY, I observe the Ass,
Who browses placidly on grass,
 Or bits of wood he will devour,
 While e'en the prickly thistle-flower
Is spicing for his garden-sass.

Last night that lovely golden mass
She called a "rarebit" proved but brass;
 And life I gaze at through a sour
  Unhappy eye.

And as this sleepless night I pass,
I learn that he who has, alas!
 An ass's judgment for his dower
 May lack the beast's digestive power.
Oh, miserie! All flesh is grass!
  Unhappy I!

Burges Johnson

MRS. SEYMOUR FENTOLIN

IT was Mrs. Seymour Fentolin who stood there, a little dog under each arm; a large hat, gay with flowers, upon her head. She wore patent shoes with high heels, and white silk stockings. She had, indeed, the air of being dressed for luncheon at a fashionable restaurant.—From a story in *The Popular Magazine*.

THE lauded lilies of the field
Who toil not—neither do they spin,
The palm sartorial must yield
To Mrs. Seymour Fentolin.

A hat, French heels, white stockings, dogs!
Not even Solomon could win
The championship for showy togs
From Mrs. Seymour Fentolin.

The two extremes of décolleté,
Of ballroom and of bathing beach,
Here meet in a bewildering way
And mingle all the charms of each.

I am no social butter-in,
I do not crave to meet her bunch,
But where does Mrs. Fentolin,
If one might venture—take her lunch?

And might one ask that peerless dame,
Without appearing impolite,
Is *Seymour* really her first name,
And has the printer spelt it right?

Oliver Herford

NURSERY RHYMES FOR THE TENDER-HEARTED

I

SCUTTLE, scuttle, little roach—
How you run when I approach:
Up above the pantry shelf,
Hastening to secrete yourself.

Most adventurous of vermin,
How I wish I could determine
How you spend your hours of ease,
Perhaps reclining on the cheese.

Cook has gone, and all is dark—
Then the kitchen is your park:
In the garbage heap that she leaves
Do you browse among the tea leaves?

How delightful to suspect
All the places you have trekked:
Does your long antenna whisk its
Gentle tip across the biscuits?

Do you linger, little soul,
Drowsing in our sugar bowl?
Or, abandonment most utter,
Shake a shimmy on the butter?

Do you chant your simple tunes
Swimming in the baby's prunes?
Then, when dawn comes, do you slink
Homeward to the kitchen sink?

Timid roach, why be so shy?
We are brothers, thou and I.
In the midnight, like yourself,
I explore the pantry shelf!

IV

I knew a black beetle, who lived down a drain,
And friendly he was, though his manners were plain;
When I took a bath he would come up the pipe,
And together we'd wash and together we'd wipe.

Though mother would sometimes protest with a sneer
That my choice of a tub-mate was wanton and queer,
A nicer companion I never have seen;
He bathed every night, so he must have been clean.

Whenever he heard the tap splash in the tub
He'd dash up the drain-pipe and wait for a scrub,
And often, so fond of ablution was he,
I'd find him there floating and waiting for me.

But nurse has done something that seems a great shame:
She saw him there, waiting, prepared for a game:
She turned on the hot and she scalded him sore
And he'll never come bathing with me any more.

Christopher Morley

BLOW ME EYES

WHEN I was young and full o' pride,
   A-standin' on the grass
And gazin' o'er the water-side,
   I seen a fisher lass.
"O, fisher lass, be kind awhile,"
   I asks 'er quite unbid.
"Please look into me face and smile"—
   And, blow me eyes, she did!

O, blow me light and blow me blow,
I didn't think she'd charm me so—
   But, blow me eyes, she did!

She seemed so young and beautiful
   I *had* to speak perlite,
(The afternoon was long and dull,
   But she was short and bright.)
"This ain't no place," I says, "to stand—
   Let's take a walk instid,
Each holdin' of the other's hand"—
   And, blow me eyes, she did!

O, blow me light and blow me blow,
I sort o' thunk she wouldn't go—
   But, blow me eyes, she did!

And as we walked along a lane
   With no one else to see,
Me heart was filled with sudden pain,
   And so I says to she:

"If you would have me actions speak
    The words what can't be hid,
You'd sort o' let me kiss yer cheek"—
    And, blow me eyes, she did!

O, blow me light and blow me blow,
How sweet she was I didn't know—
    But, blow me eyes, *she* did!

But pretty soon me shipmate Jim
    Came strollin' down the beach,
And she began a-oglin' him
    As pretty as a peach.
"O, fickle maid o' false intent,"
    Impulsively I chid,
"Why don't you go and wed that gent?"
    And, blow me eyes, she did!

O, blow me light and blow me blow,
I didn't think she'd treat me so—
    But, blow me eyes, she did!

Wallace Irwin

A CAPSTAN CHANTEY

WHAT did the captain say to the cook
When the ship went down the river?
    "I've left my girl in Melbourne town,
    Her hair was black and her eyes were brown;
And I'll love my girl for ever."
Wey-ho! We'll love the girls forever!

What did the cook to the captain say
When the ship went down the river?
    "I've left my gal in Melbourne too,
    Her hair was gold and her eyes were blue;
And I'll love my gal for ever."
Wey-ho! We'll love the gals for ever!

What did the crew at the capstan sing
As the old tank nosed the river?

"We've left our gals in Melbourne town,
  With eyes of blue and eyes of brown;
And we'll love our gals for ever."
Hey! We will forget them never!

What did the cook to the captain say
As the ship came down the river?
  "I've left my gal in London town,
  Her hair is black and her eyes are brown,
And I'll love my gal for ever."

What did the captain say to the cook
As the ship swung down the river?
  "I've left my girl in London too,
  Her hair is gold and her eyes are blue,
And I'll love my girl for ever."

What did the crew at the capstan sing?
Nothing at all but the same old thing
As the ship came down the river:
  "We've left our loves in London town,
  And some were black and some were brown,
But we'll love our loves for ever."

L'ENVOI

So blow your money, my bullies all
(The old tank's down the river),
  Blow your money and knock it down;
For some are short and some are tall,
  And some are black and some are brown,
And the world goes round for ever.

E. J. Brady

THE RAMBLING SAILOR

In the old back streets o' Pimlico
On the docks at Monte Video
At the Ring o' Bells on Plymouth Hoe
He'm arter me now wheerever I go.
An' dirty nights when the wind do blow
I can hear him sing-songin' up from sea—:

Oh! no man nor woman's bin friend to me
An' to-day I'm feared wheer to-morrow I'll be,
Sin' the night the moon lay whist and white
On the road goin' down to the Lizard Light
When I heard him hummin' behind me.

"Oh! look, boy, look in your sweetheart's eyes
  So deep as sea an' so blue as skies;
An' 'tis better to kiss than to chide her,
If they tell 'ee no tales, they'll tell'ee no lies
      Of the little brown mouse
      That creeps into the house
To lie sleepin' so quiet beside her.

"Oh! hold 'ee long, but hold 'ee light
Your true man's hand when you find him,
He'll help 'ee home on a darksome night
      Wi' a somethin' bright
      That he'm holdin' tight
In the hand that he keeps behind him.

"Oh! sit 'ee down to your whack o' pies
So hot's the stew and the brew likewise
But whiles you'm scrapin' the plates and dishes,
A-gapin' down in the shiversome sea
For the delicate mossels inside o' we
Theer's a passel o' hungry fishes."

At the *Halte des Marins* at Saint Nazaire
I cussed him, sittin' astride his chair;
An' Christmas Eve on the Mary Clare
I pitched him a-down the hatch-way stair.
But "Shoutin' and cloutin's nothin' to me,
Nor the hop nor the skip nor the jump," says he,
"For I be walkin' on every quay . . ."

"So look, boy, look in the dear maid's eyes
And take the true man's hand,
And eat your fill o' your whack o' pies
Till you'm starin' up wheer the sea-crow flies
Wi' your head lyin' soft in the sand."

                                  Charlotte Mew

DERELICT

A Reminiscence of R. L. S's. "Treasure Island" and Cap'n Billy Bones, His Song

"FIFTEEN men on the dead man's chest—
    "Yo-ho-ho and a bottle of rum!
"Drink and the devil had done for the rest—
    "Yo-ho-ho and a bottle of rum!"
The mate was fixed by the bos'n's pike,
The bos'n brained with a marlinspike
And Cookey's throat was marked belike
        It had been gripped
            By fingers ten;
        And there they lay,
            All good dead men,
Like break-o-'day in a boozing-ken—
    Yo-ho-ho and a bottle of rum!

Fifteen men of a whole ship's list—
    Yo-ho-ho and a bottle of rum!
Dead and bedamned and the rest gone whist!—
    Yo-ho-ho and a bottle of rum!
The skipper lay with his nob in gore
Where the scullion's axe his cheek had shore—
And the scullion he was stabbed times four.
        And there they lay
            And the soggy skies
        Dripped all day long
            In up-staring eyes—
At murk sunset and at foul sunrise—
    Yo-ho-ho and a bottle of rum!

Fifteen men of 'em stiff and stark—
    Yo-ho-ho and a bottle of rum!
Ten of the crew had the Murder mark—
    Yo-ho-ho and a bottle of rum!
'Twas a cutlass swipe, or an ounce of lead,
Or a yawing hole in a battered head—
And the scuppers glut with a rotting red.

And there they lay—
  Aye, damn my eyes!—
All lookouts clapped
  On paradise—
All souls bound just contrariwise—
  Yo-ho-ho and a bottle of rum!

Fifteen men of 'em good and true—
  Yo-ho-ho and a bottle of rum!
Every man jack could ha' sailed with Old Pew—
  Yo-ho-ho and a bottle of rum!
There was chest on chest full of Spanish gold,
With a ton of plate in the middle hold,
And the cabins riot of stuff untold.
  And they lay there,
    That had took the plum,
  With sightless glare
    And their lips struck dumb,
While we shared all by the rule of thumb—
  Yo-ho-ho and a bottle of rum!

More was seen through the sternlight screen—
  Yo-ho-ho and a bottle of rum!
Chartings ondoubt where a woman had been!—
  Yo-ho-ho and a bottle of rum!
A flimsy shift on a bunker cot,
With a thin dirk slot through the bosom spot
And the lace stiff-dry in a purplish blot.
  Or was she wench . . .
    Or some shuddering maid . . .?
  That dared the knife—
    And that took the blade!
By God! she was stuff for a plucky jade—
  Yo-ho-ho and a bottle of rum!

Fifteen men on the dead man's chest—
  Yo-ho-ho and a bottle of rum!
Drink and the devil had done for the rest—
  Yo-ho-ho and a bottle of rum!

We wrapped 'em all in a mains'l tight,
With twice ten turns of a hawser's bight,
And we heaved 'em over and out of sight—
  With a yo-heave-ho!
   And a fare-you-well!
  And a sullen plunge
   In the sullen swell
Ten fathoms deep on the road to hell!
  Yo-ho-ho and a bottle of rum!
       Young E. Allison

THE LANDLUBBER'S CHANTEY

(As he gazes from his office window at a ship clearing for the open sea)

HERE I drone in this human hive,
 Blow, ye sirens, blow!
And three times eight are twenty-five,
 Blow, ye sirens, blow!
Blue Peter snaps and flutters wide,
The dripping hawser slaps her side,
Out she warps on the turning tide!
 Blow, ye sirens, blow!

Three and four and a one make nine—
 Roll, ye combers, roll!
The air is sharp with windswept brine,
 Roll, ye combers, roll!
She's dropped the last low line of shore,
The furrowed seas stretch out before—
Ten thousand miles to Singapore!
 Roll, ye combers, roll!

Lawless days and thirsty knives,
 Roar, ye typhoons, roar!
Sudden ends to rum-wrecked lives,
 Roar, ye typhoons, roar!
On sunken reefs a gray sea moans
Of missing ships and dead men's bones—
Oh, blast those jangling telephones!
 Roar, ye typhoons, roar!

Debit Smith and credit Ross—
    Sigh, ye Southern seas!
Brightly burns the starry cross—
    Sigh, ye Southern seas!
A breeze with spices laden down;
A Venus done in ivory brown
Gleams through her sketchy cotton gown.
    Sigh, ye Southern seas!

Where Christians loaf and heathens sweat,
    Heave, ye rollers, heave!
There's life to live and gold to get,
    Heave, ye rollers, heave!
Beneath the ocean's sunlit green
Are pearls to grace an Eastern queen—
And eight and nine are seventeen.
    Heave, ye rollers, heave!

James Stuart Montgomery

WARM BABIES

SHADRACH, Meshach, Abednego,
Walked in de furnace to an' fro,
Hay foot, straw foot, fro an' to,
An' de flame an' de smoke flared up de flue.
Nebuchadnezzar he listen some,
An' he hear 'em talk, an' he say "How come?"
An' he hear 'em walk, an' he say "How so?
Dem babes wuz hawg tied an hour ago!"
Then Shadrach call, in an uppity way:
"A little more heat or we ain' gwine stay!"
An' Meshach bawl, so dat furnace shake:
"Landlawd, heat! fo' de good Lawd's sake!"
Abednego yell, wid a loud "Kerchoo!
Is you out to freeze us, y' great big Jew!"

Nebuchadnezzar, he rare an' ramp,
An' call to de janitor, "You big black scamp!
Shake dem clinkers an' spend dat coal!
I'll bake dem birds, ef I goes in de hole!"

He puts on de draf an' shuts de door
So de furnace glow an' de chimbly roar.
Ol' Nebuchadnezzar, he smole a smile,
"Guess dat'll hold 'em," says he, "one while."

Den Shadrach, Meshach, Abednego
Walk on de hot coals to an' fro,
Gulp dem cinders like chicken meat
An' holler out for a mite more heat.
Ol' Nebuchadnezzar gives up de fight;
He opens dat door an' bows perlite.
He shades his eyes from de glare infernal
An' says to Abednego, "Step out, Colonel."
An' he add, "Massa Shadrach, I hopes you all
Won' be huffy at me at all."

Den Shadrach, Meshach, Abednego,
Hay foot, straw foot, three in a row,
Stepped right smart from de oven door
Jes' as good as dey wuz before,
An', far as Nebuchadnezzar could find,
Jes' as good as dey wuz behind.

Keith Preston

THE DAVID JAZZ

DAVID was a Young Blood, David was a striplin',
Looked like the Jungle Boy, yarned about by Kiplin'—
Looked like a Jungle Boy, sang like a bird,
Fought like a tiger when his temper got stirred.
David was a-tendin' the sheep for his Pa,
Somebody hollered to him—that was his Ma—
"Run down to camp with this little bitta snack,
Give it to your brothers, an' hurry right back."

David took the lunch box, and off he hurried;
There he saw the Isra'lites lookin' right worried.
Asked 'em what's the matter—they pointed to the Prairie—
There he saw a sight to make a Elephant scary!

There he saw Goliath,
  Champion o' Gath,
Howlin' in his anger,
  Roarin' in his wrath;
Stronger than a lion,
  Taller than a tree—
David had to tip-toe to reach to his knee!
"Come on," says the Giant, a-ragin' and a-stridin'—
"Drag out your champeens from the holes where they're
    hidin',
Drag out your strong men from underneath their bunks,
And I'll give 'em to the buzzards, an' the lizards, an' the
    skunks! "

David heard him braggin', and he said, "I declare,
The great big lummox got 'em buffaloed for fair."
Goes to the brook, and he picks him out a pebble,
Smooth as a goose-egg an' hard as the debbil.
Starts for the giant, dancin' on his toes,
Whirlin' his sling-shot and singin' as he goes—
"Better get organized, for here I come a-hoppin',
Time's gettin' short, and hell am a-poppin'.
Hell am a-poppin' and trouble am a-brewin',
Nothin's going to save you from Big Red Ruin.
Trouble am a-brewin' and Death am distillin'—
Look out, you Philistine—there's gwineter be a killin'! "

Giant looks at David an' he lets out a laugh—
Acts like a tiger bein' sassed by a calf;
Laughs like a hyena, grins from ear to ear,
Rattles on his armor with his ten-foot spear,
Starts out for David, bangin' and a-clankin'—
"Come on, li'l infant, you're a-goin' to get a spankin'! "
David takes his sling shot, swings it round his head,
Lets fly a pebble—and the gi'nt drops dead!

MORAL

Big men, little men, houses and cars,
Widders and winders and porcelain jars—

Nothin' ain't safe from damage an' shocks,
When the neighborhood chillen gets to slingin' with rocks!

Edwin Meade Robinson

SIMON LEGREE—A NEGRO SERMON

(To be read in your own variety of negro dialect)

LEGREE'S big house was white and green.
His cotton-fields were the best to be seen.
He had strong horses and opulent cattle,
And bloodhounds bold, with chains that would rattle.
His garret was full of curious things:
Books of magic, bags of gold,
And rabbits' feet on long twine strings.
But he went down to the Devil.

Legree he sported a brass-buttoned coat,
A snake-skin necktie, a blood-red shirt.
Legree he had a beard like a goat,
And a thick hairy neck, and eyes like dirt.
His puffed-out cheeks were fish-belly white,
He had great long teeth, and an appetite.
He ate raw meat, 'most every meal,
And rolled his eyes till the cat would squeal.

His fist was an enormous size
To mash poor niggers that told him lies:
He was surely a witch-man in disguise.
But he went down to the Devil.

He wore hip-boots, and would wade all day
To capture his slaves that had fled away.
But he went down to the Devil.

He beat poor Uncle Tom to death
Who prayed for Legree with his last breath.
Then Uncle Tom to Eva flew,
To the high sanctoriums bright and new;
And Simon Legree stared up beneath,
And cracked his heels, and ground his teeth:
And went down to the Devil.

He crossed the yard in the storm and gloom;
He went into his grand front room.
He said, "I killed him, and I don't care."
He kicked a hound, he gave a swear;
He tightened his belt, he took a lamp,
Went down cellar to the webs and damp.
There in the middle of the mouldy floor
He heaved up a slab; he found a door—
And went down to the Devil.

His lamp blew out, but his eyes burned bright.
Simon Legree stepped down all night—
Down, down to the Devil.
Simon Legree he reached the place,
He saw one half of the human race,
He saw the Devil on a wide green throne,
Gnawing the meat from a big ham-bone,
And he said to Mister Devil:

"I see that you have much to eat—
A red ham-bone is surely sweet.
I see that you have lion's feet;
I see your frame is fat and fine,
I see you drink your poison wine—
Blood and burning turpentine."

And the Devil said to Simon Legree:
"I like your style, so wicked and free.
Come sit and share my throne with me,
And let us bark and revel."
And there they sit and gnash their teeth,
And each one wears a hop-vine wreath.
They are matching pennies and shooting craps,
They are playing poker and taking naps.
And old Legree is fat and fine:
He eats the fire, he drinks the wine—
Blood and burning turpentine—
Down, down with the Devil;
Down, down with the Devil;
Down, down with the Devil.

Vachel Lindsay

DE GLORY ROAD

O DE Glory Road! O de Glory Road!
I'm gwine ter drap mah load upon de Glory Road.

I lay on mah bed untell one erclock,
An' de Lord come callin' all His faithful flock.
An' He call "Whoo-ee! ", an' He call "Whoo-ee! ",
An' I knowed dat de Sabior wuz ercallin' me.
An' He call "Whoo-ee! ", an' He call "Whoo-ee! ",
An' I cry "Massa Jesus, is you callin' me? "
An' He call "Whoo-ee! ", an' He call "Whoo-ee! ",
An' I riz up f'um mah pallet, an' I cry, "Hyahs me! "

De Lawd sez, "Niggah, ain't I call yer thrice
Ter ride erlong behin' me up ter Paradise,
On de Glory Road, on de Glory Road? "
An' I clime up ter de saddle, an' I jined de load!

De hawse he wuz longer dan a thousan' mile';
His tail went lashin', an' his hoofs wuz wil';
His mane wuz flamin', and his eyes wuz moons,
An' his mouth kep' singin' Halleluyah tunes!

De Lawd sez, "Niggah, why 'n' cher look erroun'! "
An' dar we wuz flyin' over risin' groun',
Powerful hills, an' mountains too,
An' de earth an' de people wuz drapt f'um view.
An' I hyahd all 'roun me how de sperits sang,
An' de Lawd sang louder dan de whole shebang!

De Lawd sez, " Niggah, why 'n' cher look ergin? "
An' dar wuz de Debbil, on de back of Sin,
A-bangin' on de critter wid his whip an' goad,
An' boun' he gwine ter kotch us, on de Glory Road!
"O Lawdy, it's de Debbil, comin' straight f'um Hell!
I kin tell him by his roarin', an' de brimstone smell! "
But de Lawd sez, "Niggah, he ain' kotch us yit! "
An' he lashed an' He hustled, an' He loosed de bit.
Den de Debbil crept closuh, an' I hyahd him yell,
"I'm gwine ter kotch a niggah, fur ter roas' in Hell! "

An' I cried, "Lawd, sabe me! " An' de Lawd cry, "Sho! "
An' hyah it was Hebben, an' we shet de do'.

O Glory, Glory, how de angels sang!
O Glory, Glory, how de rafters rang!
An' Moses, 'n' Aaron, 'n' Methusalum,
Dey shout an' dey holler, an' dey beat de drum.
King Solomon kissed me, an' his thousan' wives,
Jes' like they'd knowed me, durin' all dey lives;
An' de Lawd sez, "Niggah, take a gran'-stan' seat.
But I 'specks youse hungry; have a bite ter eat? "
An' de ravens fed me, an' Elijah prayed,
An' de Sabed Ones gathered, while de organ played,
An' dey cry "O sinnah, come an' lose yuh load
On de Glory Road, on de Glory Road.
An' come an' dwell in de Lawd's abode,
Glory, Glory, on de Glory Road! "

Sez de Lawd, "No, sinnah, you mus' trabbel back
Ter he'p po' niggahs up de Glory Track;
Ter he'p old mo'ners an' de scoffin' coons,
By shoutin' loud Halleluyah tunes."

O come, mah breddren, won' you drap yuh load,
An' ride ter Hebben up de Glory Road?

Clement Wood

THE SWASHBUCKLER'S SONG

Three things there are, worth living for—
A kiss, a cup and a taste o' war—
Without them life's but watered ale.
As dull and drab as a twice-told tale,
While a man is young and a man is hale,
Ho, landlord, fill the bowl!

What tunes the throat to a roaring song
Like a drink that's hot and a drink that's strong?
Away with your tipples, wan and thin,
And fetch of your bravest brandy in,

That's mellow as gold and old as sin!
Ho, landlord, fill the bowl!

When the heart is young, then the heart beats **high,**
And the divil lurks in a downcast eye;
For, maids are coy but to be pursued,
And maids resist but to be subdued,
Heigh ho! 'Tis a chase that stirs the blood!
Ho, landlord, fill the bowl!

The train is laid and the breach is made!
It's pistol work and shortened blade!
The play is best when the stakes be high,
When the dice of death roll thundrous by,
And it's touch and go if you live or die!
Ho, landlord, fill the bowl!

Three loves there be, and three alone,
Born in the blood and bred in the bone!
Who follows their lead rides fast and far;
It's neck or nothing, where these three are.
So here's to woman and wine and war!
Ho, landlord, fill the bowl!

James Stuart Montgomery

THE ABBOT OF DERRY

Lines, as from a Lyttel Booke of Balettys and Dyties, enscribed to Richard Nix,
Bishoppe, by his Admyring, Faithful Friend, John Skelton, Rector of Diss:

The Abbot of Derry
   Hates Satan and Sin;
'Tis strange of him, very;
   They're both his blood-kin;
And the Devil go bury the Abbot of Derry,
   And bury him deep, say I!

The Abbot of Derry
   Has woman nor wine.
'Tis kind of him, very,
   To leave them all mine:
And the Devil go bury the Abbot of Derry,
   And bury him deep, say I!

Says the Abbot of Derry:
  "To-morrow ye die!"
"Eat, drink, and be merry!"
  Say Dolly and I:
And the Devil go bury the Abbot of Derry,
    And bury him deep, say I!

The Abbot of Derry
  Says "All flesh is grass."
Sure, the Abbot should know,
  For the Abbot's an ass!
And the Devil go bury the Abbot of Derry,
    And bury him deep, say I!

The Abbot of Derry
  Says "Love is a knave!"
I shall love when the Abbot
  Lies deep in his grave:—
And the Devil go bury the Abbot of Derry,
    And bury him deep, say I!

John Bennett

WINE AND WATER

From " The Flying Inn "

OLD Noah he had an ostrich farm and fowls on the largest
    scale,
He ate his egg with a ladle in an egg-cup big as a pail,
And the soup he took was Elephant Soup and the fish he
    took was Whale,
But they all were small to the cellar he took when he set
    out to sail;
And Noah he often said to his wife when he sat down to dine,
"I don't care where the water goes if it doesn't get into the
    wine."

The cataract of the cliff of heaven fell blinding off the brink
As if it would wash the stars away as suds go down a sink,
The seven heavens came roaring down for the throats of
    hell to drink,
And Noah he cocked his eye and said, "It looks like rain,
    I think,

The water has drowned the Matterhorn as deep as a Mendip
    mine,
But I don't care where the water goes if it doesn't get into
    the wine."

But Noah he sinned, and we have sinned; on tipsy feet
    we trod,
Till a great big black teetotaller was sent to us for a rod,
And you can't get wine at a P. S. A. or chapel, or Eisteddfod,
But the Curse of Water has come again because of the wrath
    of God,
And water is on the Bishop's board and the Higher Thinker's
    shrine,
But I don't care where the water goes if it doesn't get into
    the wine.

G. K. Chesterton

ALCIBIADES TO A JEALOUS GIRL

Slender one, white one,
You seem to marvel
With troubled brows
That I can waver
Even for a moment
In a curious choice
Between you and the wine-cup.

Listen, little one,
Listen, white one,
While I speak truth
To those small hidden
Delightful ears of yours:—
You bring a goddess
Down to earth
For tryst with me;
But the wine-cup,
Oh the wine-cup
Elevates me to be one
Of the company of all the gods!

Arthur Davison Ficke

· PERSICOS ODI

HORACE: BOOK I, ODE 38

THE pomp of the Persian I hold in aversion;
　　I loathe all those gingerbread tricks—
Those chaplets and wreathings of lindeny tree things—
　　　　　　Nix!

Boy, us for plain myrtle, while under this fertile
　　Old grapevine myself I seclude,
For you and bibacious young Quintus Horatius—
　　　　　　Stewed.

Franklin P. Adams

CHANT ROYAL OF THE DEJECTED DIPSOMA-
NIAC

SOME fools keep ringing the dumb waiter bell
Just as I finish killing Uncle Ned;
I wonder if they could have heard him yell?
A moment since I cursed at them and said:
"This is a pretty time to bring the ice!"
—Old Uncle Ned! Two times of late, or thrice,
I've thought of prodding him with something keen
But always Fate has seemed to intervene;
Last night, for instance, I was in the mood,
But I was far too drunken yestere'en—
My way of life can end in nothing good!

At Mrs. Dumple's, last week, when I fell
And spoiled her dinner party I was led
Out to a cab; they saw I was not well
And took me home and tucked me into bed.
I should quit mingling hashish with my rice!
I should give over singing "Three Blind Mice"
At funerals. Why *will* I make a scene?
Why *should* I feed my cousins Paris Green?
I am increasingly misunderstood:
When I am tactless, people think 'tis spleen.
My way of life can end in nothing good.

Why *should* one cry that he is William Tell,
Then flip a pippin from his hostess' head
That none but he can see? Why *should* one dwell
Upon the failings of the newly wed
At wedding breakfasts? *Can* I not be Nice?
I am so silly and so full of vice!
Such prestidigitator tricks, I ween,
As finding false teeth in a soup tureen
Are not real humor; they are crass and crude,
And cast suspicion on the host's cuisine:
My way of life can end in nothing good.

My wife and her best friend, a social swell,
Zoo-ward I lured to see the cobras fed;—
"We can't go home," I giggled, "for the El
Is broken, Sarah—let's elope, instead!"
I spoke of all she'd have to sacrifice,
And she seemed yielding to me, once or twice,
Until my wife broke in and said: "Eugene,
Your finger nails are seldom really clean;—
I'd loose poor Sarah's hand, Eugene, I would!"
How weak and stupid I have always been!
My way of life can end in nothing good.

I drink and doze and wake and think of hell,
My eyes are blear from all the tears I shed:
I'm pitiably bald: I'm but a shell!
I sobbed today, "I *wish* that I were dead!
I wish I *could* quit drugs and drink and dice.
I wish I had not talked of chicken lice
That Sunday that we entertained the Dean,
Nor shouted to his wife that paraffin
Would make her thin beard grow, nor played the food
Was pennies and her face a slot machine:
My way of life can end in nothing good.

That bell again: A voice: "Is your name Bryce?
These goods is C. O. D. Send down the price!"
"Bryce lives," I yell, "at Number Seventeen!"
Bryce *doesn't* live there, but I feel so mean

I laugh and lie; my tongue is harsh and rude.
—Uncle is gone! I'm phthisical and lean—
My way of life can end in nothing good!

Don Marquis

FRUSTRATE

(After an evening with Browning, Masefield, Lewis Carroll and Gertrude Stein)

I TURNED to the parlor in panic
   And blurted out, "What must you think?"
She rippled, " Then let me the canick-
      in clink!"

I soared to my feet; it was still dim. . . .
   The moon, like an opal in fright,
Leaned over and whispered, "I killed him
      Last night."

Not an hour to lose; I would save her—
   I fastened my spurs in the air
With the scent of the twilight I gave her
      To wear.

And I thought, with a shriek, of how Friday
   Would burst into corduroy pants—
And I drove like a fiend, and I cried "Day,
      Advance!"

The wind smacked its lips, "Here's a nice treat."
   The sea was a forest of flame. . . .
And so to the billowy Bye Street
      I came.

The stars at my shoulder were baying;
   I surged through a hole i' the gate;
And I knew that the Bishop was saying,
      "Too late."

.   .   .   .

They tell me that no one believed me;
   I *never* was asked to the feast. . . .
My dears, 'twas the cabby deceived me—
      The beast!

Louis Untermeyer

SPRING SONG OF A SUPER–BLAKE

(After W. H. Davies)

THE grass is green,
    The sky is blue,
The bird will preen,
    The cat will mew.
The fly has wings,
    The child a toy—
Such little things
    Do give me joy.

The tree has leaves,
    The road has miles,
And nothing grieves
    Whene'er it smiles.
The crops have sun;
    The streams close by
Do ramble on,
    And so do I.

And happy then
    My lot shall be
While rook and wren
    Build in the tree;
While ring-doves coo,
    And lions roar,
As long as two
    And two are four.

Louis Untermeyer

ANOTHER VILLON–OUS VARIATION

STINGER and Gonoph and Peterman,
    Dip and Yegg that prig and prey,
Flimp the thimble as fast as you can,
    But still in the end it doesn't pay;
Stick up a Boob or strong-arm a Jay,
    Snatch a Hanger or shove the Queer,
And square the Bulls for a getaway—
    But where are the Crooks of Yesteryear?

There's Cush in the Keck for a little span,
Fagin or Booster may have his day,
Shine with Ice like a new tin pan,
But still in the end it doesn't pay!
Lagged by the Dicks of Fate are they
Whether they lammister far or near—
The lamps of justice are bum, you say?—
But where are the Crooks of Yesteryear?

No Stool may snitch or rap your plan,
You may never be settled in Stir to stay,
You never may ride in the Hurry-up Van,
But still, in the end, it doesn't pay.
The Level Lay is the only Lay,
Take it from me as a friendly steer—
The life of the Grafter is easy and gay?—
But where are the Crooks of Yesteryear?

Ask the Gonoph whose hair is gray
And he'll tell you straight that it doesn't pay;
When he's young and flush the Gon may sneer—
But where are the Crooks of Yesteryear?

Don Marquis

BYGONES

(After W. E. Henley)

Or ever a lick of Art was done,
    Or ever a one to care,
I was a Purple Polygon,
    And you were a Sky-Blue Square.

You yearned for me across a void,
    For I lay in a different plane,
I'd set my heart on a Red Rhom*boid*,
    And your sighing was in vain.

You pined for me as well I knew,
    And you faded day by day,
Until the Square that was heavenly Blue,
    Had paled to an ashen gray.

A myriad years or less or more,
　　Have softly fluttered by,
Matters are much as they were before,
　　Except 'tis I that sigh.

I yearn for you, but I have no chance,
　　You lie in a different plane,
I break my heart for a single glance,
　　And I break said heart in vain.

And ever I grow more pale and wan,
　　And taste your old despair,
When I was a Purple Polygon,
　　And you were a Sky-Blue Square.

Bert Leston Taylor

THE LITTLE COMMODORE

(After Henry Newbolt)

IT was eight bells in the forenoon and hammocks running
　　sleek
　　(*It's a fair sea flowing from the West*),
When the little Commodore came a-sailing up the Creek
　　(*Heave Ho! I think you'll know the rest*),
Thunder in the halyards and horses leaping high,
Blake and Drake and Nelson are listenin' where they lie,
Four and twenty blackbirds a-bakin' in a pie,
　　And the *Pegasus* came waltzing from the West.

Now the little Commodore sat steady on his keel
　　(*It's a fair sea flowing from the West*),
A heart as stout as concrete reinforced with steel
　　(*Heave Ho! I think you'll know the rest.*)
Swinging are the scuppers, hark, the rudder snores,
Plugging at the Frenchmen, downing 'em by scores,
Porto Rico, Vera Cruz, and also the Azores,
　　And the *Pegasus* came waltzing from the West.

So three cheers more for the little Commodore
　　(*It's a fair sea flowing from the West*),
I tell you so again as I've told you so before
　　(*Heigh Ho! I think you know the rest*).

Aged is the Motherland, old but she is young
(Easy with the tackle there—don't release the bung),
And I sang a song like all the songs that I have ever sung
  When the *Pegasus* came sailing from the West.

                                        J. C. Squire

THE POOR OLD MAN

(After W. H. Davies)

A POOR old man
    Who has no bread,
He nothing can
    To get a bed.

He has a cough,
    Bad boots he has;
He takes them off
    Upon the grass.

He does not eat
    In cosy inns
But keeps his meat
    In salmon tins.

No oven hot,
    No frying-pan;
Thank God I'm not
    That poor old man.

                                        J. C. Squire

MAUD MULLER MUTATUR

(After J. G. Whittier)

MAUD MULLER, on a summer's day,
Powdered her nose with Bon Sachet.

Beneath her lingerie hat appeared
Eyebrows and cheeks that were well veneered.

Singing she rocked on the front piazz,
  To the tune of "The Land of the Sky Blue Jazz."

But the song expired on the summer air,
And she said "This won't get me anywhere."

The judge in his car looked up at her
And signalled "Stop!" to his brave chauffeur.

He smiled a smile that is known as broad,
And he said to Miss Muller, "Hello, how's Maud?"

"What sultry weather this is? Gee whiz!"
Said Maud. Said the judge, "I'll say it is."

"Your coat is heavy. Why don't you shed it?
Have a drink?" said Maud. Said the judge, "You said it."

And Maud, with the joy of bucolic youth,
Blended some gin and some French vermouth.

Maud Muller sighed, as she poured the gin,
"I've got something on Whittier's heroine."

"Thanks," said the judge, "a peppier brew
From a fairer hand was never knew."

And when the judge had had number 7,
Maud seemed an angel direct from Heaven.

And the judge declared, "You're a lovely girl,
An' I'm for you, Maudie, I'll tell the worl'."

And the judge said, "Marry me, Maudie dearie?"
And Maud said yes to the well known query.

And she often thinks, in her rustic way,
As she powders her nose with Bòn Sachet,

"I never'n the world would 'a got that guy,
If I'd waited till after the First o' July."

And of all glad words of prose or rhyme,
The gladdest are, "Act while there yet is time."
                                          Franklin P. Adams

GEORGIE PORGIE

(By Mother Goose and our own Sara Teasdale)

BENNIE'S kisses left me cold,
   Eddie's made me yearn to die,
Jimmie's made me laugh aloud,—
   But Georgie's made me cry.

Bennie sees me every night,
   Eddie sees me every day,
Jimmie sees me all the time,—
   But Georgie stays away.

Franklin P. Adams

THE EXQUISITE SONNET

No purple mars the chalice; not a bird
Shrills o'er the solemn silence of thy fame.
No echo of the mist that knows no name
Dims the fierce darkness of the odorous word.
The shadowy sails of all the world are stirred,
The pomps of hell go down in utter flame,
And never a magic master stands to shame
The hollow of the hill the Titans heard.
O move not, cease not, heart! Time's acolyte
Frustrates forlorn the windows of the west
And beats the blinding of our bitter tears,
Immune in isolation; whilst the night
Smites with her stark immortal palimpsest
The green arcades of immemorial years!

J. C. Squire

THE DURABLE BON MOT

WHEN Whistler's strongest colors fade,
   When inks and canvas rot,
Those jokes on Oscar Wilde he made
   Will dog him unforgot.

For gags still set the world agog
  When fame begins to flag,
And, like the tail that wagged the dog,
  The smart tale dogs the wag.

Keith Preston

THE HUMORIST

HE must not laugh at his own wheeze:
A snuff box has no right to sneeze.

Keith Preston

THE INEFFICACIOUS EGG

The egg is smooth and very pale;
It has no nose, it has no tail;
It has no ears that one can see;
It has no wit, no repartee.

If it were round or even square,
Or squat in contour like a pear;
If it were green, or blue, or black;
Or had a shell that did not crack;
One would insure its *belle tournure*.

Eggs are most futile, vapid things;
They have no soul, they have no wings;
They do not eat, they do not drink;
They do not even try to think.

Roy Bishop

EVE

Apropos de Rien

IT is not fair to visit all
The blame on Eve, for Adam's fall;
The most Eve did was to display
Contributory negligé.

Oliver Herford

MY SENSE OF SIGHT

MY sense of sight is very keen,
My sense of hearing weak.
One time I saw a mountain pass,
But could not hear its peak.

Oliver Herford

THOUGHTS ON BEING INVITED TO DINNER

Of old, all invitations ended
    With the well-known R. S. V. P.,
But now our laws have been amended
    The hostess writes
        B. Y. O. B.

Christopher Morley

THE LIMERATOMY

THE FACE

As a beauty I'm not a great star,
There are others more handsome by far,
But my face I don't mind it,
Because I'm behind it—
'Tis the folks in the front that I jar.

NOTE

In the wax works of Nature they strike
Off each minute some face for life's hike,
And of billions of mugs
On us poor human bugs—
There are no two exactly alike.

THE CONSCIENCE

With a conscience we're able to see
Just how bad we're permitted to be,
At the same time it's true
That what's wicked for you
Mightn't be half so wicked for me.

THE SNEEZE

Now the sneeze is a joy-vent, I s'pose,
When you're tickled to death in your nose—
A pleasing explosion,
Creating erosion—
But you want to watch out where it goes.

THE SMILE

No matter how grouchy you're feeling,
You'll find the smile more or less healing.
It grows in a wreath
All around the front teeth—
Thus preserving the face from congealing.

THE EARS

Now the ears, so I always had thunk,
Should bear sounds to the top of the trunk,
But from some I observe,
They seem merely to serve
As racks for the Jooler-man's junk,

THE HANDS

The hands they were made to assist
In supplying the features with grist.
There are only a few—
As a rule about two—
And are hitched to the end of the wrist.

THE ANKLE

The ankle's chief end is exposiery
Of the latest designs in silk hosiery,
Also I suspect
It was made to connect
The part called the calf with the toesiery.

Anthony Euwer

LIMERICISED CLASSICS

Anthony W. Euwer, in "The Limeratomy," deplores the fact that onr greatest poets did not make use of the Limerick form of verse. We endeavor to supply the omission, in part.

I—HOW HOMER SHOULD HAVE WRITTEN THE ILIAD

There was a young man named Achilles
Whose wrongs always gave him the willies;
So he sulked in his tent
Like a half-witted gent—
Say, wasn't them heroes the sillies?

II—SHAKESPEARE MIGHT HAVE BOILED OTHELLO

There once was a guy named Othello,
A dark, disagreeable fellow;
　After croaking his wife,
　Then he took his own life—
That bird wasn't black, he was yellow!

III—THE RUBAIYAT

"A jug and a book and a dame,
And a nice shady nook for the same,"
　Said Omar Khayyám,
　"And I don't give a darn
What you say, it's a great little game! "

IV—"TO LUCASTA, ON GOING TO THE WARS"

"Lucasta," said Terence O'Connor,
"I'm drafted—I guess I'm a goner!
　I know it will grieve you
　To death, when I leave you—
But gosh! how I'm stuck on my honor! "

V—SPOON RIVER ANTHOLOGY

I dropped my wad
Cornering cotton.　Then
I died.
Now, I guess I'm forgotten.
Well, that swell
Epitaph that I've got
Makes me laugh.
When I lived
I was certainly rotten!

Edwin Meade Robinson

PORTRAITS

EVENTS

THE queen of Egypt yawned and frowned
And twisted all her rings around,
Her thoughts were still, her pulse was slow
While kings and courtiers bowed below.
Upon a gem-encrusted throne
The queen of Egypt sat alone,
Hating her sterile gorgeous land,
When, suddenly, against her hand,
Between two curves of tortoise-shell,
A sulky little rain-drop fell.
The queen threw back her head and stared,
And on her brow the lightning flared. . . .

As Tristan and Isolde lay,
Dreaming their happiness away
Within the forest quiet-boughed,
A thrush came in a morning cloud.
And through the foliage of an oak
A silver fountain rose and broke,
Quivering leaves that drooped afar,
Still drowsing with the night's last star.
Embracing shadows grew estranged,
The dreaming of the dreamers changed;
The thrush sang on and Tristan slept,
But sad Isolde woke and wept.

Napoleon turned his horse about
And down the steepest path set out,
Letting the horse go on alone,
Picking his way from stone to stone.
The trees stood leafless on the hill,
The puddles in the clay lay still.

Napoleon set his gaze below;
The west was streaked with afterglow.
They struck the highway . . . up its side
The horse, without a warning, shied . . .
In scarlet water on the road,
Still as a sea-rock, sat a toad.

George O'Neil

QUEEN CLEOPATRA

From "Variations"

QUEEN Cleopatra, now grown old,
Watched the green grass turning brown . . .
The river is shrunk to half its size:
Now I will lay me down.

Queen Cleopatra called her slaves
And peered in the mirror with age-pearled eyes;
My lips are not so red as they were:
Not so the old leaf dies!

Light the torches, and fill the courts
With scarlet music, and bring to me
Vermilion to smear upon my lips,
And opals, that I may be

Once more what Cleopatra was
Before the woman became the queen . . .
She laughed, and backward tossed her head;
And horn, and tambourine,

Snarled at the hot and red-starred night,
While gasping dancers, one by one,
Whirled on the stone with yellow feet . . .
And when that dance was done

She poured cold poison into a cup
And watched the thick foam wink and seethe:
One black bubble upon her tongue
And she would cease to breathe.

She held the poison before her mouth . . .
And saw the dark tomb hewed in stone
Where a thousand nights would drift as one,
And she would sleep alone;

And lightly touched the goblet's rim,
And thought, with a pleased and narrowed eye,
Of this and that, and Antony,
And the laugh that will not die.

Conrad Aiken

THE FAN

LOVELY Semiramis
Closes her slanting eyes:
Dead is she long ago.
From her fan, sliding slow,
Parrot-bright fire's feathers,
Gilded as June weathers,
Plumes bright and shrill as grass
Twinkle down; as they pass
Through the green glooms in Hell
Fruits with a tuneful smell,
Grapes like an emerald rain,
Where the full moon has lain,
Greengages bright as grass,
Melons as cold as glass,
Piled on each gilded booth,
Feel their cheeks growing smooth.
Apes in plumed head-dresses
Whence the bright heat hisses,—
Nubian faces, sly
Pursing mouth, slanting eye,
Feel the Arabian
Winds floating from the fan.

Edith Sitwell

THE QUEEN OF CRETE

I SHALL make a song of the Queen of Crete
Who had nine panthers at her feet,
Who wore bright brooches in her hair—
And her private life was her own affair.

I shall also sing in a minor note
Of the thong she wore about her throat;
Of the sailor men in the Indian sea
To bring her a bed of ivory;
Of the little negro diving girls
Who burst their drums to give her pearls;
Of the hewers of stone and the hewers of wood
And the bones on which her palace stood.
But her private life was her own affair,
And she had bright brooches in her hair
And a tyrian purple robe to wear,
And a gold-encrusted robe of state,
And a lord and a slave to decapitate,
And always a lover at the gate.
And always a thong about her throat,
(But sing it still in a minor note),
A woven thong at the lady's throat.
But whether she died in her ivory bed,
Or was garroted or lost her head,
The ancient chronicler hasn't said,
But the Queen of Crete is very dead.
The queen stood here and watched the sea
And her ship come home with ivory,
And her ship come home with laden hold,
With spice and frankincense and gold,
And the sea saw all and the sea is deep,
And the sea forgets and goes to sleep.

John Grimes

THE BALLAD OF ADAM'S FIRST

Some Gypsies are like her,
Wild, dark, free!
Beads on her middle jimp
For girdle wore she.

That brown woman Lilith,
For dinner one day,
Poaching in Paradise,
Found Adam at play.

"You're some like the Father,
And some like the Snake,
Some like a sweet rarity
God's made for my sake.

"God's made me a rarity,
The very first man!
I'll be a true leman
As long as I can! "

In a mud loblolly,
Barefooted, he played—
Adam, that builded
The first bower made.

Beads on her middle jimp,
Hell-black hair—
Her beads and her beauty
Were raiment rare!

Leland Davis

EVE

AMONG the silver cornstalks
    And lantern-hanging pears
She walked, as one in dreams walks—
    In prim and virgin prayers.

The straightness of her bosom
    White fichus scarcely hid:
She bit a brown-edged blossom
    And wondered why she did.

She frowned at all the blue jays
    Her puckered little frown.
She wandered through the pathways
    And stared them up and down.

And nothing ever happened;
    And no one ever came;
And no cared a rap; and
    Each day was just the same—

And nothing seemed to matter. . . .
  Her lithe and boyish stride
Still swung beside the water
  She looked upon, and sighed;

Till there, where fruit was wanted—
  Where rivers run to rest—
He ploughed, all glowing, and planted
  The apples of her breast.

Robert L. Wolf

THE PORTRAIT OF A FLORENTINE LADY

KINGS' wares; and dreams; and April dusks;
  Out in the golden dew,
One sighing in a secret lane;—
  These wrought the look of you.

God made you out of lonely things;
  To set you at our door,
He tumbled down into the dark
  A hundred towns or more.

Lizette Woodworth Reese

MORNING SONG OF SENLIN

From "Senlin: A Biography"

IT is morning, Senlin says, and in the morning
When the light drips through the shutters like the dew,
I arise, I face the sunrise,
And do the things my fathers learned to do.
Stars in the purple dusk above the rooftops
Pale in a saffron mist and seem to die,
And I myself on a swiftly tilting planet
Stand before a glass and tie my tie.

Vine leaves tap my window,
Dew-drops sing to the garden stones,
The robin chips in the chinaberry tree
Repeating three clear tones.

It is morning. I stand by the mirror
And tie my tie once more.
While waves far off in a pale rose twilight
Crash on a white sand shore.
I stand by a mirror and comb my hair:
How small and white my face!—
The green earth tilts through a sphere of air
And bathes in a flame of space.
There are houses hanging above the stars
And stars hung under a sea . . .
And a sun far off in a shell of silence
Dapples my walls for me. . . .

It is morning, Senlin says, and in the morning
Should I not pause in the light to remember God?
Upright and firm I stand on a star unstable,
He is immense and lonely as a cloud.
I will dedicate this moment before my mirror
To him alone, for him I will comb my hair.
Accept these humble offerings, cloud of silence!
I will think of you as I descend the stair.

Vine leaves tap my window,
The snail-track shines on the stones,
Dew-drops flash from the chinaberry tree
Repeating two clear tones.

It is morning, I awake from a bed of silence,
Shining I rise from the starless waters of sleep.
The walls are about me still as in the evening,
I am the same, and the same name still I keep.
The earth revolves with me, yet makes no motion,
The stars pale silently in a coral sky.
In a whistling void I stand before my mirror,
Unconcerned, and tie my tie.

There are horses neighing on far-off hills
Tossing their long white manes,
And mountains flash in the rose-white dusk,
Their shoulders black with rains. . . .

It is morning.   I stand by the mirror
And surprise my soul once more;
The blue air rushes above my ceiling,
There are suns beneath my floor. . . .

. . . It is morning, Senlin says, I ascend from darkness
And depart on the winds of space for I know not where,
My watch is wound, a key is in my pocket,
And the sky is darkened as I descend the stair.
There are shadows across the windows, clouds in heaven,
And a god among the stars; and I will go
Thinking of him as I might think of daybreak
And humming a tune I know. . . .

Vine-leaves tap at the window,
Dew-drops sing to the garden stones,
The robin chirps in the chinaberry tree
Repeating three clear tones.

Conrad Aiken

EVENING SONG OF SENLIN

IT is moonlight.   Alone in the silence
I ascend my stairs once more,
While waves, remote in a pale blue starlight,
Crash on a white sand shore.
It is moonlight.   The garden is silent.
I stand in my room alone.
Across my wall, from the far-off moon,
A rain of fire is thrown. . . .

There are houses hanging above the stars,
And stars hung under a sea:
And a wind from the long blue vault of time
Waves my curtain for me. . . .

I wait in the dark once more,
Swung between space and space:
Before my mirror I lift my hands
And face my remembered face.

Is it I who stand in a question here,
Asking to know my name? . . .
It is I, yet I know not whither I go,
Nor why, nor whence I came.

It is I, who awoke at dawn
And arose and descended the stair,
Conceiving a god in the eye of the sun,—
In a woman's hands and hair.
It is I whose flesh is gray with the stones
I builded into a wall:
With a mournful melody in my brain
Of a tune I cannot recall. . . .

There are roses to kiss: and mouths to kiss;
And the sharp-pained shadow of death.
I remember a rain-drop on my cheek,—
A wind like a fragrant breath . . .
And the star I laugh on tilts through heaven;
And the heavens are dark and steep. . . .
I will forget these things once more
In the silence of sleep.

Conrad Aiken

EVENSONG

This song is of no importance,
I will only improvise;
Yet, maybe, here and there,
Suddenly from these sounds a chord will start
And piercingly touch my heart.

I

In the pale mauve twilight, streaked with orange,
Exquisitely sweet,—
She leaned upon her balcony and looked across the street;
And across the huddled roofs of the misty city,
Across the hills of tenements, so gray,
She looked into the west with a young and infinite pity,

With a young and wistful pity, as if to say
The dark was coming, and irresistible night,
Which man would attempt to meet
With here and there a little flickering light. . . .
The orange faded, the housetops all were black,
And a strange and beautiful quiet
Came unexpected, came exquisitely sweet,
On market-place and street;
And where were lately crowds and sounds and riot
Was a gentle blowing of wind, a murmur of leaves,
A single step, or voice, and under the eaves
The scrambling of sparrows; and then the hush swept back.

II

She leaned upon her balcony, in the darkness,
Folding her hands beneath her chin;
And watched the lamps begin
Here and there to pierce like eyes the darkness,—
From windows, luminous rooms,
And from the damp dark street
Between the moving branches, and the leaves with rain
    still sweet.
It was strange: the leaves thus seen,
With the lamplight's cold bright glare thrown up among
    them,—
The restless maple leaves,
Twinkling their myriad shadows beneath the eaves,—
Were lovelier, almost, than with sunlight on them,
So bright they were with young translucent green;
Were lovelier, almost, than with moonlight on them. . . .
And looking so wistfully across the city,
With such a young, and wise, and infinite pity
For the girl who had no lover
To walk with her along a street like this,
With slow steps in the rain, both aching for a kiss,—
It seemed as if all evenings were the same,
As if all evenings came
With just such tragic peacefulness as this;
With just such hint of loneliness or pain,
The quiet after rain.

III

Would her lover, then, grow older sooner than she,
And find a night like this too damp to walk?
Would he prefer to stay indoors and talk,
Or read the evening paper, while she sewed, or darned a sock,
And listened to the ticking of the clock:
Would he prefer it to lamplight on a tree?
Would he be old and tired,
And, having all the comforts he desired,
Take no interest in the twilight coming down
So beautifully and quietly on the town?
Would her lover, then, grow old sooner than she?

IV

A neighbor started singing, singing a child to sleep.
It was strange: a song thus heard,—
In the misty evening, after an afternoon of rain,—
Seemed more beautiful than happiness, more beautiful than
    pain,
Seemed to escape the music and the word,
Only, somehow, to keep
A warmth that was lovelier than the song of any bird.
Was it because it came up through this tree,
Through the lucent leaves that twinkled on this tree,
With the bright lamp there beneath them in the street?
It was exquisitely sweet:
So unaffected, so unconscious that it was heard.
Or was it because she looked across the city,
Across the hills of tenements, so black,
And thought of all the mothers with a young and infinite
    pity? . . .
The child had fallen asleep, the hush swept back,
The leaves hung lifeless on the tree.

V

It was too bad the sky was dark.
A cat came slinking close along the wall.
For the moon was full just now, and in the park,
If the sky were clear at all,

The lovers upon the moonlit grass would sprawl,
And whisper in the shadows, and laugh, and there
She would be going, maybe, with a white rose in her
    hair . . .
But would youth at last grow weary of these things,
Of the ribbons and the laces,
And the latest way of putting up one's hair?
Would she no longer care,
In that undiscovered future of recurring springs,
If, growing old and plain, she no longer turned the faces
And saw the people stare?
Would she hear music and not yearn
To take her lover's arm for one more turn? . . .
The leaves hung breathless on the dripping maple tree,
The man across the street was going out.
It was the evening made her think such things, no doubt.
But would her lover grow old sooner than she? . . .
Only the evening made her think such things, no doubt. . . .

VI

And yet, and yet,—
Seeing the tired city, and the trees so still and wet,—
It seemed as if all evenings were the same;
As if all evenings came,
Despite her smile at thinking of a kiss,
With just such tragic peacefulness as this;
With just such hint of loneliness or pain;
The perfect quiet that comes after rain.

Conrad Aiken

BURBANK WITH A BAEDEKER: BLEISTEIN WITH A CIGAR

BURBANK crossed a little bridge
   Descending at a small hotel;
Princess Volupine arrived,
   They were together, and he fell.

Defunctive music under sea
   Passed seaward with the passing bell
Slowly: the God Hercules
   Had left him, that had loved him well.

The horses, under the axletree
  Beat up the dawn from Istria
With even feet. Her shuttered barge
  Burned on the water all the day.

But this or such was Bleistein's way:
  A saggy bending of the knees
And elbows, with the palms turned out,
  Chicago Semite Viennese.

A lustreless protrusive eye
  Stares from the protozoic slime
At a perspective of Canaletto.
  The smoky candle-end of time

Declines. On the Rialto once.
  The rats are underneath the piles.
The Jew is underneath the lot.
  Money in furs. The boatman smiles,

Princess Volupine extends
  A meagre, blue-nailed, phthisic hand
To climb the waterstair. Lights, lights,
  She entertains Sir Ferdinand

Klein. Who clipped the lion's wings
  And fleaed his rump and pared his claws?
Thought Burbank, meditating on
  Time's ruins, and the seven laws.

T. S. Eliot

THE LOVE SONG OF J. ALFRED PRUFROCK

> *S'io credesse che mia risposta fosse*
> *A persona che mai tornasse al mondo,*
> *Questa fiamma staria senza piu scosse.*
> *Ma perciocche giammai di questo fondo*
> *Non torno vivo alcun, s'i'odo il vero,*
> *Senza tema d'infamia ti rispondo.*

LET us go then, you and I,
When the evening is spread out against the sky
Like a patient etherized upon a table;
Let us go, through certain half-deserted streets,
The muttering retreats

Of restless nights in one-night cheap hotels
And sawdust restaurants with oyster-shells:
Streets that follow like a tedious argument
Of insidious intent
To lead you to an overwhelming question. . . .
Oh, do not ask, "What is it?"
Let us go and make our visit.

In the room the women come and go
Talking of Michelangelo.

The yellow fog that rubs its back upon the window-panes,
The yellow smoke that rubs its muzzle on the window-panes
Licked its tongue into the corners of the evening,
Lingered upon the pools that stand in drains,
Let fall upon its back the soot that falls from chimneys,
Slipped by the terrace, made a sudden leap,
And seeing that it was a soft October night,
Curled once about the house, and fell asleep.

And indeed there will be time
For the yellow smoke that slides along the street,
Rubbing its back upon the window-panes;
There will be time, there will be time
To prepare a face to meet the faces that you meet;
There will be time to murder and create,
And time for all the works and days of hands
That lift and drop a question on your plate;
Time for you and time for me,
And time yet for a hundred indecisions,
And for a hundred visions and revisions,
Before the taking of a toast and tea.

In the room the women come and go
Talking of Michelangelo.

And indeed there will be time
To wonder, "Do I dare?" and, "Do I dare?"
Time to turn back and descend the stair,
With a bald spot in the middle of my hair—

(They will say: "How his hair is growing thin!")
My morning coat, my collar mounting firmly to the chin,
My necktie rich and modest, but asserted by a simple pin—
(They will say: "But how his arms and legs are thin!")
Do I dare
Disturb the universe?
In a minute there is time
For decisions and revisions which a minute will reverse.

For I have known them all already, known them all:
Have known the evenings, mornings, afternoons,
I have measured out my life with coffee spoons;
I know the voices dying with a dying fall
Beneath the music from a farther room.
   So how should I presume?

And I have known the eyes already, known them all—
The eyes that fix you in a formulated phrase,
And when I am formulated, sprawling on a pin,
When I am pinned and wriggling on the wall,
Then how should I begin
To spit out all the butt-ends of my days and ways?
   And how should I presume?

And I have known the arms already, known them all—
Arms that are braceleted and white and bare
(But in the lamplight, downed with light brown hair!)
Is it perfume from a dress
That makes me so digress?
Arms that lie along a table, or wrap about a shawl.
   And should I then presume?
   And how should I begin?

      .   .   .   .

Shall I say, I have gone at dusk through narrow streets
And watched the smoke that rises from the pipes
Of lonely men in shirt-sleeves, leaning out of windows? . . .

I should have been a pair of ragged claws
Scuttling across the floors of silent seas.

      .   .   .   .

And the afternoon, the evening, sleeps so peacefully!
Smoothed by long fingers,
Asleep . . . tired . . . or it malingers,
Stretched on the floor, here beside you and me.
Should I, after tea and cakes and ices,
Have the strength to force the moment to its crisis?
But though I have wept and fasted, wept and prayed,
Though I have seen my head (grown slightly bald) brought
      in upon a platter,
I am no prophet—and here's no great matter;
I have seen the moment of my greatness flicker,
And I have seen the eternal Footman hold my coat, and
      snicker,
And in short, I was afraid.

And would it have been worth it, after all,
After the cups, the marmalade, the tea,
Among the porcelain, among some talk of you and me,
Would it have been worth while,
To have bitten off the matter with a smile,
To have squeezed the universe into a ball
To roll it toward some overwhelming question,
To say: "I am Lazarus, come from the dead,
Come back to tell you all, I shall tell you all"—
If one, settling a pillow by her head,
   Should say: "That is not what I meant at all;
   That is not it, at all."

And would it have been worth it, after all,
Would it have been worth while,
After the sunsets and the dooryards and the sprinkled
      streets,
After the novels, after the teacups, after the skirts that
      trail along the floor—
And this, and so much more?—
It is impossible to say just what I mean!
But as if a magic lantern threw the nerves in patterns on
      a screen:
Would it have been worth while
If one, settling a pillow or throwing off a shawl,

And turning toward the window, should say:
  "That is not it at all,
  That is not what I meant, at all."

  .   .   .   .

No! I am not Prince Hamlet, nor was meant to be;
Am an attendant lord, one that will do
To swell a progress, start a scene or two,
Advise the prince; no doubt, an easy tool,
Deferential, glad to be of use,
Politic, cautious, and meticulous;
Full of high sentence, but a bit obtuse;
At times, indeed, almost ridiculous—
Almost, at times, the Fool.

I grow old . . . I grow old . . .
I shall wear the bottoms of my trousers rolled.

Shall I part my hair behind? Do I dare to eat a peach?
I shall wear white flannel trousers, and walk upon the beach.
I have heard the mermaids singing, each to each.

I do not think that they will sing to me.

I have seen them riding seaward on the waves
Combing the white hair of the waves blown back
When the wind blows the water white and black.

We have lingered in the chambers of the sea
By sea-girls wreathed with seaweed red and brown
Till human voices wake us, and we drown.

                                        T. S. Eliot

PORTRAIT OF A LADY

"Thou hast committed—
Fornication: but that was in another country, and besides, the wench is dead."—
                                        THE JEW OF MALTA

I

AMONG the smoke and fog of a December afternoon
You have the scene arrange itself—as it will seem to do—
With "I have saved this afternoon for you";
And four wax candles in the darkened room,

Four rings of light upon the ceiling overhead,
An atmosphere of Juliet's tomb
Prepared for all the things to be said, or left unsaid.
We have been, let us say, to hear the latest Pole
Transmit the Preludes, through his hair and finger-tips.
"So intimate, this Chopin, that I think his soul
Should be resurrected only among friends
Some two or three, who will not touch the bloom
That is rubbed and questioned in the concert room."

—And so the conversation slips
Among the velleities and carefully caught regrets
Through attenuated tones of violins
Mingled with remote cornets,
And begins.
"You do not know how much they mean to me, my friends,
And how, how rare and strange it is, to find
In a life composed so much, so much of odds and ends,
(For indeed I do not love it . . . you knew? you are not blind!
How keen you are!)
To find a friend who has these qualities,
Who has, and gives
Those qualities upon which friendship lives:
How much it means that I say this to you—
Without these friendships—life, what *cauchemar!*"
Among the windings of the violins
And the ariettes
Of cracked cornets,
Inside my brain a dull tom-tom begins
Absurdly hammering a prelude of its own,
Capricious monotone
That is at least one definite "false note."
—Let us take the air, in a tobacco trance,
Admire the monuments,
Discuss the late events,
Correct our watches by the public clocks,
Then sit for half an hour and drink our bocks.

II

Now that lilacs are in bloom
She has a bowl of lilacs in her room

And twists one in her fingers while she talks.
"Ah, my friend, you do not know, you do not know
What life is, you should hold it in your hands ";
(Slowing twisting the lilac stalks)
"You let it flow from you, you let it flow,
And youth is cruel, and has no remorse
And smiles at situations which it cannot see."
I smile, of course,
And go on drinking tea.
"Yet with these April sunsets, that somehow recall
My buried life, and Paris in the Spring,
I feel immeasurably at peace, and find the world
To be wonderful and youthful, after all."

The voice returns like the insistent out-of-tune
Of a broken violin on an August afternoon:
"I am always sure that you understand
My feelings, always sure that you feel,
Sure that across the gulf you reach your hand.

"You are invulnerable, you have no Achilles' heel.
You will go on, and when you have prevailed
You can say: 'At this point many a one has failed.'
But what have I, but what have I, my friend,
To give you, what can you receive from me?
Only the friendship and the sympathy
Of one about to reach her journey's end.

"I shall sit here, serving tea to friends . . ."

I take my hat: how can I make a cowardly amends
For what she has said to me?

You will see me any morning in the park
Reading the comics and the sporting page.
Particularly I remark
An English countess goes upon the stage,
A Greek was murdered at a Polish dance,
Another bank defaulter has confessed.
I keep my countenance,

I remain self-possessed.
Except when a street piano, mechanical and tired,
Reiterates some worn-out common song,
With the smell of hyacinths across the garden
Recalling things that other people have desired.
Are these ideas right or wrong?

III

The October night comes down; returning as before,
Except for a slight sensation of being ill at ease,
I mount the stairs and turn the handle of the door
And feel as if I had mounted on my hands and knees.

"And so you are going abroad; and when do you return?
But that's a useless question.
You hardly know when you are coming back,
You will find so much to learn."
My smile falls heavily among the bric-à-brac.

"Perhaps you can write to me."
My self-possession flares up for a second;
This is as I had reckoned.
"I have been wondering frequently of late
(But our beginnings never know our ends!)
Why we have not developed into friends."
I feel like one who smiles, and turning shall remark
Suddenly, his expression in a glass.
My self-possession gutters; we are really in the dark.

"For everybody said so, all our friends,
They all were sure our feelings would relate
So closely! I myself can hardly understand.
We must leave it now to fate.
You will write, at any rate.
Perhaps it is not too late.
I shall sit here, serving tea to friends."

And I must borrow ever changing shape
To find expression . . . dance, dance
Like a dancing bear,
Cry like a parrot, chatter like an ape.

Let us take the air, in a tobacco trance. . . .
Well! and what if she should die some afternoon,
Afternoon gray and smoky, evening yellow and rose;
Should die and leave me sitting pen in hand
With the smoke coming down above the house-tops;
Doubtful, for quite a while
Not knowing what to feel, or if I understand,
Or whether wise or foolish, tardy or too soon. . . .
Would she not have the advantage, after all?
This music is successful with a "dying fall"
Now that we talk of dying—
And should I have the right to smile?

T. S. Eliot

PORTRAIT D'UNE FEMME

Your mind and you are our Sargasso Sea,
London has swept about you this score years
And bright ships left you this or that in fee:
Ideas, old gossip, oddments of all things,
Strange spars of knowledge and dimmed wares of price.
Great minds have sought you—lacking someone else.
You have been second always. Tragical?
No. You preferred it to the usual thing:
One dull man, dulling and uxorious,
One average mind—with one thought less, each year.
Oh, you are patient, I have seen you sit
Hours, where something might have floated up.
And now you pay one. Yes, you richly pay.
You are a person of some interest, one comes to you
And takes strange gain away:
Trophies fished up, some curious suggestion:
Fact that leads nowhere; and a tale or two,
Pregnant with mandrakes, or with something else
That might prove useful and yet never proves,
That never fits a corner or shows use,
Or finds its hour upon the loom of days:
The tarnished, gaudy, wonderful old work;
Idols and ambergris and rare inlays.
These are your riches, your great store; and yet

For all this sea-hoard of deciduous things,
Strange woods half sodden, and new brighter stuff:
In the slow float of differing light and deep,
No! there is nothing!   In the whole and all,
Nothing that's quite your own.
                    Yet this is you.

Ezra Pound

THE ENAMEL GIRL

FEARFUL of beauty, I always went
Timidly indifferent;

Dainty, hesitant, taking in
Just what was tiniest and thin;

Careful not to care
For burning beauty in blue air;

Wanting what my hand could touch—
That not too much;

Looking not to left nor right
On a honey-silent night;

Fond of arts and trinkets, if
Imperishable and stiff,

They never played me false, nor fell
Into fine dust.   They lasted well.

They lasted till you came, and then
When you went sufficed again.

But for you, they had been quite
All I needed for my sight.

You faded.   I never knew
How to unfold as flowers do,

Or how to nourish anything
To make it grow.   I wound a wing

With one caress, with one kiss
Break most fragile ecstasies. . . .

Now terror touches me when I
Dream I am touching a butterfly.

Genevieve Taggard

CITY GIRL

BENEATH the barren artifice of red
That hides a fertile freshness on your face
I see the hypocritical embrace
Of courtesan and virgin, each in dread
Of yielding to the other, while your mouth
Reveals their secret of uneasiness.
Your mind has listened to a northern stress:
Your heart has heard old rumors from the South.
This conflict, with its plaintive undertones,
Is like an idle phantom to your soul
Whose clear aloofness sometimes sears your eyes.
The sensual games that move your youthful bones
Are still for moments, while the distant goal
Of whispering horizons lures your sighs.

Maxwell Bodenheim

OLD MAID

GOD knows how many nights upon her bed
She dreamed another Latmus, while the hot
Sweet winds of summer in her garden-plot
Kissed away tears from roses comforted.
God knows what flaming verses she had read
To keep vicarious trysts with Lancelot,
Broken with brooding over loves forgot
And lawless revels of the pagan dead.
But she has conquered all her blood's desire,
Cheated her soul of sin as misers cheat,
And now she pauses on proud, hesitant feet
At lighted rooms where men and women mix,
With amorous eyes fearful of unknown fire—
A naked nun clasping the crucifix!

J. U. Nicolson

PORTRAIT

SHE has no need to fear the fall
Of harvest from the laddered reach
Of orchards, nor the tide gone ebbing
　　From the steep beach.

Nor hold to pain's effrontery
Her body's bulwark, stern and savage,
Nor be a glass, where to foresee
　　Another's ravage.

What she has gathered, and what lost,
She will not find to lose again.
She is possessed by time, who once
　　Was loved by men.

Louise Bogan

THE CHANGED WOMAN

THE light flower leaves its little core
Begun upon the waiting bough.
Again she bears what she once bore
And what she knew she re-learns now.

The cracked glass fuses at a touch.
The wound heals over, and is set
In the whole flesh, and is not much
Quite to remember or forget.

Rocket and tree, and dome and bubble
Again behind her freshened eyes
Are treacherous.   She need not trouble.
Her lids will know them when she dies.

And while she lives, the unwise, heady
Dream, ever denied and driven,
Will one day find her bosom ready,—
That never thought to be forgiven.

Louise Bogan

A WOMAN OF WORDS

ONE sweet of hands, one starred for grace,
Should leave the heavy word alone,
Should cease to cut and carve and trace,
End the combat with a stone!

The austere sentence that you drill
Until the granite dust hangs blue,
Etched by your instrument of will
Is bitten not so deep as you.

Lettered for time, in marble told,
Your speech stands chiseled and concise;
Its surfaces are dazzling cold,
Swept clean of dust as ice.

Now hollow as a cup your cheek
In alabaster gleams—
You gave your blood that you might speak
And cut the throat of dreams. . . .

The silence softer women bring
Betrays the velvet smile of scorn;
They know a softer, stranger thing—
That there are children to be borne. . . .

Amanda Benjamin Hall

SHE–DEVIL

WHITE arms, Love, you have, and thin fingers with glit-
tering nails,
And the soft blue smoke curls up from your parted mouth!
The delicate rose of your cheeks never varies nor pales,
And your frocks and your furs are perfection—devourer
of youth!

It is thrilling to think of your room and you, wicked,
    inside—
    Adorable snake, with a snake's unflickering eyes,
And an intimate smile (to share which, fools have died)
    And lips soft as a girl's and like a siren's, wise!

Devourer of youth!   You are never alone by your fire,
    You have always a boy there, who thinks you a goddess,
    ill-used,
And adores you with passion, and brings you the gifts you
    desire—
    And the fiercer he burns, Dear, the better he keeps you
    amused!

Douglas Goldring

MARY MAGDALENE

I THINK that Mary Magdalene
Was just a woman who went to dine;
And her jewels covered her empty heart,
And her gown was the color of wine.

I think that Mary Magdalene
Sat by a stranger with shining head:
"Haven't we met somewhere? " she asked.
"Magdalene! Mary! " he said.

I think that Mary Magdalene
Fell at his feet and called his name;
Sat at his feet and wept her woe,
And rose up clean of shame.

Nobody knew but Magdalene—
Mary the woman who went to dine—
Nobody saw how he broke the bread
And poured for her peace the wine.

This is the story of Magdalene—
It isn't the tale the Apostles tell,
But I know the woman it happened to,
I know the woman well.

Leonora Speyer

TRAÜMEREI AT OSTENDORFF'S

I ATE at Ostendorff's, and saw a dame
  With eager golden eyes, paired with a red,
Bald, chilled old man. Piercing the clatter came
  Keen *Traümerei*. On the sound he bowed his head,
  Covered his eyes, and looked on things long sped.
Her white fierce fingers strained, but could not stir
His close-locked hands, nor bring him back to her.

Let him alone, bright lady; for he clips
  A fairer lass than you, with all your fire.
Let him alone; he touches sweeter lips
  Than yours he hired, as others yet shall hire.
  Leave him the quickening pang of clean desire,
Even though vain; nor taint those spring winds blown
From banks of perished bloom: let him alone.

Bitter-sweet melody, that call'st to tryst
  Love from the hostile dark, would God thy breath
Might break upon him now, through thickening mist,
  The trumpet-summons of imperial Death;
  That now, with fire-clean lips where quivereth
Atoning sorrow, he shall seek the eyes
Long turned towards earth from fields of paradise.

In vain: by virtue of a far-off smile,
  Men may be deaf a space to gross behests
Of nearer voices: for some little while
  Sharp pains of youth may burn in old men's breasts.
  But—men must eat, though angels be their guests:
The waiter brought spaghetti; he looked up,
Hemmed, blinked, and fiddled with his coffee-cup.

William Laird

CELL–MATES

Aw, quit yer cryin', kid—I know it's tough,
  But dearie, shush; nobody's gone to lynch ye;
Later ye'll find th' cops are square enough;
  It's always worse the first time that they pinch ye.

Things ain't so bad.   Now there, don't take on so—
   The matron won't do nothin' if ye shout, dear.
That's right . . . Now come an' tell me all ye know . . .
   Ain't ye got nobody to bail ye out, dear?

Well, well—. But that's a shame. A kid so cute
   An' young like youse had never ought to worry.
Gee! if they'd doll ye up, ye'd be a beaut—
   Why should ye waste yer life in work an' hurry?

Oh, there is lots o' ways it could be did—
   'Course I won't do this much for ev'rybody—
I tell ye what, I'm gone to help ye, kid,
   An' I've got infloonce, if my clo'es is shoddy.

S'posin' that I could get ye out o' here—
   Now, now; don't take on like a reg'lar baby—
Yer pretty lucky that ye met me, dear.
   What's that? No, not to-night. To-morrow, maybe.

Well's I was sayin', when I leave this hole
   I'll get my friend to go to work an' help ye—
Don't breathe this here to any livin' soul,
   Fer strangers, dear, is jest the ones to scalp ye.

Now, I've the swellest little flat uptown,
   An' jolly—somethin' doin' every minute!
There's always some live people hangin' roun';
   Ye'll never want to leave when once ye're in it.

There's lots o' dancin'—jest ye wait an' see
   The nifty rags I'll get to fit ye, dearie.
Aw, never mind the thanks—wait till you're free;
   This gratitood an' sob stuff makes me weary.

Don't worry now, an' things'll be all right;
   Ye'll only see th' folks with happy faces.
There'll be no more o' workin' noon an' night,
   An' standin' up all day behind th' laces.

Here's the address. Now, don't ye lose it, dear;
    An' come right up—don't stop to primp or tidy.
Gee! but it's lucky that ye met me here . . .
    Let's go to sleep . . . Good-night . . . an' see ye
    Frid'y.

Louis Untermeyer

PEREGRINE

LIAR and bragger,
He had no friend
Except a dagger
And a candle-end;
The one he read by,
The one scared cravens;
And he was fed by
The Prophet's ravens.
Such haughty creatures
Avoid the human;
They fondle nature's
Breast, not woman—
A she-wolf's puppies—
A wild-cat's pussy-fur:
Their stirrup-cup is
The pride of Lucifer.
A stick he carried,
Slept in a lean-to;
He'd never married
And he didn't mean to.
He'd tried religion
And found it pleasant;
He relished a pigeon
Stewed with a pheasant
In an iron kettle;
He built stone ovens;
He'd never settle
In any province.
He made pantries
Of Vaux and Arden,
And the village gentry's
Kitchen-garden.

Fruits within yards
Were his staples;
He drank whole vineyards
From Rome to Naples,
Then went to Brittany
For the cider.
He could sit any
Horse, a rider
Outstripping Cheiron's
Canter and gallop.
Pau's environs,
The pubs of Salop,
Wells and Bath inns,
Shared his pleasure
With taverns of Athens.
The Sultan's treasure
He'd seen in Turkey;
He'd known London
Bright and murky.
His bones were sunned on
Paris benches
Beset by sparrows;
Roman trenches,
Cave-men's barrows,
He liked, impartial;
He liked an Abbey.
His step was martial;
Spent and shabby
He wasn't broken;
A dozen lingoes
He must have spoken.
As a king goes
He went, not minding
That he lived seeking
And never finding.
He'd visit Peking
And then be gone soon
To the far Canaries;
He'd cross a monsoon
To chase vagaries.

He loved a city
And a street's alarums;
Parks were pretty
And so were bar-rooms.
He loved fiddles;
He talked with rustics;
Life was riddles
And queer acrostics.
His sins were serried,
His virtues garish;
His corpse was buried
In a country parish.
Before he went hence—
God knows where—
He spoke this sentence
With a princely air:
"The noose draws tighter;
This is the end;
I'm a good fighter
But a bad friend;
I've played the traitor
Over and over;
I'm a good hater
But a bad lover."

Elinor Wylie

PETER

PETER of the brothers three
Loved a life of poesy;
While they stolid bargains drove
He saw movies in the stove.

Peter was a man of peace,
Happily he tended geese;
Though his brothers, as they rose,
Ran a motor 'neath his nose.

Peter knew his limitations,—
Never needed intimations
Which tunes he was not to sing,
What new cabbage pleased the king.

Peter saw expedience
Was the way of common sense;
Sitting quiet on the down
Grabbed the princess and the crown.

Laura Benêt

THE OLD SAINT

You have stopped short of love, your May is over,
Your lips are shrivelled berries on the tree.
Earth gave you her sweet chance of being lover,—
Earth that held Eden as well as Calvary.

You may get whatever guerdon heaven carries,
But not the password to keen kissing lips,
You will never know what Helen said to Paris,
You have lost Egypt though you saved your ships.

Muriel Stuart

JUAN QUINTANA

The goat-herd follows his flock
   Over the sandy plain,
And the goats nibble the rabbit-bush
   Acrid with desert rain.

Old Juan Quintana's coat
   Is a faded purple blue,
And his hat is a warm plum-brown,
   And his trousers a tawny hue.

He is sunburnt like the hills,
   And his eyes have a strange goat-look;
And when I came on him alone,
   He suddenly quivered and shook.

Out in the hills all day
   The trees do funny things—
And a horse shaped like a man
   Rose up from the ground on wings.

And a burro came and stood
   With a cross, and preached to the flock,
While old Quintana sat
   As cold as ice on a rock.

And sometimes the mountains move,
   And the mesa turns about;
And Juan Quintana thinks he's lost,
   Till a neighbor hears him shout.

And they say with a little laugh
   That he isn't quite right, up here;
And they'll have to get a *muchacho*
   To help with the flock next year.

Alice Corbin

AN OLD MAN'S WINTER NIGHT

ALL out of doors looked darkly in at him
Through the thin frost, almost in separate stars,
That gathers on the pane in empty rooms.
What kept his eyes from giving back the gaze
Was the lamp tilted near them in his hand.
What kept him from remembering what it was
That brought him to that creaking room was age.
He stood with barrels round him—at a loss.
And having scared the cellar under him
In clomping there, he scared it once again
In clomping off;—and scared the outer night,
Which has its sounds, familiar, like the roar
Of trees and crack of branches, common things,
But nothing so like beating on a box.
A light he was to no one but himself
Where now he sat, concerned with he knew what,
A quiet light, and then not even that.
He consigned to the moon, such as she was,
So late-arising, to the broken moon
As better than the sun in any case
For such a charge, his snow upon the roof,
His icicles along the wall to keep;

And slept. The log that shifted with a jolt
Once in the stove, disturbed him and he shifted,
And eased his heavy breathing, but still slept.
One aged man—one man—can't fill a house,
A farm, a countryside, or if he can,
It's thus he does it of a winter night.

Robert Frost

HOW ANNANDALE WENT OUT

"THEY called it Annandale—and I was there
To flourish, to find words, and to attend:
Liar, physician, hypocrite, and friend,
I watched him; and the sight was not so fair
As one or two that I have seen elsewhere:
An apparatus not for me to mend—
A wreck, with hell between him and the end,
Remained of Annandale: and I was there.

"I knew the ruin as I knew the man;
So put the two together, if you can,
Remembering the worst you know of me.
Now view yourself as I was, on the spot—
With a slight kind of engine. Do you see?
Like this. . . . You wouldn't hang me? I thought not."

Edwin Arlington Robinson

CLIFF KLINGENHAGEN

CLIFF Klingenhagen had me in to dine
With him one day; and after soup and meat,
And all the other things there were to eat,
Cliff took two glasses and filled one with wine
And one with wormwood. Then, without a sign
For me to choose at all, he took the draught
Of bitterness himself, and lightly quaffed
It off, and said the other one was mine.
And when I asked him what the deuce he meant
By doing that, he only looked at me

And smiled, and said it was a way of his.
And though I know the fellow, I have spent
Long time a-wondering when I shall be
As happy as Cliff Klingenhagen is.

Edwin Arlington Robinson

IN THE VICES

GAY and audacious crime glints in his eyes,
And his mad talk, raping the commonplace,
Gleefully runs a devil-praising race,
And none can ever follow where he flies.
He streaks himself with vices tenderly;
He cradles sin, and with a figleaf fan
Taps his green cat, watching a bored sun span
The wasted minutes to eternity.
Once I took up his trail along the dark,
Wishful to track him to the witches' flame,
To see the bubbling of the sneer and snare.
The way led through a fragrant starlit park,
And soon upon a harlot's house I came—
Within I found him playing at solitaire!

Donald Evans

A MAN WHOM MEN DEPLORE

HERE lies a frigid man whom men deplore,
A presence concentrated in a frame,
A full-length portrait of the flesh of yore,
A still-life study of a death aflame,
White, unresistant, intimate and free,
The eyes a secret, hands as cold as stars,
A man who lies with his biography,
A dreaming book whose wounds have dried to scars:
There flies a thrilling soul men cultivate,
A ghostly eagle solving mysteries,
His darkest faults, graces they emulate,
Wings redolent of suns and eyes of seas:
For they who shrank from his mad human ache
Call him high Shelley now and praise his wake.

Alfred Kreymborg

SAVAGE PORTRAITS

FROGGLES

HE knows celebrities . . . or else he lies . . .
They share with him their tears, their chaff;
HE KNEW CELEBRITIES: his epitaph
Let that line be, when busy Froggles dies.
He tells you how Ben Actor dreaded fat,
He knows the oaths that Bishop Pulpit swore,
He tells you what the late Dick Author wore—
He has, indeed, a valet's eye for that.

He says Tom Bluff is losing out through drink . . .
Poor Tom, he's such a clever fellow, too!
To look at What's-his-name you wouldn't think
That he took drugs . . . alas! dear man, 'tis true!
He knew Bill Blank before success had come;
He might tell tales . . . but no, his lips are dumb!

Each dead man Froggles calls by his first name;
The living, too—provided they're not by.
Professing to defend, he spreads a lie,
Affects to cherish, while he smears, their fame.
He's rather strong on Matrimonial Stuff—
He's been the Whistles' guest, and seen their life,
And so he scarcely blames Jack Whistle's wife . . .
One sees these smash-ups coming, plain enough!

HE KNEW CELEBRITIES . . . OR DID HE LIE?
They'll carve that line some summer afternoon
Upon a stone beneath the careless sky.
Myself, I rather hope they'll carve it soon . . .
Small matter, though; for every pest you slay
Ten more rank flies pollute the breath of day.

THE GOOGS

"Precious!" says Mrs. Goog. And, "Love!" cries he,
And smacks his liar's lips against her face.
"Sweet Dove!"—and then they clinch in close embrace.
He's thirty-one, and she's turned fifty-three;

She makes him pet her when there's company.
"My Angel!" "Little Wife!"—and all men trace
The hatred crawling through his forced grimace;
Some day he'll kill her to be rich and free.

If I am on Goog's jury then, he'll hang;
I know just how he trapped the love-starved hag;
True, *she* caught *him* with coins that clinked and rang . . .
But he—I've heard that saffron cheese-rind brag!—
"My own, my Dove!" "Come, kiss me, precious pet!"—
Kiss her, you crook; it is your life-work: Sweat!

GILK

Gilk is sincere. He lets no chance get by
To tell me so, and I've no doubt he is.
Deceit moulds not nor moves that osseous phiz,
Nor ever fancy lights that opaque eye:
No bone, unhelped of brain, creates a lie.
Saints fall, and stars; erratic comets whiz
Through space; but that dead rectitude of his
Will never fail till mummies chirp and fly.

Such virtue blights my nature worse than crime—
Gilk makes me long to scream and plunge in sin!
I'd sooner writhe, outcast of Hope and Time,
Brain-sick, midst nether Hell's most impious din,
Than sit and hold Gilk's hand beside the throne,
A fellow-angel to that godly bone!

THE QUINKS

When one calls on the Quinks they always say:
"We've never quarreled, though we've been wed ten years!"
And then they quarrel, with "loves" and "pets" and
    "dears" . . .
"No, Dove!"—"Yes, Pet!"—"Sweetheart will have her
    way!"
—"Pet played the ace!"—"No, Love, I played the trey!"
If they would candidly slap mugs, pull ears,
Say "Brute!" cry "Fool!" let smiles be frankly sneers,
The sickly air might clear some honest day.

"Don't quarrel, Love!" says Pet, when Love looks gingered
Up to fling some healthy human curse.
"Be sweet, my Pet!" says Love, when Pet seems in-
    jured . . .
I can't write what I feel: I'm coarse, when terse;
But should Pet bounce a skillet off Love's sconce
I think they'd both be happier, for the nonce.

MELISSA

Melissa lisps a little bit; I wis
Melissa wisses Lillith lisped like that!
Melissa, from her instep to her hat,
Is lithe and Lillith-like . . . or thinks she is.
She is six Sirens and Semiramis,
Four Serpents, Phyrne, and a Vampire Bat,
Two Cleopatras and a Leopard Cat,
And thinks the world is dizzy for her kiss.

She'd like to have you know she's dangerous
As Venus dressed décolleté in foam—
But, really, 'Lissy never wrecked a home,
And wouldn't if she could; the whole damned fuss
Is just a literary kind of pose . . .
She writes, has bunions, and—Good God! her Nose!

Don Marquis

THE BARB OF SATIRE

THE STORY OF UG

Ug was a hairy but painstaking artist,
  Back in a simple and primitive age.
Listen, young Poet! And ere thou departest,
  Haply thou'lt learn something. (Haply thou'lt rage!)
Ug fashioned arrowheads, slowly and neatly,
  Chipping all day at the hardest of stone;
Made them symmetrical, polished them sweetly,
  Sharpened their points with a skill all his own.

Long ones and short ones and fat ones or narrow,
  Bolts of obsidian, spearheads of flint;
Some that could crash through a mastodon's marrow,
  Some that were prized for their beautiful tint;
Endless varieties told of his talents—
  All were alike in that all were acute,
All had the symmetry, finish and balance
  Arrows must have if one wants them to shoot.

And then, one day,
Ug began to notice
A distinct falling off in his trade,
And, upon inquiry, he found
That a new school of arrowhead-makers
Who made what they called "Free Arrowheads"
Was getting popular among the young men.
The arrowheads were "free"
In the sense that they had no shape,
Being mere amorphous chunks
Of flint, or sandstone or blue mud
Or any thing.
It seems that the old, shapely kind
Was felt to be monotonous and antique,
Being even on both sides,
Like a foolish old Grecian jar,

Or a butterfly, or a woman.
While the new kind
Could "express the soul" of its maker,
In looking like a piece of cheese.
You couldn't hit anything with the new kind
Because they wouldn't shoot straight;
But being purely "subjective" arrowheads,
They weren't intended to hit anything.
So Ug was neglected,
Until people began to get hungry . . .
And then, since he was the only
Skilled maker left in the country
He became
A millionaire.

Edwin Meade Robinson

TO AN UNGENTLE CRITIC

The great sun sinks behind the town
Through a red mist of Volnay wine. . . .
But what's the use of setting down
That glorious blaze behind the town?
You'll only skip the page, you'll look
For newer pictures in this book;
You've read of sunsets rich as mine.

A fresh wind fills the evening air
With horrid crying of night birds. . . .
But what reads new or curious there
When cold winds fly across the air?
You'll only frown; you'll turn the page,
But find no glimpse of your "New Age
Of Poetry" in my worn-out words.

Must winds that cut like blades of steel
And sunsets swimming in Volnay,
The holiest, cruellest pains I feel,
Die stillborn, because old men squeal
For something new: "Write something new:
We've read this poem—that one too,
And twelve more like 'em yesterday"?

No, no! my chicken, I shall scrawl
Just what I fancy as I strike it,
Fairies and Fusiliers, and all
Old broken knock-kneed thought will crawl
Across my verse in the classic way.
And, sir, be careful what you say;
There are old-fashioned folk still like it.

Robert Graves

PERPETUUM MOBILE

A PANTOUM, MORE OR LESS

PILK lauds the verse of Jobble to the skies,
And Jobble says that Bibson's Dante's peer.
Bibson is great on Pagg,—"What art!" he cries,
While Pagg is sure that Dubkin is a seer.

While Pagg is sure that Dubkin is a seer,
Dubkin swears Botchell's odes will never wane;
Botchell commands: "Watch Pimpington's career!"
Pimpington writes a book on Trodger's brain.

Pimpington writes a book on Trodger's brain,
And Trodger shrieks: "Glabb's genius stirs my soul!"
Glabb raves of Cringely's rhymes with might and main;
Cringely pens Gummit's name on glory's scroll.

Cringely pens Gummit's name on glory's scroll,
And Gummit sees in Sludd new worlds arise;
Sludd bids us hear Pilk's mighty rhythms roll;
Pilk lauds the verse of Jobble to the skies. . . .

Edith Sitwell

POST–IMPRESSIONISM

I CANNOT tell you how I love
The canvasses of Mr. Dove,
Which Saturday I went to see
In Mr. Thurber's gallery.

At first you fancy they are built
As patterns for a crazy-quilt,
But soon you see that they express
An ambient simultaneousness.

This thing which you would almost bet
Portrays a Spanish omelette,
Depicts instead, with wondrous skill,
A horse and cart upon a hill.

Now, Mr. Dove has too much art
To show the horse or show the cart;
Instead, he paints the *creak* and *strain*.
Get it? No pike is half as plain.

This thing which would appear to show
A fancy vest scenario,
Is really quite another thing,
A flock of pigeons on the wing.

But Mr. Dove is much too keen
To let a single bird be seen;
To show the pigeons would not do
And so he simply paints the *coo*.

It's all as simple as can be;
He paints the things you cannot see,
Just as composers please the ear
With "programme" things you cannot hear.

Dove is the cleverest of chaps;
And, gazing at his rhythmic maps,
I wondered (and I'm wondering yet)
Whether he did them on a bet.

Bert Leston Taylor

THE NIMBLE STAG

THE nimble stag awoke at dawn;
He had been petted when a fawn,
And nourished in a park with care
By gallant men and ladies fair.

But now he had two horns in front
And was quite old enough to hunt.

The Muddlebury Staghounds are
Exceedingly particular.
They choose the stag they think most fleet,
And then they cart it to the meet,
And hunt it up and down all day
And slaughter it when dusk is gray
(Unless, of course, it gets away).

The stag that I was speaking of,
Although it had a trifling cough,
Was otherwise quite fit and well,
And ran like—well, it ran quite well.
And after a tremendous chase
It doubled at a fearful pace
To Muddlebury Market-Place,
In which there stands an oil-cake shop,
With office buildings at the top.
The stag, whose heart went pit-a-pat,
Decided to run into that.
It ran upstairs with nimble hoof,
And somehow got onto the roof.

Of course there was a hue and cry,
And everybody said, "My eye!
Did you observe the stag come by?"
The clerks' excitement knew no bounds,
They all came out to see the hounds:
When suddenly—we can't inquire
Exactly how—the shop caught fire.
There never had been such a blaze
Since Muddlebury's earliest days.

The fire brigade with hose and spout
Did all they could to put it out.
But fearful consternation reigned
When they perceived the stag remained

High up alone upon a ledge,
Of which the flames had reached the edge.
The Master, Mr. Samuel Jape,
Went swiftly up the fire-escape,
And he was followed by the Whip,
Whose name, I think, was Reuben Tripp;
The Vicar and the Squire, as well,
Dashed bravely through the blazing hell.
They fought amidst the fiery fumes
That filled the charred and gutted rooms;
The firemen simply did not dare
To follow them, though brave they were.
Ah! how the people shouted when
That little group of stalwart men
Were finally observed to drag
Onto the fire-escape the stag,
Though since the building was so hot
They most of them were burned a lot;
They lowered it with anxious face
To Muddlebury Market-Place.
But that did not complete the task,
They gave it brandy from a flask,
And tried its feeble pulse to stir,
And stuck a glass thermometer
Into its mouth below the tongue,
Until its nerves were less unstrung.
Then when the stag at last revived,
Though not before the vet arrived,
The Master said to Reuben Tripp,
"He almost gave my hounds the slip!
Suppose he had a feed of hay,
Could we go on, d'you think, today?"
But Reuben Tripp replied with sorrow,
"Scarcely today, sir. Say, tomorrow."

So when the morrow morning came
They carted out that stag of fame,
And after an exciting run
Killed him at Little Wurzelton.
And only then did it transpire

That both the Vicar and the Squire
Were still unrescued from the fire.

E. G. V. Knox

HYMN TO MOLOCH

O THOU who didst furnish
The fowls of the air
With loverly feathers
For leydies to wear,
Receive this Petition
For blessin an aid,
From the principal Ouses
Engaged in the Trade.

The trouble's as follows:
A white-livered Scum,
What if they was choked
'Twould be better for some,
'S been pokin about an
Creatin a fuss
An talkin too loud to be
Ealthy for us.

Thou'lt ardly believe
Ow damn friendly they are,
They say ther's a time
In the future not far
When birds worth good money'll
Waste by the ton
And the Trade can look perishin
Pleased to look on:

With best lines in Paradies
Equal to what
Is fetchin a pony
A time in the at.
An ospreys an ummins
An other choice goods
Wastefully oppin
About in the woods.

They're kiddin the papers
An callin us names,
Not Yorkshire ones neither,
That's one of their games;
They've others as pleasin
An soakin with spite,
An it don't make us appy,
Ow can it do, quite!

We thank Thee most earty
For mercies to date,
The Olesales is pickin
Nice profits per crate,
Reports from the Retails
Is pleasin to read,
We certainly thank Thee
Most earty indeed.

Vouchsafe, then, to muzzle
These meddlesome swine,
An learn em to andle goods
More in their line,
Be faithful, be foxy
Till peril is past,
An plant Thy strong sword
In their livers at last.

Ralph Hodgson

WAGTAIL AND BABY

A BABY watched a ford, whereto
    A wagtail came for drinking;
A blaring bull went wading through,
    The wagtail showed no shrinking.

A stallion splashed his way across,
    The birdie nearly sinking;
He gave his plumes a twitch and toss,
    And held his own unblinking.

Next saw the baby round the spot
  A mongrel slowly slinking;
The wagtail gazed, but faltered not
  In dip and sip and prinking.

A perfect gentleman then neared;
  The wagtail, in a winking,
With terror rose and disappeared.
  The baby fell a-thinking.

Thomas Hardy

BÊTE HUMAINE

RIDING through Ruwu swamp, about sunrise,
I saw the world awake; and as the ray
Touched the tall grasses where they dream till day,
Lo, the bright air alive with dragonflies,
With brittle wings aquiver, and great eyes
Piloting crimson bodies, slender and gay.
I aimed at one, and struck it, and it lay
Broken and lifeless, with fast-fading dyes . . .
Then my soul sickened with a sudden pain
And horror, at my own careless cruelty,
That where all things are cruel I had slain
A creature whose sweet life it is to fly:
Like beasts that prey with bloody claw . . . Nay, they
Must slay to live, but what excuse had I?

Francis Brett Young

THE AFFINITY

I HAVE to thank God I'm a woman,
For in these ordered days a woman only
Is free to be very hungry, very lonely.

It is said for Feminism, but still clear
That man, more often than woman, is a pioneer.
If I would confide a new thought,
First to a man must it be brought.

Now, for our sins, it is my bitter fate
That such a man wills soon to be my mate,
And so of friendship is quick end:
When I have gained a love I lose a friend.

It is well within the order of things
That man should listen when his mate sings;
But the true male never yet walked
Who liked to listen when his mate talked.

I would be married to a full man,
As would all women since the world began;
But from a wealth of living I have proved
I must be silent, if I would be loved.

Now of my silence I have much wealth,
I have to do my thinking all by stealth.
My thought may never see the day;
My mind is like a catacomb where early Christians pray.

And of my silence I have much pain,
But of these pangs I have great gain;
For I must take to drugs or drink,
Or I must write the things I think.

If my sex would let me speak,
I would be very lazy and most weak;
I should speak only, and the things I spoke
Would fill the air a while, and clear like smoke.

The things I think now I write down,
And some day I will show them to the Town.
When I am sad I make thought clear;
I can re-read it all next year.

I have to thank God I'm a woman,
For in these ordered days a woman only
Is free to be very hungry, very lonely.

                                    Anna Wickham

THE TIRED MAN

I AM a quiet gentleman,
And I would sit and dream;
But my wife is on the hillside,
Wild as a hill-stream.

I am a quiet gentleman,
And I would sit and think;
But my wife is walking the whirlwind
Through night as black as ink.

Oh, give me a woman of my race
As well controlled as I,
And let us sit by the fire,
Patient till we die!

Anna Wickham

WOMEN

WOMEN have no wilderness in them,
They are provident instead,
Content in the tight hot cell of their hearts
To eat dusty bread.

They do not see cattle cropping red winter grass,
They do not hear
Snow water going down under culverts
Shallow and clear.

They wait, when they should turn to journeys,
They stiffen, when they should bend.
They use against themselves that benevolence
To which no man is friend.

They cannot think of so many crops to a field
Or of clean wood cleft by an axe.
Their love is an eager meaninglessness
Too tense or too lax.

They hear in any whisper that speaks to them
A shout and a cry.
As like as not, when they take life over their door-sill
They should let it go by.

Louise Bogan

LAKE SONG

THE lapping of lake water
Is like the weeping of women,
The weeping of ancient women
Who grieved without rebellion.

The lake falls over the shore
Like tears on their curven bosoms.
Here is languid, luxurious wailing,
The wailing of kings' daughters.

So do we ever cry,
A soft, unmutinous crying,
When we know ourselves each a princess
Locked fast within her tower.

The lapping of lake water
Is like the weeping of women,
The fertile tears of women
That water the dreams of men.

Jean Starr Untermeyer

DOOR–MATS

WOMEN are door-mats and have been,—
The years those mats applaud,—
They keep their men from going in
With muddy feet to God.

Mary Carolyn Davies

HERE LIES A LADY

HERE lies a lady of beauty and high degree.
Of chills and fever she died, of fever and chills,
The delight of her husband, her aunts, an infant of three,
And of medicos marveling sweetly on her ills.

For either she burned, and her confident eyes would blaze,
And her fingers fly in a manner to puzzle their heads—
What was she making?   Why, nothing; she sat in a maze
Of old scraps of laces, snipped into curious shreds—

Or this would pass, and the light of her fire decline
Till she lay discouraged and cold as a thin stalk white and
    blown,
And would not open her eyes, to kisses, to wine;
The sixth of these states was her last; the cold settled down.

Sweet ladies, long may ye bloom, and toughly I hope ye may
    thole,
But was she not lucky?   In flowers and lace and mourning,
In love and great honor we bade God rest her soul
After six little spaces of chill, and six of burning.

John Crowe Ransom

TO APHRODITE: WITH A MIRROR

HERE, Cyprian, is my jeweled looking-glass,
    My final gift to bind my final vow:
I cannot see myself as I once was;
    I would not see myself as I am now.

Aline Kilmer

THE WOMEN OF THE BETTER CLASS

The artists and writers were the first Americans to make themselves at home
in this amusing Parisian resort.   (The old Café Martin.)   And it was here too
that women of the better class first tasted the delights of café life.   It was considered quite a daring thing in the late eighties for be-cloaked and be-diamonded
women of Fifth Avenue to sit here and sip their after-dinner coffee.—*Vanity Fair*.

ONE of those queer, artistic dives,
Where funny people had their fling.
Artists, and writers, and their wives—
Poets, all that sort of thing.
Here, too, to view the vulgar herd
And sip the daring demi-tasse—
Be-cloaked, be-diamonded, be-furred—
Came women of the better class.

With its Parisian atmosphere,
It had a Latin Quarter ring.
Painters and journalists came here—
Actors, and all that sort of thing.
Here, too, to watch the great Ungroomed
And sip the dangerous demi-tasse,
Be-furred, be-feathered and be-plumed,
Came women of the better class.

Here Howells dined—Saint Gaudens, Nast,
Kipling, Mark Twain and Peter Dunne,
Nell Terry, and not least though last,
One Robert Louis Stevenson.
And mingling with that underworld,
To sip the devilish demi-tasse,
Be-cloaked, be-diamonded, be-pearled,
Came women of the better class.

Like geese to see the lions fed,
They came—be-jewelled and be-laced,
Only to find the lions fled.
"My Word!" cried they, "what wretched taste!"
Ermined and minked and Persian-lambed,
Be-puffed (be-painted, too, alas!)
Be-decked, be-diamonded—be-damned!
The women of the better class.

Oliver Herford

TWO SONNETS

ANTIGONE and Helen—would they laugh
To see La Belle Florinda shake her limbs?
How would the sacred Eleusinian hymns
Sound on the record of a phonograph?
Oh, you who cherish La Belle's autograph,
Who serve her eyebrows and her slightest whims,
Oh, you who pay her supper bills at Tims'
Who pride yourself that you can stand the gaff—
Would you be shocked beyond your puny wits
Were you to stumble on the hidden glade

Where Bacchanals and Helen danced and swayed
Nude in the moonlight? Ah, the code that fits
The glowing Broadway lights is much too staid
To tolerate such frolics in the shade!

Or is it all illusion? Do the years
Cover with glamor what was tawdry then?
Did moralists and such like thunder when
Antigone got drunk on Attic beers,
And danced too freely mid the eager leers
Of Plato's seniors, who bought up the glen
To prove to Athens that they lived like men—
And gave Antigone the college cheers?
It may be so. I should not think it strange.
Herodias, Antigone, La Belle—
One sisterhood. Perhaps we do not change
As much as some pretend to think. Ah, well—
Don't let me spoil your pleasure in the show—
For me, my vision of the long ago!

David P. Berenberg

THE MAN IN THE DRESS SUIT

ANIMAL that I am, I come to call
With soft ancestral stride, and smouldering blood,
And guarded nuances of speech that fall
Deftly within the well-bred bounds they should;
While hooded eyes, across a saucer-rim
Of Haviland, with half-insistent stare,
Or insolent slow droop, control and trim
The wick of innuendo in the air.
Pity my brother ape who cannot chat
With one whose smiles so scintillate and arch—
His belly-lusts, his brutal days, and that
Starved ignorance of opera-hats and starch:
But most—for that he crassly snares his mate
In no such spangled net of love and hate.

Robert L. Wolf

TEA

(WHAT has that woman done to you, my dear!
The elegant, the slim, whose words were wings!
That stupid tie . . . the collar big and queer . . .
Wherever do they *sell* such frumpy things!
Incredible . . . this is some crazy joke . . .
You sit there looking frightened as a rabbit . . .)
"Oh, yes, I wish you *would*—oh, please, *please* smoke!"
(It's just like having tea with George F. Babbitt!)

"Cinnamon toast and Orange Pekoe"—(why,
You don't remember! That's the final blow!
Grotesque . . . grotesque . . . I think I'm going to cry!
The room's all dark . . . maybe the Monstrous Crow! . . .)
"Your train? Of course! And Jane to pick up, too,—"
(Poor, dear, fat Jane! And now—poor, dear, fat You!)
Jacqueline Embry

CONVERSATION GALANTE

I OBSERVE: "Our sentimental friend the moon!
Or possibly (fantastic, I confess)
It may be Prester John's balloon
Or an old battered lantern hung aloft
To light poor travellers to their distress."
    She then: "How you digress!"

And I then: "Some one frames upon the keys
That exquisite nocturne, with which we explain
The night and moonshine; music which we seize
To body forth our vacuity."
    She then: "Does this refer to me?"
    "Oh, no, it is I who am inane.

"You, madam, are the eternal humorist,
The eternal enemy of the absolute,
Giving our vagrant moods the slightest twist!
With your aid indifferent and imperious
At a stroke our mad poetics to confute—"
    And—"Are we then so serious?"
T. S. Eliot

LÈSE–MAJESTÉ

THE idle chatter, rising like a fountain
  In slender gushes, sinks in silver mist
Upon white shoulders. Higgins, from his mountain
  Of watchful inattention, seems to list.

Colossus of wise butlers, for a minute
  He sways in clouds of conversation, turns
His face against small flocks of words, and in it
  I catch a lightning flash that twists and burns.

Now imperturbable he sees the lady
  Depart in warm chinchilla, thinks of her
As something set apart and is afraid he
  Might comprehend her motor's feline purr.

Herbert S. Gorman

THE SONG OF THE STRANGE ASCETIC

IF I had been a Heathen
I'd have praised the purple vine,
My slaves should dig the vineyards,
And I would drink the wine;
But Higgins is a Heathen,
And his slaves grow lean and gray
That he may drink some tepid milk
Exactly twice a day.

If I had been a Heathen
I'd have crowned Neæra's curls
And filled my life with love affairs,
My house with dancing girls;
But Higgins is a Heathen
And to lecture rooms is forced
Where his aunts, who are not married,
Demand to be divorced.

If I had been a Heathen
I'd have sent my armies forth
And dragged behind my chariots
The Chieftains of the North.

But Higgins is a Heathen
And he drives the dreary quill
To lend the poor that funny cash
That makes them poorer still.

If I had been a Heathen
I'd have piled my pyre on high,
And in a great red whirlwind
Gone roaring to the sky.
But Higgins is a Heathen
And a richer man than I,
And they put him in an oven
Just as if he were a pie.

Now who that runs can read it,
The riddle that I write,
Of why this poor old sinner
Should sin without delight—?
But I, I cannot read it
(Although I run and run)
Of them that do not have the faith
And will not have the fun.

                                        G. K. Chesterton

FANTASIA

THE happy men that lose their heads
They find their heads in heaven,
As cherub heads with cherub wings,
And cherub haloes even:
Out of the infinite evening lands
Along the sunset sea,
Leaving the purple fields behind,
The cherub wings beat down the wind
Back to the groping body and blind
As the bird back to the tree.

Whether the plumes be passion-red
For him that truly dies
By headsmen's blade or battle-axe,
Or blue like butterflies,

For him that lost it in a lane
In April's fits and starts,
His folly is forgiven then:
But higher, and far beyond our ken,
Is the healing of the unhappy men,
The men that lost their hearts.

Is there not pardon for the brave
And broad release above,
Who lost their heads for liberty
Or lost their hearts for love?
Or is the wise man wise indeed
Whom larger thoughts keep whole?
Who see life equal like a chart,
Made strong to play the saner part,
And keep his head and keep his heart,
And only lose his soul.

G. K. Chesterton

"THE MYTH OF ARTHUR"

O LEARNED man who never learned to learn,
Save to deduce, by timid steps and small,
From towering smoke that fire can never burn
And from tall tales that men were never tall.
Say, have you thought what manner of man it is
Of whom men say, "He could strike giants down"?
Or what strong memories over time's abyss
Bore up the pomp of Camelot and the crown?
And why one banner all the background fills
Beyond the pageants of so many spears,
And by what witchery in the western hills
A throne stands empty for a thousand years.
Who hold, unheeding this immense impact,
Immortal story for a mortal sin;
Lest human fable touch historic fact,
Chase myths like moths, and fight them with a pin.
Take comfort; rest—there needs not this ado.
You shall not be a myth, I promise you.

G. K. Chesterton

ELEGY IN A COUNTRY CHURCHYARD

THE men that worked for England
They have their graves at home:
And bees and birds of England
About the cross can roam.

But they that fought for England,
Following a falling star,
Alas, alas for England
They have their graves afar.

And they that rule in England,
In stately conclave met,
Alas, alas for England
They have no graves as yet.

G. K. Chesterton

SONGS OF EDUCATION

GEOGRAPHY

THE earth is a place on which England is found,
And you find it however you twirl the globe round;
For the spots are all red and the rest is all gray,
And that is the meaning of Empire Day.

Gibraltar's a rock that you see very plain,
And attached to its base is the district of Spain.
And the island of Malta is marked farther on,
Where some natives were known as the Knights of St. John
Then Cyprus, and east to the Suez Canal,
That was conquered by Dizzy and Rothschild his pal
With the sword of the Lord in the old English way;
And that is the meaning of Empire Day.

Our principal imports come far as Cape Horn;
For necessities, cocoa; for luxuries, corn;
Thus Brahmins are born for the rice-field, and thus,
The Gods made the Greeks to grow currants for us;

Of earth's other tributes are plenty to choose,
Tobacco and petrol and Jazzing and Jews:
The Jazzing will pass but the Jews they will stay;
And that is the meaning of Empire Day.

Our principal exports, all labelled and packed,
At the ends of the earth are delivered intact:
Our soap or our salmon can travel in tins
Between the two poles and as like as two pins;
So that Lancashire merchants whenever they like
Can water the beer of a man in Klondike
Or poison the meat of a man in Bombay;
And that is the meaning of Empire Day.

The day of St. George is a musty affair
Which Russians and Greeks are permitted to share;
The day of Trafalgar is Spanish in name
And the Spaniards refuse to pronounce it the same;
But the Day of the Empire from Canada came
With Morden and Borden and Beaverbrook's fame
And saintly seraphical souls such as they:
And that is the meaning of Empire Day.

G. K. Chesterton

THE HANDS–ACROSS–THE–SEA POEM

Sons of the Empire, bond and free,
    Yellow and black and brown,
I greet you all where'er you be,
    Here ere the sun goes down;
Here, while the sunset flushes red
    The waves of England's main,
I breathe the prayer our fathers said,
    And sing the song again.

The ancient song that struck the sky
    When Roman standards flew,
The song that smote the bastions high
    Of Philip's recreant crew;

The song that Drake and Nelson sang
   When Heaven flared with war,
And echoed with the shots that rang
   O'er baffled Trafalgar.

Sons of the Empire, Britain's sons,
   Here, as the darkness falls,
Over your gray Sea-Mother's guns
   The warning clarion calls;
O, and I bid you now "God speed,
   Quit you like men, be true";
Stand by us in the hour of need
   And we shall stand by you.

J. C. Squire

THE AVENGERS

WHO grafted quince on Western may,
   Sharon's mild rose on Northern briar?
In loathing since that Gospel day
   The two saps flame, the tree's on fire.

The briar-rose weeps for injured right,
   May sprouts up red to choke the quince.
With angry throb of equal spite
   Our wood leaps maddened ever since.

Then Mistletoe, of gods not least,
   Kindler of warfare since the Flood,
Against green things of South and East
   Voices the vengeance of our blood.

Crusading ivy Southward breaks
   And sucks your lordly palms upon,
Our island oak the water takes
   To war with cedared Lebanon.

Our slender ash-twigs feathered fly
   Against your vines; bold buttercup
Pours down his legions; malt of rye
   Inflames and burns your lentils up. . . .

For bloom of quince yet caps the may,
  The briar is held by Sharon's rose;
Monsters of thought through earth we stray
  And how remission comes, God knows.

Robert Graves

CANOPUS

WHEN quacks with pills political would dope us
  When politics absorbs the livelong day,
I like to think about the star Canopus,
  So far, so far away!

Greatest of visioned suns, they say who list 'em;
  To weigh it science always must despair,
Its shell would hold our whole dinged solar system,
  Nor ever know 'twas there.

When temporary chairmen utter speeches,
  And frenzied henchmen howl their battle hymns,
My thoughts float out across the cosmic reaches
  To where Canopus swims.

When men are calling names and making faces,
  And all the world's ajangle and ajar,
I meditate on interstellar spaces,
  And smoke a mild seegar.

For after one has had about a week of
  The arguments of friends as well as foes,
A star that has no parallax to speak of
  Conduces to repose.

Bert Leston Taylor

THIS VERY HOUR

MASTER, this very hour,
  Under this village sky,
Between two thieves You go,
  To die.

About our separate work,
 Ever we come and pass;
One Pilate; Andrew one;
 One scarlet Caiaphas.

Peter stoops to his bulbs,
 Under a kitchen pane;
And James halts there to talk
 Of day's luck, field or rain.

Along some brambly wall,
 Where orange haws burn hot,
His thirty coins held fast,
 Goes dark Iscariot.

Lizette Woodworth Reese

EASTER EVE

"Ses meurtriers donc ses rencontraient de bon cœur."—Alfonse Moreau

His murderers met.   Their consciences were free:
The sun's eclipse was past, the tumult stilled
In Jewry, and their duty well fulfilled.

Quoth Caiaphas:—*It wrung my heart to see*
His mother's grief, God knows.   Yet blasphemy
Was proven, the uprising imminent,
And all the church-supporting element
Demanded action, sir, of you and me.

Quoth Pilate:—*When this Nazarene denied*
Even Cæsar's rule, reluctantly I knew
My duty to the state, sir.   Still, I tried,
But found no way, to spare him yet stay true
In loyalty.ʹ . . . And still, the poor lad cried,
"Forgive them, for they know not what they do!"

James Branch Cabell

EXIT GOD

Of old our fathers' God was real,
 Something they almost saw,
Which kept them to a stern ideal
 And scourged them into awe.

They walked the narrow path of right,
    Most vigilantly well,
Because they feared eternal night
    And boiling depths of Hell.

Now Hell has wholly boiled away
    And God become a shade.
There is no place for him to stay
    In all the world he made.

The followers of William James
    Still let the Lord exist,
And call him by imposing names,
    A venerable list.

But nerve and muscle only count,
    Gray matter of the brain,
And an astonishing amount
    Of inconvenient pain.

I sometimes wish that God were back
    In this dark world and wide;
For though some virtues he might lack,
    He had his pleasant side.

Gamaliel Bradford

LIGHTEN OUR DARKNESS

ENGLAND, 1918

In the high places lo! there is no light,
The ugly dawn beats up forlorn and gray.
Dear Lord, but once before I pass away
Out of this Hell into the starry night
Where still my hopes are set in Death's despite,
Let one great man be good, let one pure ray
Shine through the gloom of this my earthly day
From one tall candle set upon a height.
Judges and prelates, chancellors and kings,
All have I known and suffered and endured,

(And some are quick and some are in their graves).
I looked behind their masks and posturings
And saw their souls too rotten to be cured,
And knew them all for liars, rogues and knaves.

Alfred Bruce Douglas

THE LOSERS

PRINCE and Bishop and Knight and Dame
　Plot and plunder and disagree!
O but the game is a royal game!
　O but your tourneys are fair to see!

None too hopeful we found our lives;
　Sore was labor from day to day;
Still we strove for our babes and wives—
　Now, to the trumpet, we march away!

"Why?"—For some one hath willed it so!
　Nothing we know of the why or the where—
To swamp, or jungle, or wastes of snow—
　Nothing we know, and little we care.

Give us to kill!—since this is the end
　Of love and labor in Nature's plan;
Give us to kill and ravish and rend,
　Yea, since this is the end of man.

States shall perish, and states be born:
　Leaders, out of the throng, shall press;
Some to honor, and some to scorn:
　We, that are little, shall yet be less.

Over our lines shall the vultures soar;
　Hard on our flanks shall the jackals cry;
And the dead shall be as the sands of the shore;
　And daily the living shall pray to die.

Nay, what matter!—When all is said,
　Prince and Bishop will plunder still:
Lord and Lady must dance and wed.
　Pity us, pray for us, ye that will!

William Young

A RIBBON TWO YARDS WIDE

THEY wind a thousand soldiers round the king,
So he may go and hear the symphony,
Square squads of rhythmic lancers fashioning
A boulevard of measured liberty,
A ribbon two yards wide whereon the thing
May prance atop a wooden steed, quite free
From any heretic outside the ring
Who might deprive him of his puppetry:
The populace applaud the miracle,
Their heads and arms, attached to hidden strings,
Acclaim the venerable vehicle
Precisely one of God's imaginings:
The king rides like a ghost on exhibition
To feed the faithful eye with superstition.

Alfred Kreymborg

"THEY"

THE Bishop tells us: "When the boys come back
They will not be the same; for they'll have fought
In a just cause: they led the last attack
On Anti-Christ; their comrades' blood has bought
New right to breed an honorable race.
They have challenged Death and dared him face to face."

"We're none of us the same!" the boys reply.
"For George lost both his legs; and Bill's stone blind;
Poor Jim's shot through the lungs and like to die;
And Bert's gone syphilitic; you'll not find
A chap who's served that hasn't found *some* change."
And the Bishop said: "The ways of God are strange!"

Siegfried Sassoon

WHEN THE DEAD MEN DIE

IN a world of battlefields there came
    Strange things abroad by night,
For the dead they have but little shame
    When their hearts are turned to white.

And we who war, and wake to sigh,
    Are apt to hear the slain,
Whose dead hearts go abroad and cry
    Not to be killed again.

For they are now in Jaques and John,
    Hans, Beppo, and the rest;
Their broken hearts are beating on
    Inside each breaking breast.

Their murdered hearts they make a moan
    For the deaths they died before,
And shattered soul with shattered bone
    Doth dread to die once more.

For many deaths their moan is made
    When the mortal charges start;
It is hard to leap the escalade
    And carry a dead man's heart!

Remember, men of guns and rhymes,
    And kings who kill so fast,
That men you kill too many times
    May be too dead at last;

That hearts may be too dead at length
    To beat again and cry,
And kings may call in vain for strength
    When the dead men die.

                              Rose O'Neill

"SAFE FOR DEMOCRACY"

    Safe for Democracy, they said.
    True; for our noblest youth are dead.

    Let but another world-war kill
    The rest, it will be safer still.

                              L. A. G. Strong

VICTORY IN THE CABARETS

THE jazz band struck up Dixie . . . I could see
A boy from Texas slipping down a trench
While some gray phantom with a grinding wrench
Twisted an arm and pulled its bayonet free.
I saw a blur of mud and flies where three
Friends from the South had joked about the stench.
And there, complaining of his lack of French,
A Richmond black felt for his missing knee.

The fife screamed Yankee Doodle . . . and the throng
Danced to a ragtime patriotic air.
The martial fervor grew as several strong
And well-shaped girls not altogether bare
Marched with toy guns and brought the flag along,
While sixteen chorus men sang Over There.

Louis Untermeyer

A HISTORY OF PEACE

(*Solitudinem faciunt, pacem appellant*)

HERE rest in peace the bones of Henry Reece,
Dead through his bitter championship of Peace
Against all eagle-nosed and cynic lords
Who keep the *Pax Romana* with their swords.

Henry was the only son of Thomas Reece,
Banker and sometime Justice of the Peace,
And of Jane Reece whom Thomas kept in dread
By *Pax Romana* of his board and bed.

Robert Graves

TO ONE WHO DENIES THE POSSIBILITY OF A PERMANENT PEACE

OLD friend, I greet you! you are still the same:
You poisoned Socrates, you crucified
Christ, you have persecuted, mocked, denied,
Rejected God and cursed Him—in God's name.

You gave monotonously to the flame
All those (whom now you honor) when the new
Truth stung their lips—for fear it might be true;
Then reaped where they had sown and felt no shame.
Familiar voice, old adversary—hail!
Yesterday's fools are now your gods.   Behold!
The generations pass and we can wait.
You slandered Shelley, Florence Nightingale;
Now a new splendor quivers in the cold
Gray shadows overhead; *still* you are late.

Margaret Sackville

MOURN NOT THE DEAD

MOURN not the dead that in the cool earth lie—
Dust unto dust—
The calm, sweet earth that mothers all who die
As all men must;

Mourn not your captive comrades who must dwell—
Too strong to strive—
Within each steel-bound coffin of a cell,
Buried alive;

But rather mourn the apathetic throng—
The cowed and the meek—
Who see the world's great anguish and its wrong
And dare not speak!

Ralph Chaplin

ART AND LIFE

WHEN Art goes bounding, lean
Up hill-tops fired green
To pluck a rose for life,

Life like a broody hen
Cluck-clucks him back again.

But when Art, imbecile,
Sits old and chill

On sidings shaven clean,
And counts his clustering
Dead daisies on a string
With witless laughter, . . .

Then like a new Jill
Toiling up a hill
Life scrambles after.

Lola Ridge

THE NEW FREEDOM

Now all the ways are open,
    And we may ramble in;
Garden and ivory temple,
    And the silken doors of sin.

No wondering by a door-step,
    No latticed mystery;
No gray portcullis guarding
    Dream's gold for you and me.

By the path into the forest
    Where four blind windows wait,
The silence has no secret,
    Down is the briared gate.

How bare the world is grown now,
    Without a bar or pin!
No little doors at twilight
    We may not enter in.

Olive Dargan

CONVENTION

THE snow is lying very deep.
My house is sheltered from the blast.
I hear each muffled step outside,
I hear each voice go past.

But I'll not venture in the drift
Out of this bright security,
Till enough footsteps come and go
To make a path for me.

Agnes Lee

CODES

THEY wove for me a little cloak
  Of worsted, brown and strong,
They wove it firm, these kindly folk
  That I might wear it long.

I, who would dance in gossamer
  With poplars on a hill,
Or wander naked with the wind,
  They clothe in worsted still.

Lois Seyster Montross

YOU PREACH TO ME OF LAWS

You preach to me of laws, you tie my limbs
  With rights and wrongs and arguments of good,
You choke my songs and fill my mouth with hymns,
  You stop my heart and turn it into wood.

I serve not God, but make my idol fair
  From clay of brown earth, painted bright with blood,
Dressed in sweet flesh and wonder of wild hair
  By Beauty's fingers to her changing mood.

The long line of the sea, the straight horizon,
  The toss of flowers, the prance of milky feet,
And moonlight clear as glass my great religion,
  And sunrise falling on the quiet street.

The colored crowd, the unrestrained, the gay,
  And lovers in the secret sheets of night
Trembling like instruments of music, till the day
  Stands marvelling at their sleeping bodies white.

Age creeps upon your timid little faces
 Beneath each black umbrella sly and slow,
Proud in the unimportance of your places
 You sit in twilight prophesying woe.

So dim and false and gray, take my compassion,
 I from my pageant golden as the day
Pity your littleness from all my passion,
 Leave you my sins to weep and whine away!

Iris Tree

SHIP NEAR SHOALS

I HAVE been so misused by chaste men with one wife
That I would live with satyrs all my life.
Virtue has bound me with such infamy
That I must fly where Love himself is free,
And know all vice but that small vice of dignity.

Come Rags and Jades! so long as you have laughter,
Blow your shrill pipes, and I will follow after.

Anna Wickham

UPSTAIRS DOWNSTAIRS

THE judge, who lives impeccably upstairs
With dull decorum and its implication,
Has all his servants in to family prayers,
And edifies *his* soul with exhortation.

Meanwhile his blacks live wastefully downstairs;
Not always chaste, they manage to exist
With less decorum than the judge upstairs,
And find withal a something that he missed.

This painful fact a Swede philosopher,
Who tarried for a fortnight in our city,
Remarked, one evening at the meal, before
We paralyzed him silent with our pity—

Saying the black man living with the white
Had given more than white men could requite.

Hervey Allen

WALLS

THE wall of his environment,
Although Chinese, was not so high
He could not see tiled roofs of kings
Like dragon-backs against the sky.
And so, spurred on by discontent,
An eagle pen that lent him wings
Transported him across the wall
To tea in gardens with the Mings.

Thus staged, his long but static fall
Made drama for ancestral ghosts,
Whose proud trangressions raised the wall
Of ego, which with echoed boasts
Had in past epochs starved their souls
With windy oats of self-applause,
Till they had met great grandpapas
Twit-tittering on the seething coals.

Hervey Allen

I CHANGE

I WONDER how it happens
    I was made
A foe of agate
    And a friend of jade,

Yet have become,
    Unwisely I'm afraid,
The friend of agate
    And the foe of jade—

So that I wish, by dying,
    To be made
Careless of agate,
    Careless of jade.

Witter Bynner

DOOM–DEVOTED

I WEEP a sight which was not seen,
  A deed which was not done at all
The murder of an unborn queen,
  The sack of an unbuilded hall.

Never a queen of Art or Song
  This doom-devoted star hath borne
Whom the protagonists of Wrong
  Did not tread down with hooves of scorn.

Stern watch those iron traitors keep
  Who crucified the Singing Child.
The unborn Christs we poets weep,
  The strangled songs, the dreams defiled.
                    Louis Golding

CREEDS

  How pitiful are little folk—
  They seem so very small;
  They look at stars, and think they are
  Denominational.
                    Willard Wattles

CREEDS

FRIEND, you are grieved that I should go
Unhoused, unsheltered, gaunt and free,
My cloak for armor—for my tent
The roadside tree;

And I—I know not how you bear
A roof betwixt you and the blue.
Brother, the creed would stifle me
That shelters you.

Yet, that same light that floods at dawn
Your cloistered room, your cryptic stair,
Wakes me, too—sleeping by the hedge—
To morning prayer!
                    Karle Wilson Baker

THE DEAD MAKE RULES

THE dead make rules, and I obey.
I too shall be dead some day.

Youth and maid who, past my death,
Have within your nostrils breath,

I pray you, for my own pain's sake,
Break the rules that I shall make!

Mary Carolyn Davies

FIRE AND ICE

SOME say the world will end in fire,
Some say in ice.
From what I've tasted of desire
I hold with those who favor fire.
But if it had to perish twice,
I think I know enough of hate
To say that for destruction ice
Is also great
And would suffice.

Robert Frost

THE CLOD

I PICKED up the clod.
"You may yet be a man," I said. "Dream on.
Are you not glad? Do you not tremble?"
But dully it looked at me.
I could swear I heard a sigh of relief.
There was no ecstasy, no joy.
"I have been a.man," the clod said.

Edwin Curran

THE SOUL SPEAKS

"HERE is Honor, the dying knight,
And here is Truth, the snuffed-out light,
And here is Faith, the broken staff,
And here is Knowledge, the throttled laugh.

And there are Fame, the lost surprise,
Virtue, the uncontested prize,
And Sacrifice, the suicide,
And here the wilted flower, Pride.
Under the crust of things that die,
Living, unfathomed, here am I."

Edward H. Pfeiffer

THE DROMEDARY

IN dreams I see the Dromedary still,
As once in a gay park I saw him stand:
A thousand eyes in vulgar wonder scanned
His humps and hairy neck, and gazed their fill
At his lank shanks and mocked with laughter shrill.
He never moved: and if his Eastern land
Flashed on his eye with stretches of hot sand,
It wrung no mute appeal from his proud will.
He blinked upon the rabble lazily;
And still some trace of majesty forlorn
And a coarse grace remained: his head was high,
Though his gaunt flanks with a great mange were worn:
There was not any yearning in his eye,
But on his lips and nostril infinite scorn.

A. Y. Campbell

AT THE AQUARIUM

SERENE the silver fishes glide,
Stern-lipped, and pale, and wonder-eyed!
As through the aged deeps of ocean,
They glide with wan and wavy motion.
They have no pathway where they go,
They flow like water to and fro,
They watch with never-winking eyes,
They watch with staring, cold surprise,
The level people in the air,
The people peering, peering there:
Who wander also to and fro,
And know not why or where they go,

Yet have a wonder in their eyes,
Sometimes a pale and cold surprise.

Max Eastman

FESTOONS OF FISHES

INCOGNITOS of masquerading moons
Refute the theories philosophers
Propound who blow their cheeks to fill balloons
And call their windy whims interpreters.
The swimming islands of the naked sun
Confound a telescope to ignorance
By dancing like oases on the run
Or delicate mirages in a trance.
The torrents of the sky reduce the earth,
A brittle stone, to powdered liquid sand;
Amuse themselves with slanting silver mirth
If hermits claim they've found the hidden hand.
Among the coral crypts that hold the sea
Festoons of fishes weave insanity.

Alfred Kreymborg

FIRST PHILOSOPHER'S SONG

A POOR degenerate from the ape,
Whose hands are four, whose tail's a limb,
I contemplate my flaccid shape
And know I may not rival him,

Save with my mind—a nimbler beast
Possessing a thousand sinewy tails
A thousand hands, with which it scales
Greedy of luscious truth, the greased

Poles and the coco palms of thought,
Thrids easily through the mangrove maze
Of metaphysics, walks the taut
Frail dangerous liana ways

That link across wide gulfs remote
Analogies between tree and tree;
Outruns the hare, outhops the goat;
Mind fabulous, mind sublime and free!

But oh, the sound of simian mirth!
Mind, issued from the monkey's womb,
Is still umbilical to earth,
Earth its home and earth its tomb.

Aldous Huxley

THE INCENTIVE

I saw a sickly cellar plant
Droop on its feeble stem, for want
Of sun and wind and rain and dew—
Of freedom!—Then a man came through
The cellar, and I heard him say,
"Poor, foolish plant, by all means stay
Contented here: for—know you not?—
This stagnant dampness, mould and rot
Are your incentive to grow tall
And reach that sunbeam on the wall."
—Even as he spoke, the sun's one spark
Withdrew, and left the dusk more dark.—

Sarah N. Cleghorn

THE SURVIVAL OF THE FITTEST

"The unfit die—the fit both live and thrive."
Alas, who say so?—They who do survive.

So, when her bonfires lighted hill and plain,
Did Bloody Mary think on Lady Jane.

So Russia thought of Finland, while her heel
Fell heavier on the prostrate commonweal.

So Booth of Lincoln thought: and so the High
Priests let Barabbas live, and Jesus die.

Sarah N. Cleghorn

THE GOLF LINKS LIE SO NEAR THE MILL

The golf links lie so near the mill
That almost every day
The laboring children can look out
And see the men at play.

Sarah N. Cleghorn

THE LAWYERS KNOW TOO MUCH

THE lawyers, Bob, know too much.
They are chums of the books of old John Marshall.
They know it all, what a dead hand wrote,
A stiff dead hand and its knuckles crumbling,
The bones of the fingers a thin white ash.
    The lawyers know a dead man's thoughts too well.

In the heels of the higgling lawyers, Bob,
Too many slippery ifs and buts and howevers,
Too much hereinbefore provided whereas,
Too many doors to go in and out of.

When the lawyers are through
What is there left, Bob?
Can a mouse nibble at it
And find enough to fasten a tooth in?

Why is there always a secret singing
When a lawyer cashes in?
Why does a hearse horse snicker
Hauling a lawyer away?

The work of a bricklayer goes to the blue.
The knack of a mason outlasts a moon.
The hands of a plasterer hold a room together.
The land of a farmer wishes him back again.
    Singers of songs and dreamers of plays
    Build a house no wind blows over.
The lawyers—tell me why a hearse horse snickers hauling
    a lawyer's bones.

Carl Sandburg

TO DIVES

DIVES, when you and I go down to Hell,
Where scribblers end and millionaires as well,
We shall be carrying on our separate backs
Two very large but very different packs;

And as you stagger under yours, my friend,
Down the dull shore where all our journeys end,
And go before me (as your rank demands)
Towards the infinite flat underlands,
And that dear river of forgetfulness—
Charon, a man of exquisite address
(For, as your wife's progenitors could tell,
They're very strict on etiquette in Hell),
Will, since you are a lord, observe, "My lord,
We cannot take these weighty things aboard!"
Then down they go, my wretched Dives, down—
The fifteen sorts of boots you kept for town,
The hat to meet the Devil in; the plain
But costly ties; the cases of champagne;
The solid watch, and seal, and chain, and charm;
The working model of a Burning Farm
(To give the little Belials); all the three
Biscuits for Cerberus; the guarantee
From Lambeth that the Rich can never burn,
And even promising a safe return;
The admirable overcoat, designed
To cross Cocytus—very warmly lined:
Sweet Dives, you will leave them all behind
And enter Hell as tattered and as bare
As was your father when he took the air
Behind a barrow-load in Leicester Square.
Then turned to me, and noting one that brings
With careless step a mist of shadowy things:
Laughter and memories, and a few regrets,
Some honor, and a quantity of debts,
A doubt or two of sorts, a trust in God,
And (what will seem to you extremely odd)
His father's granfer's father's father's name,
Unspoilt, untitled, even spelt the same;
Charon, who twenty thousand times before
Has ferried Poets to the ulterior shore,
Will estimate the weight I bear, and cry—
"Comrade!" (He has himself been known to try
His hand at Latin and Italian verse,
Much in the style of Virgil—only worse)

"We let such vain imaginaries pass!"
Then tell me, Dives, which will look the ass—
You? or myself? Or Charon? Who can tell?
They order things so damnably in Hell.

Hilaire Belloc

PART V

POEMS OF PATRIOTISM, HISTORY AND LEGEND

AMERICA THE BEAUTIFUL

O BEAUTIFUL for spacious skies,
    For amber waves of grain,
For purple mountain majesties
    Above the fruited plain!
        America! America!
    God shed His grace on thee
And crown thy good with brotherhood
    From sea to shining sea!

O beautiful for pilgrim feet,
    Whose stern, impassioned stress
A throughfare for freedom beat
    Across the wilderness!
        America! America!
    God mend thine every flaw,
Confirm thy soul in self-control,
    Thy liberty in law!

O beautiful for heroes proved
    In liberating strife,
Who more than self their country loved,
    And mercy more than life!
        America! America!
    May God thy gold refine
Till all success be nobleness,
    And every gain divine!

O beautiful for patriot dream
    That sees beyond the years
Thine alabaster cities gleam
    Undimmed by human tears!
        America! America!
    God shed His grace on thee
And crown thy good with brotherhood
    From sea to shining sea!

Katharine Lee Bates

SHADOWS OF WAR

THE VAMPIRE

1914

She rose among us where we lay.
She wept, we put our work away.
She chilled our laughter, stilled our play;
And spread a silence there.
And darkness shot across the sky,
And once, and twice, we heard her cry;
And saw her lift white hands on high
And toss her troubled hair.

What shape was this who came to us,
With basilisk eyes so ominous,
With mouth so sweet, so poisonous,
And tortured hands so pale?
We saw her wavering to and fro,
Through dark and wind we saw her go;
Yet what her name was did not know;
And felt our spirits fail.

We tried to turn away; but still
Above us heard her sorrow thrill;
And those who slept, they dreamed of ill
And dreadful things:
Of skies grown red with rending flames
And shuddering hills that cracked their frames;
Of twilights foul with wings;

And skeletons dancing to a tune;
And cries of children stifled soon;
And over all a blood-red moon
A dull and nightmare size.
They woke, and sought to go their ways,
Yet everywhere they met her gaze,
Her fixed and burning eyes.

Who are you now,—we cried to her,—
Spirit so strange, so sinister?
We felt dead winds above us stir;
And in the darkness heard
A voice fall, singing, cloying sweet,
Heavily dropping, through that heat,
Heavy as honeyed pulses beat,
Slow word by anguished word.

And through the night strange music went
With voice and cry so darkly blent
We could not fathom what they meant;
Save only that they seemed
To thin the blood along our veins,
Foretelling vile delirious pains
And clouds divulging blood-red rains
Upon a hill undreamed.

And this we heard: "Who dies for me,
He shall possess me secretly,
My terrible beauty he shall see,
And slake my body's flame.
But who denies me cursed shall be,
And slain, and buried loathsomely,
And slimed upon with shame."

And darkness fell.   And like a sea
Of stumbling deaths we followed, we
Who dared not stay behind.
There all night long beneath a cloud
We rose and fell, we struck and bowed,
We were the ploughman and the ploughed,
Our eyes were red and blind.

And some, they said, had touched her side,
Before she fled us there;
And some had taken her to bride;
And some lain down for her and died;
And some, to whom she was denied,
Who had not touched her hair,
Ran to and fro and cursed and cried
And sought her everywhere.

"Her eyes have feasted on the dead,
And small and shapely is her head,
And dark and small her mouth," they said,
"And beautiful to kiss;
Her mouth is sinister and red
As blood in moonlight is."

Then poets forgot their jewelled words
And cut the sky with glittering swords;
And innocent souls turned carrion birds
To perch upon the dead.
Sweet daisy fields were drenched with death,
The air became a charnel breath,
Pale stones were splashed with red.

Green leaves were dappled bright with blood
And fruit trees murdered in the bud,
And when at length the dawn
Came green as twilight from the east,
And all that heaving horror ceased,
Silent was every bird and beast,
And that dark voice was gone.

No word there was, no song, no bell,
No furious tongue that dream to tell;
Only the dead, who rose and fell
Above the wounded men;
And whisperings and wails of pain
Blown slowly from the wounded grain,
Blown slowly from the smoking plain;
And silence fallen again.

Until at dusk, from God knows where,
Beneath dark birds that filled the air,
Like one who did not hear or care,
Under a blood-red cloud,
An agèd ploughman came alone
And drove his share through flesh and bone,
And turned them under to mould and stone;
All night long he ploughed.

Conrad Aiken

THE CONNAUGHT RANGERS

I SAW the Connaught Rangers when they were passing by,
On a spring day, a good day, with gold rifts in the sky.
Themselves were marching steadily along the Liffey quay
An' I see the young proud look of them as if it were to-day!
The bright lads, the right lads, I have them in my mind,
With the green flags on their bayonets all fluttering in the
     wind.

A last look at old Ireland, a last good-bye maybe,
Then the gray sea, the wide sea, my grief upon the sea!
And when will they come home, says I, when will they see
     once more
The dear blue hills of Wicklow and Wexford's dim gray
     shore?
The brave lads of Ireland, no better lads you'll find,
With the green flags on their bayonets all fluttering in
     the wind!

Three years have passed since that spring day, sad years
     for them and me.
Green graves there are in Serbia and in Gallipoli.
And many who went by that day along the muddy street
Will never hear the roadway ring to their triumphant feet.
But when they march before Him, God's welcome will be
     kind,
And the green flags on their bayonets will flutter in the wind.

Winifred M. Letts

HAIL AND FAREWELL

Dogs barking, dust awhirling,
     And drum throbs in the street.
The braggart pipes are skirling
     An old tune wild and sweet.

By fours the lads come trooping
     With heads erect and high,
I watch with heart adrooping
     To see the kilties by.

And one of them is glancing
  Up to this window, this!
His brave blue eyes are dancing;
  He tosses me a kiss.

I send him back another,
  I fling my hand out free.
"God keep you safely, brother,
  Who go to die for me."

Anne Higginson Spicer

ALL THE HILLS AND VALES ALONG

ALL the hills and vales along
Earth is bursting into song,
And the singers are the chaps
Who are going to die perhaps.
    O sing, marching men,
    Till the valleys ring again.
    Give your gladness to earth's keeping,
    So be glad, when you are sleeping.

Cast away regret and rue,
Think what you are marching to.
Little live, great pass.
Jesus Christ and Barabbas
Were found the same day.
This died, that went his way.
    So sing with joyful breath.
    For why, you are going to death.
    Teeming earth will surely store
    All the gladness that you pour.

Earth that never doubts nor fears,
Earth that knows of death, not tears,
Earth that bore with joyful ease
Hemlock for Socrates,
Earth that blossomed and was glad
'Neath the cross that Christ had,

Shall rejoice and blossom too
When the bullet reaches you.
    Wherefore, men marching
    On the road to death, sing!
    Pour your gladness on earth's head,
    So be merry, so be dead.

From the hills and valleys earth
Shouts back the sound of mirth,
Tramp of feet and lilt of song
Ringing all the road along.
All the music of their going,
Ringing, swinging, glad song-throwing,
Earth will echo still, when foot
Lies numb and voice mute.
    On, marching men, on
    To the gates of death with song.
    Sow your gladness for earth's reaping,
    So you may be glad, though sleeping.
    Strew your gladness on earth's bed,
    So be merry, so be dead.

                    Charles Hamilton Sorley

1917–1919

THERE are a few things I shall not forget:
Midnight on Montmartre—Sacré Cœur—and where
The hill drops westward down that plunging stair,
The few blue lights, a fine-drawn, far-flung net
Where once the boulevards blazed; aloft, the fret
And chatter of the rotaries—and there,
There shrieks the siren, wheeling searchlights flare,
The raiders' rhythm drugs my ear-drums yet.
Midnight in Tours against some moonlight wall,
Piedmont in chestnut-time, at Rimini
Red sails a-cluster,—going to the wars,
Breasting the night-chop of the Irish Sea,
The transport's deck in darkness, over all
Lifeboats swung outboard, black against the stars!

                    Henry Martyn Hoyt

SONG OF THE DARK AGES

WE digged our trenches on the down
    Beside old barrows, and the wet
White chalk we shovelled from below;
It lay like drifts of thawing snow
    On parados and parapet:

Until a pick neither struck flint
    Nor split the yielding chalky soil,
But only calcined human bone:
Poor relic of that Age of Stone
    Whose ossuary was our spoil.

Home we marched singing in the rain,
    And all the while, beneath our song,
I mused how many springs should wane
And still our trenches scar the plain:
    The monument of an old wrong.

But then, I thought, the fair green sod
    Will wholly cover that white stain,
And soften, as it clothes the face
Of those old barrows, every trace
    Of violence to the patient plain.

And careless people, passing by,
    Will speak of both in casual tone:
Saying: "You see the toil they made:
The age of iron, pick and spade,
    Here jostles with the Age of Stone."

Yet either from that happier race
    Will merit but a passing glance;
And they will leave us both alone:
Poor savages who wrought in stone—
    Poor savages who fought in France.

                        Francis Brett Young

LITTLE SALING

On the tower of Little Saling
The leads are warm with sun,
And there along the tree-tops
You hear the breezes run,
While twenty miles of Essex wheat
Spread out to comfort one.

On the leads of Little Saling
I lay and took my rest,
And when I lost the cornlands
I watched the sky go west
Till the windy flow of Heaven
Was flame within my breast.

Down in the world below me
I heard the morning pass;
The blackbird's leisured fluting;
The elm-tree's whispering mass,
And the steely clash and rattle
Of mowing in the grass.

Yet below the blackbird's music
And the whir of the machine
And the blowing leagues of summer
That billowed in between,
I caught a sound like thunder
Behind a windy screen.

Up from the leads I started
And sought the church below.
"Out there," I said, "in Flanders,
There's more than grass to mow!"
But as I passed the pillars
I paused that I might know

What glimmer down the chancel
In golden words might be,
And there I read the legend
That "Peace" was unto me.

Yet, as I read, I seemed to hear
Faint gunfire out to sea.

.   .   .   .

It was "Liveliness in Flanders"
The morning papers said,
Which meant writhing heaps of horror
While the screaming shells o'erhead
Made corpse-stuff in the trenches
Of Things already dead.

Oh, men may do the mowing,
And men may reap the corn,
But there are women weeping
For the boys that they have borne
Who lie broken into manhood
Beneath the summer dawn.

And if Love rules in Heaven,
And if the words are true
In Little Saling chancel
Of "Peace be unto you,"
How comes it that, out seaward,
The great guns roar anew?

While old men goad the slaughter
Who are safe with hoary heads,
There are Essex boys in Flanders
Who are cold in bloody beds
Though the sun at Little Saling
Lies warm upon the leads.

Olaf Baker

THE OLD ROAD TO PARADISE

Ours is a dark Easter-tide,
And a scarlet Spring,
But high up at Heaven-Gate
All the saints sing,
Glad for the great companies
Returning to their King.

Oh, in youth the dawn's a rose,
　Dusk's an amethyst,
All the roads from dusk to dawn
　Gay they wind and twist;
The old road to Paradise
　Easy it is missed!

But out on the wet battlefields,
　Few the roadways wind,
One to grief, one to death—
　No road that's kind—
The old road to Paradise
　Plain it is to find!

(Martin in his Colonel's cloak,
　Joan in her mail,
David with his crown and sword—
　None there be that fail—
Down the road to Paradise
　Stand to greet and hail!)

Where the dark's a terror-thing,
　Morn a hope doubt-tossed.
Where the lads lie thinking long
　Out in rain and frost,
There they find their God again,
　Long ago they lost:

Where the night comes cruelly,
　Where the hurt men moan,
Where the crushed forgotten ones
　Whisper prayers alone,
Christ along the battlefields
　Comes to lead His own:

Souls that would have withered soon
　In the hot world's glare,
Blown and gone like shriveled things,
　Dusty on the air,
Rank on rank they follow Him,
　Young and strong and fair!

Ours is a sad Easter-tide,
And a woeful day,
But high up at Heaven-Gate
The saints are all gay,
For the old road to Paradise,
That's a crowded way!
                              Margaret Widdemer

AT THE FRONT

FRENCH ARMY, JANUARY–MARCH, 1918

I

Is this the front—this level sweep of life,
This pageant without pulse of haste or fear?
Can this calm exercise be mortal strife?   .
Is the last reach of passion measured here?
We looked for angry blade and poisonous breath
Striking the floor of judgment, flail and fan;
Here lurked, we thought, crude agonies of death—
But here, in one wide dignity, is man.
Others behind the conflict, safe and far,
Still wage with lips their travesty of war;
We catch the rumor when the cannon cease.
Here at the front, when most the cannon rage,
The dream-touched actors on this mighty stage
In silence play their parts, and seem at peace.

II

Framed in with battle, this weird pantomime,
This dignity of action, conjures up
Shades of old heroes—Lancelot in his prime,
Galahad, questing for the holy cup,
Beautiful Hector marching to his fate,
Tristram and Palimedes, rivals twain,
And Roland sounding his proud horn too late—
These quiet actors play these parts again.
And in the lull the critics far away,
Who have not seen, nor ever read, this play,
Who cannot act, who never trod the stage—
Their quarrel mingles with the threatening cry
Of the scene-shifters watching Roland die,
Who seize the moment for a better wage.

III

If this world be a stage, what hours we give
To tedious make-up in the tiring-room;
How simply comes at last our cue to live,
How, ere we know it, we enact our doom!
The wisdom that impels us to the play
Is patient with us while we choose our parts,
But without warning sounds our judgment day;
The curtain rises—life, the drama, starts.
How late it starts! Ere this grim curtain rose,
How long we practised attitude and pose,
Disguise of accent, costume, mood or mind!
Yet in this inventory of our art,
Living at last, we play our naked heart;
How brief a reckoning counts us with our kind.

IV

If character be fate, no need to ask
Who set the stage, who cast you for the rôle;
Put on what man you are, put off the mask,
Put on the tragic pattern of your soul.
At last be true; no gesture now let spring
But from supreme sincerity of art;
Let him who plays the monarch be a king,
Who plays the rogue, be perfect in his part.
So when this hour had rung, the scene began.
One played the rash, one played the patient man,
And one, the hero, drew the dragon's fangs;
One heard death's bugler calling and obeyed,
And one, a rose-cheeked boy, the martyr played;
One played the traitor well—see where he hangs.

V

We yet may play more rôles than we believed,
Since to himself at last each man is known,
Since now the actor studies undeceived
The part he learned, and lived, and has outgrown.
And those, the few and flawless, the sublime
Whose poignance of perfection strikes us dumb—
Even for themselves, in the surprise of time,

Doubt not another reckoning will come.
"Comrades, we shall rehearse more wisely—yea,
There shall be nobler persons in our play,
We shall rebuild the plot on kindlier laws."
So at the front they act, and see, and ponder,
And win, with simple gratitude and wonder,
Peace in themselves, which is their sole applause.

John Erskine

DREAMERS

SOLDIERS are citizens of death's gray land,
Drawing no dividend from time's to-morrows.
In the great hour of destiny they stand,
Each with his feuds, and jealousies, and sorrows.
Soldiers are sworn to action; they must win
Some flaming, fatal climax with their lives.
Soldiers are dreamers; when the guns begin
They think of firelit homes, clean beds, and wives.
I see them in foul dug-outs, gnawed by rats,
And in the ruined trenches, lashed with rain,
Dreaming of things they did with balls and bats,
And mocked by hopeless longing to regain
Bank-holidays, and picture-shows, and spats,
And going to the office in the train.

Siegfried Sassoon

FULFILMENT

WAS there love once? I have forgotten her.
Was there grief once? grief yet is mine.
Other loves I have, men rough, but men who stir
More grief, more joy, than love of thee and thine.

Faces cheerful, full of whimsical mirth,
Lined by the wind, burned by the sun;
Bodies enraptured by the abounding earth,
As whose children we are brethren: one.

And any moment may descend hot death
To shatter limbs! pulp, tear, blast
Beloved soldiers who love rough life and breath
Not less for dying faithful to the last.

O the fading eyes, the grimed face turned bony,
Oped mouth gushing, fallen head,
Lessening pressure of a hand shrunk, clammed, and stony!
O sudden spasm, release of the dead!

Was there love once? I have forgotten her.
Was there grief once? grief yet is mine.
O loved, living, dying, heroic soldier,
All, all, my joy, my grief, my love, are thine!

Robert Nichols

THE IRON MUSIC

THE French guns roll continuously,
And our guns, heavy, slow;
Along the Ancre, sinuously,
The transport wagons go,
And the dust is on the thistles
And the larks sing up on high . . .
But I see the Golden Valley
Down by Tintern on the Wye.

For it's just nine weeks last Sunday
Since we took the Chepstow train,
And I'm wondering if one day
We shall do the like again;
For the four-point-two's come screaming
Through the sausages on high;
So there's little use in dreaming
How we walked along the Wye.

Dust and corpses in the thistles
Where the gas-shells burst like snow,
And the shrapnel screams and whistles
On the Bécourt road below,
And the High Wood bursts and bristles
Where the mine-clouds foul the sky . . .
But I'm with you up at Wyndcroft,
Over Tintern on the Wye.

Ford Madox Ford

HOME THOUGHTS IN LAVENTIE

GREEN gardens in Laventie!
　　Soldiers only know the street
Where the mud is churned and splashed about
　　By battle-wending feet;
And yet beside one stricken house there is a glimpse of grass,
　　Look for it when you pass.

Beyond the Church whose pitted spire
　　Seems balanced on a strand
Of swaying stone and tottering brick
　　Two roofless ruins stand,
And here behind the wreckage where the back-wall should
　　　　have been
　　We found a garden green.

The grass was never trodden on,
　　The little path of gravel
Was overgrown with celandine,
　　No other folk did travel
Along its weedy surface, but the nimble-footed mouse
　　Running from house to house.

So all among the vivid blades
　　Of soft and tender grass
We lay, nor heard the limber wheels
　　That pass and ever pass,
In noisy continuity, until their stony rattle
　　Seems in itself a battle.

At length we rose up from this ease
　　Of tranquil happy mind,
And searched the garden's little length
　　A fresh pleasaunce to find;
And there, some yellow daffodils and jasmine hanging high
　　Did rest the tired eye.

The fairest and most fragrant
　　Of the many sweets we found,
Was a little bush of Daphne flower
　　Upon a grassy mound,

And so thick were the blossoms set, and so divine the scent,
    That we were well content.

    Hungry for Spring I bent my head,
      The perfume fanned my face,
    And all my soul was dancing
      In that lovely little place,
Dancing with a measured step from wrecked and shattered
      towns
      Away . . . upon the Downs.

    I saw green banks of daffodil,
      Slim poplars in the breeze,
    Great tan-brown hares in gusty March
      A-courting on the leas;
And meadows with their glittering streams, and silver
      scurrying dace,
      Home—what a perfect place!
                  Edward Wyndham Tennant

DEATH AND THE FAIRIES

    BEFORE I joined the Army
      I lived in Donegal,
    Where every night the Fairies
      Would hold their carnival.

    But now I'm out in Flanders,
      Where men like wheat-ears fall,
    And it's Death and not the Fairies
      Who is holding carnival.
                  Patrick MacGill

THEY WHO WAIT

    OH, the gold hills of Ireland
      The gorse blossoms on
    Are all gray with heartbreak
      Since Michael is gone.

The blue hills of Scotland
  Where heather blows gay
Are weary with crying,
  For Colin's away.

And who sees, in England,
  The daffodils dance?

. . . .

  Oh, Laddie—oh, Laddie,
    Those red fields of France!
                        Charles Buxton Going

THE STAR

Dusk made a thrust at my heart
  With a star like a sword.
I had forgotten the war
  Though the guns roared
And shells droned on and on
  In a sullen chord.

It was not the noise and the reek
  But a star in the sky
Made the black trench real again.
  Starlight, and I
Saw beauty vanished away
  And love gone by.
                        Grace Hazard Conkling

A VISION

Before the dawn-wind swept the troubled sky
  And stirred the stricken trenches far and wide,
I saw the Lord of Holiness pass by,
  With Mary at His side.

With Mary Michael passed, for I could hear
  His clashing arms, and see his spangled sword.
Loudly I cried out, "Mother!" then in fear,
  "O Mother of our Lord."

For in her eyes all human sorrow burned,
  All tenderness lay naked when she smiled;
And once she stooped to kiss and once she turned
  And shuddered like a child.

He moved through all the surge and clash of war,
  The King of Kings since Brotherhood began;
But in His still and shadowed face I saw
  The agony of Man.

Geoffrey Dearmer

CHARING CROSS

ALL through the night in silence they come and go,
The Red Cross cars with headlights low,
And maimed humanity on stretchers lain
Glides down the streets of London—while I stand
Watching this slow processional of pain.
All through the night unending flows the stream
Whence now and then a weary, bloodless hand
Answers the greeting of the silent crowd;
A pale and stricken face smiles back again
Upon the kind, dim faces that throng as in a dream.

Over them as they journey, patiently bowed
A nurse keeps watch in fear lest now at last
The fluttering spirit leave the battered cage,
And, eager for eternity, slip past
The guardian tending the poor, broken frame
With its disc and number and stencilled name.
And as I watch, a rebel thought
Stirs in my mind, for strange it seems
That down this highway of pain unending
There flow the streams
Of human traffic homeward brought,
Broken and useless, marred with terrible scars,
Eyeless and limbless and shattered, while under the stars
Flow other streams that, outward wending,
Carry the youth of the nation in splendid vigor—
And those streams flow into these at the touch of a trigger!

Long months of training that splendid humanity needed,
The toil and brain of a nation evolved it, the wealth
Of the wide world's meadows and mines was brought for its
    use,
And with careful eyes and hands it was weeded and weeded
Until it was virile with courage and perfect health;
And here is the end of it all, and we count the loss
Recording the glory, forgetting this human refuse
Left by extravagant war—borne away in the night
Swiftly and silently. God! here again at a cross
Crucified man in a dark world dies; the sight
Burns to the brain, and I cry, as once One cried—
"My God! My God! why hast Thou forsaken me?"—then
I watch with dumb anguish the endless procession of men,
The remnants picked up from the waste in the fields; they
    who died
Flow no more in the stream, they can rest; and only it
    matters
That Science should skilfully mend what it skilfully shatters.

Cecil Roberts

BROKEN BODIES

Not for the broken bodies,
    When the War is over and done,
For the miserable eyes that never
    Again shall see the sun;
Not for the broken bodies
    Crawling over the land,
The patchwork limbs, the shoddies,
Not for the broken bodies
    Dear Lord, we crave Your hand.

Not for the broken bodies,
    We pray Your dearest aid,
When the ghost of War for ever
    Is levelled at last and laid;
Not for the broken bodies

That wrought their sorrowful parts
Our chiefest need of God is,
Not for the broken bodies,
    Dear Lord—the broken hearts!

Louis Golding

A DEAD WARRIOR

HERE sown to dust lies one that drave
    The furrow through his heart;
Now, of the fields he died to save
    His own dust forms a part.

Where went the tramp of martial feet,
    The blare of trumpets loud,
Comes silence with her winding sheet,
    And shadow with her shroud.

His mind no longer counsel takes,
    No sword his hand need draw,
Across whose borders peace now makes
    Inviolable law.

So, with distraction round him stilled,
    Now let him be content!
And time from age to age shall build
    His standing monument.

Not here, where strife, and greed, and lust
    Grind up the bones of men;
But in that safe and secret dust
    Which shall not rise again.

Laurence Housman

HAPPY DEATH

BUGLE and battle-cry are still,
    The long strife's over;
Low o'er the corpse-encumbered hill
    The sad stars hover.

It is in vain, O stars! you look
  On these forsaken:
Awhile with blows on blows they shook,
  Or struck unshaken.

Needs now no pity of God or man . . .
  Tears for the living!
They have 'scaped the confines of life's plan
  That holds us grieving.

The unperturbed soft moon, the stars,
  The breeze that lingers,
Wake not to ineffectual wars
  To their hearts and fingers.

Warriors o'ercoming and o'ercome,
  Alike contented,
Have marched now to the last far drum,
  Praised, unlamented.

Bugle and battle-cry are still,
  The long strife's over;
Oh, that with them I had fought my fill
  And found like cover!

                              John Freeman

A VOLUNTEER'S GRAVE

NOT long ago it was a bird
  In vacant, lilac skies
Could stir the sleep that hardly closed
  His laughing eyes.

But here, where murdering thunders rock
  The lintels of the dawn,
Although they shake his shallow bed
  Yet he sleeps on.

Another spring with rain and leaf
  And buds serenely red,
And this wise field will have forgot
  Its youthful dead.

And, wise of heart, who loved him best
    Will be forgetting, too,
Even before their own beds gleam
    With heedless dew.

Yet what have all the centuries
    Of purpose, pain, and joy
Bequeathed us lovelier to recall
    Than this dead boy!

                    William Alexander Percy

A WHITE-THROAT SINGS

FROM ancient Edens long forgot
    He felt a breath of spring,
And in the leafless apple tree
    He heard a white-throat sing.

With fluted triplets, clear and sweet,
    The bird proclaimed its joy,
And on the withered orchard grass
    The man became a boy:

A boy who ran, a boy who dreamed,
    In April sun and rain;
Who knew all good was happiness,
    All evil only pain. . . .

Sing on, O white-throat in the tree,
    He does not hear you now!
The years are trampling on his heart
    And armies o'er his brow.

From ancient Edens long forgot
    No resurrection comes
Until the smallest sparrow's song
    Is louder than the drums!

                    Walter Prichard Eaton

THE MARCH

I HEARD a voice that cried, "Make way for those who died!"
And all the colored crowd like ghosts at morning fled;
And down the waiting road, rank after rank there strode,
In mute and measured march a hundred thousand dead.

A hundred thousand dead, with firm and noiseless tread,
All shadowy-gray yet solid, with faces gray and ghast,
And by the house they went, and all their brows were bent
Straight forward; and they passed, and passed, and passed,
      and passed.

But O there came a place, and O there came a face,
That clenched my heart to see it, and sudden turned my way;
And in the Face that turned I saw two eyes that burned,
Never-forgotten eyes, and they had things to say.

Like desolate stars they shone one moment, and were gone
And I sank down and put my arms across my head,
And felt them moving past, nor looked to see the last,
In steady silent march, our hundred thousand dead.

                                        J. C. Squire

ANTHEM FOR DOOMED YOUTH

WHAT passing-bells for these who died as cattle?
Only the monstrous anger of the guns.
Only the stuttering rifles' rapid rattle
Can patter out their hasty orisons.
No mockeries for them; no prayers nor bells,
Nor any voice of mourning save the choirs—
The shrill demented choirs of wailing shells;
And bugles calling for them from sad shires.
What candles may be held to speed them all?
Not in the hands of boys, but in their eyes
Shall shine the holy glimmers of good-bys.
The pallor of girls' brows shall be their pall;

Their flowers the tenderness of patient minds,
And each slow dusk a drawing-down of blinds.

Wilfred Owen

WHAT BIDS ME LEAVE

WHAT bids me leave thee long untouched, my lute,
Hanging so dusty, still, and mute?
Too many dreams behind these worn eyes throng
And sights too great for song.

When I was young how quick thy passions poured—
Wave on wave, chord on chord—
All simple wingèd transport and high strain
Of Earth made heaven again;

But I have seen the world, for all its wit,
Dangling on fire over the pit;
And I must dream what taught our dreamless dead
To save Man, by a thread.

Herbert Trench

THE DYING PATRIOT

. DAY breaks on England down the Kentish hills,
Singing in the silence of the meadow-footing rills,
Day of my dreams, O day!
    I saw them march from Dover, long ago,
    With a silver cross before them, singing low,
Monks of Rome from their home where the blue seas break
        in foam,
    Augustine with his feet of snow.

Noon strikes on England, noon on Oxford town,
—Beauty she was statue cold—there's blood upon her gown:
Noon of my dreams, O noon!
    Proud and godly kings had built her, long ago,
    With her towers and tombs and statues all arow,
With her fair and floral air and the love that lingers there,
    And the streets where the great men go.

By the Wood

Evening on the olden, the golden sea of Wales,
When the first star shivers and the last wave pales:
O evening dreams!
 There's a house that Britons walked in, long ago,
 Where now the springs of ocean fall and flow,
And the dead robed in red and sea-lilies overhead
 Sway when the long winds blow.

Sleep not, my country: though night is here, afar
Your children of the morning are clamorous for war:
Fire in the night, O dreams!
 Though she send you as she sent you, long ago,
 South to desert, east to ocean, north to snow,
West of these out to seas colder than the Hebrides I must go
 Where the fleet of stars is anchored, and the young star-
  captains glow.

James Elroy Flecker

BY THE WOOD

How still the day is, and the air how bright!
 A thrush sings and is silent in the wood;
The hillside sleeps dizzy with heat and light;
 A rhythmic murmur fills the quietude;
A woodpecker prolongs his leisured flight,
 Rising and falling on the solitude.

But there are those who far from yon wood lie,
 Buried within the trench where all were found.
A weight of mold oppresses every eye,
 Within that cabin close their limbs are bound;
 And there they rot amid the long profound
Disastrous silence of gray earth and sky.

These once, too, rested where now rests but one
 Who scarce can lift his panged and heavy head,
Who drinks in grief the hot light of the sun,
 Whose eyes watch dully the green branches spread,
Who feels his currents ever slowlier run,
 Whose lips repeat a silent ". . . Dead! all dead!"

Oh, youths to come shall drink air warm and bright,
   Shall hear the bird cry in the sunny wood.
All my Young England fell today in fight:
   That bird, that wood, was ransomed by our blood!

I pray you, when the drum rolls let your mood
Be worthy of our deaths and your delight.

                                    Robert Nichols

DULCE ET DECORUM

O YOUNG and brave, it is not sweet to die,
   To fall and leave no record of the race,
A little dust trod by the passers-by,
   Swift feet that press your lonely resting-place;
Your dreams unfinished, and your song unheard—
Who wronged your youth by such a careless word?

All life was sweet—veiled mystery in its smile;
   High in your hands you held the brimming cup;
Love waited at your bidding for a while,
   Not yet the time to take its challenge up;
Across the sunshine came no faintest breath
To whisper of the tragedy of death.

And then, beneath the soft and shining blue,
   Faintly you heard the drum's insistent beat;
The echo of its urgent note you knew,
   The shaken earth that told of marching feet;
With quickened breath you heard your country's call,
And from your hands you let the goblet fall.

You snatched the sword, and answered as you went,
   For fear your eager feet should be outrun,
And with the flame of your bright youth unspent
   Went shouting up the pathway to the sun.
O valiant dead, take comfort where you lie.
So sweet to live?   Magnificent to die!

                                    T. P. Cameron Wilson

ARMISTICE

How close the white-ranked crosses stand
Beneath the flag which seems to be
A soaring, hovering glory-cloud
On lily fields of Calvary!

Ours, ours they are—
Those dear, dead knights who won the golden star
  On far French hills, here in our churchyards lying,
    Or in war's wildest wreckage—yet unfound
In those torn, piteous fields which they, in dying,
      Have for us all forever sanctified.
    We can not hallow more that holy ground;
      All glory we would give them, pales beside
        The eternal splendor of those men, who thought
        But of the sacred cause for which they fought.

And now, the battles done,
They who gave all, 'tis they alone who won.
  In their great faith there was no dark misgiving;
    They saw no base self-seekers don the mask
Of high ideals, to batten on the living.
      Their vision was a world secure and just
     Won by their victory—their only task
      To crush one hideous foe; and in that trust
        They sped with eager feet, and paid the price
        Unstinting, of the last great sacrifice.

That faith they hold.
The peace for which they battled was pure gold,
  And in their splendid zeal they died unshaken.
    Knowing such sacred beauty fills their sleep,
  Shall we yet mourn, or wish they might awaken
      To find the golden peace so far debased?
    Should we not rather pray that they may keep
      Their shining vision spotless, undefaced,
        Until the world, repentant and redeemed,
        Grow to the measure of the one they dreamed?

So let them rest.
They gave for us their dearest and their best;
   They keep the holiest. Yet for their giving
    Our fittest tribute is not grief and tears,
  But the same ardent vision in our living
      As that which shone, compelling, in their eyes
    Uncowed by death and all his dreadful fears.
      Then, when at last these glorious dreamers rise,
        The world we keep for them might almost seem
        The living substance of their lofty dream!

How white the crosses—white and small!
   With what proud love the Flag appears
To mother them! And then it all
   Is blurred by the insistent tears!
                Charles Buxton Going

THE UNSCARRED FIGHTER REMEMBERS
FRANCE

That amazing holiday:
Wine and brotherhood and passion,
Paradisal in its way,
Elemental in its fashion.

Those of you that must come after,
Will not know this blithe and brave
Thing we met with vivid laughter,
Standing by an open grave.
                Kenneth Slade Alling

A. E. F.

There will be a rusty gun on the wall, sweetheart,
The rifle grooves curling with flakes of rust.
A spider will make a silver string nest in the darkest, warmest
    corner of it.
The trigger and the range-finder, they too will be rusty,

And no hands will polish the gun, and it will hang on the
wall.
Forefingers and thumbs will point absently and casually
toward it.
It will be spoken about among half-forgotten, wished-to-
be-forgotten things.
They will tell the spider: Go on, you're doing good work.

Carl Sandburg

TO MY DAUGHTER BETTY, THE GIFT OF GOD

IN wiser days, my darling rosebud, blown
To beauty proud as was your mother's prime,
In that desired, delayed, incredible time,
You'll ask why I abandoned you, my own,
And the dear heart that was your baby throne,
To dice with death.   And oh! they'll give you rhyme
And reason: some will call the thing sublime,
And some decry it in a knowing tone.
So here, while the mad guns curse overhead,
And tired men sigh with mud for couch and floor,
Know that we fools, now with the foolish dead,
Died not for flag, nor King, nor Emperor,—
But for a dream, born in a herdsman's shed,
And for the secret Scripture of the poor.

Thomas M. Kettle

LINES FOR THE HOUR

IF what we fought for seems not worth the fighting,
    And if to win seems in the end to fail,
Know that the vision lives beyond all blighting
    And every struggle rends another veil.

The tired hack, the cynic politician,
    Can dim but cannot make us lose the goal,
Time moves with measured step upon her mission,
    Knowing the slow mutations of the soul.

Hamilton Fish Armstrong

EPICEDIUM

(In Memory of America's Dead in the Great War)

No more for them shall Evening's rose unclose,
    Nor Dawn's emblazoned panoplies be spread;
Alike, the Rain's warm kiss and stabbing snows,
    Unminded, fall upon each hallowed head.
But the Bugles, as they leap and wildly sing,
Rejoice, . . . remembering.

The guns' mad music their young ears have known—
    War's lullabies that moaned on Flanders Plain;
To-night the Wind walks on them, still as stone,
    Where they lie huddled close as riven grain.
But the Drums, reverberating, proudly roll—
They love a Soldier's soul!

With arms outflung, and eyes that laughed at Death,
    They drank the wine of sacrifice and loss;
For them a life-time spanned a burning breath,
    And Truth they visioned, clean of earthly dross.
But the Fifes,—can ye not hear their lusty shriek?
They know, and now they speak!

The lazy drift of cloud, the noon-day hum
    Of vagrant bees; the lark's untrammeled song
Shall gladden them no more, who now lie dumb
    In Death's strange sleep, yet once were swift and strong.
But the Bells, that to all living listeners peal,
With joy their deeds reveal!

They have given their lives, with bodies bruised and broken,
    Upon their Country's altar they have bled;
They have left, as priceless heritage, a token
    That Honor lives forever with the Dead.
And the Bugles, as their rich notes rise and fall—
They answer, knowing all.

                                        J. Corson Miller

THE LAND

III

BE not afraid, O Dead, be not afraid:
We have not lost the dreams that once were flung
Like pennons to the world: we yet are stung
With all the starry prophecies that made
You, in the gray dawn watchful, half afraid
Of vision. Never a night that all men sleep unstirred:
Never a sunset but the west is blurred
With banners marching and a sign displayed.
Be not afraid, O Dead, lest we forget
A single hour your living glorified;
Come but a drum-beat, and the sleepers fret
To walk again the places where you died:
Broad is the land, our loves are broadly spread,
But now, even more widely scattered lie our dead.

IV

O Lord of splendid nations let us dream
Not of a place of barter, nor "the State,"
But dream as lovers dream—for it is late—
Of some small place beloved; perhaps a stream
Running beside a house set round with flowers;
Perhaps a garden wet with hurrying showers,
Where bees are thick about a leaf-hid gate.
For such as these, men die nor hesitate.
The old gray cities, gossipy and wise,
The candid valleys, like a woman's brow,
The mountains treading mightily toward the skies,
Turn dreams to visions—there's a vision now!
Of hills panoplied, fields of waving spears,
And a great campus shaken with flags and tears.

Struthers Burt

POEMS OF PLACES

APPROACHING AMERICA

CAME first, five hundred miles from port,
A perching bird of homely sort,
And next in tumbling waters gray
Nantucket's gallant lightship lay
Rocking, lonely, small and black,
A moment's friend upon the track.

And then at night from shores unseen
Shone sparsely scattered lights serene,
Sweet tokens after all the days
Shifting and void of the sea's ways:
We watched past midnight to divine
The incredible shore's uncertain line;

Then, very wakeful, went below
Thrilled a new continent to know,
Long talked about in commonplace,
Now a strange planet reached through space;
We drained the flask we dared not keep
And laughed and talked ourselves to sleep.

Chill dawn; and through the porthole's glass
Firm-circled by its rim of brass
A smoother sea, a warming fold
Of woods, browned with a year grown old:
The coast-line of an English shire
And in the midst a cosy spire.

Solent and Staten Island, these
Greet sisterly across the seas,
And in confederate kindness spread
For every stranger newly sped
From either to the other shore
Scenes he has known and loved before.

Anchored we waited. The ship stirred.
The shore went past. O dawning word
That filled our souls with silent awe!
Lovely things from heaven we saw,
Over the waters far up stream
Sublime companions of a dream:

A fair phantasmal company
Of goddesses in the morning sky,
Concourse serene of starry powers
Musing on other worlds than ours!
The water sparkled: the sun shone:
Mysteriously they were gone.

Gone: in their places fixt appearing
A mass of buildings, heightening, nearing,
A noble group fit for a great
New hemisphere's majestic gate,
Till as we slowly steamed ahead
In straggling line the cluster spread.

Each up its slice of skyway goes,
Windows in thousand chessboard rows;
Pointed and lean and broad and blunt
Behind the rusty water-front,
In random rivalry they climb
The oddest pinnacles of Time.

J. C. Squire

NEW YORK CITY

I

NEW YORK, it would be easy to revile
The flatly carnal beggar in your smile,
And flagellate, with a superior bliss,
The gasping routines of your avarice.
Loud men reward you with an obvious ax,
Or piteous laurel-wreath, and their attacks
And eulogies blend to a common sin.
New York, perhaps an intellectual grin
That brings its bright cohesion to the warm
Confusion of the heart, can mould your swarm

Of huge, drab blunders into smaller grace . . .
With old words I shall gamble for your face.

II

The evening kneels between your prisoned brick,
Darkly indifferent to each scheme and trick
With which your men insult and smudge their day.
When evenings metaphysically pray
Above the weakening dance of men, they find
That every eye that looks at them is blind.
And yet, New York, I say that evenings free
An insolently mystic majesty
From your parades of automatic greed.
For one dark moment all your narrow speed
Receives the fighting blackness of a soul,
And every nervous lie swings to a whole—
A pilgrim, blurred yet proud, who finds in black
An arrogance that fills his straining lack.
Between your undistinguished crates of stone
And wood, the wounded dwarfs who walked alone—
The chorus-girls whose indiscretions hang
Between the sentinels of rouge and slang;
The women molding painfully a fresh
Reward for pliant treacheries of flesh;
The men who raise the tin sword of a creed,
Convinced that it can kill the lunge of greed;
The thieves whose beaten vanity purloins
A fancied victory from ringing coins;
The staidly bloated men whose minds have sold
Their quickness to an old, metallic Scold;
The neatly cultured men whose hopes and fears
Dwell in soft prisons honored by past years;
The men whose tortured youth bends to the task
Of fashioning a damply swaggering mask—
The night, with black hands, gathers each mistake
And strokes a mystic freedom from each ache.
The night, New York, sardonic and alert,
Offers a soul to your reluctant dirt.

Maxwell Bodenheim

PROUD NEW YORK

By proud New York and its man-piled Matterhorns,
The hard blue sky overhead and the west wind blowing,
Steam-plumes waving from sun-glittering pinnacles,
And deep streets shaking to the million-river:

    Manhattan, zoned with ships, the cruel
      Youngest of all the world's great towns,
    Thy bodice bright with many a jewel,
      Imperially crowned with crowns . . .

    Who that has known thee but shall burn
      In exile till he come again
    To do thy bitter will, O stern
      Moon of the tides of men!

John Reed

THOMPSON STREET

    Queen of all streets, Fifth Avenue
      Stretches her slender limbs
    From the great Arch of Triumph, on—
      On, where the distance dims

    The splendors of her jewelled robes,
      Her granite draperies;
    The magic, sunset-smitten walls
      That veil her marble knees;

    For ninety squares she lies a queen,
      Superb, bare, unashamed,
    Yielding her beauty scornfully
      To worshippers unnamed.

    But at her feet her sister glows,
      A daughter of the South:
    Squalid, immeasurably mean,—
      But O! her hot, sweet mouth!

My Thompson Street! A Tuscan girl,
   Hot with life's wildest blood;
Her black shawl on her black, black hair,
   Her brown feet stained with mud;

A scarlet blossom at her lips,
   A new babe at her breast;
A singer at a wine-shop door,
   (Her lover unconfessed).

Listen! A hurdy-gurdy plays
   Now alien melodies:
She smiles; she cannot quite forget
   The mother overseas!

Samuel McCoy

BROOKLYN BRIDGE AT DAWN

OUT of the cleansing night of stars and tides,
Building itself anew in the slow dawn,   •
The long sea-city rises: night is gone,
Day is not yet; still merciful, she hides
Her summoning brow, and still the night-car glides
Empty of faces; the night-watchmen yawn
One to the other, and shiver and pass on,
Nor yet a soul over the great bridge rides.
Frail as a gossamer, a thing of air,
A bow of shadow o'er the river flung,
Its sleepy masts and lonely lapping flood;
Who, seeing thus the bridge a-slumber there,
Would dream such softness, like a picture hung,
Is wrought of human thunder, iron and blood?

Richard Le Gallienne

THE CITY'S CROWN

WHAT makes a city great? Huge piles of stone
Heaped heavenward? Vast multitudes who dwell
Within wide circling walls? Palace and throne
And riches past the count of man to tell,

And wide domain?   Nay, these the empty husk!
True glory dwells where glorious deeds are done,
Where great men rise whose names athwart the dusk
Of misty centuries gleam like the sun!
In Athens, Sparta, Florence, 'twas the soul
That was the city's bright, immortal part,
The splendor of the spirit was their goal,
Their jewel, the unconquerable heart!
So may the city that I love be great
Till every stone shall be articulate.

William Dudley Foulke

VERMONT

WIDE and shallow, in the cowslip marshes,
Floods the freshet of the April snow;
Late drifts linger in the hemlock gorges,
Through the brakes and mosses trickling slow,
   Where the mayflower,
Where the painted trillium, leaf and blow.

Foliaged deep, the cool midsummer maples
Shade the porches of the long white street;
Trailing wide Olympian elms lean over
Tiny churches where the cross-roads meet;
   Fields of fireflies
Wheel all night like stars above the wheat.

Blaze the mountains in the windless Autumn,
Frost-clear, blue-nooned, apple-ripening days;
Faintly fragrant, in the farther valleys,
Smoke of many bonfires swell the haze;
   Fair-bound cattle
Plod with lowing up the meadowy ways.

Roaring snows, down-sweeping from the uplands,
Bury the still valleys, drift them deep;
Low along the mountains, lake-blue shadows,
Sea-blue shadows, in the snow-drifts sleep;
   High above them
Blinding crystal is the sunlit steep.

Sarah N. Cleghorn

MOTHER OF MEN

MOTHER of Men, grown strong in giving
   Honor to them thy lights have led;
Rich in the faith of thousands living,
   Proud of the deeds of thousands dead—
We who have felt thy power, and known thee,
   We in whose work thy gifts avail,
High in our hearts enshrined enthrone thee,
       Mother of Men—Old Yale!

Spirit of youth, alive, unchanging,
   Under whose feet the years are cast;
Queen of an ageless empire, ranging
   Over the future and the past—
Thee, whom our fathers loved before us,
   Thee, whom our sons unborn shall hail,
Praise we today in sturdy chorus,
       Mother of Men—Old Yale!

          Brian Hooker

THE RIVER

I CANNOT sleep;—the beautiful Lynnhaven
Floods through my thoughts to-night.
Past darkling pines it moves and willows weeping
In many a cove and bight.

I cannot sleep because it gleams like silver.
Although my eyes are sealed,
Clear to my vision are its dusky shallows
And starry depths revealed.

Slowly it moves, and in a mystic silence,
It draws me wondering,
Out through its shadowy portals to the ocean
Where sails are blossoming.

On, ever on, to strange and far adventure
On waters wide and deep
The river bears me through the fragrant darkness,
And so I cannot sleep.

          Mary Sinton Leitch

VIRGINIANA

Slow turns the water by the green marshes,
In Virginia.
Overhead the sea fowl
Make silver flashes, cry harsh as peacocks.
Capes and islands stand,
Ocean thunders,
The light-houses burn red and gold stars.
In Virginia
Run a hundred rivers.
The dogwood is in blossom,
The pink honeysuckle,
The fringe tree.
My love is the ghostly armed sycamore,
My loves are the yellow pine and the white pine,
My love is the mountain linden.
Mine is the cedar.
Ancient forest,
Hemlock-mantled cliff,
Black cohosh,
Golden-rod, ironweed,
And purple farewell-summer.
Maple red in the autumn,
And plunge of the mountain brook.

The wind bends the wheat ears,
The wind bends the corn,
The wild grape to the vineyard grape
Sends the season's greetings.

Timothy, clover,
Apple, peach!
The blue grass talks to the moss and fern.

Sapphire-shadowed, deep-bosomed, long-limbed,
Mountains lie in the garden of the sky,
Evening is a passion flower, morning is a rose!

Old England sailed to Virginia,
Bold Scotland sailed,
Vine-wreathed France sailed,
And the Rhine sailed,
And Ulster and Cork and Killarney.
Out of Africa—out of Africa!
Guinea Coast, Guinea Coast,
Senegambia, Dahomey.—
Now One,
Now Virginia!

Pocahontas steals through the forest,
Along the Blue Ridge ride the Knights of the Horseshoe,
Young George Washington measures neighbor's land from
    neighbor,
In the firelight Thomas Jefferson plays his violin.
Violin, violin!
Patrick Henry speaks loud in Saint John's church.
Andrew Lewis lifts his flint-lock.—
O Fringed Hunting Shirt, where are you going?
George Rogers Clarke takes Kaskaskia and Vincennes.

They tend tobacco,
And they hoe the corn,
Colored folk singing,
Singing sweetly of heaven
And the Lord Jesus.
Broad are the tobacco leaves,
Narrow are the corn blades,
Little blue morning glories run through the cornfields.

Sumach, sumach!
Blue-berried cedar,
Persimmon and pawpaw,
Chinquepin.
Have you seen the 'possum?
Have you seen the 'coon?
Have you heard the whippoorwill?
Whippoorwill!   Whippoorwill!
Whip—poor—will!

White top wagons
Rolling westward.
Bearded men
Looking westward.
Women, children,
Gazing westward.
Kentucky!
Ohio!
Halt at eve and build the fire.
Dogs,
Long guns,
Household gear.
'Ware the Indian!
White top wagons going westward.

Edgar Allan Poe
Walking in the moonlight,
In the woods of Albemarle,
'Neath the trees of Richmond,
Pondering names of women,
        Annabel—Annie,
        Lenore—Ulalume.

Maury, Maury!
What of Winds and Currents?
Maury, Maury,
Ocean rover!
But when you come to die,
" Carry me through Goshen Pass
When the rhododendron is in bloom! "

Men in gray,
Men in blue,
Very young men,
Meet by a river.
Overhead are fruit trees.
" Water—water!
We will drink, then fight."—
" O God, why do we
Fight anyhow?

It's a good swimming hole
And the cherries are ripe!"

Bronze men on bronze horses,
Down the long avenue,
They ride in the sky,
Bronze men.
Stuart cries to Jackson,
Jackson cries to Lee,
Lee cries to Washington.
Bronze men,
Great soldiers.

The church bells ring,
In Virginia.
Sonorous,
Sweet,
In the sunshine,
In the rain.
Salvation!   It is Sunday.
Salvation!   It is Sunday,
In Virginia.
Locust trees in bloom,
Long grass in the church yard,
June bugs zooning round the roses,
First bell—second bell!
All the ladies are in church.
Now the men will follow,
In Virginia,
In Virginia!

Mary Johnston

DUSK

THEY tell me she is beautiful, my city,
That she is colorful and quaint; alone
Among the cities.   But I—I who have known
Her tenderness, her courage, and her pity;
Have felt her forces mold me, mind and bone,
Life after life, up from her first beginning—
How can I think of her in wood and stone!
To others she has given of her beauty:

Her gardens, and her dim old faded ways;
Her laughter, and her happy drifting hours;
Glad spendthrift April, squandering her flowers;
The sharp still wonder of her autumn days;
Her chimes, that shimmer from St. Michael's steeple
Across the deep maturity of June
Like sunlight slanting over open water
Under a high blue listless afternoon.
But when the dusk is deep upon the harbor,
She finds me where her rivers meet and speak,
And while the constellations gem the silence
High overhead, her cheek is on my cheek.
I know her in the thrill behind the dark
When sleep brims all her silent thoroughfares.
She is the glamour in the quiet park
That kindles simple things like grass and trees;
Wistful and wanton as her sea-born airs,
Bringer of dim rich age-old memories.
Out on the gloom-deep water, when the nights
Are choked with fog, and perilous, and blind,
She is the faith that tends the calling lights.
Hers is the stifled voice of harbor bells,
Muffled and broken by the mist and wind.
Hers are the eyes through which I look on life
And find it brave and splendid.   And the stir
Of hidden music shaping all my songs,
And these my songs, my all, belong to her.

DuBose Heyward

MY FATHERS CAME FROM KENTUCKY

I was born in Illinois,—
Have lived there many days.
And I have Northern words,
And thoughts,
And ways.

But my great-grandfathers came
To the west with Daniel Boone,
And taught his babes to read,
And heard the redbird's tune;

And heard the turkey's call,
And stilled the panther's cry,
And rolled on the blue-grass hills,
And looked God in the eye.

And feud and Hell were theirs;
Love, like the moon's desire,
Love like a burning-mine,
Love like rifle-fire.

I tell tales out of school
Till these Yankees hate my style.
Why should the young cad cry,
Shout with joy for a mile?

Why do I faint with love
Till the prairies dip and reel?
My heart is a kicking horse
Shod with Kentucky steel.

No drop of my blood from north
Of Mason and Dixon's line.
And this racer in my breast
Tears my ribs for a sign.

But I ran in Kentucky hills
Last week. They were hearth and home. . . .
And the church at Grassy Springs,
Under the redbird's wings
Was peace and honeycomb.

Vachel Lindsay

CHICAGO

HOG-BUTCHER for the world,
Tool-maker, Stacker of Wheat,
Player with Railroads and the Nation's Freight-handler;
Stormy, husky, brawling,
City of the Big Shoulders:

They tell me you are wicked and I believe them, for I have
    seen your painted women under the gas lamps luring
    the farm boys.

And they tell me you are crooked, and I answer: Yes, it is
    true I have seen the gunman kill and go free to kill
    again.

And they tell me you are brutal and my reply is: On the faces
    of women and children I have seen the marks of wanton
    hunger.

And having answered so I turn once more to those who
    sneer at this my city, and I give them back the sneer
    and say to them:

Come and show me another city with lifted head singing
    so proud to be alive and coarse and strong and cunning.

Flinging magnetic curses amid the toil of piling job on
    job, here is a tall bold slugger set vivid against the
    little soft cities;

Fierce as a dog with tongue lapping for action, cunning as
    a savage pitted against the wilderness,

    Bareheaded,

    Shoveling,

    Wrecking,

    Planning,

    Building, breaking, rebuilding,

Under the smoke, dust all over his mouth, laughing with
    white teeth,

Under the terrible burden of destiny laughing as a young
    man laughs,

Laughing even as an ignorant fighter laughs who has never
    lost a battle,

Bragging and laughing that under his wrist is the pulse,
    and under his ribs the heart of the people.

        Laughing!

Laughing the stormy, husky, brawling laughter of youth;
    half-naked, sweating, proud to be Hog-butcher, Tool-
    maker, Stacker of Wheat, Player with Railroads, and
    Freight-handler to the Nation.

Carl Sandburg

TO CHICAGO AT NIGHT

SPUTTER, city!   Bead with fire
Every ragged roof and spire;

Splash your brilliance on the sky
Till you blind the moon's round eye;

Let your jagged branding mark
Scorch across the velvet dark

Till the night beneath your sting
Shrivels like a crumpling wing.

Burst to bloom, you proud, white flower,
But remember—that hot hour

When the shadow of your brand
Laps the last cool grain of sand—

You will still be just a scar
On a little, lonesome star.
                              Mildred Plew Merryman

ELLIS PARK

LITTLE park that I pass through,
I carry off a piece of you
Every morning hurrying down
To my work-day in the town;
Carry you for country there
To make the city ways more fair.
I take your trees,
And your breeze,
Your greenness,
Your cleanness,
Some of your shade, some of your sky,
Some of your calm as I go by;

Your flowers to trim
The pavements grim;
Your space for room in the jostled street
And grass for carpet to my feet.
Your fountains take and sweet bird calls
To sing me from my office walls.
All that I can see
I carry off with me.

But you never miss my theft,
So much treasure you have left.
As I find you, fresh at morning,
So I find you, home returning—
Nothing lacking from your grace.
All your riches wait in place
For me to borrow
On the morrow.

Do you hear this praise of you,
Little park that I pass through?

Helen Hoyt

THE PAINTED HILLS OF ARIZONA

THE rainbows all lie crumpled on these hills,
The red dawns scattered on their colored sills.
These hills have caught the lightning in its flight,
Caught colors from the skies of day and night
And shine with shattered stars and suns; they hold
Dyed yellow, red and purple, blue and gold.

Red roses seem within their marble blown,
A painted garden chiseled in the stone;
The rose and violet trickling through their veins,
Where they drop brilliant curtains to the plains—
A ramp of rock and granite, jeweled and brightening,
Like some great colored wall of sudden lightning!

Edwin Curran

ON THE GREAT PLATEAU

In the Santa Clara Valley, far away and far away,
Cool-breathed waters dip and dally, linger towards another
    day—
Far and far away—far away.
Slow their floating step, but tireless, terraced down the
    great plateau.
Towards our ways of steam and wireless, silver-paced the
    brook-beds go.
Past the ladder-walled pueblos, past the orchards, pear and
    quince,
Where the back-locked river's ebb flows, miles and miles
    the valley glints,
Shining backwards, singing downwards, towards horizons
    blue and bay.
All the roofs the roads ensconce so dream of visions far
    away—
Santa Cruz and Ildefonso, Santa Clara, Santa Fé.
Ancient, sacred fears and faiths, ancient, sacred faiths and
    fears—
Some were real, some were wraiths—Indian, Franciscan
    years,
Built the kivas, swung the bells; while the wind sang plain
    and free,
"Turn your eyes from visioned hells!—look as far as you
    can see!"
In the Santa Clara Valley, far away and far away,
Dying dreams divide and dally, crystal-terraced waters
    sally—
Linger towards another day, far and far away—far away.

As you follow where you find them, up along the high
    plateau,
In the hollows left behind them Spanish chapels fade below—
Shaded court and low corrals.   In the vale the goat-herd
    browses.
Hollyhocks are seneschals by the little buff-walled houses.
Over grassy swale and alley have you ever seen it so—
Up the Santa Clara Valley, riding on the Great Plateau?

Past the ladder-walled pueblos, past the orchards, pear and
  quince,
Where the trenchèd waters' ebb flows, miles and miles the
  valley glints,
Shining backwards, singing downwards towards horizons
  blue and bay.
All the haunts the bluffs ensconce so breathe of visions
  far away,
As you ride near Ildefonso back again to Santa Fé.
Pecos, mellow with the years, tall-walled Taos—who can
  know
Half the storied faiths and fears haunting green New Mexico?
Only from her open places down arroyos blue and bay,
One wild grace of many graces dallies towards another day.
Where her yellow tufa crumbles, something stars and grasses
  know,
Something true, that crowns and humbles, shimmers from
  the Great Plateau:
Blows where cool-paced waters dally from the stillness of
  Puyé,
. Down the Santa Clara Valley through the world from far
  away—
Far and far away—far away.

                                        Edith Wyatt

SANTA BARBARA BEACH

Now while the sunset offers,
  Shall we not take our own:
The gems, the blazing coffers,
  The seas, the shores, the throne?

The sky-ships, radiant-masted,
  Move out, bear low our way.
Oh, Life was dark while it lasted,
  Now for enduring day.

Now with the world far under,
  To draw up drowning men
And show them lands of wonder
  Where they may build again.

There earthly sorrow falters,
    There longing has its wage;
There gleam the ivory altars
    Of our lost pilgrimage.

—Swift flame—then shipwrecks only
    Beach in the ruined light;
Above them reach up lonely
    The headlands of the night.

A hurt bird cries and flutters
    Her dabbled breast of brown;
The western wall unshutters
    To fling one last rose down.

A rose, a wild light after—
    And life calls through the years,
"Who dreams my fountain's laughter
    Shall feed my wells with tears."

                                    Ridgely Torrence

AS I CAME DOWN MOUNT TAMALPAIS

As I came down Mount Tamalpais,
    To north the fair Sonoma Hills
Lay like a trembling thread of blue
    Beneath a sky of daffodils;
Through tules green a silver stream
    Ran south to meet the tranquil bay,
Whispering a dreamy, tender tale
    Of vales and valleys far away.

As I came down Mount Tamalpais,
    To south the city brightly shone,
Touched by the sunset's good-night kiss
    Across the golden ocean blown;
I saw its hills, its tapering masts,
    I almost heard its tramp and tread,
And saw against the sky the cross
    Which marks the City of the Dead.

As I came down Mount Tamalpais,
  To east San Pablo's water lay,
Touched with a holy purple light,
  The benediction of the day;
No ripple on its twilight tide,
  No parting of its evening veil,
Save dimly in the far-off haze
  One dreamy, yellow sunset sail.

As I came down Mount Tamalpais,
  To west Heaven's gateway opened wide,
And through it, freighted with day cares,
  The cloud-ships floated with the tide;
Then, silently through stilly air,
  Starlight flew down from Paradise,
Folded her silver wings and slept
  Upon the slopes of Tamalpais.

Clarence Urmy

OAK AND OLIVE

I

THOUGH I was born a Londoner,
  And bred in Gloucestershire,
I walked in Hellas years ago
  With friends in white attire:
And I remember how my soul
  Drank wine as pure as fire.

And when I stand by Charing Cross
  I can forget to hear
The crash of all those smoking wheels,
  When those cold flutes and clear
Pipe with such fury down the street,
  My hands grow moist with fear.

And there's a hall in Bloomsbury
  No more I dare to tread,
For all the stone men shout at me
  And swear they are not dead;

And once I touched a broken **girl**
And knew that marble bled.

II

But when I walk in Athens **town**
    That swims in dust and sun
Perverse, I think of London then
    Where massive work is done,
And with what sweep at Westminster
    The rayless waters run.

I ponder how from Attic seed
    There grew an English tree,
How Byron like his heroes fell,
    Fighting a country free,
And Swinburne took from Shelley's **lips**
    The kiss of Poetry.

And while our poets chanted Pan
    Back to his pipes and power,
Great Verrall, bending at his desk,
    And searching hour on hour
Found out old gardens, where the wise
    May pluck a Spartan flower.

III

When I go down the Gloucester lanes
    My friends are deaf and blind:
Fast as they turn their foolish eyes
    The Mænads leap behind,
And when I hear the fire-winged feet,
    They only hear the wind.

Have I not chased the fluting Pan
    Through Cranham's sober trees?
Have I not sat on Painswick Hill
    With a nymph upon my knees,
And she as rosy as the dawn,
    And naked as the breeze?

IV

But when I lie in Grecian fields,
   Smothered in asphodel,
Or climb the blue and barren hills,
   Or sing in woods that smell
With such hot spices of the South
   As mariners might sell—

Then my heart turns where no sun burns,
   To lands of glittering rain,
To fields beneath low-clouded skies
   New-widowed of their grain,
And Autumn leaves like blood and gold
   That strew a Gloucester lane.

V

Oh well I know sweet Hellas now,
   And well I knew it then,
When I with starry lads walked out—
   But ah, for home again!
Was I not bred in Gloucestershire,
   One of the Englishmen!

James Elroy Flecker

DEVON TO ME

WHERE my fathers stood
   Watching the sea,
Gale-spent herring boats
   Hugging the lea;
There my Mother lives,
   Moorland and tree.
Sight o' the blossom!
   Devon to me!

Where my fathers walked,
   Driving the plough;
Whistled their hearts out—
   Who whistles now?

There my Mother burns
    Fire faggots free.
Scent o' the wood-smoke!
    Devon to me!

Where my fathers sat,
    Passing their bowls;
—They've no cider now,
    God rest their souls!
There my Mother feeds
    Red cattle three.
Taste o' the cream-pan!
    Devon to me!

Where my fathers sleep,
    Turning to dust,
This old body throw
    When die I must!
There my Mother calls,
    Wakeful is She!
Sound o' the west-wind!
    Devon to me!

Where my fathers lie,
    When I am gone,
Who need pity me
    Dead?   Never one!
There my Mother clasps
    Me.   Let me be!
Feel o' the red earth!
    Devon to me!

                              John Galsworthy

THE MEMORY OF KENT

KENTISH hamlets gray and old,
    The spring breeze calls you back to me;
Now I know, by weald and wold
Your primroses manifold
Glisten, and such delicate gold
    As nowhere else men see,

Through the woodways soft and brown,
    By the swollen streams,
By the cart-tracks rutted down,
        Gleams.

Sussex with wild daffodils
    Is not so dear to me:
All the cowslip-haunted hills,
All the bluebell-bordered rills,
And orchids round the high windmills
    And down the marshy lea—
One primrose from my Kentish home
    Is worth all these to me.

Edmund Blunden

THE ROLLING ENGLISH ROAD

From "The Flying Inn"

BEFORE the Roman came to Rye or out to Severn strode,
The rolling English drunkard made the rolling English road.
A reeling road, a rolling road, that rambles round the shire,
And after him the parson ran, the sexton and the squire.
A merry road, a mazy road, and such as we did tread
That night we went to Birmingham by way of Beachy Head.

I knew no harm of Bonaparte and plenty of the squire,
And for to fight the Frenchman I did not much desire,
But I did bash their baggonets because they came arrayed
To straighten out the crooked road an English drunkard
        made,
Where you and I went down the lane with ale-mugs in our
        hands
The night we went to Glastonbury by way of Goodwin Sands.

His sins they were forgiven him; or why do flowers run
Behind him; and the hedges all strengthening in the sun?
The wild thing went from left to right and knew not which
        was which,
But the wild rose was above him when they found him in
        the ditch.
God pardon us, nor harden us; we did not see so clear
The night we went to Bannockburn by way of Brighton Pier.

My friends, we will not go again or ape an ancient rage,
Or stretch the folly of our youth to be the shame of age,
But walk with clearer eyes and ears this path that wandereth,
And see undrugged in evening light the decent inn of death;
For there is good news yet to hear and fine things to be seen,
Before we go to Paradise by way of Kensal Green.

G. K. Chesterton

LONDON

Oh! London town, you are grim and gray,
Like a sad old monk in his sober gown,
Yet you touch, in your solemn surly way
The hearts of your children, London town!

You take them into your gaunt old hand,
And your stern eyes look with a darkening frown
At the cleanly air they bring from the land,
For it stirs up memories, London town!

You fling them into your squalid deeps
And whiten the faces that suns made brown,
You listen unmoved to the heart that weeps
For the quaint old homestead, London town!

You crush them into your moulds like clay
And you plaster and thump and knead them down,
Till they grow too weary with toil to pray
For the hand of death, oh! London town!

Your cold old heart is as hard as steel
While your pale lips smile—like a painted clown,
Yet deep beneath is a love that can feel
For your toiling children, London town!

Ah! London town, in your soiled old glove
Like a jewel set in an iron crown,
You hold the heart of a girl that I love—
Oh! keep it unharmed, dear London town!

T. P. Cameron Wilson

A BALLAD OF LONDON

Ah London! London! our delight,
Great flower that opens but at night,
Great City of the midnight sun,
Whose day begins when day is done.

Lamp after lamp against the sky
Opens a sudden beaming eye,
Leaping alight on either hand,
The iron lilies of the Strand.

Like dragonflies, the hansoms hover,
With jeweled eyes, to catch the lover;
The streets are full of lights and loves,
Soft gowns, and flutter of soiled doves.

The human moths about the light
Dash and cling close in dazed delight,
And burn and laugh, the world and wife,
For this is London, this is life!

Upon thy petals butterflies,
But at thy root, some say, there lies
A world of weeping trodden things,
Poor worms that have not eyes or wings.

From out corruption of their woe
Springs this bright flower that charms us so,
Men die and rot deep out of sight
To keep this jungle-flower bright.

Paris and London, World-Flowers twain
Wherewith the World-Tree blooms again,
Since Time hath gathered Babylon,
And withered Rome still withers on.

Sidon and Tyre were such as ye,
How bright they shone upon the tree!
But Time hath gathered, both are gone,
And no man sails to Babylon.

Richard Le Gallienne

PICCADILLY

Queen of all streets, you stand alway
Lovely by dusk or dark or day.
Cruellest of streets that I do know,
I love you wheresoe'er I go.

The daytime knows your lyric wonder:
Your tunes that rhyme and chime and thunder,
And exiles vision with delight
Your million-blossomed charm of night.

Sweet frivolous frock and fragrant face
Your shadow-fretted pavements trace;
And all about your haunted mile
Hangs a soft air, a girlish smile.

But other steps make echo here,
With curse and prayer and wasted tear;
And under the silver wings of sleep
Your desolate step-children creep.

Street of all fair streets fairest—say
Why thus we love you night and day;
And why we love you last and best
Whose hearts were broken on your breast!

Thomas Burke

STREETS

Church Street wears ever a smile, from having watched bright belles
  Coming home with young men, after balls, "at all hours."
Its villas don't mind; they say, "Go it, young swells,
  We've been young, too!" But Ebenezer Street glowers.

Chapel deacons live here, with side whiskers and pompous wives,
  Who play hymns on Sundays, and deeply deplore sinful acts.

They're convinced that their neighbors lead scandalous
    private lives;
  —That you and I ought to be shot, "if one knew all the
    facts."

Goreham Street's sad. Here lives old Jones the poet—
  He knew Swinburne and Watts, and has letters from "dear
    Charlie Keene."
Loo Isaacs lives here as well, and poor Captain Jowett:
  And the "Goreham Street Murder" was over at number
    thirteen.

Now George Street (E. C.) strikes a cheerful and strenuous
    note;
  It is full of live men of business, of 'buses and noise;
Of Surbiton gents, very sleek, in top-hat and fur coat;
  And earnest young clerks who perspire, and take classes
    for boys.

But Audley Street has a calm and a gently fastidious air!
  Here I shall live when I'm rich, with my wife and my car:
When we are pleased, we'll never shout nor ruffle our hair,
  And a lift of the eyebrow will show how annoyed we are.

This is where life is lived nobly and sweetly and well:
  Here are beauty, all hardly-won things, and courage and
    love.
Why people worship the slums and the poor so, I can never
    tell,
  For it's virtue and baths and good cooking go hand in
    glove!
Douglas Goldring

THE SONG OF NIDDERDALE

As I came past the Brimham Rocks
    I heard the thrushes calling,
And saw the pleasant, winding Nidd
    In peaty ripples falling.

Its banks were gay with witching flowers,
   And all the folk did hail
Me back again so cheerily
   To bonnie Nidderdale.

The blackbirds in the birchen holts
   The live-long day were singing,
Where countless azure hyacinths
   Their perfumed bells were ringing.
And Guisecliff stands in loneliness
   Between the moor and vale,
Protecting with its rocky scaur
   My bonnie Nidderdale.

And as I passed through Pateley Brigg,
   A woman carolled blithely,
And up and down the cobbled streets
   The bairnies skipped so lithely.
The sky was blue, and silken clouds,
   Each like an elfin sail,
Swept o'er the waking larchen woods
   Of bonnie Nidderdale.

Where gray-stone dykes and grayer garths
   Look down on Ramsgill village,
The thieving, gawmless, gay tomtits
   The little gardens pillage.
Gray Middlesmoor is perched upon
   The fellside azure pale,
A mist-girt, lonely sentinel
   O'er bonnie Nidderdale.

Above the dowly intake lands
   The great wide moor is calling,
Of heathered bens and brackened glens,
   Where peat-born rills are brawling.
O! land of ever-changing skies,
   Where wild winds storm and wail,
There is nowhere a land more loved
   Than bonnie Nidderdale.

                 Dorothy Una Ratcliffe

AUTUMN MORNING AT CAMBRIDGE

I RAN out in the morning, when the air was clean and new,
And all the grass was glittering and gray with autumn dew,
I ran out to the apple tree and pulled an apple down,
And all the bells were ringing in the old gray town.

Down in the town, off the bridges and the grass
They are sweeping up the leaves to let the people pass,
Sweeping up the old leaves, golden-reds and browns,
While the men go to lecture with the wind in their gowns.

Frances Cornford

HA'NACKER MILL

SALLY is gone that was so kindly,
  Sally is gone from Ha'nacker Hill,
And the Briar grows ever since then so blindly;
  And ever since then the clapper is still . . .
  And the sweeps have fallen from Ha'nacker Mill.

Ha'nacker Hill is in Desolation:
  Ruin a-top and a field unploughed.
And Spirits that call on a fallen nation,
  Spirits that loved her calling aloud,
  Spirits abroad in a windy cloud.

Spirits that call and no one answers—
  Ha'nacker's down and England's done.
Wind and Thistle for pipe and dancers,
  And never a ploughman under the Sun:
  Never a ploughman.   Never a one.

Hilaire Belloc

SHEEPSTOR

THE little granite church upholds
Four pinnacles like holy hands,
A missioner proclaiming God
To ancient unbelieving lands.

Long time it dared the indifferent hills
Child-like, half-frightened, all alone,
Lest chink of matin bell offend
The mother of its quarried stone.

Now it is proven and secure,
Yet may not sleep, remembering
How on the moor above it stand
Stone row and mound and pagan ring.

L. A. G. Strong

YATTENDON

Among the woods and tillage
That fringe the topmost downs,
All lonely lies the village,
Far off from seas and towns.
Yet when her own folk slumbered
I heard within her street
Murmur of men unnumbered
And march of myriad feet.

For all she lies so lonely,
Far off from towns and seas,
The village holds not only
The roofs beneath her trees:
While Life is sweet and tragic
And Death is veiled and dumb,
Hither, by singer's magic,
The pilgrim world must come.

Henry Newbolt

CARROWMORE

It's a lonely road through bogland to the lake at Carrow-
     more,
And a sleeper there lies dreaming where the water laps the
     shore;
Though the moth-wings of the twilight in their purples are
     unfurled,
Yet his sleep is filled with music by the masters of the
     world.

There's a hand is white as silver that is fondling with his
    hair:
There are glimmering feet of sunshine that are dancing by
    him there:
And half-open lips of faery that were dyed a faery red
In their revels where the Hazel Tree its holy clusters shed.

"Come away," the red lips whisper, "all the world is
    weary now;
'Tis the twilight of the ages and it's time to quit the plough.
Oh, the very sunlight's weary ere it lightens up the dew,
And its gold is changed and faded before it falls to you.

"Though your colleen's heart be tender, a tenderer heart
    is near.
What's the starlight in her glances when the stars are shining
    clear?
Who would kiss the fading shadow when the flower-face
    glows above?
'Tis the beauty of all Beauty that is calling for your love."

Oh! the great gates of the mountain have opened once again,
And the sound of song and dancing falls upon the ears of
    men,
And the Land of Youth lies gleaming, flushed with rainbow
    light and mirth,
And the old enchantment lingers in the honey-heart of
    earth.

A. E.

CLONARD

By lost Clonard the river meads still hold
Forgotten dreams, white memories pure as dew,
Of fragrant days when scholars wandered through
The marshy grass, and hearts had not grown old;
Beneath her purple hills a saint once told
A starry tale, a story strange and new
Brought from the dawn-lands—and all Eiré drew
Around his moat to hear the words of gold.

There stands no cross, or tower, or ancient wall
Mellow with simple peace men used to know,
And from the fields no courtly town has sprung:
Only along green banks the blackbirds call,
Just as they did a thousand years ago
In morning meadows when the world was young.

Thomas S. Jones, Jr.

SHESKINBEG

I MET the boy from Donegal, sez I, "Come here a minute,
An' tell me how is Sheskinbeg, an' were ye ever in it?"
Sez he, "I know it well, but sure 'tis awkward gettin' to it,
For there's not a road about the place but the rocks is comin'
    through it."

Och well I know the road is rough, but still my heart can
    love it,
Wi' the river runnin' at its side an' God's blue sky above it;
An' a wheen o' wee white houses sittin' there among the
    heather,
Wi' childer runnin' in an' out an' playin' all together.

If I could see the sun come up on Cloghaneely highlands,
Or drop at night like fire in the sea behind the islands;
The glow o' red upon the hills, the deep shade in the hollow,
The river slippin' through the bog an' callin' me to follow;

If I could win to Sheskinbeg an' see a turf fire burnin',
An' hear the clack o' Andy's loom and the champ o' Mary's
    churnin',
An' see the griddle hangin' wi' potato farls upon it,
There's not a road that rough but what my feet could travel
    on it.

There's hearts as hard as rock itself, there's sorrow can't
    be spoken,
I'd think a pity o' the man would say his heart was broken;
But every road is rough to me that has no friend to cheer it,
An' not a one will lead me now to Sheskinbeg, or near it.

Elizabeth Shane

A ROAD OF IRELAND

FROM Killybegs to Ardara is seven Irish miles,
   'Tis there the blackbirds whistle and the mating. cuckoos
      call,
Beyond the fields the green sea glints, above the heaven
      smiles
   On all the white boreens that thread the glens of Donegal.

Along the roads what feet have passed, could they but tell
      the story,
   Of ancient king and saint and bard, the roads have known
      them all;
Lough Dergh, Doon Well, Glen Columcille, the names are
      yet a glory,
   'Tis great ghosts in the gloaming remember Donegal.

The harbor slips of Killybegs glistened with Spanish sail
   The days Spain ventured round the world and held the
      half in thrall,
And Ardara has writ her name in the proud books of the
      Gael,
   Though sleep has fallen on them now in dream-lit Donegal.

Well, time will have its fling with dust, it is the changeless
      law,
   But this I like to think of whatever may befall:
When she came up from Killybegs and he from Ardara
   My father met my mother on the road, in Donegal.

Charles L. O'Donnell

MY BLESSING BE ON WATERFORD

MY blessing be on Waterford, the town of ships,
For it's what I love to be streeling on the quay,
Watching while the boats go out, watching them come in,
And thinking of a one I know that's sailing far away.

It's well to be in Waterford, to see the ships,
The great big masts of them against the evening sky,

Seagulls flying round, and the men unloading them,
With quare strange talk among themselves the time you're
    passing by.

I love to be in Waterford, to see the ships come in,
Bringing in their cargoes from west, and east, and south.
Some day one I love will stand there upon the quay,
He'll take my two hands in his own, and stoop to kiss my
    mouth.

Winifred M. Letts

IN FRANCE

THE poplars in the fields of France
Are golden ladies come to dance;
But yet to see them there is none
But I and the September sun.

The girl who in their shadow sits
Can only see the sock she knits;
Her dog is watching all the day
That not a cow shall go astray.

The leisurely contented cows
Can only see the earth they browse;
Their piebald bodies through the grass
With busy, munching noses pass.

Alone the sun and I behold
Processions crowned with shining gold—
The poplars in the fields of France,
Like glorious ladies come to dance.

Frances Cornford

AN AMERICAN TO FRANCE

O FRANCE, with what a shamed and sorry smile
We now recall that in a bygone day
We sought of you art, wit, perfection, style;
You were to us a playground and a play.

Paris was ours—its sudden green edged spaces
And sweeping vistas to the coming night,
Brocades and jewels, porcelains and laces—
All these we took for leisure and delight.
And all the time we should have drunk our fill
Of wisdom known to you and you alone,
Clear-eyed self-knowledge, silent courage, will;
And now too late, we see these things are one:
That art is sacrifice and self-control,
And who loves beauty must be stern of soul.

Alice Duer Miller

TO FRANCE

(MAY DAY, 1919)

MOTHER of revolutions, stern and sweet,
Thou of the red Commune's heroic days;
Unsheathe thy sword, let thy pent lightning blaze
Until these new bastilles fall at thy feet.
Once more thy sons march down the ancient street
Led by pale men from silent Père la Chaise;
Once more La Carmagnole—La Marseillaise
Blend with the war drum's quick and angry beat.
Ah, France—our France—must they again endure
The crown of thorns upon the cross of death?
Is morning here? Then speak that we may know!
The sky seems lighter, but we are not sure.
Is morning here? . . . The whole world holds its breath
To hear the crimson Gallic rooster crow!

Ralph Chaplin

PARIS: THE SEINE AT NIGHT

COME and see the chimney-pots, etched against the light!
Half-a-moon of gold above the lovely-phantomed night;
Half-a-silver-moon below, underneath a span,
Mirrored in the vaulted dark, like a jewelled fan.

Dust in dormer window-ledge, age in bolted door,
Roof-tops leaping from the dark, jumbled towards the shore;
Beauty in the shadow-lanes, like an April pain,
Hanging in the hearts of trees, lyric with the rain.

Yellow lines across the black, shimmering and pale,
Falling from the bridges' lights, undulating, frail.
Crimson lanes beside the gold, piers that lie in wait,
Crimson lamps to warn the ships, crawling homeward late.

Come and see the magic dusk, and the silver fire!
Dome and tower, turret, gate.   Moonlight on a spire.
Heart of you may wander long, through the careless day—
Soul of you that comes by night, never goes away.

                                        Charles Divine

LA RUE DE LA MONTAGNE SAINTE–GÈNE-VIÈVE

I HAVE seen an old street weeping—
Narrow, dark, ascending;
Water o'er the spires
Of a church descending;
The church thrice veiled—in rain,
In the shadow of the years,
In the grace of old design;
Dim dwellings, blind with tears,
Rotting either side
The winding passage-way,
To where the river crosses
Weeping, under gray
And limpid heavens weeping.
Gardens I have seen
Through archèd doors, whose gratings
Ever cry the keen
Dim melodies of lace
Long used and rare, gardens
With an old-time grace
Vibrating, dimly trembling
In the music of the rain.
Roses I have seen drip a faint
Perfume, and lilacs train
A quivering loveliness
From door to archèd door,
Passing by in flower carts;
While waters ever pour

O'er the white stones of the fountain,
Melting icily away
Half way up the mountain;
Where to mingle tears with tears,
Their clothes misshapen, sobbing,
Two or three old women,
In wooden sabots hobbling,
Meet to fill their pitchers,
From the stream of water leaping
Through the lips, a long time parted,
Of a face grotesquely weeping—
A carven face forever weeping.

Dorothy Dudley

MADONNA DI CAMPAGNA

MADONNA DI CAMPAGNA is the name
They christened their few hovels and a church,
And their small roads cross others in the search
For further stones to consecrate her fame;
The mountains over mountains now acclaim
A hope with which the stars, from dawn to age,
Illuminate the skies, from page to page,
In scrolls these humans fancy pray with flame!

The village has no further roundelays—
The folk are lazier, the atmosphere
Weighs drowsily beneath the golden haze:
What work have they ahead, whose path lies clear,
Except to raise some earth to shelter those
Whom the Madonna gathers for repose?

Alfred Kreymborg

SEVILLE

I KNOW not Seville,
Yet in dreams I see
The April roses
Climb from tree to tree,

And foam the houses
Till they seem to me
Great waves of blossom
From a crimson sea.

I know not Seville,
Yet in dreams I see
The drooping petals
Falling languidly,
And find the shadow
Where the grass is red
And white with roses
On a sun-warmed bed!

I know not Seville,
Yet I feel the night
Grow heavy-scented,
Starred with roses white,
And low-toned singers,
Up and down the street,
Breathe only roses,
Fallen at their feet.

L. D'O. Walters

TO F. C. IN MEMORIAM PALESTINE

Do you remember one immortal
Lost moment out of time and space,
What time we thought, who passed the portal
Of that divine disastrous place
Where Life was slain and Truth was slandered
On that one holier hill than Rome,
How far abroad our bodies wandered
That evening when our souls came home?

The mystic city many-gated,
With monstrous columns, was your own:
Herodian stones fell down and waited
Two thousand years to be your throne.

In the gray rocks the burning blossom
Glowed terrible as the sacred blood:
It was no stranger to your bosom
Than bluebells of an English wood.

Do you remember a road that follows
The way of unforgotten feet,
Where from the waste of rocks and hollows
Climb up the crawling crooked street
The stages of one towering drama
Always ahead and out of sight . . .
Do you remember Aceldama
And the jackal barking in the night?

Life is not void or stuff for scorners:
We have laughed loud and kept our love,
We have heard singers in tavern corners
And not forgotten the birds above:
We have known smiters and sons of thunder
And not unworthily walked with them,
We have grown wiser and lost not wonder;
And we have seen Jerusalem.

G. K. Chesterton

EGYPT

Egypt had cheated us,
for Egypt took
through guile and craft
our treasure and our hope,
Egypt had maimed us,
offered dream for life,
an opiate for a kiss,
and death for both.

White poison flower we loved
and the black spike
of an ungarnered bush—
(a spice—or without taste—
we wondered—then we asked

others to take and sip
and watched their death)
Egypt we loved, though hate
should have withheld our touch.

Egypt had given us knowledge,
and we took, blindly,
through want of heart,
what Egypt brought;
knowing all poison,
what was that or this,
more or less perilous,
than this or that.

We pray you, Egypt,
by what perverse fate
has poison brought with knowledge,
given us this—
not days of trance,
shadow, fore-doom of death,
but passionate grave thought,
belief enhanced,
ritual returned and magic;

Even in the uttermost black pit
of the forbidden knowledge,
wisdom's glance,
the gray eyes following
in the mid-most desert—
great shaft of rose,
fire shed across our path,
upon the face grown gray, a light,
Hellas re-born from death.

H. D.

BABYLON

IF you could bring her glories back!
You gentle sirs who sift the dust
And burrow in the mould and must
Of Babylon for bric-a-brac;

Who catalogue and pigeon-hole
The faded splendors of her soul
And put her greatness under glass—
If you could bring her past to pass!

If you could bring her dead to life!
The soldier lad; the market wife;
Madam buying fowls from her;
Tip, the butcher's bandy cur;
Workmen carting bricks and clay;
Babel passing to and fro
On the business of a day
Gone three thousand years ago—
That you cannot; then be done,
Put the goblet down again,
Let the broken arch remain,
Leave the dead men's dust alone—

Is it nothing how she lies,
This old mother of you all,
You great cities proud and tall
Towering to a hundred skies
Round a world she never knew,
Is it nothing, this, to you?
Must the ghoulish work go on
Till her very floors are gone?
While there's still a brick to save
Drive these people from her grave!

The Jewish seer when he cried
Woe to Babel's lust and pride
Saw the foxes at her gates;
Once again the wild thing waits.
Then leave her in her last decay
A house of owls, a foxes' den;
The desert that till yesterday
Hid her from the eyes of men
In its proper time and way
Will take her to itself again.

Ralph Hodgson

THE MOST–SACRED MOUNTAIN

SPACE, and the twelve clean winds of heaven,
And this sharp exultation, like a cry, after the slow six
    thousand steps of climbing!
This is Tai Shan, the beautiful, the most holy.

Below my feet the foot-hills nestle, brown with flecks of
    green; and lower down the flat brown plain, the floor of
    earth, stretches away to blue infinity.
Beside me in this airy space the temple roofs cut their slow
    curves against the sky,
And one black bird circles above the void.

Space, and the twelve clean winds are here;
And with them broods eternity—a swift white peace, a
    presence manifest.
The rhythm ceases here.   Time has no place.   This is the
    end that has no end.

Here, when Confucius came, a half a thousand years before
    the Nazarene, he stepped, with me, thus into time-
    lessness.
The stone beside us waxes old, the carven stone that says:
    "On this spot once Confucius stood and felt the small-
    ness of the world below."
The stone grows old:
Eternity is not for stones.

But I shall go down from this airy space, this swift white
    peace, this stinging exultation,
And time will close about me, and my soul stir to the rhythm
    of the daily round.
Yet, having known, life will not press so close, and always
    I shall feel time ravel thin about me;
For once I stood
In the white windy presence of eternity.

                                        Eunice Tietjens

BALLADS

A BALLAD OF A NUN

FROM Eastertide to Eastertide
   For ten long years her patient knees
Engraved the stones—the fittest bride
   Of Christ in all the diocese.

She conquered every earthly lust;
   The abbess loved her more and more;
And, as a mark of perfect trust,
   Made her the keeper of the door.

High on a hill the convent hung,
   Across a duchy looking down,
Where everlasting mountains flung
   Their shadows over tower and town.

The jewels of their lofty snows
   In constellations flashed at night;
Above their crests the moon arose;
   The deep earth shuddered with delight.

Long ere she left her cloudy bed,
   Still dreaming in the orient land,
On many a mountain's happy head
   Dawn lightly laid her rosy hand.

The adventurous sun took Heaven by storm;
   Clouds scattered largesses of rain;
The sounding cities, rich and warm,
   Smouldered and glittered in the plain.

Sometimes it was a wandering wind,
   Sometimes the fragrance of the pine,
Sometimes the thought how others sinned,
   That turned her sweet blood into wine.

Sometimes she heard a serenade
　　Complaining sweetly far away:
She said, "A young man woos a maid";
　　And dreamt of love till break of day.

Then would she ply her knotted scourge
　　Until she swooned; but evermore
She had the same red sin to purge,
　　Poor, passionate keeper of the door!

For still night's starry scroll unfurled,
　　And still the day came like a flood:
It was the greatness of the world
　　That made her long to use her blood.

In winter-time when Lent drew nigh,
　　And hill and plain were wrapped in snow,
She watched beneath the frosty sky
　　The nearest city nightly glow.

Like peals of airy bells outworn
　　Faint laughter died above her head
In gusts of broken music borne:
　　"They keep the Carnival," she said.

Her hungry heart devoured the town:
　　"Heaven save me by a miracle!
Unless God sends an angel down,
　　Thither I go though it were Hell."

She dug her nails deep in her breast,
　　Sobbed, shrieked, and straight withdrew the bar:
A fledgling flying from the nest,
　　A pale moth rushing to a star.

Fillet and veil in strips she tore;
　　Her golden tresses floated wide;
The ring and bracelet that she wore
　　As Christ's betrothed, she cast aside.

"Life's dearest meaning I shall probe;
  Lo! I shall taste of love at last!
Away!" She doffed her outer robe,
  And sent it sailing down the blast.

Her body seemed to warm the wind;
  With bleeding feet o'er ice she ran:
"I leave the righteous God behind;
  I go to worship sinful man."

She reached the sounding city's gate;
  No question did the warder ask:
He passed her in: "Welcome, wild mate!"
  He thought her some fantastic mask.

Half-naked through the town she went;
  Each footstep left a bloody mark;
Crowds followed her with looks intent;
  Her bright eyes made the torches dark.

Alone and watching in the street
  There stood a grave youth nobly dressed;
To him she knelt and kissed his feet;
  Her face her great desire confessed.

Straight to his house the nun he led:
  "Strange lady, what would you with me?"
"Your love, your love, sweet lord," she said;
  "I bring you my virginity."

He healed her bosom with a kiss;
  She gave him all her passion's hoard;
And sobbed and murmured ever, "This
  Is life's great meaning, dear, my lord.

"I care not for my broken vow;
  Though God should come in thunder soon,
I am sister to the mountains now,
  And sister to the sun and moon."

Through all the towns of Belmarie
　She made a progress like a queen.
"She is," they said, "what'er she be,
　The strangest woman ever seen.

"From fairyland she must have come,
　Or else she is a mermaiden."
Some said she was a ghoul, and some
　A heathen goddess born again.

But soon her fire to ashes burned;
　Her beauty changed to haggardness;
Her golden hair to silver turned;
　The hour came of her last caress.

At midnight from her lonely bed
　She rose, and said, "I have had my will."
The old ragged robe she donned, and fled
　Back to the convent on the hill.

Half-naked as she went before,
　She hurried to the city wall,
Unnoticed in the rush and roar
　And splendor of the carnival.

No question did the warder ask:
　Her ragged robe, her shrunken limb,
Her dreadful eyes! "It is no mask;
　It is a she-wolf, gaunt and grim!"

She ran across the icy plain;
　Her worn blood curdled in the blast;
Each footstep left a crimson stain;
　The white-faced moon looked on aghast.

She said between her chattering jaws,
　"Deep peace is mine, I cease to strive;
Oh, comfortable convent laws,
　That bury foolish nuns alive!

"A trowel for my passing-bell,
　A little bed within the wall,
A coverlet of stones; how well
　I there shall keep the Carnival!"

Like tired bells chiming in their sleep,
　The wind faint peals of laughter bore;
She stopped her ears and climbed the steep,
　And thundered at the convent door.

It opened straight: she entered in,
　And at the wardress' feet fell prone:
"I come to purge away my sin;
　Bury me, close me up in stone."

The wardress raised her tenderly;
　She touched her wet and fast-shut eyes:
"Look, sister; sister, look at me;
　Look; can you see through my disguise?"

She looked and saw her own sad face,
　And trembled, wondering, "Who art thou?"
"God sent me down to fill your place:
　I am the Virgin Mary now."

And with the word, God's mother shone:
　The wanderer whispered, "Mary, hail!"
The vision helped her to put on
　Bracelet and fillet, ring and veil.

"You are sister to the mountains now,
　And sister to the day and night;
Sister to God." And on the brow
　She kissed her thrice, and left her sight.

While dreaming in her cloudy bed,
　Far in the crimson orient land,
On many a mountain's happy head
　Dawn lightly laid her rosy hand.

John Davidson

A BALLAD OF HELL

"A LETTER from my love to-day!
    Oh, unexpected, dear appeal!"
She struck a happy tear away,
    And broke the crimson seal.

"My love, there is no help on earth,
    No help in heaven; the dead-man's bell
Must toll our wedding; our first hearth
    Must be the well-paved floor of hell."

The color died from out her face,
    Her eyes like ghostly candles shone;
She cast dread looks about the place,
    Then clenched her teeth and read right on.

"I may not pass the prison door;
    Here must I rot from day to day,
Unless I wed whom I abhor,
    My cousin, Blanche of Valençay.

"At midnight with my dagger keen,
    I'll take my life; it must be so.
Meet me in hell to-night, my queen,
    For weal and woe."

She laughed although her face was wan,
    She girded on her golden belt,
She took her jewelled ivory fan,
    And at her glowing missal knelt.

Then rose, "And am I mad?" she said:
    She broke her fan, her belt untied;
With leather girt herself instead,
    And stuck a dagger at her side.

She waited, shuddering in her room,
    . Till sleep had fallen on all the house.
She never flinched; she faced her doom:
    They two must sin to keep their vows.

Then out into the night she went,
   And, stooping, crept by hedge and tree;
Her rose-bush flung a snare of scent,
   And caught a happy memory.

She fell, and lay a minute's space;
   She tore the sward in her distress;
The dewy grass refreshed her face;
   She rose and ran with lifted dress.

She started like a morn-caught ghost
   Once when the moon came out and stood
To watch; the naked road she crossed,
   And dived into the murmuring wood.

The branches snatched her streaming cloak;
   A live thing shrieked; she made no stay!
She hurried to the trysting-oak—
   Right well she knew the way.

Without a pause she bared her breast,
   And drove her dagger home and fell,
And lay like one that takes her rest,
   And died and wakened up in hell.

She bathed her spirit in the flame,
   And near the centre took her post;
From all sides to her ears there came
   The dreary anguish of the lost.

The devil started at her side,
   Comely, and tall, and black as jet.
"I am young Malespina's bride;
   Has he come hither yet?"

"My poppet, welcome to your bed."
   "Is Malespina here?"
"Not he! To-morrow he must wed
   His cousin Blanche, my dear!"

"You lie, he died with me to-night."
    "Not he! it was a plot" . . . "You lie."
"My dear, I never lie outright."
    "We died at midnight, he and I."

The devil went. Without a groan
    She, gathered up in one fierce prayer,
Took root in hell's midst all alone,
    And waited for him there.

She dared to make herself at home
    Amidst the wail, the uneasy stir.
The blood-stained flame that filled the dome,
    Scentless and silent, shrouded her.

How long she stayed I cannot tell;
    But when she felt his perfidy,
She marched across the floor of hell;
    And all the damned stood up to see.

The devil stopped her at the brink:
    She shook him off; she cried, "Away!"
"My dear, you have gone mad, I think."
    "I was betrayed: I will not stay."

Across the weltering deep she ran;
    A stranger thing was never seen:
The damned stood silent to a man;
    They saw the great gulf set between.

To her it seemed a meadow fair;
    And flowers sprang up about her feet.
She entered heaven; she climbed the stair
    And knelt down at the mercy-seat.

Seraphs and saints with one great voice
    Welcomed that soul that knew not fear.
Amazed to find it could rejoice,
    Hell raised a hoarse, half-human cheer.

John Davidson

PETER AND JOHN

Twelve good friends
Walked under the leaves
Binding the ends
Of the barley sheaves.

Peter and John
Lay down to sleep
Pillowed upon
A haymaker's heap.

John and Peter
Lay down to dream.
The air was sweeter
Than honey and cream.

Peter was bred
In the salty cold.
His hair was red
And his eyes were gold.

John had a mouth
Like a wing bent down.
His brow was smooth
And his eyes were brown.

Peter to slumber
Sank like a stone,
Of all their number
The bravest one.

John more slowly
Composed himself,
Young and holy
Among the Twelve.

John as he slept
Cried out in grief,
Turned and wept
On the golden leaf:

"Peter, Peter,
Stretch me your hand
Across the glitter
Of the harvest land!

"Peter, Peter,
Give me a sign!
This was a bitter
Dream of mine,—

"Bitter as aloes
It parched my tongue.
Upon the gallows
My life was hung.

"Sharp it seemed
As a bloody sword.
Peter, I dreamed
I was Christ the Lord!"

Peter turned
To holy Saint John:
His body burned
In the falling sun.

In the falling sun
He burned like flame:
"John, Saint John,
I have dreamed the same!

"My bones were hung
On an elder tree;
Bells were rung
Over Galilee.

"A silver penny
Sealed each of my eyes.
Many and many
A cock crew thrice."

When Peter's word
Was spoken and done,
"Were you Christ the Lord
In your dream?"   said John.

"No," said the other,
"That I was not.
I was our brother
Iscariot."

Elinor Wylie

FROM THE DAY–BOOK OF A FORGOTTEN PRINCE

My father is happy or we should be poor,
His gateway is wide and the folk of the moor
Come singing so gaily right up to the door.

We live in a castle that's dingy and old;
The casements are broken, the corridors cold;
The larder is empty, the cook is a scold.

But father can dance and his singing is loud.
From meadow and highway there's always a crowd
That gathers to hear him, and this makes him proud.

He roars out a song in a voice that is sweet,
Of grandeur that's gone, rare viands to eat,
And treasure that used to be laid at his feet.

He picks up his robe, faded, wrinkled and torn,
Though banded in ermine, moth-eaten and worn,
And held at the throat by a twisted old thorn.

He leaps in the air with a rickety grace
And a kingly old smile illumines his face,
While he fondles his beard and stares off into space.

The villagers laugh, then look quickly away,
And some of them kneel in the orchard to pray.
I often hear whispers: "The old king is fey!"

But after they're gone, we shall find, if you please,
White loaves and a pigeon and honey and cheese,
And wine that we drink while I sit on his knees.

And then, while he sups, he will feed me and tell
Of Mother, whom men used to call "The Gazelle,"
And of glorious times before the curse fell.

At last he will sink, half-asleep, to the floor;
The rafters will echo his quivering snore . . .
I go to find cook, through the slack, oaken door.

.　　.　　.　　.　　.　　.　　.　　.　　.　　.

My father is happy or we should be poor;
His gateway is wide and the folk of the moor
Come singing so gaily right up to the door.

                                    Jean Starr Untermeyer

PATH FLOWER

A RED-CAP sang in Bishop's wood,
　　A lark o'er Golder's lane,
As I the April pathway trod
　　Bound west for Willesden.

At foot each tiny blade grew big
　　And taller stood to hear,
And every leaf on every twig
　　Was like a little ear.

As I too paused, and both ways tried
　　To catch the rippling rain,—
So still, a hare kept at my side
　　His tussock of disdain,—

Behind me close I heard a step,
　　A soft pit-pat surprise,
And looking round my eyes fell deep
　　Into sweet other eyes;

The eyes like wells, where sun lies too,
  So clear and trustful brown,
Without a bubble warning you
  That here's a place to drown.

"How many miles? " Her broken shoes
  Had told of more than one.
She answered like a dreaming Muse,
  "I came from Islington."

"So long a tramp? " Two gentle nods,
  Then seemed to lift a wing,
And words fell soft as willow-buds,
  "I came to find the Spring."

A timid voice, yet not afraid
  In ways so sweet to roam,
As it with honey bees had played
  And could no more go home.

Her home! I saw the human lair,
  I heard the huckster's bawl,
I stifled with the thickened air
  Of bickering mart and stall.

Without a tuppence for a ride,
  Her feet had set her free.
Her rags, that decency defied,
  Seemed new with liberty.

But she was frail. Who would might note
  The trail of hungering
That for an hour she had forgot
  In wonder of the Spring.

So shriven by her joy she glowed
  It seemed a sin to chat.
(A tea-shop snuggled off the road;
  Why did I think of that?)

Oh, frail, so frail!   I could have wept,—
  But she was passing on,
And I but muddled, "You'll accept
  A penny for a bun? "

Then up her little throat a spray
  Of rose climbed for it must;
A wilding lost till safe it lay
  Hid by her curls of rust;

And I saw modesties at fence
  With pride that bore no name;
So old it was she knew not whence
  It sudden woke and came;

But that which shone of all most clear
  Was startled, sadder thought
That I should give her back the fear
  Of life she had forgot.

And I blushed for the world we'd made,
  Putting God's hand aside,
Till for the want of sun and shade
  His little children died;

And blushed that I who every year
  With Spring went up and down,
Must greet a soul that ached for her
  With "penny for a bun! "

Struck as a thief in holy place
  Whose sin upon him cries,
I watched the flowers leave her face,
  The song go from her eyes.

Then she, sweet heart, she saw my rout,
  And of her charity
A hand of grace put softly out
  And took the coin from me.

A red-cap sang in Bishop's wood,
    A lark o'er Golder's lane;
But I alone, still glooming stood,
    And April plucked in vain;

Till living words rang in my ears
    And sudden music played:
*Out of such sacred thirst as hers
    The world shall be remade.*

Afar she turned her head and smiled
    As might have smiled the Spring,
And humble as a wondering child
    I watched her vanishing.

                            Olive Dargan

THE SHEPHERD OF MERIADOR

BENEATH the golden cope of dawn,
    By Laurencekirk, in Argadoe,
Amid the gorzen bush withdrawn,
    The Shepherd with his pipe would go.

The Shepherd with his pipe would pass,
    Playing a ghostly tune and pure;
The peasants trooping down to Mass,
    Stopped, smiling, at Saint Lawrence door. . . .

They stopped and listened, then passed in
    To bell-chime sweet of Holy Mass;
But he stole on to Lissadin,
    Over the golden grass. . . .

They entered in to where Christ's Body
    With rosy wounds did burn and bleed;
But he passed on to Lissadin,
    Over the dewy mead,

Treading down the Margaret Flowers,
    And treading the Lady's Fingers down,
Till he came in sight of the trembling towers
    Of old Lis Orchad's town. . . .

Trembled, trembled deep bell-chime then,
  The steeples shimmered by the stream;
He passed through the streets of Lissadin,
  Piping in a dream,

And came out on Meriador,
  Silent above the summer sea,
Where many a rune-carved granite tor
  Ruled in its ghostly company. . . .

The sun burned on the dewy flowers,
  And kissed the soft tears from their petals;
He threw his pipe away and lay
  Naked amid the stinging nettles. . . .

They burned his flesh, but left no mark,
  Then swiftly, swiftly passed the pain,
And he slept on Meriador,
  Till gently fell the summer rain,

Till gently fell the rain from Heaven,
  And soothed his weary limbs and laid
A cool kiss on his fevered brow,
  Who was the Chanter of the Maid. . . .

Down to the sandy shore he came,
  The clear waves kissed his singing feet,
His hair blew out in yellow flame,
  The winds his singing did repeat. . . .

A floating rock all isled with flowers
  Came sailing from the solemn West;
He bade farewell to citied towers,
  And leapt upon its blossomy breast,

And passed away down the path of the sea
  Into the burning azure of noon;
A thousand birds bore him company,
  Fluttering around, one living tune,

With beat of myriad-colored wings:
   He seemed, as he stood, one shaft of light,
Borne away from the crowds and the kings
   Into the World of the Infinite. . . .

And he came sailing into Syon
   About the time of the evening bell;
The stone stopped at the Gate of the Lion,
   The sky smoked like a thurible.

The banners waved from the walls of Syon,
   Vair and scarlet, purpled and palled;
Our Lord upon His throne was lying,
   Carven out of an emerald. . . .

The Shepherd knelt down before God
   On one knee and on the other knee;
Our Lord stretched out His lily-sceptre
   Unto His son full graciously. . . .

"So thou hast sailed across the Ocean,
   And washed from off thee taint of sin:
Come, sing to me songs of Meriador,
   And tales of Lissadin!

"Sing me the songs of Argadoe,
   Where linnets pipe beneath the down;
Tell me how gilded merkats go
   Through gray Lis Orchad's town. . . .

"Oft have I wandered through those lanes
   In beggar-raiment, tattering thin,
And looked up at Saint Lawrence vanes:
   Sing to me songs of Lissadin!

"The folk of Argadoe give alms
   To tattered gangrels worn and sad:
Sing, Shepherd; for much holy joy
   In those old thorpes thy Lord hath had! "

The Shepherd stood upon his feet,
   And sang such songs of rustic fairs
As caused the Angels to turn round,
   As they climbed up the crystal stairs. . . .

And one with tiny gilded wings
   Ran to Madonna, where She sat
Musing on mild and lovely things;
   She had much wonderment thereat,

To see the little Cherub run:
   "Mother," he cried, "a Shepherd sings
Of what goes on beneath the sun,
   Fond, foolish and familiar things. . . .

"There is much mirth in his sweet singing:
   My Lady, hearken and come to him! "
Mary rose up, slim as a girl,
   Lustrous and pale and slim;

She rose up in Her golden mantle,
   Cast over Her shoulders Her sky-blue cloak,
And came down to hear the exiled Shepherd
   Sing of his peasant folk. . . .

She flung a white rose toward the Shepherd;
   As weary and as wan as She
The rose was: he took it from Our Lady,
   Kneeling upon each knee. . . .

He took it and he sang his Ave,
   He sang his gladsome Salve too . . .
And woke up on Meriador,
   Drenched in the summer dew.
                      Wilfred Rowland Childe

JOHN DARROW

JOHN DARROW felt a coolness
   Across a streak of sun.
He looked into the jungle;
   Shadow there was none—

But a strange woman riding
  A tiger's velvet back,
With skin like cinnamon
  And eyes bright black.

There came a wrench of branches,
  A laugh across the sun.
Darrow stood by dazzled,
  Trailing a foolish gun.

When Darrow sprang to follow,
  People caught him back,
"You must have much magic
  To follow on that track;

"Witches have red lips
  That smile for swart men's bones.
Shall Tuan Darrow's be
  Among the wasted ones? "

Darrow's pate was addled,
  So the campong said.
The Rajah wrote to Bangkok
  Tuan Darrow had fled.

Between a dusk and moonrise
  Darrow last was seen,
Climbing a barricade
  Across a dark ravine.

The campong beat majuba
  In fearful unison.
Came a tiger's roaring;
  The Darrow man had gone.

And yet no tiger ate him.
  He wandered back, men say,
Another dreadful Lazarus
  Of calm unspeaking clay.

Where Darrow walks, comes silence,
     The hush that strikes men cold,
The curse, the hope, the beauty
     That never must be told.

Donald Davidson

THE DREAM OF ÆNGUS OG

WHEN the rose of Morn through the Dawn was breaking,
     And white on the hearth was last night's flame,
Thither to me 'twixt sleeping and waking,
     Singing out of the mists she came.

And gray as the mists on the spectre meadows
     Were the eyes that on my eyes she laid,
And her hair's red splendor through the shadows
     Like to the marsh-fire gleamed and played.

And she sang of the wondrous far-off places
     That a man may only see in dreams,
The death-still, odorous, starlit spaces
     Where Time is lost and no life gleams.

And there till the day had its crest uplifted,
     She stood with her still face bent on me,
Then forth with the Dawn departing drifted
     Light as a foam-fleck on the sea.

And now my heart is the heart of a swallow
     That here no solace of rest may find,
Forevermore I follow and follow
     Her white feet glancing down the wind.

And forevermore in my ears are ringing—
     (Oh, red lips yet shall I kiss you dumb!)
Twain sole words of that May morn's singing,
     Calling to me "Hither!" and "Come!"

From flower-bright fields to the wild lake-sedges
     Crying my steps when the Day has gone,
Till dim and small down the Night's pale edges
     The stars have fluttered one by one.

And light as the thought of a love forgotten,
  The hours skim past, while before me flies
That face of the Sun and Mist begotten,
  Its singing lips and death-cold eyes.

Eleanor Rogers Cox

CÆSAR REMEMBERS

Cæsar, that proud man,
  Sat in his tent
Weary with victory,
  With striving spent.

Where the gray Chilterns
  Coiled and slept
That hard-lipped Emperor
  Vigil kept.

In the thin starlight
  His glimmering hordes
Fought with the hard earth—
  Spades for swords.

Out on the hill-slopes
  His helmèd host
Piled stark ramparts
  Rimmed with frost.

But Cæsar cared not
  For dyke and wall,
Faint and remote
  Came the bugles' call;

Soft in the shadows
  He saw, and heard,
A Roman garden,
  A Roman bird.

"Worlds to conquer!—
  But Cæsar fails
To add one song
  To the nightingale's!"

Soft in the shadows
  The tired man heard
A woman's laughter,
  A woman's word.

. . . . .

Cæsar, shivering,
  Heard repeat
Spades on the hillside,
  Sentries' feet.

William Kean Seymour

THE PALATINE

IN THE " DARK AGES "

"HAVE you been with the King to Rome,
  Brother, big brother?"
"I've been there and I've come home.
  Back to your play, little brother."

"Oh, how high is Cæsar's house,
  Brother, big brother?"
"Goats about the doorways browse:
Night hawks nest in the burnt roof-tree,
Home of the wild bird and home of the bee.
A thousand chambers of marble lie
Wide to the sun and the wind and the sky.
Poppies we find amongst our wheat
Grow on Cæsar's banquet seat.
Cattle crop and neatherds drowse
On the floors of Cæsar's house."

"But what has become of Cæsar's gold,
  Brother, big brother?"
"The times are bad and the world is old—
Who knows the where of the Cæsars' gold?
Night comes black on the Cæsars' hill;
The wells are deep and the tales are ill.
Fire-flies gleam in the damp and mould,—
All that is left of the Cæsars' gold.
  Back to your play, little brother."

"What has become of the Cæsars' men,
        Brother, big brother?"
"Dogs in the kennel and wolf in the den
Howl for the fate of the Cæsars' men.
Slain in Asia, slain in Gaul,
By Dacian border and Persian wall;
Rhineland orchard and Danube fen
Fatten their roots on Cæsar's men."

"Why is the world so sad and wide,
        Brother, big brother?"
"Saxon boys by their fields that bide
Need not know if the world is wide.
Climb no mountain but Shire-end Hill,
Cross no water but goes to mill;
Ox in the stable and cow in the byre,
Smell of the wood smoke and sleep by the fire;
Sun-up in seed-time—a likely lad
Hurts not his head that the world is sad.
        Back to your play, little brother."

                                    Willa Cather

THE BALLAD OF WILLIAM SYCAMORE

(1790–1880)

My father he was a mountaineer,
His fist was a knotty hammer.
He was quick on his feet as a running deer,
And he spoke with a Yankee stammer.

My mother she was merry and brave
And so she came to her labor,
With a tall green fir for her doctor grave,
And a stream for her comforting neighbor.

And some are wrapped in the linen fine,
And some like a godling's scion.
But I was cradled on twigs of pine
In the skin of a mountain lion.

And some remember a white, starched lap
And a ewer with silver handles.
But I remember a coonskin cap
And the smell of bayberry candles!

The cabin logs with the bark still rough,
And my mother who laughed at trifles,
And the tall, lank visitors, brown as snuff,
With their long, straight squirrel-rifles.

I can hear them dance, like a foggy song,
Through the deepest one of my slumbers,
The fiddle squeaking the boots along
And my father calling the numbers.

The quick feet shaking the puncheon-floor,
And the fiddle squeaking and squealing,
Till the dried herbs rattled above the door
And the dust went up to the ceiling.

There are children lucky from dawn till dusk,
But never a child so lucky!
For I cut my teeth on "Money Musk"
In the Bloody Ground of Kentucky!

When I grew tall as the Indian corn,
My father had little to lend me,
But he gave me his great old powder-horn
And his woodsman's skill to befriend me.

With a leather shirt to cover my back,
And a redskin nose to unravel
Each forest sign, I carried my pack
As far as a scout could travel.

Till I lost my boyhood and found my wife,
A girl like a Salem clipper!
A woman straight as a hunting-knife
With eyes as bright as the Dipper!

We cleared our camp where the buffalo feed,
Unheard-of streams were our flagons,
And I sowed my sons like the apple-seed
On the trail of the Western wagons.

They were right, tight boys, never sulky or slow,
A fruitful, a goodly muster!
The eldest died at the Alamo.
The youngest fell with Custer.

The letter that told it burned my hand.
Yet we smiled and said, "So be it!"
But I could not live when they fenced the land,
For it broke my heart to see it.

I saddled a red, unbroken colt
And rode him into the day there,
And he threw me down like a thunderbolt
And rolled on me as I lay there.

The hunter's whistle hummed in my ear
As the city-men tried to move me,
And I died in my boots like a pioneer
With the whole wide sky above me.

And your life's easy where mine was rough,
My little clerks of the city!
But an easy body is fragile stuff
And I find you easy to pity.

I lie in the heart of the fat, black soil
Like the seed of a prairie-thistle;
It has washed my bones with honey and oil
And picked them clean as a whistle.

And my youth returns, like the rains of Spring,
And my sons, like the wild geese flying,
And I lie and hear the meadow-lark sing
And have much content in my dying.

Go play with the towns you have built of blocks,
The towns where you would have bound me!
I sleep in my earth like a tired fox,
And my buffalo have found me.

Stephen Vincent Benét

JOE TINKER

Joe Tinker was the tailor's son:
   Joe Tinker was a troublous elf
Who broke the heart of everyone—
   I don't include myself!

A ne'er-do-well, 'twere hard to find
   Another knave so bold, it's true,
But handsome, if you like that kind—
   I know there's some as do,

Though I'm not one. The devil's wit
   Had Joe—no farthing for the rest!
All day the old men used to sit
   And ripen for his jest . . .

The tailor sewed a crooked seam
   Because his fears were for the lad,
At loss to guess the sort of dream
   Joe Tinker had;—

The sort that made him shun the shop,
   That mellow room with just a door,
And window where the day would drop
   And litter sunlight on the floor,

The sort that egged him to defy
   The pious parent of his youth,
That made the rascal love a lie,
   And tell it for a truth,

And haunt the tavern ceaselessly,
   Half drunk with ale, the sturdy fool,
And with a girl upon his knee,
   Some chit just out of school,

And laughing with his brown throat bare,
   And clothes in rags, but like a king,
Wearing his crazy crown of hair
   And singing as such hoodlums sing!

He never kissed me; had he tried
   He'd soon have met his match, I trow.
I'd not have stood it, and beside
   The others suited Joe.

We played as children, but we fought
   Like cat and dog when we grew big,—
Because I told him what I thought
   He took me for a prig,

And was the readier to tell
   Of his wild pranks, with teasing quips,
Declared he meant his soul for hell,
   And spat with ruddy lips.

He sometimes poached and brought me game
   With solemn mockery and fun,
And when I scolded him for shame
   Left, whistling, with his gun,

And made sport of my innocence,
   So sinful was he to the core;
He only gave his confidence
   To make me hate him more.

Well, once too often for his good
   He bragged out of a brazen throat
About some meeting in the wood
   With some new petticoat,

And her a wedded wife, what's more;
   He told me but to rouse my ire,
For he had played with sparks before,
   But Rose MacKail was fire!

He vowed he'd meet her after dark,
   He went off laughing, flushed with drink,
And he was wayward for a lark,
   But she was worse, I think.

To swing the hammer all day long
   Was Tim's, the blacksmith's, hardy life:
You would have thought a man so strong
   Could break the metal of his wife!

Joe Tinker was her latest then—
   Oh, would the cub be never wise
And learn to walk the world of men
   With sober-seeing eyes?

The sun had passed the mountain's rim,
   The sounds of day had ceased to stir
When I resolved to punish him
   By telling tales of her,

And ran to Tim's, the blacksmith's cot,
   Threw wide the door and blundered in
Where he was supping, red and hot,
   With gravy on his chin.

"Good even', Tim!   Your Rose away?
   She's brave to roam at night, I'm told;
Joe Tinker too's a moon-mad jay—
   They'll both be young when you are old—"

I shook with palsy as I spoke,
   And yet Tim never looked at me—
I saw his fury when it woke . . .
   . . . He found them easily . . .

And when I followed him, the trees
   Had arms to guide me and the ground,
All silvery with silences,
   Seemed waiting for a sound,

And there the moonlight showed a face,
  And there Joe Tinker lay at last,
Abandoned in the milky space
  With all his future—past!

And there the scapegrace Joe lay dead,
  With tiny dew-drops on his brow:
Oh, fiercely, fiercely then I said,
  "Will you cease loving now?"

The primroses against his cheek
  Seemed not more purely pale and soft,
And then I knew he would not speak
  As I had heard him oft . . .

And anger died before his look
  That was so lovely without taint,
Like Absalom in the Holy Book,
  Or some young martyred saint.

.   .   .   .

The tailor worked with steady hand,
  And sewed his son a fitting shroud.
But who, save one, could understand
  How grief had made him proud?

Ay, 'tis Joe Tinker's grave I keep,
  And I have tended, year by year,—
Such fools we women are who weep
  For men not worth a tear!

                    Amanda Benjamin Hall

IPSWICH BAR

THE mist lay still on Heartbreak Hill,
  The sea was cold below,
The waves rolled up and one by one
  Broke heavily and slow.

And through the clouds the gray gulls fled,
  The gannet whistled past,
Across the dunes the wailing loons
  Hid from the rising blast.

The moaning wind, that all day long
  Had haunted marsh and lea,
Went mad at night, and beating round,
  Fled shrieking out to sea.

The crested waves turned gray to white,
  That tossed the drifting spar,
But far more bright the yellow light
  That gleamed on Ipswich Bar.

Old Harry Main, wild Harry Main,
  Upon the shifting sand
Had built a flaming beacon light
  To lure the ships to land.

"The storm breaks out and far to-night,—
  They seek a port to bide:
God rest ye, sirs, on Ipswich Bar
  Your ships shall surely ride.

"They see my fires, my dancing fires,
  They lay their courses down,
And ill betide the mariners
  Who make for Ipswich Town,

"For mine the wreck, and mine the gold,—
  With none to lay the blame,—
So hold ye down to-night, good sirs,
  And I will feed the flame!"

Oh dark the night and wild the gale!
  The skipper higher turned
To where, afar, on Ipswich Bar,
  The treacherous beacon burned.

With singing shrouds and snapping sheets
  The vessel swiftly bore
And headed for the guiding lights
  Which shone along the shore.

The shoaling waters told no tale,
  The tempest made no sign,
Till full before her plunging bows
  Flashed out a whitened line!

She struck, she heeled,—the parting stays
  Went by with mast and spar;
And then the wind and rain beat out
  The light on Ipswich Bar.

Gray dawn beneath a dying storm;
  A figure gaunt and thin
Went splashing through the tangled sedge
  To drag the treasure in;

For when the darkness broke away
  The lances of the moon
Had pointed where lay bow in air
  A wrecking picaroon.

What matter if the open day
  Bore witness to his shame?
'Twas his the wreck and his the gold,
  And none had seen to blame.

He did not know the eyes of men
  Were watching from afar
As Harry Main went back and forth
  The length of Ipswich Bar.

They told the Ipswich fisher folk
  Who all aghast and grim
Came running down through Pudding Lane
  In maddened search for him;

No word, no blow, no bitter jest,—
   They did not strike nor mar,
But short the shrift of Harry Main
   That day on Ipswich Bar.

They marched him out at ebb of tide
   Where lay the shattered wreck,
And bound him to the dripping rocks
   With chains about his neck.

With chains about his guilty neck
   They left him to the wave—
The lapping tide rose eagerly
   To hide the wrecker's grave.

.   .   .   .

And now when sudden storms strike down
   With hoarse and threatening tones,
Old Harry Main must rise again
   And gird his sea-wracked bones,

To coil a cable made of sand
   Which ever breaks in twain,
While echoing through the salted marsh
   Is heard his clanking chain.

When rock and shoal are white with foam,
   The watchers on the sands
Can see his ghostly form rise up
   And wring its fettered hands.

And out at sea his cries are heard
   Above the storm and far,
Where cold and still, old Heartbreak Hill
   Looks down on Ipswich Bar.

Esther and Brainard Bates

THE PURITAN'S BALLAD

My love came up from Barnegat,
   The sea was in his eyes;
He trod as softly as a cat
   And told me terrible lies.

His hair was yellow as new-cut pine
   In shavings curled and feathered;
I thought how silver it would shine
   By cruel winters weathered.

But he was in his twentieth year,
   This time I'm speaking of;
We were head over heels in love with fear
   And half a-feared of love.

My hair was piled in a copper crown—
   A devilish living thing,
And the tortoise-shell pins fell down, fell down,
   When that snake uncoiled to spring.

His feet were used to treading a gale
   And balancing thereon;
His face was brown as a foreign sail
   Threadbare against the sun.

His arms were thick as hickory logs
   Whittled to little wrists;
Strong as the teeth of terrier dogs
   Were the fingers of his fists.

Within his arms I feared to sink
   Where lions shook their manes,
And dragons drawn in azure ink
   Leapt quickened by his veins.

Dreadful his strength and length of limb
   As the sea to foundering ships;
I dipped my hands in love for him
   No deeper than their tips.

But our palms were welded by a flame
   The moment we came to part,
And on his knuckles I read my name
   Enscrolled within a heart.

And something made our wills to bend
    As wild as trees blown over;
We were no longer friend and friend,
    But only lover and lover.

"In seven weeks or seventy years—
    God grant it may be sooner!—
I'll make a handkerchief for your tears
    From the sails of my captain's schooner.

" We'll wear our loves like wedding rings
    Long polished to our touch;
We shall be busy with other things
    And they cannot bother us much.

" When you are skimming the wrinkled cream
    And your ring clinks on the pan,
You'll say to yourself in a pensive dream,
    ' How wonderful a man! '

" When I am slitting a fish's head
    And my ring clanks on the knife,
I'll say with thanks, as a prayer is said,
    ' How beautiful a wife! '

" And I shall fold my decorous paws
    In velvet smooth and deep,
Like a kitten that covers up its claws
    To sleep and sleep and sleep.

" Like a little blue pigeon you shall bow
    Your bright alarming crest;
In the crook of my arm you'll lay your brow
    To rest and rest and rest."

Will he never come back from Barnegat
    With thunder in his eyes,
Treading as soft as a tiger cat,
    To tell me terrible lies?

                                        Elinor Wylie

BALLAD OF DOUGLAS BRIDGE

On Douglas Bridge I met a man
Who lived adjacent to Strabane,
   Before the English hung him high
For riding with O'Hanlon.

The eyes of him were just as fresh
As when they burned within the flesh;
   And his boot-legs widely walked apart
From riding with O'Hanlon.

"God save you, Sir!" I said with fear,
"You seem to be a stranger here."
   "Not I," said he, "nor any man
Who rides with Count O'Hanlon.

"I know each glen from North Tyrone
To Monaghan, and I've been known
   By every clan and parish, since
I rode with Count O'Hanlon.

"Before that time," said he to me,
"My fathers owned the land you see;
   But they are now among the moors
Ariding with O'Hanlon.

"Before that time," said he with pride,
"My fathers rode where now they ride
   As Rapperees, before the time
Of trouble and O'Hanlon.

"Good-night to you, and God be with
The Tellers of the tale and myth,
   For they are of the spirit-stuff
That rides with Count O'Hanlon."

"Good-night to you," said I, "and God
Be with the chargers, fairy-shod,
   That bear the Ulster heroes forth
To ride with Count O'Hanlon."

On Douglas Bridge we parted, but
The Gap o' Dreams is never shut,
    To one whose saddled soul to-night
Rides out with Count O'Hanlon.

Francis Carlin

THE GRAY PLUME

THE long heron feather
    O'Dogherty wore,
Still sweeps o'er the heather
    But not as before;
And well may the heron
    Take pride in his plume,
With the head of O'Dogherty
    Red in the tomb.

The valleys are spurning
    Gay flowers, beneath
The purple of mourning
    Aloft on the heath;
And well may the sorrow
    Of Nature be shown,
Though the heron is happy
    In wild Innishowen.

Bright was the bonnet
    That guided his men,
But the gray feather on it
    Fell red in the glen;
And well may the Saxon
    Take pride in its fall,
While birds wear their plumage
    Above Donegal.

Ochone, that the feather
    O'Dogherty wore
Should sweep o'er the heather,
    But not as before!

Och! Och! that the heron
　　Should fly with gray plume
O'er Cahir O'Dogherty
　　Red in his tomb.

Francis Carlin

THE RETORT DISCOURTEOUS

(Italy—16th Century)

But what, by the fur on your satin sleeves,
The rain that drags at my feather
And the great Mercurius, god of thieves,
Are we thieves doing together?

Last night your blades bit deep for their hire,
And we were the sickled barley.
To-night, a-toast by the common fire,
You ask me to join your parley.

Your spears are shining like Iceland spar,
The blood-grapes drip for your drinking;
For you folk follow the rising star,
I follow the star that's sinking!

My queen is old as the frosted whins,
Nay, how could her wrinkles charm me?
And the starving bones are bursting the skins
In the ranks of her ancient army.

You marshal a steel-and-silken troop,
Your cressets are fed with spices,
And you batter the world like a rolling hoop
To the goal of your proud devices.

I have rocked your thrones—but your fight is won.
To-night, as the highest bidder,
You offer a share of your brigand-sun,
Consider, old bull, consider!

Ahead, red Death and the Fear of Death,
Your vultures, stoop to the slaughter!
But I shall fight you, body and breath,
Till my life runs out like water!

My queen is wan as the Polar snows.
Her host is a rout of spectres.
But I gave her Youth like a burning rose,
And her age shall not lack protectors!

I would not turn for the thunderclap
Or the face of the woman who bore me,
With her battered badge still scarring my cap,
And the drums of defeat before me!

Roll your hands in the honey of life!
Kneel to your white-necked strumpets!
You came to your crowns with a squealing fife
But I shall go out with trumpets!

Poison the steel of the plunging dart!
Holloa your hounds to their station!
I march to my ruin with such a heart
As a king to his coronation!

Your poets roar of your golden feats—
I have herded the stars like cattle.
And you may die in the perfumed sheets,
But I shall die in the battle!

Stephen Vincent Benét

LEPANTO

WHITE founts falling in the Courts of the sun,
And the Soldan of Byzantium is smiling as they run;
There is laughter like the fountains in that face of all men
    feared,
It stirs the forest darkness, the darkness of his beard,
It curls the blood-red crescent, the crescent of his lips,
For the inmost sea of all the earth is shaken with his ships.

They have dared the white republics up the capes of Italy,
They have dashed the Adriatic round the Lion of the Sea,
And the Pope has cast his arms abroad for agony and loss,
And called the kings of Christendom for swords about the
    Cross.
The cold queen of England is looking in the glass;
The shadow of the Valois is yawning at the Mass;
From evening isles fantastical rings faint the Spanish gun,
And the Lord upon the Golden Horn is laughing in the sun.

Dim drums throbbing, in the hills half heard,
Where only on a nameless throne a crownless prince has
    stirred,
Where, risen from a doubtful seat and half attainted stall,
The last knight of Europe takes weapons from the wall,
The last and lingering troubadour to whom the bird has
    sung,
That once went singing southward when all the world was
    young.
In that enormous silence, tiny and unafraid,
Comes up along a winding road the noise of the Crusade.

Strong gongs groaning as the guns boom far,
Don John of Austria is going to the war,
Stiff flags straining in the night-blasts cold
In the gloom black-purple, in the glint old-gold,
Torchlight crimson on the copper kettle-drums,
Then the tuckets, then the trumpets, then the cannon, and
    he comes.
Don John laughing in the brave beard curled,
Spurning of his stirrups like the thrones of all the world,
Holding his head up for a flag of all the free.
Love-light of Spain—hurrah!
Death-light of Africa!
Don John of Austria
Is riding to the sea.

Mahound is in his paradise above the evening star,
(*Don John of Austria is going to the war.*)
He moves a mighty turban on the timeless houri's knees,
His turban that is woven of the sunsets and the seas.

He shakes the peacock gardens as he rises from his ease,
And he strides among the tree-tops and is taller than the
    trees,
And his voice through all the garden is a thunder sent to
    bring
Black Azrael and Ariel and Ammon on the wing.
Giants and the Genii,
Multiplex of wing and eye,
Whose strong obedience broke the sky
When Solomon was king.

They rush in red and purple from the red clouds of the morn,
From temples where the yellow gods shut up their eyes in
    scorn;
They rise in green robes roaring from the green hells of the
    sea
Where fallen skies and evil hues and eyeless creatures be;
On them the sea-valves cluster and the gray sea-forests
    curl,
Splashed with a splendid sickness, the sickness of the pearl;
They swell in sapphire smoke out of the blue cracks of the
    ground,—
They gather and they wonder and give worship to Mahound.
And he saith, "Break up the mountains where the hermit-
    folk can hide,
And sift the red and silver sands lest bone of saint abide,
And chase the Giaours flying night and day, not giving rest,
For that which was our trouble comes again out of the west.
We have set the seal of Solomon on all things under sun,
Of knowledge and of sorrow and endurance of things done,
But a noise is in the mountains, in the mountains, and I
    know
The voice that shook our palaces—four hundred years ago:
It is he that saith not 'Kismet'; it is he that knows not
    Fate;
It is Richard, it is Raymond, it is Godfrey in the gate!
It is he whose loss is laughter when he counts the wager
    worth,
Put down your feet upon him, that our peace be on the
    earth."

For he heard drums groaning and he heard guns jar,
(*Don John of Austria is going to the war.*)
Sudden and still—hurrah!
Bolt from Iberia!
Don John of Austria
Is gone by Alcalar.

St. Michael's on his Mountain in the sea-roads of the north
(*Don John of Austria is girt and going forth.*)
Where the gray seas glitter and the sharp tides shift
And the sea-folk labor and the red sails lift.
He shakes his lance of iron and he claps his wings of stone;
The noise is gone through Normandy; the noise is gone alone;
The North is full of tangled things and texts and aching
        eyes
And dead is all the innocence of anger and surprise,
And Christian killeth Christian in a narrow dusty room,
And Christian dreadeth Christ that hath a newer face of
        doom,
And Christian hateth Mary that God kissed in Galilee,
But Don John of Austria is riding to the sea.
Don John calling through the blast and the eclipse
Crying with the trumpet, with the trumpet of his lips,
Trumpet that sayeth ha!
    Domino gloria!
Don John of Austria
Is shouting to the ships.

King Philip's in his closet with the Fleece about his neck
(*Don John of Austria is armed upon the deck.*)
The walls are hung with velvet that is black and soft as
        sin,
And little dwarfs creep out of it and little dwarfs creep in.
He holds a crystal phial that has colors like the moon,
He touches, and it tingles, and he trembles very soon,
And his face is as a fungus of a leprous white and gray
Like plants in the high houses that are shuttered from the
        day,
And death is in the phial and the end of noble work,
But Don John of Austria has fired upon the Turk.

Don John's hunting, and his hounds have bayed—
Booms away past Italy the rumor of his raid.
Gun upon gun, ha! ha!
Gun upon gun, hurrah!
Don John of Austria
Has loosed the cannonade.

The Pope was in his chapel before day or battle broke,
(*Don John of Austria is hidden in the smoke.*)
The hidden room in man's house where God sits all the year,
The secret window whence the world looks small and very
    dear.
He sees as in a mirror on the monstrous twilight sea
The crescent of his cruel ships whose name is mystery;
They fling great shadows foe-wards, making Cross and
    Castle dark,
They veil the plumèd lions on the galleys of St. Mark;
And above the ships are palaces of brown, black-bearded
    chiefs,
And below the ships are prisons, where with multitudinous
    griefs,
Christian captives sick and sunless, all a laboring race re-
    pines
Like a race in sunken cities, like a nation in the mines.
They are lost like slaves that swat, and in the skies of
    morning hung
The stairways of the tallest gods when tyranny was young.
They are countless, voiceless, hopeless as those fallen or
    fleeing on
Before the high Kings' horses in the granite of Babylon.
And many a one grows witless in his quiet room in hell
Where a yellow face looks inward through the lattice of his
    cell,
And he finds his God forgotten, and he seeks no more a
    sign—
(*But Don John of Austria has burst the battle-line!*)
Don John pounding from the slaughter-painted poop,
Purpling all the ocean like a bloody pirate's sloop,
Scarlet running over on the silvers and the golds,
Breaking of the hatches up and bursting of the holds,

Thronging of the thousands up that labor under sea
White for bliss and blind for sun and stunned for liberty.
Vivat Hispania!
Domino Gloria!
Don John of Austria
Has set his people free!

Cervantes on his galley sets the sword back in the sheath
(*Don John of Austria rides homeward with a wreath.*)
And he sees across a weary land a straggling road in Spain,
Up which a lean and foolish knight for ever rides in vain,
And he smiles, but not as Sultans smile, and settles back
    the blade. . . .
(*But Don John of Austria rides home from the Crusade.*)
                       G. K. Chesterton

PART VI

POEMS OF SENTIMENT AND REFLECTION

TO THE MODERN MAN

FROM mysteries of the Past
    The Future is prophesied.
The Actual comes and goes
    Like shadows on a tide.

Realities come and go
    Like shadows on a pool,—
The leaves are for the wise man,
    The shadows for the fool.

Out of the moment Now
    Rises the god To-Be,
The light upon his brow
    Is from eternity.

Leave dreaming to the fool
    And take things as they are;
All things are in yourself,
    Who stand upon a star

And look upon the stars,
    And yearn with deepening breath—
All things are in yourself—
    Love and Life and Death.

John Hall Wheelock

THE PHILOSOPHY OF LIFE

A CREED

I HOLD that when a person dies
   His soul returns again to earth;
Arrayed in some new flesh-disguise
   Another mother gives him birth.
With sturdier limbs and brighter brain
The old soul takes the roads again.

Such is my own belief and trust;
   This hand, this hand that holds the pen,
Has many a hundred times been dust
   And turned, as dust, to dust again;
These eyes of mine have blinked and shone
In Thebes, in Troy, in Babylon.

All that I rightly think or do,
   Or make, or spoil, or bless, or blast,
Is curse or blessing justly due
   For sloth or effort in the past.
My life's a statement of the sum
Of vice indulged, or overcome.

I know that in my lives to be
   My sorry heart will ache and burn,
And worship, unavailingly,
   The woman whom I used to spurn,
And shake to see another have
The love I spurned, the love she gave.

And I shall know, in angry words,
   In gibes, and mocks, and many a tear,
A carrion flock of homing-birds,
   The gibes and scorns I uttered here.
The brave word that I failed to speak
Will brand me dastard on the cheek.

And as I wander on the roads
  I shall be helped and healed and blessed;
Dear words shall cheer and be as goads
  To urge to heights before unguessed.
My road shall be the road I made;
All that I gave shall be repaid.

So shall I fight, so shall I tread,
  In this long war beneath the stars;
So shall a glory wreathe my head,
  So shall I faint and show the scars,
Until this case, this clogging mould,
Be smithied all to kingly gold.

John Masefield

ANOTHER GENERATION

THERE is a woman like a seed,
  There is a man in embryo,
Whose spirits, faces, sex indeed
  Their very mothers do not know.

Only their being is revealed,
  They are: all else is hid in gloom,
Fixed by authority, but sealed
  Deep in the future and the womb.

Yet they are foreordained to be
  One female, and the other male,
And they will come the light to see,
  And suck, and bite their fist, and wail,

And grow through childhood wondering still
  At all the beauties of the earth,
And learn the exercise of will,
  Mercy and truth and tears and mirth.

Season of youth! they'll live with joy
  Through all our careless days of old,
But leave behind the girl and boy
  Their dearest secrets still untold.

Separate still, they will not meet,
    Though life be light, unsatisfied;
Not finding any, wise or sweet,
    The born companions of their pride:

Till destiny disguised as chance
    Pricks out the hour with silver pin,
Decrees a dinner or a dance,
    A house, a garden, or an inn,

Where they'll be left alone a space,
    Strangers, and talk; and she will find
Him like herself, and he her face
    The language of a perfect mind.

And once again with all the rest
    They'll come together, and friends depart,
Congeniality confessed,
    Each with a trouble at the heart.

And yet once more and they will know
    A final wound; they are struck by love,
The god at last has drawn his bow,
    And sent a shaft that will not move:

And he a whole night long will wake
    Abased and helpless, framing speech,
Made desperate by his heart's fierce ache
    To ask a thing beyond his reach,

And she all trembling in her bed
    Will search his strangeness, yearn and weep,
Loving him, filled with virgin dread,
    And see the dawn, and find no sleep.

And pressed by thunder they will rise,
    And when a few more hours have gone,
Her burning cheek and languid eyes,
    Will tell him all his war is won.

Ah, but I know their months of bliss,
　Their happy silence, happy talk;
How they will roam and pause and kiss,
　Confess, discover, while they walk;

How they will stand by stream and lake,
　And go, as though exchanging sight,
Through bluebell wood and primrose brake
　Finding in all a new delight:

And watch the sunset from a gate,
　And see the evening fade, and then
All of a sudden learn to hate
　The evil that is done by men—

So they will mate, and they will get
　A wondrous child, and several more,
The prettiest, strongest, gayest set
　That mortal mother ever bore.

And love to watch this brood of theirs
　Grow up, though they grow older too,
And laugh to find their first gray hairs
　Since there is nothing else to do.

Each thought you guard, each pulse of mine
　Will wake in them, but they not guess
We shared of old the immortal wine
　Of their delight and their distress,

Who beyond question, also were
　Wisest of all the race of Man,
One only comprehending pair,
　Unique, since first the world began.

J. C. Squire

EAGLE SONNETS

III

I HAVE been sure of three things all my life.
The first is that I am—a final one
That yields no room for doubt or windy strife,—
More certain than the blazing of the sun.

The second, that I was—a fainter fact,
Broken by sudden blanks and curious lapses;
A shadow to each living thought and act,
Yet shadowed by a host of vague perhapses.
The third and last of these, that I will be:
A moment leading to a lengthening span,
A fragment formed of continuity,
A child forever growing into man.
Three things are sure. . . . O you who grope for four,
Know, man is sure of three, and never more.

VII

Flower of the dust am I: for dust will flower,
Before its final reckoning is had;
And then this dust, in a hot sudden hour,
Shall stagger, veer, and flounder, in a mad,
Tumultuous plunge into that blazing sun
—Mere dust on fire—that gave it once its birth;
And man and all his doings shall be one
With the charred cinder that was once an earth.
And then again a brief, unhurried cooling,
More flowers that walk and dream, maybe—and then
The agèd sun will end its scanted ruling
As surely as there is an end to men.
The heavens at last will end, as all things must—
To let new heavens ripple out of dust.

IX

O bitter moon, O cold and bitter moon,
Climbing your midnight hillside of bleak sky,
The earth, as you, once knew a blazing noon:
Night brings the silver hour when she will die.
We shall be cold as you are, and as bitter,
Icily circling toward a tepid fire,
Playing at life with our deceitful glitter,
Past joy, past hope, forever past desire.
Yet still the forest lifts its leafy wings,
To flutter for a while before the chill;
And still the careless heart is gay, and sings
In the green temple on the dusty hill;

And the gulls tumble; and the homing ships
Peer for the harbor; and the sand drips.

XI

When down the windy vistas of the years
Has blown the last mad hurricane of being,
When grief has gone, through lack of eyes for tears,
And life is blind, through lack of eyes for seeing;
Only the sluggish soughing of the sea
Moving, of all the bright unrest we know,
Ebbing to final immobility,
While the earth's drowsing spinning note is low,—
That is the hour to weigh each brave endeavor, . . .
The lark of hope sings in our morning air
That life is youth and shall endure forever:
While, in his breast, the maggot of despair
Feeds, in its cool, undeviating lust.
Its silence sings a dusty song of dust.

XIX

I am a tongue for beauty.   Not a day,
And not a night, but is a face of her:
The leafy surf of spring, the petal spray;
The nights when snowflakes are too stiff to stir.
She laughs in sunlit waters, and she smiles
In shivering moonlit pools that break the moon;
Her soft face shines above the herded miles
Where slums shrink from the stifling breath of noon.
Her hand is in your hand at every turning;
She slips unseen beside you in the press;
But she will break the brittle heart with yearning,
When, trembling in the glare of loneliness,
You dread to learn you are remote from worth,—
And find you are her shadow on the earth.

XX

We are the singing shadows beauty casts;
Nor shall the shadow live to see its source,
Nor her invisible sun, whose morning lasts
Long after life has spent its feeble force:

No more than waves burned silver by the moon
Shall lift to see their shining silver one,
Or her enkindling sun, whose whitest noon
Shadows some fiercer and farther sun.
Trap beauty in your net, she still is flying;
Know her, she is radiantly unknown;
Slay her, she is reborn out of her dying,
To cleave those heights only her wings have flown.
Flee her, till earth ebbs to a vanishing star,
You are her shadow: she is where you are.

Clement Wood

HEIR AND SERF

I SAY that I think for myself, but what is this Self of mine
But a chance, loose knot in the skein of life where myriad
    selves entwine?
One of my fathers died for a faith,
Another one him betrayed,
And hacked at his neck with a bigot's blade . . .
Here, in the house of my being, wraith battles with clutch-
    ing wraith. . . .

I say that I go alone, but I do not go alone:
Quivers my heart with hatreds not mine own,
And an alien madness crawls in my brain . . .
For wrongs that I never wrought I must still atone,
Blood money I pay for them that I have not slain . . .
Dust that was flesh of·mine moulders in many a tomb,
Ghosts that were sires of mine circle me here in the gloom.

I have heard cries through the night in a tongue I cannot
    speak,
And they knocked on my heart and blanched my cheek . . .
I have dreamed dreams of a temple I cannot name,
Perchance it was Bel that dwelt therein, apparelled in gold
    and flame . . .
Which is my life the more?—this visible life that seems,
Or the hours when I drift at the whim of a shade through
    the hurrying bourne of dreams?

Through cities I never saw, a slave among sullen slaves,
I am scourged with knotted whips . . .
Cairns I have raised in an unknown land over mine own
    white bones . . .
Seas that I never sailed fawn with their leaping waves,
Hailing me fellow with bitter lips,
Promising prey to the beaks of my lean, swift ships. . . .

Runes that I cannot read, I have graven on Druid
    stones . . .
Omens rush on me out of the blown sea mist,
Flash with the wheeling gulls, call to my blood and are
    gone . . .
Music I half remember the wind carries by, and I follow,
Flushed, to a tryst . . .
And I have stood shaken and glad, I have trembled and
    turned to the dawn,
Crying out to Apollo.

I say that I choose for myself, but that is an idle boast,
For here in my house of being ghost is at war with
    ghost . . .
Old loves and hates at the core of me, old doubts and
    faiths in the brain,
And salt in the stinging blood of me old lusts revive
    again . . .
I say that I am myself, but what is this Self of mine
But a knot in the tangled skein of things where chance and
    chance combine?

                                                    Don Marquis

CUPS OF ILLUSION

From this tower room above the wall
I have watched the sunworn city
And the sea.
I have seen the nights
Drain the streets
Of light and sound,
The days shrivel to thin sheets
Of wrinkled silver

On the tide.
I have seen men come
Like stippled shade along the floor,
And go, as lightly brushed,
As unremembered, as leaf shape
Tangled in a blur of glass.

I have made cups
With chisel and fire and stain;
I have made cups—
Amethyst, silver, and gold,
Emerald, agate, and bronze;
I have made cups for pride,
And cups for a woman's heart.

I have made cups
For the altars of God,
And cups for perfume and wine;
Ivory, iron and clay,
Red cups for feasting,
And cups for sacrifice;
Turquoise cups for a birthday,
Ebony cups for dice;
Cups of crystal
To pay for a bride,
And delicate cups for tears.

My cups were the pomp of kings,
And the solace of lonely men.
Long years I worked and copied
My thoughts on my colored cups,—
(Chisel and fire and crimson,
Sapphire and purple and pearl.)
But I knew as I burned and painted
The world on beautiful cups
That the world was a painted curtain
Cheating the artist's eyes;
I knew that the rainbow curtain
Hid a thing past all surmise.
Still I carved and burned and copied
On opal and copper and blue,

Wings, and the glory of woman,
And clouds,
And fishes,
And ships. . . .

I knew that beyond the curtain
Was a world of final surprise
Pure and poignant and perfect,
Passing all men's surmise.

So I said as I chiselled and carved
The world in scarlet and clay,
I can see what is there on the curtain,
Painted and seeming to stir;
But I know that behind the delusion
Are the things that really move.

I shall mock the thin confusion
Of this imaged veil of deceit;
I shall make a new cup of illusion
From a dream quite strange and complete.
I shall use not a bird, not a flower,
Not a sign from this world of defeat.
Then out of my deepest knowing
I made a new shape for a vase.
I fashioned and moulded and carved
A new line of a consummate grace—
A new shape,
A new lucent color,
And wings that shadowed a face.

Out of my deepest knowing
I painted a curious glowing,
A light of imagined sea,
But never a river or tree,
Or even the ardent going
Of birds that ever could be.
Then every one could see
A flame of figures curl and twine
About the stem;
And every one could see

A brilliant wine that seemed to fill
It to the brim and shine.

Each saw a thing most different,
Engraved upon the side;
Each saw a special vision
And looked again and cried.
Some said it was a thing of ill—
Some said it was divine.

But not again was any certain
If this world be not a curtain
Brocade with things
That seem to move,—
Or if there was a face
Upon the cup,
Shadowed with wings.

    .   .   .   .   .

Looking down
From this room above the town
I watch the days
In long retreat,
And men upon their ways
Along the street.
They are like leaves across a floor,
Like phantoms flitting past a door,—
As lightly brushed,
As unremembered,
As bird shadows on the grass.

Henry Bellamann

JOY O' LIVING

HE came with roses in his mouth,
    And kindling rubies in each vein,
Like perfume of the scented south
    Through flying arrows of the rain,
And on his goat-heels sat and played
Till we were charmed yet half afraid!

And dogs and sheep and gentle things
   Crept near, and very shy and sweet
A butterfly, on painted wings,
   Alighted softly at his feet,
And hearing him the great god Pan
Grew feeble as an old, old man.

His antics were so proud and free,
   His smiles so wilful and so rare
He should have worn eternity
   As jewels in his grape-dark hair;
And yet the burden of his song
Was that he could not linger long!

The clouds, a white-robed pilgrim lot,
   Came gathering at once they saw
Our little tangled human knot
   Attentive to his oaten straw,
Till all on tiptoe they withdrew
And let the moon adventure through.

Through evening's iridescent mist
   He saw me once and followed far;
I would that he had caught and kissed
   And set me like a burning star
To cool in some blue distant place
Till death or dawn should find my face.
Amanda Benjamin Hall

JEZEBEL

WE know she lives upon that thorny hill,
We see her lights and watch her chimneys spark—
But her we have not seen. The old wives say,
Remembering when she came, her ways were dark,
And that her only name is Jezebel.
One gray idiot tells his tale of love,
Mixing her beauty with the stars of May.

Perhaps we idly wonder if she wore
A flower in her hair, or if the beat

Of her small heels upon the sidewalk stone
Was heard at midnight through our lamplit street;
Or why it was she went away to live,
With all her perfumed satin and her lace,
In that wind-beaten, far-off place, alone.

We never wonder more of Jezebel.
We have our work to do and God is hard.
Serving the wheels or guiding straight the plow
Leaves little thought of frankincense and nard.
Yet, she is like deep waters of the Spring
Running along our minds; down at the roots,
The miracle that makes the April bough.

No man goes near that house above the town.
No man has seen her shadow on the blind,
Though through the night, till dawn, the tallow drips.
But, sometimes, when the chains of duty bind,
Because we reach too eagerly for Heaven,
Sometimes, like little bells within our sleep,
It seems we hear the music of her lips.

Then we have left what we most dearly love,
And, momentary lords of Heaven and Hell,
We have gone up through briars and the night,
And seen the secret face of Jezebel.
There, in that still confessional where she waits,
We all have had the blessing of her breast,
As over us she leaned to blow the light.

Up in that room above our godly town,
We have denied the vows we bleed to keep,
We have torn off the lying masks we wear,
And sown without the fear that we must reap.
The young, the pious, and the old alike
Have been glad penitents upon her heart—
She has absolved us by her kisses, there.

She has forgiven us and let us go,
And we have wakened in our homes again,

To hear the breathing of an earthly bride,
To watch the real world blooming on the pane.
The field, the wheel, the desk have called once more,
And we have stooped to pick the slender threads
By which we weave the patterns of our pride.

That day, we do not bargain with the sun,
To curb our pride because one angel fell—
We are the wilful brotherhood who sing!
We bend, without a thought of Jezebel,
Above our work, no longer do we drudge;
We are, awhile, like happy, armored men
God's searching whip of anger cannot sting!

Scudder Middleton

NOT THREE—BUT ONE

"And yet they are not three . . . but one."

Some of the roofs are plum-color,
Some of the roofs are gray,
Some of the roofs are silverstone,
And some are made of clay;
But under every gabled close
There's a secret hid away.

Women I know are dressed in rags,
Women I know in lace,
And one in a dusky robe of gold
With a hooded cloak of mace;
But every robe and every rag
Is a secret hiding place.

There's a road of water, a road of stone
And a road of steel as well,
And whichever one you may choose goes up
To Heaven and down to Hell;
But a secret's hidden beneath the three
No living man dare tell.

Some day, a sifted heap of dust
May lay the secret bare
Of which was woman and which was roof
And which was a thoroughfare;
But you shall not tell the gray from the gold
Or the stone from the shining hair.

Esther Lilian Duff

TRICKSTERS

I AM bewildered still and teased by elves
That cloud about me even through city streets.
One sings a stave and one a dream repeats,
One, crueller, in some old resentment delves.
I am aware they are my other selves,
Yet to what dazzling vision each entreats,
Casting a glamor over shams and cheats,
Ennobling cant, buzzing by tens and twelves!
So when my smiling grieves the passerby,
I strut in all vocations not my own,
Wearing the centuries like a baldric slung;
Whilst shabby I gawk at this splendid I.
Chronos and Momus through my lips intone,
Archangels, heroes,—rascals yet unhung!

William Rose Benét

I, WHO FADE WITH THE LILACS

I, WHO fade with the lilacs
  And with the roses fade,
Am sharing this hour with them
  Conferring in the shade.

Life has not left the wonder
  With which it first began
To make Pierrot a poet,
  In making him a man.

It has not made a rainbow
  In all the sorry years,
But was a sailing glory
  Upon a sea of tears.

Somehow life leaves one stranded
　On shores too near or far,
Hitching, forever hitching
　Ships—shallops to a star.

William Griffith

MOMENTS

MOMENTS there are when heart and brain ring clear,
When the eyes see and when the apt ears hear
More in a second's tick than in a year—
Moments at evening when the stars lean near.

And once I thought
Quick instants such as these,
That my new senses caught,
Were promises of vivid days to be
When I should stand grown up,
And brave, and full of careless, flaming song,
And free.

Those days have never come.
And now I know
That in this world of ours
Such moments never grow
Into a day—
Not even into hours—
They are as rare and brief as desert flowers.

There may be worlds where deathless shepherds lie,
Watching their starry flocks graze through the sky,
Pastures of lotus in the fields of space,
White with the tents of an eternal race.
Deep as the eye of a blue, land-locked sea
That timeless calm would seem to you and me;
Its æons short with long felicity,
But strange, how strange!
Without the yeast of change.

Give me no changeless hours, for I know
Moments of earth are sweeter that they go;

Pluck me no deathless roses from the sky;
They bloom forever, but ours wilt and die.
Earth's joys are whetted on her stone of sorrow.
Tears are real tears while we can laugh to-morrow.

Hervey Allen

HOLD FAST YOUR DREAMS

Hold fast your dreams!
Within your heart
Keep one, still, secret spot
Where dreams may go,
And sheltered so,
May thrive and grow—
Where doubt and fear are not.
O, keep a place apart,
Within your heart,
For little dreams to go!

Think still of lovely things that are not true.
Let wish and magic work at will in you.
Be sometimes blind to sorrow.   Make believe!
Forget the calm that lies
In disillusioned eyes.
Though we all know that we must die,
Yet you and I
May walk like gods and be
Even now at home in immortality!

We see so many ugly things—
Deceits and wrongs and quarrelings;
We know, alas! we know
How quickly fade
The color in the west,
The bloom upon the flower,
The bloom upon the breast
And youth's blind hour.
Yet, keep within your heart
A place apart

Where little dreams may go,
May thrive and grow.
Hold fast—hold fast your dreams!

Louise Driscoll

DREAM THE GREAT DREAM

DREAM the Great Dream, though you should dream—you,
    only,
And friendless follow in the lofty quest.
Though the dream lead you to a desert lonely,
Or drive you, like the tempest, without rest,
Yet, toiling upward to the highest altar,
There lay before the gods your gift supreme,—
A human heart whose courage did not falter
Though distant as Arcturus shone the Gleam.

The Gleam?—Ah, question not if others see it,
Who nor the yearning nor the passion share;
Grieve not if children of the earth decree it—
The earth, itself,—their goddess, only fair!
The soul has need of prophet and redeemer:
Her outstretched wings against her prisoning bars,
She waits for truth; and truth is with the dreamer,—
Persistent as the myriad light of stars!

Florence Earle Coates

PER ASPERA

THANK God, a man can grow!
He is not bound
With earthward gaze to creep along the ground:
Though his beginnings be but poor and low,
Thank God, a man can grow!
The fire upon his altars may burn dim,
The torch he lighted may in darkness fail,
And nothing to rekindle it avail,—
Yet high beyond his dull horizon's rim,
Arcturus and the Pleiads beckon him.

Florence Earle Coates

A LITTLE SONG OF LIFE

GLAD that I live am I;
That the sky is blue;
Glad for the country lanes,
And the fall of dew.

After the sun the rain,
After the rain the sun;
This is the way of life,
Till the work be done.

All that we need to do,
Be we low or high,
Is to see that we grow
Nearer the sky.

Lizette Woodworth Reese •

MEASURE ME, SKY

MEASURE me, sky!
Tell me I reach by a song
Nearer the stars:
I have been little so long.

Weigh me, high wind!
What will your wild scales record?
Profit of pain,
Joy by the weight of a word.

Horizon, reach out!
Catch at my hands, stretch me taut,
Rim of the world:
Widen my eyes by a thought.

Sky, be my depth;
Wind, be my width and my height;
World, my heart's span:
Loneliness, wings for my flight!

Leonora Speyer

WISDOM

A WISE man holds himself in check,
But fools and poets run ahead.
One must be credulous or sit
Forever with the living dead.

The wise man shuts his door at night
And pulls the bolts and drops the bars.
One must go trustful through the dark
To earn the friendship of the stars.

Scudder Middleton

NONSENSE

LIFE is a sorry *mélange* of gold and silver and stubble,
Of roses and wormword and weeds, of rubies and rubble.

I will take all life to my heart, and who knows but I may,
    ere long,
See the stubble turn gold and the wormwood bear roses
    of song?

Robert Haven Schauffler

THE ARROW

STRAIGHT from a mighty bow this truth is driven:
"They fail, and they alone, who have not striven."

Fly far, O shaft of light! all doubt redeeming;
Rouse men from dull despair and idle dreaming.

High Heaven's evangel be, gospel God-given:
"They fail, and they alone, who have not striven."

Clarence Urmy

CLAY HILLS

IT is easy to mould the yielding clay.
And many shapes grow into beauty
Under the facile hand.
But forms of clay are lightly broken;
They will lie shattered and forgotten in a dingy corner.

But underneath the slipping clay
Is rock. . . .
I would rather work in stubborn rock
All the years of my life,
And make one strong thing
And set it in a high, clean place,
To recall the granite strength of my desire.

Jean Starr Untermeyer

BUTTERFLIES

THERE will be butterflies,
There will be summer skies
And flowers upthrust,
When all that Cæsar bids,
And all the pyramids
    Are dust.

There will be gaudy wings
Over the bones of things,
And never grief:
Who says that summer skies,
Who says that butterflies,
    Are brief?

Haniel Long

THE EXAMPLE

HERE'S an example from
    A Butterfly;
That on a rough, hard rock
    Happy can lie;
Friendless and all alone
On this unsweetened stone.

Now let my bed be hard
    No care take I;
I'll make my joy like this
    Small Butterfly;
Whose happy heart has power
To make a stone a flower.

William H. Davies

RUST

IRON, left in the rain
    And fog and dew,
With rust is covered.—Pain
    Rusts into beauty too.

I know full well that this is so:
I had a heartbreak long ago.
            Mary Carolyn Davies

HOPE

WHEN I was a little boy,
I followed hope and slighted joy.
Now my wit has larger scope,
I clutch at joy and heed not hope.

At least that doctrine I profess,
For there I know lies happiness;
But hope, for all the shifts I try,
Will be my sovereign till I die.
            Gamaliel Bradford

A SONG

FOR Mercy, Courage, Kindness, Mirth,
    There is no measure upon earth;
Nay, they wither, root and stem,
    If an end be set to them.

Overbrim and overflow
    If your own heart you would know
For the spirit, born to bless,
    Lives but in its own excess.
            Laurence Binyon

COUNTERSIGN

OUT in the dark night-long
I heard the Pine Tree's song
Make secret harmonies
For frozen earth and skies—

And in the first wan light
I watched a gray gull's flight
Toward morning and the sea:
These things did counsel me

To find for Doubt a wing:
To teach Despair to sing:
To make Faith's Countersign
A gray Gull and a Pine!

Arthur Ketchum

CANDLE–LIGHTING SONG

I HAVE three candles in my room
Slender and long and white,
Their tips are buds of fire bloom
That blossom every night.

And one I light for memory,
All steady as a star;
And one burns clear for days to be,
And one for days that are.

I have three candles in my room
Slender and tall and fair;
And every one a fire bloom,
And every one a prayer.

Arthur Ketchum

THE LAST GUEST

WHY have you lit so bright a fire
   For chatterers to sit about,
While wistful at the door,
And lonely at the door,
   One waits without?

Why have you spread so rich a feast
   For careless and insatiate,
While eager at the door,
And wanly at the door,
   Waits one most delicate?

When the night deepens, and the guests
　　Have passed to some new clamorous goal,
Let in the quiet one,
Let in the longing one,—
Close to the last red embers draw
　　Your welcome soul.

Frances Shaw

FOR LIFE I HAD NEVER CARED GREATLY

For Life I had never cared greatly,
　　As worth a man's while;
　　Peradventures unsought,
　　Peradventures that finished in nought,
Had kept me from youth and through manhood till lately
　　Unwon by its style.

In earliest years—why I know not—
　　I viewed it askance;
　　Conditions of doubt,
　　Conditions that leaked slowly out,
May haply have bent me to stand and to show not
　　Much zest for its dance.

With symphonies soft and sweet color
　　It courted me then,
　　Till evasions seemed wrong,
　　Till evasions gave in to its song,
And I warmed, until living aloofly loomed duller
　　Than life among men.

Anew I found nought to set eyes on,
　　When, lifting its hand,
　　It uncloaked a star,
　　Uncloaked it from fog-damps afar,
And showed its beams burning from pole to horizon
　　As bright as a brand.

And so, the rough highway forgetting,
　　I pace hill and dale
　　Regarding the sky,

Regarding the vision on high,
And thus re-illumed have no humor for letting
My pilgrimage fail.

Thomas Hardy

THE LION-HOUSE

ALWAYS the heavy air,
  The dreadful cage, the low
Murmur of voices, where
  Some Force goes to and fro
In an immense despair!

As through a haunted brain—
  With tireless footfalls
The Obsession moves again,
  Trying the floor, the walls,
Forever, but in vain.

In vain, proud Force! A might,
  Shrewder than yours, did spin
Around your rage that bright
  Prison of steel, wherein
You pace for my delight.

And O, my heart, what Doom,
  What warier Will has wrought
The cage, within whose room
  Paces your burning thought,
For the delight of Whom?

John Hall Wheelock

THE INNER SILENCE

NOISES that strive to tear
Earth's mantle soft of air
And break upon the stillness where it dwell:
The noise of battle and the noise of prayer,
The cooing noise of love that softly tells
Joy's brevity, the brazen noise of laughter—

All these affront me not, nor echo after
Through the long memories.
They may not enter the deep chamber where
Forever silence is.

Silence more soft than spring hides in the ground
Beneath her budding flowers;
Silence more rich than ever was the sound
Of harps through long warm hours.
It's like a hidden vastness, even as though
Great suns might there beat out their measures slow,
Nor break the hush mightier than they.
There do I dwell eternally,
There where no thought may follow me,
Nor stillest dreams whose pinions plume the way.

Harriet Monroe

MENTIS TRIST

Never fear the phantom bird
Meditating in the Fens;
Night will come and quench your eyes,
Blind at last like other men's;
Never fear the tales you heard
In the rhetoric of lies.

Nothing here will challenge you,
Not the heron, tall and white,
Countersign upon the edge
Of the waterfall of night.
This is Avalon's canoe,
Eden murmurs in the sedge.

Here. My hand in pledge of rest.
Drift at random, all is well.
Twilight is a slow lagoon,
Dark will be a citadel.
Travellers who know the west
But report the waning moon.

In the citadel of peace
Hang the trophies of the world,
Yet no barons don their mail,
And no pennant is unfurled.
Daily robe, the Golden Fleece,
Daily cup, the Holy Grail.

Robert Hillyer

LIFE

LIFE is a shepherd lad who strides and sings
   Leading his flock, his brow bared to the sun,
Who knows the good grass and the hidden springs
   From whence streams of eternal beauty run.

Life is a cowherd, old, with bleeding lips,
   Driving fear-maddened cattle down a hill,
With matted hides worn raw at knees and hips,
   Knowing no sleep, no leisure to be still.

For one the dew, the hare-bell and the song;
For one the mire, the hurry and the thong.

Amory Hare

THE DAYS

I CALL my years back, I, grown old,
   Recall them day by day;
And some are dressed in cloth o' gold
   And some in humble gray.

And those in gold glance scornfully
   Or pass me unawares;
But those in gray come close to me
   And take my hand in theirs.

Theodosia Garrison

KNOWLEDGE

Now that I know
How passion warms little
Of flesh in the mould,
And treasure is brittle,—

I'll lie here and learn
How, over their ground,
Trees make a long shadow
And a light sound.

Louise Bogan

DOORS OF THE TEMPLE

MANY are the doors of the spirit that lead
   Into the inmost shrine:
   And I count the gates of the temple divine,
   Since the god of the place is God indeed.
And these are the gates that God decreed
   Should lead to His house:—kisses and wine,
Cool depths of thought, youth without rest,
   And calm old age, prayer and desire,
The Lover's and mother's breast,
   The fire of sense and the poet's fire.

But he that worships the gates alone,
   Forgetting the shrine beyond, shall see
   The great valves open suddenly,
Revealing, not God's radiant throne,
   But the fires of wrath and agony.

Aldous Huxley

TIME

TIME is God's tenderness
Told in hours and ages,
The sinner's cleansing fear,
The sure proof of sages;
Time's work is powerful,
Ingenious and true,
Making snow out of rain
And rain out of dew,
Making cities out of towns
And deserts out of cities,
Teaching by many wars
Millions of pities.

Time can lift a forest up
Where lies a bare field,
Or show the naked lie
That truth has concealed.
Goals of my long desire
Time alone can reach
And time can cure the sorrow
That finds no ease in speech.

Marguerite Wilkinson

THE TREE

I AM four monkeys.
One hangs from a limb,
tail-wise,
chattering at the earth;
another is cramming his belly with cocoanut;
the third is up in the top branches,
quizzing the sky;
and the fourth—
he's chasing another monkey.
How many monkeys are you?

Alfred Kreymborg

FROM A STREET CORNER

LIKE snails I see the people go
Along the pavement, row on row;
And each one on his shoulder bears
His coiling shell of petty cares—
The spiral of his own affairs.

Some peer about, some creep on blind,
But not one leaves his shell behind.
And I, who think I see so well,
Peer at the rest, but cannot tell
How much is cut off by my shell.

Eleanor Hammond

BLIND

THE Spring blew trumpets of color;
Her Green sang in my brain—
I heard a blind man groping
"Tap—tap" with his cane;

I pitied him in his blindness;
But can I boast, "I see"?
Perhaps there walks a spirit
Close by, who pities me,—

A spirit who hears me tapping
The five-sensed cane of mind
Amid such unguessed glories—
That I am worse than blind.

Harry Kemp

ALL BUT BLIND

ALL but blind
In his chambered hole
Gropes for worms
The four-clawed Mole.

All but blind
In the evening sky,
The hooded Bat
Twirls softly by.

All but blind
In the burning day
The Barn-Owl blunders
On her way.

And blind as are
These three to me,
So, blind to Some-one
I must be.

Walter de la Mare

FATE

ARE we mere pieces in the hand
That moves this universal Game—
Whom one by one some Power has planned
To follow some predestined aim?
Then Hope, thy burning words erase;
This world is but an abject place.

Are we a small and helpless kin
Wide-strewn upon this planet's face
Who, finding little cheer within,
Beseech some cold indifferent Grace?
Far better, then, no boon to seek
For they should perish who are weak.

O praise not him who fears his God
But show me him who knows not fear!
Who, springing from this common clod
Lives out himself; then may appear
The virtues that a whole world sees,
The by-words of the centuries.

James Fenimore Cooper, Jr.

A SERMON

THERE'S room for most things: Tropic seas,
Poll-parrots, beer, the Vicar's teas,
June nights, transparent Winter dawns,
Tulips ablaze on Summer lawns,
Queer jungle fruits of mammoth size,
And gay Brazilian butterflies;
Chalk cliffs built up of tiny shells,
Delicate mist and faint bluebells,
The sparrow's brown, the peacock's tail,
Cathedrals, Florence Nightingale,
Gaby Deslys, Paris, the small
Village tucked snugly round the Hall.—
Yes, room for all if only each
Will live content, nor strive to preach

Its own perfection as the end
Towards which the Universe should tend.
As long as daisies don't complain
The whole world's not a daisy-chain,
Or flaunting tropic birds condemn
To ridicule the sober hen;
As long as each with his own shape
Is satisfied—nor tries to ape
Another's: When the crow puts on
The peacock's plumes, his charm is gone.
Will o' the Wisp though shining bright
Won't keep your kitchen fires alight;
Tame wolves are not domestic cats,
Or fauns less fauns for bowler-hats.
Let neither Faun nor Saint reprove
Others for different ways of love,
Life and delight—there's room for wings
And feet, for wine and water-springs,
For things that walk and things that dance,
For Iceland and the South of France,
For lake and village-pump and sea,
For You—but also room for Me!

Margaret Sackville

THE FALCONER OF GOD

I FLUNG my soul to the air like a falcon flying.
I said: "Wait on, wait on, while I ride below!
    I shall start a heron soon
    In the marsh beneath the moon—
A strange white heron rising with silver on its wings,
        Rising and crying
      Wordless, wondrous things;
    The secret of the stars, of the world's heart-strings
      The answer to their woe.
Then stoop thou upon him, and grip and hold him so!"

My wild soul waited on as falcons hover.
I beat the reedy fens as I trampled past.

I heard the mournful loon
In the marsh beneath the moon.
And then, with feathery thunder, the bird of my desire
 Broke from the cover
 Flashing silver fire.
High up among the stars I saw his pinions spire.
 The pale clouds gazed aghast
As my falcon stooped upon him, and gripped and held him
fast.

My soul dropped through the air—with heavenly plunder?—
Gripping the dazzling bird my dreaming knew?
 Nay! but a piteous freight,
 A dark and heavy weight
Despoiled of silver plumage, its voice forever stilled—
 All of the wonder
 Gone that ever filled
Its guise with glory. O bird that I have killed,
 How brilliantly you flew
Across my rapturous vision when first I dreamed of you!

Yet I fling my soul on high with new endeavor,
And I ride the world below with a joyful mind.
 I shall start a heron soon
 In the marsh beneath the moon—
A wondrous silver heron its inner darkness fledges!
 I beat forever
 The fens and the sedges.
The pledge is still the same—for all disastrous pledges,
 All hopes resigned!
My soul still flies above me for the quarry it shall find!
    William Rose Benét

THE CONDUCT OF LIFE

TRIUMPHALIS

Soul, art thou sad again,
With the old sadness?
Thou shalt be glad again
With a new gladness,
When April sun and rain
Mount to the teeming brain
With the earth-madness.

When from the mould again,
Spurning disaster,
Spring shoots unfold again,
Follow thou faster
Out of the drear domain
Of dark, defeat, and pain,
Praising the Master.

Light for thy guide again,
Ample and splendid;
Love at they side again,
All doubting ended.
(Ah, by the dragon slain,
For nothing small or vain
Michael contended!)

Thou shalt take heart again,
No more despairing;
Play thy great part again,
Loving and caring.
Hark, how the gold refrain
Runs through the iron strain,
Splendidly daring!

Thou shalt grow strong again,
Confident, tender,—
Battle with wrong again,
Be truth's defender,—
Of the immortal train
Born to attempt, attain,
Never surrender!

Bliss Carman

DAYS AND NIGHTS

LIKE a king from a sunrise-land
In fair ship sailing,
With banners salt winds expand
And pennons trailing;
With wealth untold and a mind unknown,
And a power to love and make friends of his own,
And a power to leave those he likes not alone,
Each new day comes to me,—
Like king from far east sailing
Over the sea.

In a barge with golden trappings
For queen prepared,
And, against the cold, rich wrappings
And furs deep-haired,
To lands afar, by a force unguessed,
Where the face reveals what hides in the breast,
And by doubt of another no heart is distressed,
Some nights have carried me,
Like queen that homeward fared
Over the sea.

O heart, be true and strong,
That worth make thee each day's good friend;
Then thou the hours of dark shalt spend
Out there, where is no wrong.

T. Sturge Moore

A SILVER LANTERN

A SILVER lantern
   I made of my desire,
A cloudy vessel
   That dreamed of fire.

I digged my silver
   In a dark mine.
I crushed it and wrought it
   And hammered it fine;

With graven blossoms
   I made it bright,
And buds of darkness
   Dreaming of light,

Till—burnished and finished
   And marked with my name--
God blew upon it
   And gave the flame.

I carry my lantern
   Through the gusty rain:
Shielded with silver
   The light streams plain.

I carry my lantern
   Through the fierce, bald noon,
I carry my lantern
   Under the moon,

Through dark and dazzle
   Threading the ray
That picks out the climbing
   Hidden Way.

Karle Wilson Baker

BURNING BUSH

My heart, complaining like a bird,
Kept drooping on her weary nest:
"Oh, take me out under the sky,
Find me a little rest!"

I took her out under the sky,
I climbed a straggling, sandy street,
Where little weathered houses sag,
And town and country meet,

And in the corner of a yard
Unkempt, forlorn, and winter-browned,
A single sprig of Burning Bush
Thrust up from the bare ground.

It bore no leaf as yet—one flower,
Three pointed buds of pure rose-flame:
Up whirred my heart, circled in air,
Back to my bosom came.

And that was all I showed to her—
I could not find another thing—
But, "Take me home again," she cried,
"And I will sing and sing!"

Karle Wilson Baker

A PRAYER

Teach me, Father, how to go
Softly as the grasses grow;
Hush my soul to meet the shock
Of the wild world as a rock;
But my spirit, propt with power,
Make as simple as a flower.
Let the dry heart fill its cup,
Like a poppy looking up;

Let life lightly wear her crown,
Like a poppy looking down,
When its heart is filled with dew,
And its life begins anew.

Teach me, Father, how to be
Kind and patient as a tree.
Joyfully the crickets croon
Under shady oak at noon;
Beetle, on his mission bent,
Tarries in that cooling tent.
Let me, also, cheer a spot,
Hidden field or garden grot—
Place where passing souls can rest
On the way and be their best.

Edwin Markham

EXPECTANS EXPECTAVI

FROM morn to midnight, all day through,
I laugh and play as others do,
I sing and chatter, just the same
As others with a different name.

And all year long upon the stage,
I dance and tumble and do rage
So vehemently, I scarcely see
The inner and eternal me.   .

I have a temple I do not
Visit, a heart I have forgot,
A self that I have never met,
A secret shrine—and yet, and yet

This sanctuary of my soul
Unwitting I keep white and whole,
Unlatched and lit, if Thou should'st care
To enter or to tarry there.

With parted lips and outstretched hands
And listening ears Thy servant stands,
Call Thou early, call Thou late,
To Thy great service dedicate.

Charles Hamilton Sorley

PERFECTION

WHO seeks perfection in the art
Of driving well an ass and cart,
Or painting mountains in a mist,
Seeks God although an Atheist.

Francis Carlin

THE WAYS

To every man there openeth
A Way, and Ways and a Way,
And the High Soul climbs the High way,
And the Low Soul gropes the Low,
And in between, on the misty flats,
The rest drift to and fro.
But to every man there openeth
A High way and a Low,
And every man decideth
The Way his soul shall go.

John Oxenham

THE SPIRIT'S GRACE

MORE brightly must my spirit shine
Since grace of beauty is not mine;

As shaded light and converse wise
Fill with a wondering surprise

The weary traveler seeking late
A lodging at some cottage gate—

So would I that my Spirit's grace
Should beautify its dwelling place.

Janie Screven Heyward

THE PATH THAT LEADS NOWHERE

THERE'S a path that leads to Nowhere
　　In a meadow that I know,
Where an inland island rises
　　And the stream is still and slow;
There it wanders under willows,
　　And beneath the silver green
Of the birches' silent shadows
　　Where the early violets lean.

Other pathways lead to Somewhere,
　　But the one I love so well
Has no end and no beginning—
　　Just the beauty of the dell,
Just the wind-flowers and the lilies
　　Yellow-striped as adder's tongue,
Seem to satisfy my pathway
　　As it winds their scents among.

There I go to meet the Springtime,
　　When the meadow is aglow,
Marigolds amid the marshes,—
　　And the stream is still and slow.
There I find my fair oasis,
　　And with care-free feet I tread
For the pathway leads to Nowhere,
　　And the blue is overhead!

All the ways that lead to Somewhere
　　Echo with the hurrying feet
Of the Struggling and the Striving,
　　But the way I find so sweet
Bids me dream and bids me linger,
　　Joy and Beauty are its goal,—
On the path that leads to Nowhere
　　I have sometimes found my soul!
                    Corinne Roosevelt Robinson

THE JOURNEY

WHAT matter where the Apple grows?
True heroes never count the miles.
The journey leads to where it leads—
Sargasso or the Western Isles.

No one place holds the dreams of all.
Earth wears a multi-colored robe,
And there are new Hesperides
In every corner of the globe.

Some find the fruit like Hercules—
For such the moon and sun may stop;
Yet never doubt that Sisyphus
Achieved at last the mountain top.

Scudder Middleton

THREE GREEN TREES

THREE green trees marching up a hill;
Three high points of the human will.
The goals of the human will are these:
The will to be, the will to do,
The will to look into God's eyes
Like those intrepid, towering trees
Whose turrets pierce the skies.
But trees may see their dreams come true,
While man—his hill is hardly crowned
Before another hill is found!

Angela Morgan

DUE NORTH

ENOUGH: you have the dream, the flame;
   Free it henceforth:
The South has given you a name;—
   Now for the North.

Unsheathe your ship from where she lies,
   In narrow ease;
Fling out her sails to the tall skies,
   Flout the sharp seas.

Beyond bleak headlands wistful burn
   Warm lights of home;
In shutting darkness frays astern,
   Far-spun, the foam.

Come wide sea-dawns, that empty are
   Of wet sea sand;
Come eves, that lay beneath a star
   No lull of land.

And whether on faint iris wings
   Of fancy borne,
Or blown and breathed, the south wind brings
   So much to mourn!

The deep wood-shadows, they that drew
   So softly near;
The violets all veined with blue,—
   Be strong, and steer!

There is a silence to be found,
   And rested in;
A stillness out of thought, where sound
   Can never win.

There is a peace, beyond the stir
   Of wind or wave;
A sleeping, where high stars confer
   Over the brave.

The south winds come, the south winds go,
   Caressing, dear;
Northward is silence, and white snow,—
   Be strong, and steer!

For in that silence, waiting, lies,
  Untroubled, true;—
Oh, eager, clear—like love in eyes—
  The soul of you.
Benjamin R. C. Low

DUTY

WHEN Duty comes a-knocking at your gate,
Welcome him in; for if you bid him wait,
He will depart only to come once more
And bring seven other duties to your door.
Edwin Markham

TOIL AWAY

TOIL away and set the stone
That shall stand when you are gone.
  Ask not that another see
  The meaning of your masonry.

Grind the gem and dig the well,
For what? for whom?—I cannot tell.
  The stone may mark a boundary line,
  The well may flow, the gem may shine.

Be it wage enough for you
To shape them well and set them true.
  Of the future who can tell?
  Work, my friend, and so farewell.
John Jay Chapman

THE ROAD

As one who walks in sleep, up a familiar lane
  I went, my road to discover:
In my head was dark bewilderment and in my heart a pain;
  The branches hung straight over.

At the summit the sky blazed with endless stars, refired
  By the ebbing of the day;
The earth was darkly beautiful and I was very tired.
  There was my road, and nothing more to say.

John Gould Fletcher

COURAGE

Because my joy is less than joy,
  My sorrow more than pain,
I mock the grief that begs for tears
  With laughter and disdain.

I hold the sunlight in my hands
  And hurl it to destroy,
Because my pain is more than pain,
  My laughter less than joy.

When I was young with happiness
  I played at being sad,
The tears I used to mock my joy
  Were all the grief I had.

I do not play at sorrow now,
  Nor shall I weep again—
But I shall smile with less than joy,
  And laugh with more than pain.

Helen Frazee-Bower

A PROUD SONG

The saints who love the Crucified
  Are humble, for their wealth is great.
They may go royally arrayed
  In color of their high estate.

But I who am no saint at all
  And poor in every priceless thing
Put on a draggled coat of pride
  That I may face the world and sing.

Oh, I would gladly lay it by
   As cumbersome and ill to bear,
But, Father, pity poverty,—
   I have no other coat to wear.

Marguerite Wilkinson

THROWN

I'M down, good Fate, you've won the race;
   Bite deep and break a tooth in me;
Nor spit your poison in my face,
   And let me be;
Leave me an hour and come again
With insults new and further pain.

For of your tooth I'll make a pen,
   And of your slaver ink, and will
I bring a joy to being then
   To race you still:
A laughing child with feathered heels
Who shall outspeed your chariot wheels.

Ralph Hodgson

THE BUILDER

The edges of the stones are sharp
But I shall travel far
For I must seek and seek and seek
Wherever such stones are.

I am building me a secret place
With stones that cut my hands;
But I must build and build and build
Until a temple stands.

Caroline Giltinan

ANIMULA VAGULA

NIGHT stirs but wakens not, her breathings climb
To one slow sigh; the strokes of many twelves
From unseen spires mechanically chime,
Mingling like echoes, to frustrate themselves;
My soul, remember Time.

The tones like smoke into the stillness curl,
The slippered hours their placid business ply,
And in thy hand there lies occasion's pearl;
But thou art playing with it absently
And dreaming, like a girl.

A. Y. Campbell

FIRST MIRACLE

THERE was a time when Mother Nature made
My soul's sun, and my soul's shade.

A cloud in the sky could take away
The song in my heart for all day,

And a little lark in a willow-tree
Would mean happiness to me.

My woods would mirror all her whims;
Trees were my strength: their limbs, my limbs.

But, oh, my mother tortured me,
Blowing with wind, and sighing with sea.

I flamed, I withered, I blossomed, I sang,
With her I suffered pang for pang,

Until I said: "I will grow my own tree
Where no natural wind will bother me."

And I grew me a willow of my own heart's strength,
With my will for its width, and my wish for its length:

And I made me a bird of my own heart's fire,
To sing my own sun, and my own desire.

And a vast white circle came in the air,
And the winds around said, "Don't blow there."

I said, "Blow on—blow, blow, blow, blow,
Fill all the sky, above, below,
With tempest, and sleet, and silence, and snow!

"Wherever I go, no matter where,
My bird and my willow-tree are there.

" However you frown, no matter how,
I will sing as I am singing now."

Genevieve Taggard

I'LL BUILD MY HOUSE

I'LL build my house of sticks and stones,
Or lollypops and herring bones,

None other than myself to please—
Of fine, fresh straw or green sage cheese;

I'll build my house of this and that
To suit my pleasure and my cat—

(And keep a donkey and a sheep
And bring them in cold nights to sleep!)

I'll have a bean-stalk I can climb
And never get my meals on time,

But sup when stars are in the sky
On moonlight and a crust of rye,

And breakfast drowsily at noon
On heart's ease and a macaroon. . . .

I'll keep a swarm of bees at home
And live by selling honeycomb,

Or herbs to heal the old and sick,
Or anything that's ripe to pick!

I'll clothe myself in cast-off rags,
In cobwebs or in barley bags,

In oak leaves or a rabbit's skin,
Soft on my nakedness within . . .

The shabbier I am encased
The fruitier my joy will taste.

I'll set my two lips to the air
And carol to the birds' despair;

I'll tramp the lanes and sell my honey
For something more to me than money.

The housewife hiding at her blind
Will tilt the shutters of her mind,

Will call and with a furtive tear
Tell me that my wares are dear—
(But oh, the echo in her ear!)

Some musing morning as I sing
Perhaps I'll catch God listening,

From casement higher than renown
Above the little patchwork town,

In soft enchantment at His sill.
He'll tell His angels to be still,

He'll say to them in tones discreet
That there is singing in the street,

"I know not if the beggar sells
Shoestrings, thread or asphodels,

"Or toy balloons, or what the choice
But Heaven itself is in his voice—"

. . . .

I'll snap my fingers at the earth,
And find out what my song is worth!

Amanda Benjamin Hall

THE EAGLE AND THE MOLE

Avoid the reeking herd,
Shun the polluted flock,
Live like that stoic bird
The eagle of the rock.

The huddled warmth of crowds
Begets and fosters hate;
He keeps, above the clouds,
His cliff inviolate.

When flocks are folded warm,
And herds to shelter run,
He sails above the storm,
He stares into the sun.

If in the eagle's track
Your sinews cannot leap,
Avoid the lathered pack,
Turn from the steaming sheep.

If you would keep your soul
From spotted sight or sound,
Live like the velvet mole;
Go burrow underground.

And there hold intercourse
With roots of trees and stones,
With rivers at their source,
And disembodied bones.

Elinor Wylie

LET NO CHARITABLE HOPE

Now let no charitable hope
Confuse my mind with images
Of eagle and of antelope:
I am in nature none of these.

I was, being human, born alone;
I am, being woman, hard beset;
I lived by squeezing from a stone
The little nourishment I get.

In masks outrageous and austere
The years go by in single file;
But none has merited my fear,
And none has quite escaped my smile.

Elinor Wylie

FRIENDSHIP AND BROTHERHOOD

A CONSECRATION

Not of the princes and prelates with periwigged charioteers
Riding triumphantly laurelled to lap the fat of the years,
Rather the scorned—the rejected—the men hemmed in with
the spears;

The men of the tattered battalion which fights till it dies,
Dazed with the dust of the battle, the din and the cries,
The men with the broken heads and the blood running into
their eyes.

Not the be-medalled Commander, beloved of the throne,
Riding cock-horse to parade when the bugles are blown,
But the lads who carried the koppie and cannot be known.

Not the ruler for me, but the ranker, the tramp of the road,
The slave with the sack on his shoulders pricked on with
the goad,
The man with too weighty a burden, too weary a load.

The sailor, the stoker of steamers, the man with the clout,
The chantyman bent at the halliards putting a tune to the
shout,
The drowsy man at the wheel and the tired lookout.

Others may sing of the wine and the wealth and the mirth,
The portly presence of potentates goodly in girth;—
Mine be the dirt and the dross, the dust and scum of the
earth!

Theirs be the music, the color, the glory, the gold;
Mine be a handful of ashes, a mouthful of mould.

Of the maimed, of the halt and the blind in the rain and the
     cold—
Of these shall my songs be fashioned, my tale be told.
     Amen.

                                        John Masefield

BATTLE–SONG OF FAILURE

We strain toward Heaven and lay hold on Hell;
     With starward eyes we stumble in hard ways,
And to the moments when we see life well
     Succeeds the blindness of bewildered days,—
But what of that? Into the sullen flesh
     Our souls drive home the spur with splendid sting.
Bleeding and soiled, we gird ourselves afresh.
     Forth, and make firm a highway for the King.

The loveless greed the centuries have stored
     In marshy foulness traps our faltering feet.
The sins of men whom punishment ignored
     Like fever in our weakened pulses beat;
But what of that? The shame is not to fail
     Nor is the victor's laurel everything.
To fight until we fall is to prevail.
     Forth, and make firm a highway for the King.

Yea, cast our lives into the ancient slough,
     And fall we shouting, with uplifted face;
Over the spot where mired we struggle now
     Shall march in triumph a transfigured race.
They shall exult where weary we have wept—
     They shall achieve where we have striven in vain—
Leaping in vigor where we faintly crept,
     Joyous along the road we paved with pain.

What though we seem to sink in the morass?
     Under those unborn feet our dust shall sing,
When o'er our failure perfect they shall pass.
     Forth, and make firm a highway for the King!

                                   Amelia Josephine Burr

BATTLE CRY

MORE than half beaten, but fearless,
  Facing the storm and the night;
Breathless and reeling, but tearless,
  Here in the lull of the fight,
I who bow not but before Thee,
  God of the Fighting Clan,
Lifting my fists I implore Thee,
  Give me the heart of a Man!

What though I live with the winners,
  Or perish with those who fall?
Only the cowards are sinners,
  Fighting the fight is all.
Strong is my Foe—he advances!
  Snapped is my blade, O Lord!
See the proud banners and lances!
  O spare me this stub of a sword!

Give me no pity, nor spare me;
  Calm not the wrath of my Foe.
See where he beckons to dare me!
  Bleeding, half-beaten—I go.
Not for the glory of winning,
  Not for the fear of the night;
Shunning the battle is sinning—
  O spare me the heart to fight!

Red is the mist about me;
  Deep is the wound in my side;
"Coward" thou cryest to flout me?
  O terrible Foe, thou hast lied!
Here with my battle before me,
  God of the Fighting Clan,
Grant that the woman who bore me
  Suffered to suckle a Man!

                    John G. Neihardt

THE FALSE HEART

I said to Heart, "How goes it?"
Heart replied:
"Right as a Ribstone Pippin!"
But it lied.

Hilaire Belloc

I THINK OF HIM AS ONE WHO FIGHTS

You think of him as one who fails,
I think of him as one who fights,
Who goes on strange adventurous ways
Through tortured days and dangerous nights.

You know him by the fallen flesh,
The cruel trap where he was caught,
I know him by the lifted brow
And by the Cause for which he fought.

And he went first and he went far
With glorious banners lifted high—
And you and I'll have different ways
Of judging him, until we die.

For if he wins or if he falls—
I know 'tis written in God's laws
That he who fights on the right side
Shall wear the splendor of the Cause.

You know him by the grievous wound
And by the earth on which he lies—
I know him by the patient worth
And the deep sadness of his eyes.

You judge him by the hostile mood
Which was the Devil's battle shout,
I judge him by his quest for God
And by the things he prays about.

And you shall have your place of pride
And lifted banner glittering bright—
But the whole earth shall hear him speak
Of One who raised him in the night.

And you shall stay in Heaven—perchance—
With righteous souls that do not err,
But he shall come to earth again
And comfort with the Comforter.

You think of him as one who fails,
I think of him as one who fights—
Who ventures steep and perilous ways
Through tortured days and dangerous nights.

Anna Hempstead Branch

CLAVERING

I SAY no more for Clavering
    Than I should say of him who fails
To bring his wounded vessel home
    When reft of rudder and of sails;

I say no more than I should say
    Of any other one who sees
Too far for guidance of to-day,
    Too near for the eternities.

I think of him as I should think
    Of one who for scant wages played,
And faintly, a flawed instrument
    That fell while it was being made.

I think of him as one who fared,
    Unfaltering and undeceived,
Amid mirages of renown
    And urgings of the unachieved;

I think of him as one who gave
    To Lingard leave to be amused,
And listened with a patient grace
    That we, the wise ones, had refused;

I think of metres that he wrote
  For Cubit, the ophidian guest:
"What Lilith, or Dark Lady" . . . Well,
  Time swallows Cubit with the rest.

I think of last words that he said
  One midnight over Calverly:
"Good-by—good man." He was not good;
  So Clavering was wrong, you see.

I wonder what had come to pass
  Could he have borrowed for a spell
The fiery-frantic indolence
  That made a ghost of Leffingwell;

I wonder if he pitied us
  Who cautioned him till he was gray
To build his house with ours on earth
  And have an end of yesterday;

I wonder what it was we saw
  To make us think that we were strong;
I wonder if he saw too much
  Or if he looked one way too long.

But when were thoughts or wonderings
  To ferret out the man within?
Why prate of what he seemed to be,
  And all that he might not have been?

He clung to phantoms and to friends,
  And never came to anything.
He left a wreath on Cubit's grave.
  I say no more for Clavering.

               Edwin Arlington Robinson

JERICHO

Jericho, Jericho,
Round and round the walls I go
Where they watch with scornful eyes,
Where the captained bastions rise;

Heel and toe, heel and toe,
Blithely round the walls I go.

Jericho, Jericho,
Round and round the walls I go . . .
All the golden ones of earth
Regal in their lordly mirth . . .
Heel and toe, heel and toe,
Round and round the walls I go.

Jericho, Jericho,
Blithely round the walls I go,
With a broken sword in hand
Where the mighty bastions stand;
Heel and toe, heel and toe,
Hear my silly bugle blow.

Heel and toe, heel and toe,
Round the walls of Jericho . . .
Past the haughty golden gate
Where the emperor in state
Smiles to see the ragged show
Round and round the towers go.

Jericho, Jericho,
Round and round and round I go . . .
All their sworded bodies must
Lie low in their towers' dust . . .
Heel and toe, heel and toe,
Blithely round the walls I go.

Heel and toe, heel and toe,—
I will blow a thunder note
From my brazen bugle's throat
Till the sand and thistle know
The leveled walls of Jericho,
Jericho, Jericho, Jericho. . . .

Willard Wattles

IMPRISONED

I HAVE walked always in a veil.
A clinging shroud encircles me,
Steel-strong, yet yielding, and too frail
For any eye to see.

No blow can rend it, and no knife
Can slash the subtle formless thing.
It shuts me in with my own life
Past hope or questioning.

If I reach out my hand to touch
Some meeting hand of god or man,
The veil gives backward just so much
As my arm's length can span.

I cannot hope to loose its hold
Till I am free of transient suns.
I grow more separate in its fold
With every year that runs.

And yet I cannot be content.
I cry out like a lonely child;
I struggle, but my strength is spent;
I am not reconciled.

Oh, brother, whom I cannot reach,
Not willingly I pass you by!
My heart is clumsy, and my speech,
But, brother, hear my cry!

Eunice Tietjens

MAGNETS

A FAR look in absorbed eyes, unaware
Of what some gazer thrills to gather there;
   A happy voice, singing to itself apart,
   That pulses new blood through a listener's heart;

Old fortitude; and, 'mid an hour of dread,
The scorn of all odds in a proud young head;—
  These are themselves, and being but what they are,
  Of others' praise or pity have no care,
Yet still are magnets to another's need.
Invisibly as wind, blowing stray seed,
  Life breathes on life, though ignorant what it brings,
  And spirit touches spirit on the strings
Where music is: courage from courage glows
In secret; shy powers to themselves unclose;
  And the most solitary hope, that gray
  Patience has sistered, ripens far away
In young bosoms. Oh, we have failed and failed,
And never knew if we or the world ailed,
  Clouded and thwarted; yet perhaps the best
  Of all we do and dream of lives unguessed.

Laurence Binyon

SOULS

MY soul goes clad in gorgeous things,
  Scarlet and gold and blue.
And at her shoulder sudden wings
  Like long flames flicker through.

And she is swallow-fleet, and free
  From mortal bonds and bars.
She laughs, because eternity
  Blossoms for her with stars!

O folk who scorn my stiff gray gown,
  My dull and foolish face,
Can ye not see my soul flash down,
  A singing flame through space?

And folk, whose earth-stained looks I hate,
  Why may I not divine
Your souls, that must be passionate,
  Shining and swift, as mine?

Fannie Stearns Gifford

THE GLORIOUS GAME

I GO about dumbfoundedly, and show a dullard's glance,
But in my mind are spangles, and music and a dance,—
Tra-la, the hid romance!

And I suspect, O brothers (and sisters, drab and prim),
'Tis quite the same with all of you, with every her and him
That goes in masking-trim.

The whole world hides the truth; and, faith, it is a parlous
    shame
To make a pale-faced misery of such a glorious game,—
With all of us to blame.

So let us be like mummers who grin and lift their lays
And kick their heels at heaven a hundred happy ways,
Sky-larking down the days!

Richard Burton

ROSA ROSARUM

GIVE me, O friend, the secret of thy heart
    Safe in my breast to hide,
So that the leagues which keep our lives apart
    May not our souls divide.

Give me the secret of thy life to lay
    Asleep within mine own,
Nor dream that it shall mock thee any day
    By any sign or tone.

Nay, as in walking through some convent-close,
    Passing beside a well,
Oft have we thrown a red and scented rose
    To watch it as it fell;

Knowing that never more the rose shall rise
    To shame us, being dead;
Watching it spin and dwindle till it lies
    At rest, a speck of red—

Thus, I beseech thee, down the silent deep
  And darkness of my heart,
Cast thou a rose; give me a rose to keep,
  My friend, before we part.

For, as thou passest down thy garden-ways,
  Full many a blossom there
Groweth for thee: lilies and laden bays,
  And rose and lavender.

But down the darkling well one only rose
  In all the year is shed;
And o'er that chill and secret wave it throws
  A sudden dawn of red.
                              A. Mary F. Robinson

TO MY FRIEND, GROWN FAMOUS

THE mail has come from home,—
From home that still remembers,—to Japan.
My tiny maid, as faultless as a fan,
Bows in the doorway. "Honorable letters,"
She says, "have kindly come."
And smiles, knowing the fetters
That bind me still.

And all my mail to-day is full of you.
"His name," says one, "is sounding still and sounding."
And someone else, "It is astounding;
I never knew the public chatter worse.
Nineteen editions for a book of verse!"
And all the printed pages glitter, too,
With you;
With your stark vision and cold fire,
Your singing truth, your vehement desire
To cut through lies to life.
These move behind the printed echoes here,
The paper strife,
The scurry of small pens about your name,
Measuring, praising, blaming by the same

Tight rule of thumb that makes their own
Inadequacy known.
And as I read a phrase leaps clear
From your own letter: "I am tired," you say,
"Of men who talk and talk and dare not live
But take their orgasms in speech!"
Yes, that would be your way
To take the critics.   It is you who give,
Not they;
And safe beyond their reach
Huge, careless, Rabelaisian, you pass by
Watching their squirming with amusèd eye.

Here as I sit,
My paper house-side slid away
And all my chamber open to the rain,
I feel a haunting, exquisite
Gray shadow of a pain.
Beauty has part in it, and loneliness,
And the far call of home—and thoughts of you
In the rain of spring.
Here in this land of frozen loveliness,
Of artistry complete, where each small thing
Minutely, preciously, is perfect,
I have grown hungry for the sight of you
Who are not perfect,
Who are big and free
And largely vulgar like the peasantry,
And full of sorrows for mankind.
I cannot find
Your spirit in this land.   The little tree
Tortured and dwarfed—oh! beautiful I know
In the gray slanting rain,
But tortured even so—
The little pine tree in my garden close
Is symbol of the soul that grows
Within this patient cult of loveliness.
You would not understand
Would care far less
For the pale, silvered shadows of this land

That make it dear to me.
Yet when I see
Your clear handwriting march across the page,
And your brave spirit of a tonic age
Blow sharp across the spring
I smother here a little;
This conscious beauty is so light, so brittle,
So frail a thing!

But you are free!   "Go out," your letter says,
"Go drink life to the lees.
See the round world!   Watch where Lord Buddha sits
Beneath the tree; and see where Jesus walked
And talked.
See where Aspasia and Pericles
Have visited together, and where Socrates
Leaned on the wall. . . .
Go out, my friend, and see—
And then come back and tell it all to me!"

That, too, is like you; "Tell it all to me."
I feel your spirit searching hungrily
Each human being for the stuff of life,
The sharp blue flame below the smoke,
The authentic cry
That all our mouthing cannot choke.
Your hunger is for life, for life!
And you have understanding, and the power
To pierce the husk of words; to take an hour
Hot from the crisis of a soul
And live it in another, and so grow
Greater by each of us who only know
A part—and you the whole.

O friend, my friend, it's good to feel you there,
A solvent for all small hypocrisies,
A white and steady flare
That beacons over such confusing seas
To bring me truth.
It's good to know that youth

And eyes and lips are only half the tie;
That, though all listening peoples claim you now,
Your spirit still
Holds some small emptiness that I,
And only I, can fill.

So take my homage, friend, with all the rest.
It will not hurt you—you are much too wise—
And ride the world, and battle at the crest,
As at the ebb, with lies.
Yet if you weary sometimes of the praise
And greatness palls a little in the dusk,
I shall be waiting as in other days.
Then you can strip your world-ways like a husk,
And friendship will make wide her wicket gate
Of twilit gardens, sweet and intimate,
And we will talk of simple homely things,
Of flowers, of laughter, of the flash of wings. . . .

Eunice Tietjens

IMMORTALITY

BATTLES nor songs can from oblivion save,
    But Fame upon a white deed loves to build;
From out that cup of water Sidney gave,
    Not one drop has been spilled.

Lizette Woodworth Reese

PEER GYNT

WHEN he was young and beautiful and bold
We hated him, for he was very strong.
But when he came back home again, quite old,
And wounded too, we could not hate him long.

For kingliness and conquest pranced he forth
Like some high-stepping charger bright with foam.
And south he strode and east and west and north
With need of crowns and never need of home.

The Comrade

The Comrade 753

Enraged we heard high tidings of his strength
And cursed his long forgetfulness. We swore
That should he come back home some eve at length,
We would deny him, we would bar the door!

And then he came. The sound of those tired feet!
And all our home and all our hearts are his,
Where bitterness, grown weary, turns to sweet,
And envy, purged by longing, pity is.

And pillows rest beneath the withering cheek,
And hands are laid the battered brows above,
And he whom we had hated, waxen weak,
First in his weakness learns a little love.

Charles Hamilton Sorley

AN OLD STORY

STRANGE that I did not know him then,
    That friend of mine!
I did not even show him then
    One friendly sign;

But cursed him for the ways he had
    To make me see
My envy of the praise he had
    For praising me.

I would have rid the earth of him
    Once, in my pride. . . .
I never knew the worth of him
    Until he died.

Edwin Arlington Robinson

THE COMRADE

CALL me friend or foe
    Little I care!
I go with all who go
    Daring to dare.

I am the force,
  I am the fire,
I am the secret source
  Of desire.

I am the urge,
  The spur and thong:
Moon of the tides that surge
  Into song.

Call me friend or foe,
  Little care I!
I go with all who go
  Singing to die.

Call me friend or foe. . . .
  Taking to give,
I go with all who go
  Dying to live.

Lee Wilson Dodd

LOSERS

If I should pass the tomb of Jonah
I would stop there and sit for awhile;
Because I was swallowed one time deep in the dark
And came out alive after all.

If I pass the burial spot of Nero
I shall say to the wind, "Well, well!"—
I who have fiddled in a world on fire,
I who have done so many stunts not worth doing.

I am looking for the grave of Sinbad too.
I want to shake his ghost-hand and say,
"Neither of us died very early, did we?"

And the last sleeping-place of Nebuchadnezzar—
When I arrive there I shall tell the wind:
"You ate grass: I have eaten crow—
Who is better off now or next year?"

Jack Cade, John Brown, Jesse James,
There too I could sit down and stop for awhile.
1 think I could tell their headstones:
"God, let me remember all good losers."

I could ask people to throw ashes on their heads
In the name of that sergeant at Belleau Woods,
Walking into the drumfires, calling his men,
"Come on, you——! Do you want to live forever?"

Carl Sandburg

PAWNBROKERS

GOD bless pawnbrokers!
They are quiet men.
You may go once—
You may go again—
They do not question
As a brother might;
They never say
What they think is right;
They never hint
All you ought to know;
Lay your treasure down,
Take your cash and go,
Fold your ticket up
In a secret place
With your shaken pride
And your shy disgrace,
Take the burly world
By the throat again—
God bless pawnbrokers!
They are quiet men.

Marguerite Wilkinson

A LEADER

THOUGH your eyes with tears were blind,
    Pain upon the path you trod:
Well we knew, the hosts behind,
    Voice and shining of a god.

For your darkness was our day:
  Signal fires, your pains untold
Lit us on our wandering way
  To the mystic heart of gold.

Naught we knew of the high land,
  Beauty burning in its spheres;
Sorrow we could understand
  And the mystery told in tears.

A. E.

THE SERVICE

I was the third man running in a race,
And memory still must run it o'er and o'er:
The pounding heart that beat against my frame;
The wind that dried the sweat upon my face
And turned my throat to paper creased and sore;
The jabbing pain that sharply went and came.

My eyes saw nothing save a strip of road
That flaunted there behind the second man;
It swam and blurred, yet still it lay before.
My legs seemed none of mine, but rhythmic strode
Unconscious of my will that urged, "You can!"
And cried at them to make one effort more.

Then suddenly there broke a wave of sound,—
Crowds shouting when the first man struck the tape;
And then the second roused that friendly din;
While I—I stumbled forward and the ground
All wavered 'neath my feet, while men agape,
But silent, saw me as I staggered in.

As sick in heart and flesh I bent my head,
Two seized me and embraced me, and one cried,
"Your thudding footsteps held me to the grind."
And then the winner, smiling wanly, said,
"No dream of records kept me to my stride—
I dreaded you two thundering behind!"

Burges Johnson

SCATHELESS

Lord, I am humbled by the great,
  For all the great have deadly foes;
There is a worm would like to eat
  The heart of every perfect rose;

There is a crow would like to pick
  The bones of every glory bare;
My enemies are gentle souls
  And for my death they do not care.

My enemies still suffer me
  And I am scatheless to this hour.
Men hunt upon the hills of time
  A nobler quarry to devour.

Marguerite Wilkinson

THE MARKET TOWN

When I was ill in the long ago
  That lately seems so nigh,
They placed a mirror before me so
  I could see the passersby;
Market women and trading men,
  Children and ballad singers,
Farmers coming to town and then
  The noisy auction ringers

With their "Hark, ye!   Hark, ye!
At twelve o' the clock in Ballinaree—
Twenty acres of turbary land
To be sold at the fall of the hand."

Again I'm buried deep in bed,
  But in this looking glass
I see the folk who passed instead
  Of those who now may pass;

Market women and trading men,
   Children and auction ringers,
Farmers coming to town and then
   The welcome ballad singers

With their "Hark, ye!   Hark, ye!
The Blushing Rose of Ballinaree—
Twenty verses of a ballad made
For the best of the Dublin trade."

Maybe a moon in another sky
   Shall be as a mirror so
It might reflect the world which I
   Would still desire to know;
Market women and trading men,
   Children and ballad singers,
Farmers coming to town and then
   The rambling notice ringers

With their "Hark, ye!   Hark, ye!
At twelve o' the clock in Ballinaree—
A ploughing match with a guinea's prize
For the skill of your hands and eyes."

Francis Carlin

MY ESTATE

I HAVE four loves, four loves are mine,
   My wife who makes all beauty be,
Tom Squire and Master Candleshine,
   And then my gray dog Timothy.

My wife makes bramble-berry pies,
   And she is bright as bramble dew,
She knows the way the weather flies,
   And tells me everything to do.

Tom Squire he is my neighbor man,
   His apples fall upon my grass,
And in the morning, when we can,
   We say good-morning as we pass.

And Master Candleshine the True,
  Considering some fault of mine,
Says—"Had it been for me to do,
  It had been hard for Candleshine."

When I have thought all things that be,
  And drop the latch and climb the stair,
And want an eye for company,
  My gray dog Timothy is there.

My loves are one and two and three
  And four they are, good loves of mine,
Tom Squire, my gray dog Timothy,
  My wife and Master Candleshine.

John Drinkwater

THE ROAD

BECAUSE our lives are cowardly and sly,
Because we do not dare to take or give,
Because we scowl and pass each other by,
We do not live; we do not dare to live.

We dive, each man, into his secret house,
And bolt the door, and listen in affright,
Each timid man beside a timid spouse,
With timid children huddled out of sight.

Kissing in secret, fighting secretly!
We crawl and hide like vermin in a hole,
Under the bravery of sun and sky,
We flash our meannesses of face and soul.

Let us go out and walk upon the road,
And quit for evermore the brick-built den,
And lock and key, the hidden, sly abode
That separates us from our fellow-men.

And by contagion of the sun we may
Catch at a spark from that primeval fire,
And learn that we are better than our clay,
And equal to the peaks of our desire.

James Stephens

THE DRUG CLERK

THE drug clerk stands behind the counter
Young and dapper, debonair . . .

Before him burn the great unwinking lights,
The hectic stars of city nights,
Red as hell's pit, green as a mermaid's hair.
A queer half-acrid smell is in the air.
Behind him on the shelves in ordered rows
With strange, abbreviated names
Dwell half the facts of life. That young man knows,
Bottled and boxed and powdered here,
Dumb tragedies, deceptions, secret shames,
And comedy, and fear.

Sleep slumbers here, like a great quiet sea
Shrunk to this bottle's compass, sleep that brings
Sweet respite from the teeth of pain
To those poor tossing things
That the white nurses watch so thoughtfully.
And here again
Dwell the shy souls of Maytime flowers
That shall make sweeter still those poignant hours
When wide-eyed youth looks on the face of love.
And, for those others who have found too late
The bitter fruits thereof,
Here are cosmetics, powders, paints,—the arts
That hunted women use to hunt again
With scented flesh for bait.
And here is comfort for the hearts
Of sucking babes in their first teething pain.
Here dwells the substance of huge fervid dreams,
Fantastic, many-colored, shot with gleams
Of ecstasy and madness, that shall come
To some pale, twitching sleeper in a bunk.
And here is courage, cheaply bought
To cure a sick blue funk,
And dearly paid for in the final sum.
Here in this powdered fly is caught

Desire more ravishing than Tarquin's, rape
And bloody-handed murder. And at last
When the one weary hope is past
Here is the sole escape,
The little postern in the house of breath
Where pallid fugitives keep tryst with death.

All this the drug clerk knows and there he stands,
Young and dapper, debonair . . .
He rests a pair of slender hands,
Much manicured, upon the counter there
And speaks: "No, we don't carry no pomade.
We only cater to the high-class trade."

Eunice Tietjens

DRUG STORE

PARDON me, lady, but I wanta ast you,
For God's sake, stop that tappin'! I'll go nuts,
Plain bug-house if I hear that tap-tap-tap
Much longer!
      Now I went and used such language,
I got to tell you why. . . . Well, in the first place,
My business is all shot. Now drugs theirselves
Don't pay much, and the extra stuff, like candy,
Cigars and stationery and et cetery,
Don't make their keep. And that damn soda-fountain—
Excuse me, lady, but I just can't help it! . . .

Some day I'm gointa catch the guy I bought it off—
I'm losin' money every day it's here.
And soda-jerkers—now I can't get none
For love or money, so myself I got to
Mess with them malted milks, banana splits,
And slop like that. And just as doggone sure
As I start workin' on some fine prescription,
The kind I love to mix—got to be careful
The weights is hittin' on that perfect balance—
Why, then some fool wants a marshmallow sundae,
And tap-tap-tap he starts in on the show-case,
And taps and taps till I come runnin' out,

Leavin' the drugs half-done.
                                And that ain't all;
Here's the big trouble—I can't talk good grammar.
People don't think a man that mixes drugs
Can do it right and talk the way I do.
It makes me sick—why have I got to sound
Like a school-teacher?   Why, I know my stuff:
"Registered Pharmacist"—see?   I taught myself,
Workin' at night whiles I was four years clerkin';
And then I took three months down at the U,
And passed a fine exam.   But here's the thing:
I quit the public school in seventh grade,
And never paid no attention to my talk.
So it's the way I tell you—they're suspicious
Because I use such slang.   I try to stop,
But it's too late now.   I found out too late. . . .

I got a dream of what I'll do some day:
I want to quit this drug stuff altogether,
Have a nice office, with a big oak desk,
And sell just real estate.   I'd like to bet
I'd make a clean-up at it.   It'd be swell,
That office . . .
                                But this life is killin' me.
It's the fool questions they keep askin' me!
You see that clock there?   Well, just on a guess
Three times an hour some silly fish comes in here
And calls me out, and asts me, "Is that right?—
Is your clock right? "   Honest to Heaven, lady,
One day I got so sore I took a hammer
And smashed the face in.   And it cost twelve dollars
To fix it.   But I had peace for a week.
Oh, gosh, my nerves! . . . But that's the way it is.
I'm sorry I spoke so rough about that tappin',
But when I get to sellin' real estate,
They'll be no place where folks can take a coin
And tap, and tap, till I come runnin' out.
That's a man's business! . . .
                                If I ever get it. . . .
                                John V. A. Weaver

IN PASSING

THROUGH the dim window, I could see
   The little room—a sordid square
Of helter-skelter penury:
   Piano, whatnot, splintered chair:

It is so small a room that I
   Seemed almost at the woman's side:
Galled jade—too fat for vanity,
   And far too frankly old for pride.

Her greasy apron round her waist;
   The dish cloth by her on the chair:
As though, in some wild headlong haste,
   She has come in and settled there:

Grimly she bends her back and tries
   To stab the keys, with heavy hand;
A child's first finger exercise
   Before her on the music stand.

Roy Helton

A FORTUNE-TELLER

TURNING the secrets from her pack of cards,
Warning of sickness, tracing out a theft,
Guarding from danger as an omen guards,
Her hand grew withered as it grew more deft . . .

Till in the stuffy parlor where she lies,
Now to these clients, neighbors, debtors, friends,
Truest is proven of her prophecies,
"I shall be dead before December ends."

That old man, facing us, who many years
Carried the marvellous message of her art,
Now hear him how he tells us with his tears
The simpler larger wisdom of her heart.

For she was quick to share the good that came,
So that young mothers turned at last and slept
And loafers gruffly reverenced her name—
Yet more than all she gave away she kept,

Kept red geraniums on her window-sill
And a gay garden in that narrow plot
Fenced-in behind her house.   You'll find there still
Her hoe, her rake, her rusty watering-pot.

Bright, in the midst of all these dingy yards,
Her roses, hollyhocks and pansies grew;
As if some happy jester in the cards
Whispered the gayest secret that he knew.

Witter Bynner

HIGH AND LOW

HE stumbled home from Clifden fair
With drunken song, and cheeks aglow.
Yet there was something in his air
That told of kingship long ago.
I sighed—and inly cried
With grief that one so high should fall so low.

He snatched a flower and sniffed its scent,
And waved it toward the sunset sky.
Some old sweet rapture through him went
And kindled in his bloodshot eye.
I turned—and inly burned
With joy that one so low should rise so high.

James H. Cousins

THE PUDDLE

I CURSED the puddle when I found
Unseeing I had walked therein,
Forgetting the uneven ground,
Because my eyes
Were on the skies,
To glean their glory and to win
The sunset's trembling ecstasies.

And then I marked the puddle's face,
When still and quiet grown again,
Was but concerned, as I, to trace
   The wonder spread
   Above its head,
And mark and mirror and contain
The gold and purple, rose and red.

                            Eden Phillpotts

UNREST

A FIERCE unrest seethes at the core
   Of all existing things:
It was the eager wish to soar
   That gave the gods their wings.

From what flat wastes of cosmic slime,
   And stung by what quick fire,
Sunward the restless races climb!—
   Men risen out of mire!

There throbs through all the worlds that are
   This heart-beat hot and strong,
And shaken systems, star by star,
   Awake and glow in song.

But for the urge of this unrest
   These joyous spheres were mute;
But for the rebel in his breast
   Had man remained a brute.

When baffled lips demanded speech,
   Speech trembled into birth—
(One day the lyric word shall reach
   From earth to laughing earth.)—

When man's dim eyes demanded light,
   The light he sought was born—
His wish, a Titan, scaled the height
   And flung him back the morn!

From deed to dream, from dream to deed,
　　From daring hope to hope,
The restless wish, the instant need,
　　Still lashed him up the slope!

.　　.　　.　　.　　.　　.　　.　　.

I sing no governed firmament,
　　Cold, ordered, regular—
I sing the stinging discontent
　　That leaps from star to star!

Don Marquis

GOD AND THE STRONG ONES

"We have made them fools and weak!" said the Strong Ones,
　"We have bound them, they are dumb and deaf and blind,
We have crushed them in our hands like a heap of crumbling sands,
　We have left them naught to seek or find:
They are quiet at our feet!" said the Strong Ones,
　"We have made them one with wood and stone and clod;
Serf and laborer and woman, they are less than wise or human!—"
　"*I shall raise the weak!*" saith God.

"They are stirring in the dark!" said the Strong Ones,
　"They are struggling, who were moveless like the dead,
We can hear them cry and strain hand and foot against the chain,
　We can hear their heavy upward tread. . . .
What if they are restless?" said the Strong Ones,
　"What if they have stirred beneath the rod?
Fools and weak and blinded men, we can tread them down again—"
　"*Shall ye conquer Me?*" saith God.

"They are evil and are brutes!" said the Strong Ones,
　"They are ingrates of the ease and peace we give,
We have stooped to them in grace and they mock us to our face—
　How shall we give light to them and live?

They are all unworthy grace!" said the Strong Ones,
  "They that cowered at our lightest look or nod—"
"This that now ye pause and weigh of your grace may prove
    one day
   Mercy that ye need!" saith God.

"They will trample us and bind!" said the Strong Ones;
  "We are crushed beneath the blackened feet and hands,
All the strong and fair and great they will crush from out
    the state,
  They will whelm it with the weight of pressing sands—
They are maddened and are blind!" saith the Strong Ones,
  "Black decay has come where they have trod,
They will break the world in twain if their hands are on the
    rein—"
  "What is that to Me?" saith God.

"Ye have made them in their strength, who were Strong Ones,
  Ye have only taught the blackness ye have known,
These are evil men and blind?—Ay, but molded to your mind!
  How shall ye cry out against your own?
Ye have held the light and beauty I have given
  Far above the muddied ways where they must plod,
Ye have builded this your lord with the lash and with the sword—
  Reap what ye have sown!" saith God.

               Margaret Widdemer

THE CHILDREN'S GHOSTS

HEROD sitting on his throne,
Lest he should hear the children moan,
And lose awhile his careless ease,
Bade sackbuts play and psalteries,
Bade flutes and tabors take their part
To cheat the terror in his heart,
To drown the wailing of a child
That came upon the storm wind wild.

Herod, lord of armèd hosts,
Had fear of murdered babies' ghosts.
He bade his dancing girls appear
That they might dance away his fear.

He called his nobles in to dine
And drugged his sullen soul with wine.
But when at night he lay asleep
The little ghosts drew near to weep. . . .

So old and new the sacrifice
When innocents must pay the price.
Age after age the children give
Their lives that Herod still may live—
They shiver naked in the cold
That he may dress in cloth of gold.
Piteous and pale for lack of bread
They starve to keep his table spread.

Now Herod bids you turn away
Lest, through your jazz-bands loud and gay,
The Eastern wind should hear the cry
Of starving babies doomed to die.
He bids you mothers take no heed
Of all the mothers' hearts that bleed,
But turn the spectre from the door
And lay up food and clothes in store.

But if you be not Herod's kin
The little ghosts will enter in,
Will take your hands and unafraid
Tell you their tale and crave your aid:
"No longer now we suffer pain,
But let these others laugh again.
Make haste!   Before it is too late!
For Death stands knocking at the gate!"

Winifred M. Letts

THE PAWNS

PURPLE robed, with crownèd hair,
Cæsar sits in a golden chair,
And a proud cold Queen beside him there.
Knights in armor, many and tall,
And the holy Bishops throng the hall;
Why trouble your head with the pawns at all,
Iscariot?

He sits at the chess and he plays with skill
On a board far flung over river and hill,
And many a pawn works out his will.
At the chess of war to be bold is wise,
And little he recks of sacrifice:—
For what are a pawn or two in our eyes,
Iscariot?

Years agone, and a world away
Lived One who did not praise the play,
And He loved the pawns the best, men say.
And He damned the pieces for their pride:
So you sold Him to be crucified,
And bared unto the spear His side,
Iscariot.

You sold Him and you thought Him slain,
And the old proud game begins again,
And Cæsar plays with might and main.
But a hidden Player has the Black,
And the craft is foiled and the White attack,
Move by move, is beaten back,
Iscariot.

Knight nor Bishop can resist
The pawns of this Antagonist
Whose countenance is dark with mist.
The game goes on and will not wait,
Cæsar is gripped in a deadly strait—
What if the pawns should give checkmate,
Iscariot?

Frank Betts

THE TIME–CLOCK

I

" Tick-tock! Tick-tock!"
Sings the great time-clock.
And the pale men hurry
And flurry and scurry

To punch their time
Ere the hour shall chime.
"Tick-tock! Tick-tock!"
Sings the stern time-clock.

"It—is—time—you—were—come!"
Says the pendulum.
"Tick-tock! Tick-tock!"
Moans the great time-clock.
They must leave the heaven
Of their beds. . . . It is seven,
And the sharp whistles blow
In the city below.
They can never delay—
If they're late, they must pay.
"God help them!" I say.
But the great time-clock
Only says, "Tick-tock!"

They are chained, they are slaves
From their birth to their graves!
And the clock
Seems to mock
With its awful "tick-tock!"
There it stands at the door
Like a brute, as they pour
Through the dark little way
Where they toil night and day.
They are goaded along
By the terrible song
Of whistle and gong,
And the endless "Tick-tock!"
Of the great time-clock.
"Tick-tock! Tick-tock!"
Runs the voice of the clock.

II

Some day it will cease!
They will all be at peace,

And dream a new dream
Far from shuttle and steam.
And whistles may blow,
And whistles may scream—
They will smile—even so,
And dream their new dream.

But the clock will tick on
When their bodies are gone;
And others will hurry,
And scurry and worry,
While "Tick-tock! Tick-tock!"
Whispers the clock.

"Tick-tock! Tick-tock!
Tick-tock! Tick-tock!"
Forever runs on the song of the clock!

Charles Hanson Towne

THE SHOE FACTORY

Song of the Knot-Tier

THEY told me
   When I came
That this would be drudgery,
   Always the same
Things over and over,
   Day after day—
The same swift movement
   In the same small way.

Pick up,
   Place,
      Push,
         And it's tied.
Take off,
   Cut,
      And put
         It aside.

Over and over,
    In rhythmical beat—
Some say it is drudgery,
    But to me it is sweet.

Pick up,
    Place,
        Push,
            And it's tied.
Outdoors
    The sky
        Is so blue
            And so wide!

It's a joyous song
    Going steadily on,
Marching in measures
    Till the day is gone.

Pick up,
    Place,
        Push,
            And it's tied.
Soon end
    Of day
        Will bring him
            To my side.

Oh, I love the measures
    Singing so fast,
Speeding happy hours
    Till he comes at last!

                                    Ruth Harwood

THE BIRD AND THE TREE

BLACKBIRD, blackbird in the cage,
There's something wrong to-night.
Far off the sheriff's footfall dies,
The minutes crawl like last year's flies
Between the bars, and like an age
The hours are long to-night.

The sky is like a heavy lid
Out here beyond the door to-night.
What's that?   A mutter down the street.
What's that?   The sound of yells and feet.
For what you didn't do or did
You'll pay the score to-night.

No use to reek with reddened sweat,
No use to whimper and to sweat.
They've got the rope; they've got the guns,
They've got the courage and the guns;
And that's the reason why to-night;
No use to ask them any more.
They'll fire the answer through the door—
You're out to die to-night.

There where the lonely cross-road lies,
There is no place to make replies;
But silence, inch by inch, is there,
And the right limb for a lynch is there;
And a lean daw waits for both your eyes,
Blackbird.

Perhaps you'll meet again some place.
Look for the mask upon the face:
That's the way you'll know them there—
A white mask to hide the face.
And you can halt and show them there
The things that they are deaf to now,
And they can tell you what they meant—
To wash the blood with blood.   But how
If you are innocent?

Blackbird singer, blackbird mute,
They choked the seed you might have found.
Out of a thorny field you go—
For you it may be better so—
And leave the sowers of the ground
To eat the harvest of the fruit,
Blackbird.

                                    Ridgely Torrence

THE SCARLET THREAD

" Behold, when we come to the land, thou shalt bind this line of scarlet thread in the window which thou hast let us down by."—Joshua, 2:18.

RED as the lips of Rahab,
  Harlot of Jericho,
Hung the thread from her casement
  Ages on ages ago!

Over the fire and slaughter
  Shone the cord's rich flame:
Out of her ruined city
  Rahab, the shielded, came!

Swiftly the spinners of evil
  Gathered the thread and spun:
Nightly robed in its color
  Daughters of Babylon!

How its riotous tangles
  Twisted dancer and priest!
Twined the groves of Astarte;
  Girdled the emperor's feast!

Solomon, from his window,
  Watching Jerusalem,
Mused on the subtle woman
  Flaunting her scarlet hem!

Men go marching to battle—
  Suddenly flares from a door,
Deadlier than their foemen,
  Crimson that Rahab wore!

Yea, and the spindles that fashioned
  Nineveh's red attire
Spun for our present cities
  The halter of desire!

Then is the thread so woven
  Into the web of the race
That, age through age, we must bear it
  Down to the Judgment Place?

When will our spirits sicken
  Of weaving the cloth of doom?
When will the God within us
  Shatter its shuttle and loom?

Daniel Henderson

SONG OF THE NEW WORLD

I SING the song of a new Dawn waking,
  A new wind shaking the children of men.
I say the hearts that are nigh to breaking
  Shall leap with gladness and live again.
Over the woe of the world appalling,
  Wild and sweet as a bugle cry,
Sudden I hear a new voice calling—
  "Beauty is nigh!"

Beauty is nigh! Let the world believe it.
  Love has covered the fields of dead.
Healing is here! Let the earth receive it,
  Greeting the Dawn with lifted head.
I sing the song of the sin forgiven,
  The deed forgotten, the wrong undone.
Lo, in the East, where the dark is riven,
  Shines the rim of the rising sun.

Healing is here! O brother, sing it!
  Laugh, O heart, that has grieved so long.
Love will gather your woe and fling it
  Over the world in waves of song.
Hearken, mothers, and hear them coming—
  Heralds crying the day at hand.
Faint and far as the sound of drumming,
  Hear their summons across the land.

Look, O fathers! Your eyes were holden—
    Armies throng where the dead have lain.
Fiery steeds and chariots golden—
    Gone is the dream of soldiers slain.
Sing, O sing of a new world waking,
    Sing of creation just begun.
Glad is the earth when morn is breaking—
    Man is facing the rising sun!

Angela Morgan

COURAGE, ALL

OLD gods, avaunt! The rosy East is waking,
And in the dawn your shapes of clay are shaking:
Ye broke men's hearts, and now your own are breaking.

Over all lands a wingèd hope is flying:
It goes without reproof, without replying:
It bears God's courage to the dulled and dying.

The rusted chain that bound the world is broken;
A new strange star pricks down the night for token;
And the Great Word is waiting to be spoken!

Edwin Markham

RÉVEILLE

COME forth, you workers!
Let the fires go cold—
Let the iron spill out, out of the troughs—
Let the iron run wild
Like a red bramble on the floors—
Leave the mill and the foundry and the mine
And the shrapnel lying on the wharves—
Leave the desk and the shuttle and the loom—
Come,
With your ashen lives,
Your lives like dust in your hands.

I call upon you, workers,
It is not yet light
But I beat upon your doors.

Réveille

You say you await the Dawn
But I say you are the Dawn.
Come, in your irresistible unspent force
And make new light upon the mountains.

You have turned deaf ears to others—
Me you shall hear.
Out of the mouths of turbines,
Out of the turgid throats of engines,
Over the whistling steam,
You shall hear me shrilly piping.
Your mills I shall enter like the wind,
And blow upon your hearts,
Kindling a slow fire.

They think they have tamed you, workers—
Beaten you to a tool
To scoop up hot honor
Till it be cool—
But out of the passion of the red frontiers
A great flower trembles and burns and glows
And each of its petals is a people.

Come forth, you workers—
Clinging to your stable
And your wisp of warm 'straw—
Let the fires grow cold,
Let the iron spill out of the troughs,
Let the iron run wild
Like a red bramble on the floors. . . .

As our forefathers stood on the prairies
So let us stand in a ring,
Let us tear up their prisons like grass
And beat them to barricades—
Let us meet the fire of their guns
With a greater fire,
Till the birds shall fly to the mountains
For one safe bough.

Lola Ridge

COMRADE JESUS

THANKS to Saint Matthew, who had been
At mass-meetings in Palestine,
We know whose side was spoken for
When Comrade Jesus had the floor.

"Where sore they toil and hard they lie,
Among the great unwashed, dwell I.—
The tramp, the convict, I am he;
Cold-shoulder him, cold-shoulder me."

By Dives' door, with thoughtful eye,
He did to-morrow prophesy:—
"The Kingdom's gate is low and small;
The rich can scarce wedge through at all."

"A dangerous man," said Caiaphas,
"An ignorant demagogue, alas!
Friend of low women, it is he
Slanders the upright Pharisee."

For law and order, it was plain,
For Holy Church, he must be slain.
The troops were there to awe the crowd:
Mob violence was not allowed.

Their clumsy force with force to foil
His strong, clean hands he would not soil.
He saw their childishness quite plain
Between the lightnings of his pain.

Between the twilights of his end,
He made his fellow-felon friend:
With swollen tongue and blinded eyes,
Invited him to Paradise.

Ah, let no Local him refuse!
Comrade Jesus hath paid his dues.
Whatever other be debarred,
Comrade Jesus hath his red card.

Sarah N. Cleghorn

PROEM

From "Fires"

Snug in my easy chair,
I stirred the fire to flame.
Fantastically fair,
The flickering fancies came,
Born of heart's desire:
Amber woodland streaming;
Topaz islands dreaming,
Sunset-cities gleaming,
Spire on burning spire;
Ruddy-windowed taverns;
Sunshine-spilling wines;
Crystal-lighted caverns
Of Golconda's mines;
Summers, unreturning;
Passion's crater yearning;
Troy, the ever-burning;
Shelley's lustral pyre;
Dragon-eyes, unsleeping;
Witches' cauldrons leaping;
Golden galleys sweeping
Out from sea-walled Tyre:
Fancies, fugitive and fair,
Flashed with singing through the air;
Till, dazzled by the drowsy glare,
I shut my eyes to heat and light;
And saw, in sudden night,
Crouched in the dripping dark,
With steaming shoulders stark,
The man who hews the coal to feed my fire.

Wilfrid Gibson

TO THE FOUR COURTS, PLEASE

The driver rubbed at his nettly chin
With a huge, loose forefinger, crooked and black,
And his wobbly, violet lips sucked in,
And puffed out again and hung down slack:

One fang shone through his lop-sided smile,
In his little pouched eye flickered years of guile.

And the horse, poor beast, it was ribbed and forked,
And its ears hung down, and its eyes were old,
And its knees were knuckly, and as we talked
It swung the stiff neck that could scarcely hold
Its big, skinny head up—then I stepped in,
And the driver climbed to his seat with a grin.

God help the horse and the driver too,
And the people and beasts who have never a friend,
For the driver easily might have been you,
And the horse be me by a different end.
And nobody knows how their days will cease,
And the poor, when they're old, have little of peace.

James Stephens

THE BEGGAR

IF I had a farm, an' no need to be beggin' my bread,
I'd work till my fingers were all wore away to the bone.
It wouldn't be me you would see lyin' long in my bed;
I'd be out by the squeak o' the day, lookin' after my own.

But the pride of industry flies out at the raggedy holes
In a coat an' a trousers an' maybe the half of a shirt.
You rich, let you wear to a shadow your bodies an' souls;
The beggar is happy to lie on his back in the dirt.

H. L. Doak

HAWKS

AND as we walked the grass was faintly stirred;
    We did not speak—there was no need to speak.
Above our heads there flew a little bird,
    A silent one who feared that we might seek
        Her hard-hid nest.

Poor little frightened one!
    If we had found your nest that sunny day
We would have passed it by; we would have gone
    And never looked or frightened you away.

O little bird! there's many have a nest,
  A hard-found, open place, with many a foe;
And hunger and despair and little rest,
  And more to fear than you can know.

  Shield the nests where'er they be,
  On the ground or on the tree;
  Guard the poor from treachery.
                              James Stephens

UPSTREAM

THE strong men keep coming on.
They go down shot, hanged, sick, broken.
They live on fighting, singing,
          lucky as plungers.

The strong men . . . they keep coming on.
The strong mothers pulling them
          from a dark sea, a great prairie,
          a long mountain.

          Call hallelujah, call amen,
          call deep thanks.
The strong men keep coming on.
                              Carl Sandburg

THE MUSIC MAKERS

THE CITY OF THE SOUL

In the salt terror of the stormy sea
There are high altitudes the mind forgets;
And undesired days are hunting nets
To snare the souls that fly Eternity.
But we being gods will never bend the knee,
Though sad moons shadow every sun that sets,
And tears of sorrow be like rivulets
To feed the shadows of Humility.
Within my soul are some mean gardens found
Where drooped flowers are, and unsung melodies,
And all companioning of piteous things.
But in the midst is one high terraced ground,
Where level lawns sweep through the stately trees
And the great peacocks walk like painted kings.

What shall we do, my soul, to please the King?
Seeing he hath no pleasure in the dance,
And hath condemned the honeyed utterance
Of silver flutes and mouths made round to sing.
Along the wall red roses climb and cling,
And oh! my prince, lift up thy countenance,
For there be thoughts like roses that entrance
More than the langors of soft lute-playing.
Think how the hidden things that poets see
In amber eves or mornings crystalline,
Hide in the soul their constant quenchless light,
Till, called by some celestial alchemy,
Out of forgotten depths, they rise and shine
Like buried treasure on Midsummer night.

The fields of Phantasy are all too wide,
My soul runs through them like an untamed thing.
It leaps the brooks like threads, and skirts the ring
Where fairies danced, and tender flowers hide.

The voice of music has become the bride
Of an imprisoned bird with broken wing.
What shall we do, my soul, to please the King,
We that are free, with ample wings untied?
We cannot wander through the empty fields
Till beauty like a hunter hurl the lance.
There are no silver snares and springes set,
Nor any meadow where the plain ground yields.
O let us then with ordered utterance,
Forge the gold chain and twine the silken net.

Each new hour's passage is the acolyte
Of inarticulate song and syllable,
And every passing moment is a bell,
To mourn the death of undiscerned delight.
Where is the sun that made the noon-day bright,
And where the midnight moon?   O let us tell
How the white road curves down into the night.
Only to build one crystal barrier
Against this sea which beats upon our days;
To ransom one lost moment with a rhyme,
Or, if fate cries and grudging gods demur,
To clutch Life's hair, and thrust one naked phrase
Like a lean knife between the ribs of Time.

Alfred Bruce Douglas

I AM THE MOUNTAINY SINGER

I AM the mountainy singer—
The voice of the peasant's dream,
The cry of the wind on the wooded hill,
The leap of the fish in the stream.

Quiet and love I sing—
The carn on the mountain crest,
The *cailin* in her lover's arms,
The child at its mother's breast.

Beauty and peace I sing—
The fire on the open hearth,
The *cailleach* spinning at her wheel,
The plough in the broken earth.

Travail and pain I sing—
The bride on the childing bed,
The dark man laboring at his rhymes,
The ewe in the lambing shed.

Sorrow and death I sing—
The canker come on the corn,
The fisher lost in the mountain loch,
The cry at the mouth of morn.

No other life I sing,
For I am sprung of the stock
That broke the hilly land for bread,
And built the nest in the rock!

Joseph Campbell

A NOTE FROM THE PIPES

PAN, blow your pipes and I will be
Your fern, your pool, your dream, your tree!

I heard you play, caught your swift eye,
"A pretty melody!" called I,
"Hail, Pan!"—and sought to pass you by.

Now blow your pipes and I will sing
To your sure lips' accompanying!

Wild god, who lifted me from earth,
Who taught me freedom, wisdom, mirth,
Immortalized my body's worth,

Blow, blow your pipes!   And from afar
I'll come—I'll be your bird, your star,
Your wood, your nymph, your kiss, your rhyme,
And all your godlike summer-time!

Leonora Speyer

PAN–PIPES

PAN—did you say he was dead, that he'd gone, and for
    good—
Gone with the Dryads and all of the shy forest faces?
Who was it then plucked your sleeve as you came through
    the wood,
What of the whisper that waits in the oddest of places?

    Pan of the garden, the fold,
    Pan of the bird and the beast,
    Kindly, he lives as of old,
    He isn't dead in the least!

Yes, you may find him to-day (how the reeds twitter on,
Tuneful, as once when he followed young Bacchus's leop-
    ards);
Stiffer he may be, perhaps, since our moonlight has shone
Centuries long on his goat-horns—old Pan of the shep-
    herds!

    Brown are his tatters, his tan
    Roughened from tillage and toil,
    Pagan and homely, but Pan—
    Pan of the sap and the soil!

Find him, in fact, in the Park when the first crocus
    cowers;
Cockney is he when it suits him, I know that he knocks
    his
Crook at my window at times o'er sixpenn'orth of flowers,
Gives me his blessing anew with my fresh window-boxes!

    Piping the leaf on the larch,
    Piping the nymphs (in the Row),
    Piping a magic of March,
    Just as he did long ago!

Patrick Chalmers

SONG

" Convalescente di squisiti mali "

My spirit like a shepherd boy
Goes dancing down the lane.
When all the world is young with joy
Must I lie here in pain?

With shepherd's pipe my spirit fled
And cloven foot of Pan;
The mortal bondage he has shed
And shackling yoke of man.

And though he leave me cold and mute,
A traitor to his care,
I smile to hear his honeyed flute
Hang on the scented air.

V. Sackville-West

THAT HARP YOU PLAY SO WELL

O David, if I had
Your power, I should be glad—
    In harping, with the sling,
    In patient reasoning!

Blake, Homer, Job, and you,
Have made old wine-skins new.
    Your energies have wrought
    Stout continents of thought.

But, David, if the heart
Be brass, what boots the art
    Of exorcising wrong,
    Of harping to a song?

The sceptre and the ring
And every royal thing
    Will fail.   Grief's lustiness
    Must cure the harp's distress.

Marianne Moore

PETER QUINCE AT THE CLAVIER

I

JUST as my fingers on these keys
Make music, so the self-same sounds
On my spirit make a music, too.

Music is feeling, then, not sound;
And thus it is that what I feel,
Here in this room, desiring you,

Thinking of your blue-shadowed silk,
Is music. It is like the strain
Waked in the elders by Susanna:

Of a green evening, clear and warm,
She bathed in her still garden, while
The red-eyed elders, watching, felt

The basses of their beings throb
In witching chords, and their thin blood
Pulse pizzicati of Hosanna.

II

In the green water, clear and warm,
Susanna lay.
She searched
The touch of springs,
And found
Concealed imaginings.
She sighed
For so much melody.

Upon the bank she stood
In the cool
Of spent emotions.
She felt, among the leaves,
The dew
Of old devotions.

She walked upon the grass,
Still quavering.
The winds were like her maids,
On timid feet,
Fetching her woven scarves,
Yet wavering.

A breath upon her hand
Muted the night.
She turned—
A cymbal crashed,
And roaring horns.

III

Soon, with a noise like tambourines,
Came her attendant Byzantines.

They wondered why Susanna cried
Against the elders by her side:

And as they whispered, the refrain
Was like a willow swept by rain.

Anon, their lamps' uplifted flame
Revealed Susanna and her shame.

And then, the simpering Byzantines
Fled, with a noise like tambourines.

IV

Beauty is momentary in the mind—
The fitful tracing of a portal;
But in the flesh it is immortal.

The body dies; the body's beauty lives.
So evenings die, in their green going,
A wave, interminably flowing.
So gardens die, their meek breath scenting
The cowl of winter, done repenting.
So maidens die, to the auroral
Celebration of a maiden's choral.

Susanna's music touched the bawdy strings
Of those white elders; but, escaping,
Left only Death's ironic scraping.
Now, in its immortality, it plays
On the clear viol of her memory,
And makes a constant sacrament of praise.

Wallace Stevens

TO MUSIC

Ah Music, thou sweet sprite,
   Thou trammelest my feet
With blossoms of delight
   And tendrils of defeat.

Drugged by thy soft content
   I let the charmed hours pass;
Days without effort spent
   Drift by as in a glass.

Still, still thy strains allure;
   I nothing lack of peace
Save that which makes secure,
   The power to bid thee cease.

But wildered by delight
   I stumble amid flowers,
While in my Dream's despite
   The minutes run to hours.

William Kean Seymour

CHOPIN PRELUDE

Hush! Did you hear
   The cry of a flute?
The fall of a fairy tear
   On a fairy lute?

Hush! Did you mark
   Like a leaping spray
The flash of a silver lark
   In the silver day?

Hush!   Did you find—
   In the wood's deep dream—
The magic of all the wind
   By a magic stream?

Hush!   Did you hear
   The cry of a flute?
The fall of a fairy tear
   On a fairy lute?

Eleanor Norton

AT THE SYMPHONY

THE 'cellos, setting forth apart,
Grumbled and sang, and so the day,
From the low beaches of my heart,
Turned in tranquillity away.

And over weariness and doubt
Rose up the horns like bellied sails,
Like canvas of the soul flung out
To rising and orchestral gales;

Passed on and left irresolute
The ebony, the silver throat . . .
Low over clarinet and flute
Hung heaven upon a single note.

Robert Nathan

TO A SCARLATTI PASSEPIED

STRANGE little tune, so thin and rare,
Like scents of roses of long ago,
Quavering lightly upon the strings
Of a violin, and dying there
With a dancing flutter of delicate wings;
Thy courtly joy and thy gentle woe,
Thy gracious gladness and plaintive fears
Are lost in the clamorous age we know,
And pale like a moon in the lurid day;

A phantom of music, strangely fled
From the princely halls of the quiet dead,
Down the long lanes of the vanished years,
Echoing frailly and far away.

Robert Hillyer

DURING A CHORALE BY CÉSAR FRANCK

In an old chamber softly lit
  We heard the Chorale played,
And where you sat, an exquisite
Image of life and lover of it,
  Death sang a serenade.

I know now, Celia, what you heard,
  And why you turned and smiled.
It was the white wings of a bird
Offering flight, and you were stirred
  Like an adventurous child.

Death sang: "Oh, lie upon your bier,
  Uplift your countenance!"
Death bade me be your cavalier,
Called me to march and shed no tear,
  But sing to you and dance.

And when you followed, lured and led
  By those mysterious wings,
And when I heard that you were dead,
I could not weep. I sang instead,
  As a true lover sings.

To-day a room is softly lit;
  I hear the Chorale played.
And where you come, an exquisite
Image of death and lover of it,
  Life sings a serenade.

Witter Bynner

SPANISH JOHNNY

THE old West, the old time,
  The old wind singing through
The·red, red grass a thousand miles—
  And, Spanish Johnny, you!
He'd sit beside the water ditch
  When all his herd was in,
And never mind a child, but sing
  To his mandolin.

The big stars, the blue night,
  The moon-enchanted lane;
The olive man who never spoke,
  But sang the songs of Spain.
His speech with men was wicked talk—
  To hear it was a sin;
But those were golden things he said
  To his mandolin.

The gold songs, the gold stars,
  The world so golden then;
And the hand so tender to a child—
  Had killed so many men.
He died a hard death long ago
  Before the Road came in—
The night before he swung, he sang
  To his mandolin.

Willa Cather

BELLS IN THE COUNTRY

BELLS in the country,
  They sing the heart to rest
When night is on the high road
  And day is in the west.

And oh! they came to my house
  As soft as beggars shod,
And brought it nearer heaven,
  And maybe nearer God.

Robert Nathan

RESURRECTION

LET'S shake wild music from gray belfry chimes—
    And dance with ghosts and tread our youth anew:
Kissing awake old passion with young rhymes
    Until it lives again a whole night through.

Let's crown these sadder days, these colder nights
    With gold until they also flame and flare
(As once) and let us load with wine and lights
    Our frugal table—there is room to spare.

Let's sing ourselves awake!   There's no surprise
    In sleep. Of us, of us shall it be said:—
They spoke truth once—but all the rest was lies,
    Lived for a hour—then for all time were dead.

                                    Margaret Sackville

WORDS

WORDS, like fine flowers, have their colors too:
What do you say to crimson words and yellow;
And what to opal, emerald, pale blue?
And elvish gules?—he is a glorious fellow.
Think of the purple hung in Elsinore,
Or call it black, and close your eyes to see;
Go look for amber then on Lochlyn shore
And drag a sunbeam out of Arcady.
And who of Rosamund or Rosalind
Can part the rosy-petalled syllables?
For women's names keep murmuring like the wind
The hidden things that none for ever tells.
Last, to forego soft beauty, take the sword,
And see the blue steel redden at the word.

                                    Ernest Rhys

QUICKENING

SUCH little, puny things are words in rhyme:
Poor feeble loops and strokes as frail as hairs;
You see them printed here, and mark their chime,
And turn to your more durable affairs.

Yet on such petty tools the poet dares
To run his race with mortar, bricks and lime,
And draws his frail stick to the point, and stares
To aim his arrow at the heart of Time.
Intangible, yet pressing, hemming in,
This measured emptiness engulfs us all,
And yet he points his paper javelin
And sees it eddy, waver, turn, and fall,
And feels, between delight and trouble torn,
The stirring of a sonnet still unborn.

Christopher Morley

PRETTY WORDS

POETS make pets of pretty, docile words:
I love smooth words, like gold-enameled fish
Which circle slowly with a silken swish,
And tender ones, like downy-feathered birds:
Words shy and dappled, deep-eyed deer in herds,
Come to my hand, and playful if I wish,
Or purring softly at a silver dish,
Blue Persian kittens, fed on cream and curds.
I love bright words, words up and singing early;
Words that are luminous in the dark, and sing;
Warm lazy words, white cattle under trees;
I love words opalescent, cool, and pearly,
Like midsummer moths, and honied words like bees,
Gilded and sticky, with a little sting.

Elinor Wylie

MAKER OF SONGS

TAKE strands of speech, faded and broken;
Tear them to pieces, word from word,
Then take the ravelled shreds and dye them
With meanings that were never heard.

Place them across the loom.   Let wind-shapes
And sunlight come in at the door,
Or let the radiance of raining
Move in silver on the floor.

And sit you quiet in the shadow
Before the subtly idle strands.
Silence, a cloak, will weigh your shoulder;
Silence, a sorrow, fill your hands.

Yet there shall come the stirring . . . Weaver,
Weave well and not with words alone;
Weave through the pattern every fragment
Of glittered breath that you have known.

Hazel Hall

POET SONGS

I

I shall not get my poem done
Or hardly started, even;
But God will understand, I think,
And let me work in Heaven.

Or, if His plan is different
For Love, and Toil, and Art,
He'll let some red, appeasing flower
Burst from my buried heart.

II

I cast my nets in many streams
To catch the silver fish of dreams:
In vain I pant, pursue and dip—
They through the straining meshes slip.

And still I go my bootless ways
Through starry nights and striving days,
With naught to show for all my greed
But bits of shell and water-weed.

III

Dropped feathers from the wings of God
My little songs and snatches are,
So light He does not hear them fall
As He goes by, from star to star.

Dropped feathers from the wings of God
I find, and braid them in my hair;
Men heed them not—they only make
My soul unto herself more fair.

Karle Wilson Baker

PROPHET AND FOOL

FROM twigs of visionary boughs
    I gather berries red and rare.
I twine around my pallid brows
    An insubstantial dryad's hair.

Such song I hear in mission-halls,
    As Jason heard in violet seas,
While bodiless birds sing madrigals
    In tumult round my head and knees.

The draper-shops that light their jets
    To blink along the lanes of mire,
Weave splendors round the muddy sets
    And tip my feet with points of fire.

For I pursue the Golden Fleece
    Down slum-ways magical and cool;
And there I hear the flutes of peace,
    Being a prophet and a fool.

Louis Golding

ARABIA

FAR are the shades of Arabia,
    Where the Princes ride at noon,
'Mid the verdurous vales and thickets,
    Under the ghost of the moon;
And so dark is that vaulted purple
    Flowers in the forest rise
And toss into blossom 'gainst the phantom stars
    Pale in the noonday skies.

Sweet is the music of Arabia
  In my heart, when out of dreams
I still in the thin clear mirk of dawn
  Descry her gliding streams;
Hear her strange lutes on the green banks
  Ring loud with the grief and delight
Of the dim-silked, dark-haired Musicians
  In the brooding silence of night.

They haunt me—her lutes and her forests;
  No beauty on earth I see
But shadowed with that dream recalls
  Her loveliness to me:
Still eyes look coldly upon me,
  Cold voices whisper and say—
"He is crazed with the spell of far Arabia,
  They have stolen his wits away."
                               Walter de la Mare

BEFORE I STUMBLED

  BEFORE I stumbled o'er a song
    In Waterford or Kerry,
  The Winters were as long as long
    But all the Springs were merry;
  For though I could not sing myself,
    The sally-thrush was near me,
  But now my rhymes might fill a shelf
    And not a bird to cheer me.

  Before I learned these music-words
    In Ballyshunock's meadow,
  The days were happy for the birds
    Oft sang within my shadow;
  But now that I can sing a song,
    My shadow wants the thrushes,
  And the Winters are as long as long
    With neither birds nor bushes.

How long ago since I was young
  In Munster of the Music,
Is more than I could tell by tongue;
  But charming Moira Cusack,
Perchance recalls when first my words
  Made songs on her so sweetly
That all the jealous little birds
  Went off from me completely.

Francis Carlin

FLAIL

WHAT do I care for sorrow,
  What if my heart is wrung!
There are words that must be written,
  Songs that must be sung. . . .

Defoe lay down in Newgate,
  Raleigh went to gaol,
Shakespeare, Dante, many yielded
  Under sorrow's flail.

How could a little tinker
  Ever hope to sing
Without prison, or, at least,
  Grief and suffering. . . .

Travail is a bitter thing,
  Let my heart be wrung—
There are words that must be written,
  Songs that must be sung.

Power Dalton

A POET OF ONE MOOD

A POET of one mood in all my lays,
Ranging all life to sing one only love,
Like a west wind across the world I move,
Sweeping my harp of floods mine own wild ways.

The countries change, but not the west wind days
Which are my songs.   My soft skies shine above,
And on all seas the colors of a dove,
And on all fields a flash of silver grays.
I make the whole world answer to my art
And sweet monotonous meanings.   In your ears
I change for ever, bearing, for my part,
One thought that is the treasure of my years,
A small cloud full of rain upon my heart
And in mine arms, clasped, like a child in tears.

Alice Meynell

TEARS FOR SALE

I WEPT a tear
Like a little tune,
A tear for an ache to croon.

A quiet tear
That lay on grief
Like dew on a desperate leaf.

I chose cool words
That spoke of fire,
Metaphor matched desire.

I chose light words
That spoke of pain
In glib, iambic strain.

I chose two nouns
And an adjective
To make my pale tear thrive.

I urged my tear
To an unctuous rhyme,
And sold it for a dime.

I sold the tear
That wept for you;
It's a thing that poets do.

Leonora Speyer

THE POET

I TAKE what never can be taken,
  Touch what cannot be;
I wake what never could awaken,
  But for me.

I go where only winds are going,
  Kiss what fades away;
I know a thing too strange for knowing,
  I, the clay.

Haniel Long

SHE COMES NOT WHEN NOON IS ON THE ROSES

SHE comes not when Noon is on the roses—
  Too bright is Day.
She comes not to the Soul till it reposes
  From work and play.

But when Night is on the hills, and the great Voices
  Roll in from Sea,
By starlight and by candle-light and dreamlight
  She comes to me.

Herbert Trench

THE FOWLER

A WILD bird filled the morning air
  With dewy-hearted song;
I took it in a golden snare
  Of meshes close and strong.

But where is now the song I heard?
  For all my cunning art,
I who would house a singing bird
  Have caged a broken heart.

Wilfrid Gibson

PAIN

PAIN is a beckoning hand,
A voice that seems to say,
"This way!"

Pain is an opening window,
Wide wings that stretch to fly;
Beyond, the sky!

Pain is a light too near,
Blinded, I grope along—
To song!

Leonora Speyer

MY SONG

MY song that was a sword is still.
Like a scabbard I have made
A covering with my will
To sheathe its blade.

It had a flashing tongue of steel
That made old shadows start;
It would not let the darkness heal
About my heart.

Hazel Hall

FOREBODING

How shall I keep April
When my songs are done—
How can I be silent
And still feel the sun?

I, who dreaded silence,
I, who April-long
Kept my heart from breaking
With the cry of song.

How can I hold sunlight
In my hands, like gold,
And bear the pain of silence
When my songs are old?

Hazel Hall

THE SINGER

If I had peace to sit and sing,
Then I could make a lovely thing;
But I am stung with goads and whips,
So I build songs like iron ships.

Let it be something for my song,
If it is sometimes swift and strong.

Anna Wickham

ARDOR

Others make verses of grace.
   Mine are all muscle and sinew.
Others can picture your face.
   But I all the tumult within you.

Others can give you delight,
   And delight I confess is worth giving.
But my songs must tickle and bite
   And burn with the ardor of living.

Gamaliel Bradford

THE SECRET

O little bird, you sing
   As if all months were June;
Pray tell me ere you go
   The secret of your tune?

"I have no hidden word
   To tell, nor mystic art;
I only know I sing
   The song within my heart!"

Arthur Wallace Peach

THE NEW PHYSICIAN

Iᴇ I, who only sing, in other ways
Could bring refreshment to the sick-room days,
When you, who lie and listen, hear the rain
Throbbing against your window like dull pain,

Then would I change my state to many things—
A ray of golden sun, a bird that sings,
A woodland breeze, a wave-beat up the shore—
And come, a thousand memories, to your door.

Then all your weary hours would I fill
With forest odors, music of tumbling rill,
Sun, moon and stars in old Romance's land,
Gleaming where ripples kiss the lisping sand.

There many a whim in human shape should range
Across the stage in many a subtle change;
Laughter and Love—all things but Tragedy;
Beauty-with-Joy the theme of every play!

There birds should lift their matin-song, and earth
To those, her fairest children—flowers—give birth.
And you should see the wondrous forest-dawn,
And the sea's splendor ere the sun is gone.

If I, who only sing, could magic turn,
Conjure in mirror, pour from enchanted urn
Such things made even half-real, 'twere not vain
To be a poet ministering to pain!

Stephen Chalmers

BUILDERS

Wʜᴏ builds him a house of stone or brick,
With a roof against the sky,
And a base where the ivy roots spread thick,
Was born with luck in his eye;
For a house will not start, nor mortar stick,
At a wish or an oath or a sigh.

I know—for I've built as mad men do,
With wishes white and red,
But the wind gets in, the moon shines through,
And the walls shake at my tread;
Who builds him a house of a rhyme or two
Must look for the rain on his head!

Hortense Flexner

THE FLOWER

Our songs are dead, and dead in vain;
To-morrow's song is yet to sing:
Old grayness of the earthy brain,
Out of your dearth what blossoming?
.   .   .   .

It will not come for waiting long,
For asking much it will not be.
No mendicant has snatched a song
From the close palm of Poesy.

She passes, pale with scorn; her eyes
Are cold to wretchedness, her ears
Deaf to all whining. Nor none buys
Her folded ballads, it appears.

She passes, silent. The years pass.
Comes then a month, a day, an hour,
And to some unexpected lass,
Some gangling lad, she flings—*the Flower*.

Lee Wilson Dodd

THE FOILED REAPER

Death, reaping the mad world, his crimson blade
    Wearily swinging,
Saw him and all the beauty that he made,
    And heard him singing

Immortal mockery of Death, and said
    (Wearily swinging)
"Thus lay I low another dreamer's head!"
    And stilled his singing.

But his proud dreams, a lyric throng, arose
   (Ah, deathless singing!) . . .
Lo, there 'tis Death! How piteously he goes,
   Wearily swinging.
                    William Kean Seymour

HISTORY

BECAUSE a woman's lips were red,
Because a woman's breast was white,

One man went forth into the fight
Following where the battle led,
And, girded with resistless might,
He won a kingdom for his right.

Because a woman's lips were red,
Because a woman's breast was white,

One man went forth, his soul alight
With the radiance her beauty shed,
And wandering silent through the night
Dreamed of a song for her delight.

The kingdom now is dust, thereof
Nothing remains but desert sand;
The song through many a foreign land
In many a tongue proclaims its love—

How once a woman's lips were red,
How once a woman's breast was white.
                    Paul Tanaquil

A PINCH OF SALT

WHEN a dream is born in you
  With a sudden clamorous pain,
When you know the dream is true
  And lovely, with no flaw nor stain,
O then, be careful, or with sudden clutch
You'll hurt the delicate thing you prize so much.

Dreams are like a bird that mocks,
  Flirting the feathers of his tail.
When you seize at the salt-box,
  Over the hedge you'll see him sail.
Old birds are neither caught with salt nor chaff:
They watch you from the apple bough and laugh.

Poet, never chase the dream.
  Laugh yourself, and turn away.
Mask your hunger; let it seem
  Small matter if he come or stay;
But when he nestles in your hand at last,
Close up your fingers tight and hold him fast.

                                        Robert Graves

REBEL

SINCE I was a little child
My spirit has been swift and wild,
With pinions flapping hard on fate,
And burnt and blown with love and hate!
I've hated all that's mean and cold,
All that's dusty, tame, and old,
Comfortable lies in books,
Pallid Virtue's sidelong looks,
Fear that gags the jaws of Truth,
Doubt that weights the heels of Youth,
Saints who wash their hands too clean,
And walk where only Saints have been,
And mobs that blabber "Crucify!"
On him who fixes heaven too high:
All of these I seek to blast,
Love's hate shall drive me to the last.
Beyond the murk that swallows me
There is an Eye that follows me,
There is an Ear that waits and strains
To catch the echoes of my pains,
There is a Hand outstretched to take
Utmost toll for each mistake:

These Three have stalked me down the years
To mock the passion of my tears.
I fling you scorn, unholy spy!
Though living give my faith the lie,
Though loving clip the wings of Love,
Though men humanity disprove,
Though all my suns and moons go out,
Though tongues of all the ages shout
That only death may not deceive—
I'll not believe! I'll not believe!
With ardor passionate in my breath
I'll sing my undefeated faith!
O take me, break me, peaceless life!
My soul was born to welcome strife!
O sap my heart of its deep blood,
If blood be Beauty's precious food!
There is no thing I would not give,
There is no hour I dare not live,
There is no hell I'd not explore
To find a hidden heavenly door!
O loveless spy, you wait in vain,
There is no pity in my pain,
If by my living I may prove
Faith and beauty, truth and love!
Twisted, shattered, drained, and wrung,
I shall have sung! I shall have sung!

Irene Rutherford McLeod

THE QUEST

You've been a wanderer, you!
But I've been a wanderer, too!

You've seen the fine smoke rising
Like a fern uncoiled in spring;
And through the shut blind gazing
You've seen the white fire blazing;

But often I've knocked at your door
For the love I've been asking for.

You've borne, in the starlit expanses
Of the hushed night sorrowfully lying,
Gleams, like the furtive glances
Over one who is dying.

You've seen your sorrow enlarge
Like a sphere to solitude's marge;
And you've gone in need of bread
With thoughts in your heart instead.

So you think I've been filled, to be sure?
And you've never guessed how poor
My leisured safety is!

How I slake my thirst with song
To urge and lure me along,—
How I look for your melodies!

Gladys Cromwell

THE POETS

WE need you now, strong guardians of our hearts,
Now, when a darkness lies on sea and land,
When we of weakening faith forget our parts
And bow before the falling of the sand.
Be with us now or we betray our trust,
And say, "There is no wisdom but in death"—
Remembering lovely eyes now closed with dust—
"There is no beauty that outlasts the breath."
For we are growing blind and cannot see
Beyond the clouds that stand like prison-bars,
The changeless regions of our empery,
Where once we moved in friendship with the stars.
O children of the light, now in our grief,
Give us again the solace of belief.

Scudder Middleton

POETS

EARTH, you have had great lovers in your hour,
And little lovers, fearful and struck dumb;
Those who have seen you whole, as from a tower,
And others kneeling where the grass-blades come.

Age after spinning age and day by day,
They toss the dawn between them, as a ball,
Ride Beauty plunging to the whip of May,
And string the stars to light their carnival.
They will not heed the shouting, singing flood
Of lovers gone before them. Echoed cries,
Too like their own may sound, but their wild blood
Is out of hand at seas and moving skies;
The last to come will make his little tune,
And think it new—about the weary moon!

Hortense Flexner

THE POET

In the darkness he sings of the dawning.
In the desert he sings of a rose,
Or of limpid and laughing water
That through green meadows flows.

He flings a Romany ballad
Out through his prison bars
And, deaf, he sings of nightingales
Or, blind, he sings of stars.

And hopeless and old and forsaken,
At last with failing breath
A song of faith and youth and love
He sings at the gates of death.

Mary Sinton Leitch

THE POET

When I look back across the waste of years
And see how little they have left behind
Whose mighty towers, built with sweat and tears,
Are vanished as completely as the wind;
When I consider what fair years they spent
In frantic striving for a useless end,
And how, defeated in success, they went,
Leaving their sons still eager to contend,—

I say, poor lives, thus cast on empty ways!
They sought the iron crown, the place of power;
They forfeited long garlands of sweet days
To wear the diadem a little hour—
While I, at whom their grim lips curled, live on
And will be young when their last dust is gone!

Anita Grannis

MAD BLAKE

BLAKE saw a treeful of angels at Peckham Rye,
And his hands could lay hold on the tiger's terrible heart.
Blake knew how deep is Hell, and Heaven how high,
And could build the universe from one tiny part.
Blake heard the asides of God, as with furrowed brow
He sifts the star-streams between the Then and the Now,
In vast infant sagacity brooding, an infant's grace
Shining serene on his simple, benignant face.

Blake was mad, they say,—and Space's Pandora-box
Loosed its wonders upon him—devils, but angels indeed.
I, they say, am sane, but no key of mine unlocks
One lock of one gate wherethrough Heaven's glory is freed.

And I stand and I hold my breath, daylong, yearlong,
Out of comfort and easy dreaming evermore starting
    awake,—
Yearning beyond all sanity for some echo of that Song
Of Songs that was sung to the soul of the madman, Blake!

William Rose Benét

IN PRAISE OF BEAUTY

EPITAPH FOR THE POET V.

(A HYMN TO INTELLECTUAL BEAUTY)

I

It is ordained,—or so Politian said,—
That he who by some dryad-haunted brook
Or silver bathing-pool or secret glade
Shall, wandering in the dusk, suddenly look
Upon a naked goddess at her bath,—
He from that hour leaves happiness behind,
And doomed to all the splendor of her wrath
Returns as did Teiresias, smitten blind:—
Blind to the common and decaying things,
Blind to the dying summer and the dust,
Blind to the crumpled wall, the broken wings,
The yellow leaf, the sword ruined with rust;
Blind, blind to all save the wild memory
Of Beauty naked against a stormy sky.

II

For Beauty kissed your lips when they were young
And touched them with Her fatal triumphing,
And Her old tune that long ago was sung
Beside your cradle haunts you when you sing.
Wherefore there is no light in any face
To win you from these memories as you roam;
Far though you seek, you shall not find a place
Wears the mysterious twilight-glow of home.
You are an exile to those lonely lands
Far out upon the world's forsaken rim
Where there is never touch of meeting hands,—
Always you must go on, through spaces dim,
Seeking a refuge you can never know—
Wild feet that go where none save Beauty's go!

III

Beauty—what is it? A perfume without name:
A sudden hush where clamor was before:
Across the darkness a faint ghost of flame:
A far sail, seen from a deserted shore.
Out of the dust and terror it can spring
And be, for us, all that there never was:
The sun lives only to illume Her wing
Which rises, hovers, soars, and soon must pass
Into high chaos once again.   But now
While She still lingers round us in mad flight
We shall revive the vigor of our vow,
Assured that all our hopeless love was right,
And watch the wings that fade, pale, and are gone,
Knowing that they are life, and they alone.

XVII

Peculiar ghost!—great and immortal ghost! . . .
How many generations before mine
Have you not haunted? . . . I shall join the host
Of those who, when Proserpina's dark wine
Touches their lips, forget the haze they knew—
The years when—tortured, heaven-dreaming men—
They trusted sleep, the beautiful and true. . . .
We shall forget our need of sleeping, then!
Everything left behind us like a dream
Shall into an ambiguous darkness fade.
Safe, safe at last, beyond the fatal stream,
Upon our brains oblivion shall be laid. . . .
You will be waiting, on that silent shore;
And we shall speak.   We never spoke before.

Arthur Davison Ficke

I LOVE ALL BEAUTEOUS THINGS

I LOVE all beauteous things,
I seek and adore them;
God hath no better praise,
And man in his hasty days
Is honored for them.

I too will something make
And joy in the making!
Although to-morrow it seem
Like the empty words of a dream
Remembered, on waking.

Robert Bridges

WHO WALKS WITH BEAUTY

WHO walks with Beauty has no need of fear;
The sun and moon and stars keep pace with him,
Invisible hands restore the ruined year,
And time, itself, grows beautifully dim.
One hill will keep the footprints of the moon,
That came and went a hushed and secret hour;
One star at dusk will yield the lasting boon;
Remembered Beauty's white, immortal flower.
Who takes of Beauty wine and daily bread,
Will know no lack when bitter years are lean;
The brimming cup is by, the feast is spread,—
The sun and moon and stars his eyes have seen,
Are for his hunger and the thirst he slakes:
The wine of Beauty and the bread he breaks.

David Morton

THE HARVEST OF TIME

TIME winnows beauty with a fiery wind,
Driving the dead chaff from the living grain.
Some day there will be golden sheaves to bind;
There will be wonder in the world again.
There will be lonely phrases born to power,
There will be words immortal and profound;
Though no man knows the coming of the hour,
And no man knows the sower or the ground.
It may be even now the ranging earth
Lifting to glory some forgotten land
Feels there deep beauty quickening to birth,
Sprung from the sowing of a hidden hand.

Beauty endures though towering empires die.
Oh, speed the blown chaff down the smoking sky!

Harold Trowbridge Pulsifer

WILL BEAUTY COME

WILL beauty come when I am old and tired,
Too old for knowing, too old for caring much
How the heart hoped and how the eyes admired,
How the lips sang, how fingers loved to touch?

Will beauty come again when night is falling,
When eyes are dim and weary hands are still,
And call me home—Oh, will I hear her calling
Over the sea again, over the hill?

Robert Nathan

BEAUTY IS EVER TO THE LONELY MIND

BEAUTY is ever to the lonely mind
A shadow fleeting; she is never plain.
She is a visitor who leaves behind
The gift of grief, the souvenir of pain.
Yes, if a trace of loveliness remain,
It is to memory alone addressed;
That spirit looks for beauty but in vain
Which is not by an inner beauty blessed.
And, as the ebbing ocean on the beach
Leaves but a trace of evanescent foam,
So beauty passes ever out of reach,
Save to the heart where happiness is home.
There beauty walks, wherever it may be,
And paints the sunset on the quiet sea.

Robert Nathan

THE COIN

INTO my heart's treasury
I slipped a coin
That time cannot take
Nor a thief purloin,—

Oh better than the minting
   Of a gold-crowned king
Is the safe-kept memory
   Of a lovely thing.

Sara Teasdale

FROM THE PARTHENON I LEARN

FROM the Parthenon I learn
Whatever in our souls shall burn
Like the white flame of Phidias,
It shall not change, it shall not pass.

From the pyramids I know
How the stately soul may grow,
Wind and sand its enemies,
Through the embarrassed centuries.

From the Taj Mahal I see
Grief hath its own majesty;
And the Alhambra's shattered towers
Mind me of immortal hours.

That pale mountain of Milan
Flushing like a rose with dawn,
Tells how death can only be
A lovely thing we do not see.

Willard Wattles

LET ME LOVE BRIGHT THINGS

LET me love bright things
   Before my life is over . . .
Moons, and shining wings
   Of bees about the clover.

Bathers in seas;
   Cities by night;
Tall rainy trees;
   Yellow candle-light.

And long sunlit lands
   That lie anywhere;
And one with white hands
   To comb her gleaming hair!
A. Newberry Choyce

SAY NOT THAT BEAUTY

SAY not that beauty is an idle thing
And gathered lightly as a wayside flower
That on the trembling verges of the spring
Knows but the sweet survival of an hour.
For 'tis not so. Through dedicated days
And foiled adventure of deliberate nights
We lose and find and stumble in the ways
That lead to the far confluence of delights.
Not with the earthly eye and fleshly ear,
But lifted far above mortality,
We see at last the eternal hills, and hear
The sighing of the universal sea;
And kneeling breathless in the holy place
We know immortal Beauty face to face.
Robin Flower

MOMENT MUSICALE

THE round moon hangs above the rim
   Of silent and blue-shadowed trees,
And all the earth is vague and dim
   In its blue veil of mysteries.

On such a night one must believe
   The Golden Age returns again
With lyric beauty, to retrieve
   The world from dreariness and pain.

And down the wooded aisles, behold
   · What dancers through the dusk appear!
Piping their rapture as of old,
   They bring immortal freedom near.

A moment on the brink of night
They tread their transport in the dew,
And to the rhythm of their delight,
Behold, all things are made anew!

Bliss Carman

FOR THEM ALL

AT night through the city in a song
Like a cloud I drift along.

I slip into the shop-girl's room,
Soothing her eyes amid the gloom.

I smooth the wrinkles on the cheek
Of the white mother, worn and meek.

Where the laborer sits at rest,
I pour sweet dreams into his breast.

The old man and the little child
Bending o'er the page have smiled.

Into the lover's heart I stream,
Like the belovèd in a dream.

The poet and the lover, too,
I drench with beauty through and through.

I am Beauty's, and I move
Lonely amid those I love.

O poet, lover, mother, child!
For love of you my heart is wild.

Out of this very page I cry
Up to your spirits: this is I!

Are we together here at last?
O catch me up before 'tis past!

O hold me close against your breast!
There alone, at last, I rest.

John Hall Wheelock

THE STar

BEAUTY had first my pride;
But now my heart she hath,
And all the whole world wide
    Is Beauty's path!
By mountain, field and flood
I walked in hardihood;
But now with delicate pace
    Her steps I trace.

Once did my spirit dare
In fond presumptuous dream
To make her ways more fair
    That fair did seem.
But all the world became
Her ways elect, to shame
With their least lovely lot
    My loftiest thought.

Her worshipful bright fire!
Ah! Whither will it lead
My burning faint desire
    And feet that bleed?
Far in my failing view,
A pure and blazing gem,
She lights on earth the New
    Jerusalem!

Willoughby Weaving

BEAUTY

To catch some fragment from her hands
That else would fall into the sands
And lie lost and disintegrate:
For this I wait: for this I wait.

Even her casual aspects are
Vivid and lovely as a star;
Aspects that turn, retire and change
Through unimaginable range.

Is she the universe or only
An entity austere and lonely,
Whose moods are moon and colored seas;
Whose thoughts are all the mysteries?

Kenneth Slade Alling

ADVENTURE

O POSSIBLE and Probable,
  Fell jailors of my mind,
I had a way of leaping once
  And leaving you behind.

I had a way of soaring once
  Off in a maze of blue,
Tempting Unbelievable
  Until it happened true.

But now they've taken Beautiful
  And measured her a gown.
Beautiful, my Beautiful,
  Come, storm through the town

Naked on a smoking steed
  While I cry your name
And old cringing Credible
  Dies of rage and shame!

Grace Fallow Norton

BEAUTY

I FOUND no beauty on the mountain heights;
  I found no beauty where the sea-spray starts;
I found no beauty in God's days and nights;
  I found it only in my heart of hearts.

God I created, and the mountain dawn;
  My scarlet and azure colored all the charts;
Beauty, the goal whence all has come and gone,
  I too created in my heart of hearts.

In wild sea-spray I deified my soul;
  My mountain dawn uplifted all the arts;
In every part I found the glorious Whole—
  All, all, and only, in my heart of hearts.

Joel Elias Spingarn

ALOHA

I KNOW a little island
  Set in the summer sea,
Wave-washed and green and mossy
  As green can be.

Great joys are in the offing;
  And always day and night,
Putting into the harbor,
  Is some delight.

Around it sail great sorrows;
  So far it is from care
That only fleets of laughter
  May anchor there.

And only strong fair faces
  Pass always to and fro;
As in a place enchanted
  They come and go.

Once came a green sea-serpent,
  The island people say,
And in their warmth of welcome
  Basked for a day:

Basked—and with venom sweetened,
  Fled from that holy ground,
Dyeing the seas with envy
  For miles around:

With envy of the people
   Who cherish lovely things,
Such as in eld were cherished
   By queens and kings.

Stay, little island, anchored
   Far in the summer sea,
Wave-washed and green and mossy
   As green can be!

William Griffith

THE SINGERS IN A CLOUD

OVERHEAD at sunset all heard the choir.
Nothing could be seen except jewelled gray
Raining beauty earthward, flooding with desire
All things that listened there in the broken day;
Songs from freer breathers, their unprisoned fire
Out of cloudy fountains, flying and hurled,
Fell and warmed the world.

Sudden came a wind and birds were laid bare,
Only music warmed them round their brown breasts.
They had sent the splendors pouring through the air,
Love was their heat and home far above their nests.
Light went softly out and left their voices there.
Starward passed for ever all that great cry,
Burning, round the sky.

On the earth the battles war against light,
Heavy lies the harrow, bitter the field.
Beauty, like a river running through the night,
Streams past the stricken ones whom it would have healed
But the darkened faces turn away from sight.
Blind, bewildered nations sow, reap, and fall,
Shadows gather all.

Far above the birdsong bright shines the gold;
Through the starry orchards earth's paths are hung;
As she moves among them glowing fruits unfold,
Such that the heavens there reawaken young.

Overhead is beauty, healing for the old
Overhead in morning, nothing but youth,
Only lovely youth.

Ridgely Torrence

EUCLID ALONE HAS LOOKED ON BEAUTY BARE

Euclid alone has looked on Beauty bare.
Let all who prate of Beauty hold their peace,
And lay them prone upon the earth and cease
To ponder on themselves, the while they stare
At nothing, intricately drawn nowhere
In shapes of shifting lineage; let geese
Gabble and hiss, but heroes seek release
From dusty bondage into luminous air.
O blinding hour, O holy, terrible day,
When first the shaft into his vision shone
Of light anatomized! Euclid alone
Has looked on Beauty bare.   Fortunate they
Who, though once only and then but far away,
Have heard her massive sandal set on stone.

Edna St. Vincent Millay

ROMANCE

ROMANCE

WHEN I was but thirteen or so
   I went into a golden land,
Chimborazo, Cotopaxi
   Took me by the hand.

My father died, my brother too,
   They passed like fleeting dreams,
I stood where Popocatapetl
   In the sunlight gleams.

I dimly heard the master's voice
   And boys far-off at play,
Chimborazo, Cotopaxi
   Had stolen me away.

I walked in a great golden dream
   The town streets, to and fro—
Shining Popocatapetl
   Gleamed with his cap of snow.

I walked home with a gold dark boy
   And never a word I'd say,
Chimborazo, Cotapaxi
   Had taken my breath away:

I gazed entranced upon his face
   Fairer than any flower—
O shining Popocatapetl,
   It was thy magic hour:

The houses, people, traffic seemed
   Thin fading dreams by day,
Chimborazo, Cotopaxi,
   They had stolen my soul away!

W. J. Turner

GATES OF DAMASCUS

FOUR great gates has the city of Damascus,
　And four Great Wardens, on their spears reclining,
All day long stand like tall stone men
　And sleep on the towers when the moon is shining.

This is the song of the East Gate Warden
When he locks the great gate and smokes in his garden.

Postern of Fate, the Desert Gate, Disaster's Cavern, Fort
　　of Fear,
The Portal of Bagdad am I, and Doorway of Diarbekir.

The Persian Dawn with new desires may net the flushing
　　mountain spires:
But my gaunt buttress still rejects the suppliance of those
　　mellow fires.

Pass not beneath, O Caravan, or pass not singing.　Have
　　you heard
That silence where the birds are dead yet something pipeth
　　like a bird?

Pass not beneath! Men say there blows in stony deserts
　　still a rose
But with no scarlet to her leaf—and from whose heart no
　　perfume flows.

Wilt thou bloom red where she buds pale, thy sister rose?
　　Wilt thou not fail
When noonday flashes like a flail?　Leave nightingale the
　　caravan!

Pass then, pass all! "Bagdad!" ye cry, and down the billows
　　of blue sky
Ye beat the bell that beats to hell, and who shall thrust
　　ye back?　Not I.

The Sun who flashes through the head and paints the
　　shadows green and red,—
The Sun shall eat thy fleshless dead, O Caravan, O Caravan!

And one who licks his lips for thirst with fevered eyes shall
    face in fear
The palms that wave, the streams that burst, his last mirage,
    O Caravan!

And one—the bird-voiced Singing-man—shall fall behind
    thee, Caravan!
And God shall meet him in the night, and he shall sing as
    best he can.

And one the Bedouin shall slay, and one, sand-stricken on
    the way
Go dark and blind; and one shall say—"How lonely is the
    Caravan!"

Pass out beneath, O Caravan, Doom's Caravan, Death's
    Caravan!
I had not told ye, fools, so much, save that I heard your
    Singing-man.

   This was sung by the West Gate's keeper
   When heaven's hollow dome grew deeper.

I am the gate toward the sea: O sailor men, pass out from
    me!
I hear you high in Lebanon, singing the marvels of the sea.

The dragon-green, the luminous, the dark, the serpent-
    haunted sea,
The snow-besprinkled wine of earth, the white-and-blue-
    flower foaming sea.

Beyond the sea are towns with towers, carved with lions
    and lily flowers,
And not a soul in all those lonely streets to while away the
    hours.

Beyond the towns, an isle where, bound, a naked giant bites
    the ground:
The shadow of a monstrous wing looms on his back: and
    still no sound.

Beyond the isle a rock that screams like madmen shouting
in their dreams,
From whose dark issues night and day blood crashes in a
thousand streams.

Beyond the rock is Restful Bay, where no wind breathes
or ripple stirs,
And there on Roman ships, they say, stand rows of metal
mariners.

Beyond the bay in utmost West old Solomon the Jewish
King
Sits with his beard upon his breast, and grips and guards
his magic ring:

And when that ring is stolen, he will rise in outraged majesty,
And take the World upon his back, and fling the World
beyond the sea.

This is the song of the North Gate's master,
Who singeth fast, but drinketh faster.

I am the gay Aleppo Gate: a dawn, a dawn and thou art
there:
Eat not thy heart with fear and care, O brother of the
beast we hate!

Thou hast not many miles to tread, nor other foes than
fleas to dread;
Homs shall behold thy morning meal and Hama see thee
safe in bed.

Take to Aleppo filigrane, and take them paste of apricots,
And coffee tables botched with pearl, and little beaten
brassware pots:

And thou shalt sell thy wares for thrice the Damascene re-
tailers' price,
And buy a fat Armenian slave who smelleth odorous and
nice.

Some men of noble stock were made: some glory in the
    murder-blade:
Some praise a Science or an Art, but I like honorable Trade!

Sell them the rotten, buy the ripe! Their heads are weak;
    their pockets burn.
Aleppo men are mighty fools. Salaam Aleikum! Safe re-
    turn!

This is the song of the South Gate Holder,
A silver man, but his song is older.

I am the Gate that fears no fall: the Mihrab of Damascus
    wall,
The bridge of booming Sinai: the Arch of Allah all in all.

O spiritual pilgrim rise: the night has grown her single
    horn:
The voices of the souls unborn are half adream with Para-
    dise.

To Meccah thou hast turned in prayer with aching heart
    and eyes that burn:
Ah Hajji, whither wilt thou turn when thou art there, when
    thou art there?

God be thy guide from camp to camp: God be thy shade
    from well to well;
God grant beneath the desert stars thou hear the Prophet's
    camel bell.

And God shall make thy body pure, and give thee knowledge
    to endure
This ghost-life's piercing phantom-pain, and bring thee out
    to Life again.

And God shall make thy soul a Glass where eighteen thou-
    sand Æons pass,
And thou shalt see the gleaming Worlds as men see dew
    upon the grass.

And son of Islam, it may be that thou shalt learn at journey's
    end
Who walks thy garden eve on eve, and bows his head, and
    calls thee Friend.

James Elroy Flecker

THE GOLDEN JOURNEY TO SAMARKAND

PROLOGUE

I

WE who with songs beguile your pilgrimage
    And swear that Beauty lives though lilies die,
We Poets of a proud old lineage
    Who sing to find your hearts, we know not why,—

What shall we tell you? Tales, marvellous tales
    Of ships and stars and isles where good men rest,
Where nevermore the rose of sunset pales,
    And winds and shadows fall toward the West:

And there the world's first huge white-bearded kings
    In dim glades sleeping, murmur in their sleep,
And closer round their breasts the ivy clings,
    Cutting its pathway slow and red and deep.

II

And how beguile you? Death has no repose
    Warmer and deeper than that Orient sand
Which hides the beauty and bright faith of those
    Who made the Golden Journey to Samarkand.

And now they wait and whiten peaceably,
    Those conquerors, those poets, those so fair:
They know time comes, not only you and I,
    But the whole world shall whiten, here or there;

When those long caravans that cross the plain
    With dauntless feet and sound of silver bells
Put forth no more for glory or for gain,
    Take no more solace from the palm-girt wells.

When the great markets by the sea shut fast
   All that calm Sunday that goes on and on:
When even lovers find their peace at last
   And Earth is but a star, that once had shone.

EPILOGUE

At the Gate of the Sun, Bagdad, in olden time.

THE MERCHANTS (*together*)

AWAY, for we are ready to a man!
   Our camels sniff the evening and are glad.
Lead on, O Master of the Caravan:
   Lead on the Merchant-Princes of Bagdad.

THE CHIEF DRAPER

Have we not Indian carpets dark as wine,
   Turbans and sashes, gowns and bows and veils,
And broideries of intricate design,
   And printed hangings in enormous bales?

THE CHIEF GROCER

We have rose-candy, we have spikenard,
   Mastic and terebinth and oil and spice,
And such sweet jams meticulously jarred
   As God's own Prophet eats in Paradise.

THE PRINCIPAL JEWS

And we have manuscripts in peacock styles
   By Ali of Damascus; we have swords
Engraved with storks and apes and crocodiles,
   And heavy beaten necklaces, for Lords.

THE MASTER OF THE CARAVAN

But you are nothing but a lot of Jews.

THE PRINCIPAL JEWS

Sir, even dogs have daylight, and we pay.

THE MASTER OF THE CARAVAN

But who are ye in rags and rotten shoes,
  You dirty-bearded, blocking up the way?

THE PILGRIMS

We are the Pilgrims, master; we shall go
  Always a little further: it may be
Beyond that last blue mountain barred with snow,
  Across that angry or that glimmering sea,

White on a throne or guarded in a cave
  There lives a prophet who can understand
Why men were born: but surely we are brave,
  Who make the Golden Journey to Samarkand.

THE CHIEF MERCHANT

We gnaw the nail of hurry.   Master, away!

ONE OF THE WOMEN

O turn your eyes to where your children stand.
Is not Bagdad the beautiful?   O stay!

THE MERCHANTS (*in chorus*)

We take the Golden Road to Samarkand.

AN OLD MAN

Have you not girls and garlands in your homes,
  Eunuchs and Syrian boys at your command?
Seek not excess: God hateth him who roams!

THE MERCHANTS (*in chorus*)

We make the Golden Journey to Samarkand.

A PILGRIM WITH A BEAUTIFUL VOICE

Sweet to ride forth at evening from the wells
  When shadows pass gigantic on the sand,
And softly through the silence beat the bells
  Along the Golden Road to Samarkand.

A MERCHANT

We travel not for trafficking alone:
  By hotter winds our fiery hearts are fanned:
For lust of knowing what should not be known
  We make the Golden Journey to Samarkand.

THE MASTER OF THE CARAVAN

Open the gate, O watchman of the night!

THE WATCHMAN

Ho, travellers, I open.   For what land
Leave you the dim-moon city of delight?

THE MERCHANTS (*with a shout*)

We make the Golden Journey to Samarkand.
[*The Caravan passes through the gate*]

THE WATCHMAN (*consoling the women*)

What would ye, ladies?   It was ever thus.
Men are unwise and curiously planned.

A WOMAN

They have their dreams, and do not think of us.

VOICES OF THE CARAVAN (*in the distance, singing*)

We make the Golden Journey to Samarkand.
                                        James Elroy Flecker

MERCHANTS FROM CATHAY

THEIR heels slapped their bumping mules; *How that They came*
    their fat chaps glowed.
  Glory unto Mary, each seemed to wear a
    crown!
Like sunset their robes were on the wide, white
    road:
  So we saw those mad merchants come dust-
    ing into town!

Of their Beasts,

Two paunchy beasts they rode on and two
they drove before.
May the Saints all help us, the tiger-stripes
they had!
And the panniers upon them swelled full of
stuffs and ore!
The square buzzed and jostled at a sight so
mad.

And their Boast,

They bawled in their beards, and their turbans
they wried.
They stopped by the stalls with curvetting
and clatter.
As bronze as the bracken their necks and faces
dyed—
And a stave they sat singing, to tell us of the
matter.

With its Burthen

"For your silks, to Sugarmago! For your dyes,
to Isfahan!
Weird fruits from the Isle o' Lamaree.
  But for magic merchandise,
  For treasure-trove and spice,
Here's a catch and a carol to the great, grand Chan,
The King of all the Kings across the sea!

And Chorus.

"Here's a catch and a carol to the great, grand
  Chan;
For we won through the deserts to his sunset
  barbican;
And the mountains of his palace no Titan's reach
  may span
  Where he wields his seignorie!

A first Stave Fearsome,

"Red-as-blood skins of Panthers, so bright
  against the sun
On the walls of the halls where his pillared
  state is set
They daze with a blaze no man may look upon.
  And with conduits of beverage those floors
  run wet.

"His wives stiff with riches, they sit before
    him there.

  Bird and beast at his feast make song and
    clapping cheer.

And jugglers and enchanters, all walking on
    the air,

  Make fall eclipse and thunder—make moons
    and suns appear!

And a second
Right hard
To stomach

"Once the Chan, by his enemies sore-prest,
    and sorely spent,

  Lay, so they say, in a thicket 'neath a tree

Where the howl of an owl vexed his foes from
    their intent:

  Then that fowl for a holy bird of reverence
    made he!

And a third,
Which is a
Laughable
Thing.

"*A catch and a carol to the great, grand Chan!*
Pastmasters of disasters, our desert caravan
Won through all peril to his sunset barbican,
  Where he wields his seignorie!
And crowns he gave us! We end where we began:
A catch and a carol to the great, grand Chan,
  The King of all the Kings across the sea!"

We gape to
Hear them end,

Those mad, antic Merchants! . . . Their
    stripèd beasts did beat

  The market-square suddenly with hooves of
    beaten gold!

The ground yawned gaping and flamed beneath
    our feet!

  They plunged to Pits Abysmal with their
    wealth untold!

And are in
Terror,

And some say the Chan himself in anger dealt
    the stroke—

For sharing of his secrets with silly, common
    folk:

But Holy, Blessed Mary, preserve us as you may

Lest once more those mad Merchants come
    chanting from Cathay!

And dread
it is
Devil's Work!

                   William Rose Benét

THE PRAYER RUG

As supple as a tiger's skin
With wine hues and ochre blent,
It lies upon my polished floor—
Four square feet of the orient,
No more than that, yet space enough
On which to build a wonder-dream
Of that far town which, half asleep
And half a myth
Lies 'neath the crescent's golden gleam.

I see Bokhara's minarets
Like sentries o'er the housetops stand,
And far away the dropping sky
Melt in the desert's rippled sand.
Through silence born of noonday heat
And swooning radiance of the air,
I hear, from high muezzin tower
Like conscience-cry
The Moslem's solemn call to prayer.

And quick unrolling this bright rug,
I see its owner spread it down
Where'er he stands—in porch or street—
And turn his face toward Mecca's town.
On this straight line of woven flame
His knees by Allah's law must rest;
His feet and hands these squares must touch,
And in this niche
Of softened hues his brow be pressed.

And prostrate thus, he makes his plea
To Allah five times e'er the sun
A flaming chariot through the sky
Its course from dawn to dusk has run.
This much I see with half-shut eyes,
Caught in the weird rug's thralling snare,
But ah! I cannot catch the drift

Of mystic signs
That fashioned forth the Moslem's prayer.

Prayed he that to his agèd woes
The prophet's helping hand be lent,
As answering the muezzin's call
His wingèd words to Allah went?
Or yet—or yet, not old, but young—
Young with his pagan blood on fire
With life and love's eternal quest,
Prayed he instead
To gain the port of Heart's Desire?

The while, his face set toward the East,
He wore the rug smooth with his knees,
Did he recall some harem girl
Whose eyes flashed him love's dear decrees?
I cannot tell; the rug gives back
No faintest whisper of his prayer;
He may have asked his rival's blood
On whetted blade,
Or yielded him to love's despair.

I only know that o'er the leagues
Of sand that's gold, and sea that's brown
A subtle thread spins in my brain
To far Bokhara's sunlit town.
And visions haunt me like dim dreams
Whose baffling veil may ne'er be rent
I only know, or rich or poor,
I hold in fief
Four square feet of the orient.

Sara Beaumont Kennedy

THE PRINCESS

THE stone-gray roses by the desert's rim
Are soft-edged shadows on the moonlit sand,
Gray are the broken walls of Khangavar
That haunt of nightingales, whose voices are
Fountains that bubble in the dream-soft Moon.

Shall the Gazelles with moonbeam pale bright feet
Entering the vanished gardens sniff the air—
Some scent may linger of that ancient time,
Musician's song, or poet's passionate rhyme,
The Princess dead, still wandering love-sick there.

A Princess pale and cold as mountain snow,
In cool, dark chambers sheltered from the sun,
With long, dark lashes and small delicate hands:
To kiss her mouth men sighed in many lands
Until in shifting sand they buried her.

And the Gazelles shall flit by in the Moon
And never shake the frail Tree's lightest leaves,
And moonlight roses perfume the pale Dawn
Until the scarlet life from her lips drawn
Gathers its shattered beauty in the sky.

W. J. Turner

DAPHNE

WHEN green as a river was the barley,
Green as a river the rye,
I waded deep and began to parley
With a youth whom I heard sigh.
"I seek," said he, "a lovely lady,
A nymph as bright as a queen,
Like a tree that drips with pearls her shady
Locks of hair were seen.
And all the rivers became her flocks
Though their wool you cannot shear,—
Because of the love of her flowing locks . . .
The kingly Sun like a swain
Came strong, unheeding of her scorn,
Bathing in deeps where she has lain,
Sleeping upon her river lawn
And chasing her starry satyr train.
She fled, and changed into a tree—
That lovely fair-haired lady . . .
And now I seek through the sere summer
Where no trees are shady."

Edith Sitwell

LEDA

WHERE the slow river
meets the tide,
a red swan lifts red wings
and darker beak,
and underneath the purple down
of his soft breast
uncurls his coral feet.

Through the deep purple
of the dying heat
of sun and mist,
the level ray of sun-beam
has caressed
the lily with dark breast,
and flecked with richer gold
its golden crest.

Where the slow lifting
of the tide,
floats into the river
and slowly drifts
among the reeds,
and lifts the yellow flags,
he floats
where tide and river meet.

Ah kingly kiss—
no more regret
nor old deep memories
to mar the bliss;
where the low sedge is thick,
the gold day-lily
outspreads and rests
beneath soft fluttering
of red swan wings
and the warm quivering
of the red swan's breast.

H. D.

OF NICOLETTE

DREAMING in marble all the castle lay
like some gigantic ghost-flower born of night
blossoming in white towers to the moon,
soft sighed the passionate darkness to the tune
of tiny troubadours, and (phantom-white)
dumb-blooming boughs let fall their glorious snows,
and the unearthly sweetness of a rose
swam upward from the troubled heart of May;

a wingèd passion woke, and one by one
there fell upon the night, like angels' tears,
the syllables of that mysterious prayer,
and as an opening lily drowsy-fair
(when from her couch of poppy petals peers
the sleepy morning) gently draws apart
her curtains, and lays bare her trembling heart,
with beads of dew made jewels by the sun.

So one high shining tower (which as a glass
turned light to flame and blazed with snowy fire)
unfolding, gave the moon a nymph-like face,
a form whose snowy symmetry of grace
haunted the limbs as music haunts the lyre,
a creature of white hands, who, letting fall
a thread of lustre from the castle wall,
glided, a drop of radiance, to the grass—

shunning the sudden moonbeam's treacherous snare,
she sought the harboring dark, and (catching up
her delicate silk), all white, with shining feet,
went forth into the dew: right wildly beat
her heart at every kiss of daisy-cup,
and from her cheek the beauteous color went
with every bough that reverently bent
to touch the yellow wonder of her hair.

                                        E. E. Cummings

THE VENUS OF BOLSOVER CASTLE

STONE Venus, fixed and still,
holding your raven hair,
who stood you naked there?
Who carved you, tracing down those lines
each lover thought his only care,
sure that your gold lay hid in mines?

But all your gilding is the sun
who paints you with his glorious light:
your clothes, the shadows, turn and run
till hidden treasures have you none.
If with your hair a sail you make
you'll float there naked on a golden lake.

Now, working with their webbèd oars,
the swans ride near to where you float:
with steady wing a huge cloud soars
anchored in Heaven like a boat:
water and sky, above, below,
are cool and shining like a bed of snow.

Two apples tumbled from a bough
your breasts show, lying clear
and straight the swans begin to plough
till furrows do appear:
now with their beaks the fruit they try
and air, like glass, breaks with a cry.

Your legs like stems of flowers are seen
all naked from your ankles thin,
the leaves have fallen that were green
and foam lies where the flowers begin:
his plumes and white wings are no cover
and all the world can see your lover.

Gone is the cloud, the swans have flown,
waiting, you hold your raven hair,
your naked limbs by sun are shown

for human lover to climb the stair:
you stand above the fountain ledge
for all to see, without a hedge.

Know the cruel strategem to keep you safe!
Hair like a raven's wing and limbs cool white
are guarded from us, though they're still in sight.
Down pour the waters with a chillèd flood
to damp all those who are not flaming quite,
while he who carved you burns with fiery blood.

Sacheverell Sitwell

MANY WINGS

MANY wings are beating
Into the wind.
To their adventure
Earth, sea, be kind!

Dream-plumed, for voyaging,
One after one,
Into star-weather,
Out past the sun.

Wind-thrilled between worlds,
Spreads their desire. . . .
Be kind to many wings,
Air, water, fire.

Isabel Fiske Conant

ALIEN

WITHIN the still, white room that gave me birth,
My body bloomed, the counterpart of two
Who bore me; but alone, across the earth,
Miles from that place, the heart they never knew
By wise moon fairies on a far high hill
Was being woven out of threads of mist;
Its fragile beauty was a thing more still
Than any lake the wind has ever kissed.

And I have borne it secretly within,
A shy soft wonder sleeping at my breast;
And such has been dissemblance I could win
That even those who bore me have not guessed,
When misty moonlight blows from tree to tree,
How near they are at last to finding me.

Helen Frazee-Bower

WHAT DIM ARCADIAN PASTURES

WHAT dim Arcadian pastures
  Have I known
That suddenly, out of nothing,
  A wind is blown,
Lifting a veil and a darkness,
  Showing a purple sea—
And under your hair the faun's eyes
  Look out on me?

Alice Corbin

BALLAD

FOLLOW, follow me into the South,
  And if you are brave and wise
I'll buy you laughter for your mouth,
  Sorrow for your eyes.

I'll buy you laughter, wild and sweet,
  And sorrow, gray and still,
But you must follow with willing feet
  Over the farthest hill.

Follow, follow me into the South,
  You may return to-morrow
Wearing my kisses on your mouth,
  In your eyes my sorrow.

Marjorie Allen Seiffert

THE FAUN

I BRING you the scent of the earth on my body,
　The smell of the leaves in my hair;
I come with the wind and the water upon me,
　And never a care!

Haniel Long

DEAD MEN TELL NO TALES

They say that *dead men tell no tales!*

Except of barges with red sails
And sailors mad for nightingales;

Except of jongleurs stretched at ease
Beside old highways through the trees;

Except of dying moons that break
The hearts of lads who lie awake;

Except of fortresses in shade
And heroes crumbled and betrayed.

But *dead men tell no tales*, they say!

Except old tales that burn away
The stifling tapestries of day:

Old tales of life, of love and hate,
Of time and space, and will and fate.

Haniel Long

THE PEDLER

LEND me, a little while, the key
　That locks your heavy heart, and I'll give you back—
Rarer than books and ribbons and beads bright to see,
　This little Key of Dreams out of my pack.

The Song of the Ungirt Runners   843

The road, the road, beyond men's bolted doors,
  There shall I walk and you go free of me,
For yours lies North across the moors,
  And mine South. To what sea?

How if we stopped and let our solemn selves go by,
  While my gay ghost caught and kissed yours, as ghosts
    don't do,
And by the wayside this forgotten you and I
  Sat, and were twenty-two?

Give me the key that locks your tired eyes,
  And I will lend you this one from my pack,
Brighter than colored beads and painted books that make
    men wise:
  Take it. No, give it back!

Charlotte Mew

DON QUIXOTE

DEAREST of all the heroes! Peerless knight
Whose follies sprang from such a generous blood!
Young, young must be the heart that in thy fight
Beholds no trace of its own servitude.
Young, or else darkened, is the eye that sees
No image of its own fate in thy quest.
The windmills and the swine,—by such as these
Is shaped the doom of those we love the best.
Beloved knight! La Mancha's windows gleam,
Across the plain time makes so chill and gray,
With thy light only. Still thy flambeaux stream
In pomp of one who on his destined day
Put up his spear, his knightly pennon furled,
And died of the unworthiness of the world.

Arthur Davison Ficke

THE SONG OF THE UNGIRT RUNNERS

WE swing ungirded hips,
  And lightened are our eyes;
The rain is on our lips,
  We do not run for prize.

We know not whom we trust
　　Nor whitherward we fare,
But we run because we must
　　Through the great wide air.

The waters of the seas
　　Are troubled as by storm.
The tempest strips the trees
　　And does not leave them warm.
Does the tearing tempest pause?
　　Do the tree-tops ask it why?
So we run without a cause
　　'Neath the big bare sky.

The rain is on our lips,
　　We do not run for prize.
But the storm the water whips
　　And the wave howls to the skies.
The winds arise and strike it
　　And scatter it like sand,
And we run because we like it
　　Through the broad bright land.

Charles Hamilton Sorley

GIRL ATHLETES

AROUND their legs girl athletes twist
　　Their silver-chased puttees,
Or they wear half-boots, blue-embossed
　　And bound with fleur-de-lys.
　　The sun has bronzed their knees
And bosoms, so that eagle-plumes
　　Are suited to their guise,
And agates from Ohio tombs,
And textures from Algonquin looms
　　With borders of sunrise.

In waxy curls they lift their hair
　　When the night's trail has turned;
The everlasting leaves of hair

Lie close and forest-ferned
Above their brows sun-burned.
The prairie eyes, miraged and deep,
  Are filled with flowers and corn,
With smoke-fires on the edge of sleep
And secrets drifting blue-birds keep
  About the day unborn.

Who trusts the hedge of flowering quince
  To lead him far away,
The hawthornes and the hyacinths
  To take him where they play,
  Will come to them some day:
The roads are trampled by their hoofs
  Spurring to misty hills;
The roads are trampled by their hoofs
Spurring away from city roofs
  To a country pollen fills.

They are the daughters of the sun
  In polychrome and white;
And the Great Father gave each one
  To add to the delight
  Of her unswerving flight,
A cinnamon or jet-black horse.
  It is a dream to bless,
And each maid, mounted, to the source
Of the horizons on her course
  Gallops, a centauress.

In mountain pastures they play games
  Old as the first red spring,
And no one can recall the names
  Of the long ropes they fling,
  Or why they do this thing,
Or that, or the other. There they reach
  Toward goals which no one knows,
Dancing, and crying each to each
Snatches of prehistoric speech
  While the long midday grows.

They meet their lovers when day cools
    Under the upland trees,
Or by the river swimming-pools,
    Inviting at their ease
    The body-piercing breeze.
Then it is sweet as heaven to kiss,
    Enchanted and unseen;
But they think no more of love than this,
That it is something not amiss
    When leaves are long and green.

In winter, when gray clouds above
    Have exiled leaf and heat,
They keep no memory of love;
    But strapping to their feet
    White sandals, gleaming, fleet,
They fly along the frozen streams
    Half-human and half-gull.
The groves once dim with summer dreams
They now flash through with steel sunbeams
    And tunics of rose wool.

Love bores them with their ankles fleet,
    But on Antarctic shores
Gymnasia stand for their retreat
    From the rigor of outdoors.
    There on the ancient floors
Along transparent walls, the dead
    Girl athletes gleam in gold,
And tropic ferns are upwards led
To high glass arches overhead
    Which keep away the cold.

And dead girl athletes gleam in flame
    Beyond the desert trails;
Mountains are sculptured with the name
    And the recorded tales
    Of each when her day fails.
Under an arch opaque and high
    Beyond the barren verge,

With strength no centuries deny,
Rooted in rock beyond the eye,
    Their giant forms emerge.

                        Haniel Long

TARTARY

IF I were Lord of Tartary,
    Myself and me alone,
My bed should be of ivory,
    Of beaten gold my throne;
And in my court would peacocks flaunt,
And in my forests tigers haunt,
And in my pools great fishes slant
    Their fins athwart the sun.

If I were Lord of Tartary,
    Trumpeters every day
To every meal should summon me,
    And in my courtyard bray;
And in the evening lamps would shine,
Yellow as honey, red as wine,
While harp, and flute, and mandoline,
    Made music sweet and gay.

If I were Lord of Tartary,
    I'd wear a robe of beads,
White, and gold, and green they'd be—
    And clustered thick as seeds;
And ere should wane the morning-star,
I'd don my robe and scimitar,
And zebras seven should draw my car
    Through Tartary's dark glades.

Lord of the fruits of Tartary,
    Her rivers silver-pale!
Lord of the hills of Tartary,
    Glen, thicket, wood, and dale!
Her flashing stars, her scented breeze,
Her trembling lakes, like foamless seas,
Her bird-delighting citron-trees
    In every purple vale!

                        Walter de la Mare

THE DANCING SEAL

WHEN we were building Skua Light—
The first men who had lived a night
Upon that deep-sea Isle—
As soon as chisel touched the stone,
The friendly seals would come ashore;
And sit and watch us all the while,
As though they'd not seen men before;
And so, poor beasts, had never known
Men had the heart to do them harm.
They'd little cause to feel alarm
With us, for we were glad to find
Some friendliness in that strange sea;
Only too pleased to let them be
And sit as long as they'd a mind
To watch us: for their eyes were kind
Like women's eyes, it seemed to me.
So, hour on hour, they sat: I think
They liked to hear the chisels' clink:
And when the boy sang loud and clear,
They scrambled closer in to hear;
And if he whistled sweet and shrill,
The queer beasts shuffled nearer still:
But every sleek and sheeny skin
Was mad to hear his violin.

When, work all over for the day,
He'd take his fiddle down and play
His merry tunes beside the sea,
Their eyes grew brighter and more bright,
And burned and twinkled merrily:
And as I watched them one still night,
And saw their eager sparkling eyes,
I felt those lively seals would rise
Some shiny night ere he could know,
And dance about him, heel and toe,
Unto the fiddle's heady tune.

And at the rising of the moon,
Half-daft, I took my stand before

A young seal lying on the shore;
And called on her to dance with me.
And it seemed hardly strange when she
Stood up before me suddenly,
And shed her black and sheeny skin;
And smiled, all eager to begin . . .
And I was dancing, heel and toe,
With a young maiden white as snow,
Unto a crazy violin.

We danced beneath the dancing moon
All night, beside the dancing sea,
With tripping toes and skipping heels:
And all about us friendly seals
Like Christian folk were dancing reels
Unto the fiddle's endless tune
That kept on spinning merrily
As though it never meant to stop.
And never once the snow-white maid
A moment stayed
To take a breath,
Though I was fit to drop:
And while those wild eyes challenged me,
I knew as well as well could be
I must keep step with that young girl,
Though we should dance to death.

Then with a skirl
The fiddle broke:
The moon went out:
The sea stopped dead:
And, in a twinkling, all the rout
Of dancing folk had fled . . .
And in the chill bleak dawn I woke
Upon the naked rock, alone.

They've brought me far from Skua Isle . . .
I laugh to think they do not know
That as, all day, I chip the stone,
Among my fellows here inland,

I smell the sea-wrack on the shore . . .
And see her snowy-tossing hand,
And meet again her merry smile . . .
And dream I'm dancing all the while,
I'm dancing ever, heel and toe,
With a seal-maiden, white as snow,
On that moonshiny, Island-strand,
For ever and for evermore.

Wilfrid Gibson

THE CHINESE NIGHTINGALE

A SONG IN CHINESE TAPESTRIES

"How, how," he said. "Friend Chang," I said,
"San Francisco sleeps as the dead—
Ended license, lust and play:
Why do you iron the night away?
Your big clock speaks with a deadly sound,
With a tick and a wail till dawn comes round.
While the monster shadows glower and creep,
What can be better for man than sleep? "

"I will tell you a secret," Chang replied;
"My breast with vision is satisfied,
And I see green trees and fluttering wings,
And my deathless bird from Shanghai sings."
Then he lit five fire-crackers in a pan.
"Pop, pop," said the fire-crackers, "cra-cra-crack."
He lit a joss stick long and black.
Then the proud gray joss in the corner stirred;
On his wrist appeared a gray small bird,
And this was the song of the gray small bird:
"Where is the princess, loved forever,
Who made Chang first of the kings of men? "

And the joss in the corner stirred again;
And the carved dog, curled in his arms, awoke,
Barked forth a smoke-cloud that whirled and broke.
It piled in a maze round the ironing-place,

And there on the snowy table wide
Stood a Chinese lady of high degree,
With a scornful, witching, tea-rose face. . . .
Yet she put away all form and pride,
And laid her glimmering veil aside
With a childlike smile for Chang and for me.

The walls fell back, night was aflower,
The table gleamed in a moonlit bower,
While Chang, with a countenance carved of stone,
Ironed and ironed, all alone.
And thus she sang to the busy man Chang:
"Have you forgotten . . .
Deep in the ages, long, long ago,
I was your sweetheart, there on the sand—
Storm-worn beach of the Chinese land?
We sold our grain in the peacock town
Built on the edge of the sea-sands brown—
Built on the edge of the sea-sands brown. . . .

"When all the world was drinking blood
From the skulls of men and bulls
And all the world had swords and clubs of stone,
We drank our tea in China beneath the sacred spice-trees,
And heard the curled waves of the harbor moan.
And this gray bird, in Love's first spring,
With a bright-bronze breast and a bronze-brown wing,
Captured the world with his carolling.
Do you remember, ages after,
At last the world we were born to own?
You were the heir of the yellow throne—
The world was the field of the Chinese man
And we were the pride of the Sons of Han?
We copied deep books and we carved in jade,
And wove blue silks in the mulberry shade. . . ."

"I remember, I remember
That Spring came on forever,
That Spring came on forever,"
Said the Chinese nightingale.

My heart was filled with marvel and dream,
Though I saw the western street-lamps gleam,
Though dawn was brightening the western day,
Though Chang was a laundryman ironing away. . . .
Mingled there with the streets and alleys,
The railroad-yard and the clock-tower bright,
Demon clouds crossed ancient valleys;
Across wide lotus-ponds of light
I marked a giant firefly's flight.

And the lady, rosy-red,
Flourished her fan, her shimmering fan,
Stretched her hand toward Chang, and said:
"Do you remember,
Ages after,
Our palace of heart-red stone?
Do you remember
The little doll-faced children
With their lanterns full of moon-fire,
That came from all the empire
Honoring the throne?—
The loveliest fête and carnival
Our world had ever known?
The sages sat about us
With their heads bowed in their beards,
With proper meditation on the sight.
Confucius was not born;
We lived in those great days
Confucius later said were lived aright. . . .
And this gray bird, on that day of spring,
With a bright-bronze breast, and a bronze-brown wing,
Captured the world with his carolling.
Late at night his tune was spent.
Peasants,
Sages,
Children,
Homeward went,
And then the bronze bird sang for you and me.
We walked alone.   Our hearts were high and free.
I had a silvery name, I had a silvery name,

I had a silvery name—do you remember
The name you cried beside the tumbling sea? "

Chang turned not to the lady slim—
He bent to his work, ironing away;
But she was arch, and knowing and glowing,
And the bird on his shoulder spoke for him.

"Darling . . . darling . . . darling . . . darling . . ."
Said the Chinese nightingale.

The great gray joss on a rustic shelf,
Rakish and shrewd, with his collar awry,
Sang impolitely, as though by himself,
Drowning with his bellowing the nightingale's cry:
"Back through a hundred, hundred years
Hear the waves as they climb the piers,
Hear the howl of the silver seas,
Hear the thunder.
Hear the gongs of holy China
How the waves and tunes combine
In a rhythmic clashing wonder,
Incantation old and fine:
          'Dragons, dragons, Chinese dragons,
          Red fire-crackers, and green fire-crackers,
          And dragons, dragons, Chinese dragons.'"

Then the lady, rosy-red,
Turned to her lover Chang and said:
"Dare you forget that turquoise dawn
When we stood in our mist-hung velvet lawn,
And worked a spell this great joss taught
Till a God of the Dragons was charmed and caught?
From the flag high over our palace home
He flew to our feet in rainbow-foam—
A king of beauty and tempest and thunder
Panting to tear our sorrows asunder.
A dragon of fair adventure and wonder.
We mounted the back of that royal slave
With thoughts of desire that were noble and grave.

We swam down the shore to the dragon-mountains,
We whirled to the peaks and the fiery fountains.
To our secret ivory house we were borne.
We looked down the wonderful wing-filled regions
Where the dragons darted in glimmering legions.
Right by my breast the nightingale sang;
The old rhymes rang in the sunlit mist
That we this hour regain—
Song-fire for the brain.
When my hands and my hair and my feet you kissed,
When you cried for your heart's new pain,
What was my name in the dragon-mist,
In the rings of rainbowed rain? "

"Sorrow and love, glory and love,"
Said the Chinese nightingale.
"Sorrow and love, glory and love,"
Said the Chinese nightingale.

And now the joss broke in with his song:
"Dying ember, bird of Chang,
Soul of Chang, do you remember?—
Ere you returned to the shining harbor
There were pirates by ten thousand
Descended on the town
In vessels mountain-high and red and brown,
Moon-ships that climbed the storms and cut the skies.
On their prows were painted terrible bright eyes.
But I was then a wizard and a scholar and a priest;
I stood upon the sand;
With lifted hand I looked upon them
And sunk their vessels with my wizard eyes,
And the stately lacquer-gate made safe again.
Deep, deep below the bay, the sea-weed and the spray,
Embalmed in amber every pirate lies,
Embalmed in amber every pirate lies."

Then this did the noble lady say:
"Bird, do you dream of our home-coming day
When you flew like a courier on before

From the dragon-peak to our palace-door,
And we drove the steed in your singing path—
The ramping dragon of laughter and wrath:
And found our city all aglow,
And knighted this joss that decked it so?
There were golden fishes in the purple river
And silver fishes and rainbow fishes.
There were golden junks in the laughing river,
And silver junks and rainbow junks:
There were golden lilies by the bay and river,
And silver lilies and tiger-lilies,
And tinkling wind-bells in the gardens of the town
By the black-lacquer gate
Where walked in state
The kind king Chang
And his sweetheart mate. . . .
With his flag-born dragon
And his crown of pearl . . . and . . . jade,
And his nightingale reigning in the mulberry shade,
And sailors and soldiers on the sea-sands brown,
And priests who bowed them down to your song—
By the city called Han, the peacock town,
By the city called Han, the nightingale town,
The nightingale town."

Then sang the bird, so strangely gay,
Fluttering, fluttering, ghostly and gray,
A vague, unravelling, final tune,
Like a long unwinding silk cocoon;
Sang as though for the soul of him
Who ironed away in that bower dim:—
    "I have forgotten
    Your dragons great,
    Merry and mad and friendly and bold.
Dim is your proud lost palace-gate.
I vaguely know
There were heroes of old,
Troubles more than the heart could hold,
There were wolves in the woods
Yet lambs in the fold,

Nests in the top of the almond tree. . . .
The evergreen tree . . . and the mulberry tree . . .
Life and hurry and joy forgotten,
Years on years I but half-remember . . .
Man is a torch, then ashes soon,
May and June, then dead December,
Dead December, then again June.
Who shall end my dream's confusion?
Life is a loom, weaving illusion . . .
I remember, I remember
There were ghostly veils and laces . . .
In the shadowy bowery places . . .
With lovers' ardent faces
Bending to one another,
Speaking each his part.
They infinitely echo
In the red cave of my heart.
'Sweetheart, sweetheart, sweetheart,'
They said to one another.
They spoke, I think, of perils past.
They spoke, I think, of peace at last.
One thing I remember:
Spring came on forever,
Spring came on forever,"
Said the Chinese nightingale.

Vachel Lindsay

SHADOW–LAND

PREËXISTENCE

I LAID me down upon the shore
  And dreamed a little space;
I heard the great waves break and roar;
  The sun was on my face.

My idle hands and fingers brown
  Played with the pebbles gray;
The waves came up, the waves went down,
  Most thundering and gay.

The pebbles, they were smooth and round
  And warm upon my hands,
Like little people I had found
  Sitting among the sands.

The grains of sand so shining-small
  Soft through my fingers ran;
The sun shone down upon it all,
  And so my dream began:

How all of this had been before;
  How ages far away
I lay on some forgotten shore
  As here I lie to-day.

The waves came shining up the sands,
  As here to-day they shine;
And in my pre-pelasgian hands
  The sand was warm and fine.

I have forgotten whence I came,
  Or what my home might be,
Or by what strange and savage name
  I called that thundering sea.

I only know the sun shone down
　　As still it shines to-day,
And in my fingers long and brown
　　The little pebbles lay.

Frances Cornford

ATAVISM

I ALWAYS was afraid of Somes's Pond:
Not the little pond, by which the willow stands,
Where laughing boys catch alewives in their hands
In brown, bright shallows; but the one beyond.
There, when the frost makes all the birches burn
Yellow as cow-lilies, and the pale sky shines
Like a polished shell between black spruce and pines,
Some strange thing tracks us, turning where we turn.
You'll say I dream it, being the true daughter
Of those who in old times endured this dread.
Look!　Where the lily-stems are showing red
A silent paddle moves below the water.
A sliding shape has stirred them like a breath;
Tall plumes surmount a painted mask of Death.

Elinor Wylie

A STATUE IN A GARDEN

I WAS a goddess ere the marble found me.
　　Wind, wind, delay not—
Waft my spirit where the laurel crowned me!
　　Will the wind stay not?

Then tarry, tarry, listen, little swallow!
　　An old glory feeds me—
I lay upon the bosom of Apollo!
　　Not a bird heeds me.

For here the days are alien.　Oh, to waken
　　Mine, mine, with calling!
But on my shoulders bare, like hopes forsaken,
　　The dead leaves are falling.

The sky is gray and full of unshed weeping
  As dim down the garden
I wait and watch the early autumn sweeping.
  The stalks fade and harden.

The souls of all the flowers afar have rallied.
  The trees, gaunt, appalling,
Attest the gloom, and on my shoulders pallid
  The dead leaves are falling.

Agnes Lee

WHITE FEAR

I AM not afraid in April,
  I am cool enough to pass
Where robins burn like embers
  And tulips scorch the grass.

But oh when snow has fallen
  On a little city park,
I would not dream to venture
  Alone there in the dark!

For if I made one motion
  Along the muffled street,
Whole, whitened trees would tumble
  Into ashes at my feet.

The almond lamps would ripen
  In the velvet shell and fall
Upon the plush of pavements
  With no sound at all.

And, trembling in the silence,
  Like someone very old,
I would find my hair silver,
  And feel my heart cold.

Winifred Welles

FINITE

I DID not question anything
    As I went through the sun,
I watched the light wind crackle
    And the grass run;

Thin shadows huddled in my path
    When the dark came down—
Then I found myself a stranger
    In my own town.

                              Power Dalton

THE HOUSE ON THE HILL

THEY are all gone away,
    The House is shut and still,
There is nothing more to say.

Through broken walls and gray
    The winds blow bleak and shrill:
They are all gone away.

Nor is there one to-day
    To speak them good or ill:
There is nothing more to say.

Why is it then we stray
    Around the sunken sill?
They are all gone away,

And our poor fancy-play
    For them is wasted skill:
There is nothing more to say.

There is ruin and decay
    In the House on the Hill:
They are all gone away,
There is nothing more to say.

                    Edwin Arlington Robinson

MIST FORMS

THE sheets of night mist travel a long valley.
I know why you came at sundown in a scarf mist.

What was it we touched asking nothing and asking all?
How many times can death come and pay back what we saw?

In the oath of the sod, the lips that swore,
In the oath of night mist, nothing and all,
A riddle is here no man tells, no woman.

Carl Sandburg

AND OF LAUGHTER THAT WAS A CHANGELING

ALL day long I played in an orchard
Alone with a changeling child,
How should I guess that a little blue bonnet
Shaded a glance so wild?

All day long we played in the orchard
With apples russet and red,
All day long the little blue bonnet
Followed wherever I led.

Never, I think, was such mirth in an orchard
As the mirth betwixt us two,
But at dusk when I lifted her, laughing, laughing,
Over the brook—I knew.

Elizabeth Rendall

THE DUEL

ONCE I fought a shadow
In swift and gallant play.
She laughed at thrust and parry,—
That dancing wraith of gray.

Our flickering sword blades circled
In whirls of phantom light.
It was a high adventure
With such a ghost to fight.

At last, too blindly lunging,
I passed her flashing guard
And pierced her misty bosom
With my impalpable sword.

The ways of air-born women
I do not understand,
Nor how that wounded spirit
Left blood on my sword hand.

Harold Trowbridge Pulsifer

WOOD FLOWER

I FOUND a flower in the wood,
　Growing softly by some water;
Had I plucked it when I could,
　The old wild-wood's fairy daughter—
　Not thus vainly had I sought her.

So deep a spell was on me laid,
　I might not stretch my hand to take her,
So fragile she, I was afraid
　Even my lightest touch would break her—
　And now, alas, what voice shall wake her!

Richard Le Gallienne

THE KING O' SPAIN'S DAUGHTER

WHEN I leaned over a pool of black water,
I saw in the blackness the King o' Spain's daughter.

Her lips were a rose and the rose was bright red;
All the birds of the air, they flew round her head,

Her hair, it was streaming about me as light
As a boll of milkweed on soft airs of the night.

Her hands were as white as the coat of a moth,
And her gown was of gossamer spun into cloth.

There came down a wind-breath that ruffled the pool
And leaves were thrown down like the words of a fool.

I blew with my breath and cleared them away
And the wind climbed up-land to race and to play.

I looked in the pool to seek out her face
And saw but a tangle of marshweed like lace,

And never again in a pool of black water
Have I seen the blue eyes of the King o' Spain's daughter.

Jeanne Robert Foster

THE MOUNTAINY CHILDER

DOMENIC DARRAGH walked the land
Wi' a mountainy child at either hand;
They were lean an' long an' big in the eyes
An' terrible hungry for their size.
"Now where did ye pick up *them?*" said I,
"An' you wi' six o' ye're own forbye."
"'Twas up at the wee red lough," said he,
"That I found the two—or they found me;
They rose an' followed me down the track
An' sure I was feart to drive them back;
They give no tongue an' they're quare to see,
An' I don't know what they *are,*" said he.
"Would they eat," said I, "if I'd give them bread?"
An' Domenic laughed—"Is it eat?" he said,
"They would eat the two of us, heels an' head."
"It might be luck they would bring," said I.
"Och luck!" said he, "there's a week gone by
Since I've been roamin' by hill an' glen
To see could I find the mountainy men
Would take them back to their own again;
But never a one has crossed my way,
And the childer follow me night an' day,
An' beyond the crack o' a laugh," said he,
"They haven't opened their lips to me.
My corn is ripe an' my turf's to store,
Yet I darena face to my own house door,
For who's to say but there'd ill befall
Wi' the like o' them in the house at all.

I'll be to travel the hills," said he,
"Till I lose the two—or they lose me—
An' och, dear knows when that will be."
I filled his pipe an' I gave him bread,
An' the good word deep in my heart I said
For the help o' one that walked in dread.
An' down the road they went, the three;
While the crack o' a laugh came back to me.

Elizabeth Shane

THE SINGING–WOMAN FROM THE WOOD'S EDGE

WHAT should I be but a prophet and a liar,
Whose mother was a leprechaun, whose father was a friar?
Teethed on a crucifix and cradled under water,
What should I be but the fiend's god-daughter?

And who should be my playmates but the adder and the frog,
That was got beneath a furze-bush and born in a bog?
And what should be my singing, that was christened at an
        altar,
But Aves and Credos and Psalms out of the Psalter?

You will see such webs on the wet grass, maybe,
As a pixie-mother weaves for her baby,
You will find such flame at the wave's weedy ebb
As flashes in the meshes of a mer-mother's web.

But there comes to birth no common spawn
From the love of a priest for a leprechaun,
And you never have seen and you never will see
Such things as the things that swaddled me!

After all's said and after all's done,
What should I be but a harlot and a nun?

In through the bushes, on any foggy day,
My Da would come a-swishing of the drops away,
With a prayer for my death and a groan for my birth,
A-mumbling of his beads for all that he was worth.

And there sit my Ma, her knees beneath her chin,
A-looking in his face and a-drinking of it in,
And a-marking in the moss some funny little saying
That would mean just the opposite of all that he was praying!

He taught me the holy talk of Vesper and of Matin,
He heard me my Greek and he heard me my Latin,
He blessed me and crossed me to keep my soul from evil,
And we watched him out of sight, and we conjured up the
    devil!

Edna St. Vincent Millay

THE WIND ON THE HILLS

Go not to the hills of Erinn
When the night winds are about,
Put up your bar and shutter,
And so keep danger out.

For the good-folk whirl within it,
And they pull you by the hand,
And they push you on the shoulder,
Till you move to their command.

And lo! you have forgotten
What you have known of tears,
And you will not remember
That the world goes full of years.

A year there is a lifetime,
And a second but a day,
And an older world will meet you
Each morn you come away.

Your wife grows old with weeping,
And your children one by one
Grow gray with nights of watching,
Before your dance is done.

And it will chance some morning
You will come home no more;

Your wife sees but a withered leaf
In the wind about the door.

And your children will inherit
The unrest of the wind,
They shall seek some face elusive,
And some land they never find.

Where the wind is loud, they sighing
Go with hearts unsatisfied,
For some joy beyond remembrance,
For some memory denied.

And all your children's children,
They cannot sleep or rest,
When the wind is out in Erinn
And the sun is in the west.

Dora Sigerson Shorter

DEIRDRE

Do not let any woman read this verse;
It is for men, and after them their sons
And their son's sons.

The time comes when our hearts sink utterly;
When we remember Deirdre and her tale,
And that her lips are dust.

Once she did tread the earth: men took her hand;
They looked into her eyes and said their say,
And she replied to them.

More than a thousand years it is since she
Was beautiful: she trod the waving grass;
She saw the clouds.

A thousand years!   The grass is still the same,
The clouds as lovely as they were that time
When Deirdre was alive.

But there has never been a woman born
Who was so beautiful, not one so beautiful
Of all the women born.

Let all men go apart and mourn together;
No man can ever love her; not a man
Can ever be her lover.

No man can bend before her: no man say—
What could one say to her?   There are no words
That one could say to her!

Now she is but a story that is told
Beside the fire!   No man can ever be
The friend of that poor queen.

James Stephens

THREE WHITE BIRDS OF ANGUS

Last night when all the stars were still,
Upon Benn Edar's dew-gray hill
I stood, and watched where far away,
Three sea-birds cleft the moonwhite spray.
Three sea-birds like white flowers tossed
Upon the wind, now seen, now lost.
Now star-bright 'mid the sea's deep black,
Now lost amid the breakers' wrack.
Now nearer, nearer, winging yet,
Their silver course toward me set,
Their silver wings that as they came
Turned all to gold and rose-red flame,
Casting upon the air around
A music of such wondrous sound,
So sweetly strange, as on that shore
Sure mortal never heard before:
For binding each bright neck and wing
A band of silver chimes did swing,
Did swing and sway and round me fold
A tremulous thin veil of gold.
So that, as one enchanted all
I heard upon my spirit fall

A woman's voice, and where had been
The foremost bird, there shone a Queen
Poised half-way 'mid the sky and land,
A snow-white girl on either hand;
And "You, O King, shall come away
From Erin with me on a day,
Shall leave your loves and wars behind,
And ride with me the singing wind!"
She chanted, till along the sea
The feet of Morn came whisperingly.

Eleanor Rogers Cox

THE FAIRY FIDDLER

'Tis I go fiddling, fiddling,
    By weedy ways forlorn;
I make the blackbird's music
    Ere in his breast 'tis born;
The sleeping larks I waken
    'Twixt the midnight and the morn.

No man alive has seen me,
    But women hear me play
Sometimes at door or window,
    Fiddling the souls away,—
The child's soul and the colleen's
    Out of the covering clay.

None of my fairy kinsmen
    Make music with me now:
Along the raths I wander
    Or ride the whitethorn bough,
But the wild swans they know me,
    And the horse that draws the plough.

Nora Hopper

THE OTHERS

From our hidden places,
    By a secret path,
We come in the moonlight
    To the side of the green rath.

There the night through
  We take our pleasure,
Dancing to such a measure
  As earth never knew.

To dance and lilt
  And song without a name,
So sweetly chanted
  'Twould put a bird to shame.

And many a maiden
  Is there, of mortal birth,
Her young eyes laden
  With dreams of earth.

Music so piercing wild
  And forest-sweet would bring
Silence on blackbirds singing
  Their best in the ear of spring.

And many a youth entrancèd
  Moves slow in the dreamy round,
His brave lost feet enchanted
  With the rhythm of faery sound.

Oh, many a thrush and blackbird
  Would fall to the dewy ground,
And pine away in silence
  For envy of such a sound.

So the night through,
  In our sad pleasure,
We dance to many a measure
  That earth never knew.
                    Seumas O'Sullivan

THE DANCERS

FROM the gray woods they come, on silent feet
Into a cone of light.
A moment poised,
A lifting note,
O fair! O fleet!

Whence did you come in your amazing flight?
And whither now
Do you, reluctant, wistfully retreat?
Oh surely you have danced upon the hills
With the immortals.
As an arrow thrills
Through the blue air and sings,
You join with the proud wind, your fluent limbs
As tameless as his wings.
Within your hollowed hand you hold the draught
That wakes us from our lingering lethargy
To skyey joy
Like yours, luring and swift and free.
Yours is the birth in beauty that was sung
A golden age ago;
And now you come
With pipe and timbrel and the quickening drum,
Till men have hope of conquest over time
And death and tears.
Dreams know not any bars.
You leap like living music through the air
And love triumphant treads among the stars.

                            Babette Deutsch

"SHE WANDERED AFTER STRANGE GODS . . ."

O have you seen my fairy steed?
   His eyes are wild, his mane is white,
He feeds upon an elfin weed
   In cool of autumn night.

O have you heard my fairy steed,
   Whose cry is like a wandering loon?
He mourns some cloudy star-strewn mead
   On mountains of the moon.

O have you tamed my fairy horse
   To mount upon his back and ride?
He tears the great trees in his course,
   Nor ever turns aside.

'Tis he who tames a fairy thing,
  Must suffer want and bitter fate!
Deftly the bridles did I fling
  That brought him to my gate.

I soothed and fed and tendered him
  Sweet herbs and honey in a cup,
And led him in the twilight dim
  To where a spring welled up.

But there his wings they waved so bright
  Before my eyes, I drooped and slept.
When I awoke, it seemed dark night.
  I raised my voice and wept.

Alas, my lightsome fairy steed!
  I saw my pastures trampled bare
Where I had sown the springtime seed
  And planted flowers rare!

I saw my barns a mass of flame!
  His fiery wings had glanced in flight.
And me—a prey to fear and shame—
  He left, to seek the light!

                              Laura Benét

THE SPELL

As I came up the sandy road that lifts above the sea,
  Thrice and thrice the red cock crew,
  And thrice an elfin bugle blew
From the Gates of Faerie.

And riders passed me on the left, and riders on the right,
  Clad in cramoisie so fine,
  Phantom riders nine and nine,
That faded with the night.

The dawn was flushing in the east as I won to my door,
  And there within the ingle dark
  One had drawn a cantrip mark
Upon the earthen floor.

The thatch was matted o'er with weeds, the well was choked
        with stones,
    There lay a shroud upon the bed
    Draped and drawn from foot to head,
As white as dead men's bones.

I ran and shouted down the street, but none would heed
        my cry.
    I screamed across the market-place.
    Never a burgher turned his face.
In silence they passed by.

Oh, none could hear and none could see the man they used
    ›   to know.
    For he is witched for seven years,
    He who in the dawning hears
The elfin bugles blow.

As I came up the sandy road that lifts above the sea,
    Thrice and thrice the red cock crew,
    And thrice an elfin bugle blew
From the Gates of Faerie.

                                        Henry Martyn Hoyt

THE INTERPRETER

In the very early morning when the light was low
She got all together and she went like snow,
Like snow in the springtime on a sunny hill,
And we were only frightened and can't think still.

We can't think quite that the katydids and frogs
And the little crying chickens and the little grunting hogs,
And the other living things that she spoke for to us
Have nothing more to tell her since it happened thus.

She never is around for any one to touch,
But of ecstasy and longing she too knew much . . .
And always when any one has time to call his own
She will come and be beside him as quiet as a stone.

                                        Orrick Johns

DAPHNE

THEY told her she had hair the color
Of a nightingale.
They told her that her eyes were candles
Lit beneath a veil.

They praised her feet like narrow doves
Mated on the floor,
Saying there were never feet
Like her feet before.

They praised her shining voice that rang
Like stars dropped in a glass.
"Sing to thy little yellow shell!"
And so the night would pass.

But when they came too near to her
And touched her with the hand,
She drew her hair across her eyes.
She could not understand.

And when they said a thing to her
That she had never heard,
Her heart plunged into silence there
Like a hunted bird.

She caught her violet mantle close,
The Tyrian upon the white.
She quivered like a little twig.
She stepped into the night.

They called her name within the dark,
They searched beneath the sun,
But there was not a broken flower
To show where she had run.

Everything was very still,
Far too still, they said.
So they turned and went away,
Unaccompanied.

Nothing moved where they had sought,
Nothing sang or wept.
Beneath a tree that had no name,
Silence turned and slept.

Hildegarde Flanner

THE NEIGHBORS

At first cock-crow
The ghosts must go
Back to their quiet graves below.

AGAINST the distant striking of the clock
I heard the crowing cock,
   And I arose and threw the window wide;
     Long, long before the setting of the moon,
     And yet I knew they must be passing soon—
   My neighbors who had died—
Back to their narrow green-roofed homes that wait
Beyond the churchyard gate.

I leaned far out and waited—all the world
Was like a thing impearled,
   Mysterious and beautiful and still:
     The crooked road seemed one the moon might lay,
     Our little village slept in Quaker gray,
   And gray and tall the poplars on the hill;
And then far off I heard the cock—and then
My neighbors passed again.

At first it seemed a white cloud, nothing more,
Slow drifting by the door,
   Or gardened lilies swaying in the wind;
     Then suddenly each separate face I knew,
     The tender lovers drifting two and two,
   Old, peaceful folk long since passed out of mind,
And little children—one whose hand held still
An earth-grown daffodil.

And here I saw one pausing for a space
To lift a wistful face

Up to a certain window where there dreamed
A little brood left motherless; and there
One turned to where the unploughed fields lay bare;
And others lingering passed—but one there seemed
So over glad to haste, she scarce could wait
To reach the churchyard gate!

The farrier's little maid who loved too well
And died—I may not tell
How glad she seemed.   My neighbors, young and old,
With backward glances lingered as they went;
Only upon one face was all content,
A sorrow comforted—a peace untold.
I watched them through the swinging gate—the dawn
Stayed till the last had gone.

Theodosia Garrison

SHADOW TO SHADOW

If it would walk at all,
This was the very night.
I leaned out of the window while the moon
Threw down the tunneled walk a shadow-pall
Of black magnolia shade; I heard the tune
A wind sang by the ivy-mantled wall.
The west was dark but for a wisp of light,
And yet no night-birds had begun to call—
If it would walk at all, this was the night.

The quiet street lay dim beyond the gate,
And quietly its bars
Slid past each other like a gliding grate
Of ribs across the stars.

Yet, not a sound, no reassuring click
Of metal latch, and not a bird would scold,
Only the swirling darkness growing thick,
And I more cold.

The whirling darkness folded in to drape
And shroud the shape of Nothing till it stood

With bone-white moonbeams glimmering in its cape
With shadows for a hood.

And well I knew that if it spoke my name
How they would find me by the window there;
I guessed the grisly angle of the jaw,
The teeth below no nostrils, and the stare.

But not a whisper froze the waiting shadows;
No voice was added to the choir of care,
Until I croaked into a world of silence,
"How are they, over there?"

Then, like the last priest of a vanished nation,
The Shadow drew the cowl about its head,
And with a web-like hand made salutation,
And went back to the Dead.

Hervey Allen

GHOST NIGHT

A HUNDRED strange things
    Looked in at the door;
There went a soft foot
    Across the old floor.

Oh, lovely and lost,
    It was you who were there,
Wrapped round in the cloak
    Of your golden long hair!

The house grew as sweet
    As a just-lit flower,
On the edge of the rain,
    In an April hour.

Wrapped round in the cloak
    Of your golden long hair,
Oh, lovely and lost,
    It was you who were there!

I fell at your feet;
  Enough you were near,
Although but a ghost
  With the ghosts of the year!
Lizette Woodworth Reese

THE GHOST

"Who knocks?" "I, who was beautiful,
Beyond all dreams to restore,
I, from the roots of the dark thorn am hither,
And knock on the door."

"Who speaks?" "I—once was my speech
Sweet as the bird's on the air,
When echo lurks by the waters to heed;
'Tis I speak thee fair."

"Dark is the hour!" "Ay, and cold."
"Lone is my house." "Ah, but mine?"
"Sight, touch, lips, eyes yearned in vain."
"Long dead these to thine . . ."

Silence. Still faint on the porch
Brake the flames of the stars.
In gloom groped a hope-wearied hand
Over keys, bolts, and bars.

A face peered. All the gray night
In chaos of vacancy shone;
Naught but vast Sorrow was there—
The sweet cheat gone.
Walter de la Mare

GREEN CANDLES

"There's someone at the door," said gold candlestick:
"Let her in quick, let her in quick!"
"There is a small hand groping at the handle:
Why don't you turn it?" asked green candle.

"Don't go, don't go," said the Heppelwhite chair,
"Lest you find a strange lady there."
"Yes, stay where you are," whispered the white wall:
"There is nobody there at all."

"I know her little foot," gray carpet said:
"Who but I should know her light tread? "
"She shall come in," answered the open door,
"And not," said the room, "go out any more."
Humbert Wolfe

BAST

SHE had green eyes, that excellent seer,
And little peaks to either ear.
She sat there, and I sat here.

She spoke of Egypt, and a white
Temple, against enormous night.

She smiled with clicking teeth and said
That the dead were never dead;

Said old emperors hung like bats
In barns at night, or ran like rats—
But empresses came back as cats!
William Rose Benét

THE DROWNED SEAMAN

THERE came a seaman up from the sea.
"Sailor, what is your will of me?"

He rolled in his gate as seaman use,
His eye was stern that I might not choose

But fetch him 'baccy, and make him tea.
"Sailor, what is your will of me? "

He puffed at a pipe that gave no smoke,
Then this strange word from his lips there broke:

"I was drowned in the Skagger-Rack,
But we fought 'em fair, and we beat 'em back.

"Now which of these laughing lads shall be
Seamen to learn the ways of the sea? "

He looked at the lads and they left their game,
And wide-eyed over the grass they came;

And each one spoke, and thus said he:
"Sailor, what is your will of me? "

Maude Goldring

I MET AT EVE

I MET at eve the Prince of Sleep,
  His was a still and lovely face,
He wandered through a valley steep,
  Lovely in a lonely place.

His garb was gray of lavender,
  About his brows a poppy-wreath
Burned like dim coals, and everywhere
  The air was sweeter for his breath.

His twilight feet no sandals wore,
  His eyes shone faint in their own flame,
Fair moths that gloomed his steps before
  Seemed letters of his lovely name.

His house is in the mountain ways,
  A phantom house of misty walls,
Whose golden flocks at evening graze,
  And witch the moon with muffled calls.

Upwelling from his shadowy springs
  Sweet waters shake a trembling sound,
There flit the hoot-owl's silent wings,
  There hath his web the silkworm wound.

Dark in his pools clear visions lurk,
  And rosy, as with morning buds,
Along his dales of broom and birk
  Dreams haunt his solitary woods.

I met at eve the Prince of Sleep,
  His was a still and lovely face,
He wandered through a valley steep.
  Lovely in a lonely place.
                              Walter de la Mare

TO SLEEP

FRAIL Sleep, that blowest by fresh banks
  Of quiet, crystal pools, beside whose brink
  The varicolored dreams, like cattle, come to drink,

Cool Sleep, thy reeds, in solemn ranks,
  That murmur peace to me by midnight's streams,
  At dawn I pluck, and dayward pipe my flock of dreams.
                              Percy MacKaye

OLD LIZETTE ON SLEEP

BED is the boon for me!
  It's well to bake and sweep,
But hear the word of old Lizette:
  It's better than all to sleep.

Summer and flowers are gay,
  And morning light and dew;
But agèd eyelids love the dark
  Where never a light seeps through.

What!—open-eyed, my dears,
  Thinking your hearts will break?
There's nothing, nothing, nothing, I say,
  That's worth the lying awake!

I learned it in my youth—
  Love I was dreaming of!
I learned it from the needle-work
  That took the place of love.

A Wasted Day 881

I learned it from the years
  And what they brought about;
From song, and from the hills of joy
  Where sorrow sought me out.

It's good to dream and turn,
  And turn and dream, or fall
To comfort with my pack of bones,
  And know nothing at all!

Yes, never know at all
  If prowlers mew or bark,
Nor wonder if it's three o'clock
  Or four o'clock of the dark.

When the longer shades have fallen,
  And the last weariness
Has brought the sweetest gift of life,
  The last forgetfulness,

If a sound as of old leaves
  Stir the last bed I keep,
Then say, my dears: "It's old Lizette—
  She's turning in her sleep."

Agnes Lee

A WASTED DAY

I spoiled the day;
  Hotly, in haste,
All the calm hours
  I gashed and defaced.

Let me forget,
  Let me embark
—Sleep for my boat—
  And sail through the dark.

Till a new day
  Heaven shall send,
Whole as an apple,
  Kind as a friend.

Frances Cornford

MOON-MADNESS

THEY did not know that the moon had shone
　　All night across my face:
And they marvelled why I wandered alone
Picking up acorns and pebbles of stone
　　In a solitary place.

How should they know I had dreamed all night
　　With the moonbeams on my eyes
Of a goddess slender and tall and white
Who walked in a garden of strange delight
　　In the regions of Paradise?

They wondered why I was rapt and pale,
　　Haggard and ill at ease;
For they did not know I had watched a sail
Like a shimmering mist where the dream-winds fail
　　On magical, moon-bright seas.

And they questioned, "Why does he linger there
　　Where the grass is withered and dead,
With dry leaves tangled among his hair,
And fingers that tremble, and eyes astare?
　　"He is mad, quite mad," they said.

They could not know of the songs I heard
　　In the fair Moon-Gardens; nor why
I listened there for a whispered word,
And started at pipe of a sudden bird
　　Or wept when the wind went by.

Victor Starbuck

SIMPLES

*O bella, bionda
sei come l'onda*

OF cool sweet dew and radiance mild
The moon a web of silence weaves
In the still garden where a child
Gathers the simple salad leaves.

A moon-dew stars her hanging hair,
And moonlight touches her young brow;
And, gathering, she sings an air:
"Fair as the wave is, fair art thou."

Be mine, I pray, a waxen ear
To shield me from her childish croon;
And mine a shielded heart to her
Who gathers simples of the moon.

James Joyce

THE CROWNING OF DREAMING JOHN

I

Seven days he travelled
Down the roads of England,
Out of leafy Warwick lanes
Into London Town.
Gray and very wrinkled
Was Dreaming John of Grafton,
But seven days he walked to see
A king put on his crown.

Down the streets of London
He asked the crowded people
Where would be the crowning
And when would it begin.
He said he'd got a shilling,
A shining silver shilling,
But when he came to Westminster
They wouldn't let him in.

Dreaming John of Grafton
Looked upon the people,
Laughed a little laugh, and then
Whistled and was gone.
Out along the long roads,
The twisting roads of England,
Back into the Warwick lanes
Wandered Dreaming John.

II

As twilight touched with her ghostly fingers
All the meadows and mellow hills,
And the great sun swept in his robes of glory—
Woven of petals of daffodils
And jewelled and fringed with leaves of the roses—
Down the plains of the western way,
Among the rows of the scented clover
Dreaming John in his dreaming lay.

Since dawn had folded the stars of heaven
He'd counted a score of miles and five,
And now, with a vagabond heart untroubled
And proud as the properest man alive,
He sat him down with a limber spirit
That all men covet and few may keep,
And he watched the summer draw round her beauty
The shadow that fell from the wings of sleep.

And up from the valleys and shining rivers,
And out of the shadowy wood-ways wild,
And down from the secret hills, and streaming
Out of the shimmering undefiled
Wonder of sky that arched him over,
Came a company shod in gold
And girt in gowns of a thousand blossoms,
Laughing and rainbow-aureoled.

Wrinkled and gray and with eyes a-wonder
And soul beatified, Dreaming John
Watched the marvellous company gather
While over the clover a glory shone;
They bore on their brows the hues of heaven,
Their limbs were sweet with flowers of the fields,
And their feet were bright with the gleaming treasure
That prodigal earth to her children yields.

They stood before him, and John was laughing
As they were laughing; he knew them all,
Spirits of trees and pools and meadows,

Mountain and windy waterfall,
Spirits of clouds and skies and rivers,
Leaves and shadows and rain and sun,
A crowded, jostling, laughing army,
And Dreaming John knew every one.

Among them then was a sound of singing
And chiming music, as one came down
The level rows of the scented clover,
Bearing aloft a flashing crown;
No word of a man's desert was spoken,
Nor any word of a man's unworth,
But there on the wrinkled brow it rested,
And Dreaming John was king of the earth.

III

*Dreaming John of Grafton
Went away to London,
Saw the colored banners fly,
Heard the great bells ring,
But though his tongue was civil
And he had a silver shilling,
They wouldn't let him in to see
The crowning of the King.*

*So back along the long roads,
The leafy roads of England,
Dreaming John went carolling,
Travelling alone,
And in a summer evening,
Among the scented clover,
He held before a shouting throng,
A crowning of his own.*
                              John Drinkwater

HEARTH AND HOME

HOME

WHEREVER smoke wreaths
  Heavenward curl—
Cave of a hermit,
  Hovel of churl,
Mansion of merchant, princely dome—
  Out of the dreariness,
  Into its cheeriness,
  Come we in weariness
    Home.

I, too, have wandered
  Through the far lands,
Home there was their home;
  Open their hands.
Yet though all brothers, born of the foam,
  Far o'er appalling sea,
  Ever enthralling me,
  Blood still was calling me
    Home.

Men speak of jewels
  Earth holds abroad.
What can compare with
  One bit of sod,
Full of the love-gold sunk in the loam?
  There lies my holy dead,
  And there my mother shed
  Tears o'er my sleeping head—
    Home.

Home . . . where I first knew
  Day was alight;
Where I would fain be
  Ere the Long Night,
That they might write this in some old tome:
886

This earth the womb was;
This earth the room was;
This earth the tomb was.

HOME.

Stephen Chalmers

IT'S A FAR, FAR, CRY

IT's a far, far cry to my own land,
A hundred leagues or more,
To moorlands where the fairies flit
In Rosses and Gueedore
Where white maned waves come prancing up
To Dooran's rugged shore.

There's a cabin there by a holy well,
Once blessed by Columbcille,
And a holly bush and a fairy foot
On the slope of Glenties Hill,
Where the dancing feet of many winds
Go roving at their will.

My heart is sick of the level lands,
Where the wingless windmills be,
Where the long-nosed guns from dusk to dawn
Are speaking angrily;
But the little home by Glenties Hill,
Ah, that's the place for me.

A candle stuck on the muddy floor,
Lights up the dug-out wall,
And I see in its flame the prancing sea
And the mountains straight and tall;
For my heart is more than often back
By the hills of Donegal.

Patrick Macgill

NORA

WITHIN an English village yesterday
I came upon a little child at play.
I lingered by to watch the baby game,
And heard some voice call gently on her name.

Sweet she replied. How leaped my heart to hear
The pretty notes, the accent ever dear,
Shy as the wind soft singing from the South!
I, hungry, kissed the brogue upon her mouth.

Dora Sigerson Shorter

APPARITION

I

I WALKED my fastest down the twilight street;
Sometimes I ran a little, it was so late.
At first the houses echoed back my feet,
Then the path softened just before our gate.
Even in the dusk I saw, even in my haste,
Lawn-tracks and gravel-marks. "That's where he plays;
The scooter and the cart these lines have traced,
And Baby wheels her doll here, sunny days."
Our door was open; on the porch still lay
Ungathered toys; our hearth-light cut the gloam;
Within, round table-candles, you—and they.
And I called out, I shouted, "I am come home!"
At first you heard not, then you raised your eyes,
Watched me a moment—and showed no surprise.

II

Such dreams we have had often, when we stood
Thought-struck amid the merciful routine,
And distance more than danger chilled the blood,
When we looked back and saw what lay between;
Like ghosts that have their portion of farewell,
Yet will be looking in on life again,
And see old faces, and have news to tell,
But no one heeds them; they are phantom men.
Now home indeed and old loves greet us back,
Yet—shall we say it?—something here we lack,
Some reach and climax we have left behind,
And something here is dead, that without sound
Moves lips at us and beckons, shadow-bound,
But what it means, we cannot call to mind.

John Erskine

SWEET STAY–AT–HOME

SWEET Stay-At-Home, sweet Well-content,
Thou knowest of no strange continent:
Thou hast not felt thy bosom keep
A gentle motion with the deep;
Thou hast not sailed in Indian seas,
Where scent comes forth in every breeze.
Thou hast not seen the rich grape grow
For miles, as far as eyes can go;
Thou hast not seen a summer's night
When maids could sew by a worm's light;
Nor the North Sea in spring send out
Bright hues that like birds flit about
In solid cages of white ice—
Sweet Stay-at-Home, sweet Love-one-place.
Thou hast not seen black fingers pick
White cotton when the bloom is thick,
Nor heard black throats in harmony;
Nor hast thou sat on stones that lie
Flat on the earth, that once did rise
To hide proud kings from common eyes.
Thou hast not seen plains full of bloom
Where green things had such little room
They pleased the eye like fairer flowers—
Sweet Stay-at-Home, all these long hours.
Sweet Well-content, sweet Love-one-place,
Sweet, simple maid, bless thy dear face;
For thou hast made more homely stuff
Nurture thy gentle self enough;
I love thee for a heart that's kind—
Not for the knowledge in thy mind.

W. H. Davies

TO THE LITTLE HOUSE

DEAR little house, dear shabby street,
Dear books and beds and food to eat!
How feeble words are to express
The facets of your tenderness.

How white the sun comes through the pane!
In tinkling music drips the rain!
How burning bright the furnace glows!
What paths to shovel when it snows!

O dearly loved Long Island trains!
O well remembered joys and pains.
How near the housetops Beauty leans
Along that little street in Queens!

Let these poor rhymes abide for proof
Joy dwells beneath a humble roof;
Heaven is not built of country seats
But little queer surburban streets!

Christopher Morley

THE OLD HOUSE

O KINDLY house, where time my soul endows
With courage, hope, and patience manifold,
How shall my debt of love to thee be told,
Since first I heard the sweet-voiced robins rouse
The morn among thy ancient apple-boughs?
Here was I nourished on the truths of old,
Here taught against new times to make me bold,
Memory and hope the door-posts, O dear house!
Heaven's blessing rested on thy dark-gray roof,
And clasped thy children, age to lapsing age,
Birth and the grave thy tale till time's release;
Poverty did not hold from thee aloof;
Of lowly good thou wast the hermitage;
Now falls the evening light.   God give thee peace!

George Edward Woodberry

THE HOME FIRE

THE home fire's a lazy fire
    And wood it should be,
And the thoughts said about it
    Begin with we.

The home fire's a cold fire
  Time may come, and dead;
Then there's the road to go
  And the stranger's bed.

Orrick Johns

THE HOMING HEART

EACH day, dear love, my road leads far
From where you, home-contented, are.
My mood is kin to that unrest
Which sends the wild bird from its nest.

But though I have a roaming heart,
God gave me too a homing heart,—
How swift at dusk my paths run to
The lights of home, the arms of you!

Daniel Henderson

HOME

So long had I travelled the lonely road,
Though, now and again, a wayfaring friend
Walked shoulder to shoulder, and lightened the load,
I often would think to myself as I strode,
No comrade will journey with you to the end.

And it seemed to me, as the days went past,
And I gossiped with cronies, or brooded alone,
By wayside fires, that my fortune was cast
To sojourn by other men's hearths to the last,
And never to come to my own hearthstone.

The lonely road no longer I roam..
We met, and were one in the heart's desire.
Together we came, through the wintry gloam,
To the little old house by the cross-ways, home;
And crossed the threshold, and kindled the fire.

Wilfrid Gibson

THE·HEART'S LOW DOOR

O EARTH, I will have none of thee.
　Alien to me the lowly plain,
And the rough passion of the sea
　Storms my unheeding heart in vain.

The petulance of rain and wind,
　The haughty mountains' superb scorn,
Are but slight things I've flung behind,
　Old garments that I have out-worn.

Bare of the grudging grass, and bare
　Of the tall forest's careless shade,
Deserter from thee, Earth, I dare
　See all thy phantom brightness fade.

And, darkening to the sun, I go
　To enter by the heart's low door,
And find where Love's red embers glow
　A home, who ne'er had home before.

Susan Mitchell

AN OLD WOMAN OF THE ROADS

OH, to have a little house!
　To own the hearth and stool and all!
The heaped-up sods upon the fire,
　The pile of turf against the wall!

To have a clock with weights and chains
　And pendulum swinging up and down!
A dresser filled with shining delf,
　Speckled and white and blue and brown!

I could be busy all the day
　Clearing and sweeping hearth and floor,
And fixing on their shelf again
　My white and blue and speckled store!

I could be quiet there at night
   Beside the fire and by myself,
Sure of a bed and loth to leave
   The ticking clock and the shining delf!

Och! but I'm weary of mist and dark,
   And roads where there's never a house nor bush;
And tired I am of bog and road,
   And the crying wind and the lonesome hush!

And I am praying to God on high,
   And I am praying Him night and day,
For a little house—a house of my own—
   Out of the wind's and the rain's way.

Padraic Colum

THE DREAMERS

THE gypsies passed her little gate—
She stopped her wheel to see.—
A brown-faced pair who walked the road,
Free as the wind is free;
And suddenly her tidy room
A prison seemed to be.

Her shining plates against the walls,
Her sunlit, sanded floor,
The brass-bound wedding chest that held
Her linen's snowy store,
The very wheel whose humming died,—
Seemed only chains she bore.

She watched the foot-free gypsies pass;
She never knew or guessed
The wistful dream that drew them close—
The longing in each breast
Some day to know a home like hers,
Wherein their hearts might rest.

Theodosia Garrison

THE UNWILLING GYPSY

THE wide green earth is mine in which to wander;
Each path that beckons I may follow free,
Sea to gray sea.
But O, that one walled garden, small and sheltered,
Belonged to me!

High on the mountain top I watch the sunset,
Its splendid fires flare upward and burn low,
Ah, once to know
Down in the twilight lowlands dim and tender,
My own hearth-glow!

Night falls. A thousand stars look down upon me,
But though from inland plain to ocean's foam
My steps may roam,
One clear fixed star forever is denied me . . .
The light of home!

Josephine Johnson

MY MOTHER

GOD made my mother on an April day,
From sorrow and the mist along the sea,
Lost birds' and wanderers' songs and ocean spray,
And the moon loved her wandering jealously.

Beside the ocean's din she combed her hair,
Singing the nocturne of the passing ships,
Before her earthly lover found her there
And kissed away the music from her lips.

She came unto the hills and saw the change
That brings the swallow and the geese in turns.
But there was not a grief she deemèd strange,
For there is that in her which always mourns.

Kind heart she has for all on hill or wave
Whose hopes grew wings like ants to fly away.
I bless the God Who such a mother gave
This poor bird-hearted singer of a day.

Francis Ledwidge

AUTUMN

(For my mother)

How memory cuts away the years,
And how clean the picture comes
Of autumn days, brisk and busy,
Charged with keen sunshine.
And you, stirred with activity,
The spirit of these energetic days!

There was our back-yard,
So plain and stripped of green,
With even the weeds carefully pulled away
From the crooked, red bricks that made the walk,
And the earth on either side so black.

Autumn and dead leaves burning in the sharp air,
And winter comforts coming in like a pageant.
I shall not forget them:
Great jars laden with the raw green of pickles,
Standing in a solemn row across the back of the porch,
Exhaling the pungent dill;
And in the very center of the yard,
You, tending the great catsup kettle of gleaming copper
Where fat, red tomatoes bobbed up and down
Like jolly monks in a drunken dance.
And there were bland banks of cabbages that came by the
     wagon-load,
Soon to be cut into delicate ribbons
Only to be crushed by the heavy, wooden stompers.
Such feathery whiteness—to come to kraut!
And after, there were grapes that hid their brightness under
     a gray dust,
Then gushed thrilling, purple blood over the fire;
And enamelled crab-apples that tricked with their fragrance
But were bitter to taste.
And there were spicy plums and ill-shaped quinces,
And long string-beans floating in pans of clear water
Like slim, green fishes.

And there was fish itself,
Salted, silver herring from the city . . .

And you moved among these mysteries,
Absorbed and smiling and sure,
Stirring, tasting, measuring,
With the precision of a ritual.
I like to think of you in your years of power—
You, now so shaken and so powerless—
High priestess of your home.

Jean Starr Untermeyer

THE MOTHER IN THE HOUSE

FOR such as you, I do believe,
Spirits their softest carpets weave,
And spread them out with gracious hand
Wherever you walk, wherever you stand.

For such as you, of scent and dew
Spirits their rarest nectar brew,
And where you sit and where you sup
Pour beauty's elixir in your cup.

For all day long, like other folk,
You bear the burden, wear the yoke,
And yet when I look in your eyes at eve
You are lovelier than ever, I do believe.

Hermann Hagedorn

MY MOTHER'S HOUSE

"IT's strange," my mother said, "to think
Of the old house where we were born.
I can remember every chink
And every board our feet had worn.

"It's gone now. Many years ago
They tore it down. It was too old,
And none too grand as houses go,
Not like a new house, bought or sold.

"And so they tore it down. But we
Could talk about it still, and say
'Just so the kitchen used to be,
And the stairs turned in such a way.'

"But we're gone too now. Everyone
Who knew the house is dead and buried.
And I'll not last so long alone
With all my children grown and married.

"There's not a living soul can tell,
Except myself, just how the grass
Grew round the pathway to the well,
Or where the china-closet was.

"Yet while I live you cannot say
That the old house is quite, quite dead.
It still exists in some dim way
While I remember it," she said.

Eunice Tietjens

MOTHERS AND CHILDREN

Born are we of fire
And orderly desire,
And on that day
The leaves all pray
And the stars all wait
By the smallest wooden gate
To listen to the cry
Of a woman by and by.

And they gather in the door to see his little feet
And go away and whisper there are none more sweet;
And they peep in his eyes and laugh like a lord
To see another human that is not yet bored . . .
Old men and ladies, they go that way
And very, very silly are the things they say!

We are born of woman
And they say she is human

But we very soon know
She is more than so . . .
For we drink from her cup
With the top closed up
And no matter how we press
It grows no less!

And she sits by the sky where the wind comes through
And knows what we want by the things we do.
And the sound of her voice is sweeter than her milk,
And the feel of her face is like smooth white silk . . .
And a man may be ninety with a very long beard
And not be any better than his mother feared.

Orrick Johns

MY MOTHER

I KNEW her first as food and warmth and rest,
A silken lap, soft arms, a tender breast;
Then, as fear came into my world, I knew
She was a never-failing refuge too.
Then I discovered play—my playmate she,
Unwearied in gay ingenuity,
And yet at the same time in her I saw,
Scarce understood, and yet obeyed, the Law.
Time taught me more and more to comprehend
Her understanding sweetness as a friend,
And as my life's horizon grew more wide
Her meaning to myself was magnified
By vision that had grown at last to see
A love that could enfold the world—and me.
Oh, there were restive and impatient days
When wilful childhood craved its own wild ways
And flung aside the gently guiding hand—
Blind hours when I was slow to understand,
But patience and a love that would not fail
Always prevailed—how could they but prevail?
And now so well I know her that I know
The graciousness of her will always grow
Like daybreak in my spirit, and will be

Through all my life a radiant mystery
Since love like hers ever exceeds the sweep
Of mortal plummet, sound we ne'er so deep.
Eternity itself will not suffice
To fathom it.   If all through Paradise
My mother's love shall lead me wondering,
Is God's a slighter and a shallower thing?
How shall I dare to dream that I enclose
Her Maker in the mind she overflows?

Amelia Josephine Burr

THOUGHTS UPON A WALK WITH NATALIE, MY NIECE, AT HOUGHTON FARM

HERE is the same familiar land
My mother knew when she was young.
This warm earth crumbled to her hand,
She heard these very bird notes sung.

In that green meadow down the lane,
Knee-deep her pony cropped the grass,
The beaten pathways still remain
That felt her flying footsteps pass.

Beyond that willow tree the stream
Plunges forever into foam,—
Let us go there a while and dream
Of this dear place that was her home.

.   .   .   .

She must have stood here long ago
Upon this lichen-covered stone
Where we are now who loved her so;
Blood of her blood, bone of her bone.

She must have watched this sunlit pool
With wonder in her clear young eyes,
Finding within these waters cool
The mystery that never dies.

All this my heart has understood,
Dear child, or ever you were born.
The evening of her womanhood
Long held a vision of the morn.

Yet I had never hoped to see
Through these fair fields, her lambent grace,
Moving beside me on the lea,
Turning to greet me, face to face.

Now by the miracle that filled
Your slender limbs with living fire,
More than my daring spirit willed
Lies in the cup of my desire.

Long hence when you have known my grief
You will look back and understand. . . .
Now let us play awhile.   This leaf
Shall be a bark from fairyland!

We'll freight it deep with marigold,
Give it a rainbow for a sail,
Upon the deck a beetle bold
Shall lord it in his flashing mail.

Look, it is drifting down the tide,
Wind-driven from the rocky shore. . . .
Who knows what vagrant dreams may ride
On this frail ship forevermore?

Harold Trowbridge Pulsifer

A CHILD'S SONG TO HER MOTHER

THE lovely years went lightly by
    As April flowers go,
And often you would laugh or cry
    To see how I could grow.

The lonely years drift by in rain,
    As leaves in Autumn do.
I long, when we shall meet again,
    To be as tall as you.

Winifred Welles

MOTHERHOOD

MARY, the Christ long slain, passed silently,
Following the children joyously astir
Under the cedrus and the olive-tree,
Pausing to let their laughter float to her.
Each voice an echo of a voice more dear,
She saw a little Christ in every face.
Then came another woman gliding near
To watch the tender life that filled the place.
And Mary sought the woman's hand, and spoke:
"I know thee not, yet know thy memory tossed
With all a thousand dreams their eyes evoke
Who bring to thee a child beloved and lost.

"I, too, have rocked my Little One.
And He was fair!
Oh, fairer than the fairest sun,
And like its rays through amber spun
His sun-bright hair.
Still I can see it shine and shine."
"Even so," the woman said, "was mine."

"His ways were ever darling ways"—
And Mary smiled—
"So soft, so clinging! Glad relays
Of love were all His precious days.
My Little Child!
My vanished star! My music fled!"
"Even so was mine," the woman said.

Then Mary whispered: "Tell me, thou,
Of thine." And she:
"Oh, mine was rosy as a bough
Blooming with roses, sent, somehow,
To bloom for me!
His balmy fingers left a thrill
Deep in my breast that warms me still."

Then she gazed down some wilder, darker hour,
And said—when Mary questioned, knowing not:
"Who art thou, mother of so sweet a flower?"—
"I am the mother of Iscariot."

Agnes Lee

DUO

WOMAN in the garden
Where the angels came;
Nothing yet of pardon,
Nothing yet of shame;
Seraphs in her honor
To the gates repair,—
O, the sun upon her!
O, the golden air!

Woman in the green ways,—
Young roots are sweet;
In and out the glean-ways,
Brown nuts at feet;
Planting, weaving, hoarding,
Saving from the wild,
Not for self or lording,
But for us—the child.

Woman in the tower;
Moat and wall to guard,
The rare, white lady-flower
Blooming for her lord,
Whose bright sword has won her
From all knights that ride;
His to serve and honor,—
An unfading bride!

Woman 'neath the master
Of the feudal day;
For the bread he cast her
Paying life away
To him, the mighty giver,

Him, her soul and god!
A sword for who would save her,
And for her the rod!

Now by fireside singing
Here at last is home;
Over ages winging
Again the angels come.
Holy love and human
In her worship rise.
O, the light on woman
Shed from children's eyes!

To the factories feeding
Hands and soul and will;
Herded, and unheeding
She is woman still.
Trembling home in gloom light,
Home—O mock of breath!
In her eyes the loom-blight,
In her shadow, death!

Sons must pass to battle;
Armor them with prayers;
Never conflict's rattle
Reach thy straining ears;
In the home they've made thee,
Mother, sit thee down;
With their love they'll shade thee,
With their fortune crown!

Be it or here or yonder,
Where'er thy children cry,
Far as thy fairest wander,
Far as thy dearest die,—
Be thine the heart that fareth
Past every dim frontier,
Till who the last rood dareth
Shall find a mother there!

Olive Dargan

NARRATIVE AND DESCRIPTIVE POEMS

A TRAMPWOMAN'S TRAGEDY

FROM Wynyard's Gap the livelong day,
 The livelong day,
We beat afoot the northward way
 We had travelled times before.
The sun-blaze burning on our backs,
Our shoulders sticking to our packs,
By fosseway, fields and turnpike tracks
 We skirted sad Sedge-Moor.

Full twenty miles we jaunted on,
 We jaunted on,—
My fancy-man, and jeering John,
 And Mother Lee, and I.
And, as the sun drew down to west,
We climbed the toilsome Poldon crest,
And saw, of landskip sights the best,
 The inn that beamed thereby.

For months we had padded side by side,
 Ay, side by side
Through the Great Forest, Blackmoor wide,
 And where the Parret ran.
We'd faced the gusts on Mendip ridge,
Had crossed the Yeo unhelped by bridge,
Been stung by every Marshwood midge,
 I and my fancy-man.

Lone inns we loved, my man and I,
 My man and I;
"King's Stag," "Windwhistle" high and dry,
 "The Horse" on Hintock Green,

The cosy house at Wynyard's Gap,
"The Hut" renowned on Bredy Knap,
And many another wayside tap
    Where folk might sit unseen.

Now as we trudged—O deadly day,
    O deadly day!—
I teased my fancy-man in play
    And wanton idleness.
I walked alongside jeering John,
I laid his hand my waist upon;
I would not bend my glances on
    My lover's dark distress.

Thus Poldon top at last we won,
    At last we won,
And gained the inn at sink of sun
    Far-famed as "Marshal's Elm."
Beneath us figured tor and lea,
From Mendip to the western sea—
I doubt if finer sight there be
    Within this royal realm.

Inside the settle all a-row—
    All four a-row
We sat, I next to John, to show
    That he had wooed and won.
And then he took me on his knee,
And swore it was his turn to be
My favored mate, and Mother Lee
    Passed to my former one.

Then in a voice I had never heard,
    I had never heard,
My only Love to me: "One word,
    My lady, if you please!
Whose is the child you are like to bear?—
His?   After all my months o' care?"
God knows 'twas not! But, O despair!
    I nodded—still to tease.

Then up he sprung, and with his knife—
    And with his knife
He let out jeering Johnny's life,
    Yes; there, at set of sun.
The slant ray through the window nigh
Gilded John's blood and glazing eye,
Ere scarcely Mother Lee and I
    Knew that the deed was done.

The taverns tell the gloomy tale,
    The gloomy tale,
How that at Ivel-chester jail
    My Love, my sweetheart swung;
Though stained till now by no misdeed
Save one horse ta'en in time o' need;
(Blue Johnny stole right many a steed
    Ere his last fling he flung.)

Thereaft I walked the world alone,
    Alone, alone!
On his death-day I gave my groan
    And dropped his dead-born child.
'Twas nigh the jail, beneath a tree,
None tending me; for Mother Lee
Had died at Glaston, leaving me
    Unfriended on the wild.

And in the night as I lay weak,
    As I lay weak,
The leaves a-falling on my cheek,
    The red moon low declined—
The ghost of him I'd die to kiss
Rose up and said: "Ah, tell me this!
Was the child mine, or was it his?
    Speak, that I rest may find!"

O doubt not but I told him then,
    I told him then,
That I had kept me from all men
    Since we joined lips and swore.

Whereat he smiled, and thinned away
As the wind stirred to call up day . . .
—'Tis past!   And here alone I stray
     Haunting the Western Moor.
                              Thomas Hardy

GASPARA STAMPA

" Saffo de' nostri tempi alta Gaspara "

VENICE—CINQUECENTO

"I burned, I wept, I sang: I burn, sing, weep again,
And I shall weep and sing, I shall forever burn
Until or death or time or fortune's turn
Shall still my eye and heart, still fire and pain."

Like flame, like wine, across the still lagoon
The colors of the sunset stream.
Spectral in heaven as climbs the frail veiled moon,
So climbs my dream.
Out of the heart's eternal torture fire
No eastern phœnix risen—
Only the naked soul, spent with desire,
Bursts its prison.

O love, magnificent and dreadful love
At last consuming heart and brain,
Palling all days with thoughts we weary of,
Weary of pain,—
O golden city set in the sun's heart,
Isled in a golden sea,
Yet what a vague phantasmal counterpart
Of what might be,

Darkness comes down upon your domes and towers,
Dark gondolas gliding under evening bells.
Deep night spreads burning over faded hours
The hell of hells.
The shadows mock me with his step, his sigh.
The treacherous tapers flare
And flaw; but though I stare with burning eye
He is not there.

Collalto, my illustrious lord, it is
So strange! One word, one sign
Would turn, like Cana's metamorphosis,
These tears to wine,
Wine from my heart—or shall my blood be shed
To seal the crumpled scroll,
Who gave you living, who would give you dead
Body and soul?

Capitals, columns, arches, sculptures fall,
The ivy crawls on Istrian stone;
Tower and palace, chapel, drawbridge, all
Time leaves prone;
Only our Alps whose blue without one stain
Blends into higher light—
My namesake stream of the Trevisian plain—
Time finds bright.

Yet will not Time, kind to the Paduan, scroll
My name at last with yours
Vittoria, Veronica? If the soul
Of song endures
I grasp eternity. O barren bliss
Beside pomegranate flowers
Swayed in the moonlight, and one secret kiss,—
Bliss once ours.

For France is far, so far, my dearest lord,
Beyond the Alps so far, men say,
One little word, even one little word
Loses it way.
Is it not piteous then to die, to live
In death, to gasp unheard
In thirst unslaked for what one word could give,
One little word?

And for a faith to tread consuming heat
And for a love to look on death
And to go robed in fire, in fire complete,
With sharp-drawn breath,

While the trapped heart, grown frenzied with its pain,
For joy once scorning fate
Storms with wild wings, again and yet again,
Your iron gate?

The gods returned to earth when Venice broke
Like Venus from the dawn-encircled sea.
Wide laughed the skies with light when Venice woke
Crowned of antiquity,
And as with spoil of gems bewildering earth,
Art in her glorious mind
Jewelled all Italy for joy's rebirth
To all mankind.

And we were heirs, true bounden heirs of this
Epoch of glittering life and bannered love
Even as we whispered in our earliest kiss
The joy thereof,
Ere sunlight on a condottiere's lance,
A bitter trumpet blown
Scattered your words and swept your heart toward France,
Left me alone.

The hyssop on the reed, this, this to drink
In this dark hour shall seal it as the last.
No word, my lord—and no more thoughts to think
When this is past.
Titian awhile his garden walk may tread
And Sansovino keep
My words, words you may read when I am dead,
But I—would sleep.

William Rose Benét

THERE LIVED A LADY IN MILAN

There lived a lady in Milan
Wrought for a madness unto Man,
A fawn Il Moro could not tame;
Her beauty unbedecked with pearls
More than all Beatrice's girls,
Her eyes a secret subtle flame.

Brocade wherein her body dressed
Was hallowed; flowers her footstep pressed
Suspired incense ere they died.
Her father mazed with alchemy
Wrought in his cellar ceaselessly.
She lived in quiet, gentle pride.

And by her garden in his hour
Passed Leonardo, come with power
From Florence. So he saw her face
Bending above the shrivelled stalks
Of autumn on the garden walks.
And Leonardo drank her grace.

She was as if a sunset were
With fresher colors, clearer air,
And a more golden coil of cloud.
She was as if all citherns swooned
With one rich harmony myriad-tuned,
Haunting, enchanting, pure and proud.

And Leonardo said, "Ladye,
I know not what you do to me
Who have and have not, seek nor find.
The sea-shell and the falcon's feather,
Greece and the rock and shifting weather
Have taught me many things of mind.

"My heart has taught me many things,
And so have emperors, popes, and kings,
And so have leaves and green May-flies;
Yea, I have learned from bird and beast,
From slouching dwarf and ranting priest.
Yet, in the end, how am I wise?

"Though with dividers and a quill
I weave some miracle of will,—
Say, that men fly,—though I design
For peace or war a thousand things
Gaining applause from dukes and kings,—
Though soft and deft my colors shine,

"Though my quick wit breed thunderbolts
I may not loose on all these dolts,
Things they are babes to comprehend,—
Though from the crevice in stone or lime
I trace grave outlines mocking Time,—
I know when I am beaten, Friend!

"Say that there lived of old a saint
Even Leonardo dared not paint,
Even Leonardo dared not draw,—
Too perfect in her breathing prime
For colors to transmit to time
Or quill attempt,—aye, ev'n in awe!

"Say this, cold histories, and say
I looked not on her from this day
Lest frenzied I destroy my art.
O golden lily,—how she stands
Listening! Beauty,—ah, your hands,
Your little hands tear out my heart!

"Do you not know you are so fair,
Brighter than springtime in the air?
What says your mirror to your mind?"
"Phantom," she whispered, "Do you plead
With ghostly gestures? . . . Ah, indeed,
Pity a lady deaf and blind

"Since birth!" . . . Then Leonardo turned
Saluting, though the sunset burned
In nimbus round her,—went his way
In daze, repeating "God's defect,
Even he!—and masterpiece elect!"
He never saw her from that day.

William Rose Benét

KING DAVID

I

DAVID sang to his hooknosed harp:
"The Lord God is a jealous God!
His violent vengeance is swift and sharp!
And the Lord is King above all gods!

"Blest be the Lord, through years untold,
The Lord Who has blessed me a thousand fold!

"Cattle and concubines, corn and hives
Enough to last me a dozen lives.

"Plump, good women with noses flat,
Marrowful blessings, weighty and fat.

"I wax in His peace like a pious gourd,
The Lord God is a pleasant God,
Break mine enemy's jaw, O Lord!
For the Lord is King above all gods!"

His hand dropped slack from the tunable strings,
A sorrow came on him—a sorrow of kings.

A sorrow sat on the arm of his throne,
An eagle sorrow with claws of stone.

"I am merry, yes, when I am not thinking,
But life is nothing but eating and drinking.

"I can shape my psalms like daggers of jade,
But they do not shine like the first I made.

"I can harry the heathen from North to South,
But no hot taste comes into my mouth.

"My wives are comely as long-haired goats,
But I would not care if they cut their throats!

"Where are the maids of the desert tents
With lips like flagons of frankincense?

"Where is Jonathan?   Where is Saul?
The captain-towers of Zion wall?

"The trees of cedar, the hills of Nod,
The kings, the running lions of God?

"Their words were a writing in golden dust,
Their names are myrrh in the mouths of the just.

"The sword of the slayer could never divide them—
Would God I had died in battle beside them!"

The Lord looked down from a thunder-clap.
(The Lord God is a crafty God.)
He heard the strings of the shrewd harp snap,
(The Lord Who is King above all gods.)

He pricked the king with a airy thorn,
It burnt in his body like grapes of scorn.

The eyelids roused that had drooped like lead.
David lifted his great, tired head.

The thorn stung at him, a fiery bee,
"The world is wide.   I will go and see
From the roof of my haughty palace," said he.

II

Bathsheba bathed on her vine-decked roof.
(The Lord God is a mighty God.)
Her body glittered like mail of proof.
(And the Lord is King above all gods.)

Her body shimmered, tender and white
As the flesh of lilies in candlelight.

King David forgot to be old or wise.
He spied on her bathing with sultry eyes.

A breath of spice came into his nose.
He said, "Her breasts are like two young roes."

His eyes were bright with a crafty gleam.
He thought, "Her body is soft as cream."

He straightened himself like an unbent bow
And called a servant and bade him go.

III

Uriah the Hittite came to his lord,
Dusty with war as a well-used sword.

A close, trim man like a belt, well-buckled;
A jealous gentleman, hard to cuckold.

David entreated him, soft and bland,
Offered him comfits from his own hand,

Drank with him deep till his eyes grew red,
And laughed in his beard as he went to bed.

The days slipped by without hurry or strife,
Like apple-parings under a knife.
And still Uriah kept from his wife.

Lean fear tittered through David's psalm,
"This merry husband is far too calm!"

David sent for Uriah then,
They greeted each other like pious men.

"Thou hast borne the battle, the dust and the heat.
Go down to thy house and wash thy feet!"

Uriah frowned at the words of the king.
His brisk, hard voice had a leaden ring.

"While the hosts of God still camp in the field,
My house to me is a garden sealed.

"How shall I rest while the arrow yet flies?
The dust of the war is still in my eyes."

David spoke with his lion's roar.
"If Peace be a bridle that rubs you sore,
You shall fill your belly with blood and war!"

Uriah departed, calling him kind.
His eyes were serpents in David's mind.

He summoned a captain, a pliable man.
"Uriah the Hittite shall lead the van.

"In the next assault when the fight roars high,
And the Lord God is a hostile God,
Retire from Uriah that he may die.
For the Lord is King above all gods."

IV

The messenger came while King David played
The friskiest ditty ever made.

"News, O king, from our dubious war!
The Lord of Hosts hath prevailed once more!

"His foes are scattered like chirping sparrows,
Their kings lie breathless, feathered with arrows.

"Many are dead of your captains tall.
Uriah the Hittite was first to fall."

David turned from the frolicsome strings
And rent his clothes for the death of kings.

Yet, as he rent them, he smiled for joy,
The sly, wide smile of a wicked boy.

"The powerful grace of the Lord prevails!
He has cracked Uriah between His nails!

"His blessings are mighty, they shall not cease!
And my days henceforth shall be days of peace!"

His mind grew tranquil, smoother than fleece.
He rubbed his body with scented grease,
And his days thenceforward were days of peace.

His days were fair as the flowering lime
—For a little time, for a little time.

And Bathsheba lay in his breast like a dove,
A vessel of amber, made for love.

v

When Bathsheba was great with child,
(The Lord God is a jealous God!)
Portly and meek as a moon grown mild,
(The Lord is King above all gods!)

Nathan, the prophet, wry and dying,
Preached to the king like a locust crying:

"Hearken awhile to a doleful thing!
There were two men in thy land, O King!

"One was rich as a gilded ram.
One had one treasure, a poor ewe-lamb.

"Rich man wasted his wealth like spittle.
Poor man shared with his lamb spare victual.

"A traveler came to the rich man's door.
'Give me to eat, for I hunger sore!'

"Rich man feasted him fatly, true,
But the meat that he gave him was fiends' meat, too,
Stolen and roasted, the poor man's ewe!

"Hearken, my lord, to a deadly thing!
What shall be done with these men, O King?"

David hearkened, seeing it plain,
His heart grew heavy with angry pain:
"Show me the rich man, that he be slain!"

Nathan barked as a jackall can.
"Just, O King!   And thou art the man!"

David rose as the thunders rise
When someone in Heaven is telling lies.
But his eyes were weaker than Nathan's eyes.

His huge bulk shivered like quaking sod,
Shoulders bowing to Nathan's rod,
Nathan, the bitter apple of God.

His great voice shook like a runner's, spent.
"My sin hath found me!   Oh, I repent!"

Answered Nathan, that talkative Jew:
"For many great services, comely and true,
The Lord of Mercy shall pardon you.

"But the child in Bathsheba, come of your seed,
Shall sicken and die like a blasted weed!"

David groaned when he heard him speak.
The painful tears ran hot on his cheek.

Ashes he cast on his kingly locks.
All night long he lay on the rocks,

Beseeching his Lord with a howling cry:
"O Lord God, O my jealous God,
Be kind to the child that it may not die,
For Thou art King above all gods!"

VI

Seven long nights he lay there, howling,
A lion wounded, moaning and growling.

Seven long midnights, sorrowing greatly,
While Sin, like a dead man, embraced him straitly.

Till he was abased from his lust and pride
And the child was born and sickened and died.

He arose at last.   It was ruddy Day.
And his sin like water had washed away.

He cleansed and anointed, took fresh apparel,
And worshiped the Lord in a tuneful carol.

His servants, bearing the child to bury,
Marveled greatly to see him so merry.

He spoke to them mildly as mid-May weather:
"The child and my sin are perished together.

"He is dead, my son.   Though his whole soul yearn to me,
I must go to him, he may not return to me.

"Why should I sorrow for what was pain?
A cherished grief is an iron chain."

He took up his harp, the sage old chief.
His heart felt clean as a new green leaf.

His soul smelt pleasant as rain-wet clover.
"I have sinned and repented and that's all over.

"In his dealings with heathen, the Lord is hard.
But the humble soul is his spikenard."

His wise thoughts fluttered like doves in the air.
"I wonder is Bathsheba still so fair?

"Does she weep for the child that our sin made perish?
I must comfort my ewe-lamb, comfort and cherish.

"The justice of God is honey and balm.
I will soothe her heart with a little psalm."

He went to her chamber, no longer sad,
Walking as light as a shepherd lad.

He found her weeping, her garments rent,
Trodden like straw by God's punishment.
He solaced her out of his great content.

Being but woman, a while she grieved,
But at last she was comforted, and conceived.

Nine months later she bore him a son.
(The Lord God is a mighty God!)
The name of that child was SOLOMON.
He was God's tough staff till his days were run!
(And the Lord is King above all gods!)

Stephen Vincent Benêt

EYE–WITNESS

DOWN by the railroad in a green valley
By dancing water, there he stayed awhile
Singing, and three men with him, listeners,
All tramps, all homeless reapers of the wind,
Motionless now and while the song went on
Transfigured into mages thronged with visions;
There with the late light of the sunset on them
And on clear water spinning from a spring
Through little cones of sand dancing and fading,
Close beside pine woods where a hermit-thrush
Cast, when love dazzled him, shadows of music
That lengthened, fluting, through the singer's pauses
While the sure earth rolled eastward bringing stars
Over the singer and the men that listened
There by the roadside, understanding all.

A train went by but nothing seemed to be changed.
Some eye at a car window must have flashed
From the plush world inside the glassy Pullman,
Carelessly bearing off the scene forever,
With idle wonder what the men were doing,

Seeing they were so strangely fixed and seeing
Torn papers from their smeary dreary meal
Spread on the ground with old tomato cans
Muddy with dregs of lukewarm chicory,
Neglected while they listened to the song.

And while he sang the singer's face was lifted,
And the sky shook down a soft light upon him
Out of its branches where like fruits there were
Many beautiful stars and planets moving,
With lands upon them, rising from their seas,
Glorious lands with glittering sands upon them,
With soils of gold and magic mould for seeding,
The shining loam of lands afoam with gardens
On mightier stars with giant rains and suns
There in the heavens; but on none of all
Was there ground better than he stood upon:
There was no world there in the sky above him
Deeper in promise than the earth beneath him
Whose dust had flowered up in him the singer
And three men understanding every word.

The Tramp Sings

I will sing, I will go, and never ask me why
I was born a rover and a passer-by.

I seem to myself like water and sky,
A river and a rover and a passer-by.

But in the winter three years back
We lit us a night fire by the track,

And the snow came up and the fire it flew
And we couldn't find the warming room for two.

One had to suffer, so I left him the fire
And I went to the weather from my heart's desire.

It was night on the line, it was no more fire,
But the zero whistle through the icy wire.

As I went suffering through the snow
Something like a shadow came moving slow.

I went up to it and I said a word;
Something flew above it like a kind of bird.

I leaned in closer and I saw a face;
A light went round me but I kept my place.

My heart went open like an apple sliced;
I saw my Saviour and I saw my Christ.

Well, you may not read it in a book,
But it takes a gentle Saviour to give a gentle look.

I looked in his eyes and I read the news;
His heart was having the railroad blues.

Oh, the railroad blues will cost you dear,
Keeps you moving on for something that you don't see here.

We stood and whispered in a kind of moon;
The line was looking like May and June.

I found he was a roamer and a journey man
Looking for a lodging since the night began.

He went to the doors but he didn't have the pay,
He went to the windows, then he went away.

Says, "We'll walk together and we'll both be fed."
Says, "I will give you the ' other ' bread."

Oh, the bread he gave and without money!
O drink, O fire, O burning honey!

It went all through me like a shining storm:
I saw inside me, it was light and warm.

I saw deep under and I saw above,
I saw the stars weighed down with love.

They sang that love to burning birth,
They poured that music to the earth.

I heard the stars sing low like mothers.
He said: "Now look, and help feed others."

I looked around, and as close as touch
Was everybody that suffered much.

They reached out, there was darkness only;
They could not see us, they were lonely.

I saw the hearts that deaths took hold of,
With the wounds bare that were not told of;

Hearts with things in them making gashes;
Hearts that were choked with their dreams' ashes;

Women in front of the rolled-back air,
Looking at their breasts and nothing there;

Good men wasting and trapped in hells;
Hurt lads shivering with the fare-thee-wells.

I saw them as if something bound them;
I stood there but my heart went round them.

I begged him not to let me see them wasted.
Says, "Tell them then what you have tasted."

Told him I was weak as a rained-on bee;
Told him I was lost.—Says: "Lean on me."

Something happened then I could not tell,
But I knew I had the water for every hell.

Any other thing it was no use bringing;
They needed what the stars were singing,

What the whole sky sang like waves of light,
The tune that it danced to, day and night.

Oh, I listened to the sky for the tune to come;
The song seemed easy, but I stood there dumb.

The stars could feel me reaching through them;
They let down light and drew me to them.

I stood in the sky in a light like day,
Drinking in the word that all things say

Where the worlds hang growing in clustered shapes
Dripping the music like wine from grapes.

With "Love, Love, Love," above the pain,
—The vine-like song with its wine-like rain.

Through heaven under heaven the song takes root
Of the turning, burning, deathless fruit.

I came to the earth and the pain so near me,
I tried that song but they couldn't hear me.

I went down into the ground to grow,
A seed for a song that would make men know.

Into the ground from my Roamer's light
I went; he watched me sink to night.

Deep in the ground from my human grieving,
His pain ploughed in me to believing.

Oh, he took earth's pain to be his bride,
While the heart of life sang in his side.

For I felt that pain, I took its kiss,
My heart broke into dust with his.

Then sudden through the earth I found life springing;
The dust men trampled on was singing.

Deep in my dust I felt its tones;
The roots of beauty went round my bones.

I stirred, I rose like a flame, like a river,
I stood on the line, I could sing forever.

Love had pierced into my human sheathing,
Song came out of me simple as breathing.

A freight came by, the line grew colder.
He laid his hand upon my shoulder.

Says, "Don't stay on the line such nights,"
And led me by the hand to the station lights.

I asked him in front of the station-house wall
If he had lodging.   Says, "None at all."

I pointed to my heart and looked in his face.—
"Here,—if you haven't got a better place."

He looked and he said: "Oh, we still must roam
But if you'll keep it open, well, I'll call it 'home.'"

The thrush now slept whose pillow was his wing.
So the song ended and the four remained
Still in the faint starshine that silvered them,
While the low sound went on of broken water
Out of the spring and through the darkness flowing
Over a stone that held it from the sea.
Whether the men spoke after could not be told,
A mist from the ground so veiled them, but they waited
A little longer till the moon came up;
Then on the gilded track leading to the mountains,
Against the moon they faded in common gold
And earth bore East with all toward the new morning.

Ridgely Torrence

BINDLESTIFF

Oh, the lives of men, lives of men,
In pattern-molds be run;
But there's you, and me, and Bindlestiff---
And remember Mary's Son.

At dawn the hedges and the wheel-ruts ran
Into a brightening sky. The grass bent low
With shimmering dew, and many a late wild rose
Unrolled the petals from its odorous heart
While birds held tuneful gossip. Suddenly,
Each bubbling trill and whistle hid away
As from a hawk; the fragrant silence heard
Only the loving stir of little leaves;
Then a man's baritone broke roughly in:

> *I've gnawed my crust of mouldy bread,*
> *Skimmed my mulligan stew;*
> *Laid beneath the barren hedge—*
> *Sleety night-winds blew.*

> *Slanting rain chills my bones,*
> *Sun bakes my skin;*
> *Rocky road for my limping feet,*
> *Door where I can't go in.*

Above the hedgerow floated filmy smoke
From the hidden singer's fire. Once more the voice:

> *I used to burn the mules with the whip*
> *When I worked on the grading gang;*
> *But the boss was a crook, and he docked my pay—*
> *Some day that boss will hang.*

> *I used to live in a six by nine,*
> *Try to save my dough—*
> *It's a bellyful of the chaff of life,*
> *Feet that up and go.*

The mesh of leafy branches rustled loud.
Into the road slid Bindlestiff. You've seen
The like of the traveller: gaunt humanity
In stained and broken coat, with untrimmed hedge
Of rusty beard and curling sunburnt hair;
His hat, once white, a dull uncertain cone;
His leathery hands and cheeks, his bright blue eyes

That always see new faces and strange dogs;
His mouth that laughs at life and at himself.

> *Sometimes they shut you up in jail—*
>   *Dark, and a filthy cell;*
> *I hope the fellows built them jails*
>   *Find 'em down in hell.*

> *But up above, you can sleep outdoors—*
>   *Feed you like a king;*
> *You never have to saw no wood,*
>   *Only job is sing.*

The tones came mellower, as unevenly
The tramp limped off trailing the hobo song:

> *Good-bye, farewell to Omaha,*
>   *K. C., and Denver, too;*
> *Put my foot on the flying freight,*
>   *Going to ride her through.*

Bindlestiff topped a hillock, against the sky
Showed stick and bundle with his extra shoes
Jauntily dangling. Bird to bird once more
Made low sweet answer; in the wild rose cups
The bee found yellow meal; all softly moved
The white and purple morning-glory bells
As on the gently rustling hedgetop leaves
The sun's face rested.   Bindlestiff was gone.

> *Oh, the lives of men, lives of men,*
>   *In pattern-moulds be run;*
> *But there's you, and me, and Bindlestiff—*
>   *And remember Mary's Son.*
>   Edwin Ford Piper

GAMESTERS ALL

THE river boat had loitered down its way;
The ropes were coiled, the business for the day
Was done.   The cruel noon closed down
And cupped the town.

Stray voices called across the blinding heat,
Then drifted off to shadowy retreat
Among the sheds.
The waters of the bay
Sucked away
In tepid swirls, as listless as the day.
Silence closed about me like a wall,
Final and obstinate as death.
Until I longed to break it with a call,
Or barter life for one deep, windy breath.

A mellow laugh came rippling
Across the stagnant air,
Lifting it into little waves of life.
Then, true and clear,
I caught a snatch of harmony;
Sure lilting tenor, and a drowsing bass,
Elusive chords to weave and interlace,
And poignant little minors, broken short,
Like robins calling June—
And then the tune:
"Oh, nobody knows when de Lord is goin ter call,
Roll dem bones.
It may be in de Winter time, and maybe in de Fall,
Roll dem bones.
But yer got ter leabe yer baby an yer home an all—
So roll dem bones,
Oh my brudder,
Oh my brudder,
Oh my brudder,
Roll dem bones!"

There they squatted, gambling away
Their meagre pay;
Fatalists all.
I heard the muted fall
Of dice, then the assured,
Retrieving sweep of hand on roughened board.

I thought it good to see
Four lives so free

From care, so indolently sure of each to-morrow,
And hearts attuned to sing away a sorrow.

Then, like a shot
Out of the hot
Still air, I heard a call:
"Throw up your hands! I've got you all!
It's thirty days for craps.
Come, Tony, Paul!
Now, Joe, don't be a fool!
I've got you cool."

I saw Joe's eyes, and knew he'd never go.
Not Joe, the swiftest hand in River Bow!
Springing from where he sat, straight, cleanly made,
He soared, a leaping shadow from the shade
With fifty feet to go.
It was the stiffest hand he ever played.
To win the corner meant
Deep, sweet content
Among his laughing kind;
To lose, to suffer blind,
Degrading slavery upon "the gang,"
With killing suns, and fever-ridden nights
Behind relentless bars
Of prison cars.

He hung a breathless second in the sun,
The staring road before him.   Then, like one
Who stakes his all, and has a gamester's heart,
His laughter flashed.
He lunged—I gave a start.
God! What a man!
The massive shoulders hunched, and as he ran
With head bent low, and splendid length of limb,
I almost felt the beat
Of passionate life that surged in him
And winged his spurning feet.

And then my eyes went dim.
The Marshal's gun was out.

I saw the grim
Short barrel, and his face
Aflame with the excitement of the chase.
He was an honest sportsman, as they go,
He never shot a doe,
Or spotted fawn,
Or partridge on the ground.
And, as for Joe,
He'd wait until he had a yard to go.
Then, if he missed, he'd laugh and call it square.
My gaze leapt to the corner—waited there.
And now an arm would reach it. I saw hope flare
Across the runner's face.

Then, like a pang
In my own heart,
The pistol rang.

The form I watched soared forward, spun the curve.
"By God, you've missed!"
The Marshal shook his head.
No, there he lay, face downward in the road.
"I reckon he was dead
Before he hit the ground,"
The Marshal said.
"Just once, at fifty feet,
A moving target too.
That's just about as good
As any man could do!
A little tough;
But, since he ran,
I call it fair enough."

He mopped his head, and started down the road.
The silence eddied round him, turned and flowed
Slowly back and pressed against the ears.
Until unnumbered flies set it to droning,
And, down the heat, I heard a woman moaning.

DuBose Heyward

THE HORSE THIEF

THERE he moved, cropping the grass at the purple canyon's
    lip.
His mane was mixed with the moonlight that silvered his
    snow-white side,
For the moon sailed out of a cloud with the wake of a spectral
    ship.
I crouched and I crawled on my belly, my lariat coil looped
    wide.

Dimly and dark the mesas broke on the starry sky.
A pall covered every color of their gorgeous glory at
    noon.
I smelt the yucca and mesquite, and stifled my heart's quick
    cry,
And wormed and crawled on my belly to where he moved
    against the moon!

Some Moorish barb was that mustang's sire.   His lines were
    beyond all wonder.
From the prick of his ears to the flow of his tail he ached in
    my throat and eyes.
Steel and velvet grace!   As the prophet says, God had
    "clothed his neck with thunder."
Oh, marvelous with the drifting cloud he drifted across the
    skies!

And then I was near at hand—crouched, and balanced, and
    cast the coil;
And the moon was smothered in cloud, and the rope through
    my hands with a rip!
But somehow I gripped and clung, with the blood in my
    brain aboil—
With a turn round the rugged tree-stump there on the purple
    canyon's lip.

Right into the stars he reared aloft, his red eye rolling and
    raging.

He whirled and sunfished and lashed, and rocked the earth
to thunder and flame.
He squealed like a regular devil horse. I was haggard and
spent and aging—
Roped clean, but almost storming clear, his fury too fierce
to tame.

And I cursed myself for a tenderfoot moon-dazzled to play
the part;
But I was doubly desperate then, with the posse pulled out
from town,
Or I'd never have tried it. I only knew I must get a mount
and a start.
The filly had snapped her foreleg short—I had had to shoot
her down.

So there he struggled and strangled, and I snubbed him
around the tree.
Nearer, a little nearer—hoofs planted, and lolling tongue—
Till a sudden slack pitched me backward. He reared right
on top of me.
Mother of God—that moment! He missed me . . . and up
I swung.

Somehow, gone daft completely and clawing a bunch of his
mane,
As he stumbled and tripped in the lariat, there I was—up
and astride
And cursing for seven counties! And the mustang? *Just
insane!*
Crack-bang! went the rope; we cannoned off the tree;
then—gods, that ride!

A rocket—that's all, a rocket! I dug with my teeth and nails.
Why, we never hit even the high spots (though I hardly
remember things);
But I heard a monstrous booming like a thunder of flapping
sails
When he spread—well, *call* me a liar!—when he spread those
wings, those wings!

So white that my eyes were blinded; thick-feathered and
    wide unfurled,
They beat the air into billows. We sailed, and the earth
    was gone.
Canyon and desert and mesa withered below, with the world.
And then I knew that mustang; for I—was Bellerophon!

Yes, glad as the Greek, and mounted on a horse of the elder
    gods,
With never a magic bridle or a fountain-mirror nigh!
*My chaps and spurs and holster must have looked it? What's
    the odds?*
I'd a leg over lightning and thunder, careering across the sky!

And forever streaming before me, fanning my forehead cool,
Flowed a mane of molten silver; and just before my thighs
(As I gripped his velvet-muscled ribs, while I cursed myself
    for a fool),
The steady pulse of those pinions—their wonderful fall and
    rise!

The bandanna I bought in Bowie blew loose and whipped
    from my neck.
My shirt was stuck to my shoulders and ribboning out
    behind.
The stars were dancing, wheeling and glancing, dipping with
    smirk and beck.
The clouds were flowing, dusking and glowing. We rode a
    roaring wind.

We soared through the silver starlight to knock at the
    planets' gates.
New shimmering constellations came whirling into our ken.
Red stars and green and golden swung out of the void that
    waits
For man's great last adventure; the Signs took shape—and
    then

I knew the lines of that Centaur the moment I saw him come!
The musical-box of the heavens all around us rolled to a tune

That tinkled and chimed and trilled with silver sounds that
    struck you dumb,
As if some archangel were grinding out the music of the
    moon.

Melody-drunk on the Milky Way, as we swept and soared
    hilarious,
Full in our pathway, sudden he stood—the Centaur of the
    Stars,
Flashing from head and hoofs and breast! I knew him for
    Sagittarius.
He reared, and bent and drew his bow. He crouched as a
    boxer spars.

Flung back on his haunches, weird he loomed; then leapt—
    and the dim void lightened.
Old White Wings shied and swerved aside, and fled from the
    splendor-shod.
Through a flashing welter of worlds we charged. I knew
    why my horse was frightened.
He *had* two faces—a dog's and a man's—that Babylonian
    god!

Also, he followed us real as fear. Ping! went an arrow
    past.
My broncho buck-jumped, humping high. We plunged . . .
    I guess that's all!
I lay on the purple canyon's lip, when I opened my eyes at
    last—
Stiff and sore and my head like a drum, but I broke no bones
    in the fall.

So you know—and now you may string me up. Such was
    the way you caught me.
Thank you for letting me tell it straight, though you never
    could greatly care.
For I took a horse that wasn't mine! . . . But there's one
    the heavens brought me,
And I'll hang right happy because I know he is waiting for
    me up there.

From creamy muzzle to cannon-bone, by God, he's a peerless
    wonder!
He is steel and velvet and furnace-fire, and death's su-
    premest prize;
And never again shall be roped on earth that neck that is
    "clothed with thunder" . . .
String me up, Dave! Go dig my grave! *I rode him across
    the skies!*

                       William Rose Benét

NIMMO

SINCE you remember Nimmo, and arrive
At such a false and florid and far drawn
Confusion of odd nonsense, I connive
No longer, though I may have led you on.

So much is told and heard and told again,
So many with his legend are engrossed,
That I, more sorry now than I was then,
May live on to be sorry for his ghost.

You knew him, and you must have known his eyes,—
How deep they were, and what a velvet light
Came out of them when anger or surprise,
Or laughter, or Francesca, made them bright.

No, you will not forget such eyes, I think,—
And you say nothing of them.   Very well.
I wonder if all history's worth a wink,
Sometimes, or if my tale be one to tell.

For they began to lose their velvet light;
Their fire grew dead without and small within;
And many of you deplored the needless fight
That somewhere in the dark there must have been.

All fights are needless, when they're not our own,
But Nimmo and Francesca never fought.
Remember that; and when you are alone,
Remember me—and think what I have thought.

Now, mind you, I say nothing of what was,
Or never was, or could or could not be:
Bring not suspicion's candle to the glass
That mirrors a friend's face to memory.

Of what you see, see all,—but see no more:
For what I show you here will not be there.
The devil has had his way with paint before,
And he's an artist,—and you needn't stare.

There was a painter and he painted well;
He'd paint you Daniel in the lion's den,
Beelzebub, Elaine, or William Tell.
I'm coming back to Nimmo's eyes again.

The painter put the devil in those eyes,
Unless the devil did, and there he stayed;
And then the lady fled from paradise,
And there's your fact.   The lady was afraid.

She must have been afraid, or may have been,
Of evil in their velvet all the while;
But sure as I'm a sinner with a skin,
I'll trust the man as long as he can smile.

I trust him who can smile and then may live
In my heart's house, where Nimmo is to-day.
God knows if I have more than men forgive
To tell him; but I played, and I shall pay.

I knew him then, and if I know him yet,
I know in him, defeated and estranged,
The calm of men forbidden to forget
The calm of women who have loved and changed.

But there are ways that are beyond our ways,
Or he would not be calm and she be mute,
As one by one their lost and empty days
Pass without even the warmth of a dispute.

God help us all when women think they see;
God save us when they do.   I'm fair; but though
I know him only as he looks to me,
I know him,—and I tell Francesca so.

And what of Nimmo?   Little would you ask
Of him, could you but see him as I can,
At his bewildered and unfruitful task
Of being what he was born to be—a man.

Better forget that I said anything
Of what your tortured memory may disclose;
I know him, and your worst remembering
Would count as much as nothing, I suppose.

Meanwhile, I trust him; and I know his way
Of trusting me, and always in his youth.
I'm painting here a better man, you say,
Than I, the painter; and you say the truth.

Edwin Arlington Robinson

LLEWELLYN AND THE TREE

Could he have made Priscilla share
   The paradise that he had planned,
Llewellyn would have loved his wife
   As well as any in the land.

Could he have made Priscilla cease
   To goad him for what God left out,
Llewellyn would have been as mild
   As any we have read about.

Could all have been as all was not,   .
   Llewellyn would have had no story;
He would have stayed a quiet man
   And gone his quiet way to glory.

But howsoever mild he was
   Priscilla was implacable;
And whatsoever timid hopes
   He built—she found them, and they fell.

And this went on, with intervals
  Of labored harmony between
Resounding discords, till at last
  Llewellyn turned—as will be seen.

Priscilla, warmer than her name,
  And shriller than the sound of saws,
Pursued Llewellyn once too far,
  Not knowing quite the man he was.

The more she said, the fiercer clung
  The stinging garment of his wrath;
And this was all before the day
  When Time tossed roses in his path.

Before the roses ever came
  Llewellyn had already risen.
The roses may have ruined him,
  They may have kept him out of prison.

And she who brought them, being Fate,
  Made roses do the work of spears,—
Though many made no more of her
  Than civet, coral, rouge, and years.

You ask us what Llewellyn saw,
  But why ask what may not be given?
To some will come a time when change
  Itself is beauty, if not heaven.

One afternoon Priscilla spoke,
  And her shrill history was done;
At any rate, she never spoke
  Like that again to anyone.

One gold October afternoon
  Great fury smote the silent air;
And then Llewellyn leapt and fled
  Like one with hornets in his hair.

Llewellyn left us, and he said
  Forever, leaving few to doubt him;
And so, through frost and clicking leaves,
  The Tilbury way went on without him.

And slowly, through the Tilbury mist,
  The stillness of October gold
Went out like beauty from a face.
  Priscilla watched it, and grew old.

He fled, still clutching in his flight
  The roses that had been his fall;
The Scarlet One, as you surmise,
  Fled with him, coral, rouge, and all.

Priscilla, waiting, saw the change
  Of twenty slow October moons;
And then she vanished, in her turn
  To be forgotten, like old tunes.

So they were gone—all three of them,
  I should have said, and said no more,
Had not a face once on Broadway
  Been one that I had seen before.

The face and hands and hair were old,
  But neither time nor penury
Could quench within Llewellyn's eyes
  The shine of his one victory.

The roses, faded and gone by,
  Left ruin where they once had reigned;
But on the wreck, as on old shells,
  The color of the rose remained.

His fictive merchandise I bought
  For him to keep and show again,
Then led him slowly from the crush
  Of his cold-shouldered fellow men.

"And so, Llewellyn," I began—
  "Not so," he said; "not so at all:
I've tried the world, and found it good,
  For more than twenty years this fall.

"And what the world has left of me
  Will go now in a little while."
And what the world had left of him
  Was partly an unholy guile.

"That I have paid for being calm
  Is what you see, if you have eyes;
For let a man be calm too long,
  He pays for much before he dies.

"Be calm when you are growing old
  And you have nothing else to do;
Pour not the wine of life too thin
  If water means the death of you.

"You say I might have learned at home
  The truth in season to be strong?
Not so; I took the wine of life
  Too thin, and I was calm too long.

"Like others who are strong too late,
  For me there was no going back;
For I had found another speed,
  And I was on the other track.

"God knows how far I might have gone
  Or what there might have been to see;
But my speed had a sudden end,
  And here you have the end of me."

The end or not, it may be now
  But little farther from the truth
To say those worn satiric eyes
  Had something of immortal youth.

He may among the millions here
  Be one; or he may, quite as well,
Be gone to find again the Tree
  Of Knowledge, out of which he fell.

He may be near us, dreaming yet
  Of unrepented rouge and coral;
Or in a grave without a name
  May be as far off as a moral.

Edwin Arlington Robinson

PART VII

POEMS OF SORROW, DEATH AND
IMMORTALITY

A HYMN

O GOD of earth and altar,
  Bow down and hear our cry,
Our earthly rulers falter,
  Our people drift and die;
The walls of gold entomb us,
  The swords of scorn divide,
Take not thy thunder from us,
  But take away our pride.

From all that terror teaches,
  From lies of tongue and pen,
From all the easy speeches
  That comfort cruel men,
From sale and profanation
  Of honor and the sword,
From sleep and from damnation,
  Deliver us, good Lord!

Tie in a living tether
  The prince and priest and thrall,
Bind all our lives together,
  Smite us and save us all;
In ire and exultation
  Aflame with faith, and free,
Lift up a living nation,
  A single sword to thee.

G. K. Chesterton

IN THE SHADOW

THE BLACK PANTHER

THERE is a panther caged within my breast;
But what his name, there is no breast shall know
Save mine, nor what it is that drives him so,
Backward and forward, in relentless quest—
That silent rage, baffled but unsuppressed,
The soft pad of those stealthy feet that go
Over my body's prison to and fro,
Trying the walls forever without rest.
All day I feed him with my living heart;
But when the night puts forth her dreams and stars,
The inexorable Frenzy reawakes:
His wrath is hurled upon the trembling bars,
The eternal passion stretches me apart,
And I lie silent—but my body shakes.

John Hall Wheelock

THE NARROW DOORS

THE Wide Door into Sorrow
Stands open night and day.
With head held high and dancing feet
I pass it on my way.

I never tread within it.
I never turn to see.
The Wide Door into Sorrow
It cannot frighten me.

The Narrow Doors to Sorrow
Are secret, still, and low:
Swift tongues of dusk that spoil the sun
Before I even know.

My dancing feet are frozen.
I stare. I can but see.

943

The Narrow Doors to Sorrow
They stop the heart in me.

—Oh, stranger than my midnights
Of loneliness and strife
The Doors that let the dark leap in
Across my sunny life!

Fannie Stearns Gifford

HEARTBREAK ROAD

As I went up by Heartbreak Road
  Before the dawn of day,
The cold mist was all about,
  And the wet world was gray;
It seemed that never another soul
  Had walked that weary way.

But when I came to Heartbreak Hill,
  Silver touched the sea;
I knew that many and many a soul
  Was climbing close to me;
I knew I walked that weary way
  In a great company.

Helen Gray Cone

SATURDAY MARKET

Bury your heart in some deep green hollow
  Or hide it up in a kind old tree;
Better still, give it the swallow
  When she goes over the sea.

In Saturday Market there's eggs a-plenty
  And dead-alive ducks with their legs tied down,
Gray old gaffers and boys of twenty—
  Girls and the women of the town—
Pitchers and sugar-sticks, ribbons and laces,
  Posies and whips and dicky-birds' seed,
Silver pieces and smiling faces,
  In Saturday Market they've all they need.

What were you showing in Saturday Market
    That set it grinning from end to end
Girls and gaffers and boys of twenty—?
    Cover it close with your shawl, my friend—
Hasten you home with the laugh behind you,
    Over the down—, out of sight,
Fasten your door, though no one will find you—
    No one will look on a Market night.

See, you, the shawl is wet, take out from under
    The red dead thing—.   In the white of the moon
On the flags does it stir again?   Well, and no wonder!
    Best make an end of it; bury it soon.
If there is blood on the hearth who'll know it?
    Or blood on the stairs,
When a murder is over and done why show it?
    In Saturday Market nobody cares.

Then lie you straight on your bed for a short, short weeping
    And still, for a long, long rest,
There's never a one in the town so sure of sleeping
    As you, in the house on the down with a hole in your
        breast.

        Think no more of the swallow,
          Forget, you, the sea,
        Never again remember the deep green hollow
          Or the top of the kind old tree!

                Charlotte Mew

YOUR TEARS

    I DARE not ask your very all:
        I only ask a part.
    Bring me—when dancers leave the hall—
        Your aching heart.

    Give other friends your lighted face,
        The laughter of the years:
    I come to crave a greater grace—
        Bring me your tears!

                Edwin Markham

LESBIA SEWING

STITCHES over and over
  So the heart won't break,
Thrust the needle under
  For sorrow's sake.

Stitches over and over
  Till the pattern's set,
Thrust the needle under
  So the heart forget.

Stitches over and over,
  Needle hurry fast,
Till the love of beauty
  Fall from me at last.

Harold Vinal

WANDERING

VAGUE winds of sorrow blow
Across the night's wide lake;
There is a road I know,
But may not take.

There is a house of vines,
Where friendly shadows lie;
The window-candle shines,
But I pass by.

Afar my pilgrim load
I bear—yet evermore
My feet are on that road,
My hand is at the door.

Hortense Flexner

THE LONG HILL

I MUST have passed the crest a while ago
  And now I am going down—
Strange to have crossed the crest and not to know,
  But the brambles were always catching the hem of my
    gown.

All the morning I thought how proud I should be
   To stand there straight as a queen,
Wrapped in the wind and the sun with the world under me—
   But the air was dull, there was little I could have seen.

It was nearly level along the beaten track
   And the brambles caught in my gown—
But it's no use now to think of turning back,
   The rest of the way will be only going down.

Sara Teasdale

LIKE BARLEY BENDING

   LIKE barley bending
      In low fields by the sea,
   Singing in hard wind
      Ceaselessly;

   Like barley bending
      And rising again,
   So would I, unbroken,
      Rise from pain;

   So would I softly,
      Day long, night long,
   Change my sorrow
      Into song.

Sara Teasdale

THE ENCHANTED HEART

   HERE blew winter once with the snowstorms spurning
   Hill and furrow and field till all were whitened;
   Here it was the robin flew away frightened
   When I went by dreaming of spring returning.

   Now that I walk on self-same meadow and hill
   Why seems winter the fairer, happier season,
   And spring the very root of the mind's unreason?
   Why do I ponder and roam unhappily still?

What do you lack to-day that you lacked not then,
O brooding heart, that you cannot be contented?
Far away, says the heart that was enchanted,
Long ago . . . in a dream. . . . O never again!
                                    Edward Davison

THE LAND OF DREAMS

Ah, give us back our dear dead Land of Dreams!
The far, faint, misty hills, the tangled maze
Of brake and thicket; down green woodland ways
The hush of summer, and on amber streams
Bright leaves afloat, amid the foam that creams
Round crannied boulders, where the shallows blaze.
Then life ran joyous through glad, golden days
And silver nights beneath the moon's pale beams.
Now all is lost.   There glooms a dark morass
Where throbbed the thrush across the dappled lawn.
Oh, never more shall fiery pageants pass,
Nor dance of light-limbed satyr, nymph and faun,
Adrift among the whispering meadow-grass,
On wind-swept uplands, yearning toward the dawn.
                                    Henry Martyn Hoyt

PRESCIENCE

I went to sleep smiling,
    I wakened despairing—
Where was my soul,
    On what terror-path faring?
What grief shall befall me,
    By midnight or noon,
What thing has my soul learned
    That I shall know soon?
                                    Margaret Widdemer

THE GREEN RIVER

I know a green grass path that leaves the field,
And like a running river, winds along
Into a leafy wood where is no throng
Of birds at noon-day, and no soft throats yield

Their music to the moon. The place is sealed,
An unclaimed sovereignty of voiceless song,
And all the unravished silences belong
To some sweet singer lost or unrevealed.
So is my soul become a silent place.
Oh may I wake from this uneasy night
To find a voice of music manifold.
Let it be shape of sorrow with wan face,
Or Love that swoons on sleep, or else delight
That is as wide-eyed as a marigold.

Alfred Bruce Douglas

THE NEW HOUSE

Now first, as I shut the door,
    I was alone
In the new house; and the wind
    Began to moan.

Old at once was the house,
    And I was old;
My ears were teased with the dread
    Of what was foretold,

Nights of storm, days of mist, without end;
    Sad days when the sun
Shone in vain: old griefs and griefs
    Not yet begun.

All was foretold me; naught
    Could I foresee;
But I learnt how the wind would sound
    After these things should be.

Edward Thomas

DESPAIR

As I came down the hillside
    To put to sea,
I heard a girl a-singing—
    But not for me.

As we sailed past the village,
   By that last pine
A girl stood waving farewells—
   And none were mine.

She stood there long a-watching
   Our vessel's track.
But little is she hoping
   That I come back.

My mates are singing, whistling,
   Half-dead I feel.
I'm like a boat a-drifting
   With broken wheel.

They hope for lucky fishing
   And some big haul.
I once had luck past wishing—
   I've lost it all.

Edward Bliss Reed

THE END

My father got me strong and straight and slim
   And I give thanks to him.
My mother bore me glad and sound and sweet,
   I kiss her feet!

But now, with me, their generation fails
   And nevermore avails
To cast through me the ancient mould again,
   Such women and men.

I have no son, whose life of flesh and fire
   Sprang from my splendid sire;
No daughter for whose soul my mother's flesh
   Wrought raiment fresh.

Life's venerable rhythms like a flood
   Beat in my brain and blood,
Crying from all generations past,
   "Is this the last?"

And I make answer to my haughty dead,
    Who made me, heart and head,
"Even the sunbeams falter, flicker and bend—
    I am the end."

Marguerite Wilkinson

IF SOME GRIM TRAGEDY

IF some grim tragedy had smote me down
I might have risen spent
From the chastening rod, yet in some way
Magnificent.

But life moves tranquilly without event
Day after wearisome day,
Save for the little rodent cares that make
Me small as they.

Ninna May Smith

FOOTSTEPS

THEY pass so close, the people on the street;
Footfall, footfall;
I know them from their footsteps' pulsing beat;
Footfall, footfall;
The tripping, lingering, and the heavy feet;
I hear them call:

I am the dance of youth, and life is fair!
Footfall, footfall;
I am a dream, divinely unaware!
Footfall, footfall;
I am the burden of an old despair!
Footfall. . . .

Hazel Hall

THE COMFORTERS

WHEN I crept over the hill, broken with tears,
When I crouched down on the grass, dumb in despair,
I heard the soft croon of the wind bend to my ears,
I felt the light kiss of the wind touching my hair.

When I stood lone on the height my sorrow did speak,
As I went down the hill, I cried and I cried,
The soft little hands of the rain stroking my cheek,
The kind little feet of the rain ran by my side.

When I went to thy grave, broken with tears,
When I crouched down in the grass, dumb in despair,
I heard the sweet croon of the wind soft in my ears,
I felt the kind lips of the wind touching my hair.

When I stood lone by thy cross, sorrow did speak,
When I went down the long hill, I cried and I cried,
The soft little hands of the rain stroked my pale cheek,
The kind little feet of the rain ran by my side.

Dora Sigerson Shorter

FOLDED POWER

SORROW can wait,
For there is magic in the calm estate
Of grief; lo, where the dust complies
Wisdom lies.

Sorrow can rest
Indifferent, with her head upon her breast;
Idle and hushed, guarded from fears;
Content with tears.

Sorrow can bide,
With sealed lids and hands unoccupied.
Sorrow can fold her latent might,
Dwelling with night.

But Sorrow will rise
From her dream of sombre and hushed eternities.
Lifting a Child, she will softly move
With a mother's love.

She will softly rise.
Her embrace the dying will recognize,
Lifting them gently through strange delight
To a clearer light.

Gladys Cromwell

DUET

(I sing with myself)

Out of my sorrow
I'll build a stair,
And every to-morrow
Will climb to me there;

With ashes of yesterday
In its hair.

My fortune is made
Of a stab in the side,
My debts are paid
In pennies of pride;

Little red coins
In a heart I hide.

The stones that I eat
Are ripe for my needs,
My cup is complete
With the dregs of deeds;

Clear are the notes
Of my broken reeds.

I carry my pack
Of aches and stings,
Light with the lack
Of all good things;

But not on my back,
Because of my wings!

                          Leonora Speyer

HOPE'S SONG

Silent is the dark
   Before the sun-beams come,
Yet if it were not for the lark,
   The dawn would be as dumb,

And thus my soul would be
   As dark and still as night,
If 'twere not for the minstrelsy
   Of Hope that sings of Light.

Francis Carlin

THE DARK CAVALIER

CHORICOS

THE ancient songs
Pass deathward mournfully.

Cold lips that sing no more, and withered wreaths,
Regretful eyes, and drooping breasts and wings—
Symbols of ancient songs,
Mournfully passing
Down to the great white surges,
Watched of none
Save the frail sea-birds
And the lithe pale girls,
Daughters of Oceanus.

And the songs pass from the green land
Which lies upon the waves as a leaf
On the flowers of hyacinth;
And they pass from the waters,
The manifold winds and the dim moon,
And they come
Silently winging through soft Kimmerian dusk,
To the quiet level lands
That she keeps for us all,
That she wrought for us all for sleep
In the silver days of the earth's dawning—
Proserpina, daughter of Zeus.

And we turn from the Cyprian's breasts,
And we turn from thee,
Phœbus Apollon,
And we turn from the music of old,
And the hills that we loved and the meads,
And we turn from the fiery day,
And the lips that were over-sweet;

For silently
Brushing the fields with red-shod feet,
With purple robe
Searing the grass as with a sudden flame,
Death,
Thou hast come upon us.

And of all the ancient songs
Passing to the swallow-blue halls
By the dark streams of Persephone,
This only remains—
That in the end we turn to thee,
Death,
We turn to thee, singing
One last song.

O Death,
Thou art an healing wind
That blowest over white flowers
A-tremble with dew;
Thou art a wind flowing
Over far leagues of lonely sea;
Thou art the dusk and the fragrance;
Thou art the lips of love mournfully smiling;
Thou art the sad peace of one
Satiate with old desires;
Thou art the silence of beauty,
And we look no more for the morning,
We yearn no more for the sun
Since with thy white hands,
Death,
Thou crownest us with the pallid chaplets,
The slim colorless poppies
Which in thy garden alone
Softly thou gatherest.

And silently;
And with slow feet approaching;
And with bowed head and unlit eyes,
We kneel before thee:

And thou, leaning toward us,
Caressingly layest upon us
Flowers from thy thin cold hands,
And, smiling as a chaste woman
Knowing love in her heart,
Thou sealest our eyes
And the illimitable quietude
Comes gently upon us.

Richard Aldington

THE REED-PLAYER

(AFTER MACLEOD)

A HOLLOW reed against his lips
  He played a soaring strain,
That fled his dancing finger tips
Light as a swallow wheels and dips
  Above the flowing grain.

The Song of Songs it was, strange wrought
  Beyond the heather hills
From memories and dreams, and taught
By shepherd women who had caught
  Its lilt from mountain rills.

The beating of a heart I heard
  In that forlorn sweet air,
The singing of a distant bird,
A sigh, a softly uttered word
  And echoed laughter there.

"Play me a song of Death," I whispered then.
He raised his hollow reed as one who longs
To turn to dreams, and smiled, and played again,
  The Song of Songs.

Archibald MacLeish

THE DARK CAVALIER

I AM the Dark Cavalier; I am the Last Lover:
  My arms shall welcome you when other arms are tired;
I stand to wait for you, patient in the darkness,
  Offering forgetfulness of all that you desired.

I ask no merriment, no pretense of gladness,
  I can love heavy lids and lips without their rose;
Though you are sorrowful you will not weary me;
  I will not go from you when all the tired world goes.

I am the Dark Cavalier; I am the Last Lover;
  I promise faithfulness no other lips may keep;
Safe in my bridal place, comforted by darkness,
  You shall lie happily, smiling in your sleep.

Margaret Widdemer

THINGS

THINGS that are lovely
  Can tear my heart in two—
Moonlight on still pools,
  You.

Things that are tender
  Can fill me with delight—
Old songs remembered,
  Night.

Things that are lonely
  Can make me catch my breath—
The hunger for lost arms . . .
  Death.

Dorothy Dow

SONG

POPPIES paramour the girls;
  Lilies put the boys to bed;
Death is nothing else than this
  After everything is said.

They are safe and shall not fade,
  After everything is done,
Past the solace of the shade
  Or the rescue of the sun.

Haniel Long

THE GOOD HOUR

THE man who met a phalanx with their spears
  And gave his life in one sharp sacrifice,
Knew nothing of the agony of years,
  Or what man can endure before he dies.

Some men die early and are spared much care,
  Some suddenly, escaping worse than death;
But he is fortunate who happens where
  He can exult and die in the same breath.

Louise Driscoll

THE MARCH OF HUMANITY

FROM golden dawn to purple dusk,
Piled high with bales of smiles and tears,
The caravans are dropping down
Across the desert-sands of years.

And when the moonlight's kiss is sweet,
Still holds the trail a countless throng;
Betimes a weary camel halts
Before an oasis of song.

But always toward the beckoning West—
The sunset-land of heart's desire,
The caravans go down to Death
The king of Zidon and of Tyre.

J. Corson Miller

IN A MUSEUM

HERE stillness sounds like echoes in a tomb.
The light falls cold upon these antique toys
Whereby men sought to turn the scales of doom:
Jade gods, a ritual of rigid boys.
Warm blood was spent for this unwindowed stone
Tinct with the painted pleasures of the dead;
For secrets of unwithering flesh and bone—

With these old Egypt's night was comforted.
We lean upon the glass, our curious eyes
Staring at death, three thousand years remote.
And vanity, the worm that never dies,
Feeds on your silver ring and Pharaoh's coat.
And are these heartbeats, then, less perilous?
Since death is close, and death is death for us.

Babette Deutsch

TRAVELLER'S DITTY

COME day, go day,
There's sorrow at the end of it.
Turn road, wind road,
There's mystery in the bend of it.
Oh, all the winds of all the worlds
That lose themselves in starry spaces
Can never blow the secret off
That stares at us in common faces.

Life long, life short,
There's love to meet in tears or laughter.
Die soon, die late,
There's Grandsir Death to walk with, after.
And be you great or be you small,
There's no way out but going through it.
Oh, curious fate that makes us live,
But will not teach us how to do it!

Miriam Allen deFord

TWO SONNETS

I

SAINTS have adored the lofty soul of you.
Poets have whitened at your high renown.
We stand among the many millions who
Do hourly wait to pass your pathway down.
You, so familiar, once were strange: we tried
To live as of your presence unaware.
But now in every road on every side

We see your straight and steadfast signpost there.
I think it like that signpost in my land
Hoary and tall, which pointed me to go
Upward, into the hills, on the right hand,
Where the mists swim and the winds shriek and blow,
A homeless land and friendless, but a land
I did not know and that I wished to know.

II

Such, such is Death: no triumph: no defeat:
Only an empty pail, a slate rubbed clean,
A merciful putting away of what has been.
And this we know: Death is not Life effete,
Life crushed, the broken pail.   We who have seen
So marvellous things know well the end not yet.
Victor and vanquished are a-one in death:
Coward and brave: friend, foe.   Ghosts do not say,
"Come, what was your record when you drew breath? "
But a big blot has hid each yesterday
So poor, so manifestly incomplete.
And your bright Promise, withered long and sped,
Is touched, stirs, rises, opens and grows sweet
And blossoms and is you, when you are dead.

Charles Hamilton Sorley

THE LAST VOYAGE

Some morning I shall rise from sleep,
    When all the house is still and dark.
I shall steal down and find my ship
    By the dim quayside, and embark,

Nor fear the seas nor any wind.
    I have known Fear, but now no more.
The winds shall bear me safe and kind,
    Long-hoped for and long-waited for.

To no strange country shall I come,
    But to mine own delightful land,
With Love to bid me welcome home
    And Love to lead me by the hand.

Love, you and I shall cling together,
  And look long in each other's eyes.
There shall be rose and violet weather
  Under the trees of Paradise.

We shall not hear the ticking clock,
  Nor the swift rustle of Time's wings,
Nor dread the sharp dividing stroke
  Being come now to immortal things.

You of that beauty shall be fain,
  Being now no new inhabitant,
Its beauties to point out, explain,
  And all its dear delights to vaunt.

They will not end in a thousand years.
  Love, we shall be so long together
Withouten any sword to fear,
  Glad in the rose and violet weather.

With all those wonders to admire,
  And the heart's hunger satisfied,
Given at the last the heart's desire
  We shall forget we ever died.

Oh, in some morning dateless yet
  I shall steal out in the sweet dark
And find my ship with sails all set
  By the dim quayside, and embark.
                    Katherine Tynan Hinkson

THE END

AFTER the blast of lightning from the east,
The flourish of loud clouds, the Chariot throne,
After the drums of time have rolled and ceased
And from the bronze west long retreat is blown,
Shall Life renew these bodies? Of a truth
All death will he annul, all tears assuage?
Or fill these void veins full again with youth

And wash with an immortal water age?
When I do ask white Age, he saith not so,—
"My head hangs weighed with snow."
And when I hearken to the Earth she saith,
"My fiery heart sinks aching.   It is death.
Mine ancient scars shall not be glorified
Nor my titanic tears the seas be dried."

Wilfred Owen

BEFOREHAND

TRYING beforehand to make out
Has been the cause of endless trouble—
Whether we really are or not
A bubble.

If it is nowhere that we go,
It cannot be so hard to bear;
For we shall know, too late to know
Or care.

Witter Bynner

THE SWEEPER

FRAIL, wistful guardian of the broom,
   The dwelling's drudge and stay,
Whom destiny gave a single task—
   To keep the dust away!—

Sweep off the floor and polish the chair.
   It will not always last:
Some day, for all your arms can do,
   The dust will hold you fast.

Agnes Lee

A GIRL

YOU also, laughing one,
Tosser of balls in the sun,
Will pillow your bright head
By the incurious dead.

Babette Deutsch

THE WANDERER

THE ships are lying in the bay,
　The gulls are swinging round their spars;
My soul as eagerly as they
　Desires the margin of the stars.

So much do I love wandering,
　So much I love the sea and sky,
That it will be a piteous thing
　In one small grave to lie.

Zoë Akins

A GRAVE

A GRAVE seems only six feet deep
　And three feet wide,
Viewed with the calculating eye
　Of one outside.

But when fast bound in the chill loam
　For that strange sleep,
Who knows how wide its realm may be?
　Its depths, how deep?

John Richard Moreland

THE DUST

THE dust blows up and down
Within the lonely town;
Vague, hurrying, dumb, aloof,
On sill and bough and roof.

What cloudy shapes do fleet
Along the parchèd street;
Clerks, bishops, kings go by—
To-morrow so shall I!

Lizette Woodworth Reese

I SHALL BE LOVED AS QUIET THINGS

I SHALL be loved as quiet things
Are loved—white pigeons in the sun,
Curled yellow leaves that whisper down
One after one;

The silver reticence of smoke
That tells no secret of its birth
Among the fiery agonies
That turn the earth;

Cloud-islands; reaching arms of trees;
The frayed and eager little moon
That strays unheeded through a high
Blue afternoon.

The thunder of my heart must go
Under the muffling of the dust—
As my gray dress has guarded it
The grasses must;

For it has hammered loud enough,
Clamored enough, when all is said:
Only its quiet part shall live
When I am dead.

Karle Wilson Baker

VIA LONGA

IT's far I must be going,
    Some night or morning gray,
Beyond the oceans' flowing,
    Beyond the rim of day;
And sure it's not the going,
    But that I find the way.

Patrick McDonough

THE SENSE OF DEATH

SINCE I have felt the sense of death,
Since I have borne its dread, its fear—
Oh, how my life has grown more dear
Since I have felt the sense of death!
Sorrows are good, and cares are small,
Since I have known the loss of all.

Since I have felt the sense of death,
And death forever at my side—
Oh, how the world has opened wide
Since I have felt the sense of death!
My hours are jewels that I spend,
For I have seen the hours end.

Since I have felt the sense of death,
Since I have looked on that black night—
My inmost brain is fierce with light
Since I have felt the sense of death.
O dark, that made my eyes to see!
O death, that gave my life to me!

Helen Hoyt

THE LAST TOURNEY

I SHALL go forth one day to joust with death;
The brittle little chains that hold me tied
To rusted hopes, to visions cracked and dried,
Shall break, and I shall hear the trumpet's breath
Go clamoring across the barren heath,
And for a flaming moment I shall ride
The lists' brief course to meet the Undefied—
And take the blow that I shall fall beneath.
Each day, I gird my feeble soul with prayer:
May then the blood of Bayard be my own;
May I ride hard and straight and smite him square,
And in a clash of arms be overthrown;
And as I fall hear through the evening air
The distant horn of Roland, faintly blown.

Frederic F. Van de Water

LET ME LIVE OUT MY YEARS

Let me live out my years in heat of blood!
Let me die drunken with the dreamer's wine!
Let me not see this soul-house built of mud
Go toppling to the dust—a vacant shrine.

Let me go quickly, like a candle light
Snuffed out just at the heyday of its glow.
Give me high noon—and let it then be night!
Thus would I go.

And grant that when I face the grisly Thing,
My song may trumpet down the gray Perhaps.
O let me be a tune-swept fiddle string
That feels the Master Melody—and snaps!

John G. Neihardt

I ACCEPT

I shall go out as all men go,
  Spent flickers in a mighty wind,
Then I shall know, as all men know,
  What lies the great gray veil behind.

There may be nothing but a deep
  And timeless void without a name
Where no sun hangs, no dead stars sleep,
  And there is neither night nor flame.

There may be meadows there and hills,
  Mountains and plains and winds that blow,
And flowers bending over rills
  Springing from an eternal snow.

There may be oceans white with foam
  And great tall ships for hungry men
Who called our little salt seas home,
  And burn to launch their keels again.

There may be voices I have known,
  Cool fingers that have touched my hair;
There may be hearts that were my own—
  Love may abide forever there.

Who knows? Who needs to understand
  If there be shadows there, or more—
To live as though a pleasant land
  Lay just beyond an open door?

Harold Trowbridge Pulsifer

THE GREAT DIVIDE

When I drift out on the Silver Sea,
O may it be
A blue night
With a white moon
And a sprinkling of stars in the cedar tree;
And the silence of God,
And the low call
Of a lone bird,—
When I drift out on the Silver Sea.

Lew Sarett

THE WATCH

I wakened on my hot, hard bed,
Upon the pillow lay my head;
Beneath the pillow I could hear
My little watch was ticking clear.
I thought the throbbing of it went
Like my continual discontent,
I thought it said in every tick:
I am so sick, so sick, so sick;
O death, come quick, come quick, come quick,
Come quick, come quick, come quick, come quick.

Frances Cornford

SURRENDER

YOUNG and trusting, blithe and fair,
    I was the maid he took to wife . . .
But bruises on my heart I wear,
    Who wedded Life.

So reach thy lover's-arms to me—
    Burn thou my lips with eager breath:
Once will I share thine ecstasy
    With thee, O Death!

                                Ruth Guthrie Harding

FAREWELL

TELL them, O Sky-born, when I die
    With high romance to wife,
That I went out as I had lived,
    Drunk with the joy of life.

Yea, say that I went down to death
    Serene and unafraid,
Still loving Song, but loving more
    Life, of which Song is made!

                                Harry Kemp

PROTEST IN PASSING

THIS house of flesh was never loved of me!
This frail white arrogance of sounding towers,
How it has held me through the ordained hours
That I must pass to whiter dignity.
When sleep came beckoning, how I leapt, for then
I knew the low, half-flights of hampered wing,
But now there comes a surer Beckoning,
I go, nor shall endure these rooms again.
I have been held too long by closed-in walls,
By masonry of muscle, blood and bone,
This quaking house of flesh that was my own—
High roof-tree of the heart, see, how it falls!
I go . . . but pause upon the threshold's rust
To shake from off my feet my own dead dust.

                                Leonora Speyer

THE PATCHWORK QUILT

Bring to me white roses, roses, pinks, and lavender,
  Sweet stock and gillyflowers, poppies mauve and red,
Bee-flowers and mignonette, with blue forget-me-not—
  I would make a coverlet for my narrow bed.

Bring me no silken cloth, velvet sheen or satin shine,
  Gossamer of woven lace, gold and silver thread,
Purple deep and dove, and gray, through my idle fingers
    fall,
  Bidding me in patient hours make a patchwork spread.

Since I must go forth alone, far beyond the roof-tree's shade,
  Out into the open soon lonely there to lie,
What want I of silken cloth woven by the hands of men?
  Time would soon despoil me there as he passed me by.

Bring to me white roses then, roses, pinks and lavender,
  Sweet stock and gillyflowers, poppies gold and red,
Bee-flowers and mignonette and blue forget-me-not,
  So I have a coverlet for my narrow bed.
                                        Dora Sigerson Shorter

LITTLE PAGAN RAIN SONG

In the dark and peace of my final bed,
The wet grass waving above my head,
At rest from love, at rest from pain,
I lie and listen to the rain.

  Falling, softly falling,
    Song of my soul that is free;
  Song of my soul that has not forgot
    The sleeping body of me.

When quiet and calm and straight I lie,
High in the air my soul rides by.
Shall I await thee, soul, in vain?
Hark to the answer in the rain.

Falling, softly falling,
Song of my soul that is free;
Song of my soul that will not forget
The sleeping body of me.

Frances Shaw

AN EPITAPH

As shining sand-drift,
Think of me,
Warm, white and glistening
Near the sea:

Like gold-dust gleaming
Which to-day
Light-blowing sea-winds
Whirl away.

I died so long ago
That none may tell
My name, my place, my labor or my fame:
Thus I sleep well.

Margaret Sackville

EPITAPH ON A VAGABOND

CARELESS I lived, accepting day by day
The lavish benison of sun and rain,
Watching the changing seasons pass away
And come again.

Now the great harvester has stilled my breath;
In this cold house I neither hear nor see.
Though in my life I never thought of death,
Death thought of me.

Alexander Gray

SONG OF MAELDUIN

THERE are veils that lift, there are bars that fall,
There are lights that beckon, and winds that call—
Good-bye!

There are hurrying feet, and we dare not wait,
For the hour is on us—the hour of Fate,
The circling hour of the flaming gate—
   Good-bye—good-bye—good-bye!

Fair, fair they shine through the burning zone—
The rainbow gleams of a world unknown;
     Good-bye!
And oh! to follow, to seek, to dare,
When, step by step, in the evening air
Floats down to meet us the cloudy stair!
   Good-bye—good-bye—good-bye!

The cloudy stair of the Brig o' Dread
Is the dizzy path that our feet must tread—
     Good-bye!
O children of Time—O Nights and Days,
That gather and wonder and stand at gaze,
And wheeling stars in your lonely ways,
   Good-bye—good-bye—good-bye!

The music calls and the gates unclose,
Onward and onward the wild way goes—
     Good-bye!
We die in the bliss of a great new birth,
O fading phantoms of pain and mirth,
O fading loves of the old green earth—
   Good-bye—good-bye—good-bye!

T. W. Rolleston

TO ONE OF LITTLE FAITH

Put out the mourners from your heart,
   And bid your still soul rise.
It is not death, but only sleep
   That fastens down your eyes.

Return, oh Galilean days,
   Judean hands, return!
Make bloom the lily in the ash
   Of this neglected urn.

Hildegarde Flanner

FACING THE GULF

From "The Return"

FACING the sudden gulf, the silent
    Precipice where the pathways stop,
Where flame by flame the silver constant
    Lamps of our lives to darkness drop,

Life would I praise, this sentient being,
    Careless, unpraised, unplumbed delights,
Movement and speech, hearing and seeing,
    Sleep and awakening, days and nights.

Glory to Life in all things lovely,
    Birds and lithe beasts and flowers and trees,
Praise in the marvellous joy of Beauty,
    Nameless contents and ecstasies.

Praise to the power within the creature
    Creative, hand and brain and will
Toiling through endless Time in rapture,
    Failure, achievement, seeking still.

Father of Life, with songs of wonder,
    I praise Thee, even to this end,
Love unto Thee all loves surrender,
    From Whom they flow, towards Whom they tend.

Mine is Thy Will, I yield the spirit
    Still on Thine errand without cease
Gladly to run, or to inherit
    In Thine eternal dwelling peace.

Margaret L. Woods

THE DEATHLESS DEAD

I KNOW A LOVELY LADY WHO IS DEAD

I KNOW a lovely lady who is dead,
A wreath of lilies bound her charming head,
Her corn-flower eyes were closed as if in sleep,
And on her lips lay silence gay and deep.

No more the garden where she used to walk
Is filled at dusk with laughter and with talk,
No more the swaying fireflies in their glowing
Lantern to left and right her slender going.

I know a lovely lady who is dead,
And fools say there is nothingness instead.

Nothing of all this loveliness? . . . poor dear,
Beauty is not a matter of a year.

Beauty is like the surf that never ceases,
Beauty is like the night that never dies,
Beauty is like a forest pool where peace is
And a recurrent waning planet lies:
Beauty is like the stormy star that traces
His golden footsteps on the edge of rain;
When beauty has been vanquished in all places,
Suddenly beauty stirs your heart again.

She was the purport of innumerable lovers
Who down some woodland road were glad in May,
When leaves were thick and in the orchard covers
The robin and the chaffinch had their say:
She was the toll of countless men who dreamed—
The small hours heard the scratching of the mice—
In hidden room or tower until it seemed
They stood upon a lonely precipice

And felt a thin clear heady breeze that brought
The truth and peace and beauty that they sought:
She was the breath of myriad mountain pyres
That burned beneath the blueness of the dark:
Beauty is earth and air and many fires,
Runs with the water, sings with each new lark.
She was a pause upon a road that never ends,
Beauty descended on her, and descends.

I know a lovely lady who is dead,
But she was these, and these are in her stead.
. . . Out of the slime and out of endless sleeping,
Into the grayness of the earlier earth,
Crawled such a creature blind and helpless, keeping
Some unknown assignation of her birth.
Never she knew what moved her to her trying,
What would not let her be what she began,
Only a voice in the darkness crying,
Only a wish that wished itself a man.
The wish is here, the wish is ever growing:
The winds are here, the winds are ever blowing.

And her sweet years were part of all this too,
She who could catch and store each moment's aim,
Dawn when she opened windows on the blue,
And midnight when Orion marched in flame;
Kind conversation, merriment, and wit,
Old friends who knew her wit was ever kind,
And tea in winter when the logs were lit
And radiance filled the room and filled her mind;
And dogs, and games, and horses silken-throated
Along a ribboned road that danced with spring
When every hedge to green-brier is devoted,
For to her thinking all and everything
Was music; and with music soft and bright
Often she plucked the echoes from the night.
Her body was a casket white and slim.
I would that I had been her very lover,
Ah the hushed hours when, she with him,
Her young voice whispered over again and over!

Yet now when evening falls and it is late,
And a thin moon cuts clearness from the West,
And Scorpio rising by my eastern gate,
Along the rim throws high his sparkling crest,
I am no longer sorrowful but glad,
Since I was here when beauty found this niche;
Many a man great loveliness has had
But none with loveliness has been more rich.
A little, ample space was mine to know
What loveliness is, and why it cannot go.

I know a lovely lady who is dead,
Beauty is hers, and she is beauty instead.

Struthers Burt

PORTRAIT OF ONE DEAD

From "The House of Death"

THIS is the house. On one side there is darkness,
On one side there is light.
Into the darkness you may lift your lanterns—
Oh, any number—it will still be night.
And here are echoing stairs to lead you downward
To long sonorous halls.
And here is spring forever at these windows,
With roses on the walls.

This is her room. On one side there is music—
On one side not a sound.
At one step she could move from love to silence,
Feel myriad darkness coiling round.
And here are balconies from which she heard you,
Your steady footsteps on the stair.
And here the glass in which she saw your shadow
As she unbound her hair.

Here is the room—with ghostly walls dissolving—
The twilight room in which she called you "lover";
And the floorless room in which she called you "friend".
So many times, in doubt, she ran between them!—
Through windy corridors of darkening end.

Here she could stand with one dim light above her,
And hear far music, like a sea in caverns,
Murmur away at hollowed walls of stone.
And here, in a roofless room where it was raining,
She bore the patient sorrow of rain alone.

Your words were walls which suddenly froze around her.
Your words were windows—large enough for moonlight,
Too small to let her through.
Your letters—fragrant cloisters faint with music.
The music that assuaged her there was you.

How many times she heard your step ascending,
Yet never saw your face!
She heard them turn again, ring slowly fainter,
Till silence swept the place.
Why had you gone? . . . The door, perhaps, mistaken . . .
You would go elsewhere. The deep walls were shaken.

A certain rose-leaf, sent without intention,
Became, with time, a woven web of fire—
She wore it, and was warm.
A certain hurried glance, let fall at parting,
Became, with time, the flashings of a storm.

Yet there was nothing asked, no hint to tell you
Of secret idols carved in secret chambers
From all you did and said.
Nothing was done, until at last she knew you.
Nothing was known, till, somehow, she was dead.

How did she die?   You say she died of poison.
Simple and swift.   And much to be regretted.
You did not see her pass
So many thousand times from light to darkness,
Pausing so many times before her glass.

You did not see how many times she hurried
To lean from certain windows, vainly hoping,
Passionate still for beauty, remembered spring.

You did not know how long she clung to music,
You did not hear her sing.

Did she, then, make the choice, and step out bravely
From sound to silence—close, herself, those windows?
Or was it true, instead,
That darkness moved—for once—and so possessed her? . . .
We'll never know, you say, for she is dead.

Conrad Aiken

THE MASQUERADER

You were no more to me than many others,
    I never thought you beautiful or bright,
And yet I find your memory returning
    Many a night.

Again I hear your strange, heart-broken laughter,
    Laughter more pitiful than any tears;
Again I see your gallant head uplifted
    Through heavy years.

You held so tight the fragile toy you wanted,
    And when it broke you would not let it go;
You would not let us guess your heart broke with it—
    You played you did not know.

Now you are gone we see how well you suffered,
    We see the valiant way you struggled on.
Can you forgive our foolish condescension,
    Now you are gone?

Aline Kilmer

ELEGY

Let them bury your big eyes
In the secret earth securely,
Your thin fingers, and your fair,
Soft, indefinite-colored hair,—
All of these in some way, surely,
From the secret earth shall rise;
Not for these I sit and stare,
Broken and bereft completely:

Your young flesh that sat so neatly
On your little bones will sweetly
Blossom in the air.

But your voice,—never the rushing
Of a river underground,
Not the rising of the wind
In the trees before the rain,
Not the woodcock's watery call,
Not the note the white-throat utters,
Not the feet of children pushing
Yellow leaves along the gutters
In the blue and bitter fall,
Shall content my musing mind
For the beauty of that sound
That in no new way at all
Ever will be heard again.

Sweetly through the sappy stalk
Of the vigorous weed,
Holding all it held before,
Cherished by the faithful sun,
On and on eternally
Shall your altered fluid run,
Bud and blossom and go to seed;
But your singing days are done;
But the music of your talk
Never shall the chemistry
Of the secret earth restore.
All your lovely words are spoken.
Once the ivory box is broken,
Beats the golden bird no more.

                    Edna St. Vincent Millay

AN EPITAPH

SHIFTLESS and shy, gentle and kind and frail,
  Poor wanderer, bewildered into vice,
You are freed at last from seas you could not sail,
  A wreck upon the shores of Paradise.

                    J. C. Squire

TO ——

They could not shut you out of heaven
Although the sins you'd sinned were seven:

Not all the saints and souls in glory
Could exile you to Purgatory:

For this is true:—they need your eyes
To light the ways of Paradise.

Katharine Morse

REQUIESCAT

She should have had the state
Of a king's daughter,
Or a hut of willow branch
Near running water.

Or a scaled silver armor
For a breast cover,
Or a sweet lie in her mouth
For a lying lover.

Since she had none of these,
But a song instead,
She has well hidden herself
With the beaten dead.

Since for lack of these things
She knew herself lost,
She has well chosen silence
With her hands crossed.

Katherine Anne Porter

A WIND ROSE IN THE NIGHT

A wind rose in the night, .
  (She had always feared it so!)
Sorrow plucked at my heart
  And I could not help but go.

Softly I went and stood
  By her door at the end of the hall.
Dazed with grief I watched
  The candles flaring and tall.

The wind was wailing aloud:
  I thought how she would have cried
For my warm familiar arms
  And the sense of me by her side.

The candles flickered and leapt,
  The shadows jumped on the wall.
She lay before me small and still
  And did not care at all.

Aline Kilmer

THE ADVENTURER

He came not in the red dawn,
  Nor in the blaze of noon,
And all the long bright highway
  Lay lonely to the moon.

And nevermore, we know now,
  Will he come wandering down
The breezy hollows of the hills
  That gird the quiet town.

For he has heard a voice cry
  A starry-faint "Ahoy!"
Far up the wind, and followed
  Unquestioning after joy.

But we are long forgetting
  The quiet way he went,
With looks of love and gentle scorn
  So sweetly, subtly blent.

We cannot cease to wonder,
  We two who loved him, how
He fares along the windy ways
  His feet must travel now.

But we must draw the curtain
And fasten bolts and bars
And talk, here in the firelight,
Of him beneath the stars.

Odell Shepard

SANDY STAR

No more from out the sunset,
    No more across the foam,
No more across the windy hills
    Will Sandy Star come home.

He went away to search it
    With a curse upon his tongue:
And in his hand the staff of life,
    Made music as it swung.

I wonder if he found it,
    And knows the mystery now—
Our Sandy Star who went away,
    With the secret on his brow.

William Stanley Braithwaite

TWENTY STARS TO MATCH HIS FACE

TWENTY stars to match his face,
    All the winds to blow his breath.
In the dark no eye can trace
    Life or death.

The word came, and out he went,
    Heard the unseen flutterings
Of wings that showed the dream he sent,
    The song he sings.

Twenty stars to match his face,
    The sea-foam, his permanence—
There is no wind can mark his place
    Here, or hence.

William Stanley Braithwaite

TO–DAY I SAW BRIGHT SHIPS

To-day I saw bright ships come swinging home
In the proud, magic beauty of their bows;
I will not say again that dust can house
You who were singing with them through the foam.
You loved them once, for blue ways they would roam,
Hazarding great wild winds upon their prows,
And rough old seas that would with them espouse—
For silks and jade, red wine and honeycomb.
I will not wrong so your adventurous soul,
Thinking you lie in dreams and do forget
White spume across the deck, wind in the spars.
Death was a harbor and a transient goal
Wherefrom you pass now, with your skysail set
For ports beyond the margin of the stars.

Eloise Robinson

TO ONE WHO DIED IN AUTUMN

He watched the spring come like a gentle maid,
Suffused with blushes at her lover's call,
Her radiant figure swaying, slim and tall,
Her white arms decked with carven gold and jade;
And in her steps new grass with tender blade
Sprang up, and flowers whose faces sweet and small
Wove patterns like a rare old Persian shawl,
And carpets for the wanton summer laid,
Where she with dancing feet and passionate
Warm breasts lured autumn, purple robed and red,
Who brought blue swallows, yellow butterflies,
Calm streams, clear stars and death inviolate;
While like a seamless garment overhead
Stretched endlessly the blue, unclouded skies.

Virginia McCormick

THE ROAD TO BABYLON

"How far is it to Babylon?
—Threescore miles and ten.
Can I get there by candle-light?
Yes, and back again."

And while nurse hummed the old, old rhyme,
Tucking him in at evening time,
He dreamed how when he grew a man
And travelled free, as big men can,
He'd slip out through the garden gate
To roads where high adventures wait
And find the way to Babylon,
Babylon, far Babylon,
All silver-towered in the sun!

He's travelled free, a man with men;
(Bitter the scores of miles and ten!)
And now face down by Babylon's wall
He sleeps, nor any more at all
By morning, noon or candle-light
Or in the wistful summer night
To his own garden gate he'll come.
—Young feet that fretted so to roam
Have missed the road returning home.

Margaret Adelaide Wilson

A PHANTASY OF HEAVEN

PERHAPS he plays with cherubs now,
　Those little, golden boys of God,
Bending, with them, some silver bough,
　The while a seraph, head a-nod,

Slumbers on guard; how they will run
　And shout, if he should wake too soon,—
As fruit more golden than the sun
　And riper than the full-grown moon,

Conglobed in clusters, weighs them down,
　Like Atlas heaped with starry signs;
And, if they're tripped, heel over crown,
　By hidden coils of mighty vines,—

Perhaps the seraph, swift to pounce,
　Will hale them, vexed, to God—and He
Will only laugh, remembering, once
　He was a boy in Galilee!

Harry Kemp

THE SON

(Southern Ohio Market Town)

I heard an old farm-wife,
    Selling some barley,
Mingle her life with life
    And the name "Charley."

Saying: "The crop's all in,
    We're about through now;
Long nights will soon begin,
    We're just us two now.

"Twelve bushel at sixty cents,
    It's all I carried—
He sickened making fence;
    He was to be married.

"It feels like frost was near—
    His hair was curly.
The spring was late that year,
    But the harvest early."

Ridgely Torrence

SAUL

"*And they put his armor in the house of Ashtoreth.*"—
SAMUEL, XXXI, 10

WEEP for the one so strong to slay, whom One has taken at
    last!
Mourn for the mail that rings no more and the ruin un-
    forecast!
This was he of the flaming heart and the deep, heroic breath,
Whose sword is laid and his armor hung in the House of
    Ashtoreth.

Weep for the one so swift to slay, whose knees have bent to
    the night!
Dust is thick on his thresholds now, though trumpets call
    to the fight.

Slinger and bowman gather fast, but our strong man does not come.
Captains long for his counsels now, but the sated lips are dumb.

Cry his name in the citadel, sending the runners forth:
The South gives back no rumor of him; in vain they question the North.
Seek him not where the wall is held or the spears go in to death,
Whose shield is laid and his armor hung in the House of Ashtoreth.

This was he grown mighty in war, but her war is otherwise:
Swords that flash from her bosom bared, arrows cast from her eyes.
Who shall stoop from her javelin thrown, who from her singing dart?
Her sudden shaft is hot in his loins, her steel in his maddened heart.

Deep in the still and altared dusk her lamp glows small and red,
Mirrored clear in the great cuirass, like the rubies of her bed;
Blood of light on his burnished helm, on the belt and the greaves, one saith
Whose spear is laid and his armor hung in the House of Ashtoreth.

Tho Gath go up to the threshing-floors, or hosts assemble at Tyre,
Wait no more for your prince's word, who has taken his desire.
Cities and fields and given hearts, honor and life were weighed,
The balance shown and the end foreseen and the deep decision made.

Weep for the one so strong in war, whose war is now of the Dark!

Well he harnessed his breast with steel, but her arrows
find their mark.
Her hands have loosened the brazen belt and her breath has
found his breath
Whose sword is laid and his armor hung in the House of
Ashtoreth.

George Sterling

EPITAPH

HERE lies the flesh that tried
  To follow the spirit's leading;
Fallen at last, it died,
  Broken, bruised, and bleeding,
Burned by the high fires
Of the spirit's desires.

It had no dream to sing
  Of ultimate liberty;
Fashioned for suffering,
  To endure transiently,
And conscious that it must
Return as dust to dust.

It blossomed a brief hour,
  Was rosy, warm and strong;
It went like a wilted flower,
  It ended like a song;
Someone closed a door—
And it was seen no more.

The grass is very kind;
  (It knows so many dead!)
Those whom it covers find
  Their wild hearts comforted;
Their pulses need not meet
The spirit's speed and heat.

Here lies the flesh that held
  The spirit prisoner—
A caged thing that rebelled,
  Forced to subminister;

Broken it had to be
To set its captive free.

It is very glad to rest,
  It calls to roots and rain,
Safe in its mother's breast,
  Ready to bloom again.
After a day and an hour
'Twill greet the sun a flower.

Louise Driscoll

THE TERRIBLE DEAD

WE pity; we should dread
The terrible dead.
These things of flesh and bones
Ascend now to their thrones!
From whence they judge, unjustly, all we do.
We have no law but what they thought and knew,
Wished and preferred, deemed evil and deemed true.
We are free or prisoned, as their word is said.
We pity; we should dread
The terrible dead. . . .

Mary Carolyn Davies

PITY NOT

PITY not the dead;
They are comforted.

Should they wake not,
All is forgot.

If they rise again,
Love folds them then.

William H. Simpson

DIRGE

TUCK the earth, fold the sod,
Drop the hollow-sounding clod.
Quiet's come; time for sleeping,

Tired out of mirth and weeping,
Calmed at last of mirth and weeping.
Tuck the earth, fold the sod;
Quiet's here, maybe God.

William Alexander Percy

NOT DEAD

WALKING through trees to cool my heat and pain,
I know that David's with me here again.
All that is simple, happy, strong, he is.
Caressingly I stroke
Rough bark of the friendly oak.
A brook goes babbling by: the voice is his,
Turf burns with pleasant smoke;
I laugh at chaffinch and at primroses.
All that is simple, happy, strong, he is.
Over the whole wood in a little while
Breaks his slow smile.

Robert Graves

THE WATCHER

SHE always leaned to watch for us,
    Anxious if we were late,
In winter by the window,
    In summer by the gate;

And though we mocked her tenderly,
    Who had such foolish care,
The long way home would seem more safe
    Because she waited there.

Her thoughts were all so full of us,
    She never could forget!
And so I think that where she is
    She must be watching yet,

Waiting till we come home to her,
    Anxious if we are late—
Watching from Heaven's window,
    Leaning from Heaven's gate.

Margaret Widdemer

COMFORT

Ah! if we only dreamed how close they stand
Who were our flesh and blood once, and are still
A part of us in sympathy and will,
We should not grieve so, thinking death had banned
All sweet communion with life's spirit-land,
But fancy in each faint delicious thrill
That stirs us when Heaven's cisterns overfill,
Droppings of comfort some near love had planned.
Death brings them nearer to us: human sense,
Earth-dulled, is all the barrier that hides
The adjacent country where each one abides;
And we shall wonder, when we too pass hence,
Our hearts were thwarted by so frail a fence,
And could not break the weak wall that divides.

May Doney

DIFFUGERE NIVES, 1917

The snows have fled, the hail, the lashing rain,
  Before the Spring.
The grass is starred with buttercups again,
  The blackbirds sing.

Now spreads the month that feast of lovely things
  We loved of old.
Once more the swallow glides with darkling wings
  Against the gold.

Now the brown bees about the peach trees boom
  Upon the walls;
And far away beyond the orchard's bloom
  The cuckoo calls.

The season holds a festival of light
  For you, for me,
But shadows are abroad, there falls a blight
  On each green tree.

And every leaf unfolding, every flower
    Brings bitter meed;
Beauty of the morning and the evening hour
    Quickens our need.

All is reborn, but never any Spring
    Can bring back this;
Nor any fullness of midsummer bring
    The voice we miss.

The smiling eyes shall smile on us no more;
    The laughter clear,
Too far away on the forbidden shore,
    We shall not hear.

Bereft of these until the day we die,
    We both must dwell;
Alone, alone, and haunted by the cry:
    "Hail and farewell!"

Yet when the scythe of Death shall near us hiss,
    Through the cold air,
Then on the shuddering marge of the abyss
    They will be there.

They will be there to lift us from sheer space
    And empty night;
And we shall turn and see them face to face
    In the new light.

So shall we pay the unabated price
    Of their release,
And found on our consenting sacrifice
    Their lasting peace.

The hopes that fall like leaves before the wind,
    The baffling waste,
And every earthly joy that leaves behind
    A mortal taste.

The uncompleted end of all employ,
    The wasted store,
The aftertaste of every mooted joy
    Vex them no more.

Without them the awakening world is dark
    With dust and mire;
Yet as they went they flung to us a spark,
    A thread of fire

To guide us while beneath the somber skies
    Faltering we tread,
Until for us like morning stars shall rise
    The deathless dead.

Maurice Baring

SENTINEL SONGS

TO L. H. B.

[LESLIE HERON BEAUCHAMP, 1894–1915]

LAST night for the first time since you were dead
I walked with you, my brother, in a dream.
We were at home again beside the stream
Fringed with tall berry bushes, white and red.
"Don't touch them; they are poisonous," I said.
But your hand hovered, and I saw a beam
Of strange, bright laughter flying round your head
And as you stooped I saw the berries gleam.
"Don't you remember?   We called them Dead Man's
    Bread!"
I woke and heard the wind moan and the roar
Of the dark water tumbling on the shore.
Where—where is the path of my dream for my eager feet?
By the remembered stream my brother stands
Waiting for me with berries in his hands.
"These are my body.   Sister, take and eat."

Katherine Mansfield

TO WILLIAM BLAKE

[1757–1827]

*(When an original copy of "Songs of Innocence," etched
and colored by the author, was left overnight on my pillow)*

BE a god, your spirit cried;
Tread with feet that burn the dew;
Dress with clouds your locks of pride;
Be a child, God said to you.

Then with blood a wild sea-wave,
Then while Death drew near to look,
Firm your fingers grew and gave
Man and me this gentle book.

993

Dream that burns the dreamer mad
Swept you through and did not sere;
Forth you looked, a little lad;
Sang the songs that all may hear.

Bright you go, with dewy fire
Of your music flowing fleet;
Drifting lower, drifting higher,
With the winds beneath your feet.

And I'll take the way I find
With no thought of footing sore.
Stones are tender, thorns are kind,
Where your piping goes before.

Olive Dargan

RUPERT BROOKE

[1887–1915]

I

YOUR face was lifted to the golden sky
Ablaze beyond the black roofs of the square
As flame on flame leapt, flourishing in air
Its tumult of red stars exultantly
To the cold constellations dim and high:
And as we neared the roaring ruddy flare
Kindled to gold your throat and brow and hair
Until you burned, a flame of ecstasy.
The golden head goes down into the night
Quenched in cold gloom—and yet again you stand
Beside me now with lifted face alight,
As, flame to flame, and fire to fire, you burn. . . .
Then, recollecting, laughingly you turn,
And look into my eyes and take my hand.

II

Once in my garret—you being far away,
Tramping the hills and breathing upland air,
Or so I fancied—brooding in my chair,
I watched the London sunshine feeble and gray

Dapple my desk, too tired to labor more,
When, looking up, I saw you standing there
Although I'd caught no footsteps on the stair,
Like sudden April at my open door.
Though now beyong earth's farthest hills you fare,
Song-crowned, immortal, sometimes it seems to me
That, if I listen very quietly,
Perhaps I'll hear a light foot on the stair
And see you, standing with your angel air,
Fresh from the uplands of eternity.

III

Your eyes rejoiced in color's ecstasy,
Fulfilling even their uttermost desire,
When, over a great sunlit field afire
With windy poppies streaming like a sea
Of scarlet flame that flaunted riotously
Among green orchards of that western shire,
You gazed as though your heart could never tire
Of life's red flood in summer revelry.
And as I watched you, little thought had I
How soon beneath the dim low-drifting sky
Your soul should wander down the darkling way,
With eyes that peer a little wistfully,
Half-glad, half-sad, remembering, as they see
Lethean poppies, shrivelling ashen gray.

IV

October chestnuts showered their perishing gold
Over us as beside the stream we lay
In the Old Vicarage garden that blue day,
Talking of verse and all the manifold
Delights a little net of words may hold,
While in the sunlight water-voles at play
Dived under a trailing crimson bramble-spray,
And walnuts thudded ripe on soft black mould.
Your soul goes down into a darker stream
Alone, O friend, yet even in death's deep night
Your eyes may grow accustomed to the dark.

And Styx for you may have the ripple and gleam
Of your familiar river, and Charon's bark
Tarry by that old garden of your delight.

Wilfrid Gibson

VERNON CASTLE

[1887–1918]

DEAD dancer, how is this?—the laurel here
      Upon your bier?
The brazen wings, the sword—and the shrill tone
      Of bugles blown?

Why do you wear, light-footed one—O proud!—
      The flag for shroud?
Where have you danced? from what high-spherèd dome
      Have you come home?

Bravo!—you trod the measure gallantly,
      Swiftly flew free!
Goodbye—perhaps your flight has just begun
      Under the sun.

Harriet Monroe

EDITH CAVELL

[1872–1915]

THE world hath its own dead; great motions start
In human breasts, and make for them a place
In that hushed sanctuary of the race
Where every day men come, kneel, and depart.
Of them, O English nurse, henceforth thou art
A name to pray on, and to all a face
Of household consecration; such His grace
Whose universal dwelling is the heart.
O gentle hands that soothed the soldier's brow
And knew no service save of Christ's the Lord!
Thy country now is all humanity.
How like a flower thy womanhood doth show
In the harsh scything of the German sword,
And beautifies the world that saw it die!

George Edward Woodberry

ADELAIDE CRAPSEY

[1878–1914)

AMONG the bumble-bees in red-top hay, a freckled field of
   brown-eyed Susans dripping yellow leaves in July,
   I read your heart in a book.

And your mouth of blue pansy—I know somewhere I have
   seen it rain-shattered.

And I have seen a woman with her head flung between her
   naked knees, and her head held there listening
   to the sea, the great naked sea shouldering a load
   of salt.

And the blue pansy mouth sang to the sea:
   Mother of God, I'm so little a thing,
   Let me sing longer,
   Only a little longer.

And the sea shouldered its salt in long gray combers hauling
   new shapes on the beach sand.
                                        Carl Sandburg

ERNEST DOWSON

[1867–1900]

O BROTHER, what is there to say to you,
Now that your feet have passed beyond the sun!
Now is the twilight waned, the dark begun,
And the consoling memories fall like dew.
Alas, what has your dreaming brought you to!
O brother—what is this that you have done!
But peace, these are no things to think upon,—
And evening brings the immortal stars to view.
As one might lay his palm upon your breast
And feel the pleading of your heart's demand,
While yet it throbbed for life, though fain to weep;
Now, when the stars have gathered you to rest,
O inconsolable friend, I lay my hand
Upon this page, and hear it, though you sleep.
                                        John Hall Wheelock

CÉSAR FRANCK

[1822–1890]

To grasp it; say that you have seized that hour
   Choking with music like a bright smoke; say
That you have crushed it as you crush a flower
   Because it dies to-day;

To breathe it in, a brilliant dizziness
   Glittering, overwhelming, battering sense
Down, and beating in a radiant press
   Of wings up to the tents

Of the pavilioned spirit!—so you shall reach
   The slow white width of peace, and for a while,
Even for a while, hear an exalted speech
   And know Death by his smile.

Joseph Auslander

JULIAN GRENFELL

[1888–1915]

BECAUSE of you we will be glad and gay,
Remembering you, we will be brave and strong;
And hail the advent of each dangerous day,
And meet the last adventure with a song.
And, as you proudly gave your jewelled gift,
We'll give our lesser offering with a smile,
Nor falter on that path where, all too swift,
You led the way and leapt the golden stile.
Whether new paths, new heights to climb you find,
Or gallop through the unfooted asphodel,
We know you know we shall not lag behind,
Nor halt to waste a moment on a fear;
And you will speed us onward with a cheer,
And wave beyond the stars that all is well.

Maurice Baring

AN ELECTRIC SIGN GOES DARK

[ANNA HELD, 1877–1918]

POLAND, France, Judea ran in her veins,
Singing to Paris for bread, singing to Gotham in a fizz at
    the pop of a bottle's cork.

"Won't you come and play wiz me" she sang . . . and
    "I just can't make my eyes behave."
"Higgeldy-Piggeldy," "Papa's Wife," "Follow Me" were
    plays.

Did she wash her feet in a tub of milk?   Was a strand of
    pearls sneaked from her trunk?   The newspapers
    asked.
Cigarettes, tulips, pacing horses, took her name.

Twenty years old . . . thirty . . . forty . . .
Forty-five and the doctors fathom nothing, the doctors
    quarrel, the doctors use silver tubes feeding twenty-
    four quarts of blood into the veins, the respects of a
    prize-fighter, a cab driver.
And a little mouth moans: It is easy to die when they are
    dying so many grand deaths in France.

A voice, a shape, gone.
A baby bundle from Warsaw . . . legs, torso, head . . . on
    a hotel bed at The Savoy.
The white chiselings of flesh that flung themselves in somer-
    saults, straddles, for packed houses:
A memory, a stage and footlights out, an electric sign on
    Broadway dark.

She belonged to somebody, nobody.
No one man owned her, no ten nor a thousand.
She belonged to many thousand men, lovers of the white
    chiseling of arms and shoulders, the ivory of a laugh,
    the bells of song.

Railroad brakemen taking trains across Nebraska prairies,
    lumbermen jaunting in pine and tamarack of the
    Northwest, stock ranchers in the middle west, mayors of
    southern cities
Say to their pals and wives now: I see by the papers Anna
    Held is dead.

Carl Sandburg

THOMAS HOOD

[1799–1845]

THE man who cloaked his bitterness within
This winding-sheet of puns and pleasantries,
God never gave to look with common eyes
Upon a world of anguish and of sin:
His brother was the branded man of Lynn;
And there are woven with his jollities
The nameless and eternal tragedies
That render hope and hopelessness akin.
We laugh, and crown him; but anon we feel
A still chord sorrow-swept,—a weird unrest;
And thin dim shadows home to midnight steal,
As if the very ghost of mirth were dead—
As if the joys of time to dreams had fled,
Or sailed away with Ines to the West.

Edwin Arlington Robinson

A COMRADE RIDES AHEAD

[EMERSON HOUGH, 1857–1923]

TIME brings not death, it brings but changes;
    I know he rides, but rides afar,
To-day some other planet ranges
    And camps to-night upon a star
    Where all his other comrades are.

For there were those who rode before him,
    As there are these he leaves behind;
Although from us time's changes bore him,
    Out there our comrade still will find
    The kinship of the comrade mind.

Time brings us change and leaves us fretting;
   We weep when every comrade goes—
Perhaps too much, perhaps forgetting
   That over yonder there are those
   To whom he comes and whom he knows.

I would not hold our loss too lightly;
   God knows, and he, how deep the pain;
But, friends, I see still shining brightly
   The brightest link in all our chain
   That links us with a new domain.

For this I swear, because believing:
   Time breaks no circle such as this.
However hurt, however grieving,
   However much a friend we miss,
   Between the worlds is no abyss.

For friendship binds the worlds together—
   World over there, world over here.
From earth to heaven is the tether
   That brings the earth and heaven near
   And makes them both a bit more dear.

Not weaker now our chain, but stronger;
   In all our loss and all our ill
We now shall look a little longer
   At every star above the hill
   And think of him, and have him still.

Whatever vales we yet may wander,
   What sorrow come, what tempest blow,
We have a friend, a friend out yonder,
   To greet us when we have to go—
   Out yonder someone that we know.

To all eternity he binds us;
   He links the planet and the star;
He rides ahead, the trail he finds us,
   And where he is and where we are
   Will never seem again so far.

Douglas Malloch

JOYCE KILMER

[1886–1918]

SURELY the saints you loved visibly came
To welcome you, that day in Picardy—
Stephen whose dying eyes beheld his Lord,
Michael, a living blade of crystal flame,
And all the flower of heavenly chivalry
Smiling upon you, calling you by name.
Leaving your body like a broken sword
You went with them—and now, beyond our sight,
Still in the ranks of God you sing and fight,
For death to you was one more victory.

Amelia Josephine Burr

IN MEMORIAM: FRANCIS LEDWIDGE

[1891–1917]

SOLDIER and singer of Erin,
What may I fashion for thee?
What garland of words or of flowers?
Singer of sunlight and showers
 The wind on the lea;

Of clouds, and the houses of Erin,
Wee cabins, white on the plain,
And bright with the colors of even,
Beauty of earth and of heaven
 Outspread beyond Slane!

Slane, where the Easter of Patrick
Flamed on the night of the Gael,
Guard both the honor and story
Of him who has died for the glory
 That crowns Inisfail.

Soldier of right and of freedom,
I offer thee song and not tears.

With Brian, and Red Hugh O'Donnell,
The Chiefs of Tyrone and Tyrconnell,
    Live on through the years!
Norreys Jephson O'Conor

THE LINCOLN–CHILD

[1809–1865]

Clearing in the forest,
In the wild Kentucky forest,
And the stars, wintry stars strewn above!
O Night that is the starriest
Since Earth began to roll—
For a Soul
Is born out of Love!
Mother love, father love, love of Eternal God—
Stars have pushed aside to let him through—
Through heaven's sun-sown deeps
One sparkling ray of God
Strikes the clod—
(And while an angel-host through wood and clearing sweeps!)
Born in the Wild
The Child—
Naked, ruddy, new,
Wakes with the piteous human cry and at the mother-
      heart sleeps.

To the mother wild berries and honey,
To the father awe without end,
To the child a swaddling of flannel—
And a dawn rolls sharp and sunny
And the skies of winter bend
To see the first sweet word penned
In the godliest human annal.

Frail Mother of the Wilderness—
How strange the world shines in
And the cabin becomes chapel
And the baby reveals God—
Sweet Mother of the Wilderness.

New worlds for you begin,
You have tasted of the apple
That giveth wisdom starred.

Do you dream, as all Mothers dream,
That the child at your heart
Is a marvel apart,
A frail star-beam
Unearthly splendid?
Ah, you are the one mother
Whose dream shall come true,
Though another, not you,
Shall see it ended.

Soon in the wide wilderness,
On a branch blown over a creek,
Up a trail of the wild coon,
In a lair of the wild bee,
The wilding boy, by Danger's stress,
Learnt the speech the wild things speak,
Learnt the Earth's eternal tune
Of strife-engendered harmony—
Went to school where Life itself was master,
Went to church where Earth was minister—
And in Danger and Disaster
Felt his future manhood stir!

All about him lay the land,
Eastern cities, Western prairie,
Wild, immeasureable, grand;
But he was lost where blossomy boughs make airy
Bowers in the forest, and the sand
Makes brook-water a clear mirror that gives back
Green branches and trunks black
And clouds across the heavens lightly fanned.

Yet all the Future dreams, eager to waken,
Within that woodland soul—
And the bough of boy has only to be shaken
That the fruit drop whereby this Earth shall roll

A little nearer God than ever before.
Little recks he of war,
Of national millions waiting on his word—
Dreams still the Event unstirred
In the heart of the boy, the little babe of the wild—
But the years hurry and the tide of the sea
Of Time flows fast and ebbs, and he, even he,
Must leave the wilderness, the wood-haunts wild—
Soon shall the cyclone of Humanity
Tearing through Earth suck up this little child
And whirl him to the top, where he shall be
Riding the storm-column in the lightning-stroke,
Calm at the peak, while down below worlds rage,
And Earth goes out in blood and battle-smoke,
And leaves him with the sun—an epoch and an age! . . .

And lo, as he grew ugly, gaunt,
And gnarled his way into a man,
What wisdom came to feed his want,
What worlds came near to let him scan!
And as he fathomed through and through
Our dark and sorry human scheme,
He knew what Shakespeare never knew,
What Dante never dared to dream—
That Men are one
Beneath the Sun,
And before God are equal souls—
This truth was his,
And this it is
That round him such a glory rolls—
For not alone he knew it as a truth,
He made it of his blood, and of his brain—
He crowned it on the day when piteous Booth
Sent a whole land to weeping with world-pain—
When a black cloud blotted the sun
And men stopped in the streets to sob,
To think Old Abe was dead.
Dead, and the day's work still undone,
Dead, and war's ruining heart athrob,
And earth with fields of carnage freshly spread—

Millions died fighting,
But in this man we mourned
Those millions, and one other—
And the States to-day uniting,
North and South,
East and West,
Speak with a people's mouth
A rhapsody of rest
To him our beloved best,
Our big, gaunt, homely brother—
Our huge Atlantic coast-storm in a shawl,
Our cyclone in a smile—our President,
Who knew and loved us all
With love more eloquent
Than his own words—with Love that in real deeds was
     spent. . . .

Oh, to pour love through deeds—
To be as Lincoln was!—
That all the land might fill its daily needs
Glorified by a human Cause!
Then were America a vast World-Torch
Flaming a faith across the dying Earth,
Proclaiming from the Atlantic's rocky porch,
That a New World was struggling at the Birth!

Ah, is this not the day
That rolls the Earth back to that mighty hour
When the sweet babe in the log-cabin lay
And God was in the room, a Presence and a Power?—
When all was sacred—even the father's heart—
And the stirred Wilderness stood still,
And roaring flume and shining hill
Felt the working of God's Will?
O living God, O Thou who living art,
And real, and near, draw, as at that babe's birth,
Into our souls and sanctify our Earth—
Let down Thy strength that we endure
Mighty and pure
As mothers and fathers of our own Lincoln-child—

Make us more wise, more true, more strong, more mild.
That we may day by day
Rear this wild blossom through its soft petals of clay;
That hour by hour
We may endow it with more human power
Than is our own—
That it may reach the goal
Our Lincoln long has shown!
O Child, flesh of our flesh, bone of our bone,
Soul torn from out our Soul!
May you be great, and pure, and beautiful—
A Soul to search this world
To be a father, brother, comrade, son,
A toiler powerful,
A man whose toil is done
One with God's Law above:
Work wrought through Love!

James Oppenheim

LINCOLN

I

LIKE a gaunt, scraggly pine
Which lifts its head above the mournful sandhills,
And patiently, through dull years of bitter silence,
Untended and uncared for, starts to grow.

Ungainly, laboring, huge,
The wind of the north has twisted and gnarled its branches;
Yet in the heat of midsummer days, when thunder-clouds
    ring the horizon,
A nation of men shall rest beneath its shade.

And it shall protect them all,
Hold everyone safe there, watching aloof in silence;
Until at last one mad stray bolt from the zenith
Shall strike it in an instant down to earth.

II

There was a darkness in this man; an immense and hollow
    darkness,

Of which we may not speak, nor share with him, nor enter;
A darkness through which strong roots stretched downwards
    into the earth
Towards old things;

Towards the herdman-kings who walked the earth and spoke
    with God,
Towards the wanderers who sought for they knew not what,
    and found their goal at last;
Towards the men who waited, only waited patiently when
    all seemed lost,
Many bitter winters of defeat;

Down to the granite of patience,
These roots swept, knotted fibrous roots, prying, piercing,
    seeking,
And drew from the living rock and the living waters about
    it
The red sap to carry upwards to the sun.

Not proud, but humble,
Only to serve and pass on, to endure to the end through
    service;
For the axe is laid at the roots of the trees, and all that bring
    not forth good fruit
Shall be cut down on the day to come and cast into the fire.

III

There is silence abroad in the land to-day,
And in the hearts of men, a deep and anxious silence;
And, because we are still at last, those bronze lips slowly
    open,
Those hollow and weary eyes take on a gleam of light.

Slowly a patient, firm-syllabled voice cuts through the end-
    less silence
Like laboring oxen that drag a plow through the chaos of
    rude clay-fields:
"I went forward as the light goes forward in early spring,
But there were also many things which I left behind.

"Tombs that were quiet;
One, of a mother, whose brief light went out in the darkness,
One, of a loved one, the snow on whose grave is long falling,
One, only of a child, but it was mine.

"Have you forgot your graves?   Go, question them in
     anguish,
Listen long to their unstirred lips.   From your hostages to
     silence,
Learn there is no life without death, no dawn without sun-
     setting,
No victory but to him who has given all."

IV

The clamor of cannon dies down, the furnace-mouth of the
     battle is silent,
The midwinter sun dips and descends, the earth takes on
     afresh its bright colors.
But he whom we mocked and obeyed not, he whom we
     scorned and mistrusted,
He has descended, like a god, to his rest.

Over the uproar of cities,
Over the million intricate threads of life wavering and
     crossing,
In the midst of problems we know not, tangling, perplexing,
     ensnaring,
Rises one white tomb alone.

Beam over it, stars,
Wrap it round, stripes—stripes red from the pain that he
     bore for you—
Enfold it forever, O flag, rent, soiled, but repaired through
     your anguish;
Long as you keep him there safe, the nations shall bow to
     your law.

Strew over him flowers:
Blue forget-me-nots from the north, and the bright pink
     arbutus

From the east, and from the west rich orange blossoms,
But from the heart of the land take the passion-flower;

Rayed, violet, dim,
With the nails that pierced, the cross that he bore and the
    circlet,
And beside it there lay also one lonely snow-white mag-
    nolia,
Bitter for remembrance of the healing which has passed.

John Gould Fletcher

LINCOLN

BIRTH seems like chance, and life appears uncertain:
All living things express a force unbidden.
Unconscious Nature never lifts the curtain:
Men fumble at her door—the key is hidden.
They call chance blind, and they themselves are blind:
Great Nature's forces, unrestrained and free,
Produced, by chance, this giant of mankind,
And challenge man to solve his mystery.
Spontaneous! Inspired! The perfect flower
Of chance, he was by liberal Nature sent
To lead man nobly, with unconscious power,
And justify the law of accident.
Titanic seer!   And poet lovable!
His life links Shakespeare's with the probable.

Rembrandt William B. Ditmars

HORSE IN A FIELD

[TO KATHERINE MANSFIELD]

*"And there was a Horse in the King's Stables; and the name
    of the Horse was Genius."*—ARABIAN NIGHTS.

WE sat and talked. It was June, and the summer light
Lay fair upon ceiling and wall as the day took flight.
Tranquil the room—with its colors and shadows wan,
Cherries, and china, and flowers: and the hour slid on.
Dark hair, dark eyes, slim fingers—you made the tea,
Pausing with spoon uplifted, to speak to me.
Lulled by our thoughts and our voices, happy were we!

And musing, an old, old riddle crept into my head,
"Supposing I just say 'Horse in a field,'" I said,
"What do you *see*?" And we each made answer: "I,
A roan, long tail, and a red-brick house, near by."
"I—an old cart-horse and rain!" "Oh no, not rain:
A mare with a long-legged foal by a pond—oh, plain!"
"And I—a hedge—and an elm—and the shadowy green
Sloping gently up to the blue, to the West, I mean.". . .

And now. On the field that I see night's darkness lies.
A brook brawls near: there are stars in the empty skies.
The grass is deep: and dense, as I push my way,
From sour-nettled ditch sweeps fragrance of clustering may.
I come to a stile. And lo, on the further side,
Beneath still, umbrageous, night-black fronds, spread wide,
A giant cedar broods. . . . And in crescent's gleam—
A horse, milk-pale, sleek-shouldered, strange as a dream,

Startled, it lifts its muzzle, deep eyes agaze,
With silk-plaited mane . . .
                "Whose pastures are thine to graze?
Creature delicate, lovely, with womanlike head,
Sphinx-like, gazelle-like. . . . Where tarries thy rider?"
    I said.
And I scanned by that sinking slip's thin silver shed
A high-pooped saddle of leather, night-darkened red,
Stamped with a pattern of gilding; and over it thrown
A cloak, chain-buckled, with one great glamorous stone
Wan as the argent moon when o'er fields of wheat
Like Dian she broods, and steals to Endymion's feet.
Interwoven with silver that cloak from seam to seam.
And at toss of the head from its damascened bridle did beam
Mysterious glare in the dead of the dark. . . .
                "Thy name,
Fantastical Steed? And thy pedigree?
Peace out of Storm, is the tale: or, *Beauty—of Jeopardy?*"

The water weeps. Not a footfall. And midnight here.
Why tarries Darkness's bird? Spiced and clear
Slopes to yon hill with its stars the moorland sweet.

There sigh the airs of far heaven. And the dreamer's feet
Scatter the leagues of paths secret to where at last meet
Roads called Wickedness, Righteousness, broad-flung or
      strait,
And a third that leads on to the Queen of fair Elfland's gate.

This then the horse that I see: swift as the wind;
That none may master or mount; and none may bind;
But she, his Mistress; cloaked, and at throat that gem—
Dark head, dark eyes, slim shoulder . . .
      God speed, K. M.

Walter de la Mare

THE POET OF GARDENS

FOR   THE   TERCENTENNIAL   YEAR   OF   ANDREW   MARVELL

[1621–1678]

MARVELL, still your fragrant rhyme
Prospers on the bough of time!
Far beyond Nunappleton
Have your lovely lyrics run:
Backwards to Theocritus,
Forward to the hearts of us!

Walk this new world, splendid ghost!
Watch Manhattan's surging host!
Would you dream our hearts are closes
For your tulips and your roses?
That your lilies and rosemary
Give our souls a sanctuary?
That the bird of silver wing
Nests in our remembering?

Time will dull us; life will harden!
But our thoughts shall keep your garden
Green as when you taught a maid
Latin verses in its shade!
Green as when its wall shut out
Roundhead brawl and royal rout!

Green as when there came to birth
Milton's heaven, Marvell's earth!

Poet, see your sylvan view
Fresh with an eternal dew!

Daniel Henderson

REPETITIONS

[1886–1916]

THEY are crying salt tears
Over the beautiful beloved body
Of Inez Milholland,
Because they are glad she lived,
Because she loved open-armed,
Throwing love for a cheap thing
Belonging to everybody—
Cheap as sunlight,
And morning air.

Carl Sandburg

OF A POET PATRIOT

[WILLIAM ROONEY]

HIS songs were a little phrase
    Of eternal song,
Drowned in the harping of lays
    More loud and long.

His deed was a single word,
    Called out alone
In a night when no echo stirred
    To laughter or moan.

But his songs new souls shall thrill,
    The loud harps dumb,
And his deed the echoes fill
    When the dawn is come.

Thomas MacDonagh

RONSARD

[1524–1585]

Four hundred urgent springs and ripened summers,
Four hundred winters sharp beneath the moon:
And still your delicate and moulded tune,
Like wind-carved waters, through your land of France
Runs in a singing dance,
Over whose waves the insect pipes and drummers
Die in an afternoon.

Miriam Allen deFord

SAGAMORE

[THEODORE ROOSEVELT, 1858–1919]

At Sagamore the Chief lies low—
Above the hill in circled row
The whirring airplanes dip and fly,
A guard of honor from the sky;—
Eagles to guard the Eagle. Woe
Is on the world. The people go
With listless footstep, blind and slow;—
For one is dead—who shall not die—
     At Sagamore.

Oh, Land he loved, at last you know
The son who served you well below,
The prophet voice, the visioned eye.
Hold him in ardent memory,
For one is gone—who shall not go—
     From Sagamore!

Corinne Roosevelt Robinson

"THE SAD YEARS"

[DORA SIGERSON SHORTER, 18— –1919]

You whom I never knew,
Who lived remote, afar,
Yet died of the grief that tore my heart,

Shall we live through the ages alone, apart,
Or meet where the souls of the sorrowful are
Telling the tale on some secret star,
How your death from the root of my sorrow grew—
You whom I never knew.

Nay, perhaps in the coming years,
Down here on our earth again,
We shall meet as strangers on some strange shore,
And dream we have known one another before,
In a past life, weeping over the slain—
Because of a thrill and a throb of pain,
And eyes grown suddenly salt with tears . . .
Perhaps . . . in the coming years. . . .

Eva Gore-Booth

SAINT R. L. S.

[1850–1894]

SULTRY and brazen was the August day
    When Sister Stanislaus went down to see
    The little boy with the tuberculous knee.

And as she thought to find him, so he lay:
    Still staring, through the dizzy waves of heat,
    At the tall tenement across the street.

But did he see that dreary picture?   Nay:
    In his mind's eye a sunlit harbor showed,
    Where a tall pirate ship at anchor rode.

Yes, he was full ten thousand miles away!
    —The Sister, when she turned his pillow over,
    Kissed "Treasure Island" on its well-worn cover.

Sarah N. Cleghorn

TO MY FATHER

[SIR HERBERT BEERBOHM TREE, 1853–1917]

I CANNOT think that you have gone away,
You loved the earth—and life lit up your eyes,
And flickered in your smile that would surmise
Death as a song, a poem, or a play.
You were reborn afresh with every day,
And baffled fortune in some new disguise.
Ah! can it perish when the body dies,
Such youth, such love, such passion to be gay?
We shall not see you come to us and leave
A conqueror—nor catch on fairy wing
Some slender fancy—nor new wonders weave
Upon the loom of your imagining.
The world is wearier, grown dark to grieve
Her child that was a pilgrim and a king.

Iris Tree

TRELAWNY LIES BY SHELLEY

(IN THE PROTESTANT CEMETERY, ROME)

TRELAWNY lies by Shelley, and one bed
Of violets covers Keats and Severn, so
The friends who went life's way together know
No parting of the ways now they are dead.
Young Shelley, like a spirit, spoke and fled,
And Keats, before his youth began to blow;
Trelawny counted eighty winters' snow,
And eighty winters fell on Severn's head.
Yet here they lie, like poppies at one stroke
Cut by the selfsame blade in the summer sun;
The poets, and the friends who heard their song,
Believed and waited till the morning broke,
Then told their candle that the night was done;
When Friendship rested in the daytide strong.

Charles L. O'Donnell

VILLIERS DE L'ISLE–ADAM

UP from the darkness on the laughing stage
A sudden trap-door shot you unawares,
Incarnate Tragedy, with your strange airs
Of courteous sadness.   Nothing could assuage
The secular grief that was your heritage,
Passed down the long line to the last that bears
The name, a gift of yearnings and despairs
Too greatly noble for this iron age.
Time moved for you not in quotidian beats,
But in the long slow rhythm the ages keep
In their immortal symphony.   You taught
That not in the harsh turmoil of the streets
Does life consist; you bade the soul drink deep
Of infinite things, saying: "The rest is naught."

Aldous Huxley

TO A PORTRAIT OF WHISTLER IN THE BROOK-LYN ART MUSEUM

[1834–1903]

WHAT waspish whim of Fate
    Was this that bade you here
Hold dim, unhonored state,
    No single courtier near?

Is there, of all who pass,
    No choice, discerning few
To poise the ribboned glass
    And gaze enwrapt on you?

Sword-soul that from its sheath
    Laughed leaping to the fray,
How calmly underneath
    Goes Brooklyn on her way!

Quite heedless of that smile—
    Half-devil and half-god,
Your quite unequalled style,
    The airy heights you trod.

Ah, could you from earth's breast
    Come back to take the air,
What matter here for jest
    Most exquisite and rare!

But since you may not come,
    Since silence holds you fast,
Since all your quips are dumb
    And all your laughter past—

I give you mine instead,
    And something with it too
That Brooklyn leaves unsaid—
    The world's fine homage due.

Ah, Prince, you smile again—
    "My faith, the court is small!"
I know, dear James—but then
    It's I or none at all!

Eleanor Rogers Cox

THE DEAD POET

[OSCAR WILDE, 1856–1900]

I DREAMED of him last night, I saw his face
All radiant and unshadowed of distress,
And as of old, in music measureless,
I heard his golden voice and marked him trace
Under the common thing the hidden grace,
And conjure wonder out of emptiness,
Till mean things put on beauty like a dress
And all the world was an enchanted place.
And then methought outside a fast-locked gate
I mourned the loss of unrecorded words,
Forgotten tales and mysteries half said,
Wonders that might have been articulate,
And voiceless thoughts like murdered singing birds.
And so I woke and knew that he was dead.

Alfred Bruce Douglas

O WORLD INVISIBLE

MIRACLES

From "The Jig of Forslin"

I

TWILIGHT is spacious, near things in it seem far,
And distant things seem near.
Now in the green west hangs a yellow star.
And now across old waters you may hear
The profound gloom of bells among still trees,
Like a rolling of huge boulders beneath seas.

Silent as thought in evening contemplation
Weaves the bat under the gathering stars.
Silent as dew we seek new incarnation,
Meditate new avatars.
In a clear dusk like this
Mary climbed up the hill to seek her son,
To lower him down from the cross, and kiss
The mauve wounds, every one.

Men with wings
In the dusk walked softly after her.
She did not see them, but may have felt
The winnowed air around her stir;
She did not see them, but may have known
Why her son's body was light as a little stone.
She may have guessed that other hands were there
Moving the watchful air.

Now, unless persuaded by searching music
Which suddenly opens the portals of the mind,
We guess no angels,
And are contented to be blind.
Let us blow silver horns in the twilight,
And lift our hearts to the yellow star in the green,

To find perhaps, if, while the dew is rising,
Clear things may not be seen.

II

Under a tree I sit, and cross my knees,
And smoke a cigarette.
You nod to me: you think perhaps you know me
But I escape you, I am none of these;
I leave my name behind me, I forget . . .

I hear a fountain shattering into a pool;
I see the gold fish slanting under the cool;
And suddenly all is frozen into silence.
And among the firs, or over desert grass,
Or out of a cloud of dust, or out of darkness,
Or on the first slow patter of sultry rain,
I heard a voice cry "Marvels have come to pass,—
The like of which shall not be seen again!"

And behold, across a sea one came to us,
Treading the wave's edge with his naked feet,
Slowly, as one might walk in a ploughed field.
We stood where the soft waves on the shingle beat,
In a blowing mist, and pressed together in terror,
And marvelled that all our eyes might share one error.

For if the fisher's fine-spun net must sink,
Or pebbles flung by a boy, or the thin sand,
How shall we understand
That flesh and blood might tread on the sea-water
And foam not wet the ankles?   We must think
That all we know is lost, or only a dream,
That dreams are real, and real things only dream.

And if a man may walk to us like this
On the unstable sea, as on a beach,
With his head bowed in thought—
Then we have been deceived in what men teach:
And all our knowledge has come to nought;
And a little flame should seek the earth,

And leaves, falling, should seek the sky,
And surely we should enter the womb for birth,
And sing from the ashes when we die.

Or was the man a god, perhaps, or devil?
They say he healed the sick by stroke of hands;
And that he gave the sights of the earth to the blind.
And I have heard that he could touch a fig-tree,
And say to it, "Be withered!" and it would shrink
Like a cursed thing, and writhe its leaves, and die.
How shall we understand such things, I wonder,
Unless there are things invisible to the eye?

And there was Lazarus, raised from the dead:
To whom he spoke quietly, in the dusk,—
Lazarus, three days dead, and mortified;
And the pale body trembled; as from a swoon,
Sweating, the sleeper woke, and raised his head;
And turned his puzzled eyes from side to side . . .

Should we not, then, hear voices in a stone,
Talking of heaven and hell?
Or if one walked beside a sea, alone,
Hear broodings of a bell?—
Or on a green hill in the evening's fire,
If we should stand and listen to poplar trees,
Should we not hear the lit leaves suddenly choir
A jargon of silver music against the sky?—
Or the dew sing, or dust profoundly cry?—

If this is possible, then all things are:
And I may leave my body crumpled there
Like an old garment on the floor;
To walk abroad on the unbetraying air;
To pass through every door,
And see the hills of the earth, or climb a star.

Wound me with spears, you only stab the wind;
You nail my cloak against a bitter tree;
You do not injure me.

I pass through the crowd, the dark crowd busy with murder,
Through the linked arms I pass;
And slowly descend the hill, through dew-wet grass.

Conrad Aiken

THE AWAKENING

I

OUTWARD from the planets are blown the fumes of thought,
And the breath of prayer drifts out and makes a mist
    between the stars;

The void shall be void no longer,
And the caverns of infinity shall be fulfilled of spirit;

For in the wilderness between the worlds a sentience strug-
    gles to awaken,
Passions and ghosts and visions gather into a Form.

The God that we have worshipped for a million years begins
    to be,
And he whom we have prayed to creates himself out of the
    stuff of our prayers.

His wings are still heavy with chaos,
And his pinions are holden down as with a weight of slumber;

His face is ambiguous,
His countenance is uncertain behind the veils of space;

He has not speech,
He has but only thunder for his voice;

But the mornings gather to shape his eye,
And the fire of many dawns has thrilled his twilight with a
    prescience of vision.

II

From myriad altars a reek of incense,
And outward from the constellations there leaps the flame
    of burning prophets;

There goes forth the breath of lovely purpose,
As a south wind bearing seeds over a meadow it goes forth
across the firmament;

There arises a dew from the bruised foreheads of martyrs,
And the broken hearts of the just, of them that have loved
justice, are dissolved into a bloody dew;

Out from the populated spheres a mist,
And from the peopled worlds a breeding fog:

And in the mist a God gathers unto Himself Form, and ap-
parels himself in Being,
For them that have desired a God create him from the stuff
of that desire.

III

In the nebular chasms there is a shaping soul,
And a light begins to glow in the dark abyss;   .

That which is to be draws to itself what has been and what is,
He drinks up the hopes of them that were as a sun sucks
up water;

He builds himself out of the desperate faith of them that have
sought him,
And his face shall be wrought of the wish to see his face.

Man has lifted his voice unto the hollow sky and there was
no answer but the echo of his voice,
But out of many echoes there shall grow a word.

There is a cry from the peaks of Caucasus,
From the throat of Prometheus a hoarse shout of agony
and courage and defiance;

Answer, O you stars! and make reply, you rushing worlds!
Have you not always chained your Titans where the vultures scream about the bloodied rocks?
Have you not thrust your beaks into the livers of them
that loved you?

There is a cry goes forth from all the stars,
The voice of rebels and great lovers;

Out of agonies and love shall God be made,
He is wrought of cries that meet between the worlds,
Of seeking cries that have come forth from the cruel spheres
    to find a God and be stilled.

Answer, you populations,
And make reply, you planets that are red in space:
Do not ten thousand broken Christs this hour cry their
    despair?

Are not Golgothas shaken this hour and the suns shamed?
Goes there not forth a manifold wailing of them that cry,
"My God, my God, why hast thou forsaken me?"

These cries have wandered out along the waste places,
And these despairs have met in the wilderness of chaos,
And they have wrought a God;

For he builds himself of the passion of martyrs,
And he is woven of the ecstasy of great lovers,
And he is wrought of the anguish of them that have greatly
    needed him.

Don Marquis

OBERAMMERGAU

RICH man, poor man, beggar-man, thief,
Over the hills to the mountain folk,
Doctor, lawyer, merchant, chief,
Across the world they find their way;
Christ will be crucified to-day.

Christ will hang high and we are here,
Villager, are there beds for us?
Soup and bread and a pot of beer?
—Weary Gentile, Turk and Jew,
Lord and peasant, Christian too.—

Who called His Name?   What was it spoke?
Perhaps I dreamed.   Then my walls dreamed!
I saw them shaking as I woke.
The dawn tuned silver harps, and there
The Star hung singing in the air.

"Rich man, rich man, drawing near,
Have you not heard of the needle's eye?
Beggar, whom do you follow here?
Did you give to the poor as He bade you do?
Proud sir, which of the thieves are you?

"Doctor, lawyer, whom do you seek?
Do you succor the needy and ask no fee?
Chief, will you turn the other cheek?
Merchant, there is a story grim
Of money-changers scourged by Him!"

The Star leaned lower from the sky;
"O men in holy orders dressed,
Hurrying so to see Him die,
Important as becomes your creed,
Why bring you dogma for his need?"

.   .   .   .

The streets of Oberammergau
Are waking now, are crowding now,
The Star has fallen like a tear,
There is a tree with a waiting bough
Not far from here.

Rich man, poor man, beggar and thief,
Over the hills to the mountain folk,
Doctor, lawyer, merchant, chief,
Magdalene, Mary, great with grief,
And Martha walking heavily . . . . . .

Doubter . . . . . . dreamer . . . . . . Which am I?
Lord, help thou mine unbelief.

Leonora Speyer

A PAGAN REINVOKES THE TWENTY–THIRD PSALM

I KNOCK again and try again the key,
I, who, enraged, fled from Thy temple's trees
Because the presence of my enemies
Around the table there offended me. . . .
I, who laid up so long and bitterly
Complaints and old reproaches, on my knees
Offer regret for years misspent as these,
And wonder how such folly came to be.
Anoint again my head and let me walk
The valley of the shadow, with the rod
Thou hast afforded for my comfort, God:
My soul restored, and singing through my veins.
Forgive the years of idle, foolish talk:
The cup that runneth over still remains.

Robert Wolf

SONG OF A FACTORY GIRL

IT's hard to breathe in a tenement hall,
So I ran to the little park,
As a lover runs from a crowded ball
To the moonlit dark.

I drank in clear air as one will
Who is doomed to die,
Wistfully watching from a hill
The unmarred sky.

And the great trees bowed in their gold and red
Till my heart caught flame;
And my soul, that I thought was crushed or dead,
Uttered a name.

I hadn't called the name of God
For a long time;
But it stirred in me as the seed in sod,
Or a broken rhyme.

Marya Zaturenska

GOD, THE ARCHITECT

Who thou art I know not,
　But this much I know:
Thou hast set the Pleiades
　In a silver row;

Thou hast sent the trackless winds
　Loose upon their way;
Thou hast reared a colored wall
　Twixt the night and day;

Thou hast made the flowers to blow,
　And the stars to shine;
Hid rare gems of richest ore
　In the tunneled mine—

But, chief of all thy wondrous works,
　Supreme of all thy plan,
Thou hast put an upward reach
　In the heart of Man.

Harry Kemp

GOD IS AT THE ANVIL

God is at the anvil, beating out the sun;
　Where the molten metal spills,
　At His forge among the hills
He has hammered out the glory of a day that's done.

God is at the anvil, welding golden bars;
　In the scarlet-streaming flame
　He is fashioning a frame
For the shimmering silver beauty of the evening stars.

Lew Sarett

PRODIGALS

I saw this eve the wandering sun—
　Spent was his purse of gold—
Sink at his father's door, foredone,
　As the day grew old.

Then from within the western wall
  Such floods of glory spread—
"They keep," I thought, "high carnival
  For one they held as dead."

And I thought of how Love's Prodigal
  Came home on bloodless feet
To His Father's house and festival
  And the right-hand seat.

Charles L. O'Donnell

THE EYES OF GOD

I SEE them nightly in my sleep.
The eyes of God are very deep.
There is no cave, no sea that knows
So much of unplumbed depth as those,
Or guards with walls or specters dumb
Such treasures for the venturesome.

I feel them burning on my back.
The eyes of God are very black.
There is no substance and no shade
So black as God his own eyes made;
In earth or heaven no night, no day
At once so black, so bright as they.

I see them wheresoe'er I turn.
The eyes of God are very stern.
The eyes of God are golden fires
That kindle beacons, kindle pyres;
And where like slow moon-rays they pass
They burn up dead things as dry grass.

They wait, and are not hard to find.
The eyes of God are very kind.
They have great pity for weak things
And joy in everything with wings;
And glow, beyond all telling bright,
Each time a brave soul dares a flight.

Hermann Hagedorn

BARTER

IF in that secret place
Where thou hast hidden it, there yet is lying
Thy dearest bitterness, thy fondest sin,
Though thou hast cherished it with hurt and crying,
Lift now thy face,
Unlock the bolted door and let God in
And lay it in His holy hands to take. . . .

(How such an evil gift can please Him so
I do not know)
But, keeping it for wages, He shall make
Thy foul room sweet for thee with blowing wind
(He is so serviceable and so kind)
And set sweet water for thy thirst's distress
Instead of what thou hadst, of bitterness:

And He shall bend and spread
Green balsam boughs to make a scented bed
Soft for thy lying
Where thine own thorns pricked in . . .

Who would not pay away his dearest sin
To let such service in?

Margaret Widdemer

HARVEST

THOUGH the long seasons seem to separate
Sower and reaper or deeds dreamed and done,
Yet when a man reaches the Ivory Gate
Labor and life and seed and corn are one.

Because thou art the doer and the deed,
Because thou art the thinker and the thought,
Because thou art the helper and the need,
And the cold doubt that brings all things to naught,

Therefore in every gracious form and shape
The world's dear open secret shalt thou find,
From the One Beauty there is no escape
Nor from the sunshine of the Eternal Mind.

The patient laborer, with guesses dim,
Follows this wisdom to its secret goal.
He knows all deeds and dreams exist in him,
And all men's God in every human soul.

Eva Gore-Booth

OVERNIGHT, A ROSE

THAT overnight a rose could come
   I one time did believe,
For when the fairies live with one,
   They wilfully deceive.

But now I know this perfect thing
   Under the frozen sod
In cold and storm grew patiently
   Obedient to God.

My wonder grows, since knowledge came
   Old fancies to dismiss;
And courage comes. Was not the rose
   A winter doing this?

Nor did it know, the weary while,
   What color and perfume
With this completed loveliness
   Lay in that earthly tomb.

So maybe I, who cannot see
   What God wills not to show,
May, some day, bear a rose for Him
   It took my life to grow.

Caroline Giltinan

THE UNSEEN BRIDGE

THERE is a bridge, whereof the span
Is rooted in the heart of man,
And reaches, without pile or rod,
Unto the Great White Throne of God.

Its traffic is in human sighs,
Fervently wafted to the skies;
'Tis the one pathway from Despair,
And it is called the Bridge of Prayer.

Gilbert Thomas

O GOD, HOW MANY YEARS AGO

O GOD, how many years ago,
  In homes how far away,
A people I shall never know
  Have humbled them to pray!

Not once or twice we cry to thee,
  Not once, or now and then,—
Wherever there is misery,
  Wherever there are men.

Frederick W. H. Myers

THE PASSIONATE SWORD

TEMPER my spirit, oh Lord,
  Burn out its alloy,
And make it a pliant steel for thy wielding,
  Not a clumsy toy;
A blunt, iron thing in my hands
  That blunder and destroy.

Temper my spirit, oh Lord,
  Keep it long in the fire;
Make it one with the flame. Let it share
  That up-reaching desire.
Grasp it, Thyself, oh my God;
  Swing it straighter and higher!

Jean Starr Untermeyer

A PRAYER

Lord, make my childish soul stand straight
To meet the kindly stranger, Fate;
Shake hands with elder brother, Doom,
Nor bawl, nor scurry from the room.

William Laird

FAITH

When the night kneels down by your bed
    In the time of your sadness,
Remember O child of the mountains
    This word of the law:
The night is the shadow of God
    Who made you for gladness,
And your sorrows are less than your strength
    Which He foresaw.

Preston Clark

SHE ASKS FOR NEW EARTH

Lord, when I find at last Thy Paradise,
Be it not all too bright for human eyes,
Lest I go sick for home through the high mirth—
For Thy new Heaven, Lord, give me new earth.

Give of Thy mansions, Lord, a house so small
Where they can come to me who were my all;
Let them run home to me just as of yore,
Glad to sit down with me and go out no more.

Give me a garden, Lord, and a low hill,
A field and a babbling brook that is not still;
Give me an orchard, Lord, in leaf and bloom,
And my birds to sing to me in a quiet gloom.

There shall no canker be in leaf or bud,
But glory on hill and sea and the green wood;
There, there shall none grow old but all be new,
No moth or rust shall fret nor thief break through.

Set thou a mist upon Thy glorious sun;
Lest we should faint for night and be undone;
Give us the high clean wind and the wild rain,
Lest that we faint with thirst and go in pain.

Let there be Winter there and the joy of Spring,
Summer and Autumn and the harvesting;
Give us all things we loved on earth of old,
Never to slip from out our clinging hold.

Give me a little house for my desire,
The man and the children to sit by my fire,
And friends to be crowding in to our lit hearth—
For Thy new Heaven, Lord, give me new earth!

Katherine Tynan Hinkson

THE LIVING CHALICE

THE Mother sent me on the holy quest
Timid and proud and curiously dressed
In vestures by her hand wrought wondrously;
An eager burning heart she gave to me.
The Bridegroom's Feast was set and I drew nigh—
Master of Life, Thy Cup has passed me by.

Before new-dressed I from the Mother came,
In dreams I saw the wondrous Cup of Flame;
Ah, Divine Chalice, how my heart drank deep,
Waking I sought the Love I knew asleep.
The Feast of Life was set and I drew nigh—
Master of Life, Thy Cup has passed me by.

Eyes of the Soul, awake, awake and see
Growing within the Ruby Radiant Tree,
Sharp pain hath wrung the Clusters of my Vine;
My heart is rose-red with its brimmèd wine.
Thou hast new-set the Feast and I draw nigh—
Master of Life take me, Thy Cup am I.

Susan Mitchell

"IN NO STRANGE LAND"

" The Kingdom of God is within you."

O WORLD invisible, we view thee:
  O world intangible, we touch thee:
O world unknowable, we know thee:
  Inapprehensible, we clutch thee!

Does the fish soar to find the ocean,
  The eagle plunge to find the air—
That we ask of the stars in motion
  If they have rumor of thee there?

Not where the wheeling systems darken,
  And our benumbed conceiving soars—
The drift of pinions, would we harken,
  Beats at our own clay-shuttered doors.

The angels keep their ancient places—
  Turn but a stone, and start a wing!
'Tis ye, 'tis your estrangèd faces
  That miss the many-splendored thing.

But (when so sad thou canst not sadder)
  Cry;—and upon thy so sore loss
Shall shine the traffic of Jacob's ladder
  Pitched betwixt Heaven and Charing Cross.

Yea, in the night, my Soul, my daughter,
  Cry,—clinging Heaven by the hems;
And lo, Christ walking on the water
  Not of Genesareth, but Thames!
                   Francis Thompson

LILIUM REGIS

O LILY of the King! low lies thy silver wing,
And long has been the hour of thine unqueening;
And thy scent of Paradise on the night-wind spills its sighs,
Nor any take the secrets of its meaning.

O Lily of the King! I speak a heavy thing,
O patience, most sorrowful of daughters!
Lo, the hour is at hand for the troubling of the land,
And red shall be the breaking of the waters.

Sit fast upon thy stalk, when the blast shall with thee talk,
With the mercies of the king for thine awning;
And the just understand that thine hour is at hand,
Thine hour at hand with power in the dawning.
When the nations lie in blood, and their kings a broken
      brood,
Look up, O most sorrowful of daughters!
Lift up thy head and hark what sounds are in the dark,
For His feet are coming to thee on the waters!

O Lily of the King! I shall not see, that sing,
I shall not see the hour of thy queening!
But my song shall see, and wake, like a flower that dawn-
      winds shake,
And sigh with joy the odors of its meaning.
O Lily of the King, remember then the thing
That this dead mouth sang; and thy daughters,
As they dance before His way, sing there on the Day,
What I sang when Night was on the waters!
                                        Francis Thompson

DEUS NOSTER IGNIS CONSUMENS

To Him be praise who made
    Desire more fair than rest:
Better the prayer while prayed,
    Than the attained request!
Man goes from strength to strength
    Fresh with each draught of pain,
Only to fail at length
    Of heights he could not gain.

The soul of live desire,
    How shall it mate with dust?
To whom was given fire,—
    For ashes shall be lust?

Man's tenure is but breath,
   His flesh, a vesture worn:
Let him that fears not death
   Fear not to rest unborn.

The crown entails the curse;
   Here all the fame that's won,
A harvest for the hearse,
   Falls withered to the sun.
There, weary of reward,
   The victor strips his wreath;
There, sick with deaths, the sword
   Sighs back into the sheath.

Laurence Housman

OUR LORD AND OUR LADY

NOËL

On a winter's night long time ago
    (*The bells ring loud and the bells ring low*),
When high howled wind, and down fell snow
    (Carillon, Carilla).
Saint Joseph he and Notre Dame,
Riding on an ass, full weary came
From Nazareth into Bethelehem.
    And the small child Jesus smile on you.

And Bethlehem inn they stood before
    (*The bells ring less and the bells ring more*),
The landlord bade them begone from his door
    (Carillon, Carilla).
"Poor folk" (says he), "must lie where they may,
For the Duke of Jewry comes this way,
With all his train on a Christmas Day."
    And the small child Jesus smile on you.

Poor folk that may carol hear
    (*The bells ring single and the bells ring clear*),
See! God's one child had hardest cheer!
    (Carillon, Carilla).
Men grown hard on a Christmas morn;
The dumb beast by and a babe forlorn.
It was very, very cold when our Lord was born.
    And the small child Jesus smile on you.

Now these were Jews as Jews must be
    (*The bells ring merry and the bells ring free*),
But Christian men in a band are we
    (Carillon, Carilla).
Empty we go, and ill be-dight,
Singing Noël on a Winter's night.
Give us to sup by the warm firelight,
    And the small child Jesus smile on you.
                      Hilaire Belloc

CHRISTMAS CAROL

LACKING samite and sable,
　Lacking silver and gold,
The Prince Jesus in the poor stable
　Slept, and was three hours old.

As doves by the fair water,
　Mary, not touched of sin,
Sat by Him,—the King's daughter,
　All glorious within.

A lily without one stain, a
　Star where no spot hath room.
Ave, gratia plena—
　Virgo Virginum!

Clad not in pearl-sewn vesture,
　Clad not in cramoisie,
She hath hushed, she hath cradled to rest, her
　God the first time on her knee.

Where is one to adore Him?
　The ox hath dumbly confessed,
With the ass, meek kneeling before Him,
　Et homo factus est.

Not throned on ivory or cedar,
　Not crowned with a Queen's crown,
At her breast it is Mary shall feed her
　Maker, from Heaven come down.

The trees in Paradise blossom
　Sudden, and its bells chime—
She giveth Him, held to her bosom,
　Her immaculate milk the first time.

The night with wings of angels
　Was alight, and its snow-packed ways
Sweet made (say the Evangels)
　With the noise of their virelays.

Quem vidistis, pastores?
  Why go ye feet unshod?
Wot ye within yon door is
  Mary, the Mother of God?

No smoke of spice is ascending
  There—no roses are piled—
But, choicer than all balms blending,
  There Mary hath kissed her child.

Dilectus meus mihi
  Et ego illi—cold
Small cheek against her cheek, He
  Sleepeth, three hours old.

              May Probyn

THE BALLAD OF THE CROSS

MELCHIOR, Gaspar, Balthazar,
  Great gifts they bore and meet;
White linen for His body fair
  And purple for His feet;
And golden things—the joy of kings—
  And myrrh to breathe Him sweet.

It was the shepherd Terish spake,
  "Oh, poor the gift I bring—
A little cross of broken twigs,
  A hind's gift to a king—
Yet, haply, He may smile to see
  And know my offering."

And it was Mary held her son
  Full softly to her breast,
"Great gifts and sweet are at Thy feet
  And wonders king-possessed,
O little Son, take Thou the one
  That pleasures Thee the best."

It was the Christ-Child in her arms
  Who turned from gaud and gold,
Who turned from wondrous gifts and great,
  From purple woof and fold,

And to His breast the cross He pressed
   That scarce His hands could hold.

'Twas king and shepherd went their way—
   Great wonder tore their bliss;
'Twas Mary clasped her little Son
   Close, close to feel her kiss,
And in His hold the cross lay cold
   Between her heart and His!

                        Theodosia Garrison

BALLAD OF THE EPIPHANY

WHEN Christ was born in Bethlehem,
   Pan left his Sussex Downs,
To see three kings go riding by,
   All in their robes and crowns;
And, as thy went in royal state,
   Pan followed them, unseen,
Though tiny tufts of grass and flowers
   Showed where his feet had been.

And when to Bethlehem they came,
   Birds sang in every tree,
And Mary in the stable sat,
   With Jesus on her knee;
And while the oxen munched their hay,
   The kings with one accord
Placed gold and frankincense and myrrh
   Before their infant Lord.

And when Pan peeped upon the scene,
   The Christ-Child clapped His hands,
And chuckled with delight to see
   The god of pasture lands;
And Mary sang "*Magnificat*"
   Above the kneeling kings,
And angels circled overhead
   On rainbow-colored wings.

And many a little singing bird
  Flew past the open door
To hop and chirrup in the straw
  Above the stable floor;
Wrens, robins, linnets, greenfinches,
  And many another one,
Flew in to show good fellowship
  With Mary's newborn Son.

Then Pan stood up and played his pipes
  Beside the manger-bed,
And every little bird went near
  And raised its faithful head;
And one, most beautiful to see,
  A fair and milk-white dove,
Arose and hovered in the air
  To testify its love.

But when the kings looked up to find
  Who made the piping sound,
They only saw white lilies shine,
  Fresh-gathered, on the ground,
And through the doorway, and beyond,
  A shaggy wild goat leap;
And, in its gentle mother's arm,
  The Baby fast asleep.

Charles Dalmon

HOW FAR IS IT TO BETHLEHEM

How far is it to Bethlehem?
  Not very far.
Shall we find the stable-room
  Lit by a star?

Can we see the little Child,
  Is He within?
If we lift the wooden latch
  May we go in?

May we stroke the creatures there,
  Ox, ass, or sheep?
May we peep like them and see
  Jesus asleep?

If we touch His tiny hand
  Will He awake?
Will He know we've come so far
  Just for His sake?

Great Kings have precious gifts,
  And we have naught;
Little smiles and little tears
  Are all we brought.

For all weary children
  Mary must weep.
Here, on His bed of straw,
  Sleep, children, sleep.

God, in His Mother's arms
  Babes in the byre,
Sleep, as they sleep who find
  Their heart's desire.

Frances Chesterton

A CAROL

MARY the Mother
  Sang to her Son,
In a Bethlehem shed
  When the light was done.

"Jesus, Jesus,
  Little son, sleep;
The tall Kings are gone,
  The lads with the sheep.

"Jesus, Jesus,
  My bosom is warm;
And Joseph and I
  Will keep You from harm."

Mary the Mother
  Sang to her son,
In Bethlehem town
  When the light was done.

                                              Lizette Woodworth Reese

A CHRISTMAS FOLK–SONG

THE little Jesus came to town;
The wind blew up, the wind blew down;
Out in the street the wind was bold;
Now who would house Him from the cold?

Then opened wide a stable door,
Fair were the rushes on the floor;
The Ox put forth a hornèd head:
"Come, little Lord, here make Thy bed."

Uprose the Sheep were folded near:
"Thou Lamb of God, come, enter here."
He entered there to rush and reed,
Who was the Lamb of God indeed.

The little Jesus came to town;
With ox and sheep He laid Him down;
Peace to the byre, peace to the fold,
For that they housed Him from the cold!

                                              Lizette Woodworth Reese

THE OXEN

CHRISTMAS EVE, and twelve of the clock.
  "Now they are all on their knees,"
An elder said as we sat in a flock
  By the embers in hearthside ease.

We pictured the meek mild creatures where
  They dwelt in their strawy pen,
Nor did it occur to one of us there
  To doubt they were kneeling then.

So fair a fancy few would weave
  In these years!   Yet, I feel,
If someone said on Christmas Eve,
  "Come; see the oxen kneel

"In the lonely barton by yonder coomb
  Our childhood used to know,"
I should go with him in the gloom,
  Hoping it might be so.

Thomas Hardy

A LEGEND OF CHERRIES

Now St. Joseph's cottage stood
Close beside a cherry wood;
And when all the trees were red
With their dangling fruit, 'tis said
Jesus, at His mother's gown,
Begged to have the branches down.
All in vain she made reply,
"Mother cannot reach so high,"
For He begged them none the less,
In His perfect childishness.

Joseph, in his workshop near,
Heard the Babe, and would not hear—
Heard the Blessed Virgin say,
"Joseph, pull them down, I pray!"
But he answered, with a frown,
"*Let His Father pull them down!*"
Then, to Joseph's wonderment,
Every cherry branch was bent;
And Our Lady sweetly smiled,
Picking cherries for her Child.

Charles Dalmon

IN THE CARPENTER'S SHOP

MARY sat in the corner dreaming,
  Dim was the room and low,
While in the dusk the saw went screaming
  To and fro.

Jesus and Joseph toiled together,
  Mary was watching them,
Thinking of Kings in the wintry weather
  At Bethlehem.

Mary sat in the corner thinking,
  Jesus had grown a man;
One by one her hopes were sinking
  As the years ran.

Jesus and Joseph toiled together,
  Mary's thoughts were far—
Angels sang in the wintry weather
  Under a star.

Mary sat in the corner weeping,
  Bitter and hot her tears—
Little faith were the angels keeping
  All the years.

Sara Teasdale

JOSES, THE BROTHER OF JESUS

Joses, the brother of Jesus, plodded from day to day
With never a vision within him to glorify his clay;
Joses, the brother of Jesus, was one with the heavy clod,
But Christ was the soul of rapture, and soared, like a lark, with God.
Joses, the brother of Jesus, was only a worker in wood,
And he never could see the glory that Jesus, his brother, could.
"Why stays he not in the workshop?" he often used to complain,
"Sawing the Lebanon cedar, imparting to woods their stain?
Why must he go thus roaming, forsaking my father's trade,
While hammers are busily sounding, and there is gain to be made?"
Thus ran the mind of Joses, apt with plummet and rule,
And deeming whoever surpassed him either a knave or a fool,—

For he never walked with the prophets in God's great
   garden of bliss—
And of all mistakes of the ages, the saddest, methinks, was
   this
To have such a brother as Jesus, to speak with him day by
   day,
But never to catch the vision which glorified his clay.

Harry Kemp

CRADLE-SONG

MADONNA, Madonnina,
Sat by the gray road-side,
Saint Joseph her beside,
And Our Lord at her breast;
Oh they were fain to rest,
Mary and Joseph and Jesus,
All by the gray road-side.

She said, Madonna Mary,
"I am hungry, Joseph, and weary,
All in the desert wide."
Then bent a tall palm-tree
Its branches low to her knee;
"Behold," the palm-tree said,
"My fruit that shall be your bread."
So were they satisfied,
Mary and Joseph and Jesus,
All by the gray road-side.

From Herod they were fled
Over the desert wide,
Mary and Joseph and Jesus,
In Egypt to abide.

The blessèd Queen of Heaven
Her own dear Son hath given
For my son's sake; his sleep
Is safe and sweet and deep.

Lully . . . Lulley . . .
So may you sleep alway,
My baby, my dear son:
Amen, Amen, Amen.

My baby, my dear son.
Adelaide Crapsey

OUR LORD AND OUR LADY

THEY warned Our Lady for the Child
   That was Our blessed Lord,
And She took Him into the desert wild,
   Over the camel's ford.

And a long song She sang to Him
   And a short story told:
And She wrapped Him in a woolen cloak
   To keep Him from the cold.

But when Our Lord was grown a man
   The Rich they dragged Him down,
And they crucified Him in Golgotha,
   Out and beyond the Town.

They crucified Him on Calvary,
   Upon an April day;
And because He had been her little Son
   She followed Him all the way.

Our Lady stood beside the Cross,
   A little space apart,
And when She heard Our Lord cry out
   A sword went through Her Heart.

They laid Our Lord in a marble tomb,
   Dead, in a winding sheet,
But Our Lady stands above the world
   With the white Moon at Her feet.
Hilaire Belloc

COURTESY

Of Courtesy, it is much less
Than Courage of Heart or Holiness,
Yet in my Walks it seems to me
That the Grace of God is in Courtesy.

On Monks I did in Storrington fall,
They took me straight into their Hall;
I saw Three Pictures on a wall,
And Courtesy was in them all.

The first the Annunciation;
The second the Visitation;
The third the Consolation,
Of God that was Our Lady's Son.

The first was of Saint Gabriel;
On wings a-flame from Heaven he fell;
And as he went upon one knee
He shone with Heavenly Courtesy.

Our Lady out of Nazareth rode—
It was Her month of heavy load;
Yet was Her face both great and kind,
For Courtesy was in Her Mind.

The third it was our Little Lord,
Whom all the Kings in arms adored;
He was so small you could not see
His large intent of Courtesy.

Our Lord, that was Our Lady's Son,
Go bless you, People, one by one;
My Rhyme is written, my work is done.

Hilaire Belloc

I SEE HIS BLOOD UPON THE ROSE

I SEE His blood upon the rose
And in the stars the glory of His eyes,
His body gleams amid eternal snows,
His tears fall from the skies.

I see His face in every flower;
The thunder and the singing of the birds
Are but His voice—and carven by His power
Rocks are His written words.

All pathways by His feet are worn,
His strong heart stirs the ever-beating sea,
His crown of thorns is twined with every thorn,
His cross is every tree.

Joseph M. Plunkett

THE STICK

To failing strength a stick is given—
A kindly prop acceptable!—
Thy Cross upon my road to Heaven
Upholds me well.

On wood, the dear Creator hung,
On wood I lean for second strength—
I who have found too young—too young
The road's gray length!

O honest friend of simple guise—
Plain wood, no fluted gold's emboss—
I hold thee and my thoughts arise
To Christ, His Cross!

May O'Rourke

COMRADES OF THE CROSS

I CANNOT think or reason,
I only know He came
With hands and feet of healing
And wild heart all aflame.

With eyes that dimmed and softened
At all the things He saw,
And in his pillared singing
I read the marching Law.

I only know He loves me,
Enfolds and understands—
And oh, his heart that holds me,
And oh, his certain hands—

The man, the Christ, the soldier,
Who from his cross of pain
Cried to the dying comrade,
"Lad, we shall meet again."

Willard Wattles

THE NEW GHOST

" And he, casting away his garment, rose and came to Jesus."

AND he cast it down, down, on the green grass,
Over the young crocuses, where the dew was—
He cast the garment of his flesh that was full of death,
And like a sword his spirit showed out of the cold sheath.

He went a pace or two, he went to meet his Lord,
And, as I said, his spirit looked like a clean sword,
And seeing him the naked trees began shivering,
And all the birds cried out aloud as it were late spring.

And the Lord came on, He came down, and saw
That a soul was waiting there for Him, one without flaw,
And they embraced in the churchyard where the robins play,
And the daffodils hang down their heads, as they burn away.

The Lord held his head fast, and you could see
That he kissed the unsheathed ghost that was gone free—
As a hot sun, on a March day, kisses the cold ground;
And the spirit answered, for he knew well that his peace was
    found.

The spirit trembled, and sprang up at the Lord's word—
As on a wild, April day, springs a small bird—
So the ghost's feet lifting him up, he kissed the Lord's cheek,
And for the greatness of their love neither of them could
 speak.

But the Lord went then, to show him the way,
Over the young crocuses, under the green may
That was not quite in flower yet—to a far-distant land;
And the ghost followed, like a naked cloud holding the
 sun's hand.

Fredegond Shove

SYMBOL

My faith is all a doubtful thing,
 Wove on a doubtful loom,—
Until there comes each showery spring,
 A cherry-tree in bloom;

And Christ who died upon a tree
 That death had stricken bare
Comes beautifully back to me
 In blossoms, everywhere.

David Morton

HYMN FOR A HOUSEHOLD

Lord Christ, beneath thy starry dome
We light this flickering lamp of home,
And where bewildering shadows throng
Uplift our prayer and evensong.
Dost thou, with heaven in thy ken
Seek still a dwelling-place with men,
Wandering the world in ceaseless quest?
O Man of Nazareth, be our guest!

Lord Christ, the bird his nest has found,
The fox is sheltered in his ground,
But dost thou still this dark earth tread
And have no place to lay thy head?

Shepherd of mortals, here behold
A little flock, a wayside fold
That wait thy presence to be blest—
O Man of Nazareth, be our guest!

Daniel Henderson

IN THE NAME OF JESUS CHRIST

In the name of Jesus Christ—
　To whom the sea is as a drop of water,
　And a fleck of dust the land;
To whom the pinions of an eagle are a fan,
　And the shadow of a mountain as the shadow of his hand.

I asked for wings in the morning;
　Plumed they were, like an eagle for a great ascent;
I asked for wings at night,
　And they were folded like a flag when the wind is spent.

I asked in the morning for power,
　And it crashed like the tide of the sea over the reverberant
　　floor;
In the evening I asked for peace,
　And it rested like the shadow of a mountain upon a quiet
　　shore.

For I asked in the name of Jesus Christ,
To whom the sheaves of shining stars
　Are but a harvest ripe for reaping;
To whom the four winds of Heaven
　Are but a lullaby for sleeping.

Claudia Cranston

THE JEW TO JESUS

O man of my own people, I alone
Among these alien ones can know thy face,
I who have felt the kinship of our race
Burn in me as I sit where they intone
Thy praises,—those who, striving to make known
A God for sacrifice, have missed the grace

Of thy sweet human meaning in its place,
Thou who art of our blood-bond and our own.
Are we not sharers of thy Passion? Yea,
In spirit-anguish closely by thy side
We have drained the bitter cup, and, tortured, felt
With thee the bruising of each heavy welt.
In every land is our Gethsemane.
A thousand times have we been crucified.

Florence Kiper Frank

THE BUILDER

SMOOTHING a cypress beam
  With a scarred hand,
I saw a carpenter
  In a far land.

Down past the flat roofs
  Poured the white sun;
But still he bent his back,
  The patient one.

And I paused surprised
  In that queer place
To find an old man
  With a haunting face.

"Who art thou, carpenter,
  Of the bowed head;
And what buildest thou?"
  "Heaven," he said.

Willard Wattles

GABRIEL

MARY walked in the daisies
Along a winding way;
The wind came by and touched her,
Her face was glad and gay;
Something nestled in her heart, . . .
The sad Christ smiled that day.

For God had grown so lonely
On his throne,
He put his staff on his shoulder
And set off alone;
Among the scornful brambles
He laid his head on a stone.

Mary bore the daisies
Home in her two hands,
Daisies of white petals
For all the lonely lands,
That will not fade or vanish
While the arch of Heaven stands.

Willard Wattles

TO FELICITY WHO CALLS ME MARY

You go singing through my garden on little dancing feet,
Crying "Mary, Mary, Mary," with laughter shrill and
    sweet;
And the lily bud grows paler and the passion flower flames,
As light upon the wandering breeze you toss the name of
    names.

When I was but a tiny child, they chose for me a saint,
Fulfilled of Christian charity and heavenly restraint;
But you have called me Mary, and oh! I joy to hear
The name of God's own Mother come so gaily on the air.

What though my arms be empty, and hers for ever press
The eternal Child who touches you with such divine caress,
Here's another love, Felicity, and oh, sweetheart, drink deep,
That you may laugh more easily, and I forget to weep.

For you have called me Mary, making bitter waters sweet,
Oh little soul of happiness, oh little dancing feet;
And I grow bold in honor, that all my spirit shames,
As light upon the wandering breeze you toss the name of
    names.

Frances Chesterton

CAROL NAÏVE

Was never none other
Like our God's Mother.

I sing the Lady of all most fair,
Of all most dainty and debonair,
She to whose feet the angels come,—
Lady Mary of God's Kingdom!

I sing the Lady of all most good,
Immaculate Lady of Motherhood,
She that holdeth our hearts in fee,—
Lady Mary of God's City!

I sing the Lady of all most dear,
She that cherished us yesteryear,
She that will cherish when this world dies,—
Lady Mary of Paradise!

Yet was never none so fair,
Yet was never none so good,
On the green earth anywhere
As our Lady of Motherhood.—

Yet never none other
Like our God's Mother.

John McClure

LA MADONNA DI LORENZETTI

Perhaps she watches where a silver bay
Curves like a twisted moon between the hills,
Her mild eyes lowered while the angels play
Their soft-tongued trumpets, and a music fills
The sky and sea.   Perhaps her wistful soul
Steals back to that sweet hour when Gabriel
Bore her the swaying lily to unroll
The mystic plans of God.   I cannot tell,
And yet it seems not so. . . . I see her stand

At dusk beneath some rich, dull olive grove,
Pensive with thoughts of motherhood and love,
Her slender body like a flower swayed
To hold her child, watching the blue sea fade,
And neighbors toiling up the terraced land.

John Williams Andrews

A FLEMISH MADONNA

HERE is no golden-crowned, celestial queen
Such as Angelico would fitly paint,
With pink-white cheek and haloed smile serene,
Enringed by many a cherub, many a saint.
This is a peasant woman worn by toil,
Her cheeks are hollow as with child-bed's trace;
A poor, plain creature of the common soil,
Yet wearing godhead on her earnest face.
Well have you wrought, good painter, that could show
So pure a spirit in so rude a shrine.
The dullest soul that looks on this will know
That motherhood has loveliness divine.
  What greater power than this has brush or pen:
  To bring the thought of God to simple men?

Charles Wharton Stork

CHRIST IN THE UNIVERSE

  WITH this ambiguous earth
His dealings have been told us.   These abide:
The signal to a maid, the human birth,
The lesson, and the young Man crucified.

  But not a star of all
The innumerable host of stars has heard
How He administered this terrestrial ball.
Our race have kept their Lord's entrusted word.

  Of His earth-visiting feet
None knows the secret, cherished, perilous,
The terrible, shamefast, frightened, whispered, sweet,
Heart-shattering secret of His way with us.

No planet knows that this
Our wayside planet, carrying land and wave,
Love and life multiplied, and pain and bliss,
Bears, as chief treasure, one forsaken grave.

Nor, in our little day,
May His devices with the heavens be guessed,
His pilgrimage to thread the Milky Way,
Or His bestowals there be manifest.

But, in the eternities,
Doubtless we shall compare together, hear
A million alien Gospels, in what guise
He trod the Pleiades, the Lyre, the Bear.

O, be prepared, my soul!
To read the inconceivable, to scan
The million forms of God those stars unroll
When, in our turn, we show to them a Man.

Alice Meynell

INDEX OF AUTHORS

Selections from the earlier work of the poets whose names are starred will be found in THE HOME BOOK OF VERSE.

INDEX OF FIRST LINES

A

INDEX OF TITLES

1107